ENCYCLOPEDIA OF THE MODERN OLYMPIC MOVEMENT

Edited by John E. Findling and Kimberly D. Pelle

GREENWOOD PRESS
Westport, CT • London

Library of Congress Cataloging-in-Publication Data

Encyclopedia of the modern Olympic movement / edited by John E. Findling and Kimberly D. Pelle.
    p. cm.
  Includes bibliographical references and index.
   ISBN 0–313–32278–3 (alk. paper)—ISBN 0–275–97659–9 (pbk. : alk. paper)
    1. Olympics—History—Encyclopedias. I. Findling, John E. II. Pelle, Kimberly D. III.
Historical dictionary of the modern Olympic movement.

   GV721.5.H546   2004
   786.48—dc21   2003049205

British Library Cataloguing in Publication Data is available.

Library of Congress Catalog Card Number: 2003049205

ISBN: 0–313–32278–3
    0–275–97659–9 (pbk.)

First published in 2004

Greenwood Press, 88 Post Road West, Westport, CT 06881
An imprint of Greenwood Publishing Group, Inc.
www.greenwood.com

Printed in the United States of America

The paper used in this book complies with the
Permanent Paper Standard issued by the National
Information Standards Organization (Z39.48–1984).

10 9 8 7 6 5 4 3 2 1

Copyright Acknowledgment

The editors and publisher gratefully acknowledge permission for use of the following material:

The chapter "Mexico City, 1968" was previously published in "Hosting the Summer Olympic Games"
in *Sport in Latin America and the Caribbean*, ed. Joseph L. Arbena and David G. La France (Wil-
mington, DE: Scholarly Resources, 2003), 133–43.

For Micah and Jody
Janet and Fred

CONTENTS

Contents

Contents

PREFACE

John E. Findling and
Kimberly D. Pelle

The *Encyclopedia of the Modern Olympic Movement* is a revised and expanded edition of our 1996 book, *Historical Dictionary of the Modern Olympic Movement.* In this new edition, we have made a number of changes and additions to make it an even more useful reference book for students and general readers with an interest in the Olympic movement. We have updated most of the articles, both textually and bibliographically, and have asked a number of additional specialists to write new entries on some of the Summer and Winter Games. In addition, we have added new essays on the forerunners of both the Summer and Winter Games, on the Olympics and television, and on electronic sources for Olympic Games research. Finally, we have brought the history of the Olympic movement forward to include essays on the completed Nagano, Sydney, and Salt Lake City Games, and on the planned Games in Athens, Torino, Beijing, and Vancouver.

Many reference books have been published about the Olympic Games, but virtually all of them emphasize the athletic achievements of top performers at the Games: the medal winners, the world record times, distances, and weights, and the nations whose athletes have performed the best. Like the earlier edition, this book deals instead with the historical context in which the modern Olympic Games have taken place. The entries emphasize such matters as site selection and development, political questions or controversies, collateral events, programmatic changes, and political and/or economic consequences, while keeping discussions of winners and losers to a minimum. Each entry also includes a substantial bibliographical essay for readers interested in the best primary and secondary sources on each Game, and the book concludes with an extensive general bibliography, which covers works of a topical or biographical nature and works that touch on several different Games. A number of appendixes include essays covering the International Olympic Committee and its eight presidents, the U.S. Olympic Committee, and Olympic feature films.

ACKNOWLEDGMENTS

This book originated with a suggestion from our editor, Cynthia Harris, at Greenwood Press, who sought a reference book on the Olympics that was similar in format and style to our *Historical Dictionary of World's Fairs and Expositions* (1990). Many people have helped us in the preparation of this book. Bob Barney and Bob Barnett gave us some valuable suggestions as we began the project, and Bob and Ashleigh Barney were genial hosts on a trip to the Centre for Olympic Studies in London, Ontario. The library staff at Indiana University Southeast was, as always, very helpful in facilitating interlibrary loan requests and helping us in many other ways. The office staff of the Division of Social Sciences at Indiana University Southeast, especially Brigette Colligan, assisted with word processing and other clerical chores, often on short notice, and we thank them. Brook Dutko also handled some important word-processing duties, and Lee Bruce dug out some elusive bibliographical information. The computer wizards at I.U.S., notably Kevin Hostetler, saved us much grief with their ability to turn disks full of mysterious symbols into readable WordPerfect.

We are also grateful to many individuals who helped us find much of the information that is in this book. Maynard Brichford and his staff at the University of Illinois archives facilitated our trip into the massive Avery Brundage collection. Gisela Terrell introduced us to the Olympic material at the National Track and Field Hall of Fame Historical Research Library at Butler University in Indianapolis. Cindy Slater of the U.S. Olympic Committee provided a careful description of that organization's archival holdings, as did Wayne Wilson of the Amateur Athletic Foundation in Los Angeles. Max Howell of the University of Queensland put us in touch with various Australian sport history archives and libraries, and Greg Blood and Melissa Petherbridge graciously responded to our requests for information. We are grateful to the staffs of the Centre for Olympic Studies and the main library at the University of Western Ontario in London for making sure we saw all of their holdings.

We also want to thank Karel Wendl of the International Olympic Committee's research center for making it possible to examine the many materials held at the IOC library and archives in Lausanne. Thanks to Michele Veillard, the archivist, Denis Echard and Laura Davies, the editor and assistant editor of *Olympic Review*, Jean-Francois Pahud, the curator of the Olympic Museum, Alexandra Leclef Mandl, director of the photographic department, and Fekrou Kidane, *chef du cabinet* of the IOC, for sharing their time and knowledge with us. Also, we thank Swantje Scharenberg at the Institut für Sport-Wissenschaften at Georg-August-Universitat in Göttingen, Karl Lennartz at the Carl-Diem-Institut in Cologne, and Ulrike Merke at the Sportbibliothek of the Technische Universitat in Munich for their assistance.

Finally, Joe Arbena, Bruce Kidd, Nancy Bouchier, Douglas Brown, Gordon MacDonald, Scott Martyn, Norm Baker, James Riordan, Yvonne Condon, and Allen Guttmann all provided various kinds of help or encouragement along the way, and we thank them for that. Likewise, our spouses, Carol Findling and Jay Pelle, and our children bore our joys and frustrations willingly; their part in bringing this project to completion was, as always, very important.

ACKNOWLEDGMENTS FOR SECOND EDITION

As with the first edition, Cynthia Harris, our editor at Greenwood, has been a model of patience and helpfulness. Liz Kincaid of Greenwood was of great assistance in arranging for many of the photographs in this book. We wish to acknowledge gratefully the photographic contributions of two of our authors, Larry Maloney and Ed Goldstein, as well as Kevin Wamsley at the University of Western Ontario, Katia Bonjour at the International Olympic Committee archives in Lausanne, and Maynard Brichford at the University of Illinois Archives. Linda Brizzolara of the Torino 2006 Organizing Committee was helpful in getting information to us about the 2006 Games, and Ana Belen Moreno was a courteous host during a visit to the Centre d'Estudis Olimpics at the Universitat Autonoma de Barcelona. Heather Dichter led us to the Douglas F. Roby Papers at the University of Michigan and provided useful information on some of the Games.

Finally, we wish to thank the staffs of the Office of Admissions and the School of Social Sciences at Indiana University Southeast, our coworkers, who were always sympathetic, and all of our authors, who collectively made this book possible.

John E. Findling
Kimberly D. Pelle

INTRODUCTION

John A. Daly

> Within the Olympic idea there inevitably develops [a] . . . conflict of the past
> with the future and of reality with the ideal.
>
> —Carl Diem

The Olympic Games are the foremost sporting event in the world, attracting young men and women to compete together in a spirit of honor and fellowship. Athletes consider the Games to be special because of the idealism attached to them and the moral code that is demanded of them as competitors. These qualities make them different from world championships, though both events seek to discover and acclaim the best in their field of endeavor. The claim of Pierre de Coubertin, the creator of the modern Olympic Games, that it is as important to take part as it is to win and that the athletes should compete in an honorable gathering respecting the rules of sport and the efforts of others, is more than a popular cliché; it is a heroic ideal accepted by most Olympians. Indeed it is this specialness of the event that provides much of its public appeal and has guaranteed its growth from a quaint idea of the 1890s to a major world event every four years. John MacAloon, writing of Coubertin and the origins of the modern Olympic Games, suggested that the Games "have grown from a fin-de-siècle curiosity of regional interest to an international cultural [and sporting] performance of global proportion."

The first "Games of the modern era," those held in Athens in 1896, were contested by only 300 athletes from 11 countries. In contrast, the Olympic Games in Sydney in the year 2000 attracted 10,000 athletes from nearly 200 countries. Some 15,000 media representatives went to Australia to cover the Games, which were viewed on television by well over half the world's population. Television rights to the Sydney Olympics cost more than $1 billion, and the estimated cost of the Games was more than $3 billion. The Olympic Games have become, in a century, "the Mount Everest of sport," as Olympic historian John Lucas describes them.

THE IDEAL VERSUS THE REALITY

Coubertin believed that the Games would encourage a community among athletes that would overshadow their national differences:

> To ask the peoples of the world to love one another . . . is childishness. [But] to ask them to respect one another is not in the least utopian. [However] in order to respect one another it is first necessary to know one another . . . through sport.

The Games, he argued, would also be a display of physical and moral excellence that would be an inspiration to the young and aspiring. The fact that the Olympic Games are of such importance would indicate that Coubertin was successful.

The twentieth-century growth and conduct of the Olympic Games, however, has not been without criticism. Indeed the Games have been criticized from the very beginning. A colleague (but later antagonist) of Coubertin, Georges Herbert, suggested in a letter in 1911 to the *renovateur* of the Games that he was "deluding" himself "as to their importance." They are, he asserted, "exclusively . . . [an] exhibition of international athletes"—nothing more, that is, than another international contest. Herbert argued that there was nothing educational about them, nothing of a higher moral order that would appeal to the general populace, as Coubertin had claimed. John Lucas quite rightly adjudges that by 1911, the Games had "ceased to be 'games' or an ideal place in which to 'play.' " Nevertheless, they were seen still as "arenas of honor"; Herbert was incorrect in his assessment that they would not appeal to the general public. He wrote his letter to Coubertin on the eve of the 1912 Games in Stockholm, where more than 2,500 athletes representing 28 countries competed. If any further evidence of their appeal was needed, the resumption of the Olympics after the Great War (1914–18) attested to their resilience and perceived significance.

Their significance, of course, was viewed differently depending on whether one was an athlete or a politician. The 1936 Games in Berlin confirmed the political value of the Olympics, but they were not the first to be used in this way. Excellence in both organization and athletic performance had become a measure of national status in the Olympic Games conducted in Amsterdam (1928) and Los Angeles (1932), as well as Berlin. R. M. Goodhue is correct in his assertion that "one cannot detach 1936 from the previous Olympic Games. [These Games] were not an aberration. The conditions that made 1936 possible were apparent in the development of the Games from 1900 to 1932."

Despite the significance of the Games, however, to those who would use them to confirm their identity or indicate their development, athletes have persisted in viewing them in the idealistic light of their founder. They were arenas of honor, contests with dignity. Without really being aware of it, the athletes of the twentieth century endorsed the values of the classical era. The Greeks called their games *agones*, from which our word *agony* stems. It is the anguish of the struggle that reveals the essence of the person in the sporting contest.

Still, despite the value of the Games to contemporary athletes and their appeal to those who would witness the human struggle in the world's greatest arena, criticism of the Games continues, especially when an incident creates controversy and calls into question the idealism that is meant to suffuse the Olympic contests. This is the contradiction of the Games—their agony and ecstasy. The popularity and growth of the modern Olympic Games, with their espoused idealism, have been both their strength and their weakness. There is no doubting the appeal of the Games and the words of Coubertin. The language of the Olympic philosophy grips the heart and stirs the soul—certainly of those who believe in the heroic nature of sport. Olympic words and phrases suggest a value for sport contests beyond simple exercise, and this sentiment is the source of the power of the idealistic Olympic message. Coubertin explained Olympism thus:

> The Olympic idea ... is a strong culture based in part on the spirit of chivalry ... [which we call] "fair play" ... a love of sport for itself, for its high educative value, for the pursuit of human perfection.

The problem for the Olympic movement has been that any controversial incidents that occur are counterpoised against the idealistic words of Coubertin and the keepers of the flame who followed him. Ideological differences, racism, gender issues, illicit behavior including the use of drugs, commercial and political exploitation: at various times, all of those have focused attention on the relevance of the heroic ideals in the face of apparent discountenance. Indeed, when the incidents are significant enough to cause general unease, the question of continuing the Games is raised. Coubertin was aware of the problems and the criticism. He knew that his "Olympic idea" was considered "utopian and impractical." In a letter in 1931, to Liselott Diem, the wife of Carl Diem, and a longtime German Olympic leader, he declared that "at every Olympiad I have read that it was going to be the last." It has been so since his death in 1937 despite the incredible growth of his idea.

CONTINUE THE GAMES?

The continuance of the Games is still questioned. "The Games must end!" was the headline in a world press appalled at the use of a sporting arena for political terrorism when 11 Israeli athletes were murdered at the athletes' village in Munich in 1972. *Time* magazine reported a cynic as saying, "The only time people get into uniform is for war or the Olympics." A "Five-Ring Circus" was the phrase used to describe the Olympics and the U.S.-led political boycott of the Moscow Games in 1980. Retaliation by the Eastern bloc countries four years later in 1984 and the unease felt by many about the commercialization of the Games in Los Angeles did little to stem the tide of criticism. British journalist Ian Wooldridge declared in a radio interview in 1984 that the International Olympic Committee (IOC) had "all but handed over the games to Walt Disney" and commercial interests. They were called the "MacDonald Games" or the "Coca Cola Games" depending on where the television images were coming from—the swimming pool or the athletic arena.

At least those Games made a profit. In 1976, Montreal went into long-term debt to pay for its Olympic facilities. It is no wonder that the first arrivals to the Olympic city were treated to the disconcerting spectacle of local citizens' driving in a motorcade around the fence of the village urging, "Olympian, go home! We don't want you here!"

In Seoul in 1988, the poor and their shantytown were displaced to make way for the Olympic facilities on the Han River. Where did they go? Critics of the Games vehemently argue that the Olympic flame is kept alight often at the expense of pressing social issues that should take precedence in host cities. Jean-Marie Brohm criticizes the modern Olympics for being a gross commercial spectacle and asserts:

> If a balance sheet is drawn up of the last four or five Olympic Games the sorry conclusion must be that they form part of an economic system of waste, uncontrolled affluence and the large display of luxury, while the rest of the planet is sunk in famine and ignorance.

The debate about whether to hold the Games while there is social unrest or to spend valuable resources on sport where there are blatant inequities still to be addressed causes much soul searching during an Olympic festival by both critics and supporters of Coubertin's idea. It is inappropriate to discuss it here but it must be acknowledged as a cause of concern and disquiet as the Games grow in size and presentation.

The idea that the growth of the modern Games into a Hollywood spectacle would please their founder is at odds with a plea that Coubertin made in the 1930s: "My friends, I have not laboured to restore the Olympic Games for you to make a spectacle of them . . . to use them for business or political ends." He was quite clear about their moral and educational value and is on record as saying, "Sport must decide whether it is to be a market or a temple!"

In some circumstances there is no division between those who admire the Olympic philosophy and the critics—for example, no disagreement between antagonists or protagonists about condemning the use of ergogenic aids in a "chivalrous" Olympian contest that advocates "a freely exercised morality" as an inspiration to the young. The incidence of drug taking to boost athletic performance is deplored by both Olympic proponents and critics alike. The fact that the Olympic ideals stress fair play and promote the contest as an illustration of "an ever more highly aspiring, bolder and purer humanity" means that whenever there is a breach of Olympic morality, there is appropriate condemnation of the athlete (Carl Diem, *The Olympic Idea: Discourses and Essays*, 1970, p. 22). When the incidence of drug taking seems to be widespread, then cynicism about the honesty of all Olympic athletes is openly expressed, along with justifiable concern that if the high ideals expected of Olympians cannot be ensured, then the Games themselves lose the special moral value that sets them apart from other sporting events. Carl Diem, Coubertin's German disciple, argued that "the true sportsman finds his standard of behavior within himself . . . and the Games are a reminder of sporting ideals" to be honored. This is one of the appealing aspects of the Games for athlete and spectator alike, the quality that sets the Games apart—that makes them special.

When the Canadian sprinter Ben Johnson was disqualified for drug use after winning the 100-meter sprint in Seoul in 1988 and his coach, Charlie Francis, declared at the inquiry in Canada that "as many as 80 percent of the world's leading athletes may be using steroids to improve their . . . performances," many expressed the opinion that the Olympic Games could no longer be considered a special illustration of human excellence in honorable competition. Kevin Doyle, editor of *Maclean's*, Canada's weekly newsmagazine, writing of the "national disgrace," concluded, "And the Olympics, once the grandest spectacle in international sports, have now been reduced to the status of mud-wrestling."

Supporters of the Olympic philosophy share the concern of the critics about the apparent decline in sporting morality and the suggestions of widespread drug use.

They feel let down by athletes like Johnson, but not enough to give in to the cry to abolish the Games. They argue that because a few athletes cannot uphold the ideals of fair competition in an Olympic arena, others should not suffer the implied assertions of immorality and lose their opportunity for "noble competition." They should not be denied their quest for excellence in the world's greatest sporting event. Indeed, fellow athletes in Seoul felt so enraged and betrayed by Johnson and his apparent cheating that they affixed a notice to the door of his room in the Olympic Village that declared he had gone from "Hero to Zero!"

Carl Diem was right when he suggested that the morality inherent in Olympic competition "finds a deep place in the soul" of the genuine Olympian. He was also astute enough though to observe that "within the Olympic idea there inevitably develops . . . a conflict . . . between reality and the ideal."

The attachment to the philosophy of Olympism and the effort to preserve what are thought to be worthwhile sporting ideals are the reasons that supporters of the Games refuse to be swayed by the social arguments of the critics of the modern Olympic athlete and sports administrator. It is an example of those who, aware of the problems of contemporary Games, still advocate their continuance, and indeed believe that the Games are "one of the greatest leavening forces for good" in an imperfect world. As Roger Bannister, the British Olympic athlete, put it:

> It may seem paradoxical that, despite all the problems, I believe in the Olympic Games . . . as one of the great causes in the world which are capable of engaging the most serious determination of our young people and harnessing much of that . . . idealism which is latent in human beings . . . We should not give up an ideal because it has not been attained. (J. Segrave and D. Chu, *Olympism*, 1981, p. 145)

No doubt the Games and their professional philosophy and idealism are seriously questioned and sometimes threatened (some would argue compromised) by the contemporary realities of commercialism, technology, and political events that seem to affect them. But the threats to the Olympic ideals are in no way due to the differences in time between Coubertin's era and the present. Sport philosopher Robert Osterhoudt reminds us that

> Coubertin was by inclination and by influence very much more fully swayed by the idealistic optimism and purposive certainty of the nineteenth century than he was by the contrary sentiment that governs the current epoch. . . . Olympism is trapped in the conjunction between the nineteenth and twentieth centuries.

This is not to suggest though that the idealistic philosophy of Coubertin and the Olympic movement have no contemporary relevance. They do. Despite those who would argue the irrelevance of the Olympic Games and erosion of Coubertin's ideals or suggest that these nineteenth-century ideals have been overtaken by and are at odds with modern values and attitudes, countless others point to the Games as a constant reminder of the heroic possibilities of sport. The fact that the Olympic ideals appear to conflict with reality does not negate the ideals themselves.

Robert Osterhoudt contends that Olympism embodies the highest principles of sport's promised odyssey and as such is unique among modern sporting institutions. No other institution has "stood so steadfastly" against the dehumanizing abuses of contemporary elite competition or been so insistent on combining sporting excellence with "good and virtuous conduct." He concludes that because "Olympism has brought sport nearer its fully human possibilities than any other modern event," the Games should, indeed must, be preserved.

The Olympic ideal encourages chivalrous contest. Humanity needs such heroic illustrations in the education of its youth as a counterpoint to the negative and sometimes degenerative effects of contemporary sport spectacles. Olympic contests with their Coubertin philosophy present a heroic view of humanity that our young and aspiring can identify with. Heroes and heroines renew the faith of these youngsters in the quality of the human spirit. American poet Wallace Stevens warned that

> Unless we believe in the hero,
> What is there to believe?
> Indecisive what, the fellow
> Of what good?

Carl Diem, explaining the apparent disparity between Olympic ideals and contemporary reality, suggested that the Olympic Games were "a regulative force in sport. Like a gyroscope they keep it pointing toward its true [humanizing] goal. This gyroscope, too, may be buffeted by the gale. . . . but there is the test. . . . Sport teaches us that no victory can be won without a battle and the Olympic idea will have to go on battling" to combat the critics—those who would discontinue the Olympic Games because the sporting ideals inherent in the philosophy are too difficult to live (or play) by or are sometimes broken in a world that seems to be less concerned with honor (Diem, *Olympic Idea*, p. 22).

The fact that the Olympics have moved into another century after the 2000 Games in Sydney bears eloquent testimony to their resilience and ability to counter contemporary criticism. They are valued for their idealism and for the moral code they demonstrate in heroic sporting contests.

PROLOGUE: THE ANCIENT GAMES

Robert K. Barney

Throughout the modern world, sport is a cultural value etched indelibly into the lives of most people. Concern for personal health and fitness, dispositions towards particular sports, participation in international competitions, and collective pride in athletic accomplishment are all embodiments of this fact. Deeply ingrained into this worldwide fascination with sports, of course, is an intense interest in the Modern Olympic Games, whether witnessing them as spectators in Olympic venues or from thousands of miles away as television viewers. Of the world's approximately 6 billion people, for instance, well over half were "touched" in some way by the occurrence of the Games of the XXV Olympiad in Barcelona in 1992. And, of some 200 countries in the world today, 170 of them were represented in Barcelona.

The beginning of the historical explanation of this global cultural phenomenon evolves from the experience of the ancient Greek world, the birthplace of much of Western culture. None of the great civilizations that preceded Greece in chronological time served as a model for its development. With the Greeks, something new evolved in the world: an evolution of spirit and initiative that the modern world has come to recognize and respect as having had no equal in the long path of human progress. History has yet to find a greater historian than Thucydides, greater philosophers than Plato and Aristotle, or greater poets than Homer and Pindar. Greece promoted a new world from one that issued dark confusions. The Greece of antiquity, of course, is assigned its place in the ancient world by chronology. In truth, though, it was modern; different from any of its contemporaries. What other culture in its time placed so much value on sport and glorification of the human body, a place and glorification that has taken over two thousand years for contemporary humans to approach once again. The record demonstrates that the Greeks enjoyed sport on a grand scale. They played with a sense of joy, commitment and, above all, a feeling of celebration. And, nowhere in antiquity was such celebration more evident than at Olympia.

Crucial for an understanding of sport and the Olympic Games in antiquity is the ancient Greek context in which they evolved. Early Greek culture was markedly military in character. Keen rivalries and competition for commercial dominance and protection of self-interests often led to confrontation between various factions. War was often the final arbiter of disputes. Beyond doubt, there was a striking connection between military training and sporting competition. The description of one such connection has provided the Western world with two of its earliest and most enduring sport literature commentaries—passages from Homer's *Iliad* and *Odyssey*. A brief discussion of Homer's works, particularly his descriptions of funeral contests, gives us a good idea of sport festival preludes leading to the establishment of the Olympic Games.

According to Greek tradition, sometime near the middle of the thirteenth century a major military episode occurred. Events leading to the war between a confederation of Achaean states and Troy, episodes surrounding the war's ten year struggle, its final outcome, and adventures encountered by warriors returning to their homelands afterwards, all provided grist for enduring oral legend. For some five centuries the tales of the war were transmitted orally. Somewhere around the middle of the eighth century B.C.E. the Greek poet Homer set the tales to recited verse. Homer's grand epic, probably recorded in written form after 700, is read by us today in the form of two poems. One of them, the *Iliad*, focuses on the war itself: its causes, preparations, battles, sieges, and conclusion. The *Odyssey* narrates a great warrior's ten-year, adventure-laden return journey to his island home of Ithaca in the Ionian Sea. In antiquity the *Iliad* and *Odyssey* became the reading and recitation standard for every Greek lad. Almost three thousand years after their composition they are read in various languages by millions of people the world over. They provide the basis for our understanding how athletic competition in great festival context rose in the ancient world.

The events Homer described probably occurred somewhere around 1250 B.C.E. Since Homer composed the poems some five hundred years after the fact, the modern world looked upon them as pure fiction, unsupported as his descriptions were by corroborating archaeological evidence. In the latter part of the nineteenth century, however, the dilettante German archaeologist, Heinrich Schliemann, carried out extensive excavations in Anatolian Turkey near the south shore of the Dardanelles. Not only did Schliemann locate and uncover ruins and priceless artifacts dated to Troy's time, but he also found ample evidence of cultures existing on the site well before and after the demise of Troy itself. The scientific and literary world greeted his finds with elaborate acclaim. Thus, the historical value of Homer's epic poems gained some veracity, enhanced even further by later archaeological discoveries at other early Greek sites.

The twenty-third book of the *Iliad* provides a glorious example of military physical skills transferred to competitive sport. What we really have with Homer is the first description of what correctly can be termed a type of sport tournament, a precursor to the Olympic Games, in which athletes competed for prestige and prizes, where rules governed various events, competitive strategies were pondered, exhortations and argument among spectators noted, the aid of divine spirits cultivated, and both sportsmanlike and unsportsmanlike conduct witnessed. These qualities are all facets of modern sport competition, and yet, they were all present some three thousand years ago. Homer versified the latter stages of the Achaean siege of Troy. The Achaean prince, Patroclus, is slain in battle by the Trojan warrior, Hector. Patroclus's friend and military comrade, the renowned Achilles, seeks revenge against Hector. After slaying Hector, Patroclus's funeral celebration is organized.

One dimension of the funeral celebration is a series of sporting contests. Achilles does not compete; instead, he is the organizer of the contests as well as their patron. He provides valuable prizes to the victors. Most competitors are of noble birth, the sons of kings. They are well trained in military skill, and transfer that skill to the various athletic events. We are told of a chariot race (in great detail), contests in boxing, archery, weight-throwing (discus), javelin, wrestling, running, and, most dangerous of all, a fight in full armor with spears.

In the *Iliad* Homer tells us that a great crowd of spectators gathers on a plain near the sea to witness the funeral games. Diomedes wins the two-horse chariot race, besting four other competitors. Each gains a prize for his efforts, with Diomedes winning the most coveted, a young maiden and an ornate tripod, spoils of war from Achaean victories over Trojan forces. Homer's account of the chariot race, in particular, suggests all sorts of modern sporting parallels. Before the race gets underway, Antilochus of Pylos receives sage strategy and counsel from his father, King Nestor, once a great athlete himself at funeral games held many years earlier. We are told also of an official stationed at the racecourse's turning post to report any attempts at turning short of the mark. Angry verbal confrontations, nearly resulting in blows, occur among the spectators. King Idomeneus of Crete and Aias of Locris are such spectatorial antagonists. Nor were the athletes above devious attempts to achieve victory. Antilochus, displaying rough and unsportsmanlike tactics, forces Menelaus's chariot off the course near the turning point.

The drama and excitement generated by the chariot race extended to the other subsequent events. A brash young prince, Epeios, won at boxing, making good his threat to all rivals "that he would tear their bodies into pieces and break their bones." Epeios decisively whipped the only individual who dared to oppose him—Euryalus of Thebes. In the wrestling match, Odysseus, of whom we shall hear more, drew with Aias of Salamis. They agreed to share the prize, a large tripod cauldron and a girl skilled in handicraft. Aias of Locris, the bellicose spectator previously noted, joined Odysseus and Antilochus in the running race. Aias looked like a sure winner, but he slipped in oxen dung short of the finish post. He recovered to finish second, gaining the runner-up prize—a large bull. Odysseus, the winner, won a much coveted silver bowl from Phoenicia. Antilochus, earlier berated for his unsportsmanlike conduct in the chariot race, finished third and last. This time, he was a model of decorum, complimenting Odysseus on his victory and at the same time pocketing a half talent of gold as a reward for his conduct. The weight throwing contest (it has been called a discus throw by many interpreters) resulted in Polypoites besting Aias of Salamis with a throw of such distance that onlookers were held in a spell of amazement. The iron ingot thrown by Polypoites was given to him as his victory prize. It was touted by Achilles as sufficient enough to provide its owner with enough first-class iron for five years. For the archery contest Achilles ordered a ship's mast planted in the sandy soil with a pigeon tied to its upright end by one foot. For sheer drama the ensuing contest surpassed all. There were two entrants: Teucrus and Meriones. Teucrus shot first. His arrow was near the mark; in fact, it severed the cord that secured the pigeon. The freed pigeon flew away. Meriones snatched the bow from his fellow competitor, hastily strung an arrow, and shot the flying target through the chest. The mortally wounded bird landed at the slayer's feet. In the javelin, or spear throwing contest, Agamemnon, King of Mycenae and commander in chief of the Achaean forces, was matched against Meriones of Crete. Fresh from his dramatic victory in the archery contest,

Meriones was clearly keen for still another triumph. However, Achilles cancelled the contest and accorded the first prize of a flower-decorated cauldron to Agamemnon, it being well known to all that he had no equal in the skill. The disappointed Meriones received a bronze lance. Aias and Diomedes squared off against each other in the armed spear duel, the aim being to penetrate the opponent's defense and draw blood from a lance "touch." Each attacked three times, Aias jabbing at his opponent's shield and Diomedes trying to get above the shield to Aias's throat. Not wishing to see a warrior's death as the outcome of the contest, the onlookers requested Achilles to end the event. Achilles agreed, dividing the prizes between Aias and Diomedes; but Diomedes gained the most cherished article—a large silver-adorned sword of Thracian origin.

Aside from the *Iliad*'s description of athletic sport in Achaean times, Homer's second poem, the *Odyssey*, also contributes insights. In essence, the *Odyssey* is a tale of Odysseus's adventures on the long journey home to his island of Ithaca. Near the latter part of the ordeal Odysseus is shipwrecked and cast up on the shores of a land called Phaeacia. No one is certain exactly where Phaeacia was in the greater Greek world—if it was a real place. Odysseus was taken in by the Phaeacians, provided with food and accommodations, indeed, treated like an honored guest. At a banquet in his honor Odysseus's host arranged for entertainment featuring music, dance and athletic activities, including throwing the discus. The Phaeacians perceived that Odysseus had an athletic body despite the privations encountered at sea for a lengthy period of time. He was invited to try his hand at besting the Phaeacian locals in throwing the weight (discus). Odysseus, having witnessed the Phaecians throwing and knowing that they were far inferior to his own skill, politely refused the invitation, claiming that his long sea voyage home had robbed him of any chance to train. Heckled and ridiculed by one Phaeacian athlete in particular, he took up a discus heavier than any yet thrown in the contest and proceeded to heave it further than all marks. His startling athletic achievement established his noble status among the Phaeacians. Such is the prestige that attends athletic achievement then and now.

Homer's descriptions of early Greek sport deserve further commentary and analysis. How much may the status and context of sport during Homer's actual lifetime have influenced his verse? We shall probably never know the definitive answer to this question. We can only base our judgment on that evidence before us— Greek archaeological recovery wedded to Homer's literary works based on several centuries-old oral tradition. During Homer's lifetime in Greek history, however, sport and athletics were in their infancy when compared to a century or two later. The record of what in time became known as the ancient Olympic festival had barely evolved by Homer's time. This gives us the idea that perhaps oral tradition was of greater consequence in shaping Homer's narrative than was the actual world about him in the eighth century B.C.E. Most certainly, we know that a Greek world existed during the time about which Homer wrote, a world in which people were bonded by strong cultural commonalities. Among the most evident of these were a common religious worship of anthropomorphic gods and goddesses, an early Greek language, and an appreciation for and practice of sport in ceremonial, celebration, recreation, and competition context. Competitive sporting activities were largely associated with contests featuring basic military expertise of the times— running, throwing, hand-to-hand combat, chariot driving, and archery.

We shall probably never know whether or not the common Greek man sported. Homer's tales involve mostly aristocratic warriors—kings and the sons of kings.

Such a privileged individual was described in the Greek language as *agathos*, a man trained for war and therefore brave. *Agathos* contrasted to *kakos*, an ordinary man, untrained and therefore cowardly and bad. A stronger derivative of the term *agathos* was *agathos ex agathon*, brave among the brave. A further extension was *aristos*, high-born. The qualities of *agathos* and *aristos* can be summed up in the word *arete*, a term Homer used for qualities inherent in a warrior—strength, skill, bravery, and heroism. It was the responsibility of a father to see to it that his sons developed in such a way as to strive for *arete*, to become heroic and godlike and, in time, to assume a leadership role in society. Although we have no exact counterpart of the word *arete*, we can be satisfied with "excellence." Thus, a quest for excellence in ancient times was the responsibility of all leaders in society. Several of Homer's warriors were personifications: Achilles and Odysseus, for example. Many fell far short of the ideal. But it is the pursuit of the ideal that translates into progress and achievement, not particularly one's attainment of the goal. The quest for excellence in all things military, of course, overlapped into other areas of human endeavor—wisdom, intelligence, eloquence. The quest for athletic excellence in competition against others is seeded in the ideology of *arete*.

THE ANCIENT OLYMPIC GAMES

A legitimate place from which to commence an investigation of Greek athletics and the evolution of the ancient Olympic Games is the religious sanctuary called Olympia. The ancient site of Olympia was located in the northwest Peloponnese in the district presided over by the town of Elis. Archaeological evidence demonstrates that Olympia was inhabited during Achaean times. Achaean cult objects devoted to nature, fertility, and vegetation gods have been found there. When the Achaeans' successors (later Greeks, sometimes called Dorians) settled on the Peloponnese, the site of Olympia claimed their attention as a religious sanctuary where both old Achaean gods and new Dorian deities were worshipped. In time, with the ascendance of the Olympian family in Greek religion, Zeus became the chief figure worshipped at Olympia. We simply will never know for sure what type of athletic activities, if any, might have been celebrated at Olympia as part of early Dorian religious sacrifice and ceremony.

History, however, has assigned the date 776 B.C.E. as the first record of athletic activity at Olympia. The date is etched into the record because the ancient Olympic victor list commences from that year. Surely athletic activities in keeping with older traditions were carried out at the site long before 776, indeed, just as archaeological evidence tells us that religious activity definitely occurred at Olympia well before 776. Based on ancient theories, various points of view exist that attempt to explain the rejuvenation of athletics as part of the religious festival at Olympia. In consistent fashion, they point to athletics being closely connected with religious events. For instance, Pindar (518–446 B.C.E.) stated that the Olympic Games originated during the late Achaean period honoring the victory of the god Heracles over King Augeas of Elis. Thus, the sanctuary of Olympia originally may have been a celebration site for Heracles, with Zeus later evolving in influence following the rise of Dorian prominence. Pindar's view was supported in later times by the noted Greek scholars Lysias and Aristotle. The Roman poet Strabo (63 B.C.E.–21 C.E.) stated that the original Olympic religious festival evolved from the initiative of the Elean citizen, Oxylus, in celebration of his peoples' return to Elis after being forced by severe drought conditions to move westward to Aetolia for a period. Strabo's notation gives an 1104 B.C.E. date. An explanation rendered by the historian Phlegon of Tralles, writing in 138 C.E., recounts that Iphitus of Elis, Lycurgus of Sparta, and Cleisthenes of Pisa, all Dorians, visited the great oracle at Delphi to gain an answer for purging their lands of famine and pestilence. The word conveyed to them was that Zeus was angry because the one-time athletic dimension of the religious celebrations at Olympia had ceased. A revival of athletics was said to have taken place in order to please Father Zeus and restore good times.

Two anecdotal tales are perhaps of less consequence in explaining the origin of athletics at Olympia but, nevertheless, form an interesting aside. One such tale points to the establishment of athletic and religious festivals at Olympia in commemoration of the Olympian victory over the rival Titans. The supreme Olympian God, Zeus, vied with his father, Cronus, sovereign leader of the Titans. The Olympians triumphed. Zeus bade that the citizens of the Elean district establish a religious festival in his honor. Zeus is said to have commemorated his father's memory by naming a small mountain near the sanctuary site after him. The "Hill of Kronus" may be viewed today, abutting the northeast boundary of the sanctuary's archaeological remains. The other anecdotal story etched in mythology alludes to an earlier time, two or three generations before the Achaean siege of Troy. King Oenomaus of Pisa was the proud father of a lovely daughter. He offered the young lady's hand in marriage to the first suitor to escape with her in his chariot. The story goes that various young men accepted the challenge, but all were pursued and killed by Oenomaus and his men, that is, until the hero Pelops (after whom the Peloponnese is named) secretly tampered with his prospective father-in-law's chariot, causing a wheel to come off during the chase. The mishap resulted in the King's death and his daughter, Hippodamia, was claimed by Pelops as his bride. Pelops, the myth tells us, celebrated his victory and marriage with a festival, of which a chariot race was one celebratory function. Some ancient interpreters of the myth have changed the story to relate that a festival with chariot racing was established upon Pelops's death, thus making such an occasion a funeral event, akin to that for Patroclus described by Homer in the *Iliad*.

Regardless of which version is closest to the mark, we know that a quadrennial religious celebration (perhaps originally celebrated every eight years) and attendant competitive sporting events evolved at Olympia. The festival at Olympia, called the Olympic Games, was the oldest, most enduring athletic festival in the ancient Greek world. It was also the most conservative and resistant to change. As an athletic festival it had no peer, being by far the most prestigious. Finally, the athletic affairs at Olympia became models for the rise of other athletic festivals.

The first recorded victor at the ancient Olympic Games was apparently a simple cook, an Elean by the name of Koroebus. The event was a one-length sprint of the racecourse, which in earlier times may have been laid out between two altars. The event became known as the stadium run (*stade*). For over 50 years (12 succeeding Olympiads) the *stade* was the sole athletic event. By 676 B.C.E., a set program of events at Olympia had evolved. Besides the *stade*, it included the *diaulos* (two lengths of the running course), *dolichos* (multiple lengths of the running course), wrestling, boxing, pankration, pentathlon, and chariot racing. Athletic events for boys were introduced in 632. At various times experimentation with other forms of events occurred, including a race in armor and equestrian contests for foals (colts) and mule carts. For almost a thousand years Olympia's athletic program stood in place, the supreme model for others to emulate.

In its early years the Olympic festival was attended by athletes residing solely on the Peloponnese, attesting to the festival's local character at its outset. Indeed, we do not learn of an Olympic victor from outside the Peloponnese until 720, when Orsippos of Megara won the *stade*. In 696 we note an Athenian victor in the stadium run, the first in a long list of Olympic victors from Greece's most glorious city. By the early part of the sixth century the Olympic victor list abounds with winners from Greek colony city-states located across the entire Mediterranean basin. Joining the perennial Peloponnesian athletic powers Sparta, Elis, and Messene, are Thessaly and Larisa in the north; Kroton and Syracuse in Italy; Sicily, Rhodes, Crete, and Mytilene in the Aegean; Miletos, Ephesus, Pergamon and Halicarnassus in Anatolia; and Alexandria in Egypt.

Other religious sanctuaries and city-states copied Olympia's athletics program, modifying the slate of events to suit their needs and desires. A number of these deserve our attention. Delphi, home of Apollo, the virtuous son of Zeus, had long been a religious sanctuary of unrivalled importance in the Greek world. Delphi commenced an athletic program in about 586. Delphi's Pythian Festival, named after Apollo's feat of killing a menacing python during mythological times, occurred once every four years, two years before and two years after each Olympic festival. The Isthmian Games, celebrating Poseidon (Zeus's brother, and god of the sea), evolved in 582. A festival at Nemea, a few kilometers from the ancient Achaean city of Mycenae, was still another athletic/religious event of importance. Originating in 573, the Nemean festival honored Zeus, even though its earliest lineage as a religious site can be traced to another of Heracles's victories in Greek myth, this time over a livestock-ravaging lion. Both the Nemean and Isthmian festivals were held every other year, the Nemean in the odd-numbered years, and the Isthmian in the even. The four great festivals—Olympian, Pythian, Nemean, and Isthmian—formed what became known as the Pan-Hellenic Crown Games. To all Greeks they were the most important festivals. To win at any was a cause for great celebration by an athlete's city-state, as well as by the athlete himself, for he most certainly could look forward to commensurate enrichment for his efforts. And, to win at Olympia was the most rewarding of all.

The Pan-Hellenic Festivals were certainly not the only athletic meetings in the Greek world. Athens organized one of the most flamboyant civic athletic festivals anywhere in ancient Greece. Aside from religious sacrifice surrounding the celebration of her patron goddess, Athena, the Pan-Athenaic Festival featured religious pomp and pageantry as well as spirited athletic competition. There were various categories of athletic events: ones for non-Athenian athletes, for Athenian male adults, for military cadets, and for boys. Prizes at the Athenian games were of significant value. We shall hear more about them later. By the middle of the fifth century other athletic festivals of note had evolved in Greece proper. On the Peloponnese alone, athletic meetings were organized at Tegea, Argos, Corinth, Epidaurus, Sicyon, Pellene, Pheneus, Clitor, and Parrhesia, and in central Greece at Plataea, Eleusis, and Megara. In Africa, Cyrene hosted games, and in Italy, Kroton. On the Aegean Islands of Delos and Rhodes, prestigious festivals were held regularly. Later, under Alexander's influence, the penchant for organizing and staging athletic festivals was multiplied in Greek communities located in Asia Minor.

Greek athletes were not unlike their modern counterparts. They trained ardu-ously, benefitted from sports trainers and coaches, were adored by an admiring public, and more often than not were rewarded handsomely for their efforts. Olympic athletes had to be citizens of pure Greek parentage, although this restric-tion may well have been relaxed in later times when the Greek world spread to include a conglomerate of ethnic strains. A participant at Olympia must have trained under local supervision for a period of almost a year. One month before the Olympic festival commenced prospective competitors presented themselves to a council of judges (*Hellanodicae*), who judged and supervised their final preparations. If any were found to be unworthy of the Olympic tradition of athletic excellence, they were sent away. Only the most deserving vied at Olympia.

An athlete's training was carried out in a *gymnasium*, or, if he specialized in com-bat events, in a *palaestra*. He was supervised by a cadre of overseers including a coach (*gymnastes*), anointers, masseurs, and other support staff. Runners ran and practiced starts and turns around a post. Wrestlers, boxers, and pankratiasts drilled on various techniques of offensive and defensive maneuvers and engaged in weight training to build strength and body mass. Pentathletes practised the subdisciplines of their events—sprinting, jumping, throwing the discus and javelin, and wrestling. Equestrian activities were not seen in the *gymnasium*. Such events, especially char-iot racing, remained the province of the wealthy until well after athletics in ancient Greece had become democratized to include participants from all strata of life. The training was intensive, prolonged, and specialized. In this regard, as well as in the matters of prize consideration and social prestige, there is little to distinguish the ancient Greek athlete from today's professional or quasi-professional athlete.

Most athletic/religious festivals were carried out over a period of several days. We know that at Olympia the events were held during a five-day period. The first day and a portion of the last were given over to religious sacrifice and ceremony. The remaining time focused on athletic competition and celebration of individual sporting achievement.

The remains of ancient Greek athletic stadiums tell us that spectators by the thousands viewed the agonistic struggles of ancient athletes. At Olympia some 40,000 may have gathered to worship and spectate. Olympia featured one of the simplest, most unadorned stadiums in the Greek world; individuals simply arranged themselves on the grassy slopes of artificially-constructed embankments. At Delphi the onlookers at the athletic events were about 7,000 in number. Unlike at Olympia, however, they sat on beautifully constructed tiers of stone seats built in Roman times. The grandest stadium anywhere in the ancient Greek world is at Aphrodisias, high in the mountains of Anatolian Turkey. That magnificent stadium accommodated over 80,000. Following their conquest of Greece, the Romans used one end of the Aphrodisias stadium as an amphitheater in which to stage activities much more violent than Greek athletics.

Spectators journeying to Olympia to pay homage to Zeus and to witness supreme athletic endeavor were protected by a so-called Olympic Truce, which guaranteed their passage against harm from warring Greek factions and other types of harassment, including bandits. Violators of the truce, if apprehended, were fined heavily. There was more to the festival than religious and sporting activity. The assembly of large numbers of Greeks, many of them powerful and influential, pro-vided opportunities for all sorts of sociopolitical action. Military and commercial agreements might be struck, one's political and philosophical views on a number of subjects voiced, and proficiency displayed in Greek cultural endeavors—art, public speaking, and music. Indeed, the greatest festivals in antiquity were places where people came not only to see, but also to be seen. Olympia, of course, was the most important forum for these kinds of activities. The spectator's lot was not always comfortable. Spectators most often had to sleep in rustic bivouac fashion, subsisting on those supplies brought with them or purchased from vendors nearby. Sports onlookers sat for hours under the hot sun, slapping and fanning at innumerable insects, and listening to or being involved in the types of arguments and confrontations that invariably arise among zealous sports fans. We noted one such incident in Homer's account. To watch competitions between local athletes at local festivals was one thing; to watch confrontations between the best athletes drawn from all over the Greek world was quite another experience. Olympia held the greatest attraction for both athlete and spectator.

Homer's description of the prizes bestowed on athletes at the funeral games tells us that they were of significant utilitarian value. Without exception Achilles's prizes prompted intense competition. There is enough evidence to suggest that the value of competitive prizes grew in intensity as sport in ancient Greek society became more institutionalized. True, we hear of the simple olive wreath being given to the victor of events held at Olympia, a laurel wreath at Delphi, pine at Isthmia, and celery at Nemea, but these were merely symbolic awards. What might be bestowed on the victorious athlete when he returned home was certainly more than the term symbolic connotes. In fact, the result was most often a grand expansion of the tradition related by Homer. We have many examples to guide our understanding on this point. Early in the sixth century, the Athenian lawmaker Solon decreed that Athenian victors at the Isthmian Games receive 100 drachmas from the public treasury. More grandly compensated, a victory at Olympia was worth 500 drachmas. The annual wage of an ordinary seaman in the employ of the Athenian merchant fleet was at that time 100 drachmas. We hear also of such gratuities to the victorious athlete as immunity from paying taxes, honored seats at civic and religious functions, free repasts at the civic messes, glorious statues struck in his honor, poetry composed, and orations delivered on his behalf. At Aphrodisias, in the first century A.D., a prize money list for specific athletic events has survived. The inscription tells us that the winner of the pentathlon garnered a prize of 500 dinar, 750 dinar for the *dolichos*, 1,000 for the *diaulos*, 1,250 for the *stade*, 2,000 each for boxing and wrestling, and 3,000 for the brutal pankration. As the wage of a common laborer at the time was approximately one dinar per day, one can readily see the wisdom of pursuing athletics as a profession. The inscription tells us something else also: the tamer, less violent events were the least rewarded; the more violent ones commanded huge purses. This phenomenon was most probably a reflection of Roman influence in Greek culture.

On the subject of athletic prizes in ancient Greece, no record is perhaps as graphic as that rendered by an Athenian inscription from the first half of the fourth century B.C.E. The message from the inscription is irrefutable. First-place winners in various athletic events of the great Athenian civic festival, the Pan-Athenean, were awarded prizes in the form of amphoras of olive oil. Both oil and amphora were of significant value in the Athenian economy. The amphoras were large, beautifully executed, and exquisitely painted with sporting motifs. The following table underscores in graphic terms the attractiveness of pursuing athletics as a profession in one's physically active years. (The equivalencies in earning power have been suggested by David Young.)

Table 1
Pan-Athenaic Prizes in the Classical Period

		PRIZE IN AMPHORAS OF OIL	DRACHMA VALUE (12 drachmas per amphora)	NUMBER OF DAYS WAGES at 1.417 DRACHMA PER DAY (skilled)	NUMBER OF YEARS FULL EMPLOYMENT (at 30 days)
STADE					
men	first	100	1,200	847	2.82
	second	20	240	169	.56
youths	first	60	720	508	1.69
	second	12	144	102	.34
boys	first	50	600	423	1.41
	second	10	120	85	.28
PENTATHLON					
men	first	60	720	508	1.69
	second	12	144	102	.34
youths	first	40	480	339	1.13
	second	8	96	68	.23
boys	first	30	360	254	.85
	second	6	72	51	.17
WRESTLING					
men	first	60	720	508	1.69
	second	12	144	102	.34
youths	first	40	480	339	1.13
	second	8	96	68	.23
boys	first	30	360	254	.85
	second	6	72	51	.17
BOXING					
men	first	60	720	508	1.69
	second	12	144	102	.34
youths	first	40	480	339	1.13
	second	8	96	68	.23
boys	first	30	360	254	.85
	second	6	72	51	.17
PANKRATION					
men	first	80	960	678	2.26
	second	16	192	136	.45
youths	first	50	600	423	1.41
	second	10	120	85	.28
boys	first	40	480	339	1.13
	second	8	96	68	.26
EQUESTRIAN EVENTS Chariot race					
	first	140	1,680	1,186	3.95
	second	40	480	339	1.13

It would appear that remuneration for victories at athletic festivals increased commensurately with the increase of wealth across the wide sphere of Greek influence in the Mediterranean area. Compensation for athletic success some 2,000 years ago and earlier, and that noted today, together with the translation of such earnings to buying power then and now, appear to reflect little difference. This has not, in general, been the message passed to us by the earliest scholars of sport in Greek antiquity. There is much to be admired and be thankful for in the writings of Gardiner, Harris, and other post-Victorian British investigators, but their consensus that Greek athletes in antiquity were the counterpart of virtuous English amateurs of the late nineteenth and early twentieth centuries is off target. Ancient Greek athletes were motivated by the same forces that stimulate gifted, higher-level athletes of today—recognition, prestige, status and, above all, the chance for a big payday.

Even though Homer described wrestlers in the *Iliad* as athletes wearing loincloth girdles, a startling characteristic of later Greek culture was the fact that athletic exercise was carried out in the nude. One theory is that this phenomenon evolved from attempts by early Greek artists to reflect legendary tales in graphic perspective; heroic subjects were often presented in naked form. The mythological personality most favored for nude presentation was Heracles. In mythology Heracles alone was allowed to appear before Zeus and the other gods in nude fashion. Because of his image as a warrior-athlete, Heracles had an early association with Olympia. Heracles became a cult symbol for athletes and physical exercisers alike, all of whom trained and competed in the nude, just as they envisioned their patron.

The events that formed the core of the athletic competitions were different in many ways from what we know of the same types of exercises in modern context. On the other hand there are innumerable similarities. Modern Greeks in the late nineteenth century, in part, used knowledge of ancient competitions to select and frame rules for some of the contests in the first Modern Olympics held in Athens in 1896.

The *stade* run in ancient times, a length of the stadium sprint, needs little description. Competitors, crouched slightly at the start with toes of each foot resting in starting grooves cut in stone sills arranged across the racecourse, ran in a straight line to the end of the stadium (usually about 200 yards). The *diaulos* (the equivalent of the modern 400 meters) was a bit different. A turn had to be made at the far end of the stadium, necessitating a return to the starting line. The start was the same as in the *stade*. Our best evidence for the turn maneuver suggests that all runners turned around a central turning post in a counterclockwise direction. Negotiation of the turn made for some tricky navigation. The *dolichos* was a long-distance running event, perhaps a race of between 1,500 and 3,000 meters. Runners turned around central turning posts situated at each end of the stadium. The *dolichos*'s greater distance probably made for a more strung-out field of competitors; thus excitement at the turns was probably diminished as the race progressed because of less crowded conditions. From time to time other types of running races occurred also, including the race in armor and torch races. In the race in armor a competitor wore a helmet and carried a shield; at times he wore greaves (leg guards). The length of the race was most often a *diaulos*, but at Nemea it was a double *diaulos*. At Plataea, in commemoration of the Greek victory over the Persians at Marathon, a battle in which Plataeans were participants, the race in armor was 15 *stades* in length, well over one and one-half miles. The torch races, when held, were probably associated with religious ritual. We observe sixth and fifth century vase paintings displaying youthful runners passing the torch to a teammate, perhaps an ancient forerunner of the relay race.

The combative events had particular appeal to most spectators; tests of strength and fortitude under trying circumstances usually do. Wrestling involved trying to throw one's opponent to the ground. It appears to have been a grappling exercise, carried on in upright fashion, similar to modern Greco-Roman wrestling. Interpreters have suggested that a three-out-of-five fall format comprised a match. Vase painting wrestling scenes attest that the ancients employed most of the maneuvers seen in modern forms of wrestling. The pankration was an event often misinterpreted by contemporary writers to be wrestling or boxing. It was a particularly brutal exercise, exhibiting elements of both boxing and wrestling. Unlike boxers, however, pankratiasts did not wear boxing thongs on their fists. Much of the match featured grappling on the ground, such as in modern freestyle wrestling. The brutal aspects of the pankration related to the fact that the rules permitted such violent tactics as throat holds and kicking actions, and the bending of fingers, arms and legs until they were broken or badly injured. The aim of the pankratiast was to render his opponent unconscious or reduce him to such a state that he voluntarily gave up. The submissive signal of the defeated individual was an upheld arm with extended index finger. Only gouging of the eyes and biting appeared to be prohibited by the referee who supervised the event from close perspective. Violators of the rules were at times flogged by the official to encourage a halt to such conduct. Boxing was simpler. Pugilists wore leather thongs for protection of their hands. Over the centuries the "glove" became more sophisticated in form, finally covering the hand completely. The gloves' later character resulted in a potentially lethal, punishment-inflicting item rather than one used solely for protection. There were neither rounds nor weight classifications. Opponents fought until one was knocked out, rendered incapable of continuing, or voluntarily gave up. Competitors in wrestling, pankration, and boxing progressed through a series of elimination bouts until two athletes remained, each then vying in a final match for the symbolic victory wreath and the rewards that were conferred on him at a later time.

The pentathlon event consisted of five components. Three of them occurred only in the pentathlon. Called the "triad" disciplines, they were the jump, hurling the discus, and the javelin throw. The remaining two events were the *stade* run and wrestling. Greeks were of different opinions on the stature of the pentathlon. One school of thought, represented by Aristotle's opinion, looked upon the pentathlon as the supreme example of athletic ability in that it displayed versatility and harmony. On the other hand, Plato and those who agreed with him thought the event to be one for "second raters," athletes who were not good enough to win in any of the other events on the program. The evidence clearly supports Plato's contention. In the almost one thousand years of recorded ancient Olympic Games history, not once is it noted that a Greek won both the pentathlon and another event as well in the same festival. In fact, the pentathlon event itself was conspicuously absent from the Olympic victor lists as early as the late Hellenistic Period. Each competitor in the discus and javelin threw from a *balbis,* an open-ended rectangular area similar to the modern javelin throwing area. Throws were measured for distance. We do not know how many tries athletes were allowed. The javelin was thrown with the aid of an *ankule,* a thong looped around the shaft near the center of gravity, which added a slinging action to the spear. The pentathlon jump has prompted argument among scholars of Greek athletic events, but the thesis that appears to best satisfy the ancient evidence supports a multiple jumping exercise of five successive leaps along the jumping pit (*skamma*). We know that small weights (between 3 and 10 pounds), called *halteres*, were gripped in both hands of the jumper throughout the exercise. Scholars believe that the swinging action of the *halteres* added distance to the jump over what might be accomplished if they were not used. We do not know how many tries a pentathlete jumper received, nor what was actually required to win the overall event. The best analysis appears to support a notion that an athlete had to win three of the subdisciplines in order to be declared the champion. The triad events were first (discus, jump, and javelin), followed by the *stade*. Wrestling, if necessary, was last. If one competitor won all of the triad events, the pentathlon was ended, he having won the necessary three subevents. If the results of the triad event competitions produced two or three different winners, then those competitors proceeded to run and wrestle in order to determine a pentathlon champion.

The remaining events of the athletic festival's program were equestrian in nature. Of these chariot racing was by far the most important. Chariot racing was usually the province of the aristocratic faction of Greek society. They alone owned the means to support the breeding, care, and training of animals, as well as the maintenance of drivers. At times a consortium of less wealthy individuals sponsored chariot teams. Most teams had four horses. The prize and distinction for winning always went to the owner, never the driver, who was usually a simple domestic groomsman serving in the aristocrat's stable. Kings and tyrants were known to celebrate chariot victories by striking coins with racing scenes stamped on them. Chariot racing occurred over a course laid out across level ground. Turning barriers were installed at each end of the racing venue. At Olympia the racecourse was situated on the floodplain of the Alpheus River.

Of absorbing interest to contemporary sports fans are the exploits of famous Olympic athletes: Jim Thorpe, Paavo Nurmi, Jesse Owens, Wilma Rudolph, and Carl Lewis, for example. Many of the most notable are etched in modern history as sport heroes, celebrated in literature, sports halls of fame, indeed, in oral tradition. Ancient Greece was no different. Sport heroes abounded. We have previously noted those about whom Homer wrote. There were many others of later Greek times. The greatest in legend and deed was Milon of Kroton. Kroton, located in southern Italy, became noted in the late sixth and early fifth centuries for the Olympic achievements of its athletes. Milon was a wrestler. As a boy he won at Olympia in 540 B.C.E.; as an adult he captured five Olympic wrestling crowns (532, 528, 524, 520, and 516). He was denied a seventh Olympic crown in 512, being defeated by his disciple, the Kroton wrestler Timasitheos, a youth of 28. Added to Milon's wrestling feats at Olympia were his 7 titles won at Delphi, 9 at Nemea, and 10 at Isthmia. Six times Milon was *periodonikes*, winner of crowns at Olympia, Delphi, Nemea, and Isthmia in the period of one Olympiad (four years). Leonidas of Rhodes was antiquity's most renowned sprinter and middle-distance runner. In the Olympic Games of 164 he won three crowns—*stade*, *diaulos*, and race in armor. In 160 and 156 he duplicated the feat. In 152, at age 36, Leonidas was accorded heroic status in Rhodes for once again capturing his favorite "triple." Leonidas finished his career with 12 Olympic crowns, the most in history, ancient or modern.

Of a host of other noted athletes and their achievements in ancient Greek sport, Theagenes of Thasos deserves mention. He first triumphed in boxing at Olympia in 480; then he turned his attention to the pankration, which he won at the Games of 476. These two feats in themselves do not tell the whole story about Theagenes. Theagenes became what modern history would call the consummate professional athlete, touring the Greek world for years participating in the sporting festivals of various cities. When he finally retired he had won some 1,300 victories, 9 of them the coveted crown at Nemea, 10 at Isthmia, and several more at Delphi. Except for one, all were gained in the pankration or boxing events. Competing at games held in Phthia, the home of Homer's Achilles, he entered the *dolichos*, motivated by a desire to gain victory in a footrace held in the homeland of the swiftest of the most ancient of athletic heroes. His quest was achieved. After Theagenes's death Thasos erected a huge statue in his honor; he became embossed in Thacian legend.

Finally, we should note perhaps the noblest athletic hero in ancient history—Diagoras, the Rhodian boxer. Diagoras was descended from royal lineage. His great-grandfather was Damagetos, King of Ialysos. A huge man for his time (well over six feet), he owned "a fine face, proud step, and statuesque stance." Diagoras was called *euthymaches* (fair fighter) because he never stepped aside, stooped, or shied away from an opponent. He fought with dignity, pride, and sportsmanlike bearing, qualities that ancient Greeks appreciated then as we revere them now. Diagoras won the boxing at Olympia in 464, gained two Nemean and four Isthmian crowns, and won competitions several times at games held on the Greek mainland and on various Aegean islands. His eldest son, Damagetos, won the Olympic pankration in 452 and 448; his second eldest son, Akousilaos, the boxing in 448. One can imagine Diagoras's joy and pride at witnessing both his oldest sons being crowned victors at Olympia in 448. Legend has it that his sons presented their father with their crowns and carried him on their shoulders out from among the spectators onto the running course. An ovation of recognition and adoration erupted. Issuing from the spectators came the shouted voice of a Spartan: "Die now, Diagoras, there is nothing left for you but to ascend to Olympos." We are told that Diagoras heard the voice, and from the shoulders of his sons, bent his wreath-crowned head, and breathed his last. If the legend of Diagoras's demise is true then he was deprived of perhaps even greater joy: living to witness three consecutive Olympic pankration titles won by his youngest son, Doreius, in 432, 428 and 424. Diagoras's sports achievement record, and those of his sons, are authenticated. The particulars of his death may or may not have occurred. Nevertheless, sport legends in ancient Greece were embellished with as many glorifying twists as locker-room tales are today. A large bronze statue of Diagoras borne aloft on the shoulders of his two sons can be viewed today on the grounds of the International Olympic Academy adjacent to the ancient stadium of Olympia where the legendary occurrence was supposedly witnessed.

To this point, the narrative has been void of remarks about women in the sphere of sport, exercise, and the body in ancient Greece. In our modern world, of course, vigorous participation in all types of sport at all levels by women is a natural and expected phenomenon. Female competitions at the Modern Olympic Games, for instance, form one of the most interesting and exciting dimensions of the entire festival. A parallel state of affairs was certainly not the case in antiquity. Aside from Spartan society (which will be discussed shortly), women were excluded from the sporting and body exercise venues of males. In general, women did not exercise and train for athletics; neither did they spectate. During the great religious and athletic celebrations for Zeus, women were not permitted in the vicinity of Olympia.

A possible explanation for women not being allowed to participate in male athletic festivals was that many such festivals, particularly at Olympia, were traditionally linked to a celebration of Heracles. Heracles, of course, was associated with war and sporting vigor. Female presence at an athletic site was felt to diminish the power and strength necessary to triumph. The evidence of antiquity emphatically supports this view. Women attended various religious festivals along with men, but not those that were associated with Heracles and sport performance. One religious festival reserved exclusively for girls was the Heraia, which celebrated the Goddess Hera, sister and wife of Zeus. The Heraia festival was held at the same Olympia sanctuary site where men celebrated games for Zeus. The temple of Hera within the sanctuary has been dated an earlier structure than the more massive and dominating Temple of Zeus. At the Heraia there was one exhibition of athleticism, a single running race for unmarried girls. A final comment on this subject: women pursued *arete*. Instead of glory and wealth from war and sport, a woman's prescription for *arete* involved domestic affairs—how well children were raised, how well household staff was managed, how well a husband was cared for, in effect, the maintenance of the home and family environment. We today are not too far removed from a time when a woman's role in life was primarily the same as in antiquity. Many moderns, men and women alike, might wince at this observation; but women in antiquity would not do so. The female role was well defined, as was the male's. Women pursued their goals with as much zeal, determination, and quest for excellence as did men.

EPILOGUE

Sport, indeed the Olympic Games, continued to be present throughout the Greek world until the time of Christ and much later. Although we have noted that Homer and Pindar were outstanding examples of Greeks who glorified sport in the 300 year period between 750 and 450, Greek writers of later periods, although favorably disposed to the value of physical education and physical exercise, often rendered severe criticisms against the specialization and brutality of athletes, as well as the status they were accorded in society. Euripedes, noted as an eternal pessimist, viewed athletes as "a worthless race." Xenophanes not only railed against the athlete's lofty social position, but stated that the recompense he received was out of keeping with his accomplishments. The noted sixth century Ionian philosopher also enunciated that "wisdom is better than the strength of men and horses." Aesop stated that there was "no glory in defeating a weaker opponent, skill is the real measurement." Plato and Aristotle were also vigorous critics of the specialization of athletes, a phenomenon that went hand in hand with a noted rise in professionalism. Plato scorned athletics as producing "hardness and savagery, violence and disharmony." In the same vein Aristotle decried the one-sidedness of the overtrained and specialized, a characteristic in opposition to pursuing a versatile, liberally oriented life.

Despite growing criticism of athletics and athletes emanating from the fourth century on, sport festivals continued to have wide popular appeal throughout the Greek world. Sport tournaments and festivals proliferated, finding new glorification in the magnified Greek empire in the Middle East established by Alexander in the second half of the fourth century.

By the time of Christ, several factors had become apparent in the slow erosion of Greek athletics and the Ancient Olympic Games. Prominent among them was the influence of Rome. Rome had reduced Greece to an occupied province by the middle of the second century. The Roman penchant for cruel and barbarous dimensions of sport, reflected in wild beast fights and human gladiatorial combat, began to filter into the Greek consciousness. Track and field activities, the foundation of ancient Greek festivals, declined in favor of violent, combative events of Roman character.

In general the portrait of Greece during the Roman era of influence was one that exhibited a greater spectatorial phenomenon and less energetic physical exercise. The hardy physical exercises of the *gymnasium* were replaced at times by the rise of still another Roman institution—luxurious and lengthy bathing. In effect, a sweeping sedentarianism developed, weakening a human race that was once the epitome of physical action.

Aside from the effect of the aforementioned phenomena on the decline of sport in the world of Ancient Greece, the most damaging factor, by far, was the rise of Christianity. Christianity offered hopes and dreams for something better than the degradation characteristic of later Roman civilization. Actions by some Christian leaders were initiatives aimed at reducing the trappings of Greek and Roman paganism. In time, Greek and Roman temples were razed. Cathedrals and places of Christian worship rose on the very foundations of the ancient temples of Zeus, Apollo, Poseidon, and the other gods and goddesses of antiquity. Sport, associated from its very beginning with the gods of antiquity, was one such pagan trapping that received its share of scrutiny and derision from early Christians. Over a period of some 400 years after the birth of Christ, the growth and influence of Christianity took its toll. What once had been a vast Greek domain in the Mediterranean and Middle East, succeeded in time by Roman conquest and cultural influence, slowly became Christianized. By the late fourth century C.E., the Christian envelopment was complete. The ancient festival at Olympia had also ceased. Even though the last recorded event at Olympia occurred in 369, the victory lists are silent of any activity from 281 to 365. The Christian emperor Theodosius I issued a decree in 393, which abolished in word what had in fact disappeared in deed over a century before—the ancient Olympic Games, supreme emblem of ancient paganism.

From time to time athletic games continued to be held in sporadic fashion in Greek cities of the eastern Mediterranean world, faint reminders of once glorious times for sport. In increasingly severe measures, Christian emperors sought to eradicate them from cultural memory. In general, attempts of the new religion to disassociate itself completely from most pagan reminders were successful.

Five hundred years after Christ, sport in the ancient Greek world had reached the end of a life cycle. The life cycle's birth and infant stage can be seen in the sporting culture of the Achaeans, about which Homer rhapsodized. The formative adolescent, maturing, and productive years were reflected in the glory of Greece's Classical and Hellenistic Ages. Finally, sport reached its twilight years, a withering period featured by erosion of interest, participation, and celebration. Yet sport in ancient Greece never experienced mortal death. Like our own genealogical process, which sees the essence of us passed on to our children and grandchildren, so, too, was the cultural legacy of sport and the Olympic Games in ancient Greece passed to future generations. Inspiration from that legacy has provided much of the initiative that brought about the modern Olympic Movement. It gave rise to a thriving, contemporary fitness ethic and germinated body concepts that today have important overtones for healthy lifestyles geared to movement rather than sedentarianism. This cultural phenomenon began with the ancient Greeks. Consequently, we should study their history with dedication and appreciation. Perhaps then, we will become more in tune with the message inscribed above the entrance to the ancient temple of Apollo at Delphi, which all Greeks noted as they entered to worship: "Know thyself."

BIBLIOGRAPHICAL ESSAY

A study of sport and the Olympic Games in antiquity has to begin with an examination of the literary comment made by the ancient Greeks themselves. In this regard, Homer's *Iliad* and *Odyssey* are fundamental. The works of Herodotus, Philostratus, Thucydides, and Plutarch, among others, provide important commentary from the context of being viewed as original sources. For the best of modern surveys of ancient sources on the history of Greek athletics and the ancient Olympic Games, the reader is referred to the following: Nigel B. Crowther, "Studies in Greek Athletics," *Classical World* 78, 79 (1985); Stephen G. Miller, *Arete: Ancient Writers, Papyri, and Inscriptions on the History and Ideals of Greek Athletics and Games* (Chicago, 1979); and Rachel Sargent Robinson, *Sources for the History of Greek Athletics* (Cincinnati, 1955). For the best scholarly surveys of sport and physical education in Greek antiquity, see the following: Clarence A. Forbes, *Greek Physical Education* (New York, 1929); E. Norman Gardiner, *Greek Athletic Sports and Festivals* (London, 1910); Donald G. Kyle, "Directions in Ancient Sport History," *Journal of Sport History* (Spring 1983); Vera Olivova, *Sports and Games in the Ancient World* (London, 1984); Thomas F. Scanlon, "The Ecumenical Olympics: The Games in the Roman Era," in *The Olympic Games in Transition* (Champaign, IL, 1988); Waldo Sweet, *Sport and Recreation in Ancient Greece* (New York, 1987); Nicholaos Yalouris, *The Eternal Olympics* (New York, 1976); W. Rushke (ed.), *Archaeology of the Olympics* (Madison, WI, 1988); and M. I. Finley and H. W. Pleket, *The Olympic Games: The First Thousand Years* (London, 1976). Newer titles include Ulrich Sinn, *Olympia: Cult, Sport, and Ancient Festival* (Princeton, NJ, 2000); Mark Golden, *Sport and Society in Ancient Greece* (Cambridge, UK, 1998); and Judith Swaddling, *The Ancient Olympic Games* (Austin, TX, 2000). Finally, a useful videotape, *The Ancient Olympics*, that makes excellent use of ancient Greek art, was produced by New Step recordings in collaboration with the Institute for Mediterranean Studies in 1996.

There are scores of scholarly treatments on specific aspects of the world of ancient Greek athletics. On the subject of prizes and awards, see: N. W. Pleket, "Games, Prizes, Athletes, and Ideology," in *Stadion* 1 (1975): 49–89; and David C. Young, *The Olympic Myth of Greek Amateur Athletics* (Chicago, 1984). On nudity, see: John Mouratidis, "The Origin of Nudity in Greek Athletics, *Journal of Sport History* 12 (1985): 213–32. On combat sports, see: Nigel B. Crowther, "Rounds and Byes in Greek Athletics," *Stadion* 18 (1992): 68–74; Michael Poliakoff, *Combat Sports in the Ancient Greek World: Competition, Violence, and Culture* (New Haven, CT, 1987); and Thomas F. Scanlon, "Greek Boxing Gloves: Terminology and Evolution," in *Stadion* (1982–1983): 31–46. On the pentathlon and its subevents, see: Robert Knight Barney, "The Ancient Greek Pentathlon Jump: A Preliminary Reinterpretive Examination," in Fernand Landry and W. A. R. Orban, eds., *Philosophy,*

Theology, and History of Sport and Physical Activity (Miami, 1978); Joachim Ebert, *Zum Pentathlon der Antike* (Berlin, 1963); and Harald Schmid and Norbert Muller, "New Recognition of Theories of the Long Jump in Ancient Greece," in *Proceedings: 1988 Seoul Olympic Scientific Congress* (Seoul, 1988). On running competition, see: Stephen G. Miller, "Turns and Lanes in the Ancient Stadium," in *American Journal of Archaeology* 84 (1980): 161–66. For information on the Pan-Athenaean Games in Athens, a civic festival rivaling the quadrennial Olympic Games, see: Donald G. Kyle, *Athletics in Ancient Athens* (Leiden, 1987).

Finally, for general treatments of Greek cultural dispositions on the subject of sport, see: Edith Hamilton, *The Greek Way* (New York, 1963); Michael Poliakoff, "Stadium and Arena: Reflections on Greek, Roman and Contemporary Social History," in *Olympika: The International Journal of Olympic Studies* 2 (1993): 67–78; David Sansone, *Greek Athletics and the Genesis of Sport* (Berkeley, CA, 1988); James G. Thompson, "Ancient Greek Attitudes on Athletics," in *Canadian Journal of History of Sport* (December 1974): 159–66; and John T. Powell, *Origins and Aspects of Olympism* (Champaign, IL, 1994).

I | THE SUMMER GAMES

OLYMPIC GAMES BEFORE COUBERTIN

Joachim K. Rühl

Like all their predecessors on more or less national levels, the modern Olympic Games were not intended to be a historically genuine revival of the Olympic Games of classical antiquity when they were inaugurated in 1896. Baron Pierre de Coubertin, the creator of the modern games, was not interested in reinstituting them in their heathen and pre-Christian setting. From the very start he had them staged on an international level, an unhistorical construct that had no predecessor in antiquity when only Greek citizens and—at a later date—only vassals of the Greco-Roman Empire were permitted as active participants. Heathen rituals and rites, which had governed all the Pan-Hellenic Games in classical antiquity, were entirely cut out in the nineteenth century. What was retained from the classical Games were a few athletic events, such as the discus throw that had been part of the classical pentathlon, the Olympiad between the Games, and the idea of the *Ekecheiria*, which was falsely interpreted as having constituted a sort of "Olympic Truce" governing the whole empire at the time of the Games, in a modernized form.

All the Olympic Games—before, at the time of Coubertin, and thereafter—were mere grand sport festivals and spectacles with a contemporary or an intended archaic sport program, which had next to nothing to do with classical sport events, a fact that modern writers and Olympic enthusiasts ignore. All organizers of Olympic Games took advantage of the *epitheton ornans* "Olympic" to secure more importance for and to convey more splendor to their ventures. The focus of organizers was not on classical antiquity; on the contrary, they strove to assemble a program of events that met contemporary tastes. And this holds for the modern Olympic Games that Coubertin inaugurated in 1896.

Although Coubertin was far from being the first person to pick up the idea of a reinstituting the Olympic Games, he was the most successful one. He was, more or less, the last in a long line—a fact he reluctantly conceded before the turn of the century but never fully acknowledged in the ensuing years. Coubertin first proclaimed this idea in 1892 at the fifth anniversary of the *Union des Societés francaises de sports athletiques* (USFSA); the audience widely approved of his proposal. However, nobody fully understood his concept, and his venture petered out completely. Not until 1894 was he able to successfully launch his grand vision.

ROBERT DOVER'S "OLIMPICK GAMES" (1612–2003)

Captain Robert Dover revived and/or instituted these Games, also known as the Cotswold Games, on Dover's Hill between Weston-sub-Edge and Chipping Campden in Gloucestershire, England, in 1612. After a possible (second) interruption from 1622 to 1624 they were revived in 1625. The only contemporary source is M. Walbancke's *Annalia Dubrensia* (1636), a collection of thirty-three poems and laudatory verses about Dover, compiled by members of his family, professional friends, and eminent poets of the day. Several poems show a remarkable knowledge of the ancient Pan-Hellenic festivals, and some abound in classical allusions to them. The Games were staged annually on Thursdays and Fridays in Whitsun Week. According to this source, "Mr. Robert Dover's Olimpick Games vpon [*sic*] Cotswold-Hills," with their classical touch and paraphernalia, had been instituted to revive and preserve the old English folk festivals and to resist the influence of the Puritans who were trying to crush all merrymaking and pastimes of an alleged "Non-Christian" origin throughout England. The landed gentry of the vicinity favored Royalist tendencies and subsidized and assisted Dover in his endeavors. With the support of his most influential friends, such as the large-estate owners Sir B. Hicks and E. Porter, the two monarchs, James I and Charles I, as well as Bishop G. Goodman of Gloucester, widely acclaimed for his obstinacy against the Puritans, Dover was able to set up a program with sporting events for all social strata. For the landed gentry there were horse races on a two-and-one-half-mile racecourse around Dover's Hill, coursing, hunting by scent, and chess. The lesser ranks could indulge in irish, cent, balloon, and shovelboard. Townspeople enjoyed wrestling, running at the quintain, and fighting at the barriers. The largest number of events was staged for the rural population: the cudgel-play, shin-kicking, running, jumping, throwing the sledgehammer and the javelin, tossing the bar, football, tumbling, skittles, dancing, and pipe and tabor music. Most of these events are depicted on the frontispiece of the *Annalia Dubrensia*. Dover was a clever attorney and notary who knew how to attract clients and customers with his advocacy of old customs and sport and of people's right to play them. In his "A Congratvlatory [*sic*] Poem to My Poetical and Learned Noble Friends, Compilers of this Booke" [*Annalia Dubrensia*], Dover hinted at the reasons he inaugurated his Games. He observed that the ancient Greeks, after they abandoned their Olympic and other Pan-Hellenic festivals, had become physically and politically insignificant and not able to defend themselves against the invading Turks. In his opinion the Puritans' policy was leading England to a similar disaster; the country was in danger of abandoning its preparedness for war and the art of national self defense. His final two lines read: "Yet, I was bold, for better recreation, / T'invent these sports, to countercheck that fashion."

With the outbreak of the English Civil War, the Games came to a premature end in 1642. However, they were taken up again as "Dover's Meeting" shortly after 1660, when the monarchy was restored, and were organized by the innkeepers of the vicinity. In the late seventeenth and the entire eighteenth century there are sporadic references to Dover's Games in contemporary literature and local newspapers. As a rural folk-festival, they are on record for the years 1725, 1740, 1773, 1779, and 1797. After 1803 they were staged again at irregular intervals, and there were notices and posters advertising them in 1806, 1812, 1814, 1818, 1819, 1821, 1825, and 1826. From 1826 to 1852 an account book of the union of fieldsmen of Weston-sub-Edge shows entries of sums for rentals of Dover's Hill where the Games were staged at yearly intervals. Because the grounds were to be enclosed, the last Games took place in 1852. In 1928 Dover's Hill became the property of the National Trust, and in 1951 a token revival was attempted during the Festival of Britain, but it was not until 1963 that a "Robert Dover's Games Society" was established to again stage the Games under the name "Robert Dover's Games" at yearly intervals with a completely revised, "modern" sport program. These Games are still being celebrated today.

THE DREHBERG "OLYMPIC GAMES" (1776–99, 1840–42, 1989–2003)

Prince Leopold Friedrich Franz (1740–1817) of the small principality of Dessau in Germany was a well-known humanist, pedagogue, and philanthropist who traveled in England and lived in Rome where he came into contact with archaeologists and the sites of classical antiquity that inspired him to aim at a revival of such styles at home. In the 1770s as a modern prototype of the Age of Enlightenment—and following classical models like the round tomb of Theodoric—he built for himself and his wife a princely burial vault, the so-called "Drehberg," between Dessau and Woerlitz. The round vault was sited on a small hill and was encircled with rows of seats and six recesses in trapezoid shapes, which were used for dancing, as well as by an outer ring (surrounded by a wall), which formed the track for foot races. Here, in deliberate imitation of the spirit of antiquity and its funeral games, he intended the rural inhabitants of his principality to enjoy sporting activities to strengthen their bodies. Thus the interior of the vault was decorated with depictions of all sorts of gymnastic exercises. In 1774 in Dessau the sovereign also founded the first *Philanthropinum*, a model school for citizens where regular physical exercises were taught for the first time in Germany. Thereafter Dessau became a place of pilgrimage for modern sport pedagogues. When one of the most famous ones, Johann Christoph Friedrich Gutsmuths (1759–1839) from the *Philanthropinum* in Schnepfenthal, saw the games staged around the Drehberg, he wrote a detailed description of the various events, thereby greatly contributing to their denomination as "Olympic Games."

The First Phase (1776–99)

The Games were staged at yearly intervals from 1776 until 1799. They took place on September 24, the birthday of the prince's wife. As in the modern Olympic Games, the sovereign opened the games in person with a welcoming speech, the various village delegations occupied their recesses, whereupon ten selected maidens were decorated, dressed in bridal gowns, and given 150 *reichsthalers* by the princess. There were only two major events, again in deliberate imitation of antiquity. The first was the horse race and the second was the foot race for mature lads and lasses. "Hundreds of foreign visitors" are reported to have attended.

A 2.5 kilometer racecourse was built on a poplar avenue for the horse race. Both the start and finish (with a taut rope) was at the entrance of the vault. Thus the riders (without saddles!) had to cover 5.0 kilometers. The prince and high court officials acted as judges. In the individual heats the winners were given a bunch of flowers by the princess and a hat with golden galloons (a kind of braid or band) by the master of ceremonies. Those coming in second received ribbons and streamers. The overall winner earned a prize worth 20 to 30 thalers. Because horse breeding in Dessau was held in high esteem in those days, the best horses were sold to the highest bidders on the spot. Since horses and riders had undergone a harsh training for the race, veterinarians and practitioners were at hand, and the prince himself went to see the injured.

After the horse race, the foot race for men and women took place on the circular racetrack around the Drehberg. The track was between 150 and 200 meters long. Recorded performances for 1780 were 25 or 26 seconds for the best men and 28 or 29 seconds for the women. The young son of the prince arranged the order of the runners; he, or the prince himself, gave the starting signals. The winners of the men's heats received a hat with silver galloons, those coming in second silk mufflers and neck ribbons. There were finals to determine the winners of two different age groups. The winners in the heats for the older women were given some ells of silk goods; those who came in second received a bunch of flowers, a silk scarf, and handkerchiefs. The princess decorated the winners of the heats for the younger women with a garland and gave them small silk scarves. Those who placed second were given a bunch of flowers.

At the same time the children, under the supervision of their teachers, indulged in dancing on the Woerlitz market square, which—in imitation of the Circus Maximus in Rome—was rearranged in the shape of a (small) hippodrome. Throughout the day there was dancing and singing as well as free meals and drinks offered in tents and booths. The model for such generosity was the classical *leiturgia*, the banquet staged in the *prytaneion* in ancient Olympia.

The Second Phase (1840–42)

It is not known why the Games were discontinued after 1799. The Drehberg was not used as a burial vault after the prince and the princess died, and it fell into decay. In 1826 it was pulled down and used as a stone pit. On the initiative of the people, the Games were revived on August 10, 1840, the centennial of the prince's birthday. In 1841 his nephew, Duke Leopold Friedrich, appeared in person promising financial help for the future, but that promise was not kept. A third, and last, revival took place in 1842, on the twenty-fifth anniversary of the duke's accession. The events and the festivities were the same as before—at the expense of the local rural community. Contests with the crossbow for the elderly as well as bowling, rope skipping, and ball games for the youth were added.

The Present State

From the 1930s on, the Nazis (mis)used the Drehberg for their purposes, staging yearly summer camps for their Hitler Youth and May Day celebrations. They covered the top of the Drehberg with a wooden booth and built kitchens, outhouses, and a swimming pool. In 1985 the district government entered into consultations about reconstructing the Drehberg because Leipzig was campaigning to win the bid for the 2000 Olympic Games. On September 23, 1989, the scholars of the *Philanthropinum* of Dessau started a revival of the Games, which was subsequently carried on by Heike Brueckner of the Bauhaus Dessau who inaugurated the yearly "Farmers' Olympics." Popular sports dominated these new Olympics: bicycle races, three-legged races, relay races, races over 10 and 20 kilometers, wheelbarrow races round the Drehberg, pole- and long-jump, tug-of-war, volleyball, and a variety of traditional folklore events. Since 1989 the Drehberg Olympic Games have been staged annually.

OLYMPIC GAMES OF RAMLOESA (1834, 1836)

Shortly after 1800, and especially after the loss of Finland in 1809, strong reactionary forces in Sweden campaigned for a national rebirth, a strengthening of Sweden's defensive power, an improved preparedness for war of Sweden's youth, and a romantic recourse to Sweden's glorious past. With respect to physical prowess, Per Henrik Ling (1776–1839) admired and espoused the classical model of antiquity and the Olympic Games. His pupil Gustaf Johan Schartau (1794–1852), also a staunch supporter of the Olympic Games and Ling's successor as fencing master at the University of Lund (1814–34), eagerly adopted these new ideas, founding an "Olympic Club" in 1833, the aim of which was to "revive the Olympic Games of Antiquity." He selected the racecourse of Ramloesa, a suburb of Helsingborg, as the site for his venture. Ramloesa was Sweden's most prestigious summer spa, and after 1831 it was the center of Swedish horse racing. The local press questioned the usefulness of horse races in Sweden's military preparedness and asked for more practical physical involvement of the youth and the working classes.

Encouraged by local newspaper owners and sponsored by wealthy local citizens, Schartau staged his first Olympic Games on July 17, 1834, one day after the horse races. These first Olympic Games attracted only 43 competitors, all of whom belonged to the lower social strata. No officers, members of the military, or nobility entered. There were four events: gymnastics, foot races, wrestling, and climbing the mast. The gymnastic event, with seven competitors, consisted of a set of flexibility and balance exercises, high jump, pole vault, and jumping over a live horse. In the races, four runners competed in each of the five heats over 237.5 meters. In the final race, those who had placed first in the heats ran 505 meters. There were seven competitors in wrestling, but there are no records of the types of matches or the results. The nine participants in mast climbing drew lots to determine their order. The prize, a silver coin, was affixed atop a ten-meter mast, which was greased with soap, and the first competitor to reach the top won the event. After the Olympic Games, the press spoke very favorably of them and criticized only the "chaotic organization," of the Games.

The second Olympic Games of Ramloesa were staged on August 4, 1836, again one day after the races. The events and prizes listed were exactly the same as in 1834, except that a gold ring replaced the silver coin as the prize in mast climbing. In addition there was an essay contest on the topic of "The Olympic Games of Antiquity in Comparison to Chivalric Events and Tournaments of the Middle Ages and the Benefit of a Revival of the Contests in Our Times." As in 1834, the Olympic Games of 1836 attracted a large number of spectators, but no record of the Games themselves survives.

These Games were never held again, and there is no indication of the reason for their premature end. The Olympic Club disappeared in the same year, the old race-course was abandoned, and after 1950 the national railway used (and is still using!) the premises as a freight yard. What still reminds us of the Olympic Games are the names *Olympiaden* for the neighborhood and for a firm on the site today, and the streets named Raennarbanan, Faektmeastaregatan, and Kapploepningsgatan.

LOCAL OLYMPIAN GAMES AT MUCH WENLOCK (1850–2003), REGIONAL OLYMPIAN GAMES IN SHROPSHIRE (1860–62, 1864), AND NATIONAL OLYMPIAN GAMES IN ENGLAND (1866–68, 1874, 1877, 1883)

Since these English Olympian Games at the three different levels are very closely interlinked and interdependent, they should be discussed as a sort of unit. The mutual link is their founder, William Penny Brookes. Brookes, a medical doctor, became active in the political, business, and intellectual life of Much Wenlock. In 1850, he instituted a Wenlock Olympian Class (WOC) that staged 11 *Annual Meetings*, or *Much Wenlock Olympian Games* (WOG), between 1850 and 1860. The objectives of these Games were to encourage outdoor recreation and to award prizes for "skill in Athletic exercises and proficiency in intellectual and industrial attainments." Some 44 diverse and colorful events comprised the program, including everything from cricket to foot races to archery to a wheelbarrow race. Other events, such as a Bible history contest, knitting, and an essay contest, were less athletic in character. Some events were restricted to inhabitants, but others were open to all and attracted competitors from as far away as London and Liverpool. When Brookes heard of Evangelis Zappas's planned Olympic Games in Athens, he corresponded with the Greek organizers in 1858, was sent the program, and donated the Wenlock Prize worth £10 for the winner of the tilting event in 1859. In November 1860 he became president of the Wenlock Olympian Society (WOS), which evolved from the WOC. In March 1860, after consultations with members of the WOC, Brookes formally inaugurated the Shropshire Olympian Society (SOS) in 1861 that staged three Shropshire Olympian Games (SOG) in Wellington (1861), Much Wenlock (1862), and Shrewsbury (1864).

The four Shropshire Olympian Games were quite similar to the Wenlock Olympic Games, with only small differences in the program. However, by this time, Brookes was corresponding with the Greek organizers of the Zappas Games and began to adorn his Much Wenlock Olympian Games with a pseudo-Hellenic varnish.

The WOG were staged on the Olympian Field; Greek inscriptions decorated the ribbons; victors were crowned with laurel and olive wreaths; bronze, silver, and gold medals were coined, the latter with the effigy of Nike, the Greek goddess of victory, encircled by a Greek passage taken from Pindar. The javelin (in 1859) and three pentathlons (in 1868 and 1869) were added to the program. After 1861, numerous new events were added to the program, including such obviously non-Greek-inspired competitions as a brass band contest, a tricycle race, a sword exercise, and something called a Zulu contest. Many of these events made only one appearance at the Games. Initially these events were open to amateurs only, but professionals appeared from 1868 onward, and betting on the Games started in 1869.

In 1865 Brookes helped found the National Olympian Association (NOA) that between 1866 and 1883 staged six National Olympian Games (NOG). However, one of its objectives, to "form a center of union for the different Olympian, Athletic, Gymnastic, Boating, Swimming, Cricket, and other similar Societies," incurred the wrath of the Amateur Athletics Association (AAA) and led to the demise of the NOG after nearly 18 years.

The first NOG, staged in London in 1866, featured swimming events, as well as track and field and gymnastics events, and drew a reported 10,000 spectators and competitors. Winners in all events received silver medals. Entry was free, but NOA membership was obligatory. A banquet at the Crystal Palace and a torchlight procession completed the program. Later NOGs were held in various locations in England, but the basic program changed relatively little over the years, although as noted above, a number of odd events appeared from time to time. Financial exigencies caused the Games to be held somewhat irregularly in the 1870s and 1880s. Finally in 1883, the AAA's rule that all athletes "competing at sports held under rules not approved by the AAA will render themselves ineligible to compete at meetings held by associated clubs" dealt the death blow to the NOGs.

Brookes also was active in the international Olympic movement. His endeavors in the autumn of 1880 to organize an "International Olympian Festival, to be held in Athens," met with no support. In October 1890, the 81-year-old Brookes staged an autumn meeting in honor of the young Pierre de Coubertin, who came to England to learn more about athletics, physical education, and school sport. Two months later Coubertin wrote that it had been through Brookes's inspiration that the Olympic Games survived. Brookes and Coubertin continued to correspond, and Coubertin invited Brookes to the 1894 Congress in Paris. Brookes declined because of failing health, although he did write to the Greek prime minister asking him to support Coubertin. Brookes died in 1895, months before the Athens Games of 1896. The WOG were discontinued during the early twentieth century, were revived briefly in 1950, were taken up again in 1977, recently welcomed eminent visitors of the Olympic community, and presently offer a modern sport program. They are still a popular event.

OLYMPIC FESTIVALS IN LIVERPOOL (1862–67) AND MORPETH (1871–1958)

In Liverpool Olympic Festivals were held annually between 1862 and 1867. Organized by the Liverpool Athletic Club under the leadership of club president Charles Pierre Melly and his friend John Hulley, these festivals were initially one-day affairs held at different Liverpool locations (and one time in Llandudno, Wales). The later festivals ran for three or four days. Only so-called Gentlemen Amateurs could compete, and while there were medals for the winners, there were no cash prizes. The inaugural festival included 22 disciplines, mostly in track and field and gymnastics, but also including a sword fight, fencing, boxing, and wrestling. John Hulley acted as director of the events, assisted by several policemen. Military bands supplied entertainment for the 7,000 to 10,000 spectators while they watched 209 competitors from Liverpool and Manchester.

Subsequent festivals replicated the first one, although Hulley gradually added more festivities, such as fireworks, and crowds increased. The program of events did not change much over the six festivals, although by the time of the third in 1864, the *Liverpool Mercury* had to reassure its readers that Hulley was not moving Liverpool back "towards the Paganism of the ancient Greeks . . . the festival has no religious significance." After the sixth festival in 1867, Hulley ran into financial difficulty. The Liverpool Athletic Club, whose membership fees underwrote the events, was not growing, and Hulley did not know how to market his festival properly.

Morpeth is located in Northumberland, and beginning in the 1870s, athletic contests were held there. In 1873 a former wrestler, Edmond Dobson, inaugurated a series of Games that were strictly for professional athletes, who vied for cash prizes in several different events, including horseshoes, wrestling, and an assortment of track and field competitions. By the end of the decade, the champion wrestlers were receiving nearly £40 as a prize, and the Games were attracting substantial crowds.

After 1882 these games were called the Olympic Games at Morpeth (MOG), although the origins of that phrase are unknown. These one-day Games were held annually and were very successful, with continually increasing numbers of competitors, increased prize money, and more spectators. In 1890, for example, some 17,000 spectators attended, and the champion wrestler received £86.

In 1896, the MOG moved to Grange House Field, a more spacious outdoor arena, in which organizers built a new wrestling ring and an excellent track. Prize money was increased once again, and a record number of competitors entered, including 175 in wrestling and 119 in the 120-yard handicap race, where runners started from different points, depending on their past performances. Ironically, the local press made no mention at all of the Olympic Games in Athens that year.

The MOG prospered in subsequent years. Two afternoons were needed in 1912 after more athletic events had been added. The Games were interrupted during World War I, reinstituted in 1919, and staged on Mount Haggs Field from 1921 to 1939. In 1922 there were 280 entries for the 120-yard handicap, and in 1935 boxing was introduced. The MOG were suspended during World War II, and in 1946 they were moved back to Grange House Field. A total of 36 heats in the 80-yard handicap were run in 1952. The MOG were staged in 1958 for the last time after the death in 1957 of its president, John Nicholson.

So far the MOG have been utterly neglected by sport historians. Strictly professional, the Games hosted six world wrestling championships at various times, and no prominent amateur ever seems to have had the slightest chance of winning. In 1934 the famous Australian exhibition runner, M. Dunn, did not survive his first heat in the 110-yard handicap when he started from scratch. In 1950, Barney Ewell, world sprint champion from the United States, was eliminated in the first heats of the 110-yard and the 80-yard handicaps.

OTHER NINETEENTH-CENTURY "OLYMPIC" EVENTS

There were another eight "Olympic" events, which are difficult to classify. These were either of a primarily local character or have not been thoroughly researched, and they are simply listed here in chronological order:

1. 1796: "Olympic Games" in Paris in the framework of revolutionary festivals.
2. 1820/1850/1852: "Olympic Games" in the framework of the "Oktoberfest" in Munich.
3. 1832–1952: "Olympic Games" for school boys in Rondeau and Montfleury, France.
4. 1844: "Olympic Games" lasting two days in Montreal, Canada.
5. 1853: "Olympic Games" in an indoor circus (five-month run) in New York, United States.
6. 1866: "Grand Olympic Festival" in Leicester, England on the grounds of a lunatic asylum.
7. 1877: "Modern Olympic Games" in Athens, staged by a crew in Piraeus Harbour.
8. 1880–1940: "Olympic Games" at Lake Palic in Subotica, Hungary.

EVANGELIS ZAPPAS'S OLYMPICS (1859, 1870, 1875, 1888–89)

After Greece won its independence from Turkey in 1830, a number of people considered reviving the Olympic Games in combination with the rise of national patriotic festivals. Among these individuals was the editor of the newspaper *Ilios*, Panagiotis Soutsos. Soutsos wrote a memorandum to King Otto I in which he described his plan, modeled on the Pan-Hellenic games of antiquity, to stage an annual eight-day festival rotating among four Greek cities. In 1837, King Otto decreed that a "Committee for the Furtherance of National Economy" be created; this committee took charge of staging physical competitions at national trade fairs.

Evangelis Zappas, a veteran of the Greek war for independence and a wealthy land owner, heeded Soutsos's plea to revive the Olympic Games, offering to pay for a stadium in which to stage Games in 1857. Although that year was too soon to be practical, in 1858 the government authorized the formation of a Committee for the Olympics. This committee was charged with organizing Olympic Games every four years to coincide with the national exposition of agricultural and industrial products.

The first of Zappas's Olympic Games took place in November 1859. Attendees included the Greek king, the military, and eminent personalities in rows of seats, as well as nearly half of the inhabitants of Athens in the stands. The official program included such events as a stadium race, discus, javelin, long jump, climbing the greased mast, and the *askoliasmos*, an event in which contestants balanced on a greased animal skin that was filled with some sort of liquid. The winner of the longest race received Brookes's Wenlock Prize of £10. Although the press lauded the Games as being "positive," they were a disappointment to thousands of Athenians who could not see anything from the stands and who did not understand the old sport events—most of the track and field events had not yet made their way to Greece. The site was unsuited for the events, and the weather was too cold.

Evangelis Zappas died in 1865. On August 11 of that year a Committee for the Olympics and the Zappas Foundation was established by royal decree, and a site was selected for the future stadium, to be known as the *Zappeion*. In July 1869, the dates of the 1870 Olympics were announced, followed by organizational plans and proposals about which events to include. The committee paid for participating athletes to undergo three months of training prior to the Games. This training was held in the old Panathenian stadium, which had been cleaned and leveled, furnished with pits for jumping, a wrestling ring, masts, and tracks. An ample wooden grandstand was reserved for the royal family, government officials, the diplomatic corps, and other official guests. On November 1, the Games were officially opened with patriotic speeches, but the athletic events were postponed until November 15 because of bad weather. Moreover, all of the nautical events, the horse races, and the shooting events had to be canceled. Some 20,000 to 25,000 people watched 31 athletes who had previously qualified compete in a variety of events. Before competition started, the athletes, who were all clad alike, were asked to swear that they would compete in a fair manner. Every discipline was announced by a trumpet flourish, and later, every winner's name and birthplace was announced by a herald. As in 1859, winners received a cash prize; in addition, the first three winners received wreaths of the olive tree and small branches of the olive tree and laurel.

Competition in the arts was also integral to the great Greek exposition, and the Olympics in 1870 featured 59 sculptures, 48 paintings, 9 poems, and 5 architectural drawings. The press unanimously praised the excellent organization and deemed the Olympics as a great Greek success.

Planning for the 1875 Olympics began in 1871, and in 1873, the foundation stone for the Zappeion was laid. Ioannis Fokianos (1845–96), in charge of all the state-owned sporting facilities in Athens, was entrusted with the overall organization. To prevent participation by working-class people, Fokianos admitted only students over 17 to his training program. These Olympics were planned as part of the great Greek exposition with 1,200 national and 72 foreign exhibitors, the largest Greece had ever seen.

After the official opening on May 4, the shooting events began on May 11, 1875, with 34 civilians and soldiers. The track and field events were staged on May 18 in the Panathenian stadium. Twenty-four athletes who had attended Fokianos's training camp, all clad in white shirts and shorts with blue belts, participated in a variety of events. Since not all of the scheduled exercises on the parallel and the high bar could be executed, no awards were given in gymnastics. The press heavily criticized the lack of organization and the disorder in the stadium as well as the fact that the organizers admitted only the "better" classes as competitors. In addition, newspapers referred to the youths' performances as "theatre games" and "amusements" that ridiculed the memory of Greece's former glory. Fokianos became so embittered that he resigned as overall leader of the Olympics. Once again, however, the artistic competitions proved a great success: 25 composers won awards in music, and 18 sculptors and painters were honored.

After an extended period of litigation between the Greek government and a group of Zappas's relatives over Zappas's bequests, Konstantinos Zappas secured the execution of Evangelis's will. The government used Zappas's money to complete the *Gymnasterion*, a central gym, in 1878 and to continue work on the Zappeion, begun in 1873 and frequently interrupted. The Zappeion officially opened on October 20, 1888, in time for the next Olympic Games. As he had done in 1875, Fokianos, assisted by two young sport instructors, took charge of the sporting events, which were postponed until April 30, 1889, and staged in *Gymnasterion*. Because of the large crowds, the competition had to be interrupted and continued on May 8. Thirty athletes competed in a variety of disciplines, including discus, pole long leap (over a ditch), weight lifting, mast climbing, and rope climbing, among others. All participants were clad alike, and 100 students from two schools in Athens gave a demonstration of their gymnastic skills, which the press praised for its military organization and for its exhibition of the fitness of the youth. Fokianos finally secured public recognition for his work. With their donations, wealthy Greek citizens from abroad contributed significantly to the success of the art competitions, which by far surpassed the sporting events and the agricultural and industrial expositions.

The Zappas Olympics of the year 1888–89 were the last ones because of lack of funding. When Konstantinos Zappas died in January 1892, his relatives renewed and won their lawsuit against the Greek state. On June 22, 1890, a royal decree, signed by Crown Prince Konstantinos and the Foreign Minister Stefanos Dragoumis, announced that the Olympics would be staged at four-year intervals starting with those of 1888. The next Olympics were officially announced for 1892. However, the death of Konstantinos Zappas interrupted this series of national Greek Olympics for good and left the Greek state without the necessary financial backing to continue. Nevertheless, the Zappas Olympic Games paved the way for the advent of Coubertin's Olympics Games in 1896.

BIBLIOGRAPHICAL ESSAY

The first outline of Olympic Games before Coubertin was compiled by Gerald Redmond, "Prologue and Transition: The 'Pseudo-Olympics' of the Nineteenth Century." In *Olympism*, Jeffrey Segrave, Donald Chu, eds. (Champaign, IL, 1981): 7–21. The best comprehensive treatment in English is David C. Young, *The Modern Olympics: A Struggle for Revival* (Baltimore, MD, 1996), which contains an excellent bibliography. Joachim K. Rühl, "The Olympian Games at Athens in the Year 1877: A Unique Effort of British Naval Officers," *Journal of Olympic History* 5, no. 3 (1997): 26–34 also lists journal articles, which deal with the topic and the individual Olympic Games. Additionally, most of them are outlined and illustrated by diverse authors in Wolfgang Decker, Georgios Dolianitis, Karl Lennartz, eds., *100 Jahre Olympische Spiele: Der neugriechische Ursprung* (Würzburg, 1996), a compendium, which also has a list of primary sources and an excellent bibliographical chapter. Most of the individual Olympic Games have been investigated in their mother tongues, in German by myself, or in diploma theses under my supervision (indicated as "s. J.K. R."). Because these are parts of diploma examinations, they are unpublished. Local press articles of the periods in question are also excellent sources.

THE INDIVIDUAL OLYMPIC GAMES BEFORE COUBERTIN

Robert Dover's "Olimpick Games"

Christopher Whitfield, *Robert Dover and the Cotswold Games. Annalia Dubrensia* (London, 1962). David Burns, *ANNALIA DUBRENSIA. Vpon the yeerely celebration of Mr. ROBERT DOVERS Olimpick Games vpon Cotswold-Hills; with a History of the Cotswold Games* (MA diss., Sheffield University, 1960). Joachim K. Rühl, *Die "Olympischen Spiele" Robert Dovers 1612–1969* (Heidelberg, 1969).

The Drehberg "Olympic Games"

Erhard Hirsch, "'Olympischen Spiele' am Drehberg in Anhalt-Dessau zur Goethezeit," *Nikephoros* 10 (1997): 265–88. Heike Brückner, *Der Drehberg im Dessau-Wörlitzer Gartenreich* (Dessau, 1991). Lutz Petri, *Die Geschichte der Drehbergspiele zu Wörlitz* (diploma thesis; s. J.K. R., Cologne, 1997).

Olympic Games of Ramloesa

Johan Pape, "Olympiska Spelen i Hälsingborg på 1830-talet—Ett blad ur svenska idrottens historia." In *Kring Kärnan. Hälsingborgs Museums Årsskrift 1951* (Hälsingborg, 1952): 11–36. Åke Svahn, "*Olympiska Spelen" i Ramlösa 1834 och 1836* (Helsingborg, 1984). Ansgar Molzberger, *Geschichte und Entwicklung der Olympischen Spiele in Ramlösa von 1834–1836* (diploma thesis; s. J.K. R., Cologne, 1998).

Olympian Games at Much Wenlock, in Shropshire, and England

Sam Mullins, *British Olympians: William Penny Brookes and the Wenlock Games* (London, 1986). Benno Neumüller, *Die Geschichte der Much Wenlock Games 1850–1895* (diploma thesis; s. J.K. R., Cologne, 1985). David C. Young, "The Origins of the Modern Olympics. A New Version," *IJHS* 4 (1987): 271–300. David C. Young, *The Modern Olympics* (1996). Don W. Anthony, *Minds, Bodies and Souls. An A to Z of the British Olympic Heritage Network* (London, 1995). Ian Stuart Brittain, *The History and Development of the National Olympian Association 1865–1886* (MSc diss., Univ. of Leicester, 1997).

Olympic Festivals in Liverpool

Roy Rees, "The Development of Sport and Recreation in Liverpool in the 19th Century" (M.Ed. diss., Univ. of Liverpool, 1968): 60–75. Annette Keuser, "Die Geschichte der 'Liverpool Olympics' (1862–1867) und ihre Bedeutung für die Wiederbelebung der Olympischen Spiele" (diploma thesis; s. J.K. R.; Cologne, 1991). Joachim K. Rühl, Annette Keuser, "Olympic Games in 19th-century England with Special Consideration of the Liverpool Olympics." In *Contemporary Studies in the National Olympic Games Movement*, ed. Roland Naul (Frankfurt am Main, 1997): 55–70.

Olympic Games at Morpeth

These Olympic Games have been brought back to mind by Frederick C. Moffatt, *Turnpike Road to Tartan Track: The Story of Northern Foot Handicaps* (privately printed, Morpeth,

1979). Apart from Moffatt, original material is only available in the local newspapers. Jürgen Thielgen, *Entstehung und Entwicklung der "Morpeth Olympic Games" von 1873–1958* (diploma thesis; s. J.K. R., Cologne, 1996). Joachim K. Rühl, "The History and Development of the Morpeth Olympic Games 1871–1958." In *Proceedings of the 6th Congress of the ISHPES, 14–19 July, 1999 in Budapest, Hungary* (Budapest, 2002): 197–203.

"Olympic Games" in Paris

These games have been dealt with only marginally by Otto Schantz, "Französische Festkulturals Wegbereiter der Modernen Olympischen Spiele," *Stadion* 21/22 (1995/1996): 64–85. The games themselves are still waiting for a detailed investigation.

"Olympic Games" in the Oktoberfest in Munich

So far they have only been treated recently in an interesting essay by Karl Lennartz, "Das Münchener Oktoberfest—ein Ursprung der Olympischen Spiele!" In *Proceedings of the 6th Congress of the ISHPES, 14–19 July, 1999 in Budapest, Hungary* (Budapest, 2002): 185–6.

"Olympic Games" in Rondeau and Montfleury

These *Jeux olympiques* are of interest to Olympic historians because father Henri Didon, who devised the motto *citius, altius, fortius*, was an "Olympic winner" when he was a pupil at this school. The most original treatments are in French: Henry Rousset, *Les Jeux Olympiques au Rondeau. 1832–1893* (Grenoble, 1894); Alain Arvin-Bérod, "*Et Didon créa la devise des Jeux Olympiques" ou l'histoire oublié des Jeux Olympiques du Rondeau: Grenoble 1832–1952* (Echirolles, 1994); Alain Arvin-Bérod, *Les enfants d'Olympie* (Paris, 1996); Michael Schwind, *Die Geschichte der "Olympischen Spiele" von Rondeau 1832–1905* (diploma thesis; s. J.K. R., Cologne, 1997); Tim Stapel, *Die Geschichte der "Olympischen Spiele" von Rondeau 1906–1952* (diploma thesis; s. J.K. R., Cologne, 2002). The last two theses contain many colored illustrations and complete lists of the winners.

"Olympic Games" in Montreal

These games were staged by the Montreal Olympic Club. They are dealt with by Gerald Redmond, "Prologue and Transition." In *Olympism* (1981): 14–15. The main source is the *Montreal Gazette*, 29 August, 1844.

"Olympic Games" in New York

They were run for five months in an indoor circus. Cf. Gerald Redmond, "Prologue and Transition." In *Olympism* (1981): 13–14. The main source is the *New York Times*, March 25 to September 2, 1853.

"Grand Olympic Festival" in Leicester

The two original sources are the *Leicester Advertiser,* May 26, 1866, and *The Chronicle and Mercury United*, May 26, 1866. The games are outlined by Joachim K. Rühl, "Das *Grand Olympic Festival* auf dem Irrenanstaltsgelände, Leicester 1866." In Wolfgang Decker, Georgios Dolianitis, Karl Lennartz, eds. *100 Jahre Olympische Spiele* (1996): 65.

"Modern Olympian Games" in Athens

They are dealt with in detail by Joachim K. Rühl, "The Olympian Games at Athens." In *Journal of Olympic History* 5, no. 3 (1997): 27–34. The main sources are the log of H. M. S. Research and a contemporary drawing.

"Olympic Games" at Lake Palic in Subotica, Hungary

The "Palic Olympics" are still fairly unknown outside Hungary and Yugoslavia (now Serbia). Apart from articles in Hungarian, the only essay in English is Branko Mrkic, "Olympiads at Palic—Subotica from 1880 to 1914: The Origin of the Olympic Movement and Modern Sports in Yugoslavia." In: *Proceedings of the ICOSH Seminar 1988, The Olympic Movement 'Past, Present and Future,' 13–19 June 1988* (Sarajevo, 1989): 208–21. Available at the end of 2003: Victoria B. Timar, *Geschichte und Entwicklung der Palic-Spiele in Ungarn von 1880 bis 1914* (diploma thesis; s. J.K. R., Cologne, 2003).

Evangelis Zappas's Olympics

Apart from David C. Young, *The Modern Olympics* (1996) and extensive works by Greek authors, the best publications are: Konstantinos Georgiadis, *Die ideengeschichtliche Grundlage der Erneuerung der Olympischen Spiele im 19. Jahrhundert in Griechenland und ihre Umsetzung 1896 in Athen* (Kassel, 2000), which is a dissertation of 737 pages including 431 original documents; Anastasios Kivroglou, *Die Olympien im 19. Jahrhundert in Griechenland: Entstehung, Gründung und wirtschaftspolitische Aspekte bei der Einführung der hellenischen Nationalfeste* (Ph.D. diss., Cologne, 2002; in print), with 300 pages and a copious bibliography.

ATHENS 1896

Karl Lennartz and Stephen Wassong

THE GAMES OF THE FIRST OLYMPIAD

In 393 C.E. the Roman emperor Theodosius I decreed that all heathen cultures were to be prohibited, including the Agone in Olympia whose long tradition was only barely alive. In the following centuries earthquakes and floods buried beneath layers of mud all that had remained intact of ancient Olympia. Due to those layers early excavation attempts often failed. Promising and directive excavation plans for later expeditions to Olympia were provided by Johann Joachim Winckelmann. He declared his intentions in 1767 in the first part of his *Anmerkungen über die Geschichte der Kunst des Alterthums*. But even if Winckelmann had not been killed on April 8, 1768, in Trieste and had pursued his plans, he would not have been credited with the rediscovery of Olympia. The English archaeologist Richard Chandler had already discovered Olympia during his travels through Greece two years earlier.

After Chandler, French and English archaeologists traveled to Olympia every few years. But even with growing public interest in the ancient site, plans to excavate the site systematically—apart from those of Winckelmann—emerged only during the Greek struggle for independence. In addition to the military force the French government sent in support of the Greek battle for independence, a scientific expedition to Morea was launched. The archaeologists of this *Expédition scientifique de Morée* started digging in Altis on May 10, 1829. Although the remaining relics of the Zeus temple were exposed after only a few weeks, further excavations by the French were forbidden. The Greek government wanted to prevent the removal of antique Greek pieces of art to France.

Eventually the excavation of Olympia became the task of German archaeologists whose increased engagement in Greece manifested itself only after the termination of the Greek war of independence in 1829 and the election of Otto of Bavaria as king of Greece. In Germany the idea of the excavation of Olympia was initiated by Ernst Curtius, who had seen and cherished Olympia for the first time as a student. Curtius, who had been offered an appointment as a professor in Berlin in 1844 and was a teacher of Prince Friedrich Wilhelm of Prussia, described the results of his investigations in his work *Peleponnes, eine historisch-geographische Beschreibung der Halbinsel.* The plan to excavate Olympia completely probably occurred to Curtius in September 1851. Before then he had not made any comments concerning such excavation plans. Only four months later, on January 10, 1852, Curtius proposed the excavation of Olympia in a long lecture held before the *Wissenschaftlicher Verein zu Berlin.* Although this idea was positively received, Curtius did not receive the funds to carry out his plan. One of Curtius's detailed accounts on the excavation of Olympia was received so enthusiastically by the Prussian government that negotiations with the government of Greece ensued. However, the ratification of the treaty was blocked in 1854 because of Greece's involvement in the Crimean War and the resulting domestic political problems that resulted in the downfall of the king.

The negotiations between the Prussian crown prince and the new Greek king, George I, gave rebirth to the excavation plans. However, the Franco-Prussian War in 1870–1871 shattered these plans. New negotiations with the Greek government begun in April 1873 eventually led to Curtius traveling to Greece in the spring of 1875 in order to sign the German-Greek treaty concerning the excavation of Olympia. After six expeditions between 1875 and 1881, the complete Altis was exposed. After the scientific examination of the objects found, plaster copies were made of the pieces of art, thus enabling the originals to be kept in Olympia—as arranged in the 1875 treaty. From 1876 to 1881 Curtius and his colleagues published five volumes of the main work *Olympia. Die Ereignisse der Deutschen Reich veranstalteten Ausgrabungen.* The first volume, which describes the history of Olympia, was published as the sixth and last volume in 1897. Curtius was working on this volume until his death on July 11, 1896.

Athens 1896—Unidentified gymnast on rings. Courtesy of International Centre for Olympic Studies, University of Western Ontario.

Although Curtius never expressed his opinion on Pierre de Coubertin's plans to revive the Olympic Games, it can be assumed that he knew of the plans of the French baron. Of course, Coubertin, whose knowledge of ancient Greece constantly comes through in his writings and lectures, had heard of the archaeological works and objects found in Olympia. But although Coubertin appreciated the exposure of Olympia, it would be too one-sided to see this as the only impulse for his plans to renew the Olympic Games in a contemporary era. Coubertin did not develop the plan to reintroduce the Olympic Games merely to stage an ancient play, but rather to offer the youth of the world the possibility of peacefully competing every four years. The youth were to develop maturity of character, enabling them to cope with the social, political, and economic challenges of the coming twentieth century.

On the one hand, Olympic sport was regarded as a means of educating young people to be responsible and democratic citizens. The objective was to transfer the moral and social virtues gained in sport such as fairness, self-assertiveness, teamwork, self-discipline, and conscientiousness to areas of life outside of sport. On the other hand, Coubertin and his supporters regarded the Olympic Games as a possibility for "international contacts" offering the possibility of a dignified representation of one's country, as well as getting to know other nations. This process of mutual contact taking place on both the athletic and spectator levels was intended to promote the reduction of hostility, distrust, and prejudice among nations, thus decreasing the possibility of war. Nationalism and internationalism did not, in Coubertin's opinion, exclude each other. Coubertin thought that, properly understood, peaceful internationalism not only corrected narrow-minded nationalism but also acknowledged the differences and characteristics among nations.

Coubertin endorsed bringing together representatives of different nations and cultures through sport, since sport activities aroused worldwide interest. By reviving the Olympic Games, Coubertin wanted to extend the interest in international competitions. The word "Olympic" was to remind people of the events of antiquity:

> Modern, very modern, will be these restored Olympian Games. There is no question of reviving the old-time dress and manners; and those who suppose that they will be upon some sacred hill and to revived tones of the "Hymn of Apollo," that the contest will be waged have only their own imaginations to thank for the mistake. There will be no tripods, no incense; those things are dead, and dead things do not revive.

From June 16 to 24, 1894, an international sport congress was held at the Parisian university, the Sorbonne. Coubertin organized and financed this congress with the cooperation of the Englishman Charles Herbert and the American William M. Sloane. On the agenda was international standardization of the rules of amateurism as well as a discussion concerning a possible revival of the Olympic Games. Sloane had undertaken the task of publicizing the congress on the American continent, Coubertin in continental Europe, and Herbert in Great Britain and its colonies. As secretary of the Amateur Athletic Association, Herbert had a multitude of international contacts that he could make use of in his preparation for the congress. Coubertin utilized the Union des Sociétés Francaises de Sports Athlétiques as an administrative body. He had already tried to win supporters of the Olympic project during a trip to the United States in 1893 and a short stay in England in February 1894. At this point, however, he was able only to convince Sloane in the United States, Herbert, the Prince of Wales, and John Astley in Britain of the worthiness of his Olympic plans.

As general secretary of the Union des Sociétés Francaises de Sports Athlétiques, Coubertin had already sent informal announcements to all sport associations he knew of both in France and overseas on January 15, 1894. While the congress was still announced as Congrés International de Paris pour l'étude et la propagation des principles d'amateurisme, the congress was called Congrés International de Paris pour le Rétablissement des Jeux Olympiques on the official invitations sent out in mid-May 1894. This gave Coubertin's intention of reintroducing the Olympic Games a formal emphasis.

Some scholars allege that Coubertin was led by tactical considerations concerning this swap of terms and that he used the amateur topic only as a bait in order to realize his actual aim—namely the reintroduction of the Olympic games—more quickly. With the fast spread of professionalism in sport, the announcement of a congress on the topic of the standardization of amateurism to protect sport appeared to be more effective in gaining first letters of acceptance. This procedure was probably due to Coubertin's experiences in 1892 when, on the occasion of the five-year jubilee of the Union des Sociétés Francaises de Sports Athlétiques in November, Coubertin had for the first time publicly announced his intentions of reestablishing the Olympic Games.

About 2,000 participants attended the congress in 1894. Among this crowd, however, only 37 sport associations with 78 sport leaders were present. The foreign participation was restricted to 20 sport leaders from eight countries. Among these was the cosmopolitan Greek Dimitrios Vikelas, then living in Paris, who stood in for Ioannis Fokianos, the president of the Greek gymnastics association. Initially Vikelas had planned to perform this unexpected task with great restraint. At the end of the congress, however, Vikelas was to contribute considerably to its success.

The conference was split into two commissions that met in a festive atmosphere that climaxed with performances of the *Hymn to Apollo*, whose score had been found a short time before in Delphi. While Vikelas was the chairman of the commission dealing with the reestablishment of the Olympic Games, the commission dealing with the standardization of amateur ruling was chaired by the president of the Racing Club de France, Michel Godinot, who was supported in his work by Sloane. The recommendations of the commissions were put to a vote in a plenary assembly. While the proposals of the consulting commission on the reintroduction of the Olympic Games were accepted without any discussion, consensus on the amateur question was not so easily achieved. An elitist-oriented ruling excluding workers from amateur competitions was rejected after the protest of the English Amateur Rowing Association. Whether formal decisions were held concerning the composition of the Comité International, renamed in 1898 the Comité International Olympique (IOC), cannot be deduced from minutes, although there is evidence that Vikelas suggested forming such a committee. A list of the 13 committee members is printed in the *Bulletin de Comité International des Jeux Olympiques* that was published in July 1894. Since Vikelas was the president of this committee, he became the first president of the IOC.

Coubertin, who was not a member of either commission and dealt primarily with the organizational management of the congress, had proposed to hold the first Olympic Games during the international exposition planned for Paris in 1900. However, the participants pressed for a swift realization of the Olympic project and decided to take up Vikelas's proposal to hold the first Olympic games in 1896 in Athens. Vikelas had received news that the Greek royal family supported the idea to hold the first modern Olympic Games in Athens.

The decision to hold the Olympic Games in Athens led to great enthusiasm in Greece among the general public and the Greek press. In governmental quarters, the decisions of the Sorbonne congress were received less warmly, since some did not see how it would be possible to organize and host such an international sport event, given that recent crop failures and the ongoing war against the Turks had brought on a high national debt. Vikelas went to Athens in September 1894 to negotiate with Prime Minister Charilaos Trikoupis but had to return to Paris early because his wife was dying. In November, Coubertin traveled to Greece to continue the talks with the Greek government.

However, Coubertin could not win more than moral support from the Greek prime minister. Trikoupis did not want to burden the weakened Greek budget additionally with a project that appeared unimportant to him. Thus he rejected Coubertin's proposed budget of 200,000 drachmas. Eventually Coubertin found an advocate in Crown Prince Constantine. Together they created an organizing committee chaired by the crown prince. But while Coubertin was traveling back to Paris, committee members loyal to Trikoupis resigned. Although this was a setback, Vikelas returned to Athens, where he managed to form a Committee for the Olympic Games on January 25, 1895, three days after Trikoupis had tendered his resignation. The new prime minister was Theodoros Diligiannis, an Olympic Games supporter.

Government support was now secured, but funds for the organization of the Games were still lacking. This time the Greek government showed itself cooperative. It waived postal charges for the Committee of the Olympic Games, and the Greek national bank granted a loan of 400,000 drachmas. The profits of a national lottery, the sale of a special issue of Olympic stamps, and the patronage of wealthy Greeks brought in additional revenue. The Greek merchant Georgios Averoff donated more than a million gold drachmas for the renovation of the ancient stadium that had been excavated by the German Ernst Ziller in 1869–70. Due to the short building time and a hard winter, not all construction was completed. But the stadium still provided seats for almost 70,000 spectators. In honor of the donor a marble statue of Averoff was ceremoniously unveiled in front of the stadium on the day before the opening ceremony.

While the competitions in athletics, gymnastics, weight lifting, and wrestling were held in the stadium, a concrete bicycle racing course was constructed, modeled on a Danish-built course in Calithea that measured 400 meters in length and 120 meters in width. Inside the cycling stadium, two tennis courts were also built and used for the tennis competition. The Zappeion, a pavilion completed in 1888 and named after Evangelios Zappas, was used for the fencing competition. The Zea Bay near Piraeus was used for the swimming events.

It was difficult during the short preparation time to complete the construction of the venues so that they could be used not only for sport competitions but also for advertising the Olympic Games. Moreover, arranging for the participation of athletes in Athens caused problems. The members of the IOC and the Athens organizing committee sent invitations to sport associations, clubs, and individuals known to have a sporting background. Although this organizational effort was vast, the number of foreign athletes agreeing to come to Greece remained very small. During the preparation of the Games it became clear that a majority of competitors would be Greeks. In the end 262 athletes from 13 nations participated, including 76 foreign athletes.

Coubertin even had problems persuading French athletes to make the journey to Athens. What was called the French team consisted of two cyclists, two runners, and some fencers. The Netherlands and Belgium did not send any athletes at all. In both Hungary and Germany, the question of whether an Olympic team should be sent had become a political issue. Since no Olympic team was formed in Austria and just three athletes decided to go to Athens on their own, Hungary decided to select an official Olympic team for political reasons. Hungary doubtless wanted to demonstrate its own independence within the Austrian-Hungarian dual monarchy. In Germany the gymnasts decided against participating in the Olympic Games. They justified their refusal superficially on the fact that Coubertin had not invited gymnasts to the Parisian congress. The actual reason for the German gymnasts' rejection of the Olympic Games was probably based on the fact that the organization of the games was mainly in French hands. Statements made by the Greek ambassador in Berlin that the old as well as the new Olympic Games were not French but Greek were overheard. Dr. Willibald Gebhardt spoke out against this narrow-minded nationalism and tried to send a highly qualified team to Athens. At the time of the founding of the Olympic committee, Gebhardt had good use for the support rendered by Wilhelm II, since Prince Constantine of Greece was married to Sophie, sister of the Kaiser. The German chancellor made his son, hereditary prince Philip Zu Hohenlohe-Schillingfüst, chair of the National Olympic Committee. The chancellor himself had previously been Bavarian legate in Greece. His son was married to a daughter of the Greek nobility. Among the German Olympic participants who traveled to Athens under the leadership of Gebhardt were 11 gymnasts who German gymnastic officials called traitors to their home country.

Apart from the host country Greece, England sent the largest team among the other participating European countries, which included Bulgaria, Denmark, Sweden, Russia, Italy, and Switzerland. One of the members of the British team was the successful long-distance runner Edwin Flack, who actually was an Australian member of the London Sports Club. Apart from one athlete competing for Chile and apparently living in Paris, the only athletes from the Western Hemisphere came from the United States. Sloane recruited four Princeton University students who, together with nine athletes from Boston, formed the U.S. Olympic team. Sloane himself refrained from going to Athens with his wife and donated the money he would have spent to a fund for financing the U.S. team. The Americans regretted that the Games were to be held from April 6 to April 15 because this was the examination period at American universities. This prevented many qualified college athletes from traveling to Athens. For the Greeks, however, there could not have been a better time.

The Games of the First Olympiad took place from April 6 to April 15, 1896, according to the Gregorian calendar. The difference between the Gregorian and the Julian calendar, led to confusion among the Americans concerning the beginning of the Games. The Greeks used the Julian calendar, according to which the Games started on March 25. The American team reached Athens just in time. The Games were opened on a Greek national holiday. Before the king opened the Games in the packed stadium using the now traditional phrase, "I hereby declare the opening of the first international games in Athens," the crown prince delivered a speech and the orchestra played the Olympic hymn, composed by Spiridon Samaras with lyrics by Kostis Palams.

The Olympic program consisted of competitions in track and field, gymnastics, fencing, shooting, sailing, swimming, cycling, equestrian sports, and tennis. The variety of the sport program as well as the fact that all sport disciplines were put on the same level were signs of modernity in the Olympic games. The program was a compromise between the associations' interests, the interests of the competing nations, and Coubertin's ideas concerning the arrangement of events. The rules by which the various competitions were held were also a compromise. The amateur ruling drawn up at the Sorbonne congress was complemented in various disciplines by rules specified by their associations. These included the rules of the Union Sociétés Francaise des Sports Athlétiques, valid for the running events, those of the English Amateur Athletic Foundation for the throwing events, those of the Parisian Société d'encouragement de l'escrine for the fencing events, and the rules of the Rowing Club Italiano for the rowing events. In the cycling competitions the rules of the International Cyclists' Association were employed, and in tennis the rules of the All England Lawn Tennis Association were used.

The track-and-field events that were the center of interest were dominated by the American athletes. They won 16 of the possible 37 first three places and won 9 out of 12 competitions. Thomas Burke won the 100-meter and 400-meter runs, Thomas Curtis won the 110-meter hurdles, James Connolly won the triple jump, Ellery Clark won the high jump and long jump, William Hoyt won the pole vault, and Robert Garret won the shot put and discus. The series of victories by the American athletes was broken only by Edwin Flack, who won the middle-distance races over 800 meters and 1,500 meters, and the Greek Spyridon Loues, who won the marathon race. This race had been included in the competition program because of a proposal by the French philologist Michel Bréal. On the historic stretch from Marathon to Athens the foreign runners, including Flack, dropped out one after another. Apart from the Hungarian Gyula Kellner, only Greeks reached the finish line. Winning the marathon race was especially important to the Greeks since all other track-and-field events had been won by foreign athletes. Loues reached the finish line in about three hours and became a popular national hero. He had received promises of financial, material, and idealistic rewards in case of victory. As long as it went no further than promises, the Greeks did not violate the amateur code that they demonstrably did not interpret too precisely.

Similarly successful as the American athletes in track and field were the Germans in gymnastics and the Greeks in the shooting contests. However, few good foreign shooters participated in these shooting events, apart from the two American brothers who easily won the pistol disciplines. The level performed at the cycling competitions was also rather low. Two Frenchmen, unknown in their home country, won four cycling events. An Austrian won the 12-hour track race. As in track and field, the host nation won only a long-distance victory. Aristides Konstantinidis won the cycling road race from Athens to Marathon and back to Athens. However, the Greeks were more successful in the fencing disciplines that the French dominated. The swimmers competing over the distances of 100 meters, 500 meters, and 1,200 meters suffered in the icy seawater of the bay. The Greek organizing committee had refused to spend the money necessary to host the swimming competitions in a specially constructed stadium. The rowers' competitions were cancelled due to storms and rain.

Teams consisting of athletes of different nationalities were present in Athens. Accordingly, the tennis doubles were won by the Englishman John Boland and the German Fritz Traun. Boland also won the singles. Another characteristic of the Olympic Games of 1896 that would be unthinkable in today's Games is that athletes at the 1896 games did not always restrict themselves to their specific discipline. Edwin Flack not only competed in the marathon race but also ran in the middle-distance races and played in the tennis tournament. The German Carl Schuhmann won four events—three in gymnastics and one in wrestling.

Unlike contemporary Olympic Games, only the flag of the victorious athlete's nation was hoisted after the competitions. As was usual until 1928, the presentation ceremony was part of the closing ceremony. George I personally presided at the ceremony, handing each athlete a memorial medal; the winners silver medals, a diploma, and an olive twig; and runners-up copper medals and a laurel twig. At the end of the ceremony all victorious athletes formed a procession led by Spyridon Loues around the arena, accompanied by the applause of the spectators.

In spite of all the organizational difficulties concerning the preparations for the Games and the relatively scant participation of foreign athletes who often were not their countries' best, the Games in Athens were the first success of the modern movement. However, expressions of thanks towards Coubertin and his French supporters, who made the event possible from the start, were muted at the Athens Games. Furthermore, a petition to stage the Olympic Games permanently in Greece did not please Coubertin. Despite the fact that the Americans had signed this petition along with the Greeks, Coubertin held fast to his concept of staging the Games in different places. The attacks from the Greek press that called him a thief, and the fact that the remarkable organizational efforts made by Coubertin and his colleagues prior to the Games were forgotten, must have been painful for him.

BIBLIOGRAPHICAL ESSAY

Olympic researchers have turned only lately towards serious work on the events in Athens in 1896. Since it has been assumed that all valuable documents on the Games of 1896 were burned in the Melas House, researchers had long depended on secondary sources. More intense recent research has, however, contributed to getting past the jungle of anecdotes, fairy tales, and myths concerning the first modern Olympic Games. The special status of the Games in Athens becomes clear in the reprint of the official report: Spyridon Lambros, *Politis, Nicolaus: Die Olympischen Spiel 776 v Chr.—1896 n.Chr. Erster Theil. Die Olympischen Spiele im Altertum.* (Athens and Leipzig, 1896). No other official report has been reprinted so far. Primary and secondary literature of the modern Olympic Games can be found in particular with Bill Mallon, *The Olympics: A Bibliography* (New York, 1984) and in Karl Lennartz, ed., *Die Olympischen Spiele 1896 in Athen. Erläuterungen zum Neudruck des Offiziellen Berichtes* (Kassel, Germany, 1996). Additional facts and data are presented in Lennartz's other works that have been cited by various authors writing about the introduction of the modern Olympic movement. Standard older works include John MacAloon, *The Great Symbol: Pierre de Coubertin and the Origins of the Modern Olympic Games* (Chicago, 1981) and Richard Mandell, *The First Modern Olympics* (Berkeley, CA, 1976). See also Ath. Tarasoulleas, *Olympic Games in Athens, 1896–1906* (Vironas, Greece, 1988), a day-by-day account of the Games, illustrated with period postcards and containing summaries and winners of each event. Newer works on this topic are the monographs by David C. Young, *The Modern Olympics: A Struggle for Revival* (Baltimore, MD, 1996); Bill Mallon, *The 1896 Olympic Games* (Jefferson, NC, 1998), and Andreas Morbach, *Dimitrios Vikélas: Patriotischer Literat und Kosmopolit. Leben und Wirken des ersten Präsidenten des Internationalen Olympichen*

Komitees (Würzburg, Germany, 1998). The papers by Dietrich Quanz, "Classical Schools and History of Modern Olympic Sports," and Stephan Wassong, "US-Patronage for the First Games and the Role of the American School of Classical Studies" are also very informative. These may be found in Manfred Messing and Norbert Müller, eds. *Blickpunkt Olympia: Entdeckungen, Erkenntnisse und Impulse* (Kassel, Germany, 2000).

Among contemporary articles regarding the Games, consult Pierre de Coubertin, "The Olympic Games of 1896," *Century Magazine* 53 (1896): 39–53 and "The Logical Culmination of a Great Moment," reprinted in *Olympic Review* 161 (1981): 243 for his views on the Games, and Rufus Richardson, "The Revival of the Olympic Games," *Scribner's Magazine* 19 (April 1896): 452–59. Other contemporary accounts include James B. Connelly, *Olympic Victor: A Story of the Modern Games* (New York, 1908); James S. Murray, *Souvenir of the Olympic Games at Athens* (Boston, 1896); Ellery H. Clark, *Reminiscences of an Athlete: Twenty Years on Track and Field* (Boston, 1911); and Burton Holmes, *The Olympian Games in Athens, 1896: The First Modern Olympics* (New York, 1984), a book originally published as a travelogue in 1901.

PARIS 1900

Andre Drevon
Translated by Dominique Leblond

THE GAMES OF THE SECOND OLYMPIAD

Sport histories, and particularly those published in France, have generally criticized the second Olympic Games held in Paris in 1900, suggesting that Paris could only offer Olympism a modest place amid an array of uninteresting fairground attractions. Most of these histories are inspired by the accounts given by Pierre de Coubertin in his memoirs published in 1909 and 1931, who after calling the Games at the time "an impressive sport manifestation whose influence on athletics would be beneficial," later passed the harshest judgment on these Games he had not organized. That opinion, so commonly held for nearly a century, even called into question whether these Games were Olympic. Interest in the Paris Games is very recent.

What happened in Paris in 1900? Specifically there were the *Concours internationaux d'exercices physiques et de sports* (international competitions of physical exercises and sports) that took place under the auspices of the Paris Universal Exposition of 1900, which had been identified by Coubertin as the Games of the Second Olympiad. This recognition was probably first expressed in June 1900, during a meeting between Daniel Mérillon, director of these international competitions, Coubertin, and two other members of the International Olympic Committee: the Italian Brunetta d'Usseaux and the Greek Dimitrius Vikelas. The other members of the committee were immediately informed and mobilized to act for these international competitions/Olympics Games.

However, it is noteworthy that this competition, whose scale was much greater than that of Athens, would never claim the title given by Coubertin. The term Olympics does not appear on any official documents, nor on the many posters put up on the walls of Paris during the event. It is true that in 1900 the idea of the Olympics Games was practically unknown to the public, in spite of Athens, but this fact was especially the result of the conflict between Pierre de Coubertin and Alfred Picard, general director of the universal exposition, during the preparation of the event. The situations in Paris in 1900 and in Athens in 1896 were very different: in Greece, Coubertin had to convince a government to organize a sport competition, but in Paris, in contrast, he saw the government already working at such an event.

In fact the plan of the Olympic Games imagined by Coubertin and the plan of *Concours internationaux*, decided by the organizers of the universal exhibition, were born at the same time. The former one, as we know, was approved during the congress of the Union of French Athletics Sport Societies (USFSA) held in June 1894 at the Sorbonne. The latter was first proposed in 1893 and was organized in September 1894, by a committee presided over by the minister in charge of the exhibition.

At the 1894 congress, Coubertin had wanted the first Games to coincide with the Paris 1900 universal exhibition, but the congress had chosen Paris to host the second Games, a choice confirmed at the end of Athens games.

Both plans had the same purpose: to organize "international competitions, real world championships in which all sports and physical exercises practiced today would be represented," matching Coubertin's definition of Olympics. The one, to be repeated every four years, would become legendary, while the other, tied to a very important but specific single event, would be forgotten, despite the event's great success. Besides having the same purpose, they both faced a major challenge; at that time no real international sport organizations existed, except in cycling, which was already a professional sport, and in rowing. Nevertheless, the goal would be reached: in Paris, during the mild 1900 summer, the first great international sport meeting was held, bringing together nearly all the sports practiced in the world at the time, with athletes from all the countries where sport was practiced.

The figures are self-evident: At Paris in 1900, there were 30 countries, 34 sports, and 58,731 participants (both latter numbers still stand as records in the Olympic Games' history), with 1,587 foreigners. By contrast, at Athens in 1896 there were 9 sports, 13 countries, and 262 participants, with 76 foreigners.

First of all, both plans responded to educational purposes. Coubertin had always linked the Olympic Games, even when at their peak, with his idea of educational reform. International competitions were a direct result of the concern for "physical revival" and had become a political issue in France since the 1870 war with Prussia. Additionally, physical education had become compulsory in primary school in 1882.

Clearly, the government's plan for 1900 was to encourage both students and the general population to engage in physical exercise and to support societies working at "improving the physical strength and moral energy of the country." For the first time in France, the role played by physical exercise and sports societies was officially acknowledged.

However, the competition's organizers did not limit themselves to military-related activities such as shooting or to the very popular and patriotic gymnastics then prevailing in schools. All physical activities and sports were on the program, including traditional sports such as fencing and modern ones such as cycling—in 1900 the leading French sport. The variety of sports clearly shown on the program gives a picture of the diversity of the physical activities at the beginning of the twentieth century.

> **Section I:** Athletic games: track and field, football rugby, soccer football, cricket, lawn tennis, croquet, bowling, *longue paume*, tug-of-war, *pelote basque*, golf, baseball (demonstration)
>
> **Section II:** Gymnastics

Section III: Fencing

Section IV: Shooting: rifle shooting, balltrap, pigeon shooting, archery, pistol shooting

Section V: Horse riding: horse show, polo

Section VI: Cycling

Section VII: Automobilism

Section VIII: Water sports: rowing, yachting, motorboating, swimming, water polo, fishing

Section IX: Life saving

Section X: Aerostatics: balloon races, carrier pigeon racing

Section XI: Military preparatory exercises (national contest)

Section XII: School competitions (national contest)

Section XIII: Hygiene and physiology committee: (scientific observations under the direction of the scientist Etienne Jules Marey)

Leaders of all these activities had been invited to organize *international competitions*, or *world championships*. The performance of elite athletes, people were discovering, was considered the best way "to prove [the] importance and utility of these exercises" and to encourage their development throughout the country. Gymnastics, although it had 8,000 participants at its national festival, had to organize an individual "international championship." This meant a contest, contrary to its traditional culture, based on collective movements; this was the reason why French gymnasts had refused to participate in Athens. "We live in an excessive sport period," the head of Aerostatics regretfully said, as he was compelled to set up balloon races modeled on sports.

France had organized universal exhibitions since 1855. The 1900 exposition was a supreme achievement of its kind, with nearly 50 million visitors from all over the world. This event stood as a hymn to progress and modernity and confirmed the new century under the sign of faith in the future—all values also contained in sport. With this exposition, France would reaffirm its leading role in art, culture, and science. It would also promote its economic dynamism in order to "give French industry a new impulse and expand its exports." In bringing together all the industrial nations of the time, the 1900 universal exhibition explicitly expressed the internationalist trend of early twentieth-century economic trade—a sort of early globalization. In addition, the 1900 exhibition aimed at asserting "pacific intentions" and set itself up as an opening to the world.

In such a context, the idea to organize world championships, at the same time and in the same place, was born in France. The idea responded to the intimate and narcissistic nature of sport, in other words the need to designate the best ever, at the very moment when the exposition opened France to the world. The social development of sports provided a powerful and idealized picture of this internationalism displayed at the universal exhibition. As Coubertin noted, "Internationalism had slipped behind . . . sport." In the Paris of the 1890s, it was possible to imagine a future for sport.

Simultaneously with international competitions in major sports, open competitions were organized in many other disciplines, which accounts for the large number of participants. A number of these disciplines, aiming at gaining recognition, set up street shows and parades, adding to the festive character of the event. The exhibition's organizers wished to open it up to people from every walk of life; their democratic determination went as far as requesting an angling contest since this was one of the few working-class activities. The universal exhibition was implemented by the "radical" Waldeck Rousseau's government, elected on a program of "defense of the Republic." Women made the most of this context; they were unreservedly accepted and for the first time participated in the Olympic Games. Women took part in tennis and golf, two sports traditionally practiced, as well as in nine other events.

How did Coubertin respond to this official plan? Common sense and efficiency certainly required him to reach an agreement with Alfred Picard, but how could such an agreement be possible between the resolutely determined republican director of an exhibition entirely dedicated to modernity and a young baron who apparently proposed to restore ancient Games? Coubertin actually never even tried to compromise; he wrote in his memoirs, "I had understood I had nothing to expect from Mr. Alfred Picard for the Olympic Games." Coubertin figured that the Paris Games were his own business, to the point that he had not even mentioned the issue at the Olympic Congress at Le Havre in 1897. In 1900, Coubertin initiated a hopeless conflict in order to impose his own plan.

As a consequence, Coubertin found support only among the aristocracy, shown by the composition of the committee he set up. With the Vicomte de La Rochefoucauld as president, this committee was soon labeled the "*comtes* and *marquis*" committee. At a time of national political crisis, caused by the recent Dreyfus affair, Coubertin's elitist committee gave the conflict with Picard a political tone.

The Rochefoucauld committee suggested a program based on that of Athens, one far different from that of Picard and Mérillon. Picard considered this program "very cheap and unfit to represent the nation."

As expected, sports organizations, including the USFSA and the La Rochefoucauld committee, which had disbanded after the USFSA's defection, had rallied to the call for international competitions. Entirely isolated then, Coubertin could only acknowledge the validity of Picard's international competitions and support them. With the conflict ended, however, Coubertin could not hope for any favors from the intransigent general director of the universal exhibition. But all things considered, this was just a trivial issue, a minor disagreement between French organizers, and the Games went forward.

Events that constituted the Games of the II Olympiad stretched from May 14 to October 28, 1900, with at least one and often several events daily until August 20 and then several a week through September. The final ten events took place in October. Events were held at 24 venues in Paris and its suburbs, except for yachting, which was contested in the English Channel at Le Havre. The principal venue was a wooden stadium and velodrome built in Vincennes with room for 4,000 spectators. Track and field events were held at the Racing Club of France in the Bois du Boulogne.

The U.S. team, the largest foreign contingent, dominated the track and field events, despite the fact that team members refused to compete on Sunday for religious reasons. Alvin Kranzlein won four events—the 60-meter dash, the 110-meter hurdles, the 200-meter hurdles, and the running long jump—and Ray Ewry, a former polio victim, won the standing high jump, the standing long jump, and the standing hop, step, and jump. Altogether, six world records were broken, and all of Athens's track and field times or distances were bettered, except in the marathon.

A British tennis player, Charlotte Cooper, was the first woman to win an Olympic event when she defeated Helene Prevost of France, 6–4, 6–2. Cooper also won the mixed doubles with her partner Reginald Doherty. Margaret Abbot, from Chicago, was an art student in Paris during the Olympics. A top golfer in the Chicago area, she heard about the golf event, entered, and shot a 47 in the nine-hole event to win.

The immense success of the competition was described as "grandiose" by Brunetta d'Usseaux, who had come to Paris and participated in its organization, as had most of the IOC members. The Games of the second Olympiad clearly took place in Paris in 1900. The colorful and enchanting manifestation, so long forgotten, shows how sport entered the twentieth century. A journalist described these second Olympic Games some days after their closing:

> Indeed, since the time when every four years Olympic Games aroused in Greece and throughout the antic [*sic*] world extreme emotion, never has the sport been so honored than this year, never has it gathered such a crowd [. . . .] Sport has definitively become a new religion. (*L'auto-velo*, November 27, 1900)

BIBLIOGRAPHIC ESSAY

There is generally considered to be no official record of the 1900 Paris Games. Three reports related to the exposition, however, may serve as virtual official reports. *Exposition universelle international de 1900 à Paris. Concours internationaux d'excercises physiques et sport. Rapports* (Paris, 1901), produced under the direction of Daniel Mérillon, contains a summary of the result of the athletic competition and includes photographs and tables. Alfred Picard, *Exposition universelle de 1900 à Paris. Rapport general administratif et technique* (Paris, 1903) gives a more general report on the exposition. Another exposition document, *Direction general de l'exploitation. Reglaments et programmes des concourse nationaux et internationaux d'exercises physiques et de sports* (Paris, 1901) contains information on the rules and schedules of the various events and discusses some of the events, such as ballooning, which were not subsequently sanctioned by the IOC. For a similar program description in English, see Ferdinand Peck, *Programme of the International Contests of Physical Exercise and Sports* (New York, 1900). For an official U.S. report, see A. G. Spalding, "Report of the Director of Sport," in *Report of the Commission General for the United States of America at the International Paris Exposition, 1900* (Washington, D.C., 1901).

A Paris magazine, *La vie au grand air 1900*, published interesting summaries and photographs of sports at the exposition, including photographs of Coubertin's friend Father Didon, who gave the movement its *Citius, Altius, Fortius* (Faster, Higher, Stronger) slogan; the professional athletes; the cycling championships; and much more. Coubertin's view of the Games is contained in his article, "The Mystery of the Olympian Games," *North American Review* (June 1900): 806–9.

Various secondary works shed light on the history of the Games. André Drevon, *Les jeux Olympiques oublies. Paris 1900* (Paris, 2000) is a general study. Bill Mallon, *The 1900 Olympic Games: Results for All Competitors in All Events with Commentary*

(Jefferson, NC, 1998) sorts out the myriad events and their winners. Karl Lennartz and Walter Teutenberg, *Die Olympische Spiele 1900 in Paris* (Kassel, Germany, 1995) is another general history. John J. MacAloon, *This Great Symbol* (Chicago, 1981) describes Coubertin's personal life during this time, including his family tragedy and psychological turmoil. Richard Mandell, *Paris 1900: The Great World's Fair* (Toronto, 1967) is a good history of the exposition but includes little about the Olympics. A more succinct history of the exposition is Robert W. Brown, "Paris 1900," in John E. Findling and Kimberly D. Pelle, eds., *Historical Dictionary of World's Fairs and Expositions, 1851–1988* (Westport, CT, 1990). Reet Howell and Max Howell, *Aussie Gold: The Story of Australia at the Olympics* (Albion, Queensland, 1986) uses correspondence and interviews of competitors and their descendants to describe the Games from an Australian perspective. Finally, Andre Drevon has produced a 30-minute documentary film on the Paris Games: *Les jeux Olympiqués retrouvé, Paris 1900* (1998).

ST. LOUIS 1904

C. Robert Barnett

THE GAMES OF THE THIRD OLYMPICS

Historians consider the third Olympic Games, held in St. Louis, to have been the worst in the history of the Olympic movement. Originally awarded to Chicago, the Games were moved to St. Louis, where the events were caught up in the promotional hoopla of a world's fair. The St. Louis Olympic Games were bathed in nationalism, ethnocentrism, controversy, confusion, boosterism, and bad taste. They were, in short, a clear reflection of American sport, if not America itself, shortly after the turn of the century.

From the very beginning of the Olympic movement, Chicago was a prime candidate to be the first American city to host the Olympic Games. The fiasco that was the Paris Games influenced Baron Pierre de Coubertin's ideas about where the next Olympic Games should be held and sparked the interest of two prominent figures in American sport who had observed the 1900 Games.

St. Louis 1904—Photo of judge's automobile. Courtesy of International Olympic Committee, IOC Museum Collections.

James E. Sullivan, the secretary of the powerful Amateur Athletic Union (AAU), was an influential figure in American amateur sport. A meticulous organizer, record keeper, and somewhat skilled public relations man, Sullivan had been appalled by the disorganized state of the Paris Games. Amos Alonzo Stagg was the well-known football and track coach at the University of Chicago. He had taken the University of Chicago track and field team to Paris to participate in the Games and later used his experiences there to help promote the Chicago Olympic effort.

A May 1901 article in the *Chicago Tribune* about the 1904 Olympic Games stirred an interest in bringing the competition to Chicago. University of Chicago president William Rainey Harper formed a committee of eight, chaired by prominent attorney Henry J. Furber and including Stagg, to study the question of bidding for the 1904 Games. With encouragement from Coubertin and promises for funding from Chicago merchants, the committee decided to bid for the Games.

When the International Olympic Committee (IOC) met in Paris in May 1901 to select the site for the 1904 Games, the only two cities to put forward serious bids were St. Louis and Chicago. The St. Louis bid had problems. The plan was to tie the Games into the scheduled 1903 world's fair. Coubertin adamantly opposed both: linking the Games with another world's fair and moving them back to 1903.

The Chicago bid held much more appeal for Coubertin. He had been extremely impressed with the city during his visit to the 1893 World's Columbian Exposition and liked the idea that the Games would be associated with the University of Chicago. The city's main selling point, however, was that local merchants had promised $200,000 to support the event. With Coubertin's enthusiasm for Chicago and the promise of financial support, a favorable vote from the IOC members was a forgone conclusion. On May 21, 1902, the Chicago Olympic Committee received a telegram from Coubertin: "Chicago Wins."

Over the next two years, a series of circumstances occurred that allowed St. Louis to steal the Olympic Games. On March 3, 1901, Congress passed the Louisiana Purchase Exposition bill, which authorized funding for the St. Louis fair. The exposition company then had little more than two years to organize the fair before the proposed opening date of May 1, 1903. When construction delays and the likelihood of only a small number of exhibits threatened financial disaster, the Louisiana Purchase Exposition Company received congressional authority to postpone the opening of the fair for one year. The one-year extension and the redoubling of the efforts of the exposition company to secure exhibits and attractions put the world's fair and the Chicago Olympic Games on a collision course.

Meanwhile, the Chicago Olympic Committee continued to promote the Games. In August 1902, it released a letter of support from President Theodore Roosevelt. At the same time, the organizers of the Louisiana Purchase Exposition began serious consideration of ways to acquire the Olympic Games as an added attraction for the exposition. In early October, exposition officials requested a preliminary meeting with Furber concerning the Games; two weeks later exposition president David Francis traveled to Chicago to talk with the members of the Chicago Olympic Committee.

After the meeting, Furber informed Coubertin that the St. Louis exposition organizers felt that the Olympic Games in Chicago would threaten their enterprise, and if the Olympics were not switched to St. Louis, they would put on their own athletic events. This, wrote Furber, could damage the Games seriously. Furber concluded that if Coubertin wished to change the site, the Chicago committee would raise no objection.

The controversy placed Coubertin and the IOC in a difficult dilemma. If Coubertin forced Chicago to live up to its commitment to hold the Games in 1904, they might be so overshadowed by the St. Louis events that they would attract few athletes and little public attention. Worse, Chicago could back out of its agreement at the last minute, and the Games would have to be cancelled. Equally distasteful to Coubertin was the transfer of the Games to St. Louis, where they would be only a sideshow attraction to the much larger international exposition.

Apparently Coubertin decided that St. Louis was the less harmful choice, for when the IOC met in Paris on December 23, 1903, it voted to transfer the 1904 Games to St. Louis. Shortly afterward, Coubertin wrote to Walter Liginger, president of the AAU, asking that he and James E. Sullivan take charge of the events. Liginger quickly accepted.

St. Louis, Missouri, sits on the flood plain of a great curve in the Mississippi River, and in 1900 was the fourth largest city in the United States, with a population of 575,238. St. Louis was a Midwestern city with a foreign-born population of 19.4 percent. About 10 percent of the residents had been born in Germany, and many more were first-generation German-Americans.

In 1901 the Louisiana Purchase Exposition Company had been incorporated to produce a world's fair that would bring prestige to and focus on St. Louis. David R. Francis, the former mayor of St. Louis and governor of Missouri, was elected president of the company, which decided to locate the exposition in Forest Park, a wooded park on the western side of the city. The groundbreaking ceremony was held on December 20, 1901.

On Saturday, April 20, 1904, a beautiful sunny day, the Louisiana Purchase Exposition opened. The crowd of 187,793 was treated to a parade of hundreds of dignitaries from the United States and foreign governments, military units, and bands. Promptly at 1:06 P.M., President Roosevelt, in Washington, D.C., pressed a gold telegraph key that "unfurled the flags and put in motion all of the tremendous engines of the Exposition."

The Louisiana Purchase Exposition had three major objectives, as did most other world's fairs of that period: to promote St. Louis and to demonstrate the city's ability to establish and administer a first-class expedition; to provide an attractive spectacle to draw enough people to break even financially, a difficult task with $19.6 million at stake; and to demonstrate progress, a term many felt was synonymous with civilization as represented by the industrialized Western nations. Consequently the exposition devoted much of its space to industrial and commercial exhibits, particularly those demonstrating modern technology.

The exposition was massive, covering two square miles and including more than 200 buildings, virtually a city unto itself. It had its own railway, bank, post office, electrical generators, hotel, and restaurants and could accommodate daytime crowds of more than 100,000. The Renaissance-style architecture, the grand water basin, and the many lagoons were reminiscent of the 1893 Chicago fair, but it was twice as large and cost twice as much to build as the earlier fair.

Organizationally, the fair was divided into sixteen departments. One of these, the Department of Physical Culture, reinforced the belief in the superiority of Western industrial society. In general, the Physical Culture Department exhibits demonstrated the progress made by modern people in attaining better health. The exhibits, including athletic events by various clubs and educational institutions, fulfilled educational objectives, and the department was used to attract professional meetings to the fair.

Moreover, exposition organizers used athletic events as inexpensive attractions, and the free publicity that these events received on sports pages, both locally and nationally, was invaluable in promoting the fair. As plans for the fair became more grandiose, so did the scope of the Physical Culture exhibit. The most important boost to the exhibit occurred when the opening of the fair was postponed from 1903 to 1904, enabling the Louisiana Purchase Exposition to steal the Olympic Games from Chicago.

The securing of the Olympic Games necessitated the hiring of James E. Sullivan as chief of the Department of Physical Culture. Sullivan's wide-ranging background made him an ideal choice for the job. He had worked at the U.S. pavilion at the Paris Exposition in 1900 and had been director of athletics at the Pan-American Exposition at Buffalo in 1901. At the time of his appointment as chief, Sullivan was the secretary of the AAU and president of its Metropolitan Athletic Association (New York City). He had owned and published *Sporting Times* and in 1904 was the owner of the American Sports Publishing Company, which published the *Spalding Athletic Guide Series* and many other books about physical education and athletics.

The Department of Physical Culture was housed in a permanent, three-story building later used as a gymnasium by Washington University. The department was also responsible for the Olympic stadium, which held 10,000 spectators and had a one-third-mile track rather than the standard one-quarter-mile track. All of the athletic events, including the Olympic events, were held out-of-doors, in the infield of the stadium, with the exception of two basketball games, which were played in the gymnasium because of rain.

Sullivan used his numerous contacts to promote the Physical Culture exhibit by attracting professional meetings, scheduling championship athletic events, and recruiting participants for the Olympic Games. Sullivan staged more than forty different athletic events, which by his own estimate drew an astonishing 9,476 participants. At that time the IOC did not have an established program of Olympic events. The selection of events was left to the organizers of the Games, and Sullivan at one time or another referred to every one of the events he scheduled as Olympic, creating tremendous confusion. The Physical Culture Department events began on May 14 with a track meet for Missouri high schools and dragged on for six months before concluding on November 26 with an Olympic College Football game in which Carlisle beat Haskell 34 to 4 in a contest between two Native American schools.

The most popular events were the gymnastics exhibitions and competitions held by the German Turner Clubs. A mass exhibition on June 23 drew 3,500 participants, and a July event drew 140 competitors, many of whom traveled from Germany to participate. Other successful events were the public school basketball and track championships, the YMCA championships, and a demonstration of Bohemian gymnastics by 1,000 American Sokol Club members. The least successful events were the Olympic roque tournament (a croquet-like game) and lacrosse tournaments, each of which drew three teams.

The 1904 Olympic Games was an athletic sideshow to the world's fair in much the same way that the 1900 Olympic Games in Paris had been. Coubertin had suspected as much and did not even make the trip to St. Louis to attend the Games.

Sullivan organized about sixteen different athletic events that could now be considered Olympic because they were open to all competitors, had foreign entries, or are current Olympic events. The program was spread out over five months, beginning on July 4. On that day, a ten-event AAU track and field competition was held, and the winner, Thomas Kiely, is listed in most sources as the Olympic decathlon champion. The events continued through mid-November, concluding with a three-team soccer tournament that was won easily by the Galt (Canada) Football Club over two hastily organized, inept St. Louis teams.

Few European athletes bothered to travel to St. Louis to compete. Americans were virtually the only competitors in many events, including boxing, wrestling, roque, tennis, tug-of-war, gymnastics, and archery (the only event for women). In fact, athletes from the United States swept every medal in every event in those sports, most of which also served as U.S. championship events. All the athletes wore the uniforms of their athletic club rather than that of their country. The most spirited competition in the Games was between the New York and Chicago Athletic Clubs. Two events drew some foreign athletes: golf and fencing. The golf tournament attracted a handful of Canadians among the eighty-five entrants (one-third of whom were from local St. Louis clubs). George Lyon, the 1903 Canadian champion, beat H. Chandler Egan, the defending U.S. champion, 3 and 2, in the final round of match play. The fencing competition, which drew only nine participants (one German, two Cubans, and six Americans), was dominated by Ramón Fonst and Manuel Díaz, both Cubans.

The swimming events were the most internationally competitive, with good swimmers from Hungary and Germany as well as swimmers from both the Chicago and New York Athletic Clubs. The outstanding swimmers were Zolton Holomay of Hungary, Charles Daniels of the New York Athletic Club, and Emil Rausch of Germany, each of whom won two gold medals.

The 1904 Olympic Games were noted for two bizarre events: the marathon race and a set of events for primitive people known as Anthropology Days, that have helped mark the 1904 Games as possibly the worst Olympic Games of all time.

The marathon was run under horrible conditions, with the apparent winner having ridden in an automobile and the actual winner having openly been given stimulants during the race. The race started in mid-afternoon in 90-degree August heat over rutted, dusty, dirt roads with only one water stop. Only fourteen of the thirty-one starters were able to complete the race, which Thomas Hicks won in a time of 3 hours, 28 minutes, 53 seconds, the worst winning time ever in Olympic marathon history. During the race, Hicks was openly given strychnine (which in large doses is lethal but in small doses is a stimulant), the first known example of drug-enhanced performance used in the Olympic Games. Hicks's victory was not immediately apparent, however, because of a hoax pulled by Fred Lorz. Lorz, an experienced marathoner, dropped out of the race at the 13-mile mark because of cramps and was picked up by an official's car. After several miles, the car in which Lorz was riding ran off the road and into a tree. Unhurt, Lorz decided to run on to the stadium. As he did, he passed the leader, entered the stadium, circled the track, and broke the tape as the apparent winner. Just as he was about to be presented the silver cup as the marathon winner, Lorz admitted that he had ridden part of the way in a car and had broken the tape as a joke. The AAU had no sense of humor and suspended him for life for his prank. He was later reinstated, however, and won the 1905 Boston Marathon. Comic relief abounded in the marathon, in part provided by Felix Carvajal, a Cuban mail carrier, who ran in street clothing, stole fruit from a farmer's orchard, lay down to rest for part of the race, and still finished fourth.

Anthropology Days, or primitive people's Olympic Games, was a two-day series of athletic events cosponsored by the Physical Culture and Anthropology departments at the fair. The event was a scientific attempt to prove the theory that primitive people had extraordinary physical ability because they led a life that demanded a high level of physical performance. Actually the event was a bizarre exhibition in which Sullivan took untrained, unmotivated people who had been sedentary for four or five months and ran them through a series of athletic events. When their performances did not measure up to those of modern athletes, Sullivan made disparaging remarks about the participants.

The Anthropology Days were consistent with the fair's goals of drawing spectators and providing evidence of the supremacy of Anglo-Saxon civilization. One of the ways the fair attempted to demonstrate that supremacy was to juxtapose the exhibits of modern technology with those of primitive people, and there were many primitive people in their natural setting: Cocopa Indians from Mexico; Kwakiutl Indians from Vancouver Island, Canada; Ainu from Japan; Patagonians from Argentina; pygmies from Africa; various Philippine tribes; Native Americans; South Africans; Asians; and Turks.

The first day's events were mostly standard track and field events, including the 100-yard dash, shot put, running broad jump, baseball throw, and 56-pound weight throw. None of the performances by the participants was particularly good. The second day's activities included events supposedly geared to primitive activities. The day began with a telegraph pole climbing contest and included a javelin throwing (for accuracy) contest, tug-of-war, a one-mile run, and archery. The pygmies concluded the day's activities with a demonstration of their version of "shinny," and then they divided up for a "mud fight."

At the end of this *scientific* demonstration, Sullivan concluded that primitive people had neither good natural athletic skills nor the intelligence to make team sports work. However, W. J. McGee, the head of the fair's Anthropology Department, believed that the primitive people would become proficient in a short time if they were properly trained and instructed. In the end, the event proved nothing and was at best only a bizarre sideshow of the fair.

In retrospect, Pierre de Coubertin made the most prophetic statement of the time concerning Anthropology Days: "As for that outrageous charade, it will of course lose its appeal when black men, red men, and yellow men learn to run, jump, and throw and leave the white man far behind them."

BIBLIOGRAPHICAL ESSAY

The 1904 Olympic Games, despite being held in the United States, present considerable confusion for researchers. Part of the problem is due to the fact that there was no set program and that James E. Sullivan, the Games director, referred to every event as Olympian. Moreover, the results of the Games do not fit well into the modern record summaries, nor do they mesh with modern conceptions of what the Games should include. Most modern popular accounts tend to repeat the lowlights and myths of the Games, such as the marathon, the involvement of President Roosevelt, and Anthropology Days with journalistic enthusiasm, but with varying degrees of accuracy. Bill Mallon, however, has carefully researched each of the events and detailed the results in his authoritative *The 1904 Olympic Games: Results for All Competitors in Events with Commentary* (Jefferson, NC, 1999).

The Missouri Historical Society (MHS) in St. Louis has the best collection of primary source material on the 1904 Olympic Games. It holds the official records of the Louisiana Purchase Exposition Company, including the records of the Department of Physical Culture, complete with a finding aid. Excellent sources in this collection are Mark Bennitt, ed., *History of the Louisiana Purchase Exposition* (St. Louis, 1905); David R. Francis, *The Universal Exposition of 1904* (St. Louis, 1913); and various fair bulletins and programs. The MHS Department of Prints and Photographs archives has a number of photographs of the Olympic Games. The University of Chicago Archives holds the papers of William Rainey Harper and Amos Alonzo Stagg, both of whom were on the Chicago Olympic Committee. The U.S. Olympic Committee archives in Colorado Springs, Colorado, has scrapbooks of clippings on the Games from a variety of newspapers.

A short history of the exposition is Yvonne Condon, "St. Louis 1904," in John E. Findling and Kimberly D. Pelle, eds., *Historical Dictionary of World's Fairs and Expositions, 1851–1988* (Westport, CT, 1990). See also the chapter on the exposition in Robert Rydell, *All the World's a Fair* (Chicago, 1984), which has an excellent description and analysis of Anthropology Days.

The Games committee did not prepare an official report for the IOC, but James E. Sullivan, ed., *Spalding's Official Athletic Almanac for 1905: Special Olympic Number, Containing the Official Report of the Olympic Games of 1904* (New York, 1905), constitutes the official account of the Games. This work contains the results of all of the athletic events staged in the Olympic stadium, a narrative description of Anthropology Days, and more than 100 photographs.

Another contemporary account of the Games is Charles J. P. Lucas, *The Olympic Games 1904* (St. Louis, 1905), an eyewitness description of the track and field events, with a chapter devoted to the marathon, in which Lucas served as a trainer for the winner and observed the entire race from an automobile following the lead runner. A German account is Theodor Lewald, *Denkschrift uber Deutschlands Beteiligung an der Weltausstellung von St. Louis 1904* (Berlin, 1905). The *St. Louis Globe-Democrat* and *St. Louis Dispatch* covered almost every event at the fairgrounds in some detail, while the *New York Times* and *Chicago Tribune* presented extensive though uneven coverage of the site controversy and athletic competition.

Modern accounts of the Games include Carl A. Posey, *The III Olympiad: St. Louis 1904. Athens 1906* (Los Angeles, 2000), a richly illustrated, accurate, and well-written account of the Games. Allen Guttmann, *The Olympics: A History of the Modern Games* (Champaign, IL, 2002) places the St. Louis Games in the context of the early modern Olympic Games. See Mark Dyreson, "The Playing Fields of Progress," *Gateway Heritage* (Fall 1993): 5–23, John E. Findling, "World's Fairs and the Olympic Games," *World's Fair* 11 (October-December 1990): 13–15; and Robert K. Barney, "Born from Dilemma: American Awakens to the Modern Olympic Games, 1901–1903," *Olympika* 1 (1992): 92–135, for other perspectives on the Games. John A. Lucas, "Early Antagonists: Pierre de Coubertin versus James E. Sullivan," *Stadion* 3 (1977): 264–66, discusses the struggle between Chicago and St. Louis to host the Games. Other accounts of the 1904 Games are Lew Carlson, "Giant Patagonians and Hairy Aino: Anthropology Days at the St.

Louis Olympics," *Journal of American Culture*, 12, 3 (1989): 19–26, and Peter Andrews, "The First American Olympics," *American Heritage*, 39, 4 (1988): 39–46. Jack McCallum, "The First Olympic Basketball Tournament: Could Be the Start of Something Big," *Sports Illustrated*, 91, 21 (1999): 96–98, is a semi-fictionalized account of the Games, focusing on the basketball competition.

Frank Cosentino and Glynn Leshon, *Olympic Gold: Canada's Winners in the Summer Games* (Toronto, 1975), provides information about the Canadian gold medal-winning lacrosse and soccer teams and biographical data on Etienne Desmarteam and George Lyon, Canada's individual gold medal winners.

ATHENS 1906

Bill Mallon

THE INTERCALATED OLYMPIC GAMES

In 1906, special Olympic Games were conducted in Athens outside of the usual pattern of holding the Games of the Olympiad only every four years. They are known by various names—Intercalated Olympic Games, Intermediate Olympic Games, and International Olympic Games in Athens. The 1906 Olympics are controversial, as their status remains debated, and to this day, the International Olympic Committee does not accord them official Olympic status. However, many Olympic historians and statisticians (notably David Wallechinsky, Volker Kluge, Karl Lennartz, and Erich Kamper) do consider the 1906 Games to have been Olympic. In fact, they may have saved Coubertin's nascent Olympic Movement and should be considered among the most important of Olympic Games.

After the 1896 Olympic Games, the Greeks wanted all future modern Olympic Games to be held in Greece. At a reception on April 12, 1896, King Georgios I expressed the hope that his country would be nominated the "permanent and continuous arena of the Olympic Games." His speech noted:

> Greece, who has been the mother and nurse of the Olympic Games in ancient times and who had undertaken to celebrate them once more today, can now hope, as their success has gone beyond all expectations, that the foreigners, who have honored her with their presence, will remember Athens as the peaceful meeting place of all nations, as the tranquil and permanent seat of the Olympic Games.

The Greeks did not support Coubertin's idea of spreading the Olympics around to various cities; in fact, they firmly opposed it. And they had support for this opposition, notably from the Americans and the Germans.

Shortly after the 1896 Olympic Games, the American athletes who had competed in Athens wrote a letter to *The New York Times* stating that all Olympic Games should be held in Greece. King Georgios I of Greece and the Greek cabinet supported the idea of holding future Olympic Games in Greece. Coubertin suggested to the king a compromise in which, in between the standard cycle of Olympics, Pan-Hellenic Games would be held in Athens every four years alternating with the Olympic Games, such that one or the other would be held every two years. The Greeks wanted these to be termed Olympic Games, but Coubertin initially did not accord them that privilege.

There was some support for holding the first of these Games in 1898. But the idea was stalled by the Thirty Days' War that occurred between the Greeks and the Turks in 1897. At the 1901 International Olympic Committee (IOC) Session, held in Paris from May 21 to 23, the three German members of the IOC (Willibald Gebhardt, Duke de Talleyrand-Perigord, and Edouard de Salms-Horstmar) suggested to the entire IOC that a second series of Olympic Games should be organized in between the regular series of Olympic Games.

A record of the Greek proposal still exists. The proposal noted:

> In the year 1902 a session of our committee is to take place in Athens, [at] which an exact schedule and program for future Olympic Games is to be established—with special consideration for those to be held in the future in Athens. The international competitions will take place every two years, alternating between Athens and other large cities of the cultured states, such that every four years these Olympic Games will be celebrated in the Greek capital. In the year 1906 the second Olympic Games will take place in Athens, the third in 1910, etc.

The details of what exactly happened over the next few years now become murky. Karl Lennartz has noted, "At the 1901 session in Paris the IOC resolved that the Games would take place every two years, alternating between Athens and other cities." However, Wolf Lyberg has stated, "It would therefore be foolish for the IOC to lend its growing good name to such an adventure. Such games should rather be organized on a national basis instead of an international." (Lyberg, *The History of the IOC Sessions. I. 1894–1939* [Lausanne, 1994], p. 26). But Lennartz has noted that Coubertin eventually acquiesced and gave tacit support to the plan.

It is known for certain that Coubertin by this time was no longer in ironclad control of the IOC. John A. Lucas has written that Coubertin's position as leader of the Olympic Movement by then was quite tenuous. Lucas noted that Coubertin's loss of control came as the result of four problems: 1) his resignation and loss of control over the 1900 Olympics, 2) Greek nationalists who, through the newspaper *Messager d'Athènes*, labeled Coubertin as an interloper into the idea of Olympic Games, which they labeled as a purely Greek notion, 3) the challenge to Coubertin's authority by American sport officials, notably James E. Sullivan, and 4) internal defections within the IOC in which many of the people supporting Coubertin resigned.

In 1905, an Olympic Congress, which doubled as the Sixth IOC Session, was held in Brussels from June 9 to 14. Although Coubertin had put off the decision of what to do about the 1906 Olympics in Athens until this Congress, little is really mentioned about it as the Congress was split into three commissions whose agendas were: 1) pedagogy, 2) sports, and 3) physical education. But the Greek IOC member, Alexandros Merkati, announced at the Brussels Congress that the Committee for the Olympic Games at Athens had been formed and would begin holding the Olympic Games every four years beginning in 1906. Coubertin appears to have resigned himself to the idea by now as he later noted that the IOC would "support additional Greek games in the year 1906." In addition, a letter from Coubertin to Jiří Guth of Bohemia cites the decision of the IOC members in Brussels to accept "the Olympic Games of Athens." Thus it appears that the IOC and Coubertin did agree to hold Olympic Games in Athens in 1906.

Coubertin did not attend the 1906 Olympic Games, but other members of the IOC did come to Athens. The Spalding report noted, "In attendance at the Olympic Games were many members of the International Committee, and they held several conferences during their stay in Athens. Among those who were very prominent in such affairs were: Dr. W[illibald] Gebhardt, Colonel [Viktor Gustaf] Balck, Count [Clarence] de Rosen, Count [Eugenio] Brunetta d'Usseaux, Dr. Jiří Guth, Count Alex[andros] Mer[k]ati, Baron [Frederik Willem Christiaan Hendrik] van Tuyll [van Serooskerken]."

The 1906 Olympic Games began on Sunday, April 22 [April 9 on the Julian Calendar then used by the Greeks]. These Opening Ceremonies were important in the history of the Olympic Movement because they featured several innovations that are now standard portions of the Opening Ceremonies. Notably, all the athletes marched in together in the first Parade of Nations. In addition, the athletes' teams were preceded by a flag bearer carrying the flag of their nation.

Over 60,000 spectators crowded the Panathenaic Stadium for the Opening Ceremonies. The royal procession began the ceremonies, preceded by both the Greek and British national anthems, entering the stadium at about 3:15 P.M. A carriage containing King Georgios and his sister, Queen Alexandra of Great Britain; King Edward VII of Great Britain and his sister-in-law, the Greek queen, Olga; and the Prince of Wales with his wife, Princess Mary, then entered the stadium, followed by members of the Greek royal family and representatives of various European courts. The royal family passed through the *foustanellofori*, or *evzoni*, a group of soldiers serving as the king's bodyguards, who formed two long lines in front of the stadium, with a lane for the royalty about 10 feet wide. After the entrance of the royal families, Crown Prince Konstantinos then stood in front of the box and addressed the king of Greece as follows:

Your Majesty, the Committee whose president I am induced by the law that gave us the charge and the preparation of the Olympic Games, has invited to the Stadium, which was rebuilt in its ancient beauty by a patriotic Greek citizen, all the nations that regard athletic and gymnastics as the progress and inducement of civilization. We are grateful today seeing that our pains have been crowned with success by the presence of international teams, which are set before your Majesty and the King of the strong United Kingdom of England.

Greece opens its arms to receive the best in rank in physical education, those who came here from all over the civilized world. The Stadium is broadened during these days into a universal Stadium, whose victory will spread its laurels on the heads of the best of the nations. And whatever country the victors will carry their prize of their worthy victory, we hope they will not forget that we have crowned their head with laurels from Olympia, that have grown on the banks of the Alpheus. Let them not forget they have been applauded and crowned as Olympic victors on the sacred ground of Athens by the descendants of ancient Greece, who recognize as brothers those of the art of Athletics, the noble daughter of Greece has wrought up its victors. Leaving Athens as victors, let them consider themselves as other Athenians since they have been crowned by Athenian prizes. Under such good omen I have the honor to ask your Majesty to proclaim the openings of the Olympic Games of 1906.

King Georgios of Greece stood up and proclaimed the formal opening of the Olympic Games, after which the athletes began the Parade of Nations. They marched around the ancient Greek track in rows of four led by the flag bearer of each nation. As the flag bearer passed the royal box all of them lowered their flag as a salute to King Georgios and King Edward. While the athletes marched, four choirs played music, including the Olympic hymn, composed in 1896 by Spyros Samaras.

The 1906 Olympic Games continued from April 22 through May 2 [April 9–19]. There was competition in 13 sports and 74 events, much smaller than the bloated programs of 1900 and 1904, but much better organized. Many of the events took place in the Panathenaic Stadium (athletics, gymnastics, tug-of-war, weightlifting, wrestling). Other venues included the Zappeion for fencing, the Neo Phaliron Velodrome for cycling and the football matches, the Neo Phaliron Bay for rowing, swimming, and diving, the Kallithea Shooting Stand for the shooting events, and the Athens Lawn Tennis Club at Illisos for tennis.

Twenty nations competed at the 1906 Olympic Games with 847 athletes competing. Women competed only in singles and mixed doubles lawn tennis, with Marie Décugis of France joining five Greek women in the competition.

The star of the athletics events was the American weightman, Martin Sheridan. Sheridan was primarily a discus thrower, but in Athens he won five medals, with golds in the discus and shot put, and silvers in the standing high jump, long jump, and stone throw. He was also a heavy favorite in the Ancient Pentathlum event, modeled after the ancient Greek Pentathlon, but he had to withdraw with an injury.

Paul Pilgrim of the United States pulled off a rare Olympic double, winning the 400 and 800 meters, even though he had been added to the American team only as an afterthought and he had to pay his own way to Athens. His double feat was not matched at the Olympics until 1976 when Cuba's Alberto Juantorena won the same events at Montréal. Several American athletes defended their Olympic titles in Athens. Archie Hahn had won the 60 meters, 100 meters, and 200 meters at St. Louis in 1904. He had only the 100 meters to contest in Athens, but he won the gold medal again. James Lightbody also defended his title in the 1,500 meters. In the standing jumps, Ray Ewry again won the high jump and long jump, as he had in 1900 and 1904. He had also won the standing triple jump in those years, but it was not contested in Athens.

The Greeks were hoping to produce the champion of the marathon footrace, as Spyridon Loues had done in 1896 at the first Olympic Games of the modern era. But it was not to be. The race was won by the Canadian, William Sherring, who had traveled to Athens on his own two months prior to the Olympics and had trained daily on the Olympic course. The best Greek, Ioannis Alepous, finished fifth. When Sherring entered the Panathenaic Stadium, he was met by Prince Georgios, who ran alongside him to the finish, as he had done in 1896 with Loues.

The most important feature of the athletics competitions was its international nature. In fact, there were 19 competing nations in the athletics, with eight teams entering more than 10 competitors. It was the most representative international sporting competition contested to that date.

In the cycling competitions, Italy's Francesco Verri won three gold medals on the track—in the match sprint, the one lap (333 1/3 meters) time trial, and the 5,000-meter race. As in 1896, the cycling road race was conducted on the same course as the marathon footrace, but with the riders beginning in Athens, riding to Marathon, and then retracing their route back to Athens. The French swept the medals in this event, led by Fernand Vast.

In gymnastics, there was a team competition and two individual all-around events, one with five events and one with six events. France's Pierre Payssé won both of the individual all-around competitions, with Alberto Braglia (Italy) winning the silver and Georges Charmoile (France) the bronze in both. The team event went to Norway. A rope climbing event was also conducted, won by George Aliprantis, a Greek athlete based in Constantinople.

The aquatic competitions were conducted in the Neo Phaliron Bay. On April 25–26 [April 12–13], the weather played havoc with the competitions, as bitter cold and high winds forced the postponement of several events. Eventually the entire programs for both sports were finished. In rowing, crews from the Italian club Bucintoro Venezia won three competitions—the coxed pairs at 1,000 meters, the coxed pairs at one mile, and the coxed fours. Three members of this club won gold medals in all three events—Enrico Bruna, Emilio Fontanella, and the coxswain, Giorgio Cesana. There were four swimming events and a diving competition conducted in 1906. Charles Daniels of the United States won the 100-meter freestyle, narrowly defeating the 1904 champion, Hungary's Zoltán von Halmay.

There were 12 shooting events conducted at the Kallithea Shooting Stand, which allowed shooters to earn multiple medals. Primary among these were Léon Moreaux (France), who won five medals, including two gold, and his countryman Louis Richardet, who won three gold medals. Another Frenchman, Max Décugis, won three gold medals on the tennis courts—the singles, the men's doubles (with Maurice Germot), and the mixed doubles (with his wife Marie).

Greece's Dimitrios Tofalos won the two-hand barbell lift, defeating the favorite, Josef Steinbach of Austria. The barbell that was used for the winning lift of 142.4 kgs. was actually owned by Tofalos. This and the judging greatly upset Steinbach. He wished to use the continental style, in which the lifter moved the weight to his waist and then stopped before moving it to his shoulders. However, the style required at the Olympics insisted that the weight be moved continuously to the shoulders without touching the body before then. The rule read as follows:

> c) It is forbidden to let the weight rest on the knees or on the stomach in lifting it to the shoulder. But, if in carrying it from the shoulder above the head, the bar touches the chest of the competitor, the lifting is taken into consideration.

After he had lost the competition and Tofalos won, Steinbach returned to the lifting platform and picked up the winning weight in his own style, moving it to his shoulders in two movements, and then jerked it overhead six times in succession. The Greek crowd, unaware of the rules, initially thought that Steinbach had been cheated of victory. British writers, however, thought that Steinbach had been quite unsportsmanlike.

Although the scheduled competitions had concluded with the marathon race on Tuesday afternoon, one additional event was held in the morning of May 2 [April 19], a 3,000-meter walk competition. This was added to the schedule at the last minute because of a controversy that occurred when George Bonhag had won the 1,500-meter walk event, with several other competitors having been disqualified.

Many people thought that Bonhag, who was primarily a runner and had never competed in a walking competition previously, should have been disqualified for running. The additional supplementary walk event was won by György Sztantics of Hungary. As in the 1,500-meter walk, the first- and second-place finishers, Robert Wilkinson and Eugen Spiegler, were both disqualified.

Early in the afternoon of May 2 [April 19], the Closing Ceremonies of the 1906 Intercalated Olympic Games were held. The prizes, which included medals as well as an olive wreath, were given on this day from the sacred Altis in Olympia. Crown Prince Konstantinos presented a bronze statuette of a wolf suckling Romulus and Remus to the "Italian athletes Roman and Olympian Games committee." Manager Matthew Halpin rounded up the American team and led a three-cheers for the Royal Family of Greece. Gymnastic exercises were given by 6,000 Greek school-children for the spectators. All participants were also given a souvenir medal. The Games were closed by King Georgios at about 3:30 P.M. That evening a reception was given for the athletes and the officials by the Greek committee at the Zappeion. At this reception, King Georgios made the following speech:

> I feel the greatest joy in seeing around me the representatives of almost all the nations that take an interest in gymnastics and athletics. It is a great honor for Greece that everyone has striven to gain the reward of victory in Athens. The recollections of ancient times, the patriotism of Averof, and the zeal of the Greek nation have proved that my capital is by way of excellence the best city that can with courage entertain strangers who have an aspiration of getting athletic laurels. It is from you, who represent the international ideas about gymnastics and the different athletic games, it is from you that we expect to hear whether these games, organized according to the laws of the Greek kingdom by a committee presided over by my son, the Crown Prince of Greece, have proved to be successful. One thing, however, that I consider to be my duty and my pleasure is to extend the expression of my sincere thanks for your kindness in coming here from all over the world in response to the invitation by Greece. You can be sure, gentlemen, and I beg you to transmit this from my part to all the governments, committees, clubs and societies, that you may represent that the royal family of Greece and the Greek nation have been exceedingly happy in having you with them during these beautiful days. Also, they will feel the same pleasure every four years, when according to the laws of the Greek kingdom, Greece will have an opportunity to renew the bonds of peace with all the nations with whom she is happy to cooperate for the good of civilization and of progress.

The Intercalated Athens Olympics of 1906 were not supposed to be an isolated event. It was expected that the Greeks would hold the games again in 1910, 1914, and then quadrennially thereafter. But it never came to pass. Greece and its Balkan neighbors were basically fighting wars the entire time, based on their former imperial land claims. Greece did make tentative plans for Intercalated Olympic Games in 1910, going so far as to form an organizing committee, with Alexandros Merkati as its head. However, its 1907–1908 war with Turkey over Crete and its militaristic globalization beginning in 1910 in an effort to ward off the Ottoman Empire prevented the nation from putting much emphasis on sporting contests. The Balkan Wars of 1913 and 1914 and the onset of World War I in the region in 1914 eliminated any chance of Intercalated Olympic Games in 1914, although again an organizing committee had been formed. The ongoing conflagration of World War I into 1918, much of it fought in the Balkans and particularly in the Macedonian area, eliminated any chance of 1918 Intercalated Olympic Games. The Greek economy of the era, which was tenuous, and with most of its budget devoted to defense, also obviated the hosting of an Olympic Games. After 1920, the special series of Greek Olympic Games was never mentioned again. There is no suggestion in the historical record, however embryonic, to hold them in 1922 or ever after.

So the question now is asked: were the 1906 competitions truly Olympic Games? To most historians, it appears that they were. The IOC gave them their approval, with Coubertin's approval. He discussed them as Olympic Games several times in the *Bulletin of the IOC*, the forerunner of *Olympic Review*. All of the world's media referred to the 1906 Athens events as "Olympic." All of the material printed by the Athens Organizing Committee in 1906 refers to the "Olympic Games" or the name in another language.

But Coubertin had not been overly supportive of the idea and it appears that the IOC approved this distinction against his wishes. He went along, as it seems he had to, as his control of the IOC was less firm than it had once been. Lennartz has noted that at the IOC Session in Athens in 1906, for which Coubertin was not present, a palace coup of sorts was attempted, with the members offering the IOC chairmanship to the Greek Crown Prince. When the members returned from Athens, he had correspondence from several of them and was able to stay in control, though barely. It is obvious that Coubertin had little love lost for the 1906 Olympic Games.

In fact, in his writings after 1906, he would refuse to list them as a formal Olympic Games, even though they certainly had that title in April 1906. Based on his writings, beginning as early as 1908, he ignored the 1906 Olympics. Once he overcame this seeming insurrection from the 1906 IOC Session, the IOC was ruled quite autocratically by Coubertin and, to some extent, can be considered Coubertin's ideas and decisions almost solely. It appears that the eventual IOC policy of not including the 1906 Olympics on its list of Olympic Games is based solely on Coubertin's refusal to acknowledge them as such.

However, the IOC did make an official ruling concerning the status of the 1906 Olympic Games. At the 41st IOC Session in London in 1948, Dr. Ferenc Mező, a Hungarian member, made a proposal that the Intermediate Games in Athens (1906) should be accepted as the IIIB Olympic Games. It was decided that this proposal would be placed in the hands of the Brundage Commission. The Brundage Commission was a three-man commission headed by future IOC President Avery Brundage of the United States. The other members were Sidney Dawes of Canada and Miguel Angel Moenck of Cuba. They met in New Orleans, Louisiana, in January 1949.

In its report, the Brundage Commission noted, "It is not considered that any special recognition that the IOC might give to participants in these Games at this late date would add any prestige, and the danger of establishing an embarrassing precedent would more than offset any advantage." They presented their report at the 42nd IOC Session in Rome in 1949. Their report dealt with 32 items, the fourth of which was the 1906 Olympic Games. The item was listed as "Acceptance of the Intermediate Games 1906," and the Brundage Commission conclusion was "Rejected." But it is quite obvious from reading the minutes that the decision was made only by referring to Coubertin's writings and not looking at any primary sources from circa 1906.

In contradistinction to this IOC position, it appears that the Athens Olympic Games were considered official Olympic Games in 1906. In fact, all of the international newspapers termed this sporting festival of 1906 as "Olympic Games," using their native language for the appellation. They should maintain this designation, for they deserve it. They were very important Olympic Games. After the problems that occurred in Paris in 1900 and St. Louis in 1904, these successful Athens Games of 1906 helped resurrect the flagging Olympic Movement. The Games were the most international to date, they were the best-held to date, and they had the most international media attention of any of the Games since the 1896 Olympics in Athens. These were the 1906 Olympic Games.

BIBLIOGRAPHIC ESSAY

The Official Report for the 1906 Olympic Games was edited by Panagiotis S. Savvidis, and the title transliterates to *Leukoma ton en Athenais B' Diethnon Olympiakon 1906 (ΛΕΥΚΩΜΑ ΤΩΝ ΕΝ ΑΘΗΝΑΙΣ Β' ΔΙΕΘΝΩΝ ΟΛΥΜ-ΠΙΑΚΩΝ ΑΓΩΝΩΝ)* (Athens, 1907). Unfortunately, it is available only in the original Greek version and is thus difficult for many Western researchers. The Greek organizing committee also published Official Programs, complete Entry Lists, and, after the Games, Official Results. The results had titles in both Greek and French and were entitled *Diethnais Olympiakoi Agones 1906. Episema Apotoloesmata/Jeux olympiques internationaux 1906. Resultats officials.*

There are two useful modern studies of these Games. Karl Lennartz and Walter Teutenberg published *Die Olympischen Spiele 1906 in Athen* (Kassel, Germany: 1992), which is in German and includes reproductions of a number of primary documents and photographs from the Games. More recently, Bill Mallon published *The 1906 Olympic Games: Results for All Competitors in All Events, with Commentary* (Jefferson, NC, 1999). This contains virtually complete results with some background in sociopolitical history and an index of all competitors at the 1906 Olympic Games.

More recently, a subcommittee of the International Society of Olympic Historians (ISOH) has completed work on a document submitted to the IOC requesting that full Olympic status be granted to the 1906 Olympic Games. The subcommittee consisted of Lennartz, Mallon, and David Wallechinsky, although the document was primarily written by Lennartz. Entitled "The 2nd International Olympic Games in Athens 1906," it was published in the decennial issue of the *Journal of Olympic History* (Vol. 10, Dec 2002/Jan 2003) and then again as a special issue consisting only of this article that was distributed to the members of the IOC.

Several other sources exist in various languages from circa 1906. In English, James Sullivan published *The Olympic Games at Athens 1906* (New York, 1906), as part of his Spalding Athletic Library. Karl Johannes Haagensen wrote *Athenfærden 1906. Nordmæden Deltagelse i de Olympiske Lege* in Norwegian (Kristiania [Oslo], 1907). In Swedish, Baltazar Roosval wrote *Med svenskarne til Athen* (Stockholm, 1906), and Viktor Gustaf Balck wrote *Olympiska Spele i Athén. Redogorelse for sveriges Deltagande* (Stockholm, 1906). Perhaps the best-known contemporary European effort was by Carl Diem in German, *Die Olympischen Spiele 1906* (publishing data unknown).

Prior to Lennartz's recent study of the 1906 Olympic Games, few journal articles existed that discussed them in any detail. Notable among these are John A. Lucas's "American Involvement in the Athens Olympic Games of 1906: Bridge Between

Failure and Success," in *Stadion* 6 (1981): 217–228. Fritz K. Mathys wrote "Those Controversial Games of 1906," which was published in *Olympic Review* 146 (December 1979): 694–695. For the IOC's discussions about the 1906 Games, see Wolf Lyberg, *The History of the IOC Sessions. I. 1894–1939* (Lausanne, 1994).

The Games are described in most standard Olympic histories. More recently, Athanassios Tarassouleas wrote *Olympic Games in Athens: 1896–1906* (Athens, 1988), which devotes almost 100 pages to the 1906 Olympics.

LONDON 1908

James Coates

THE GAMES OF THE FOURTH OLYMPIAD

As the Games of the 1908 Olympiad approached, the host country, England, steeped in sporting tradition and one of the most economically powerful nations in the world, was beset with problems of funding, politics, partisanship, competition, and weather. The 1908 Olympic Games had originally been awarded to Rome, Italy. This was to be an opportunity for the Italian government to show that it was truly one of the world's great powers, but when Mount Vesuvius erupted in 1906, the government found that it did not have the resources to bring about recovery and finance the Olympic Games. In order to prevent the Italian economy from collapsing, the government relinquished the right to host the 1908 Games, which were then awarded to London.

London 1908—Women's archery competition. Courtesy of International Olympic Committee, IOC Museum Collections.

In the face of England's problems, the British Olympic Organizing Council prepared for the staging of the games of the fourth modern Olympiad. With or without sufficient funding, the London organizers were set to host teams from Australia, Austria, Belgium, the Bahamas, Canada, Denmark, France, Germany, Greece, Holland, Hungary, Italy, Norway, Russia, Sweden, South Africa, Switzerland, and the United States.

As late as July 1, 1908, Lord Desborough, president of the organizing council, issued a call to British citizens to contribute additional funds to ensure that the Olympic Games maintained their "high standards." With the start of the Games scheduled for July 13, the council had only £15,000 of the £65,000 Desborough indicated it needed. In an effort to solicit funds from all possible sources, Desborough chided government officials by revealing that for the 1896 Games, Greece, the host country, had appropriated £125,000 and pointing to the lack of funding from the British government for the 1908 Games. In the end, the only revenue the British Olympic Council was assured of was a one-fourth share of the gross gate receipts. The remainder was to go to the Franco-British Exposition, on whose grounds the Games were being held.

Lacking financial support, Desborough and his Council members were forced to abandon several activities slated for the athletes. Included among these activities were a reception and excursions to a few of the historical sites and cities of Great Britain. Without the generosity of the general public, explained Desborough, the hospitality afforded the British at previous Olympic Games would not be able to be returned in England.

Despite the lack of financial support, organizers of the London Games openly welcomed the British royalty and many other heads of state attending the opening ceremonies on July 13. Included among this cast of dignitaries were King Edward VII of Great Britain, who officially opened the Games, accompanied by Queen Alexandra; King Georgios of Greece; King Haakon of Norway; Crown Prince Gustav Adolph of Sweden; and officials from all 19 participating countries.

Leaving Buckingham Palace just a little after three o'clock, King Edward arrived at the stadium for the opening ceremonies at 3:30. Upon his arrival, the King was officially greeted by Lord Desborough, Baron Pierre de Coubertin, founder of the modern Olympic Games, the members of the International Olympic Committee, and three members of the British Olympic Association, Lord Selby, Lord Blythe, and M. Imre Kiralfy.

The king remained at the opening activities for almost two hours. His interest in the Games was no surprise, given that he was a prolific sportsman. The British press assured readers that King Edward was the most appropriate person to open the Games and that England, with its fine tradition in field sports, was the right country to host the event known for bringing peace to nations of the world rather than war.

Although the government's financial support for the Games was weak, receptions for the foreign leaders and international Olympic officials were hosted by prominent citizens on behalf of the British Government. The hospitality and flowery speeches at these events mitigated somewhat the lack of financial support on the part of the government.

Taking center stage at these 1908 Games, along with a lack of funding, was the weather and attendance. Throughout the Games, the weather ranged from fair to poor. And while no one can control the weather, criticism of weather conditions was constant. The [London] *Times* noted that at its best in mid-July, the British weather is not very good. From the opening day of the Games, it was frequently rainy and chilly. On only a few occasions was the weather excellent. For example, on the day of the marathon, the crowd enjoyed the best weather of the Games and turned out in record numbers. The large crowds on the last two days of the Games were a blessed sight for Olympic officials. The early attendance at the Games had been so poor that organizers reduced the price of admission into the stadium.

Although the weather cleared for the marathon, it helped to magnify another of the major flaws of the London Games: rule disputes. During the marathon one of the many controversies occurred. After entering the stadium well ahead of his closest competitor, Pietri Dorando of Italy, struggling and in pain, more than likely unable to finish the race, was aided by British officials. This was a clear violation of the rules concerning attendants on the course. Dorando's condition was so bad that rumors that he had died persisted after the day's events were completed.

The next runner entering the stadium after Dorando was an American, John J. Hayes. As the rules required, Hayes completed the race on his own power, and then, under instructions from U.S. officials and coaches, filed a protest against the actions of the British officials. The governing body ruled in favor of the American runner and disqualified Dorando, enabling the United States to capture three of the first four places in the race. The officials running the Games believed that Italy's Dorando should have been declared the marathon winner and that the Americans were being poor sportsmen. With Lord Desborough, recognized as a very fair and honest person, firmly concurring that officials had been wrong to aid Dorando, the hearing committee had little choice but to allow Hayes's protest.

Controversy was a constant companion of the London Olympic Games, and the marathon affair only served to enhance the belief of many Americans that the British officials were willing to go to almost any lengths to prevent a U.S. victory. Anglo-American friction had begun with the opening day ceremonies, when the American, Swedish, and Finnish flags were not displayed. In protest, some Swedes left the games. Finland, under Russian domination, could not afford to do much in protest. When Ralph Rose, a shot-putter and flag bearer refused, as a customary courtesy, to dip the American flag when passing before King Edward VII, the remaining activities were held with open animosity. The marathon was no exception.

The marathon protest was just one of several launched by the Americans; others were made in the tug-of-war, the 400-meter run, and the pole vault. In addition, several nations were concerned with the scoring system being utilized.

The tug-of-war rules used at the Games had been written by the British Olympic Association. The rules prohibited participants from wearing specially prepared boots or shoes or boots or shoes with any projecting nails, tips, springs, or points. According to the Americans, not all the competing teams were made to comply with these rules. Of the 19 countries competing in the Games, only 2 entered teams in the tug-of-war. The host country, England, had three teams in the event, and the Americans had one team. The American team first competed against a team from Liverpool, wearing heavy boots with steel rims around the heels, a clear violation of the stated rules. The Americans, in regular street shoes, protested but were told that the shoes were acceptable because they were the type normally worn by the Liverpool policemen who comprised the team.

Despite believing that they were being unfairly treated, the Americans decided to compete against the Liverpool team. The Americans, however, made no effort to win. By making no effort, they wanted to show that the use of the boots against street shoes was unsportsmanlike and gave the Liverpool team an unfair advantage.

The Liverpool team easily defeated the Americans. Matthew Halpin, the American team manager, told event officials that if the rules were not adhered to his team would not continue. The officials ignored this protest, and the American team left the field. After hearing of the incident, James E. Sullivan, commissioner of the American contingent, formally protested to the British Olympic Association. The British association referred the case to the Amateur Athletic Association, which ruled that the decision was fair.

During the second week of the Games, another of the many Anglo-American disputes arose. While running the 400-meter race, John C. Carpenter of the American team was accused of fouling another runner and was disqualified. The disqualification came despite a rule providing that in the case of any boring (fouling), the race would be rerun a half-hour later. Running in the finals of this race were three Americans—Carpenter; John B. Taylor, a black man from the University of Pennsylvania; and William C. Robbins of Cambridge, Massachusetts; and one British runner, Lieutenant Wyndham Halswelle, the British champion.

The controversy began when Carpenter was called for fouling Halswelle. The two men had traded the lead back and forth during the latter stage of the race, but British officials came onto the track and declared the race over before the runners reached the finish line. All the runners continued, except Taylor who stopped when informed by the officials. Spectators argued whether a foul had been committed. The Amateur Athletic Association held a hearing on the situation, getting testimony from the British officials and Halswelle. Not one American official or runner was asked to testify before the association. After Carpenter's disqualification, the race was rerun two days later, but Carpenter's American teammates refused to compete, allowing Halswelle to win in a walkover. The hostility between the British officials and the American contingent intensified.

In part because of the many controversies that plagued the London Games, Olympic officials declined to present an overall team championship trophy to any nation. The chief concern was the scoring system used for the Games. Another concern was the inclusion of events in which few, if any, countries other than Great Britain participated. These issues combined with the disputes over questionable officiating led the Games committee to declare that an overall championship trophy would not be given. Only individual event winners were recognized.

Even the closing ceremonies caused concern. As Queen Alexandra was presenting awards, she paid special attention to Italy's Dorando. She presented him with a personal gift, a cup, as well as an Olympic wreath. Considering that he was not a winner, some of the Americans felt that this was a slight to John Hayes and the United States.

Hayes, as well as the rest of the American team, heard from President Theodore Roosevelt. Upon the team's arrival back in the United States, they were received by the president at his home in Oyster Bay, New York. He congratulated the team for their victories on behalf of the nation.

Officials and athletes from many of the 19 participating countries complained of the handling of the fourth modern Olympic Games. Prior to these Games, each nation understood that the management of each event would be handled by the association governing that sport in Great Britain. That association would be responsible both for providing all officials and for the conduct of the athletes. Foreign representatives taking part in the Games had no part in their management.

Having local associations with sole responsibility over their respective events caused much of the confusion over the conduct of the Games. The scoring system at the London Games also caused much confusion. British officials scored the contests by awarding one point to each victory and nothing to second- and third-place finishers. Events both inside and outside the stadium were scored. The contests inside the stadium included track-and-field events. Events outside the stadium included regatta, lacrosse, and tennis. This system placed Great Britain well ahead of all other nations, since very few of them participated in activities outside of the stadium.

The United States's scoring system, used in previous Games, was to award five points for first place, three points for second place, and one point for third place. The Americans calculated their scores only for the stadium events. Like most other teams, the United States sent athletes to participate mainly in stadium events, while Great Britain, not having to travel, had athletes in all events.

What each of these nations and their athletes recognized, however, was that the host city and country, London, England, made certain that the Games themselves were the feature attraction. This had not been the case with either the 1900 Games in Paris or the 1904 Games in St. Louis, where a world's fair had been the main event and the Olympic Games just a minor sideshow.

Organizers of the Franco-British Exhibition were strong advocates of the Olympic movement and sought to make the Games the featured attraction in 1908. The track-and-field stadium seated 68,000 people and had been paid for by the Franco-British Exhibition organizers. As a consequence, the economic success of the 1908 London Olympics was of little concern for the Games organizers. Regardless of the attendance or sponsorships, they did not have to worry about their largest capital expenditure.

Attendance for most of the Games was poor. For only a few events did the crowds meet or exceed expectations. In addition to the poor weather, the cost of admission was a major contributor to the poor attendance. Ticket prices ranged from 70 cents to five dollars. Although the organizers intended to double these prices on the day of the marathon, the poor attendance forced them to reduce prices prior to the marathon. Despite the controversial nature of the 1908 London Olympics, most observers and participants agreed that the Games were helpful for the future of the Olympics. These Games served as a vehicle for ways in which future Games could be structured. No longer would local officials and host countries have sole responsibility for scoring, officiating, or judging the events. No longer would the Games take a subordinate status to other events. The London Games aided the Olympic movement in becoming a worldwide spectacle with international cooperation on all issues of concern.

BIBLIOGRAPHICAL ESSAY

Some archival records of the 1908 London Olympics may be found at the International Olympic Academy in Athens and at the International Olympic Committee archives in Lausanne. The official report is Theodore A. Cook, ed., *The Fourth Olympiad: Being the Official Report of the Olympic Games of 1908 Celebrated in London under the Patronage of His Most Gracious King Edward VII and by the Sanction of the International Olympic Committee* (London, 1909). The rules and regulations governing the competition are spelled out in *The Rules of Sport: Being the International Code for All Competitions in the Olympic Games* (London, 1908). See also Max Howell and Reet Howell, *The Olympic Movement Restored: The 1908 Games* (Quebec, 1976) and Ossi Brucker, "Die Tragoedie den Marathonlaufers Dorando Pietri," *Olympische Feuer* 33 (1983): 46–58.

Other books that may be helpful for the history of the 1908 Games are David Chester, *The Olympic Games Handbook: An Authentic History of Both the Ancient and Modern Olympic Games* (New York, 1975) and Endre Kahlich, *Olympic Games 1896–1972* (Budapest, 1972). For a comparison of the way the Games were viewed on both sides of the Atlantic, see George R. Matthews, "The Controversial

Olympic Games of 1908 As Viewed by the *New York Times* and the *Times* of London," *Journal of Sport History* 7, 2 (summer 1980): 40–53. Bruce Kidd, *Tom Longboat* (Don Mills, Ontario, 1980) is a biography of the great Canadian Indian long-distance runner who competed in the controversial marathon at the 1908 Games.

The Theodore Roosevelt Papers at the Library of Congress, Washington, D.C., contain some references to the 1908 Games. The primary newspaper source is, of course, the *Times* [London], especially the July 11 to July 28 daily and weekend issues, although the *New York Times*, the *Los Angeles Times*, and the *Washington Post* also contain articles of interest.

STOCKHOLM 1912

Ulf Hamilton

THE GAMES OF THE FIFTH OLYMPIAD

In Sweden the Olympic Games of 1912 are often referred to as "the Sunshine Olympiad." The Swedish organizers were lucky with the weather—constant sunshine through July when the Games took place. The usual conditions—considerably colder and with rain from time to time—would have probably diminished the glorious impression the Olympic Games gave to people like the young Avery Brundage and George S. Patton, the German sports leader Carl Diem, the king of Sweden, and others. The V Olympic Games in Stockholm were, however, a combination of luck, excellent planning, and a smooth operation.

During the first years of the twentieth century, the planning of the Olympic Games was in some jeopardy. The Games of 1908 were at first given to Rome, but owing to the eruption of Mount Vesuvius in 1906 the Games were handed over to London on rather short notice. After London, the International Olympic Committee

Stockholm 1912—Before Olympic villages were built specifically for each set of Games, athletes were housed in existing facilities. For the Stockholm Games of 1912, athletes stayed in the Military College, shown here. Courtesy of International Olympic Committee, IOC Museum Collections.

(IOC) wanted more long-term planning of the Games, which were steadily growing in numbers of participating athletes and nations. Bidding for the 1912 Games was declared open, with Berlin, Germany, in a strong position to get the Games. In spite of this, Sweden, through its IOC member Viktor Balck, started to plan for a possible Olympic Games in Stockholm.

Even if it was a small and somewhat remote nation, Sweden occupied a relatively strong position in the Olympic movement. Balck had been a member of the IOC from 1894, and had good connections with the chairman and soul of the Olympic idea, Baron Pierre de Coubertin. In 1900 Sweden sent an additional member to the IOC, Count Clarence von Rosen, even though the usual membership was one person per nation. Moreover, Sweden had competed successfully in the Olympic Games in Athens 1906 and London 1908, and its strong gymnastic tradition—with gymnasts such as Per Henrik Ling and his son Hjalmar—added to the nation's prestige.

Returning from the IOC meetings to Sweden, the efficient Balck at once started to explore the possibilities of bringing the Games to Stockholm. Balck's inquiries met with great interest. The national athletic associations wanted to take part, and the royal family—headed by the active tennis player King Gustaf V—wanted to be involved. Most importantly, the Swedish government, through a special state lottery, could financially support the Games.

In Germany the planning had been less successful; the main problem being the financing of the Games. At the IOC meeting in Berlin in 1909, Balck was able to present his proposal. When Coubertin then argued strongly in favor of Sweden's proposal, Germany withdrew its candidacy. Accordingly the Games of 1912 were given to Stockholm, and two years later the IOC fulfilled its long-term planning goal by giving the 1916 Games to Berlin.

The Swedish Organization Committee (SOC)—headed by Balck and the industrialist and former athlete Sigfrid Edström (the future president of the IOC)—and the IOC began a long and complicated negotiation regarding the Olympic program. Sweden wanted a smaller program of Games than the London 1908 program and offered to organize only four sports: track and field (with tug-of-war), wrestling, swimming, and gymnastics, a tiny number, compared with London's 22 sports. The IOC at once added sailing, rowing, and fencing. The point of view of both Sweden and the IOC was that the London program had been too extensive. Winter sports—London had an ice skating competition—were rejected, along with programs with apparent Anglo-Saxon roots like polo, rackets, lacrosse, and motorboat racing. Sweden argued intensively against boxing, because it was not legal in the country. Sweden also rejected soccer. Denmark and Great Britain, however, argued strongly in favor of those two programs, and as a compromise, boxing was excluded but the SOC arranged a soccer competition (in which England beat Denmark in the final). The content of the program of gymnastics also led to some arguments. Sweden—as the native country of P. H. Ling— wanted gymnastics on the program, but the IOC's view was that gymnastics were for display only and not competitive. Again, the negotiations led to a compromise, with an extensive gymnastics program as a demonstration event—in which some women's national teams took part—and limited official competition to three gymnastic events.

The 1912 Games initiated some new programs. The cavalryman and Swedish IOC member von Rosen shaped and endorsed a comprehensive equestrian program with an upper class touch, in which only military officers on active duty were allowed to compete, and in which Sweden dominated the prize lists.

Through ideas and endorsement from Coubertin himself, other new programs were included. To broaden the Olympic ideal, Coubertin wanted a *concourse d'art*, or a program where artists would compete in literature, sculpture, painting, architecture, and music. The SOC delegated this program to Swedish groups connected to the relevant cultural domains. In the end, however, the IOC organized the arts program.

Coubertin also introduced the new program of modern pentathlon—a combination of riding, swimming, fencing, running, and shooting. The SOC found it an interesting challenge and organized a program with some 20 sportsmen from 9 different nations. The young American army officer George S. Patton shot poorly in the competition and finished in fifth place behind four Swedish competitors.

As the Olympic program began to take shape, the question of women's competition was discussed. Generally, Coubertin, the American athletic leader James E. Sullivan, and others, were against women participating. Women did not fit in their conception of the Olympic ideal. The same attitude was taken by the feminist Rose Scott on other grounds. According to Scott, women in swimsuits would invite voyeurism—especially if the athletes were attractive. The SOC maintained a conservative but indifferent attitude. Unlike the Games at London, where women had only participated in a few tennis and swimming events, the Games at Stockholm increased their opportunities for competition. Women took part in the gymnastic displays, and the number of female participants in tennis and swimming—owing to more events for women—increased from 36 in London to 57 in Stockholm.

With respect to shaping the program of the Olympic Games in Stockholm, it is clear that the host nation and its national athletic associations had considerable impact. This was seen in the near exclusion of soccer from the Olympic program, for no substantial reason. Nor was there an explanation for the exclusion of core Anglo-Saxon sports such as cricket, baseball, American football, or rugby. One can understand that motor sport was not suitable, since it had no connection to ancient Greece, but no explicit reason for its exclusion was ever given.

Step by step the SOC put together the program and planned sites for the different events. The central issue, already in Balck's mind when bidding for the Games in 1909, was the need for a new sports arena. Instead of expanding an existing sports facility in Stockholm, the SOC decided to build a new one and leave the nearby existing arena for training purposes. The commission for the design of the new arena was given to the leading Swedish architect Torben Grut. Grut designed an art nouveau stadium in brick and granite to accommodate about 22,000 spectators, located close to the center of the city. The building—still used as a sports arena—has been very well maintained.

Building the stadium was an expensive undertaking for the SOC. To meet the costs of the remaining program sites, the SOC had only limited resources. To some extent Stockholm could take advantage of its location on the water. Commercially, Stockholm was known as "The Venice of the North." The rowing and swimming programs could take place close to the center of the city. The sailing program took place outside Nynäshamn on the Baltic coast some 70 kilometers south of Stockholm. The tennis, modern pentathlon, fencing, shooting, and equestrian programs all occurred in buildings or on grounds at Norra Djurgården close to the stadium and the site of the swimming and rowing programs. In addition, this sports environment included an amusement park named Olympia, for the participant's diversion. This was a part of an extensive social program for the atheletes. On behalf of the royal family, the SOC, and Viktor Balck, a series of receptions and dinners was arranged for the atheletes and officials. A tour of the famous outdoor museum, Skansen, was a happy memory for many of the participants as well.

No Olympic Village was planned. Instead, the SOC arranged lodging in schools, military barracks, and a variety of hotels. The American team stayed on the ship that brought them over the Atlantic.

The official invitations to the Games were sent out in late autumn, 1910. Application forms were distributed in spring 1912 and had to be returned before June 6. The opening ceremonies of the Games took place one month later. Regarding invitations, the SOC had to face some delicate diplomatic issues. The problem was that the IOC had its own definition of nation. According to the IOC and Coubertin, a nation could be a part of another sovereign state, as in the case of Finland being a part of Russia, or Hungary and Bohemia being parts of Austria. As long as the nations had an athletic tradition, they were allowed to have their own representatives in the IOC and were accordingly looked upon as independent nations. During the first Olympic Games this had not been an issue of importance. After London 1908, and the growing international interest in the Olympic Games, Russia and Austria started a campaign to change the IOC definition of nation. Other complications included the problem of Iceland being a part of Denmark, and Ireland being a part of Great Britain, even though Canada, South Africa, and Australia, also parts of the British Commonwealth, competed independently.

Despite the diplomatic controversy, invitations were sent to 41 nations based on the IOC's national definition. Twenty-seven of them sent teams, an increase of five teams over the London Games. The number of participating athletes, including those in the gymnastic display, was well over 3,000, with a thousand more who were expected but did not attend. Among invited nations that did not participate were China, India, Cuba, and Persia (Iran). New participating nations included Chile, Egypt, Japan, and Turkey. The Bahamas took part in 1908 but was not invited to Stockholm. Finland said it was sending a considerable team of 204 athletes—much larger than the Russian team—a situation that threatened renewed controversy. Through diplomatic intervention, it was decided that the Finnish team would be part of the Russian contingent but could display the country's name, Finland, under a Russian flag. In the parade during the opening ceremonies, the Finnish team created a gap between their athletes and the Russian athletes, raised a Finnish flag, and marched on, giving the impression Finland was a sovereign nation. Russian officials reacted strongly, and Swedish authorities promptly confiscated the flag. Finland was, however, very successful in the Games and finished in fourth place, beating out countries such as Germany and France.

With respect to ceremonies and prizes, the SOC adhered to established rules and traditions from earlier Games. Gold, silver, and bronze medals were designed, produced, and distributed accordingly. In addition, a number of challenge trophies were donated by Coubertin, the king of Greece, the emperor of Germany, the English Soccer Union, and others. The American athlete Jim Thorpe won not only two gold medals, but also challenge trophies from the king of Sweden and the emperor of Russia. The opening ceremony on July 6 was a mix of Olympic and Swedish tradition. With the royal family present and the crown prince as honorary—but very active—chairman of the SOC, the king of Sweden declared the Games open. The music had a Swedish touch, but the parade of athletes was traditional. To that was added prayer and psalm singing, presumably an unusual experience for athletes from Japan or Egypt.

The rules for amateur athletics were complied with in full detail by the SOC. Even if different amateur rules existed for nearly all the sports—a special publication on the subject concerning amateur athletics was printed on the behalf of SOC—the basic regulation was the same. As an amateur, one could not earn money from one's sport, one could not compete with professionals, one could not instruct in athletics for money, and one could not sell one's prizes or display them for money. These rules were added to the application forms.

A significant event regarding the amateur rules of the 1912 Games was the Jim Thorpe affair. As mentioned above, the American athlete Thorpe—of Irish but mostly Native American stock—won the pentathlon and decathlon by wide margins and he was declared the best athlete in the world by the Swedish king. In the autumn of 1912, however, the American press reported that Thorpe had played baseball and had been paid for it. This scandalous information was immediately addressed by the Amateur Athletic Union (AAU) of the United States. Thorpe was declared a professional athlete and the decision was sent to the SOC. As a possible explanation, the AAU noted in its letter of January 27, 1913, "In some justification of his [Thorpe's] position, it should be noted that Mr. Thorpe is an Indian of limited experience and education in the ways of other than his own people." The issue was settled with an IOC decision in May 1913, directing Thorpe to return his medals. The consequences were substantial not only for Thorpe, who was personally hurt and never understood the punishment, but also for the United States. If the amateur issue was taken seriously in the beginning of the century and endorsed by future IOC presidents Edström and Brundage, another view was developed towards the end of the century. Accordingly, Thorpe's punishment was posthumously lifted by the IOC, and the gold medals were returned to his children during the 1980s.

The SOC did not want to have international officials at the Games and instead argued for Swedish ones. In the IOC some delegates were worried about the outcome of this decision on the grounds of justice, interpretation of international rules, language problems, and so on. The IOC, however, went along with the SOC. This system was supplemented by an international organization. Compared with earlier Olympic Games, the Swedish model worked out very well, and the Games had no scoring or judging controversies.

The Olympic program started with an indoor lawn tennis program in early May followed by an outdoor tournament just before the opening of the Games. The track and field program attracted the most public interest. Here, the SOC was able to introduce electronic timing and a photo finish camera to some of the track and field events. Because of the Ling ideal—to develop the whole body—javelin, discus, and shotput were contested with athletes using their right hand and then their left hand. The prestigious marathon was run on a very hot day, which led to great misfortune for the SOC. K. K. McArthur from South Africa won in 2 hours, 36 minutes, and 55 seconds, but about half of the athletes did not finish the race. Among them, the Portuguese Francisco Lazaro was felled by sunstroke and later died at a hospital. In tug-of-war five national teams were expected, but only two—England and Sweden—showed up. Overall, the Americans dominated track and field ahead of Sweden and Finland. Compared with London 1908, times were significantly improved. In wrestling, the competition was dominated by the Finns and the Swedes. Oddly, the outcomes of matches were decided only on the pinning of one's opponent—no points or rounds were counted—which meant that many of the matches went on for several hours.

Together with the competitive programs, there were many demonstration events. The most popular were the gymnastic demonstrations with some 1,000 athletes preforming on different national teams. There were other demonstrations as well. Special events of medieval origin from the Swedish island of Gotland in the Baltic were shown together with old fashioned wrestling from Iceland. To give the Scandinavian spectators something exotic, a demonstration of baseball was arranged as well.

The Stockholm Olympic Games were in many respects a hit. With no connection to a world's fair as had been the case in Paris in 1900 and St. Louis in 1904, Stockholm showed that the Olympic Games could be a worldwide attraction on its own. This development was due in large part to excellent planning. Sweden's political neutrality, the generosity of the royal family, and a strong arts program all helped to foster Coubertin's idea of brotherhood across national borders. This was also reflected in the improved competition of the Games, in which Sweden and Finland performed well. The entire program more closely resembled Coubertin's ideas and pointed toward the future of the Olympic Games. Through the success of the Games in Stockholm in the hot summer of 1912, the Olympic Movement survived the First World War and made an easy comeback at Antwerp in 1920. As a legacy of that success, the doors were now open for Sigfrid Edström to become the dominant leader of IOC into the 1950s.

BIBLIOGRAPHICAL ESSAY

The most thorough written source about Stockholm 1912 is Erik Bergvall, ed., *Officiell redogörelse för olympiska spelen i Stockholm 1912* (Stockholm, 1913) which is a close description—in 1068 pages—of the planning, carrying through, and legacies of the Games. It was published by the Stockholm organizing committee and reflects to some extent a homeland attitude toward the Games. An English translation has been done by Evert Adams Ray. Carl Cederström, *Den femte olympiaden: Olympiska spelen i Stockholm 1912 i ord och bild* (Stockholm, 1912), and Gustaf G-son Uggla, *Olympiska spleen i Stockholm 1912* (Stockholm, 1912), contain a multitude of illustrations from the Games. The amateur rules at the beginning of the century are dealt with in Eric Frick, *Reglen och allmänna bestämmelser för allmän idrott vid olympiska spelen i Stockholm 1912* (Stockholm, 1911). Many records concerning the Games are housed in different Swedish archives, chiefly the National Archives.

Carl Diem, *Die olympischen spiele 1912* (Berlin, 1912; reprinted, 1990), is a valuable unofficial resource for the Stockholm Games. Diem wrote the book immediately after the Games. He was a professional sports leader and as he was concerned with the coming Berlin Games, he made close observations. The problem between the IOC and states like Russia and Austria is discussed in Juhani Paasivirta, *Finland och de olympiska spelen i Stockholm. Diplomatin bakom kulisserna* (Ekenäs, Finland, 1963). A semi-official U.S. report is James E. Sullivan, ed., *The Olympic Games, Stockhom, 1912* (New York, 1912). Sullivan was the secretary-treasurer of the Amateur Athletic Union and President William H. Taft's official representative to the Games. Another source in English is Ferenc Mezo, *The Stockholm Olympiad 1912* (Budapest, 1955). In Allan Guttman, *The Games Must Go On. Avery Brundage and the Olympic Movement* (New York, 1984), the American view of the Games is recorded along with the young Avery Brundage's impressions of Stockholm 1912. The Jim Thorpe affair is discussed in Joseph B. Oxendine, *American Indian Sports Heritage* (1988).

BERLIN 1916

William Durick

THE GAMES OF THE SIXTH OLYMPIAD (NEVER HELD)

On their return trip from the first modern Olympics in Athens, German Olympic committee officials discussed the prospect of holding the Olympic Games in Berlin. Germany felt an important link with the ancient Olympics. Long before the unification of Germany in 1871, the Germans viewed themselves and their vigorous culture as the reincarnation of the ancient Greeks. This attachment to the Hellenics was manifested in the excavation attempts of the ancient site of Olympia by German archaeologists. In the mid-eighteenth century, Johann Joachim Winckelmann planned an expedition to Olympia to exhume the ancient stadium. The plan was suspended with Winckelmann's death in 1767 but not forgotten.

A century later, Ernst Curtius, a professor at the University of Berlin, actively pursued Winckelmann's objectives. In 1875, four years after the formation of the German Empire, Curtius led an expedition to Olympia, Greece. Within six years, Curtius unearthed the *altis*, where the ruins of the Temple of Zeus and Hera were uncovered. The German archaeologist's success could be attributed to the active support of Kaiser Wilhelm's son Frederick, who would succeed his father in 1888 and who saw the methodical excavation as a great cultural undertaking. The German Reichstag generously financed Curtius's ambition from the state treasury. The German effort resulted in the unveiling of the ancient Olympic site where for a thousand years the Olympic Games had been held.

The German activity in Olympia and information about the discoveries themselves were published in scientific journals throughout Europe between 1890 and 1897 and helped to acquaint the Western world with the idea of reviving the Olympic Games. The Germans were able to bring to life the knowledge of Olympia, painting a clear and certain picture of the Olympic site and the procedures of the Games. Ernst Curtius suggested that a suitable undertaking for the intellectuals and educators of the late nineteenth century might be the revival of the Olympic Games.

This challenge was heard by many Germans but actively pursued by Frenchman Baron Pierre de Coubertin. In 1894, delegates from 12 countries met at the Sorbonne in Paris and agreed upon the revival of the Olympic Games. It was agreed that the Games would be held every four years, would embrace all modern sports, and the Olympics would be allotted to different countries instead of always being held at one location, as in ancient times. The first Olympic Games of the modern era was held in Athens in 1896. After the 1896 Games, the International Olympic Committee (IOC), which controlled the Olympic Games, awarded the second Games to Paris, the home of Coubertin and the site of an Exposition Universelle scheduled for the summer of 1900.

Preparations for a Berlin Olympic Games began in earnest at the turn of the century. In 1901, at the Olympic Congress in Paris, German IOC member Dr. Willibald Gebhardt made a bid for the Olympic Games to be held in Berlin. The German Imperial Board for the Olympic Games was then established on a permanent basis to organize national Olympic Games in the German Empire, to prepare participants for the international Olympic Games, and to achieve a more universal representation by uniting the various German organizations that promoted gymnastics. This board consisted of Berlin sport leaders and individual gymnasts, who did not permit themselves to be contaminated by their colleagues' hostility toward competitive sport.

The German Imperial Board for the Olympic Games established a committee to raise money and secure a location for the construction of a suitable arena for the future games. An attempt to secure land from the German government failed, and a public collection fared only slightly better, raising only 1,000 marks. The committee members continued their search, and their attention eventually focused on a piece of land that the Berlin Union Club was leasing from the Prussian office of forest management. On this land, at the edge of the Grunewald forest, the Berlin Union Club had constructed a horse-racing track. General Graf von der Asseburg, president of the German Imperial Board for the Olympic Games and member of the Berlin Union Club, convinced the imperial board that an athletic arena could be built on the natural depression within the oval track. Asseburg deduced that since the track and the arena would still be used for racing, the contract with the Prussian government would not be violated. While the imperial board was busy securing a location for the Berlin stadium, the IOC awarded the 1904 Olympic Games to St. Louis.

Shortly after the St. Louis Games, the IOC met in London. The German bid for the 1908 Olympic Games was rejected on the claim that it lacked evidence of governmental support at either the municipal or state level. Rome, which had the support of the Italian government and sport federations, was selected over Berlin. The selection was short lived. In 1906, Mount Vesuvius erupted, killing 2,000 people and devastating the Italian economy. The Italian Olympic Organizing Committee withdrew Rome as the Olympic site. The IOC, meeting in Athens at the time of the announcement, invited Great Britain, rather than Germany, to take over the organization of the 1908 Games, and the British Olympic Association accepted. This rejection did not diminish the German desire to host the Olympic Games.

In 1909, the IOC met in Berlin to decide the site for the 1912 Games. Berlin and Stockholm both presented their credentials. Stockholm received the majority of delegates' ballots and was awarded the Games. According to Carl Diem, member of the German Olympic committee, the IOC members left Berlin very impressed with German athletic attitudes and informed the German committee that it should begin serious planning for the 1916 Olympic celebration.

This announcement inspired German action. Shortly after the IOC meeting in Berlin, a first phase of stadium construction began with the building of a forecourt under the Grunewald horse track to house dressing rooms, a police station, and a first-aid station. That same year, Asseburg died and the presidency of the German Imperial Board for the Olympic Games passed to General Victor von Podbielski. Podbielski had been actively involved in German sport and had served with the Prussian government as postmaster general and later as minister of the interior. Podbielski's government connections helped to further the building of the stadium. He was able to arrange a loan of 2.75 million gold marks from the German government and to secure the notable architect Otto March to draw blueprints and direct construction.

The second phase of stadium construction called for the leveling of the floor of the natural depression in order to build a 400-meter footrace track. Around the perimeter of this track a 600-meter cycle track was constructed. Stands for 34,000 spectators were built into the sides of the depression, stopping slightly above the arena floor. At the northern edge of the arena a 100-meter pool was built surrounded by bleachers with seating for 4,000 spectators. To accommodate the predicted overflow crowds, a terrace was constructed around the top of the stands. All construction was below ground level so as not to impede the spectator's view of the horse racing that took place at ground level. The German Imperial Olympic Committee was intent on creating a stadium that would exceed both London's and Stockholm's in accommodations for athletes and spectators and in architectural design.

As the building of the stadium continued, official word arrived in 1911 that the IOC had selected Berlin to host the VI Olympics. The excitement and confidence of this news, however, turned to disappointment with the inferior athletic performances turned in by the German team at the 1912 Olympic Games. German athletes were lagging behind those of other European powers and the United States. Sport in Germany could not keep pace with the nation's commercial and military achievements. Through the first five Olympiads, the Germans had not won a gold medal in any track or field event. The Germans believed that if the 1916 Berlin Olympics were going to be a success, athletic reform in Germany was necessary.

Every host nation had done extremely well in its Olympic Games, and Germany did not want to be an exception. The German Imperial Olympic Committee, responsible for organizing the Berlin Games, was intent on correcting the mistakes of the past and making the best possible showing at the Berlin Games. The German committee concluded that German training techniques were lacking in effectiveness, and since American college athletes were the world's best in most track-and-field events, they viewed the American athletic system as an excellent model to follow. In 1913, the German committee sent a four-man contingent to the United States to learn American training methods with the idea of adapting them to Germany.

The German commission, consisting of Dr. Carl Diem, secretary-general of the German Imperial Board for the Olympic Games; Lieutenant Walter von Reichenau, representing the Ministry of War; Joseph Wartzer, a prominent athletic coach in Germany; and Martin Berner, a young German sportsman and writer, spent almost two months in the United States. They visited U.S. military academies and universities in the Midwest and hired Dr. Alvin C. Kraenzlein, a former Olympic gold medalist who knew German, as a coach for the German team.

Kraenzlein was expected to do for German athletics what Field Marshal Helmuth von Moltke had done for the army in 1871: organize victory. To accomplish this task, the German Imperial Olympic Committee gave Kraenzlein complete control of German athletics. After his arrival in Germany, Kraenzlein told a *New York Times* correspondent that he witnessed a great athletic renaissance. He told the reporter that the Germans firmly believed their national life could only benefit from the healthy enthusiasm and rivalry found in athletic competition and in Olympic sports. This new athletic enthusiasm had been first manifested on June 8, 1913, when Kaiser Wilhelm dedicated the new Berlin Stadium in celebration of his 25th anniversary as head of the German state. The dedication of the Grunewald Stadium was hailed as the "greatest athletic exhibition Europe had ever witnessed," a combination of religious fervor and German military pomp. Some 30,000 athletes paraded around the stadium. The program consisted of games and the demonstration of athletic skills in honor of the Kaiser. The closing speech, given by General von Podbielski, urged the three million members of German athletic societies to organize for victory in the upcoming Olympic games. The encouragement of the Olympic Games by the Kaiser, like that by Adolf Hitler 20 years later, conformed with German political policy and was looked upon by both leaders as an excellent instrument in which to carry out the German plan to impress the world with the achievements and accomplishments of the fatherland.

Many of the delegates to the IOC Congress held at Lausanne in May 1913 had recognized this German enthusiasm and energy. The talk of the Congress concerned the astounding thoroughness and organization of the Berlin Games conducted by the German organizing committee. An example of this thoroughness was the organizing committee's attempt to remedy a problem plaguing earlier Olympic organizing committees: how to house the hundreds of athletes participating in the Olympic Games.

The German Organizing Committee developed a novel plan. They offered private training camps to all participating nations. The committee asked each nation to bear a proportion of the expense necessary for the construction of athletes' quarters near the stadium, and they then secured a large plot of land in the Grunewald pine forest for the purpose of building these dwellings. This location would afford each participant the opportunity to reside in seclusion within walking distance of the Olympic stadium. Each facility would include all the comforts of home, including private cooks specializing in that country's foods and an adjacent athletic field. The Swedes were first to take advantage of the German offer, and they paid to erect a traditional Swedish country house for their athletes. The organizing committee, aware that many countries did not want to incur the cost of a building for a limited stay, also offered an alternate plan to house athletes in special portable barracks during their stay in Berlin.

Meanwhile, late in 1913, the German Imperial Parliament supplemented the private donations received by the German Imperial Board for the Olympic Games with an additional $75,000 in order to provide the German athletes and coaches with all ingredients necessary to guarantee victory in 1916. With a new stadium and a very supportive government, the 1916 Berlin Games looked as if they would be the best ever.

On June 4, 1914, the IOC met at the Sorbonne in Paris to celebrate the 20th anniversary of the revival of the Olympic Games. At this meeting, the program for the 1916 Berlin Games was put into final form and the symbolic, five-ringed Olympic flag was unfurled for the first time. Robert Thompson, president of the American Olympic Committee, left the conference convinced "the Berlin Games would be the greatest ever held" because of the thoroughness of its preparation and organization and the lack of political controversy despite the nationalism and militarism building in Europe.

On June 28, 1914, while the Sorbonne Congress was still in session, a Serbian assassin shot and killed Archduke Franz Ferdinand, heir to the Austro-Hungarian throne, in the Bosnian capital of Sarajevo. A month later Austria-Hungary declared war on Serbia. Days later Germany sided with Austria-Hungary and declared war on Russia and France. By August 1914, Europe became engulfed in a war that touched all aspects of life.

Coubertin, the IOC president, believed that the power of the Olympic movement was such that the Germans, who had wanted the Games since their revival, would reduce their belligerent conduct and complete their plans for the VI Olympics. He was wrong: Germany invaded neutral Belgium in August, and Britain joined the Allied Powers and entered the war against Germany.

The British also fought the Germans on the Olympic front. The British IOC contingent opposed Coubertin's insistence that Berlin be retained as the Olympic site for 1916. Theodore Cook, a British member, demanded the expulsion of the German members from the IOC. When his motion was defeated, Cook resigned from the committee in protest. According to Coubertin, the dream of Olympia had to be preserved, and Berlin would host the Games in 1916.

Others believed differently. Days before Germany declared war, Alvin Kraenzlein and his staff, fearing a devastating struggle in Europe, sailed back to the United States. Three months later, another American trainer, Jim McCoughlin, who had been hired by Denmark, returned to the United States because Danish Olympic officials were convinced that it would be impossible for the Germans to hold the Olympic Games in 1916.

The Germans disagreed. The German Imperial Board for the Olympic Games anticipated a short war and continued with their ambitious plans for the VI Olympics. As the war progressed, the status of the Berlin Games remained in limbo. The German Olympic committee firmly stated that Berlin was the only site for the 1916 Games and that they would be held as planned. In November 1914, two months after the battle of the Marne, the IOC met in Lyons, France. Germany was not represented. Some Allied and neutral Olympic members called for moving the Games to a different site, but the Germans stood their ground. In March 1915, the German Imperial Olympic Committee reported to IOC members that Germany was still making official preparations for the Berlin Games and that only nations allied with Germany and neutral countries would be invited. Comte Justinien de Clary, president of the French Olympic Committee, promptly dismissed the German claim and said that he thought there could be no Olympics before 1920.

Many U.S. cities, however, believed otherwise. Offers to host the 1916 Games arrived from Chicago, New York, Newark, Cleveland, San Francisco, and Philadelphia. Despite the protests of Comte de Clary and the growing movement to change the Olympic site, the Germans continued to claim that Berlin was the only possible site for the next Olympic Games. Coubertin expressed his feelings concerning the 1916 Berlin Games in a March 1915 letter to the Associated Press:

> The IOC has not the right to withdraw the celebration of the Olympic Games from the country to which the celebration was given without consulting that country. The Sixth Olympic Games remain and will remain credited to Berlin, but it is possible that they will not be held. In olden times it happened that it was not possible to celebrate the games but they did not for this reason cease to exist. I consider all that is said and written on this subject now to be useless; the IOC will not allow its hand to be forced. (Quoted in *New York Times*, March 19, 1915)

Throughout 1915, battle followed battle as the war reached a stalemate. The German Imperial Olympic Committee continued to insist, however, that the Olympics would take place in Berlin at the end of the war. The summer of 1916 found European civilization at the brink of destruction and the Berlin stadium vacant. The Olympic flag of peace was not seen in Berlin. The flag of peace in Europe was not seen for another two years and the Olympic flag for another four years.

The fact that Berlin was selected as the city to host the VI Olympic Games was a recognition of the tremendous growth of interest in sport in Germany. The founding of German associations for bowling, cycling, swimming, skating, fencing, and lawn tennis during the late nineteenth century supported the new feeling in Germany of the importance of the spirit of competition and the pursuit of athletic records as opposed to the traditional views of the German Gymnastic Union. The Olympic Games provided Imperial Germany an opportunity to demonstrate to the world that Germans were as successful in the realm of sport as they had become industrially and commercially. Through the first five Olympiads, however, the Germans did not achieve the athletic success they had anticipated. To remedy this situation, Imperial Germany attempted to "Americanize" German sport by adapting American athletic ideas and methods for its sport associations. The year 1916 was to have been Germany's year to demonstrate its athletic prowess and its ability to stage the best Olympic Games ever held. The German Imperial Olympic Committee had selected a team that it hoped was destined for Olympic victory, while the German organizing committee, with help from the imperial government, constructed Olympic facilities never seen before at Olympic Games. Imperial Germany's chance to shine athletically disappeared with World War I. Germany would have to wait until 1928 to participate in the Olympic Games and would once again be given the opportunity to host the Games eight years later. The preparations and the interest in sport spawned by the VI Olympiad scheduled for Berlin in 1916 culminated in the success of the 1936 Berlin Olympic Games.

BIBLIOGRAPHICAL ESSAY

In the hundreds of books written about the Olympic Games since their revival by Baron Pierre de Coubertin in 1896, the 1916 Games are almost always neglected. Some books devote a page to the Games but most address the contest with a simple statement such as "the Great War of 1914–18 precluded the conducting of the

Games at Berlin in 1916." Although neglected, there are materials available that will provide the reader with information and insight into the VI Olympiad.

Despite the fact that the Games never took place, the organizing committee did prepare an official report for the IOC, titled *Denkschrift zur Vorbereitung der VI. Olympiade, veranstaltet im Deutschen Stadion zu Berlin* (Berlin, n.d.), as well as *Olympische Spiele in Berlin 1916. Programm und allgemeine Beststimmungen* (Berlin, 1916), in German, French, and English editions.

Carl Diem, a leading advocate of sport in Imperial, Weimar, and National Socialist Germany, in *Weltgeschichte des Sports und der Leibeserziehung* (Stuttgart, Germany, 1960) offers insight into the early German involvement in the Olympic movement, the formation of the German Olympic Committee, and the political and economic aspects of the Sixth Olympiad. Diem's *Sport in Amerika* (Berlin, 1931) is an excellent source for information about his visit to the United States in 1913.

Karl Lennartz, a noted Olympic historian and director of the Carl-Diem-Institut in Cologne, has written a history of the 1916 Games, *Die VI. Olympische Spiele—Berlin 1916* (Cologne, 1978). See also Lennartz's article, "Die VI. Olympischen Spiele Berlin 1916," *Stadion* 6 (1980): 229–50. A book previewing the 1916 Games is Adolf Petienz's *Olympia 1916* (Berlin, 1914).

The *Olympic Games News Service*, published by the German organizing committee for the 1936 Games, was helpful because of its background material on the 1916 Games. Additional material for the 1916 Games was also found in the *Official Guide Book to the Celebration of the XI Olympiad* and *The XI Olympic Games, Berlin, 1936: Official Report* (Berlin, 1937), published in English by the German Organizing Committee. These sources reflected on the cancelled 1916 Berlin Games because of their impact on the 1936 Games.

The *New York Times* and *Times* (London) published statements made by IOC members during the war years of 1914–15.

ANTWERP 1920

Roland Renson

THE GAMES OF THE SEVENTH OLYMPIAD

No other Olympic Games started their preparations with less time than did the VII Olympic Games, held in Antwerp, Belgium, in 1920. The so-called Great War had ended only twenty months before, and yet Baron Pierre de Coubertin was able to convince the cruelly damaged Belgian nation to host the first Olympic Games in eight years.

Situated on the Scheldt River, Antwerp is one of the most important seaports in the world. It lies in the Flemish part of Belgium. At the time of the seventh Olympiad, the population of Antwerp, like many other Flemish cities, was still characterized by an outspoken sociocultural and economic division between a dominantly Francophone elite on the one hand and a Flemish-speaking lower- and lower-middle-class majority on the other hand.

The first Gymnastics Society of Belgium was founded in 1839 in Antwerp. The city was the major gymnastics stronghold of the country, with Nicolaas J. Cupérus, the founding president of the Fédération Européenne de Gymnastique (FEG) in 1881, as one of its most influential exponents. Typical British sports such as rowing and association football had been adopted by some members of the Antwerp elite as early as 1851 and 1870, respectively. Sports like track and field, fencing, field hockey, equestrian events, and polo maintained a very exclusive social status in the host country at that time. The popular physical activities among the lower and lower-middle classes were professional cycling, in which several Belgians had excelled internationally; gymnastics; boxing; wrestling; and the traditional games of archery and *kaatsen* (*balle pelote*). Association football was quickly gaining in popularity. Although the war had seriously hampered regular competition, many of the best players had had a chance to play while serving in the military. The so-called Front Wanderers, a selection of Belgian soccer players, had competed behind the lines against British and French army teams, from which they had learned a lot.

In 1912, at the 13th International Olympic Committee (IOC) Session in Basel, the president of the Belgian Olympic Committee (BOC), Baron Edouard de Laveleye, made a bid for Belgium to host the 1920 Games. Originally it was intended that the Games would take place in the Belgian capital, Brussels, but Charles Cnoops, the vice president of the Belgian Fencing Association, and others led a successful campaign on behalf of Antwerp. By 1914, when the site decision for the 1920 Games was to be decided, Antwerp had replaced Brussels as the preferred Belgian site.

Although the final decision was delayed because of the outbreak of World War I, French and Belgian representatives signed an agreement that Antwerp would host the Games if that city was liberated by 1920. Shortly after the armistice in November 1918, Coubertin approached the Belgian government to host either the 1920 or 1924 Games. Although the Belgians were skeptical at first, they agreed to host the 1920 Games after the Antwerp Provisory Committee pledged 1 million Belgian francs to help cover expenses. The final decision was made on April 5, 1919, at the 17th IOC Session in Lausanne, just sixteen months before the official opening of the Games. It was obvious that the choice of Antwerp was a political option, intended to give moral support to Belgium.

As a result of the late decision, the organization of the Games relied more on bravado and improvisation than on sound planning. On April 7, 1919, the BOC convened the Belgian sports federations in order to obtain their collaboration. Alfred Verdyck, the man who would become the major engineer of the Antwerp Games, was not glowing with enthusiasm when he was invited to this assembly. He and his colleague R. W. Seeldrayers had mixed feelings toward the whole operation. This was due to the fact that Count Henri de Baillet-Latour, influenced by some Antwerp sportsmen, had obtained the seventh Olympic Games for Antwerp, but, in doing so, he had failed to consult the Belgian sports federations. After his return to Belgium, he organized an assembly of the sports federations. Verdyck and Seeldrayers, representing the Royal Belgian Football Association, were both convinced that it would be impossible to set up, in one year, an organization for which other countries—unaffected by war—had needed no less than four years. However, when they left the meeting, Verdyck had been appointed general secretary and Seeldrayers secretary-rapporteur of a committee under the presidency of Baillet-Latour.

The first stone of the transformed Beerschot Stadium was laid by mayor Jan De Vos on July 4, 1919, and the Olympic Stadium was officially inaugurated on Sunday, May 23, 1920, with demonstrations of the Antwerp Gymnastics Section and a choir of 1,200 singers. Since the official report mentions May 1 as opening date, there must have been two separate semi-official openings, as confirmed later by the Antwerp newspaper *De Nieuwe Gazet*.

The entire Olympic enterprise is generally considered a magnificent piece of work on the part of the Belgians. Coubertin stated in his opening speech at the 18th IOC Session on August 17 in Antwerp that "In addition to the record of national honour, won in 1914, Belgium has now succeeded in setting a record of intelligent and rapid organization or—if I am allowed to speak in less academic but more expressive terms—a new record for its skill in improvisation" (Coubertin, *L'idée olympique*, p. 81). Nevertheless, because of the lack of time, money, and materials, the standards of the 1912 Stockholm Games were not met. Although the stadium had been rebuilt and the running track had been newly constructed, there were many complaints. The silver medallist in the 1,500-meter race, Philip Noel-

Baker, wrote that the track was slow and heavy. Rains left ruts and depressions in its surface, causing the runners constant worry. And it rained almost constantly during those August days of 1920.

Whereas the official report stressed the good accommodations provided for the visiting teams, this view was shared by only a minority of the participants. As spokesman for the British team, Noel-Baker described the accommodation in the Antwerp city schools, the catering, and the food as very good. Contradictory comments were heard from the mutinous American athletes, who had already rioted on board the *Princess Matoika* during their crossing. Whereas the athletes who had served in the navy were transported on board the cruiser *S.S. Frederick*, the majority of the army and civilian athletes were shipped on the *S.S. Princess Matoika*. There was nothing regal about the *Princess*. It was a rusty old troop carrier that had been called in at the last minute to replace the broken-down *Great Northern*. It became a stirring crossing, known in American Olympic history as the "mutiny of the Matoika." While the female athletes and a few officials had cabins on the top deck, 108 male athletes were placed in troop quarters below decks. The sea was rough, the food was terrible, and the cream of the athletic world turned slightly sour. The American Olympic Committee was roundly denounced. Weight thrower Pat McDonald and swimmer Norman Ross acted as spokesmen for the riotous athletes. The only cheerful note was provided by Duke Kahanamoku, the Hawaiian swimmer who, together with fellow Hawaiians, sang on deck while strumming a ukulele.

Unfortunately, things did not improve on arrival in Antwerp, where the male athletes were accommodated in a city school, while the women stayed at the YWCA Hostess House. The men complained about the lack of privacy and the absence of hot showers in their schoolrooms. Most outspoken was the Irish-American hammer thrower Pat Ryan, who spread around the news that all athletes would get "cauliflower ears" sleeping on hard bunks with hay-filled pillows. Similar criticism was voiced by Swedish team members on their way home from Antwerp. When these allegations appeared in Dutch and German newspapers, the Antwerp sports magazine *Sport-revue* launched a counterattack, responding with reports about the behavior of Olympic participants outside the stadium. It accused some athletes, who had complained about Antwerp's high prices, of misbehavior in night bars and "mingling with venus kittens" (*Sport-revue*, September 21, 1920, p. 163).

Coubertin's opinion that the swimming pool was a "model of its kind" in the Report of the American Olympic Committee was shared by the local population but certainly not by the American swimmers. Aileen Riggin recalled that she had never seen anything like it; it was just a ditch that had been dug with an embankment on one side for protection in case of war. The water was entirely black and the coldest the American swimmers had ever encountered. The divers brought woollen stockings, socks, and mufflers to keep warm and gave each other rubdowns between dives.

Against the will of the Antwerpians, the soccer matches were played in several other Belgian cities, which wanted their share of the VII Olympic Games. The final match, however, pitting the host Belgian team against the Czechoslovakians, was played in the Olympic Beerschot Stadium in Antwerp before 40,000 spectators.

Boxing and wrestling, both very popular in the harbor city of Antwerp, were staged in the auditorium of the Antwerp Zoological Society near the central train station and drew large crowds. The rowing contests were held on the canal of

Willebroek near Brussels. Even Coubertin qualified it as an "anti-Olympic setting": amid reservoirs, oil storage tanks, and walls of factories, the location was so horrid that any attempt to hide its ugliness was abandoned. Yachting was moved to Ostend at the North Sea coast. Shooting events were held at the army camp of Beverloo, about 60 kilometers from Antwerp, except for running deer shooting and trapshooting, which were staged near Antwerp. Next to track and field, there were more rifle and pistol shooting medals awarded than in any of the other twenty-two events in Antwerp. A reporter from the *Echo de Paris* observed that "not even at Verdun were so many rifle shots heard."

During the Antwerp Games, the scars of the Great War were still omnipresent. For these first postwar Games, the Olympic ceremonies had been revised and highly ritualized. In the morning of the official opening day, August 14, 1920, a religious service was held in Antwerp Cathedral in remembrance of those who had lost their lives in the war.

For the first time in Olympic history, the Olympic flag was raised at the Opening Ceremony. According to Coubertin, this flag had been first displayed in Paris during the celebration of the twentieth anniversary of the reorganization of the Olympic Games in June 1914, but it had never appeared at an Olympic gathering. The five entwined multicolored circles, on a white background, symbolize the five parts of the world united by Olympism and, at the same time, reproduce the colors of every nation. This novelty became a favorite object for souvenir hunters. Wilfred Kent Hughes, who competed as a hurdler for the Australian team in Antwerp, remembered how the road leading to the stadium was bedecked with Olympic flags, "one of which, by some strange chance, was among my baggage on return to England" (Donald and Selth, eds., *Olympic Saga*, p. 34). During the IOC Session in Sydney in 2002, the 103-year-old former U.S. platform diver and bronze medalist Harry Prieste returned an Olympic flag that he had stolen in Antwerp in 1920. For the first time the Olympic oath was recited, spoken aloud by the Belgian fencer Victor Boin, a former Olympic medalist and war pilot. A flight of doves, symbolizing the ideals of brotherhood and world peace, was ironically accompanied by the firing of a gun salute.

Germany and its former allies were not present. Although Coubertin had refused to exclude the former aggressors from the Olympic movement, he had worked out a diplomatic solution, leaving the task of the invitation to the organizing country. He believed that it would be unwise to let a German team appear in the Games before 1924. It was not long ago that the last German soldiers had left Belgian soil, and hostile feelings against the former invaders were still very high. On June 13, two months before the official opening of the Olympics, Antwerpians had watched a demonstration against the return of Germans. Soldiers and Boy Scouts were charged with the security tasks in the stadium, in which soldier-athletes of the victorious allied nations wore their army uniforms during the opening ceremony. Although the weather at the opening day had been warm and sunny, attendance remained far below expectations. Photographs clearly show that the stadium was far from filled. King Albert, who had presided at the opening ceremony, remarked, "All this is quite nice . . . , but it certainly lacks people" (*Les Sports*, August 19, 1920).

The 1919 Interallied Games in Paris showed how the war had hampered the progress of sport. At these strictly military games, the Americans won almost half of the competitions. One year later in Antwerp, however, American supremacy in track and field was seriously challenged by the remarkable achievements of the Finnish athletes. The legendary Paavo Nurmi, who made his first Olympic appearance in Antwerp, won the 10,000-meter and the 8-kilometer cross-country races. He was beaten in the 5,000-meter race by the eccentric Frenchman Joseph Guillemot, a victim of poison gas in the war, who took revenge for the defeat of his compatriot Jean Bouin at the 1912 Stockholm Games. The "grey eminence" of track and field, Hannes Kolehmainen of Finland, took the lead in the marathon at 30 kilometers and held it to the end. It made him the most popular sport hero at Antwerp.

The brash American sprinter, Charles Paddock, won a gold medal in the 100-meter dash with a spectacular leap at the finish line. Only four years later, in Paris, the American hegemony in the sprint events would be broken by the British athlete Harold Abrahams. Contrary to the story told in Hugh Hudson's film *Chariots of Fire*, Abrahams participated at Antwerp. He ran the 100-meter and 200-meter races but did not qualify for the finals. He also was a member of the British 4 × 100-meter relay team, which finished in fourth place.

America ruled the waves in the icy cold Antwerp swimming pool. Hawaiian Duke Kahanamoku repeated his Stockholm victory in the 100-meter freestyle, and his fellow Hawaiian Warren Paoa Kealoha won the 100-meter backstroke. Norman Ross, who had impersonated the role of Captain Bligh during the mutiny on board the *Princess Matoika*, won gold in the 400-meter and 1,500-meter freestyle events. American Ethelda Bleibtrey excelled among her swimming peers. She was the first female contestant to win three gold medals: 100-meter and 200-meter freestyle and 4 × 100-meter relay. Fourteen-year-old Aileen Riggin won the springboard diving from both the 1-meter and 3-meter boards and thus became the youngest Olympic champion in history. Belgium lost in the water polo final against Great Britain, 3–2. Belgian fans, quite unhappy with the decisions of the Swedish referee, started booing when the band played "God Save the King."

Belgian medals were rather scarce, except for archery, in which Hubert Von Innis won four gold and two silver medals. Archery then still included popinjay shooting. Van Innis had also won this event, which involves shooting at a moving bird target at the top of a 33-meter mast, at the 1900 Paris Games. Along with the tug-of-war, popinjay shooting would not reappear on the Olympic program after 1920.

One of three American gold medal winners in boxing was Edward Eagan, a Yale student, who won the light-heavyweight event. Twelve years later, Eagan would make a unique Olympic comeback as a member of the winning American bobsled team at the Lake Placid Winter Games.

The Belgian public showed only scant interest in the whole Olympic happening. Some of the events, such as ice hockey and rugby, had never been seen before and appeared as exotic curiosities to the astonished spectators. Only swimming, boxing, and wrestling drew large crowds. But 40,000 invaded the stadium for the football final between Belgium and Czechoslovakia. A group of boys even dug a tunnel under a fence to gain entry. Belgium took an early lead through a penalty and scored a second goal in the 28th minute. The Czech players were very upset about the officiating by the British referee John Lewis, and the game got rougher. After a foul was called against one of their players, the Czech team left the field some minutes before the half. The Czechoslovakian team was disqualified, and the Belgians were declared Olympic champions. No victory had been more enthusiastically acclaimed since the end of the war in Belgium. The spontaneous outburst of public joy that overtook the stadium acted as a catharsis for a battered population that regained some of its pride through football. From that point, football grew in popularity to become the premier sport in Belgium.

In a formal address on August 17, 1920, in the Antwerp city hall, Coubertin had warned of the danger of "mercantilism," which had already begun to menace sport. These words turned out to be prophetic, not only for the financial disaster of the Antwerp Games, but also for the further evolution of the Olympic Games. In 1913, during the very first initiative to obtain the Games, the amount of 1 million Belgian francs had been promised by the Provisory Committee in order to place Antwerp in the pole position among the possible candidates. These promises were never kept and when the final accounts were made, a deficit of 626,022,500 Belgian francs was recorded. What had happened? Two rival factions had developed within the Provisory Committee. Opposing the Executive Committee was the so-called Festivities Committee, a consortium of Antwerp ship owners, exporters, and diamond traders, which had been formed to raise the promised million. This committee, consisting of "personalities absolutely alien to sport," according the official report of the Games, managed to appropriate the prospective capital for its own aims. Moreover, the official report also noted that the committee had scheduled a series of pre-Olympic events, which had prematurely drained away the interest and money of the public from the actual Games. The official report also blamed the Belgian press, and especially the Brussels press, for its boycott of the Games. However, an analysis of fifteen Belgian and four foreign newspapers does not lend support to these contentions. On the contrary, it appeared that the four foreign newspapers covered the Games less fully than the Belgian papers did. In the face of these facts, the validity and objectivity of the official report of 1920 can seriously be doubted. On many occasions, the report appears as a plea written in defense of the brave but deceived men, who had courageously taken up a task too heavy for their shoulders. It is not their integrity at fault here, but rather their naive misreading of the economic situation in Belgium in 1920. At that time, the Olympics were still very much a symbol of conspicuous consumption. This lack of insight on the part of the organizers was clearly put into words by *Sport-revue*: "They have failed to understand that sport resides more in the soul of the people than in the higher circles" (August 15, 1920). The whole Olympic enterprise was probably most accurately summarized in the weekly Flemish magazine *Ons Volk*: "The Olympiads (*sic*) of Antwerp seem to have been successful with regard to the participation of the contestants. They failed with regard to the public interest" (September 4, 1920).

BIBLIOGRAPHICAL ESSAY

Primary sources for the first postwar Olympic Games are almost as scarce as genuine coffee and real butter must have been during the war years. The official report of the Belgian Olympic Committee is *Rapport officiel des Jeux de la 7ième Olympiade*, edited by Alfred Verdyck (Brussels, n.d.) but it is inaccurate and incomplete. This inspired Bill Mallon to publish *The Unofficial Report of the 1920 Olympics* (Durham, NC, 1992), which is the most comprehensive compilation of the results of the Games, although it does not touch their political or sociocultural aspects.

Some of the more interesting primary sources are the official reports of several national Olympic committees, such as the extensive *Report of the American Olympic Committee: Seventh Olympic Games Antwerp, Belgium 1920* (Greenwich, CT, 1920).

There are no official reports from the British or French Olympic committees, but one can find reports from Sweden, Denmark, Finland, Italy, and Japan, all in the language of those countries. Another interesting source is the very nicely edited brochure *Aurons nous la VIIe Olympiade à Anvers en 1920?*, which was published in 1914 as part of Antwerp's bid for the 1920 Games. Another primary source was published as part of the Spalding Athletic Library, *VIIth Olympic Games: Antwerp 1920* (New York, 1920). Originals of the latter two works, together with original copies of the Belgian *Rapport officiel* and the Swedish and the Finnish reports, are held in the Sportmuseum Vlaanderen in Leuven, Belgium. For Coubertin's views, see his *L'Idée olympique* (Stuttgart, Germany, 1967).

Daily newspapers, magazines, and, of course, sport publications are most valuable primary sources. Wilfried Mostinckx undertook a comparative quantitative analysis of fifteen Belgian newspapers and four foreign newspapers during the 1920 Games period. These results were published in 1983 in his licentiate thesis (under the supervision of Roland Renson) at the K.U. Leuven, Belgium, titled "De Olympische Spelen van Antwerpen en hun receptie in de pers."

The most important secondary work on the Antwerp Games is Roland Renson, *The Games Reborn: The VIIth Olympiad Antwerp 1920* (Antwerp, 1996). Other secondary sources of interest are Keith Donald and Don Selth, *Olympic Saga: The Track and Field Story, Melbourne 1956* (Sydney, 1957), which discusses track and field competition at Olympic Games through Melbourne; John Lucas, "American Preparations for the First Post World War Olympic Games," *Journal of Sport History* 10 (Summer 1983): 20–44; and Roland Renson, "From the Trenches to the Track: The 1920 Antwerp Olympic Games," in Norbert Muller and Joachim K. Ruehl, eds., *Olympic Scientific Congress 1984 Official Report: Sport History* (Niederhausen, Germany, 1985, pp. 234–244).

For the Interallied Games of 1919, see J. Mills Hanson, ed., *The Interallied Games: Paris, 22nd June to 6th July, 1919* (n.p., n.d.). A general account of the Olympics is Alexander Weyand, *The Olympic Pageant* (New York, 1952), notable because Weyand was a member of the U.S. Greco-Roman wrestling team in 1920 but failed to win a medal.

PARIS 1924

Mark Dyreson

THE GAMES OF THE EIGHTH OLYMPIAD

The 1920 Olympic Games rescued the Olympic movement from the shadows of the Great War, but scars remained. In Antwerp, the former Central Powers (Germany, Austria, and Turkey) and the new Soviet regime in Russia were banished beyond the Olympic pale. Germany and Austria were also excluded from the new League of Nations. Some observers suggested that the Olympic movement itself be turned over to the League. The lingering wounds of economic dislocation and national rivalry clouded the Olympic future. As the Games of the VIII Olympiad approached, it became clear that the Olympics needed a grand venue, a larger roster of participating nations, and dazzling performances in order to recapture the international prestige that the Games had enjoyed before the war.

Baron Pierre de Coubertin and the International Olympic Committee (IOC) had fled France for Switzerland during the war. From his new Olympic capitol in Lausanne, the Baron plotted the future of the Olympic movement while announcing in 1921 that he would soon retire from the IOC presidency. Coubertin wanted to leave the Olympic movement on a solid foundation by staging a mammoth Olympic celebration in 1924 as his farewell gesture. He also dreamed of a triumphant return to his homeland. At the 1921 IOC Congress, where he broke the news that he would soon step down as the IOC's leader, Coubertin requested that members cede the Games of the VIII Olympiad to his beloved Paris, although Amsterdam, Barcelona, Los Angeles, Prague, and Rome also had aspirations to win the 1924 Games.

In order to guarantee the Games for Paris Coubertin shrewdly promised that in 1928 the Games would depart from the stadiums of the Allied victors in the Great War and move to "neutral" Holland. The majority of delegates succumbed to the Baron's maneuver and voted for Paris in 1924 and Amsterdam in 1928. Coubertin's clever stratagem made Paris the first city to host the Olympic Games twice. The Italians, incensed that the Olympics would not be headed to Rome, stormed out of the meetings. The Americans, angered that the new coliseum they were building in Los Angeles to attract the Olympics had been spurned, groused to the press about European parochialism.

The Parisian victory in the battle to serve as Olympic host signaled that in the wake of the Great War, nationalism would remain the central conflict in the Olympic movement. During the 1920s new states pressed to have their flags included in the Olympic parade while the losers of the Great War lobbied for re-entry. The IOC sought to expand its reach into the developing nations by sanctioning a series of regional sporting contests in Africa, Asia, and Latin America. Nationalism also shaped the struggle to include winter sports in the Olympics, which began with an experimental "International Sports Week" in early February 1924 at the alpine resort of Chamonix, France. Those contests were later rechristened as the first Olympic Winter Games.

Nationalism continued to create intense struggles over which men's and women's sports would be included in the summer program. The 1921 IOC Congress had altered the program for the 1924 Games. They increased the opportunities for women swimmers, adding the 100-meter backstroke and the 200-meter breaststroke. They also added women's fencing to the slate of events. The Congress eliminated the tug-of-war, the 3,000-meter walk, the 56-pound weight throw, archery, and golf. More significant than the additions and deletions, the IOC also made basic structural changes in administering the various sports in order to limit nationalistic rancor over judging standards and competition rules that had plagued previous Olympic Games. The IOC Congress sought to standardize competitions by assigning to the international sport federations the responsibility for running contests rather than charging the host nation's organizing committee with that task. The IOC hoped that its modernization efforts would diminish problems with national chauvinism and breed international harmony. Results from the Paris Games would reveal that even with international federations handling the events, nationalistic outbursts would continue to rage.

In 1923, nationalism nearly scuttled the Paris Games when France sent troops into Germany's industrial Ruhr valley to force the payment of war reparations. France's economy, dependent on reparations for capital as it recovered from the war with Germany, had plunged into a deep recession, precipitating the decision to strip the Germans of resources by force. The portent of war again darkened European horizons. Fear of a general European economic collapse spread. The winter of 1923 also brought a major flood to Paris. The Seine River burst its banks and damaged large sections of the city. In the wake of the flood, the Ruhr crisis, and the faltering economy, French government authorities suddenly decided that they could not guarantee the economic and security resources necessary to host the Olympics. A worried Coubertin quietly made arrangements to ship the 1924 Olympics to Los Angeles if war or financial collapse ravaged Europe. The emergencies passed. Paris readied itself for an Olympian celebration. Repaying American loyalty, Coubertin made sure that the IOC gave Los Angeles the 1932 Games.

The political and economic crises that threatened to derail the Paris Games nearly undid Baron de Coubertin's skillful lobbying of the French government for support. Recalling the French government's meddling in the 1900 Paris Olympics, Coubertin had managed to secure pledges from national leaders that the 1924 Games would be a showcase for the French republic. The government nationalized the enterprise by placing the French Olympic Organizing Committee (FOOC) under the direction of the Ministry of Foreign Affairs, and the national government appropriated 20 million francs to stage the Games.

French intellectuals also embraced the Olympics. Novelists, poets, and essayists filled newspapers and magazines with odes to athletic endeavors. One of the major innovations of the Paris Games was the inclusion in the Olympic festivities of an international artistic and literary competition run by the French Ministries of Foreign Affairs and Fine Arts. This "great season of art," as the official invitations dubbed it, kicked off the Olympic celebration. Medals were offered in five categories: architecture, literature, music, painting, and sculpture. Luminaries such as the composers Igor Stravinsky and Maurice Ravel agreed to judge the musical entries. Nobel prize winners Selma Lagerlöf and Maurice Maeterlinck served on the literary jury. Hungary's Alfréd Hajós won a silver medal in architecture for a stadium design to add to his two Olympic swimming gold medals at Athens in 1896. The huge public attention devoted by the government, the intelligentsia, and the common folk to the Olympics convinced observers in Great Britain and the United States that an Olympian fever had consumed France.

Paris ultimately proved a wise choice for the Games of the VIII Olympiad. The city had escaped the Great War relatively unscathed. While many areas in the provinces remained rubble-strewn wastelands marked by the huge graveyards that held a generation of European manhood, Paris boomed in the postwar period. The crucible of Western cultural life in the 1920s and a refuge for many expatriate artists, Paris was a vibrant city filled with modern conveniences and one of the centers of an emerging global culture. As the American poet Gertrude Stein claimed, "Paris was where the twentieth century was."

Paris possessed an existing infrastructure of exhibition halls for staging boxing, wrestling, fencing, and other indoor sports. Initially, French organizers considered using Pershing Stadium, which the United States had built in 1919 for the Inter-Allied Games, as the main venue. FOOC inspections soon revealed that Pershing Stadium would need major renovations in order to serve as the headquarters of the Games. It was also located in an undesirable location. Organizers quickly changed plans, selecting a site near the Seine River in the industrial suburb of Colombes for the construction of a new stadium. When the promised funds from the national government failed to materialize quickly, Comte Justinien de Clary, president of the FOOC, turned to banks for construction loans. Financial problems and the Ruhr crisis put the project behind schedule. The French finally finished Olympic Stadium on May 1, 1924, just a few days before the rugby football matches were scheduled to open the Games. The new stadium seated 20,000 spectators and provided standing-room accommodations for 40,000 more. The stadium also housed state-of-the-art timing and measuring devices set up by the French Congress of Chronometry. In addition to a new stadium, the FOOC spent eight million francs to construct a first-rate swimming pool with seats for 10,000 spectators.

With the facilities in place, France prepared to welcome the nations of the world—or at least those that the IOC allowed to compete. Olympic officials, over the objections of Coubertin, continued the ban on the Soviet Union and Germany. Germany's partners in the Great War, the Austro-Hungarian and Ottoman Empires, were allowed to compete in their new national identities as Austria, Bulgaria, Hungary, and Turkey. In an effort to limit nationalism, and especially to stymie American chauvinism, Baron de Coubertin and the IOC rejected U.S. calls for an official scoring system to anoint an overall Olympic champion and refused to endorse national medal counts. IOC rules at the time did allow for national medal counts in particular sports, however, and a contentious argument broke out between American and French representatives over how to score the Olympic track-and-field meet.

Angry words about scoring systems turned into open hostility as the American and French rugby teams met in the new stadium in a May preview to the main Olympic events scheduled for July. The French press and fans had condemned American rugby players for "hoodlumism" in a first-round match against Romania. Tempers flared at the rugby final between the United States and France after the French press warned that the Americans planned to play "'rough neck' football" in the championship. When the U.S. squad defeated the favored French team to win Olympic gold, catcalls and curses cascaded from the stands. Fights erupted between small bands of American and French spectators in the crowd of 30,000. French fans and even security police booed as the American flag rose and the American national anthem blared to signal the victory. French Olympic officials and rugby players apologized for their countrymen's behavior, but the French press blamed American arrogance for the demonstrations. The rugby final provided an ominous portent for the main events to be held six weeks later.

The featured contests began in July. More than 3,000 athletes (2,956 men and 136 women) from 44 nations gathered in Paris to compete in the Games of the VIII Olympiad. A huge U.S. team, more than 350 strong, arrived in France on the liner *America*, specially outfitted for training on the transatlantic voyage. A contingent of U.S. Navy athletes steamed to France in the newly launched battleship *West Virginia*. French organizers offered collective housing—though not yet an "Olympic village"— near the stadium for athletes. The American team rejected the lodgings as inferior and quartered in several alternative locations. As they had in 1900 when they attempted to impose a Sabbatarian ban on an earlier Parisian Olympics, U.S. Olympic officials tried to Americanize Paris. With prohibition in effect in the U.S., American managers demanded that the French close all saloons and take down all signs advertising alcohol in the American zone. Stunned French officials refused to accede to what they considered a typically parochial American request. The sparring over liquor did little to ease the tensions raised between France and the U.S. by the rugby match.

The main events commenced on July 6. The parade of nations marched past the box of French president Gaston Doumergue and his guests, including the Prince of Wales, the crown princes of Sweden and Romania, the Regent of Abyssinia, and the commander of American forces in Europe during the Great War, General John J. "Black Jack" Pershing. Several nations made their Olympic debut, including the Latin American countries of Argentina, Ecuador, Mexico, and Uruguay, as well as the new European states of Ireland, Latvia, Lithuania, Poland, Romania, and Yugoslavia. The Philippines, still an American protectorate, competed under its own flag for the first time. French organizers employed Father Henri Didon's phrase, *citius, altius, foritius* (faster, higher, stronger), as the Olympic motto for the first time. They could have added hotter, since the main events were contested during a torrid July heat wave that brought temperatures as high as 113 degrees Fahrenheit. The brutal conditions particularly affected the distance running events.

National heat ultimately proved a more powerful force at the Paris Olympics than summer swelter. Outbursts of chauvinism ignited in many of the competitions. Officials in boxing decided to experiment with placing the referee in a seat outside of the ring. Some boxers took advantage of that situation. French middleweight Roger Brousse was initially given a victory over the defending Olympic champion, Britain's Harry Mallin, in a controversial decision in which clear bite marks on Mallin's chest indicated that the French fighter had exceeded the allowable level of pugilistic assault. A British appeal overturned the decision and disqualified Brousse. French fans had to be restrained by the police from charging the ring. Mallin went on to win the gold medal in front of a French crowd that booed his efforts vociferously. The rancor spread beyond Anglo-French hostilities. Two Italian pugilists withdrew from the tournament in a protest against the officiating after a British judge disqualified an Italian for illegal holding. Italian fans pelted the judge with coins. Argentine fans staged a demonstration after one of their boxers lost a decision to a Belgian boxer. Belgian partisans launched a counterdemonstration. The gendarmes were called in to restore order.

Other combat sports also produced bitter enmity toward officials. An official decision in wrestling favoring a Swedish competitor over a French favorite was overturned by a jury of appeals after considerable hometown pressure. Incensed by the reversal, the Swedes contemplated withdrawing from the competition. In fencing, the Italian team quit the competition after an incident in the team foil competition in which an Italian fencer was disqualified by a Hungarian judge for abusive language. The episode led to accusations that the Italian-born coach of the Hungarian team had supported the claim of abusive language because he feared that the team from his homeland would defeat his Hungarian charges in the next round. Feeling that his honor had been besmirched, the aged coach challenged the captain of the Italian team to a real duel. After the Olympics the coach's son demanded his right to fight in his father's place and wounded the Italian captain grievously with a saber before the duel was stopped. Another dispute between the Hungarians and the Italians, involving the same judge who had overseen the team foil competition, broke out in the individual saber. Once again, it led to a formal duel between the Hungarian judge and a disqualified Italian fencer. For his role in the contentious affair, the Italian fencer was barred from Olympic competition for life.

While nationalistic rancor proved a global habit, much of the enmity at Paris emerged from incidents between French spectators and the American team. For their part, the French were troubled by what they perceived as American arrogance as the U.S. team dominated the competitions and by American insults of France's staging of the Games. The earlier incidents at the rugby final were not an anomaly. French fans regularly booed American victories and sought to drown the strains of the "Star-Spangled Banner." When American women divers swept the medals in the "fancy" diving contest, the French crowd threatened to throw the judges into the pool. The French even booed the feats of American swimming star Johnny Weissmuller, winner of three gold medals. In tennis, the American sweep of all five events (men's singles and doubles, women's singles and doubles, and mixed doubles) irritated French crowds who had hoped that even in the absence of French star Suzanne Lenglen, other French players could wrest the laurels away from Helen Wills and the rest of the American team. American players, officials, and reporters responded in kind—denouncing the condition of the courts, criticizing the Parisian atmosphere, and even claiming that French carpenters had left the women's locker room unfinished so that they could peep at the American women as they changed for matches.

National rancor and national ranking provided the focus for media coverage of the Paris Games. The international press corps ignored IOC protocol and spent a great deal of time constructing tables of national power based on overall Olympic performance. Daily calculations of national standing appeared on the front pages of American newspapers. The home team, France, registered victories in water polo, fencing, and cycling, mollifying Parisians to some degree. Finland commanded Greco-Roman Wrestling and made a strong showing in track and field–especially in distance running. The U.S. dominated tennis, swimming and diving, shooting, and rugby. The American team also won the most track-and-field events. The final medal count showed the United States on top with 45 gold medals, 27 silver medals, and 27 bronze medals. Finland finished second with 14 gold, 13 silver, and 10 bronze medals. France was third with 13 gold, 15 silver, and 10 bronze medals. Great Britain finished fourth with 9 gold, 13 silver, and 12 bronze medals.

President Calvin Coolidge radioed the American team in France after its victory. "Our pride was stirred as reports reached us of your successive victories over what was described as the most impressive international group of athletes ever assembled for the revival of the ancient Greek games," the president declared. Given the hyperbole that accompanied the American expedition to Paris, not all the critics were satisfied with the strength of its showing. Indeed, *Current Opinion* magazine published a revised set of national standings assessing how well each country did based on its population. Norway led in per-capita medal production with 84.5 points. Finland finished second with 76.5, Sweden was third with 50.5, and Switzerland was fourth with 49. The United States ended up fourteenth in *Current Opinion*'s rankings with 6.1 points. The magazine credited Scandinavia's more democratic system of sport for the masses for clobbering the elitist American system.

Winning huge numbers of medals or besting the rest of the world in the per-capita counts of medal production were not the only routes to consecrating national identity through the Paris Olympics. Uruguay won only one medal in 1924, a gold in the association football (soccer) tournament. Their surprising triumph over supposedly superior European teams sparked patriotic celebrations in the tiny South American nation. Uruguayan essayist Eduardo Galeano claimed that the 1924 Olympic soccer championship was the defining moment in shaping Uruguayan nationhood. "The sky-blue shirt [the symbol of the national team] was proof of the existence of the nation: Uruguay was not a mistake," declared Galeano. Football fever, and the impassioned nationalism it produced, quickly spread throughout the continent. Olympic football contests paved the way for the creation of the World Cup. Uruguay's repeat as Olympic champion in 1928 earned it the honor of hosting the inaugural World Cup in 1930. Uruguay's championship game win over Argentina in the first World Cup solidified its rank as the world's leading football power of the era.

Demonstrations of national prowess at the Paris Olympics made for compelling international theater. Several Olympians who turned in sterling performances were transformed into heroes in their homelands and into media stars on the international stage. Uruguay's José Andrade, labeled "the Black Pearl" by reporters who marveled at his skills and his status as the first player of African descent to play on an Olympic pitch, launched his career as one of the first international football stars in Paris. American Helen Wills continued her ascent as the most recognized female athlete of the 1920s by dominating the tennis matches. The press focused on the sexual appeal of Wills and other female athletes, selling them as attractive commodities to readers. Reporters also frequently speculated on how women's performances compared to men's feats. American women swimmers and divers, who dominated their events, were marketed as the "beauty queens" of the Paris Games. Correspondents also marveled at their fast times, especially at the performances of Sybil Bauer, who held the world record in the 440-yard backstroke for both women and men. Two years after the Paris Games, Gertrude Ederle, who won two bronzes in individual swimming events and a gold in the relay, earned international acclaim as the first woman to swim the English Channel. Her time in the Channel swim set a world record for either gender. Male swimmers also earned renown in Paris. Andrew "Boy" Charlton became a national idol in Australia by winning the 1,500-meter freestyle in world record time. American swimmer Johnny Weissmuller's victories in the 100-meter and 400-meter freestyle, and his anchoring of the victorious U.S. 800-meter freestyle relay team, catapulted him to celebrity status and a career that would culminate in international fame as Hollywood's Tarzan.

While swimming and other Olympic sports in Paris captured more public attention than ever before, track and field remained the most popular feature of the spectacle for global audiences. On the 500-meter track and in the field of Olympic Stadium, athletes set 6 new world records and equaled or surpassed 13 Olympic records. The U.S. squad dominated the field events in earning a surprisingly close team victory over Finland. Harold Osborn won the high jump and the decathlon. Clarence "Bud" Houser won the shot put and discus. William DeHart Hubbard became the first African American gold medalist in U.S. history when he won the long jump. The U.S. also won the pole vault, hammer throw, the 4 × 100-meter relay, the 4 × 400-meter relay, the 110-meter hurdles, the 400-meter hurdles, and the 200-meter dash. British athletes upset favored Americans in several of the shorter races. Harold Abrahams took the 100-meter dash. Eric Liddell, the Scottish missionary whose Sabbatarian convictions led him to withdraw from the 100-meters rather than run on a Sunday, triumphed in the 400-meter race. Douglas Lowe won at the wire in the 800-meter run to complete Great Britain's strong showing in track athletics.

Finland's genius for track and field became one of the leading stories of the Paris Olympics. Finnish athletes took gold medals in the pentathlon, javelin, and in every foot race of 1,500 meters or longer. Vilho Ritola triumphed in the 10,000 meters. Albin Stenroos won the marathon. The brightest media star of the Games, Paavo Nurmi, won the 1,500 meters, the 5,000 meters, the 10,000-meter cross country, and led the Finnish team to victories in the 3,000 meter and 10,000-meter cross-country team races. Although Nurmi later became famous for proclaiming, "I ran for myself, not for Finland," his domination of distance running in Paris brought global attention to Finland and made him the most famous Finn in the world. In glowing accounts from the world press corps, Nurmi became the embodiment of *sisu*, the Finnish national virtue that combined endurance and will. Nurmi and his fellow flying Finns made *sisu* the emblem of Finland's global reputation.

Theories to explain Finnish superiority in distance running filled the media—mirroring later speculations about Kenyan domination of endurance racing. The hypotheses ranged from claims of their Nordic racial superiority, to support for their robust diets of raw fish and black bread and affinities for cold baths, to the endorsement of their compulsory system of government-supported mass physical education, to faith in their traditional rural social values, to the notion that their rigorous climate and environment produced a nation of hardy runners. American sportswriter Grantland Rice pointed to the fact that the two nations that dominated track and field, Finland and the United States, both practiced prohibition.

More cynical reporters revealed that neither Nurmi and the Finns nor the American athletes had reputations as teetotalers.

In late July 1924, as the Paris Games concluded, the IOC commended French organizers for staging a remarkable Olympic Games. The IOC also conferred the honorary title of perpetual president on Baron de Coubertin. The Baron would officially leave the IOC's helm in 1925. Although Coubertin lived until 1937, these would be the last Olympic Games that he would attend. With Belgian Count Henri Balliet-Latour at the helm, the IOC moved into a new era. The Paris Games set the stage for the post-Coubertin period. They also revealed the problems the Olympic movement would face for the rest of the twentieth century—rampant nationalism and money issues. The Paris Olympics ended with a budget deficit. The program had dragged on for close to four months. Although crowds at events were often large, free passes rather than ticket purchases drew many of the fans. At the next IOC Congress in Prague, American diplomat and IOC member Charles Sherrill resurrected the Sabbatarian controversy that had plagued Paris in both 1900 and 1924 when he sought the elimination of all Sunday competitions in future Olympic Games. His motion failed, but the IOC did cut back on Sunday morning contests.

Sherrill's efforts were tied to Anglo-American national customs. In spite of the rhetoric of Olympism, there was little that the IOC could do to remove nationalism from contests where national uniforms, national flags, and national anthems dominated the pageantry. Indeed, one of the legacies of the Paris Games was to cement the use of the Olympic Games to establish national rankings and national identities, as the next three Olympics in Amsterdam, Los Angeles, and Berlin would readily reveal. Some observers found the nationalistic fervor that accompanied the Olympics disturbing. The English press was especially critical. The *Times* of London went so far as to propose a ban on future Olympic Games. "The peace of the world is too precious to justify any risk—however wild the idea may seem—of its being sacrificed on the altar of international sport," concluded the *Times*.

Newspapers in other parts of the world scoffed at the English suggestion. A French publication labeled the *Times* the "enemy of France." In the United States, the *New York Times* sneered that a "few squabbles" were insufficient grounds on which to abandon such an important global movement. The *New York Herald Tribune* noted the Olympics were not held in "utopia" and that "there were bound to be disagreeable incidents in the keen athletic rivalry of many nations." A few problems, believed the American press, should not scuttle such dramatic and glorious international competitions—particularly when the United States ranked at the top of the Olympic world.

The "keen athletic rivalry" of the nations at Paris demonstrated that nationalism had become the central appeal of the Olympics. While paeans to Olympic internationalism sometimes obscured that reality, much of the world paid attention to the Olympics because they provided such an important locus for modern patriotism. Victors from the United States, Finland, Uruguay, and other nations went home to ticker-tape parades and demonstrations of national pride. Mexico's failure to win any medals in Paris was treated by the Mexican press as a national disgrace. Great Britain's Harold Abrahams, Eric Liddell, and Douglas Lowe became national heroes in spite of the disdain among certain sections of the English fourth estate for the Olympics. Even the popular cinematic treatment of the 1924 Olympic Games, *Chariots of Fire* (1981), wrapped in the typical romantic gauze and historical laxity of both Hollywood epics and Olympic myths, could not obscure the fact that national rivalry was at the heart of the modern Olympic experience.

In 1924 Paris provided the Olympics with a grand venue, a larger roster of national teams than ever before, and dazzling athletic performances. The Paris Games recaptured global attention for the Olympics. They expanded the global reach of sport. They fed audiences around the world a new crop of athletic heroes. The presence of Hollywood movie stars Douglas Fairbanks and Mary Pickford in the American Olympic traveling party underscored the links between sport and entertainment in the popular culture of the 1920s. With increased attention came more opportunities for shrewd promoters and athletes to make money from their burgeoning fame. Johnny Weissmuller's ascent to a global icon began in Paris. Paavo Nurmi's feats in Paris earned him not only notoriety as the world's greatest runner but a reputation as the globe's most highly paid "amateur" athlete.

Global attention brought problems as well as possibilities. After the Paris Games the IOC and the international sporting federations battled over amateur standards and definitions as athletes such as Weissmuller and Nurmi began to cash in on their Olympian fame. At the same time the renewed popularity of the Olympics brought more intense challenges from groups that promoted workers' Olympics and women's Olympics as alternatives to what critics regarded as the IOC's bourgeois and patriarchal traditions. The success of an expanded program of contests for women at Paris helped to move the IOC to co-opt Alice Milliat's women's Olympic movement by increasing the number of women's sports in the Olympic program— particularly by adding track and field.

The efforts to modernize the Olympics had created a vast, imposing, and chauvinistic spectacle. If it was not exactly what Baron de Coubertin and the IOC had intended, it had become a major world event that nations were desperate to stage for a variety of reasons. In the following decades, more nations would join the fray and more political fights would rage as the Olympics grew even more gigantic. The Olympics had become a front-page story for the world's newspapers. Olympic medals had become a desired commodity for nation-states. They would remain fulcrums for nationalism for the rest of the twentieth century.

BIBLIOGRAPHICAL ESSAY

English language newspaper coverage of the Paris Olympic Games was fairly extensive. Major urban dailies in the United States, Canada, Great Britain, and Australia provided thorough reporting while concentrating on their own national teams. Especially strong coverage in the United States can be found in the *New York Herald Tribune, New York Times, Chicago Tribune, Los Angeles Times, Atlanta Constitution,* and *Pittsburgh Press.* The national editions of African American newspapers such as the *Chicago Defender* and *Pittsburgh Courier* illuminate important alternative views of the Olympics. For solid reporting on the Paris Games by American magazines see *American Magazine, American Review of Reviews, Current Opinion, The Independent, Literary Digest, The Outlook, The Playground,* and *The World's Work.* Other good sources on U.S. participation include Spalding Athletic Library, *Spalding's Official Athletic Almanac–1925* (New York, 1925) and the official AOC report edited by Robert M. Thompson, *Report on VIII Olympiad: Paris, France, 1924* (New York, 1924).

Official IOC, NOC, and French organizing committee reports are useful. The official report on the Games is the French Olympic Committee's *Les Jeux de la VIIIème Olympiade Paris 1924, Rapport officiel du Comité Olympique français* (Paris, n.d.). English language reports include the British, F. G. L. Fairlie, ed., *The Official Report of the VIII Olympiad, Paris, 1924* (London, 1925); and the Canadian, J. Howard Crocker, ed., *Report–Canadian Olympic Committee 1924 Games* (n.p., 1925). An interesting Spanish language report is Argentina's *La participacion de los Atletas Argentinos en los torneos de la VIIIa Olimpidia–Paris 1924* (Buenos Aires, 1924). Scandinavian reports include the Norwegian, *Beretning om Norges deltagelse i de Olympiske leker sommeren 1924 i Paris og vinteridrettsstevnet i Chamonix 1924* (Oslo, 1924); and the Swedish, Erik Bergvall, ed., *VIII Olympiaden: Berattelser over olympiska spelen i Paris 1924* (Stockholm, 1924). Although the Germans did not participate, some German language works exist including Willy Meisl, *Die olympischen 1924 in Wort, Bild, Statistik* (Oldenburg, Germany, 1924).

A useful overview of the Paris Games is Ellen Phillips, *The VIII Olympiad: Paris, 1924; St. Moritz, 1928,* (Los Angeles, 1996) in the USOC's series on the modern Olympics. Solid journal articles on American participation in the Paris Games include John A. Lucas, "Architects of the Modernized American Olympic Committee, 1921–1928: Gustavus Town Kirby, Robert Means Thompson, and General Douglas MacArthur," *Journal of Sport History* 21 (spring 1995): 38–45; Mark Jenkins, "An American Coup in Paris," *American Heritage* 40 (July–August 1989): 66–71; and Mark Dyreson, "Scripting the American Olympic Story-Telling Formula: The 1924 Paris Olympic Games and the American Media," *Olympika: The International Journal of Olympic Studies* 5 (1996): 45–80. On women's roles in the Paris Games see Sheila Mitchell, "Women's Participation in the Olympic Games, 1900–1926," *Journal of Sport History* 4 (summer 1977): 208–28; and Mary H. Leigh, "The Pioneering Role of Madame Alice Milliat and the FSFI in Establishing International Track and Field Competition for Women," *Journal of Sport History* 4 (spring 1977): 72–83.

Interpretations of Scandinavian views of the Paris Games are included in Per Jørgensen, "From Balck to Nurmi: The Olympic Movement in the Nordic Nations," *International Journal of the History of Sport* 14 (December 1997): 69–99, and Matti Goksøyr, "The Popular Sounding Board: Nationalism, 'the People' and Sport in Norway in the Inter-War Years," *International Journal of the History of Sport* 14 (December 1997): 100–14. Insightful sources on Latin American entry into the Olympic movement at Paris include Cesar R. Torres, "Tribulations and Achievements: The Early History of Olympism in Argentina," *International Journal of the History of Sport* 18 (September 2001): 59–92; Richard V. McGehee, "The Origins of Olympism in Mexico: The Central American Games of 1926," *The International Journal of the History of Sport* 10 (December 1993): 313–32; and Joseph L. Arbena, "Nationalism and Sport in Latin America, 1850–1990: The Paradox of Promoting and Performing 'European Sports,'" *International Journal of the History of Sport* 12 (August 1995): 210–19; and "Sport, Development and Mexican Nationalism, 1920–1970," *Journal of Sport History* 18 (winter 1993): 350–64. A brief but illuminating section on Uruguayan identity and the Olympic soccer championship can be found in Eduardo Galeano, *Soccer in Sun and Shadow*, trans. Mark Fried (London, 1998).

AMSTERDAM 1928
Edward S. Goldstein

THE GAMES OF THE NINTH OLYMPIAD

The Netherlands is a little country whose people do very big things. In the span of a few centuries, the citizens of this "lowlands" west European nation built an extensive canal and dike system to reclaim thousands of acres of land from the sea, including much of the land in the "polder" region of the country that includes the capital city of Amsterdam. Holland was also for much of the seventeenth century the most powerful seafaring nation in the world. The worldwide expansion of Dutch commerce that began during this period fueled the growth of Amsterdam as a center of trade, industry, and artistic creativity and paved the way for the International Olympic Committee (IOC) to select this beautiful city of canals, bridges, and tree-lined streets as the host of the IX Olympic Games in 1928.

One other good reason Amsterdam followed Paris in the honor roll of Olympic hosts is that Dutch people relish physical activity. A visitor to the Netherlands today will observe people of all ages using bicycles as their primary mode of transportation. Another example of the Dutch people's strong sporting heritage is the 124-mile ice skating race called the Elfstedenstacht that finds thousands of Dutch men and women gliding across canals that link the 11 cities of the northern province of Friesland. In the summer of 1928, the Amsterdam Games (July 28–August 12) were centered around a new 40,000-seat track-and-field stadium built on reclaimed marshlands in the new Amsterdam south region. This area had been the focus of a large-scale building effort in the early 1900s to meet demand for industrial worker housing. Next to the main stadium was an outdoor swimming pool seating 1,500 and gymnasiums where the boxing, wrestling, and fencing competitions took place. While building the stadium on the soft, spongy lowland soil highlighted Dutch ingenuity and industriousness in using every parcel of land in their small country, some participating athletes thought the track surface, which was composed of the same soil, was too soft for international competition. To remedy the problem, Dutch engineers worked feverishly in the days before the Games to provide a more solid footing to the running track. When the issue first came up, Major General Douglas MacArthur, the head of the American Olympic Committee (AOC), struck an upbeat note: "On the battlefield never believe reports of disaster. Leave it to Dutch engineering genius to produce a proper field for the Games."

There were problems at the swimming stadium as well. At the pool, the water appeared to run uphill because of faulty construction. Because the swimming stadium was located in a swampy area and the necessary piling had not been used in the foundation, one end of the pool had sunk about six inches. Olympic venues that did work well included the fencing pavilion, whose "eight fine strips provided perfect lighting overhead and underfoot," the equestrian facility at Hilversum, and the rowing venue in the Sloten Canal that found 10,000 cheering fans and assorted cows and sheep lining its banks for the dramatic eight-oared shell with coxswain race on the next to last day of the competition.

For these Games, there was no need to construct an Olympic Village as many of the teams, including the United States, stayed on ships moored in Amsterdam harbor. Other participating nations were housed in many of the city's splendid hotels.

The Opening Ceremonies for the Games of the Ninth Olympiad took place on a Saturday afternoon under gray Dutch skies in front of a record-breaking 40,000 spectators at the track-and-field stadium. Adding a splash of welcome color to the events of the day were the nattily-clad parading athletes from 46 participating nations, an increase of 2 from the Paris Games. Among the most sartorially splendid marchers were the South Africans, who were decked out in brilliant scarlet blazers and matching caps; the fez-wearing Turks; the pink-clad Belgians; and the American men with blue jackets with white trousers and straw hats and their female counterparts in white dresses. Drawing special notice from the crowd was the first German contingent to compete in the Olympics since World War I. The German squad "looked like ship stewards" with their Eton jackets and stiff shirts but were very impressive with their precise order of march. Also displaying a military bearing was the Italian team, whose members wore army green and gave the Benito Mussolini regime's Fascist salute as they passed the royal reviewing stand.

The American team was also watched closely for their etiquette as they marched passed the reviewing stand. Led by AOC head MacArthur, the Yankee squad continued the American custom of refusing to bow to or salute any foreign monarch and gave a correct right dress as they passed in front of IOC President Count Henri Baillet-Latour and Holland's Prince Consort Henry. The Netherlands' reigning monarch, Queen Wilhelmina, did not attend the Opening Ceremonies. Her absence was reportedly due to her religiously-based objection to the fact that the competition would begin on the Sabbath.

Also absent from the Opening Ceremonies was the entire French contingent. The day before the Games began, a cantankerous gatekeeper refused to let French track-and-field athletes into the main stadium for a practice run. Following a few choice insults, the gatekeeper came to blows with Paul Mericamp, the general secretary of the French Athletic Federation. When the French team found out that the offending gatekeeper was still at his post the next day, they decided on the spot to boycott the Opening Ceremonies and threatened to withdraw from the Games. The former Dutch foreign minister was brought in to negotiate this burgeoning crisis with the French minister to the Hague. After an official apology was issued and a bottle of champagne was presented to the French as a peace offering, the French decided that the gatekeeper's offense was not severe enough to force their absence from the Games. What the French did miss at the Opening Ceremonies was a spectacle of artillery salvos, bands, and hundreds of pigeons as well as a colorful overflight of several airplanes.

In the competition, the men's track-and-field events were dominated by the "Flying Finns." Paavo Nurmi, the 1924 Olympic star, duplicated his 10,000-meter run victory, this time setting an Olympic record, and also finished second in the 3,000-meter steeplechase. Harry Larva, Vilho Ritola, Toivo Loukola, and Paavo Yrjola added to the Finnish victory parade in the 1,500-meter, 5,000-meter, and 3,000-meter steeplechase and decathlon events. Canada's diminutive sprinter, Percy Williams, was the Games' individual star with victories in the 100- and 200-meter sprints. Japan's Mikio Oda became the first Olympic track victor from Asia, with a leap of 49 feet and 11 inches in the hop, step, and jump event (now the triple jump).

In the marathon, Boughera El Ouafi, an Algerian who ran dispatches for the French Moroccan army behind the lines of the desert chieftain Abd El Krim in 1926, won a stirring race against more than 100 competitors in a 2:32.37 time "across the typical Dutch landscape, between grim dikes and beside desolate marshes, punctured with tiny flower-decked windmills, under heavy watery skies through which the sun was unable to cast a single cheering ray" (*New York Times*, August 6, 1928). Ouafi's life would later have a tragic end; he was shot to death sitting in a Parisian café in 1959.

The American men's track-and-field squad was somewhat of a disappointment. Prior to the Games, MacArthur predicted team members would sew up "nine [individual] firsts" and stated "This is the greatest team in our athletic history. Americans can rest serene and assured." In the end, the Americans fell three short of the predicted medal count with six individual victories, along with two world records in the 4 × 100-meter and 4 × 400-meter sprint relays. The *London Evening Standard* speculated that the lackluster American performance could be blamed on "too much ice cream and lavish feeding" enjoyed by the U.S. athletes on board their ship the *President Roosevelt*. The *Standard* noted that the British athletes, including popular 400-meter hurdle victor Lord David Burghley, had consumed "hearty green salads" at their hotel. Hearing of this affront to the U.S. team's home base, T. V. O'Connor, chairman of the powerful U.S. Shipping Board, disclaimed any responsibility for diets on the *President Roosevelt*. "The principal complaint [of the English press] seems to be 'too lavish feeding.' This is a rather unique complaint about an ocean liner," noted O'Connor about shipboard fare of the time, which was certainly not up to the standards enjoyed on modern cruise ships. MacArthur, who was already developing the keen sense of public relations that would serve him well during World War II, cabled O'Connor: "The American athletes have not only not failed, but have achieved a brilliant success compared to those of past Olympics. Guests who were entertained on board the *Roosevelt* were served the same fare always served to passengers. The standard of living on American ships is very high—much higher than on competing lines, perhaps. However, this is not a matter of reproach, but of gratification" (*New York Times*, August 11, 1928). Then he released the contents of the cable to the press.

Food was not an issue in the women's events. Rather, the very fact that women were competing in track and field was a novelty. The IOC had long opposed the participation of women in track-and-field competition, with the aristocratic leaders holding to prejudices about "amazon" female athletes or to Victorian notions about the propriety of men watching scantily clad women compete. Even the Roman

Catholic Church weighed in on the subject, with Pope Pius XI avowing that female athletic competitions "should not be made a public display" (*New York Times*, May 3, 1928). Even after the Games, the Vatican stated, "Athletic competitions for girls offend the Christian sentiments and the customs of our civilization" (*New York Times*, November 16, 1928). But the IOC was forced to change with the times, especially after the Federation Sportive Feminine Internationale was formed and put on a highly successful track-and-field championship for women in Paris in 1922 and planned a "Women's Olympics" for 1926. The IOC took note of the growing popularity of women's athletics, and on April 5, 1926, voted to accept the recommendation of the International Amateur Athletic Federation (IAAF) that women be permitted to compete in gymnastics and track and field (women were already competing in Olympic swimming and diving events). The number of track-and-field events were limited to five (100-meter dash, 800-meter run, 4 × 100-meter relay, high jump, and discus), which prompted a boycott by the British women.

In the first women's track event to be contested, Betty Robinson, a 16-year-old sprinter from Chicago, set a world record of 12.2 seconds in the 100-meter dash. In the high jump, Canada's Ethel Catherwood, the "Saskatoon Lily," pleased the crowd with her five-feet-two-inches winning performance. The women's 800-meter run, however, was the most consequential event of the Games. In the race, won by Germany's Frau Lina Radke, six of the nine contestants faltered at the end of a furious sprint to the finish line. Florence MacDonald of the United States was woozy for several minutes after the race, and even the second-place finisher, Kinue Hitomi of Japan, required medical attention before leaving the field.

Antifeminists in the press and in the IAAF seized on the race as evidence that women should be banned from running in events longer than 200 meters. For example, the *London Daily Mail* quoted doctors who said that female participants in 800-meter races and other such "feats of endurance" would become old too soon. IOC President Baillet-Latour joined the chorus and spoke out in favor of eliminating all women's sports from the Olympics and returning to the Greek custom of male-only competition. Representing women athletes before a special meeting of the IAAF in Amsterdam, Britain's Lady Heath rebutted Baillet-Latour's argument about women not having participated in the ancient Greek games. She retorted that neither were the hop, step, and jump; fencing; and pistol shooting a part of the Greek Olympiads. Lady Heath then urged the IAAF members to "Let us help you raise your banners on the Olympic pole. We are now your comrades in industry, commerce, in the arts and sciences, why not in athletics? If you approve of athletics for women at all you must approve of participation in the Olympics. For women need the stimulus of matching their prowess against the world's best athletes quite as much as the men" (*New York Times*, August 8, 1928). Another proponent of female participation in the Games was a Dr. Bergmann who as the "examining physician" of women athletes in Berlin presented the IAAF leadership the astounding evidence based on 10 years of experience that women athletes married and bore children just like nonathletes.

The protective males who governed the IAAF ended up deciding that the 800-meter event was too taxing for the "frail feminine gender," a decision that would last until the 1960 Games. Also shunted aside for the time being were the women's long jump, shot put, and 200-meter race; the events that remained were the 100-meter dash and 4 × 100-meter relay, the 80-meter hurdles, the high jump, discus, and javelin throw.

Controversy was also part of the mix, as it is at many Olympic Games, in the boxing hall. Decisions of referees led to raucous scenes following several of the bouts. After Belgium's Marcel Santos won a disputed decision over U.S. flyweight (112 lbs.) Hyman Miller, U.S. boxing coach Jacob Stumpf wanted to take the entire team out of the competition, but MacArthur curtly replied, "Americans never quit." And when Holland's Lambertus van Klaverens was awarded a decision over Argentina's Victor Peralta in the featherweight competition, the unhappy Argentine fans in the hall decided to shower a few fisticuffs on the Dutch police.

A clear victor in the field hockey event was the team from India, which had begun international competition in the sport just two years prior to the Games. The Indian squad swept all its matches in Amsterdam and went on to an incredible 30-game winning streak in the next six Olympics before losing to Pakistan in the final match of the 1960 Games.

Two American athletes who went from Amsterdam to further glory were swimmers Johnny Weissmuller and Clarence "Buster" Crabbe. Weissmuller lowered his Olympic record in the 100-meter freestyle, shared in a world record in the 4 × 200-meter freestyle relay, and was also on the U.S. water polo team. Weissmuller turned his Olympic victories into fame on the silver screen as he became the first of the movie Tarzans. Crabbe finished only third in the 1,500-meter freestyle but also headed to Hollywood, where he would take on the larger-than-life roles of Tarzan, Flash Gordon, and Buck Rogers.

On the water, the most exciting event in the Games may have been the men's eight-oared with coxswain rowing final between the United States, represented by the University of California at Berkeley and England, represented by the Thames Rowing Club. The U.S. squad beat the English eight by half of a boat length in a race witnessed by 10,000 along the Sloten Banks. *New York Times* sportswriter Wythe Williams was most impressed by the performance of U.S. coxswain Don Blessing, who displayed "one of the greatest performances of demoniacal howling ever heard on a terrestrial planet. . . . He gave the impression of a terrier suddenly gone mad. But such language. And what a vocabulary! . . . One closed his eyes and waited for the crack of a cruel whip across the backs of the galley slaves" (*New York Times*, August 11, 1928). In contrast to Blessing's strong language, the British coxswain George Sulley futilely encouraged his rowers on with the more sedate call of "Up, up, up."

The Games came to an end with a ceremony at the track-and-field stadium. This time, the stadium was graced by the presence of Queen Wilhelmina, even though the ceremonies were held on a Sunday. The queen had actually warmed up to the competition after hosting a state dinner for the official Olympic party, and she had made one appearance at the stadium to witness an exhibition of the Dutch national sport of korfball. At the Closing Ceremonies, Wilhelmina shared the royal box with members of her family and various members of the Norwegian and Swedish royal families. The press was told that Wilhelmina was greatly interested in all things military and wanted to watch the conclusion of the Olympic equestrian competition, which resulted in a tie between the Dutch and Polish teams. The queen also presented medals to the winning athletes. And with the sound of bugles, cannons, and a band playing a final hymn filling the air of Amsterdam, the participants and the spectators headed home, knowing the athletes of the world would next assemble in a distant and relatively young city beside the Pacific Ocean named Los Angeles.

BIBLIOGRAPHICAL ESSAY

Records of the 1928 Summer Olympics may be found at the Municipal Archives of Amsterdam, Amsteldijk 67, 1074 HZ Amsterdam, The Netherlands, and at the Dutch Sportsfederation Library, Laan van de Poort 361, 2566 DA Den Haag, The Netherlands. Additional information is available at the IOC Archives in Lausanne, Switzerland, and in the Avery Brundage Collection at the University of Illinois Archives, Urbana, Illinois.

The official report of the Amsterdam organizing committee is George van Rossem, ed., *The Ninth Olympiad; Being the Official Report of the Olympic Games Celebrated at Amsterdam Issued by the Netherlands Olympic Committee* (Amsterdam, 1930). French and Dutch editions were also published simultaneously. The committee also published *Rapport sur la preparation de l'organisation des Jeux de la IXe Olympiade a Amsterdam en 1928* (Amsterdam, 1927); *Catalogue de l'exposition au Musee municipal d'Amsterdam. 12 juin—12 aout* (Amsterdam, 1928); a catalog of the art competition accompanying the Games; and a variety of daily programs and booklets detailing the rules and regulations of the competition.

The American Olympic Committee report is *Report of the American Olympic Committee; Ninth Olympic Games, Amsterdam, 1928. Second Olympic Winter Sports, St. Moritz, 1928* (New York, 1928); the Canadian report is M. M. Robinson, ed., *The Official Report of the IXth Olympiad 1928* (Hamilton, Ontario, 1929). The British version, edited by Harold M. Abrahams, is *The Official Report of the IXth Olympiad, Amsterdam, 1928* (London, 1928). The French Olympic Committee published *La Participation francaise aux jeux de la IXe Olympiade Amsterdam 1928* (Paris, 1928), and the Germans celebrated their return to Olympic competition in *Bericht uber die Beteiligung Deutschlands an den IX. Olympischen Spielen Amsterdam und St. Moritz 1928* (Berlin, 1928). Sport medicine scholars may wish to consult F. J. J. Buytendijk, *Ergebnisse der sportartlichen Untersuchungen bei den IX. Olympishe Spielen 1928 in Amsterdam* (Berlin, 1929), a collection of papers dealing with sport medicine published after the Games and based in part on data collected at the Games. Excellent daily coverage of the Games can be found in the *New York Times*, whose correspondent, Wythe Williams, provided detailed, colorful reports of the events and pageantry of the Games from the American team's perspective. Williams was one of the few American correspondents on the scene, and his dispatches covered all of the major activities of the Games. As a passenger accompanying the team on the *President Roosevelt*, he had access to American Olympic Committee president Major General Douglas MacArthur and other U.S. officials and athletes. MacArthur's role in the AOC and the Amsterdam Games is detailed in John A. Lucas, "USOC President Douglas MacArthur and His Olympic Moment," *Olympika* 3 (1994): 111–15.

Finally, the demonstration sport of korfball is described in Anthony Th. Bijkerk, "Korfball at the Olympic Games," *Citius, Altius, Fortius* 2, 2 (May 1994): 20–23.

LOS ANGELES 1932

Doris Pieroth

THE GAMES OF THE TENTH OLYMPIAD

When the International Olympic Committee (IOC) named Los Angeles the site for the 1932 Games at its meeting in Rome in 1923, no one could have foreseen economic disaster ahead. William May Garland, Los Angeles real estate baron, civic booster, and member of the IOC, made the case for Los Angeles in Rome. He returned home to his booming and optimistic city where work soon began to renovate and expand the Coliseum in Exposition Park into an Olympic Stadium.

In 1925, California voters approved a $1 million bond issue to underwrite the Games. That same year the Los Angeles Organizing Committee for the Games of the X Olympiad (LAOC), chaired by Garland, rejected the possibility of replacing Amsterdam as host city in 1928. With sights still set on 1932, the city of Los Angeles voted a $1.5 million supporting bond issue.

By the end of the decade, however, boom had become bust, economic despair was settling over the world, and the organizing committee faced a gloomy prospect. War, its aftermath, and political boycotts have canceled or diminished Olympic Games, but Garland's committee refused to give in to the devastation of the Great Depression. Olympic planners worked against constant, draining reminders of the Depression, including record unemployment in California and the daily arrival of refugees from the plains states, where severe drought had made farming impossible. Some of the soup kitchens serving the destitute of Los Angeles were in the shadow of the Coliseum. Sentiment ran against the usual frivolity of the Games. Pickets at the capitol in Sacramento called for them to be canceled, but the power and influence of the Los Angeles civic and business elite prevented that.

The Herbert Hoover administration offered no help. The president himself declined to open the Games, breaking the tradition of heads of state presiding at the Opening Ceremony that dated back to King Georgios of Greece in 1896.

Other nations, feeling hard-pressed economically, hesitated to commit their teams to this longest Olympic journey to date. In mid-April 1932, with ticket sales and guarantees of participation near zero, Zack Farmer, general secretary of the LAOC, offered a plan for housing all athletes in an "Olympic Village." When he had proposed this idea earlier, other nations rejected it, preferring secrecy and opposing fraternization among competitors. This time, however, by reducing the cost of feeding and housing an athlete to two dollars a day, the Olympic Village proved, literally, to be the salvation of the Games.

A short three months before the scheduled opening, an athletes' village of 500 cottages rose west of the Coliseum on 250 acres in the undeveloped Baldwin Hills section of Los Angeles. Organizers persuaded steamship and rail lines to cut fares on their nearly empty carriers; teams could then afford to travel from Europe, Asia, and South America.

The movie colony lent its prestige and charisma to the Olympic cause. In mid-July, Mary Pickford and Douglas Fairbanks, whose popularity knew no bounds, broadcast worldwide invitations to come for the Games, and the press began to report positively on preparations. Although it had hardly seemed possible ninety days earlier, 101,000 people paid two dollars each to crowd into the Coliseum for the Opening Ceremony. Thousands more milled around outside.

One episode clouding the pre-World War II international political scene had some impact on the Olympic picture. Early in 1932, Japan had moved into the Chinese province of Manchuria and created the puppet state of Manchukuo; it then sought to send athletes from its pawn to the Games in Los Angeles. The IOC rejected the move, but the bid did spur China to send one lone athlete—Chung Cheng-Liu, an unsuccessful competitor in the men's 200 meters.

Most political discord surrounding the 1932 Games was domestic, consisting of internal bickering in the American Olympic Association (AOA). Until then, the Olympic Games had been considered Eastern or elitist by most Americans who had heard anything at all about them. Easterners, who predominated in AOA affairs, openly doubted the ability of Californians to oversee the planning and conduct of the Games. After the Association's executive committee tentatively approved the formation of the LAOC in June 1929, Avery Brundage, president of the AOA, succeeded in muting further criticism and preventing true animosity from building. Final approval of the organizing committee, which the IOC required, came at the quadrennial meeting of the AOA in Washington, on November 19, 1930. In a final echo of discord after the Games had ended, Californians contended that the Easterners had let them down in fund-raising.

The spotlight of Olympic politics focused on two issues—amateur purity and the participation of women. Half a century later, with women's events firmly established and Olympic athletes paid for medal-winning efforts, both elements seem quaintly dated.

Baron Pierre de Coubertin, in acclaiming the classical Greek athletic ideal of the young male athlete in the ultimate contest, saw no place for women in the modern Olympic movement. Nevertheless, women's golf had appeared once in the Games, at Paris in 1900; women's tennis had been played in 1900 and from 1906 to 1924; women's swimming had entered the Olympic program in Stockholm in 1912; and women's fencing began at Paris in 1924, remaining on the program in 1928.

Both swimming and fencing enjoyed a measure of acceptance in the mid-1920s, when expectations and ideas of what was proper for women still had a heavy Victorian cast. Track and field, however, bore marginal if not negative status. Intense championship competition for women in any sport drew condemnation in the United States, especially from physical education professionals and from the Women's Division of the National Amateur Athletic Federation (NAAF).

At Amsterdam in 1928, five women's track-and-field events made an Olympic debut on an experimental basis—100- and 800-meter races, 4×100-meter relay, high jump, and discus. The collapse of exhausted runners at the end of the 800 meters amplified criticism. In an attempt to prevent women from competing in Los Angeles, the Women's Division of the NAAF petitioned the IOC in April 1930 to drop women's track and field. Their appeal followed a 1929 proposal by new IOC president, Count Henri de Baillet-Latour, to eliminate all women's events as one way to trim the burgeoning program of the Games.

The IOC deferred final action until it met in Barcelona in 1931. By that time, Avery Brundage, already a key American in Olympic affairs, had been enormously impressed by a women's track-and-field demonstration at the 1930 Olympic Congress in Berlin. Brundage was a representative to the International Amateur Athletic Federation (IAAF) and a member of its committee on women's sports, which recommended retaining women's events. Finally, in April 1931, the IOC called for the upcoming X Olympic Games to include women's swimming, fencing, and track and field, with the javelin throw replacing the 800 meters.

The issue of women's participation was settled in 1931, but the matter of amateurism was not resolved until the day before the 1932 Opening Ceremony. Acting on allegations that Paavo Nurmi, the brilliant and popular Finnish runner, had accepted financial rewards for races, the IAAF executive board ruled him a professional and barred him from competing in what would have been his fourth Olympic Games. Judging this a blow to the Games' prospects and drawing power, one journalist wrote that the Games would now be "like Hamlet without the celebrated Dane in the cast." The outraged Finns threatened to withdraw the rest of their team from the Games.

On the media front, radio made its Olympic debut in the summer of 1932. Multimillion-dollar bidding wars for broadcast rights to the Games would have staggered the imaginations of Games planners in 1932. Individual stations and networks were not permitted to broadcast directly from the Coliseum or any other venue. Listeners settled for summaries of each day's events and occasional interviews with medalists. The largest gathering of movie newsreel cameramen yet assembled for an international event covered every phase of the Olympic Games. Their films provided audiences worldwide with a taste of Olympic excitement in 1932, and they serve today as a priceless early record in celluloid.

By the time of the Nurmi decision, athletes from thirty-nine nations had arrived to warm California welcomes. Sizable parties of Japanese-Americans greeted the large contingent from Japan, including its powerful team of male swimmers. No team had a more enthusiastic reception in Los Angeles than Germany's, met by an overflow crowd at the Santa Fe Station where two bands led hundreds in singing "Deutschland Uber Alles" at every opportunity.

Even though the country remained locked in the Depression, spectators flocked to Los Angeles. Cars with out-of-state license plates filled the city, and trains daily brought swarms of Olympic visitors. An occasional group even landed at Mines Field, the small municipal airport west of Inglewood that would become the Los Angeles International Airport. The organizing committee's fears that it might be throwing a party no one would attend proved groundless.

The Los Angeles facilities surpassed any previously provided by Olympic hosts. Four of the principal venues were clustered near Exposition Park—Olympic Stadium, Swimming Stadium, the State Armory, and the Los Angeles Museum of History, Science and Art, which housed entries in the arts competition.

Facilities at the Olympic Village included a small hospital, complete with X-ray and laboratory equipment. The bungalows of the Olympic Village drew magnanimous raves from the world's male athletes and team officials. In presenting the Olympic Village plan, Farmer had made clear that women would be excluded. They were housed separately in the Chapman Park Hotel just off Wilshire Boulevard near the Ambassador Hotel.

Usually critical American sports reporters employed such terms as "breathtaking" and "an architectural marvel" in assessing the refurbished Olympic Stadium. Renovations included new seating for 105,000, improvements to the dirt track surface, and the installation of a 20-by-30-foot scoreboard. Addition of a 107-foot high torch to burn throughout the Games made possible the inauguration of that Olympic tradition.

The newly completed swimming stadium, with its state-of-the-art pool, stood in stark contrast to earlier sites that ranged from barely adequate to nearly unacceptable. The swimming stadium had permanent seating for 10,000 and temporary seats for 2,000 more.

The armory, which housed fencing competition, could accommodate 1,000. The 10,000-seat auditorium in the heart of the city was the venue for the boxing, wrestling, and weightlifting events. Pasadena's Rose Bowl hosted cycling. Rowing took place at Long Beach Marine Stadium, which offered permanent and temporary seats as well as two miles of enclosed standing room along the course. The equestrian events were held at the Riviera Country Club near Beverly Hills, and yachting events took place off Los Angeles Harbor.

No track team could use the Coliseum track for training. Each morning during the week of July 25, busses arrived at the Chapman Park Hotel and the Olympic Village to transport athletes to various practice locations—high school fields, playgrounds, and athletic facilities at the University of Southern California and the University of California at Los Angeles. Such planning was a welcome departure from previous years when nations often had to arrange for their own training sites.

During the week before the opening of the Games, teams trained in the swimming stadium pool at designated times; water polo and diving claimed morning hours. The Los Angeles Playground and Recreation Department reserved mornings for Olympic practice at such locations as Griffith Pool on Riverside Drive near Griffith Park and West Los Angeles Pool on Stoner Avenue. Teams also used the private pools of such landmarks as the Ambassador Hotel and the Hollywood, Pasadena, and Los Angeles athletic clubs.

In his presentation to the IOC in 1923, William May Garland had exploited the movie capital's worldwide celebrity by labeling Los Angeles a suburb of Hollywood. The crowded Olympic social calendar that greeted officials and athletes reflected the Hollywood connection along with the more formal bent of the civic elite.

Ballrooms and banquet halls at the Ambassador Hotel on Wilshire and the imposing Biltmore Hotel downtown provided sites for gala Olympic functions. Japan's Olympic committee, for example, hosted its American counterpart at an elegant banquet at the Ambassador. The formal Ball of All Nations honored athletes as special guests in the Coconut Grove nightclub at the Ambassador, and Junior Olympic Hostesses entertained athletes at another ball in the Biltmore's Sala de Oro. The Coconut Grove regularly attracted athletes, movie moguls and stars, Olympic dignitaries, and civic leaders.

Motion pictures captivated the world in the 1930s. Even had 1932 not seen the release of gold-medal swimmer Johnny Weissmuller's first Tarzan film, Olympians would have reveled in social activities with a Hollywood link. The movie colony redeemed pledges of help made to Garland's committee and entertained the visitors royally. Radio's immensely popular "The Breakfast Club" hosted Olympians at a broadcast, and athletes delighted in small gatherings at stars' homes. A star-studded luncheon and tour of the Fox Studios hosted by humorist Will Rogers was a social highlight for the women athletes. Mary Pickford and Douglas Fairbanks had supported the Olympic Games since 1924 when they cheered their friend Charlie Paddock to a silver medal in Paris. Star-struck athletes coveted an invitation to "Pickfair," their English Regency mansion, and the popular pair hosted a reception there for Olympians toward the end of the Games. The Hollywood connection helped assure positive and widespread publicity. Olympic stars became familiar names, and the Games themselves enjoyed greater popularity in the United States that year.

The Olympic Fine Arts Exhibition, mounted in the Los Angeles Museum of History, Science and Art, drew more than 348,000 visitors. It contained over 1,100 works by artists of 32 nations, including painting, sculpture, architecture, graphic arts, literature, and music. Two giants in American letters, William Lyon Phelps and Thornton Wilder, judged the literary entries. It is worth noting that they awarded honorable mention to Avery Brundage's essay "The Significance of Amateur Sport." Prize-winning paintings, watercolors, prints, and drawings bore such titles as "Struggle," "Jackknife," and "Stadium." An honorable-mention award went to "Indian Ball Game," by Native American artist Blue Eagle. First prize for sculpture was awarded Mahonri Young of the United States for "The Knockdown." Venerable Canadian sculptor R. Tait McKenzie's "Shield of the Athletes" placed third among medals and reliefs. Architectural design awards of lasting interest included second prize for Yale's Payne Whitney Gymnasium in New Haven, Connecticut, and honorable mention for the Stanford Stadium, in Palo Alto, California. Awards in fine arts competition received ceremonial announcement in the Stadium just as those for athletic events did. The victory stand, with medal ceremonies at the conclusion of each event, first appeared in 1932.

Nearly perfect weather graced the entire run of the Games in Los Angeles. This happy reality, together with improved facilities and conditions, virtually guaranteed that Olympic records would fall, and fall they did.

On Saturday, July 30, a capacity crowd settled into their seats in the Coliseum under a blazing California sun. The Opening Ceremony established patterns and precedents for pageantry and showmanship. In the opinion of blasé New York columnist Damon Runyon, the games "opened in the most amazing setting and with the most impressive ceremonies in all the history of sports." Hundreds of flags flew above the Coliseum. National banners and the five-ringed Olympic flag flanked the peristyle at the east end. The peristyle itself bore Coubertin's expression of the Olympic spirit: "The important thing in the Olympic Games is not winning, but taking part. The essential thing is not conquering, but fighting well."

A 250-piece band and a choir of 1,200 voices delivered impassioned music. With the delegation from Greece at its head, the parade of athletes marched crisply from the Coliseum's main tunnel, drew up in columns across the field, and stood at attention. Vice President Charles Curtis proclaimed the Games officially open. Artillery rounds saluted the lighting of the Olympic torch; the choir rendered the Olympic hymn; the Olympic standard rose to the top of the flagpole; and 2,000 pigeons flew to freedom. Following the Olympic Oath, the athletes exited the stadium. The huge crowd remained seated. Although they stayed in response to a request to allow the athletes to clear the area, they had also been deeply moved by this most impressive of Olympic opening ceremonies.

The 1932 Games proved salutary for the future of women in the Olympics and for women athletes in general. Women's events enjoyed significant popularity in Los Angeles. The women won the admiration of spectators and, through the press, the entire world. This was due in no small part to the publicity surrounding the performances of Mildred "Babe" Didrikson, the phenomenal all-around athlete from Texas. Generally conceded to have been the outstanding individual competitor of the Los Angeles Games, Didrikson went on to immortality as a pioneer and pace-setter in women's golf. In 1932, the versatile 21-year-old electrified spectators in the first women's event of the Games with her world-record-breaking first javelin throw. She won gold medals in two of the three events for which she qualified—the javelin and the 80-meter hurdles. The third event, the high jump, created one of the more enduring Olympic controversies. Women's rules in 1932 mandated crossing foot-first over the bar. The judges ruled that Didrikson's rolling, horizontal jump was a headfirst dive that disqualified her in a jump-off with teammate Jean Shiley, who won the gold medal.

For the X Olympic Games, officials went to great lengths to assure confidence in timing of events. They paid $6,000 each for 32 Swiss government-certified watches used by timers. In many respects, the Los Angeles Games represent a quantum leap forward, but electronic timing's day had not yet arrived. The United States used electrical timers at the men's Olympic trials that year, but the IAAF rules committee chose to stay with handheld stop watches for the Games themselves. The committee did approve the semi-official use of the new Kirby photo-electric timer, a primitive device that may have provoked more controversy than it resolved.

At its July meeting on timing devices, the rules committee dealt another technological setback to sprinters when they continued their ban on starting blocks. Use of blocks had been under discussion since Amsterdam, but in Los Angeles sprinters again carried trowels to the track to dig starting holes.

Olympic controversies, protests, and complaints about judging date back at least to the contentious London Games of 1908. Dispute marked many of the highlights of the 1932 Games but did nothing to mar their luster.

United States sprinters Eddie Tolan and Ralph Metcalfe finished so nearly even in the 100 meters that several judges and most spectators disputed the award of gold to Metcalfe. Tolan himself thought he had lost and congratulated Metcalfe before the final ruling was made. The popular Didrikson figured in another dispute when she took the 80-meter hurdles gold medal from Chicago's Evelyne Hall in what many considered a dead heat.

Dispute reached a high-water mark with the water polo match between Brazil and Germany. That 7–3 victory for the Germans ended in a minor riot at the swimming stadium. Brazilian players, incensed by their forty fouls in contrast to four called on Germany, charged at referee Bela Komjadi of Hungary, whose work had been roundly booed by spectators. Los Angeles police were summoned to protect Komjadi and to quell the melee that erupted.

Entrants in the 3,000-meter steeplechase were more sanguine in the face of a judging lapse. Finland's Volmari Iso-Hollo ran an extra lap to capture the gold medal because a substitute official neglected to flag the field on the final lap. During the officials' two-hour delay in reaching a decision, no runner exercised his privilege of demanding a rerun of the tortuous grind.

Fortunately that contest for first place was not close. However, Iso-Hollo's teammate, world-record holder Lauri Lehtinen, figured in a men's 5000-meter controversy that had uglier overtones. Lehtinen twice swerved into a lane ahead of Ralph Hill, blocking the Oregonian's attempts to pass during the last 50 meters. The crowd roared its outrage when the judges awarded first place to the Finn. That judges' decision also required a two-hour delay and carried the suspicion that, in the wake of the Paavo Nurmi affair, no judge dared risk further offense to Finland.

Rowing and the marathon provided memorable thrills without controversy. Some 80,000 people lining the course at Long Beach saw the University of California crew continue U.S. eight-oared domination with its thrilling come-from-behind victory over Italy. The runner in the lead when twenty-eight marathoners left the stadium still led when twenty returned, waving his white hat to the appreciative, roaring crowd. Juan Carlos Zabala, invariably labeled as a "20-year-old newsboy from the Argentine," had cut a full minute from the record set at Antwerp in 1920.

The water polo imbroglio aside, swimming saw little discord. Excepting Clarence "Buster" Crabbe's gold medal for the United States in the 400-meter freestyle, Japan virtually swept the men's events. Helene Madison, the premiere female freestyler of the day, took three gold medals home to Seattle. New York's backstroker Eleanor Holm and all the American divers won medals and notoriety, which would escalate for Holm en route to Berlin four years later, when she was dismissed from the U.S. team for violating training rules on the transatlantic voyage to Europe.

The Games of the X Olympiad, begun in doubt, ended triumphantly. The August 14 Closing Ceremony paled but little beside the brilliant opening two weeks earlier. A crowd of 87,000 filled the Coliseum that Sunday. A parade of nations' flags replaced the parade of athletes, many of whom had left Los Angeles immediately after their events in order to save money. Trumpet fanfare and artillery salutes marked the lowering of the five-ringed Olympic flag, which the mayor of Los Angeles accepted for safekeeping until it would rise in Berlin in 1936. The huge crowd joined massed bands and a thousand-voiced chorus in an emotion-filled moment, singing "Aloha" as the sun dropped below the horizon.

Approximately 1,250,000 people had paid $1.5 million to attend events over the sixteen days. Optimism and tenacity had triumphed over a depressed economy to produce a financial profit for the Games and reward the Games planners with untold personal satisfaction. Los Angeles had staged a celebration that endowed the Olympics with much of the organization, color, and pageantry that have become traditions of the Games.

BIBLIOGRAPHICAL ESSAY

Essential to any work on the 1932 Games are Frederick Granger Browne, ed., *The Games of the Xth Olympiad, Los Angeles, 1932: Official Report* (Los Angeles, 1933), the report of the Los Angeles Organizing Committee (LAOC), and Frederick W. Rubien, ed., *American Olympic Committee Report: Games of the Xth Olympiad, Los Angeles, 30 July—14 August 1932. IIIrd Olympic Winter Games, Lake Placid, New York, 4–13 February, 1932* (New York, 1933). There is no collection extant of papers of the LAOC, but its 700-page report has superb photographs, a complete record of the competition, and details relating to housing, practice sites, and the like.

Five major libraries in the Los Angeles area have holdings relating to the 1932 Games. Varying in size and scope, collections can be found at the Los Angeles Public Library, in the Special Collections of the University of Southern California and University of California at Los Angeles, at the Paul Ziffren Sports Resource Center Library of the Amateur Athletic Foundation, and among papers housed in the Bill Henry Room of the Occidental College Library.

The Ziffren Center library holds transcripts of interviews with Olympians taped as part of the Athletic Foundation's oral history program. Videotapes made from 1932 films of some events can be viewed. Other helpful items to be found there include a complete collection of the 39 daily editions of the *Official Program, Games of the Xth Olympiad, Los Angeles, 1932*, a complete set of the booklets that contain official regulations for the Games, and bound copies of 1932 editions of the *Los Angeles Times* and the *Los Angeles Herald-Examiner.* The *New York Times* is an excellent press source, but for the 1932 Games, the *Los Angeles Times* should be considered the newspaper of record.

Bill Henry and Patricia Henry Yeoman, *An Approved History of the Olympic Games* (New York, 1984), a general history first published in 1948, has special significance for the X Olympiad. Henry served as "technical adviser" and public address announcer for the Games in Los Angeles, and his daughter, Patricia Yeoman, continued efforts to keep the 1932 legacy alive.

The Los Angeles County Museum published *Olympic Competition and Exhibition of Art: Catalogue of the Exhibit* (Los Angeles, 1932) to accompany its contribution to the X Olympiad.

The Vance Bibliographies Series published Glenna Dunning, *The Olympic Games of 1932 and 1984: The Planning and Administration of the Los Angeles Games* (Monticello, IL, 1985). It is intended for use by urban planners and historians and, as the title implies, entries relate to planning and administration.

Al J. Stump, "The Olympics That Almost Wasn't," *American Heritage* 33, 5 (1982): 65–71 presents a short overview of the 1932 experience. The background of the Games is chronicled by John Lucas, "Prelude to the Games of the Tenth Olympiad in Los Angeles, 1932," *Southern California Quarterly* 64, 4 (1982): 313–17. A slender pamphlet by Franklin Kjorvestad, *The 1932 Los Angeles Xth Olympiad: Its Development and Impact on the Community* (n.d.) focuses on community impact.

Two books produced at the time of the 1984 Games contain material relating to 1932: Paul Zimmerman, *Los Angeles the Olympic City, 1932–1984* (Hollywood, CA, 1984), and Delmar Watson and Miseki L. Simon, eds., *Xth Olympiad, Los Angeles, 1932* (South San Francisco, CA, 1984), the latter of which contains an impressive collection of photographs.

A number of books contain interviews with or biographical material about individual 1932 Olympians. These include William O. Johnson, *All That Glitters is Not Gold: The Olympic Games* (New York, 1972); Lewis H. Carlson and John J. Fogarty, *Tales of Gold* (Chicago, 1987); William O. Johnson and Nancy P. Williamson, *"Whatta Gal": The Babe Didrikson Story* (Boston, 1977); and Betty Lou Young, *Our First Century: the Los Angeles Athletic Club, 1880–1980* (Los Angeles, 1980). See also Arthur E. Grix, *Olympische Tage in Los Angeles* (Berlin, 1932), a diary of the Olympic Games by a German boxer then living in New York.

The archives of the Amateur Athletic Foundation of Los Angeles has a 31-minute videotape of Pathe newsreel coverage of the 1932 Games, made directly from 35-mm film footage. In 1982, noted Olympic filmmaker Bud Greenspan produced *Time Capsule: The Los Angeles Olympic Games of 1932*.

BERLIN 1936

Annette Hofmann and Michael Kruger

THE GAMES OF THE ELEVENTH OLYMPIAD

The Olympic Games that took place from August 1 to 16, 1936, in Berlin, Germany, are known in history as the "Spiele unterm Hakenkreuz" (Games under the Swastika). They are an example of the political instrumentation of sports and the Olympic Games, of the many meanings of sports, and of the symbolic meaning of sport events, forms, and rituals. In these Olympic Games everything came together that the world of sport had to offer in the 1930s: the variety of different sports and disciplines that until then had been organized in most civilized countries of the world in federations, outstanding athletic achievements by both men and women, the Olympic movement as the accepted center of world sports, and the Olympic Games as a worldwide media event.

The Olympic Games that were planned for 1916 in Berlin became a victim of World War I, for which the Germans were held responsible. For this reason they were not allowed to participate in the 1920 Antwerp and 1924 Paris Games. In 1928 the Germans were invited to participate at the Olympic Games in Amsterdam. At the IX Olympic Congress in May 1930, Berlin introduced its candidacy for 1936. Besides Berlin, Alexandria, Barcelona, Budapest, Buenos Aires, Cologne, Dublin, Frankfurt/Main, Helsinki, Nüremberg, and Rome had applied to host the Games. At the 29th IOC organizational session one year later in Barcelona, all the cities except Barcelona and Berlin had withdrawn. Due to the Spanish revolution, only 20 of the then 67 IOC members participated; therefore it was not possible to choose the next host city. However, at the following postal ballot, 43 votes were in favor of Berlin and 16 for Barcelona. Thus, Berlin was chosen to hold the XI Olympic Games, and the Germans were anxious to use this opportunity to make up for the cancelled Games of 1916.

On January 24, 1933, the Organizing Committee for the Olympic Games in Berlin was officially founded. But the political developments in Germany, the victory of the National Socialists in 1932, and finally the "Machtergreifung" (assumption of power) by Adolf Hitler and his "Nationalsozialistische Arbeiterpartei" (National Socialist Workers Party) at the end of January 1933, a few weeks after the founding of the Organizing Committee, threatened to ruin everything. It was clear that the international Olympic Games and their idea would not be in accordance with the ideological principles of the National Socialists. Equality, democracy, peace, and internationalism were not to be united with the militarism, chauvinism, racism, and anti-Semitism of the National Socialists. Their followers were against the Games and initially tried to prevent their taking place in Germany. The NS Press agitated against the Olympic Games and against persons who supported the Games.

These attacks ended after German IOC member and president of the Organizing Committee, Theodor Lewald, and General Secretary Carl Diem were able to

convince Hitler and his propaganda department, led by Joseph Goebbels, on March 16, 1933, of the propagandistic effects of the Games. On October 16, 1934, Hitler took on sponsorship of the Games. Lewald and Diem were able to keep their positions on the Organizing Committee.

As a result, Diem and the Organization Committee had practically unlimited financial and propagandistic means for their plans. Instead of the originally planned extension of the old Olympic Stadium, a new one was built that offered room for over 100,000 spectators. The budget for the Games originally amounted to approximately five million reichmarks; now it had been raised to about 500 million reichsmarks. All facilities—the "Reichssportfeld," as the stadium including the huge marching field were called; a 20,000-seat hockey rink; a 16,000-seat swimming pool; the regatta

Berlin 1936—Shooting the diving sequence for the official film, *Olympia*, by Leni Riefenstahl. Courtesy of International Olympic Committee, IOC Museum Collections.

course; the sailing facilities in Kiel; and the ski and ice-skating stadium in Garmisch-Partenkirchen, where the Winter Games took place; and housing for the athletes—could now generously be planned and finished in time. The organizers had the full support of the Führer. Well-known German artists and architects were engaged. The architect Werner March planned the stadium, the sculptor Josef Thorak designed his enormous "Faustkämpfer" (Fist Fighter), and Josef Waderle, his "Rosseführer" (Horse Leader), which were placed in front of the Marathon Tor (Marathon Gate) on the Reichssportfeld. The size and power of the Third Reich, the supremacy of the German Herrenrasse (master race), and the military will of the nation were to be demonstrated by these symbols. Richard Strauss composed music for a dance, "The Olympic Rings," for the Opening Ceremony of the Games, and Mary Wigman danced to Diem's "Weihespiel," for which Carl Orff and Werner Erg wrote the music.

Finally, Leni Riefenstahl was commissioned to make an Olympic movie to preserve the Games for eternity in pictures. Riefenstahl's two-part film (*Fest der Völker, Fest der Schönheit*), which also came out in French and English in 1938 and is still known today not only in Germany but also abroad, is a typical example of National Socialistic propagandistic film art.

The National Socialist leadership was counting on the propagandistic effects of the Olympic Games both on the world and within the German population. With the taking over and perfect organization of the Olympic "Games of Peace," they could demonstrate to the world their regime's love of peace. Suspicious foreign countries could convince themselves of how peaceful and hospitable the Germans were. The world could see that criticism of the National Socialist regime was unfounded and aimed against the Germans by international Judaism, as the National Socialistic press claimed. The demonstration of love of peace would consciously cover the real warlike goals of the regime, since, in the opinion of the military and the NS leadership, the Reich was not yet ready for a war at that point in time.

The second goal with regard to foreign politics that could be fulfilled through the Olympic Games was the demonstration of the struggle and effectiveness of the regime and its loyalty to the people. Therefore it was very important to the rulers that the organization be perfect, that no impression of weakness show up, and that the enthusiasm of the German population be shown. Another goal was that the German Olympic athletes should rank especially well, if possible as winners of the competitions.

The Olympic Games were also a tool for propaganda within Germany, with which to stifle the growing doubts of the population towards the regime, doubts that had arisen after the first persecution of Jews and the passage of the Nürnberger Rassengesetze (Nuremberg Race Laws) of 1935, which included decisive steps in the discrimination, persecution, and ultimate destruction of the Jews. With the planned Games they could demonstrate to their people the strength of the National Socialist rulers, who were capable of organizing such a huge festivity and leading the German athletes to victory. The identification with winning athletes could be transferred to the regime itself.

At the same time they could demonstrate to the German population that Germany was not isolated from the world, as was partly the case during the Weimar Republic, when Germany was not allowed to participate in the Olympic Games. On the contrary, now that a strategy of strength was being followed with respect to foreign countries, the world was coming to Germany to be its guests.

These propagandistic goals of the National Socialists were mirrored in their engagement in the preparation, organization, and political evaluation of the Games. But one cannot overlook the fact that there were major obstacles to this propaganda. The biggest one was the Olympic idea itself and the Olympic Charter; these are set IOC rules that are valid for all Games, covering everything from the competition and the nomination of the participants to the ceremonies that accompany the Games.

The IOC supervises all of this. It gives the Games not to a country or a nation, but to a city, in this case, Berlin. The head of that country is not allowed to do more than declare the Games open in a formula of one single sentence. Through this,

Pierre de Coubertin originally wanted to avoid the misuse of the Games for the nationalistic interests of single states or a regime. Thus, on the basis of Coubertin's principles the IOC has repeatedly emphasized that the Games must not have a "political" character and that no one should be excluded or discriminated against because of racist or religious reasons. Athletic achievement alone is the decisive factor—as long as the athlete is an amateur—in determining whether he or she may participate. To guarantee these Olympic rules and principles was the intention of the Belgian IOC president, Comte Henri de Baillet-Latour, who had followed Coubertin in office in 1925. He threatened to withdraw the Games from Berlin if the Germans could not guarantee adherence to the Olympic rules. "The government of the Reich should . . . give a written guarantee that it will not hinder the most careful observation of the Olympic rules," wrote the Belgian count to his German colleagues a month before the decisive session of the IOC in June of 1933 in Vienna, where the situation in Germany was again to be discussed.

At this session, Lewald, the German IOC member, was able to give Baillet-Latour a written guarantee by the German minister of interior affairs, Wilhelm Frick. However, the American IOC members remained suspicious. Only a conversation of the IOC president with Hitler could convince the IOC members to hold the XI Olympic Games in Berlin and the Winter Games in Garmisch-Partenkirchen, because the required conditions would be respected by the German Olympic Committee.

The point the foreign countries complained about most and which was the basis of the American boycott movement was the question of whether Jews should participate at the Games or not. In the United States, many public figures were against a participation of American athletes in Berlin. The Rassenhetze (racism) of the Germans meant major discrimination, especially against Jewish athletes, and would not be in agreement with the Olympic Charter. America did not want to compromise itself through participation of its athletes in National Socialist Germany; it required the observance of the principles of the Olympic movement: equal chances, equality of the races, and human dignity. It also required specifically that in Germany, Jewish athletes should have equal opportunity to participate in the games.

But since 1933, Jewish athletes had been excluded from the German Turn- and Sportvereine (gymnastic and sport clubs); since then they had had no possibilities of preparing themselves for the Olympic Games. They were not allowed to train in public sport facilities or to compete against Aryan athletes; thus they had no chance at all of being nominated by a federation or the German Olympic Committee.

An example is the German-Jewish high jumper Gretel Bergmann from Stuttgart. Despite this discrimination she was able to show the best pre-Olympic results. Nevertheless, with the agreement of the German IOC member and the Führer of the Track-and-Field Division of Nazi Sport, Dr. Karl Ritter von Halt (member of the NSDAP and the SA since 1932), she was not nominated for the Olympic team. Only the half-Jewish fencer Helen Mayer, who lived in the United States, ended up being on the German team. This was only possible because in compliance with the regulations of the Nürnberger Gesetze, the participation of half-Jews was still allowed. The German Olympic organizers and NS propaganda, too, exploited the participation of Helene Mayer in Berlin and the half-Jewish ice hockey player Rudolf Ball at the Winter Games in Garmisch-Partenkirchen as a sign of good will.

The American boycott movement was unsuccessful, first, because the German Olympic officials Diem, Lewald, and von Halt were able to calm down their

Olympic friends again and again. After the Games Lewald even went so far as to accuse himself in front of the American consul, George Messersmith, of lying to the IOC. And second, the boycott was a failure because of the behavior of the IOC and also some important officials in the United States, who massively tried to suppress the boycott movement in their own country.

The most important role was played by Avery Brundage, at that time president of the American Olympic Committee and the American Athletic Union (AAU), since 1946 vice-president, and, from 1952 to 1972, president of the IOC. He was able to succeed against the supporters of the boycott, whose leader was Jeremiah Mahoney, subsequently his successor as president of the AAU, and Ernst Lee Jahncke, the third American IOC member. Brundage won the decisive ballot by a close majority. Beforehand, a delegation had traveled to Germany to get an impression of the political situation and mainly of the oppression of Jewish people. The American Olympic team went to Berlin, and Brundage, who, at that time, was known to be anti-Semitic and racist, was appointed to the IOC instead of Jahncke.

By the way, Coubertin, too, who, since his retirement from the IOC in 1925 had not visited the Olympic Games nor an IOC session, made a statement about the Games in Berlin, after he had been courted by the Germans, and Diem and Lewald visited him in the summer of 1935. Coubertin gave a radio speech in which he emphasized his confidence in the preparation of the Games in accordance with the Olympic spirit.

Since Coubertin and the Olympic Games in Athens in 1896, the festive settings and the Olympic ceremonies have become a fixed part of the Olympic Games. Their purpose is to show that the Olympic Games are not only the sum of athletic competition, but the realization of a huge idea as well. Gradually the official ceremonies had been expanded, so that part of the ceremonies and the Olympic Games are the Opening and Closing Ceremonies, the presentation ceremonies, the Olympic oath, the Olympic greeting, the Olympic flag with its five rings, the Olympic flame, and the Olympic hymn and fanfare.

Especially the German organizers, headed by Carl Diem, revolutionized and enlarged upon the ceremonies, which also fitted into the concept of the Nazi Games. Some examples are as follows: The Olympic greeting was almost involuntarily misinterpreted. Since the 1924 Games in Paris it was common for the athletes to hold their arms to the right when they marched into the stadium. In Berlin the German athletes entered the stadium with the German greeting, arm held in front of the body, while passing the Führerloge, as did the Austrians. When the French team marched in with the Olympic greeting, the 100,000 spectators rejoiced, because they thought the French were using the German greeting. Accordingly, this scene can be seen in Riefenstahl's Olympic film, which was interpreted by the media as a success with regard to foreign politics.

The Olympic fanfare, which traditionally is blown at the hoisting of the Olympic flag at the Opening Ceremony, resounded when the Führer entered the Stadium. The Olympic oath has been a fixed part of the Olympic ceremonies since 1920. According to the classical model and custom, one athlete, representing all athletes, promises to adhere to the rules during the Games. The speaker of this oath has to hold his national flag during his speech. In Berlin this oath was sworn by the German weight lifter and Olympic gold medallist of 1932, Rudolf Ismayrs. While he spoke the oath he held the Swastika flag, which was the new German national flag, not only for Germany but for National Socialist Germany. In general, it was not the Olympic flag with the Olympic rings symbolizing internationalization and cosmopolitanism—until today the most typical characteristic inherent to the Olympic movement—which symbolized this festivity, but the Swastika.

The Olympic fire, or the Olympic flame, was used by Carl Diem and the National Socialists to create a kind of solstitial celebration. The torch relay from Olympia to Berlin was the work of Diem, based on a suggestion by Goebbels's ministry. Since the German track-and-field athlete Fritz Schidlgen lit the Olympic fire in 1936 at the Marathon Tor in Berlin, this torch relay has become a fixed part of the Olympic ceremonies.

The presentation ceremony is an old Olympic symbol at which the winners are presented with medals, a diploma, and even an olive tree or laurel branch. In Berlin the winners additionally received oak foliage and a small oak tree, which they were to plant in their home country as a "symbol of German character, German strength, and German hospitality."

Beyond this Olympic ceremony, which was less a Germanization in Berlin than a Nazification in the sense of the NS state, the National Socialist symbolism was especially manifested in the architecture and art. Since Hitler was the builder and sponsor of the Games, all Olympic buildings were planned in a very monumental way, mirroring the National Socialist interpretation of art. The Olympic arena became the Reichssportfeld, which was to be more than an Olympic sport facility; it became a monumental center of the cult of the German people: extending out in front was the Maifeld, a huge marching field, and behind it the Langemarckhalle with the Führerturm, and the huge bell, inscribed by Diem with the words "Ich rufe die Jugend der Welt" (I am calling the youth of the world).

The connection of sport with the National Socialist death cult was obviously created in the festival performance, "Olympische Jugend," which Diem had written for the Opening Ceremony. The cheerful game of youth ended in the fourth scene with the theme "Heldenkampf und Totenklage" (Fight of the Heroes and Death Moaning). In the "Schwertertanz der Jünglinge" (Dance of the Swords of the Young Males), a hero-like fight of young soldiers takes part, which ends in the sacrifice of life and women moaning—danced by Mary Wigman and the avant-garde of German dance. With the sacrifice of the lives of the heroes, a huge dome of spotlights arched over the stadium, created by special lights, and 15,000 singers sang Schiller's and Beethoven's "Ode an die Freude."

The reinterpretation of the symbols of the Olympic Games into a National Socialist death cult and cult of sacrificing had nothing to do with the Olympic idea of a festival of peace, friendship, and understanding among nations.

Through this ambiguous symbolism, the 1936 Olympic Games was both a highlight in the history of the modern Games and, at the same time, the beginning of the biggest crisis of Olympism—a crisis related to the fact that after the Berlin Games the world had to wait for 12 years until the Olympic Games could again take place, but a deeper crisis involving confidence in and the trustworthiness of the ideals of Olympic sport. The Olympic movement had allowed itself to be deceived, blinded, corrupted, and misused, and the men responsible in the IOC had neither the strength nor the will to meet this danger.

Some 49 teams with 3,963 athletes, of which 328 were women, participated in the 1936 Olympic Games in Berlin. The German hosts presented the largest team with 427 athletes, followed by America with 367 participants. Altogether there were 19 different sports (basketball, bicycling, boxing, canoeing, fencing, gymnastics, handball, hockey, rowing, soccer, swimming, track and field, wrestling/weight lifting, modern pentathlon, polo, sailing, and shooting) that included 129 disciplines. Baseball and gliding were demonstrated. The cultural program consisted of 15 art competitions.

In the medals table the Germans won, followed by the Americans and Hungarians. National Socialist leaders interpreted this success as a sign of Aryan superiority. However, the star of the Games was the African American athlete Jesse Owens. Owens set a series of world records, among them the 100-meter and 200-meter dashes, then another one in the long jump, and together with his team in the 400-meter relay. German superiority was also questioned by the victories of the Korean Kiteo Son in the marathon and the Hungarian Jew Iboya Csá, who won the high jump event for women (by the way, at the same height that excluded Bergmann from participation in the Games). The German fencer and half-Jew Helene Mayer also was able to win a silver medal.

Besides Owens with his four gold medals, among the most successful athletes was the German gymnast Konrad Frey, who won three gold, one silver, and two bronze medals; the Dutch Henrika Wilhemina Mastenbroek, with her four gold and one silver medal in swimming; the German gymnast Alfred Schwarzmann, with three gold and two silver medals; and the French cyclist Robert Charpernier, with three gold medals.

Berlin 1936 was a landmark in the history of the modern Olympic Games. It had become obvious that sport, as it was presented and celebrated in Berlin, had become an undeniably integral element of modern culture and civilization. But the price that had to be paid was high: the loss and defeat of the boycott movement in the United States led to a years-long, deep crisis and cleavage of organized sports there, as Allen Guttmann mentioned in his biography on Brundage. The Männerorden IOC was not only accused of having made a pact with the devil in Germany, but also of having betrayed its own holy Olympic principles. The German Olympians Diem, Lewald, and von Halt were also suspected not only of having allowed the misuse of the Olympic Games in Berlin, but of having actively supported it. They had chummed up with the National Socialists, it was said, and had delivered the knowhow that helped to make the Games into a triumphal staging of the Third Reich. This show had helped to deceive the world, veiling the true political and military aims of the National Socialists: the preparations for the world war, and the annihilation of the Jews.

In contrast to this were not only the opinions of Diem and Brundage, who argued that the Games had been a great success primarily for Olympic sport and not for National Socialist Germany, but also that of the British Olympic participant and silver medalist, Nobel Peace prize winner Philip Noel-Baker, a member of Parliament and labor minister under Clement Attlee. He himself did not go to Berlin in 1936 and had supported the American and English boycott movements against the Games. Later, in connection with the boycott movement of the 1980 Moscow Games, Noel-Baker argued that he regretted not having traveled to Berlin in 1936, because those Games had meant a tremendous defeat for Hitler. They had showed the world and especially the German public that Hitler's racism and his militaristic Games were "false, stupid, and obscene." The message was that the greatest athletes in the world were black men. Here he was referring to American athlete Jesse Owens with his four gold medals, Williams, Woodruff, and others. The message was that chosen competitors of all the nations were one great happy family, inspired by the same ideal of sportsmanship, bound together by ties of common interest and friendship. In Philip Noel-Baker's opinion, this message of the Games disproved the National Socialist ideology and politics "to anyone with eyes to see." Unfortunately not all—or only a few—people used their eyes to see the truth and stand up for it.

BIBLIOGRAPHICAL ESSAY

The history of sport and physical education in the period of the German National Socialistic government is presently one of the best-explored epochs and topics in German sport history. Peiffer/Spitzer have published an elaborate bibliography ("Sport im Nationalsozialismus—im Spiegel der sporthistorischen Forschung," *Sozial- und Zeitgeschichte des Sport* [1990]: 1, 35–74) with comments. One of the pioneers was Hajo Bernett, who did extensive research in this field.

It is not possible to mention all the publications that deal with the 1936 Olympic Games; in the following the most important works are mentioned. There are uncounted Olympic overview books or general publications on sport history that include chapters on the 1936 Olympic Games in Berlin, such as those by Michael Krüger, *Einführung in die Geschichte der Leibeserziehung und des Sport. Teil 3* (Schorndorf, Germany, 1993) and Hajo Bernett and Hans Joachim Teichler, "Olympia unter dem Hakenkreuz," in Manfred Lämmer, ed., *Deutschland in der Olympischen Bewegung* (Frankfurt, 1999). Christiane Eisenberg dedicates one chapter in her book on *English Sports und Deutsche Bürger. Eine Gesellschaftsgeschichte 1800–1939* to the 1936 Olympic Games, in which she describes the ambivalent memories of these Games. The German Volker Kluge has listed all Olympic competitions and results of the 1936 Games in *Olympische Sommerspiele. Die Chronik 1. Athen 1896–Berlin 1936* (Berlin, 1997). In *The Olympics: A History of the Modern Games* (Urbana, IL, 2002), Allen Guttmann devotes one chapter to the 1936 Games. He not only summarizes the most important facts, but also gives insight into the American boycott movement and the role of Avery Brundage, as he did earlier in his *The Games Must Go On: Avery Brundage and the Olympic Movement* (New York, 1984). The American and British boycott movements are also central themes in Arnd Krüger's *Die Olympischen Spiele 1936 in Berlin und die Weltmeinung. Ihre außenpolitische Bedeutung unter besonderer Berücksichtigung der USA* (Berlin, 1972), which deals with the significance of the Games with respect to foreign politics. Hans Joachim Teichler, *Internationale Sportpolitik im Dritten Reich* (Schorndorf, Germany, 1991) also mentions the National Socialist propagandistic sport politics and its effects on England. See also the entry on the Berlin 1936 Games in the first edition of this dictionary.

Only a few monographs on the Berlin Games have been published, among them Richard Mandell, *The Nazi Olympics* (New York, 1971), which has been translated into German. The content reaches from the description of sport in classical Greece—the Nazis viewed their sporting program as an integral part of their cultural renaissance—to the narrating of the actual athletic events in 1936. Separate chapters discuss the role of three outstanding athletes (Jesse Owens, Helen Stephens, Kitei Son) as well as the villains and victims of the Games. Duff Hart-Davis shows the British perspective in *Hitler's Games: The 1936 Olympics* (New York, 1986). Other works in English include Judith Holmes, *Olympiad 1936: Blaze of Glory for Hitler's Reich* (New York, 1971). A bilingual approach (English and German) has been edited by Reinhard Rürup, *1936. Die Olympischen Spiele und der Nationalsozialismus/The Olympic Games and National Socialism* (Berlin, 1996). This book, which includes a variety of photos of the Games, gives an overview on the German sport movement, the political situation in Germany, and the Nazification of sports. It also takes up the preparation, competitions, reception, and manipulation of the 1936 Games, among other topics.

A number of essays in various international journals and books have been published, among them Bruce Kidd, "The Popular Front and the 1936 Olympics," *Canadian Journal of the History of Sport and Physical Education* 11 (1980): 1–18; D. A. Kass, "The Issue of Racism at the 1936 Olympics," *Journal of Sport History* 3, 3 (winter 1976): 223–35; Carolyn Marvin, "Avery Brundage and American Participation in the 1936 Olympic Games," *American Studies* 16 (1982): 81–106; Moshe Gottlieb, "The American Controversy over the Olympic Games," *American Jewish Historical Quarterly* 61 (March 1972): 181–213; Horst Ueberhorst, "Spiele unterm Hakenkreuz. Die Olympischen Spiele von Garmisch-Partenkirchen und Berlin 1936 und ihre politischen Implikationen," *Aus Politik und Zeitgeschichte. Beilage zur Wochenzeitung 'Das Parlament'* 31 (1986) 3–15; and Alkemeyer, Thomas, *Gewalt und Opfer im Ritual der Olympischen Spiele 1936*, in W. Dressen, ed., *Selbstbeherrschte Körper. Berliner Topografien 6* (Berlin, 1986): 60–77. Among the German authors, Hans Joachim Teichler is a specialist on the Berlin Games and National Socialistic sport. Among his essays are "Berlin 1936—ein Sieg der NS-Propaganda? Institutionen, Methoden und Ziele der Olympia propaganda Berlin 1936," *Stadion* 2 (1976): 265–306; "1936 – ein olympisches Trauma. Als die Spiele ihre Unschuld verloren," in Manfred Blödorn, ed. *Sport und Olympische Spiele* (Reinbeck, Germany, 1984): 47–76; and "Zum Ausschluss der deutschen Juden von den Olympischen Spielen 1936," *Stadion* 15, 1 (1989): 45–64.

Quite a number of biographies and autobiographies of athletes or officials who participated in these Games are available. Besides the above-mentioned publication of Allen Guttmann on Avery Brundage, examples are William J. Baker, *An American Life. Jesse Owens* (New York, 1986) or the Master's thesis by C. Diederix, "Die Judenfrage im Sport. Eine Untersuchung am Beispiel des Lebenswegs der jüdischen Sportlerin Gretel Bergmann" (Universität Stuttgart, Germany, 1993).

Just before the Games Friedrich Mildner published his *Olympia 1936 und die Leibesübungen im nationalsozialistischen Staat Berlin* (Buchvertrieb Olympiade, 1936), in which he lends detailed insight into German sport and the preparation of the German athletes for the 1936 Olympic Games. In the aftermath of the Games the book, *Olympia 1936. Band II. Die XI Olympischen Spiele in Berlin 1936*, edited by Walter Richter and the Cigaretten-Bilderdienst (Hamburg, 1936) was published, mainly listing the result of the athletic competitions. Photoprints of the Games, which one could buy in cigarette packs, could be glued into the book.

For further research with original documents on sports in National Socialist Germany, the following archives can be recommended: the Bundesarchiv in Koblenz contains important documents of the Reichsministerium. Additional material can be found in the "Politische Archiv des Auswärtigen Amts" in Bonn and the "Geheimes Staatsarchiv" in Munich. Personal files on National Socialist sport leaders are in the Berlin Document Center. The Avery Brundage Collection, available on microfilm at Cologne and at the Centre for Olympic Studies at the University of Western Ontario in Canada gives insight into the American Olympic and boycott movement during the 1930s. For research on Carl Diem, the Carl-Diem-Institut at the Deutsche Sporthochschule in Cologne is very valuable.

TOKYO/HELSINKI 1940

Sandra Collins

THE GAMES OF THE TWELFTH OLYMPIAD (NEVER HELD)

If the modern Olympic Games was the Great Symbol of the belief in internationalism at the turn of the twentieth century, the Games had become the Great Symptom of the breakdown of the world system by the 1930s. Although the IOC espoused claims to international goodwill and political neutrality, it could not escape the tense contradictions emerging among fascist, communist, and capitalist nation-states that struggled for supremacy in an uncertain era. The IOC not only permitted the sensational self-aggrandizement of Nazi Germany in the 1936 Berlin Olympics but also supported Tokyo's bid for the 1940 Games despite Japan's imperialist war in China. Eventually Japan's dreams for the first Asian Olympics could not be sustained as it continued its war in China, and Helsinki soon replaced Tokyo as the Olympic host site for 1940. Although the IOC continued to promote the 1940 Games when Great Britain declared war against Germany in 1939, the Russian invasion of Finland in the winter of 1939 forced the IOC to officially cancel the 1940 Games entirely. The history of the 1940 Olympic Games is symptomatic of how the IOC could not escape the onslaught of what would become World War II.

When Tokyo won the right to host the 1940 Olympic Games in 1936, it became the first Asian nation to both seek and win the honor of holding the Olympics. Although Baron Pierre de Coubertin originally conceived of the Games as being "'ambulatory' to win true international standing," they had up to then only been hosted in Europe and the United States. Capitalizing on the absence of any non-Western Olympic site, Tokyo officials began in 1930 to promote their city as the most capable Eastern Olympic host for 1940. The idea of a Tokyo Olympics became a powerful banner for Japan during the 1930s, as Japan sought to orient many Western institutions to the world of the East. At the same time, a majority of members of the International Olympic Committee also considered the idea of a

Tokyo Olympics an attractive symbol for the universalization of the Olympic Movement. Despite this appeal, the battle for the 1940 Games was intense, and Japan amazed the world when Tokyo emerged victorious against such established Western cities as Rome, London, and Helsinki.

The bidding campaign for the 1940 Games began in earnest at the IOC Session before the 1932 Los Angeles Olympic Games. There were a total of twelve cities that presented their candidacies: Alexandria, Barcelona, Budapest, Buenos Aires, Dublin, Helsinki, Milan, Montreal, Rio de Janeiro, Rome, Tokyo, and Toronto. IOC President Count Henri Baillet-Latour considered the numerous bids for the 1940 Games as proof that the "Olympic idea is stronger now than ever." The general consensus at the time, however, was that the 1940 Games belonged to Rome, given its proximity to other European nations that dominated the Olympic community and its earlier cancellation of the 1908 Olympic Games due to the unfortunate volcanic eruption of Mt. Vesuvius in 1906. Italian Premier Benito Mussolini's love for sports was world-renowned, and the elaborate Palace of Sport in Rome and especially the Stadium of Marbles were viewed as grand locations for a future Olympic site. Although the Tokyo proposal was exotic and Helsinki's earnest, many believed that Tokyo and Helsinki were second-tier candidates compared to Rome.

The Helsinki bid to be a host city was first submitted in 1927 when it applied for the 1936 Games. The success of the Finnish track and field athletes, especially the famous Paavo Nurmi, earned the small nation of Finland worldwide acknowledgement as a formidable sports nation. In 1927, Finnish IOC member Ernst Krogius offered Helsinki as a candidate for the 1936 Games, with the assumption that Berlin would win the 1932 Games. The success of William Garland's campaign to bring the 1932 Games to Los Angeles changed the timing for Helsinki and Berlin, and Helsinki was forced to submit its candidacy for 1940 instead. Helsinki campaigners for the 1940 Games openly countered the dream of Pierre de Coubertin that the Games would be truly universal: the Finns argued that the 1940 Games should be retained in Europe "to which they of right belong." Perhaps the Eurocentrism was less an assault against the threat of the East and more of an argument to hold the Games in Europe after the expensive 1932 voyage to Los Angeles.

Of all the candidates for the 1940 Games, not only was the Tokyo bid considered the most exotic, it would also become the most controversial Olympic campaign up to that time in IOC history. Tokyo Mayor Hidejiro Nagata boasted that 1940 was the perfect time for Tokyo to bring the Olympics east given that it was the 2,600th anniversary of the founding of Japan as a nation and would concur with the planned World Exhibition for that year. The Tokyo City Assembly unanimously endorsed the Tokyo campaign as a means to stimulate the economic redevelopment of Tokyo through international tourism, after the disastrous 1923 Kanto earthquake. Other Japanese were not as forthcoming in their support of the Tokyo Olympics. Japanese IOC members Jigoro Kano and Seiichi Kishi did not believe that the international community would support Tokyo because of Japan's recent debut in the Olympic Games. After years of negotiating with Tokyo officials, the pair agreed to submit the Tokyo invitation at the 1932 Los Angeles IOC Session almost one year after the Japanese army's invasion of Manchuria. With the incident in China, the Japanese national government declined to provide any public official support. In order to convince the national government, the Tokyo bid committee members fashioned the Olympics as a forum of Japanese "popular diplomacy" for Japan after its 1933 withdrawal from the League of Nations. The Japanese national government remained uncommitted to the Tokyo campaign, until the 1935 sensational show of support for the Tokyo bid given by the premier of Italy, Benito Mussolini.

The bid tactics adopted by the Japanese campaigners in their pursuit for the Olympic Games stood in stark contrast to the campaign protocols of the IOC. The newest IOC members from Japan, Yotaro Sugimura and Count Michimasa Soyeshima, initiated the first state-to-state negotiations for an Olympic host city. As the Japanese ambassador to Italy, Sugimura arranged for him and Soyeshima to meet with Mussolini in early 1935 before the Oslo IOC Session. After Count Soyeshima pleaded Japan's case and begged Mussolini to rescind Rome's proposal, Mussolini agreed and vowed to support Tokyo for 1940 if Japan would support Rome for 1944. The Japanese believed that Mussolini agreed to rescind the candidacy of Rome as a friendly gesture. Mussolini understood that the year was the commemoration year for Japan; he was also moved by the zeal of Soyeshima, who was very ill when he visited the prime minister with the request for Rome's withdrawal. The Japanese national government followed Mussolini's gesture by passing bills endorsing the Tokyo bid on the eve of the opening of the 1935 Oslo IOC Session.

Just as the Tokyo campaign was finally becoming a national priority for Japan, it was also becoming the center of controversy for the IOC. The aggressive Japanese campaign activities, culminating in the successful negotiations with Mussolini, forced the Olympic community to articulate many of its unspoken assumptions about the received traditions and protocols of the Olympic Games. The Italian National Olympic Committee (CONI) and the Italian IOC delegate Alberto Bonacossa protested Mussolini's decision to decide the fate of Rome's candidacy. Moreover, the IOC president, Henri Baillet-Latour, argued against the authority of behind-the-scenes negotiations with state officials as interfering with the right of the IOC to decide any Olympic matter. Ultimately, the inability of the IOC to resolve many issues during the 1935 Oslo IOC Session forced the postponement of the selection of the host for the 1940 XII Olympiad for the first time in Olympic history. Rome's proposal would later be withdrawn from the IOC, as dictated by Mussolini.

In another unprecedented tactic in host-city campaigning, Tokyo bid officials invited Baillet-Latour on a three-week, all-expense-paid trip to Japan to investigate Tokyo as a possible Olympic site. Japanese sports officials described the IOC president as being "sympathetic towards Japan only as a curious object of exoticism, like one would love a cute pet. In his innermost thoughts, he does not think that Japan could be called a strong Olympic host candidate despite the fact that Japan is a top-ranked sports nation." So as not to violate any Olympic protocols, Baillet-Latour coached the Tokyo bid committee to publicize his tour as a "private trip" and asked the city of Tokyo to pay his estimated travel expenses of 15,000 yen ($7,500) in November 1935. The highly controversial nature of the inspection tour required the utmost discretion of the Japanese government and the IOC president. The extra cost and work of the trip proved to be worth the effort for the campaign officials, for at some point during his three-week tour of Japan in March 1936, Baillet-Latour became an enthusiastic supporter of Tokyo under several stipulations. He encouraged the Tokyo bid officials to offer a one-million-yen ($500,000) travel subsidy to the Olympic delegations, to hire an IOC-appointed technical advisor and a staff of translators, and to guarantee the cost of room and board of the Olympic delegations.

In order to remain neutral in the eyes of the IOC, the IOC president also planned another "personal" trip for Finland in June 1936. In a private letter to Pierre de Coubertin, Baillet-Latour confided that he was traveling to Finland "in order to not be accused of partiality" to Japan. Baillet-Latour remained impressed with Japan, declaring "I came back from Japan, enthusiastic about the very Olympic sportsmanship of the Japanese. They deserve the Games; besides it would be an excellent thing to give the so-called sportsmen of Europe and America the opportunity to see what a nation can do, a nation that has not been contaminated by our evils [of professional sport]." Baillet-Latour and fellow IOC delegate Theodor Lewald arrived in Finland on June 3, 1936, and stayed for only five days. While the tour of the IOC president was enthusiastically received by the Finnish people and exhaustively covered by the Finnish press, the IOC President left Finland only to promote Tokyo.

The sensational state-to-state negotiations between Japan and Italy regarding the 1940 Games and the international publicity surrounding Baillet-Latour's favorable opinion of Tokyo seemed to secure the future success of the Tokyo bid. In an act of protest against Tokyo as the first Asian Olympic host, the Lord Mayor of London and the British Olympic Association (BOA) decided to seek the 1940 Games and announced the candidacy of London on June 19, 1936. The London bid caught many IOC members unaware, as the announcement followed Baillet-Latour's letter of June 18, 1936, asking members to vote for either Tokyo or Helsinki. The unexpected London bid forced yet another round of aggressive campaign maneuvers not just from the representatives of the Tokyo bid but also from the IOC president himself. Although Baillet-Latour had previously denounced the Japanese negotiations with Mussolini, he was uncommonly silent about Japan's negotiations with British politicians. Convinced that the London bid was submitted due to cultural misunderstandings by the English, IOC member Count Soyeshima arrived in London ready to initiate another series of behind-the-scenes negotiations. Soyeshima continued his meetings with British Olympic and state officials explaining the national importance of 1940 as the anniversary of the founding of Japan as a nation. Sir Robert Vansittart, the Permanent Under Secretary, representing the British government, decided not to complicate British foreign policy with Japan in the Far East and agreed to convince London and the BOA to withdraw the London bid.

The selection of the 1940 host was scheduled to take place on July 29, 1936, at the IOC Session before the Berlin Olympic Games were to open. British IOC member Lord Aberdare dutifully withdrew the London bid. Baillet-Latour used his influence as IOC president to ensure the success of the Tokyo bid by declaring that he felt "justified in recommending Tokyo as the choice for his colleagues, a choice which would mean the extension of the Olympic ideals to this part of the world." The president's support and lengthy discussion of the Tokyo bid contrasted sharply with the brief presentation of the Helsinki delegation. Many IOC delegates perceived that voting for Tokyo was symbolically linked to universalizing the Olympic Games while voting for Helsinki was tied to increasing the participation of smaller European nations. An informal vote conducted by members of the Tokyo bid committee revealed that IOC members in the following nations supported Tokyo: Belgium, Canada, China, Czechoslovakia, Egypt, England, France, Germany, Hungary, India, Italy, Iran, New Zealand, South Africa, and the United States. With a final vote of thirty-six to twenty-seven, the Games of the XII

Olympiad were awarded to Tokyo, which responded by declaring a three-day festival in order to mark the momentous occasion.

After the joyous news of the Tokyo bid's success reached Japan, the planning for the Games proved particularly difficult, given the domestic and international climate of 1930s Japan. As the military campaigns in China intensified in 1936 and 1937, the ideological value of the Tokyo Olympics became intensely debated by the Japanese elite, who argued whether hosting the 1940 Olympics was appropriate for a nation battling China. Many Japanese ideologues argued that the Tokyo Olympics were less about international sportsmanship than about promoting a positive national image for Japan. In the imagination of some Japanese, a Tokyo Olympics would force the West to acknowledge the true rank of Japan as a world power. Others disagreed and stressed that Japan adhere to Olympic protocols so as to prove Japan a modern nation capable of remaining in the international system. The IOC also grew increasingly alarmed over the nationalistic tenor of the Japanese debates over the 1940 Olympics and strongly cautioned Japanese Olympic officials to stop associating the Tokyo Games with the promotion of national politics.

These ideological debates were not the biggest obstacles to successfully organizing the Games for Japan. The labor- and time-intensive Japanese style of brokering intricate agreements among different political factions not only delayed the creation of the Japanese Olympic Organizing Committee, but also hindered many decisions required to organize the Tokyo Games. For example, although the location of the Tokyo Olympic complex was identified as the Meiji Shrine Outer Gardens in the 1932 Tokyo invitation and during the 1936 visit to Japan by Baillet-Latour, various Japanese officials began to protest the location. The Tokyo city government began to criticize the Meiji plan because the estimated renovation cost of over two million yen was too prohibitive. The Shrine Bureau of the Ministry of Home Affairs also objected that the colossal construction would destroy the "scenic beauty" of the sacred space dedicated to the memory of the Japanese emperor—which was really the concern over ritual pollution of the sacred space given the large number of foreign athletes expected to compete. After one and a half years of intense debate, the organizing committee acquiesced on March 29, 1938, to the Tokyo plans to develop a new Olympic complex in Komazawa Golf Park, given that the city was accountable for the majority of the construction costs. In addition to the main stadium, the Japanese hotly contested the route of the Olympic torch relay. In order to perpetuate the torch relay from Athens as an Olympic tradition, Carl Diem consulted famed explorer Sven Hedin to design a plan for the relay along the historic Silk Route from Olympia to Tokyo. The Japanese Organizing Committee disagreed over whether the torch relay should take an international route or a more national circuit through Japan. The constant delays fueled worldwide doubts about whether the Tokyo Olympic Games would actually take place at all and led to the fate of the Tokyo Olympics being decided by the IOC at the controversial 1938 Cairo IOC Session.

Not all aspects of planning for the 1940 Tokyo Games remained debated. Complete plans for the Olympic stadium complex were drafted and included approved budgets and construction start dates, most of which were after October 1938. The Toda rowing course and the Shibaura cyclodrome were both completely finished, and the 650-room Dai-Itchi Hotel, the largest hotel in Asia, was completed in April 1938. The program for the Tokyo Games was modeled on that of the Berlin Games and incorporated suggestions made by international sport federations to include track and field, fencing, hockey, canoeing, football, gymnastics, yachting, shooting, basketball, handball, rowing, and cycling. New track and field events—the men's 10,000-kilometer walk and the women's 200-meter race, broad jump, and shot put—were also included in the Tokyo program.

As the debates over the planning of the Tokyo Olympics continued, the international community began to threaten to boycott the 1940 Olympic Games if Tokyo remained the Olympic host. Not only did the Japanese themselves debate whether it was appropriate to host the Olympic Games while Japanese youths were battling for their lives in China, other nations also voiced concern about whether Japan as a nation ostensibly at war should or could host the Games. Just before the IOC Session was to open in Cairo in March 1938, the British Olympic Committee voted on February 1, 1938, to boycott the Games if the Japan-China incident continued, and it was soon joined by William J. Bingham of Harvard University, who led members of the American Olympic community. Chengting T. Wang, the IOC member in China, also called upon his IOC colleagues to transfer the Games away from Tokyo. American IOC member Avery Brundage, the staunch supporter of separating politics and the Olympic Games, clarified that the issue was not about the conflict between Japan and China but whether Tokyo had made adequate preparations. IOC president Baillet-Latour also supported the Tokyo Games and cited IOC Olympic protocol established during the planned 1916 Berlin Games, which specified that if the organizing committee does not voluntarily forfeit the Games, the IOC cannot take the Games away. The IOC president did, however, instigate a series of behind-the-scenes maneuvers to prepare for the voluntary forfeiture of the Tokyo Games by Japan. First, the IOC president asked all present at the IOC Session to confirm that the IOC executive committee would be "given full power in case Tokyo should drop out as places [sic] of the next Olympic Games. The executive committee was charged to take immediately the necessary steps to insure the possibility of having the Games in 1940, in one of the cities which are prepared to do so." At an IOC executive committee meeting on March 17, 1938, Baillet-Latour asked the committee members "what action could be taken if Tokyo should not be able to stage the Games." Although IOC member Lord Aberdare stated that London could take over the 1940 Games "in a state of emergency," the IOC president informed the executive committee that he would inquire about the situation in Helsinki. In a highly secret conversation, the IOC president asked Finnish IOC member Ernst Krogius if Helsinki could be prepared within six months to celebrate the 1940 Games. Krogius responded enthusiastically and informed the president that the recently built Helsinki stadium could easily be renovated to accommodate 50,000 to 60,000 spectators.

Despite the IOC's support for the Tokyo Games as late as March 1938, the situation was rapidly deteriorating in Japan. With the announcement of the government's "New Austerity Plan" on June 23, 1938, the financial bonds and steel resources required by the Tokyo Games became uncertain. When Minister of Finance and Commerce Shigeaki Ikeda announced the startling decision to postpone the international exhibition indefinitely, the fate of the Olympics also seemed to be sealed. Japanese Welfare Minister Koichi Kido canceled the 1940 Games on July 15, 1938, by announcing "I do not think that you can separate the Olympic Games from the International Exposition. The time has come for the Government to decide what to do with both. In a time when the whole nation is preparing for war, I think that it cannot host the [Olympics] and it cannot be helped." Minister Kido did not confer with the organizing committee before announcing the decision of the Japanese government, and the committee felt that it was left with no possibility for further discussion. The Tokyo organizing committee had no recourse but to forfeit voluntarily the 1940 Games under the counsel of the Japanese national government, and it did so by forwarding a telegram to the IOC on July 16, 1938. The mayor of Tokyo also announced to the IOC that it would apply for the 1944 Games at the 1939 IOC Session in London.

Upon the notification that the Tokyo Olympic Organizing Committee voluntarily forfeited the 1940 Games, Ernst Krogius accepted Baillet-Latour's invitation to organize the Helsinki Games on July 16, 1938, as they had previously agreed. The Games were officially awarded to Helsinki on July 19. With only eighteen months to go, the Finnish people enthusiastically prepared to host the 1940 Games. Some 250 million Finnish marks ($5 million) were allocated to finance the 1940 Games, of which a large part was to prepare the national infrastructure of railways, communications, and cable systems to host the Games. The city of Helsinki bore the burden of providing 125 million Finnish marks ($2.5 million) for the construction of the Olympic complex. Finnish workmen were enlarging the Helsinki Olympic stadium's seating from 30,000 to 60,000; construction on the swimming stadium and velodrome began in December 1938 and on the Olympic Village in January 1939; and twenty-one ocean liners were to be docked around Helsinki as floating hotels. During his inspection tour in November 1939, Carl Diem remarked that the distinguishing feature of the Helsinki Games would be the close proximity of all the venues. A total of 132 events were scheduled for the official 1940 Olympic program, including the new sport of gliding that had been demonstrated at the Berlin Games. The Helsinki program included thirty-three events in track and field, eight in gymnastics, sixteen in swimming and water polo, seven in rowing, four in yachting, nine in canoeing, fourteen in wrestling, five in weight lifting, eight in boxing, five in shooting, seven in fencing, six in riding, and two in gliding, as well as soccer and the modern pentathlon. The handball, hockey, polo, basketball, and women's gymnastics events of the Berlin program were eliminated and replaced with the men's 10,000-meter walk and the women's shot put, broad jump, and 200-meter race; two shooting competitions; and gliding events. Sixty-four IOC member nations were formally invited to the 1940 Olympic Games, including Palestine, Lithuania, and Slovakia, all of which were invited for the first time to any Olympic competition. At the time the Games were canceled, thirty-nine nations had submitted their entries to the 1940 Games.

When Great Britain declared war against Germany, the IOC executive committee was forced to review whether the Games should be held, allowing only neutral countries to participate, or whether they should be canceled altogether. On November 25, 1939, Baillet-Latour announced the cancellation of the V Winter Games in Garmisch-Partenkirchen, Germany. During the following month, Russia launched attacks against Finland and put the future of the 1940 Games into further doubt. In the end, the IOC waited for the Helsinki organizing committee to forfeit the Games, which it did on April 29, 1940. The IOC then announced on May 6, 1940, that "In accordance with the Fundamental Principle No. 2 of the Olympic Charter the XII Olympiad will not be celebrated." As Chinese IOC member Chenting T. Wang lamented upon hearing the news, "Instead of building up youth and goodwill among nations, we see now but death to the young and bitter struggle between the nations." In the last analysis, the fate of the 1940 Olympic Games was tied to the 1930s world system, which could not overcome the deep political and economic conflicts that would soon lead to another world war.

BIBLIOGRAPHICAL ESSAY

Official reports, publications, and documents for the 1940 Olympic Games can be found at His Imperial Majesty Prince Chichibu Memorial Library in Tokyo, Japan; the Amateur Athletic Foundation of Los Angeles; the Avery Brundage Collection at the University of Illinois Champaign-Urbana Archives, in Urbana, Illinois; the Sports Library of Finland, the Sports Archives of Finland, and the City of Helsinki Archives; and the IOC archives in Lausanne, Switzerland. The Japanese language version of the official report as well as the monthly magazine published by the Japanese National Olympic Committee (then named the Japanese Amateur Athletic Association) *Orinpikku* (*The Olympics*) can also be found at the Japanese National Olympic Committee library and archive in Tokyo, Japan. Personal letters of Count Michimasa Soyeshima to fellow IOC members can be found at His Imperial Highness Prince Chichibu Memorial Sports Museum and Library in Tokyo, Japan. The Ministry of Foreign Affairs archive in Tokyo also houses letters and telegrams related to Japan in the Olympic Movement, including the 1940 Games. In Cologne, Germany, there are some autobiographical materials and letters at the Carl Diem Archives at the National Sports Library. All are accessible to qualified researchers.

The official reports and publications for Tokyo include the monthly newsletter from the Organizing Committee, *Tokyo Olympic News, XIIth Olympiad, 1940*, May 10, 1937–August 25, 1938, and the official report published after the Japanese forfeiture of the Games, which includes an overview of the bid for the Games, letters to and from the IOC, detailed maps and blueprints of the proposed Olympic venue locations, and photographs of various Committee members: *The Olympic Games XIIth, Tokyo 1940, Report of the Organizing Committee on Its Work for the XIIth Olympic Games in 1940 in Tokyo until the Relinquishment* (Tokyo, 1938). Also see the pamphlet that accompanied the 1932 bid, which includes rare photographs of Tokyo and Japanese culture, *Tokyo: The Sports Center of the Orient* (1933); another photographic album, *Scenic Japan* (1935); the pamphlet created for the 1936 IOC Session, pictorially presenting the Tokyo candidacy, *The Olympic Spirit in Tokyo, XIIth Olympic Games to the Far East* (1936); the pamphlet published for the 1938 Cairo IOC Session, *We Call the Youth of the World, XIIth Olympiad* (1938); and *The Twelfth Olympiad Tokyo, 1940: General Rules and Programme* (1938). For Helsinki, the official report, *XIIth Olympiad Helsinki, 1940*, and the monthly newsletter, *XIIth Olympiad: Helsinki, 20ᵗʰ July–4ᵗʰ August 1940*, provide glimpses into the accelerated preparations for the Helsinki Games.

There is a small body of secondary research on the 1940 Games available in English. Sandra Collins has written an in-depth history of the 1940 Games from the Japanese perspective, *Orienting the Olympics: Japan and the Games of 1940* (Chicago, 2002). The unexpected London bid and subsequent concerns over British-Japanese diplomacy have been meticulously researched by Martin Polley, "Olympic Diplomacy: The British Government and the Projected 1940 Olympic Games," in *The International Journal of the History of Sport* 9, 2 (1992): 169–187. The role of IOC member Count Soyeshima in the Japanese decision to cancel the

1940 Tokyo Olympics is addressed by Junko Tahara, "Count Michimasa Soyeshima and the Cancellation of the XIIth Olympiad in Tokyo: A Footnote to Olympic History," *The History of Sport* 9, 3 (1992): 467–472. The diplomatic role of the first IOC-appointed technical adviser, Werner Klingeberg, is questioned by the unpublished article of Garth Paton, "Letters From the Spy Left Out in the Cold: Werner Klingeberg and the I.O.C.," (n.p., n.d.). The *New York Times* provides an interesting historical view into the unfolding events of the 1940 Olympic Games.

There are two historical treatments of the failed Games in German. Hajo Bernett, "Das Scheitern der Olympischen Spiele von 1940," *Stadion* 6 (1980): 251–290 addresses the role of the Japanese-Chinese and Russo-Finnish wars on the 1940 Games; also see Kumihiko Karaki, *Die aufgegebenen Olympische Spiele in Tokio 1940* (n.p., 1982).

LONDON 1944

Martin Manning

THE GAMES OF THE THIRTEENTH OLYMPIAD (NEVER HELD)

The XIII Olympic Summer Games did not take place because of World War II, "the suicide of a culture," as Avery Brundage observed. The Summer Games were scheduled for London, while the VI Winter Games were awarded to Cortina d'Ampezzo, Italy. The International Olympic Committee (IOC) chose London over Athens, Budapest, Detroit, and Lausanne in the late 1930s.

On August 7, 1939, a gigantic Olympic preview was held at White City stadium, outside of London, where Americans won 8 of the 14 events. Less than a month later, on September 1, German troops invaded Poland and athletic festivals became less important. Preparations for 1940 were dominated by the Tokyo-Helsinki competition for the Summer Games. Berlin viewed Tokyo's eventual success as evidence of an Anglo-Japanese alliance, especially after London withdrew its half-hearted bid for the Games. The fact that London withdrew in order to obtain the 1944 Games made less of an impression on Germany than the fact that Japan was the immediate beneficiary of the British decision.

Japan did not hold the award long. In 1937, the beginning of the Sino-Japanese war demonstrated that Japan was committed to a major military adventure in Asia. Under such circumstances, the Japanese returned the Games to the IOC, which conferred them on Helsinki, a replacement city suggested even before Japan gave up the Games. Japan held an all-Japan meet instead, and planned later events that would include all the areas under the jurisdiction of the Greater East Asian Co-Prosperity Sphere.

The Winter Games, which ended up in Garmisch-Partenkirchen, were canceled because of Germany's belligerency, but there was still hope, at least in America, that the Summer Games would be held in Helsinki, even though Finland had recently emerged from its 100 days of war with the Soviet Union. However, in April 1940, the Finnish Olympic Committee officially announced that it was necessary to cancel the Games. With the continuation of the war long past the date when any kind of preparations could be made for the 1944 Games, they too were canceled.

World-class athletes were deprived of their chance to compete in the 1944 Olympics, but some semblance of a hypothetical U.S. team can be seen from a list of members of the All-American track-and-field team: 100-meter dash, Claude Young; 200-meter dash, Charles Parker; 400-meter run, Elmore Harris; 800-meter run, Robert Kelley; 1-mile run, Gilbert Dodds; 3-mile run, Oliver Hunter; 10,000-meter run, Norman Bright; marathon, Charles Robbins; 120-yard hurdles, Owen Cassidy; 440-yard hurdles, Arky Erwin; 3,000-meter steeplechase, Forest Efaw; 50,000-meter walk, Walter Fleming; high jump, Fred Sheffield; long jump, Barney Ewell; hop, step, and jump, Donald Barksdale; pole vault, Cornelius Warmerdam; shot put, Earl Audet; hammer throw, Henry Dreyer; discus throw, Hugh Cannon; javelin throw, Martin Biles; and decathlon, Irving Mondschein.

In 1944, the fiftieth anniversary of the revival of the modern Olympic Games was celebrated at the IOC headquarters in Lausanne. London hosted the Games of the Fourteenth Olympiad in 1948, undertaking their second Olympic Games with more advance notice but more severe problems than was the case in 1908. The 1944 Games, it might be said, were merely postponed four years, giving London time to begin to recover from the war and allowing Helsinki until 1952 to prepare for an Olympic Games promised since 1938.

BIBLIOGRAPHICAL ESSAY

The IOC archives in Lausanne have some material on the XIII Olympiad, including the candidature reports, which describe events leading to the selection of London for the 1944 Games. There are no references to the 1944 London games in the printed guide to the Avery Brundage Collection at the University of Illinois.

A few more general histories of the Olympics discuss the World War II years and the efforts of the IOC to keep the movement alive during difficult times. See Allen Guttmann, *The Olympics: A History of the Modern Games* (Urbana, IL, 2002), and Alexander M. Weyand, *The Olympic Pageant* (New York, 1952), which has a chapter on the lost years.

LONDON 1948

Norman Baker

THE GAMES OF THE FOURTEENTH OLYMPIAD

In the immediate aftermath of World War II, it was by no means a certainty that the Games of the XIV Olympiad would take place in 1948. Journalists on both sides of the Atlantic questioned the wisdom of such a rapid resumption of the Games. The most severe critics even argued against any resumption of the Olympics, largely on the grounds that they engendered more international hostility than goodwill. The experience of Berlin in 1936 provided the primary rationale for such allegations. More pragmatic opposition rested on the belief that there would not be time by 1948 for international sporting competition to regain prewar standards and therefore 1952 was a more suitable date for the revival of the Games.

These various reservations were overwhelmed by the widespread desire to return life to peacetime normalcy as rapidly as possible. There were many potential measurements for assessing the attainment of normal, but for many people the resumption of the calendar of major sporting events was among the most significant. Thus, when a meeting of the IOC Executive Committee was convened in London in August 1945, the enthusiasm displayed by the three members present for a 1948 Olympics reflected not only personal choice but also a very broad-based sentiment regarding postwar life.

The choice of London as a site stemmed in part from the fact that the British capital had earlier been awarded the ill-fated 1944 Games. This motivation was reinforced by the fact that the majority of alternative host cities were located in the United States, and there were severe doubts about the practicalities and costs of trans-Atlantic travel and the impact that this could have on the number of participants. This was a serious consideration in an era when, numerically, European nations predominated within the Olympic movement. From the time of the August 1945 meeting of the executive committee it was generally assumed that London would host the 1948 Games. Nevertheless, it was not until February 1946 that the British Olympic Committee, through the Lord Mayor of London, issued the official invitation. The nearly six months of delay was the product of several influences. These included the postwar need to reconstitute the governing bodies of British sport, concerns over the short time available for preparation, and the need to receive assurances of government cooperation in overcoming postwar shortages and controls. Such government support, which did not involve direct financial aid, was forthcoming largely because of the expected boost that the Games would give to tourism and thus hard currency earnings, most particularly U.S. dollars.

In early 1946, the British organizers did not underestimate the difficulties of the task ahead. However, neither they, nor anyone else, including the government, anticipated the depth of Britain's postwar economic problems. These were to complicate greatly the Organizing Committee's task and to bring about significant changes to their original plans. When Britain's economic difficulties were at their most severe in the late summer of 1947, they provoked a public campaign for the abandonment of the Games headed by the prominent conservative politician and newspaper proprietor, Lord Beaverbrook. Twice the government had to assure the Organizing Committee of the continuation of their support. This commitment was based on the extent of preparations already undertaken and the fear of loss of national and political prestige that would arise from the abandonment of the Games.

While publicly the Organizing Committee, particularly its chairman, Lord Burghley, displayed consistent optimism, behind the scenes there was great uneasiness. The nervousness of the committee is understandable given the range of problems they encountered. Wembley Stadium was preferred as the primary site over the White City, which had filled that role in 1908. This choice had, in part, been based on the number of events that was expected could be staged within the one complex, thus simplifying logistical arrangements. Shortages of materials and control of labor resulted in an inability to undertake new construction. This, in turn, served to reduce the degree to which events could be concentrated at Wembley. The resulting dispersion, accompanied by scheduling complications, led to confrontation with the international governing bodies of various sports, most notably FINA (Federation Internationale de Natation). Wembley Stadium itself was regularly used for greyhound and motorcycle racing. Both were very profitable for the company that ran the facility. Therefore, in order to minimize the interruption to these activities, a finished surface for the running track could only be laid in the last two weeks before the Games. There was concern that this would allow an insufficient time for the track to settle and that performances would thus be adversely affected. Such fears were not fulfilled, and most commentary on the track was positive.

Plans for the housing and feeding of Olympic competitors and officials not only involved organizational difficulties but also was a delicate public relations exercise. The rationing of food and a critical shortage of housing persisted for much longer after the war than had been anticipated and thus became the objects of a volatile public debate. To accord too much privilege to foreign visitors would garner hostility from an austerity-stricken British public. On the other hand, to expose competitors to the full rigors of postwar British life would surely provoke international controversy. After protracted deliberation involving the Organizing Committee and the government, compromises were struck. Any idea of a specially constructed Olympic Village was abandoned and the majority of male Olympians were housed in adapted Army and Air Force camps reasonably close to Wembley. Women visitors were boarded in more widely dispersed college dormitories that had been vacated for the summer holidays. During competition, athletes were fed specially extended rations normally reserved for workers in heavy industry and, within limits, each competing nation was allowed to bring in its own supplementary supplies. By taking ample advantage of that concession, the Americans provoked considerable resentment and security concerns.

The provision of accommodation for foreign tourists was less well planned. This was so, even though an anticipated boost to tourism had furnished the government with its primary motive in backing the Games. Two problems emerged. First, there were a number of demarcation disputes between the various government departments involved. Second, with Americans mainly in mind, the focus of preparation had been on hotel accommodation. However, many European visitors had been subject to currency controls imposed by their own governments and were thus not able to afford hotel accommodation. At the last minute, an urgent appeal had gone out to homeowners in the vicinity of Wembley to provide bed and breakfast at low rates. Fortunately, this plea stimulated a significant response and another potential crisis was averted.

In addition to the problems presented by the condition of the domestic economy, the Organizing Committee faced uncertainties arising from the state of international relations in the postwar era. The first concerned the participation of the defeated Axis powers. There existed a body of opinion, of which Avery Brundage was widely believed to be part, that held that the exclusion of Germany and Japan would contravene the principle of separation between sport and politics. Against this argument was arrayed a majority view that, particularly in light of the atrocities committed by both powers, it was simply too soon to let them back in to international sporting competition. In the end, something of a compromise solution was reached. Germany and Japan were excluded but on the technical grounds that they had not reconstituted national Olympic Committees. While there had been some hostility toward Italian participation in the 1946 IAAF (International Amateur Athletic Federation) Games in Oslo, it proved a minority position, and no significant opposition was raised to their inclusion in the London Olympics.

Substantial doubt surrounded the Olympic participation of the former ally, the Soviet Union. Initially, the British Organizing Committee appeared to favor Soviet inclusion, at least in part on the grounds that it would swell the numbers of competitors and add to the prestige of the Games. Others, notably Avery Brundage, were far less enthusiastic over the prospect of the Russians coming to London. State sponsorship of athletes and the promise of cash payments if records were broken raised serious questions about Soviet compliance with prevailing standards of amateurism. The Soviets certainly gave the appearance of playing upon the divisions of opinion in the West, alternately raising and dashing hopes that they would participate. Their fluctuating actions exasperated even their erstwhile supporters in the West who claimed indifference when the Soviets failed to meet the entry deadline.

The participation of the Soviets would have further complicated what was already becoming a contentious issue, namely, the development of an appropriate and workable definition of amateurism. The Winter Games in St. Moritz, Switzerland, had been thrown into jeopardy by the presence of two U.S. ice hockey teams, representing different governing bodies of the sport, each with a distinct view regarding amateurism. Prior to the Summer Games, debate focused on the acceptability of broken time payments as consistent with amateurism. Could an athlete be compensated for loss of earnings arising from his or her preparation for, and participation in, international competition and still retain amateur status? The Swedes had been prominent in the effort to have such payments legitimized. Their efforts to effect reform within the IAAF were frustrated by the British, headed by Lord Burghley, and their American ally Avery Brundage, who succeeded in delaying any decision until after the 1948 Games. Even the British were not unanimous in their opposition to change. As Britain's record in postwar international sporting competition went from bad to worse and the Games approached there was significant journalistic debate over a related issue: what was the appropriate length and intensity of preparation for international competition? As competitors were believed to be adopting more and more rigorous training methods could, or should, the British adhere to their traditionally more casual approach? Such discussion was not without precedent and it certainly continued into the future. Nevertheless it was given particular edge as Britain prepared to host the 1948 Olympics.

The onset of the Berlin Blockade and the consequent heightening of international tension coming only a few weeks before the start of the Games posed a serious threat to the fulfillment of the Organizing Committee's plans. A substantial share of tickets for the major events had been allocated to the Americans. Concerns over the international situation resulted in the return of large numbers of tickets both from American tourists and U.S. forces serving in Europe. As ticket sales constituted the primary source of revenue with which to cover the expenses the committee had incurred, the shadow of financial loss hung over the Games. Fears thus provoked were the more intense because the British public appeared to be very slow in developing much enthusiasm for the Games. For months the British press, when it had turned its attention to the Olympics, only did so to bewail the popular preoccupation with the staples of British sport and the related indifference to the upcoming international sporting event. Consequently there were serious doubts as to whether the British public would be interested enough to buy up the excess of tickets that had suddenly been created. It was only at the last minute that these concerns were put to rest as the public suddenly warmed to the Games and bought up most of the available tickets. The unhappy prospect of a loss disappeared and a small profit was made on the Organizing Committee's outlay of about £750,000.

The London Games of 1948 were judged by most contemporaries to have been a success. With hindsight there is no major reason to contest this opinion, particularly when one takes into account the range of difficulties faced by the organizers. One of the principal measures of success for a particular Olympics is the emergence of memorable performances and moments of intense drama, both triumphal and catastrophic. On this account, London was by no means lacking. In winning four gold medals, Fanny Blankers-Koen of the Netherlands turned in one of the most notable individual Olympic performances of all time. Referred to by the British press as "the lanky Dutch housewife," Blankers-Koen, a mother of three, won medals in all four of the track events for women and did not even compete in the long jump for which she held the world record. For Americans, the decathlon victory of 17-year-old Bob Mathias was probably the most notable individual performance. However, in the long term, the African American dominance of the sprints and the gold medal Alice Couchman won in the high jump were of greater significance. Also in anticipation of the future was the emergence of the Czech Emil Zatopek, whose victory in the 10,000 meters was but an appetizer for greater things to come in Helsinki in 1952. For drama, nothing could match the painful progress of the Belgian Etienne Gailly, who was the first marathon runner to enter the stadium but was passed as he staggered round the last lap, first by the eventual winner, Argentinean Delfo Cabrera and then by the silver medallist, Welshman Tom Richards.

Fears that the level of performance would not reach the standards of prewar Games were not fulfilled to any significant degree. While recognizing that in many instances the vagaries of weather and the condition of course or track make comparisons unreliable, some sense of rising or falling performance can be gained by reviewing the winning times, heights, and distances achieved by gold medallists at successive Games. In the 21 men's track-and-field events held at all four Olympics between 1932 and 1952 there is some evidence of a lower standard of performance in 1948 as compared to 1936 and 1952. In 12 of the 21 events, winning times, heights, or distances, were inferior in 1948 to those recorded in 1936 and 1952. However, if performance in 1948 is compared to 1932, then the postwar athletes did better than their Los Angeles predecessors in 14 of 21 events. If overall competitiveness is measured in terms of the ability of one country to dominate, then there is little variation over the four Olympiads considered here. The United States won 11 track-and-field events in 1932, the same number in 1936, and again in 1948. They became even more dominant in 1952, winning 14 gold medals. With respect to the six track-and-field events for women in which there was competition in all four Olympics, the pattern is similar in terms of winning performances. In three of the six events the gold medallists of 1948 did less well than those of both 1936 and 1952 and in the other three they equaled performances in Berlin and Helsinki. However, performance was better in London than in Los Angeles in four of the six events. American domination at home in 1932, with five wins, soon evaporated with only two in 1936 and one each in London and Helsinki. This happened despite the fact that there were more events for women in both the postwar Games.

In men's swimming there was a steadier pattern of improvement over the four Olympics than was the case in track and field. Here there was no postwar decline in winning times. Improvement occurred between 1936 and 1948 in four of six events and between 1948 and 1952 in five of the six. There was almost total American domination in both London and Helsinki. The overall pattern in women's swimming was similarly one of improvement. In London, winning times were better than they had been in Berlin in four of five events. Performance in weight lifting was less likely to be influenced by variable conditions than was the case with either track and field or swimming. It is thus interesting to note that winning lifts improved consistently through all four Olympics and for all five weight divisions. On this limited basis it can be suggested that the interruption of competition caused by the war did not have an excessively adverse impact on performance in 1948. Contemporary pessimism over the standards likely to be achieved was not warranted. Taking into account the absence of the Germans and Japanese, who between them had won 38 gold medals in Berlin, then it can be claimed that the level of performance among the countries that did compete in London showed no clear decline as a result of the war.

The Games of 1948 were not without blemishes and not everyone was satisfied with the competitive outcome. It would indeed have been surprising if some element of international politics had not intruded into the Games themselves as they had into the period of preparation. Of the two principal examples occurring immediately before and during the Games, one arose from a new political situation, the other from a longer-standing dispute. When invitations to the Games had been sent out and acceptances received, Palestine had been among the expected participants. However by the time of the Games themselves, Israel had replaced Palestine. When Egypt threatened to withdraw if the Zionist flag was flown at the Games, the IOC extricated itself by declaring that Israel could not simply take over the invitation issued to Palestine and that, without an Olympic Committee of its own, Israel was ineligible. With a certain irony, Israel was thus placed in the same non-Olympic category as Germany. Disputes between Britain and the Republic of Ireland, or Eire, over athletes born in Northern Ireland dated back to the 1930s. These had reemerged in the period leading up to the Games and erupted into a full-blown controversy as competition began in July 1948. A number of contending parties were involved, including the IOC, the British Olympic Association, the international governing bodies of individual sports, pro-Irish groups in the United States, and two rival organizations claiming to represent Irish sporting interests. The result of this mix was considerable confusion and acrimony. Eventually, two members of the Irish swimming team who came from Northern Ireland were banned by the IOC, and in response the whole swimming team withdrew from the Games. Before doing so, they and the soccer team protested over their designation as representatives of Eire rather than Ireland.

Although the general level of sportsmanship displayed during the Games was widely hailed, there were some exceptions. Boxing was cited as providing "a partial exception to the blessed rule of good temper and good sense." The supporters of a defeated boxer from Uruguay staged a wild demonstration protesting what they deemed to be the injustice of the result. Though extreme in their response, this group was not alone in its dissatisfaction with the judging. Early in the competition, five referees and seven judges were dropped from the roster of officials. The frequency of fouls and ejections threatened to give water polo a reputation similar to that of boxing. A fight broke out in a basketball game between Canada and Uruguay. The team from Argentina temporarily walked out of the fencing competition, disputing a hit awarded to a Belgian competitor. American women divers protested that the boards were too firm and criticized what they viewed as outdated restrictions on the type of dives they were allowed to perform. The Americans themselves were the targets of criticism over their swimmers' practice of inhaling oxygen before a race. Allegations were made that some of the canoes competing at Henley had illegal keels.

One particular incident was potentially embarrassing for the British organizers and threatening for the 1952 Helsinki Games. Despite the Organizing Committee's efforts to control distribution and discourage what they termed touting, foreign athletes and officials were found to be selling tickets outside some of the main venues. No punishment was imposed when it was discovered that the tickets were being sold only at face value and that the largest single group of vendors were Finns who had been denied any currency exchange privileges by their own government and needed funds to subsist. Among them were officials already appointed to the Organizing Committee for 1952. After the Games were over, the Italians banned the showing of the Olympic film because it failed to cover any of their eight victories. Also in retrospect, the British press raised two issues that anticipated future controversy. It was forecast that medical examinations would be required at subsequent Games in order to verify the gender of competitors and solve the problem of "half-sexed" entrants. European cyclists were allegedly stimulated by drugs, "much in the manner of racehorses."

Except for some lengthy delays during the first day of track-and-field competition, the overall organization of events drew extensive praise. However, the nature and location of accommodation for the athletes was subject to some criticism. American and Australian women complained of the hardness of the beds and the lack of mirrors at Southlands College where they were housed. The coach of the British swimming team protested when the men and women who had trained together were placed in accommodations distant from each other and the women were assigned rooms on the eighth floor of a building whose elevator was not working. Some national teams, which had arrived early, were moved on the eve of the Games into different housing. Others found themselves lodged at a distance from their training facilities and thus dependent on unreliable transportation. While the Organizing Committee might have been a legitimate target of some of these criticisms, they could hardly be held accountable for the rowdy behavior that some athletes claimed kept them awake long into the night.

The British themselves experienced the greatest disappointment of the Games, and it was caused by the overall competitive failure of their athletes. The only three gold medals won by the host nation came in rowing and sailing, events staged far away from the main focus of attention in London. In track and field and swimming, viewed as the two most important sports, Britain won no gold medals. That the women's track-and-field team won five silver medals provided little consolation for a grieving press, which displayed throughout the Games its general indifference and, in some cases, positive hostility toward female athletes, even though they accounted for less than 10 percent of all competitors. Disappointment was particularly acute in boxing and cycling where expectations had been high. In some of the minor sports, such as basketball and water polo, British performance was humiliatingly poor. Perhaps the greatest disappointment of all came over the men's 4×100 relay staged on the last day of track-and-field competition. Britain appeared to have won the gold when the American team was disqualified for an illegal exchange. Three days later, examination of the official film showed that the Americans had exchanged correctly so Britain had to be satisfied with the silver. In the end, the hosts had to seek consolation in the praise that many visitors conferred on them for both their organizational achievements and the sportsmanship displayed by the spectators. The British were given credit for the friendly atmosphere that generally prevailed in 1948, which was often compared favorably to Berlin in 1936.

If the clock is stopped at any given point in time during the evolution of an institution such as the Olympic Games, evidence can be found of both the perpetuation of past practices and attitudes and the anticipation of those of the future. Inevitably this was true of the London Games of 1948. The general adherence to amateurism and the cautious approach toward media coverage and commercial sponsorship reflected a continuing attachment to the past. Still dominated athletically and administratively by Western Europe and North America and not yet feeling the full extent of Cold War rivalries, the London Olympics might, ironically, be described as the last prewar Games. On the other hand, as isolation from international politics became increasingly hard to maintain, as the first Eastern European athletes defected to the West, and as traditional amateur practices and ideals came to be called into question, some of the contentious characteristics of the Olympic future were beginning to emerge. A search for the most particular feature of the 1948

Games might very well conclude with the simple fact that they were held at all so soon after the destruction and turmoil of World War II.

BIBLIOGRAPHICAL ESSAY

For anyone wishing to develop an in-depth knowledge of the 1948 Games, the best place to start is the library at the British Olympic Association offices in Wandsworth, London. The extensive collection of secondary sources on the London Games and Olympic history in general includes the association's own official report on the Games, edited by Cecil Bear, and that of the Organizing Committee, edited by Lord Burghley. Also available are daily programs, visitor's guides, and team handbooks. Further official materials are to be found in the IOC's own archives in Lausanne.

A number of national Olympic committees and associations published reports on the Games. These include Nelson C Hart, Robert Kerr, and Alex Muir, eds., *Canada Competes at the Olympic Games 1948: Official Report of the Canadian Olympic Association, 1938–1948* (Montreal, 1948); Johann Bernhard, ed., *Iceland's Olympic Team at the Games in London 1948* (Reykjavik, 1949); Kurt Gassman, ed., *Rapport sur la participation Suisse aux Jeux Olympiques de Londres 1948* (Lausanne, 1948); Asa S. Bushnell, ed., *Report of the United States Olympic Committee: XIV Olympiad, London 1948; V Winter Olympic Games, St. Moritz, Switzerland* (New York, 1949).

Two collections of private papers offer significant insight into the preparatory process and much that went on behind the scenes. The Avery Brundage Collection in the archives of the University of Illinois in Champaign-Urbana provides a mine of information particularly through Brundage's correspondence with those active on the Organizing Committee, notably Lord Burghley and Evan Hunter. The papers of Phillip Noel-Baker are housed in the archives at Churchill College Cambridge. An Olympic competitor before and after World War I, Noel-Baker remained active in a number of athletic organizations while pursuing his political career. This background, combined with the fact that he held office in the postwar Labour Government, provided him with many valuable insights into the preparations for the 1948 Games.

Government documents in the Public Record Office at Kew, London, shed light on the role that its officials played in negotiating the many practical and political problems faced by the Organizing Committee. A number of departments were involved including the Cabinet Office, the Foreign Office, the Home Office, the Ministry of Food, the Board of Trade, and the Ministry of Works.

Those involved in organizing the Games frequently complained of the failure of the British press to generate public expectations about, and thus interest in, the Games. In order to assess the validity of this charge, a range of different papers can be consulted at the British Library collection at Colindale, London. Because it is indexed, the *Times* is one of the easier papers to access, but some of the more popular papers should be included in such a review, particularly the *Evening Standard* and the *Daily Express*, which were critical of the commitment to the Games. A different perspective can be obtained from the *New York Times*, which like its London counterpart has the advantage of being indexed. A number of periodicals such as the *Economist*, the *Spectator*, and the *Picture Post* provide a different perspective, though their coverage of the Games was limited.

HELSINKI 1952

Vesa Tikander

THE GAMES OF THE FIFTEENTH OLYMPIAD

When the International Olympic Committee (IOC) met in Stockholm in June 1947 to select the host city of the Games of the Fifteenth Olympiad, the political situation in Europe had become precarious. Manifestations of inter-Allied friendship of the immediate postwar years had given way to the distrustful atmosphere of the cold war. The Soviet Union was tightening its grip on Eastern Europe and was actively seeking ways of increasing its influence in world affairs. In the world of sports, Soviet athletes began to make appearances in selected international competitions, and the entry of the USSR into the IOC was considered imminent. This was a cause of great concern for the committee, decidedly anti-communist by persuasion and deeply suspicious of what state-sponsored athletes might do to amateur Olympic sport. There were five American cities among the candidates for the 1952 Games: Chicago, Detroit, Los Angeles, Minneapolis, and Philadelphia. The two European entrants were Amsterdam and Helsinki.

Finland had dreamed of hosting the Olympic Games ever since the halcyon days of the 1920s, when Paavo Nurmi and his teammates reigned supreme in track and field. Helsinki lost the vote for the 1940 Games to Tokyo, but in 1938 the IOC asked it to stand in after the Japanese had to forfeit the Games. The Finns were more than happy to comply, and Olympic preparations were well along when World War II broke out in September 1939. Two moths later the Soviet Union invaded Finland, and in the ensuing Winter War, Finland lost a substantial part of its territory. Peace was made in March 1940, but as war went on elsewhere in Europe, Helsinki had to renounce the Olympic Games. The official telegram to that effect was sent to the IOC on April 29, 1940. In June 1941 war resumed, as Finland joined Germany in its offensive against the Soviet Union in order to regain its lost territory. This undertaking failed, and in September 1944 Finland bailed out of the World War by signing an armistice with the USSR and its allies.

If there were an award for a person most responsible for the success of an Olympic Games, Erik von Frenckell would be a strong contender. A man of inherited wealth, aristocratic upbringing, suave manners, and ruthless ambition, he had carved out for himself a personal empire in Finnish sports administration. As a sports-minded businessman and aspiring politician, he had been advocating for a Helsinki Olympic bid ever since the 1910s and chaired the foundation set up in 1927 for building an Olympic stadium. As a rising star in international sports circles, he was actively involved in the initial unsuccessful bid for the 1940 Games. As deputy mayor of Helsinki in charge of construction works and (later) of financial matters he oversaw preparations for those Games, most notably the construction of the stadium, which was inaugurated in 1938. Undaunted by wars and cancellations, von Frenckell put himself in charge of another Olympic bid almost as soon as peace returned.

Helsinki 1952—Bob Mathias, U.S. decathlon winner, accepting his medal at awards ceremony, Helsinki Games, 1952. Courtesy of University of Illinois Archives, Avery Brundage Collection.

The new Olympic project took place in a totally new political climate. Finland was not occupied after the war, but the country was put under the inspection of the Allied Control Commission, dominated by the Soviet representative Andrei Zhdanov, until the signing of the peace treaty in 1947. Communists, banned before the war, were included in a broad-based coalition government, and in the 1945 elections they won 23 percent of the votes. Nervousness grew as similar situations led to complete communist takeovers in several Eastern European countries. Finnish foreign policy, led by President Juho Kusti Paasikivi, was a careful balancing act: the Soviets were to be kept as happy and as distant as possible. Moscow was conciliated as much as reasonable to keep it from encouraging domestic communists. Any signs of understanding and moral support from the West were meanwhile most welcome. The Olympic Games would provide that understanding and support.

Finnish sport politics was subject to similar considerations. Finnish representatives in various international sports organizations were actively propagating for the USSR to be accepted as a member; von Frenckell did his part in the International Football Federation (FIFA). There were domestic concerns as well. The Finnish sports scene had been divided into two antagonistic camps ever since the civil war of 1918. Affiliates of the bourgeois Finnish Gymnastics and Sports Federation

(SVUL) had the sole right of representing Finland in international sport organizations, and athletes of the socialist Workers' Sports Federation (TUL) were excluded from the Olympic Games. The two federations had worked out an agreement that would have enabled TUL athletes to participate in the 1940 Helsinki Games, but after the war there was no agreement in force. The situation was complicated by an ongoing battle inside the TUL, where communists were trying to wrest control of the federation from Social Democrats. One of the first matters that von Frenckell had to attend to was to solicit a truce that would create a united Finnish front behind the Helsinki Olympic bid. The bid project had a huge public appeal, and federation leaders finally saw the wisdom of not becoming the ones who betrayed Finnish Olympic dreams by political bickering. A compromise cooperation agreement between the federations was signed in March 1947, and von Frenckell led a united bidding team to the IOC Session in Stockholm in June.

The Finnish press was not optimistic about the IOC vote, even if Stockholm had already renounced its own bid in favor of Helsinki. Von Frenckell gave a spirited speech, however, in which he evoked Finland's glorious athletic past and the grave injustice suffered by Helsinki in 1940. He said that as a neutral country Finland would be an excellent place for athletes of East and West to meet in peaceful competition. There was another crucial point that von Frenckell did not fail to emphasize: "In order to correct possible misunderstandings I should mention that Finland is a free, independent country." Von Frenckell's arguments fell on fertile ground. If the Olympic movement was going to act as a conciliating force in world politics it could be better done on neutral ground than in an American city. Many IOC members felt sympathy for Finland for the lost 1940 Games and wished to lend it support in its present political situation. Not to be overlooked, finally, was von Frenckell's personal diplomacy. He provided sumptuous entertainment for the IOC members and knew his way in their aristocratic circles, in stark contrast to the casually attired spokesmen of the rival American cities. On the first ballot Helsinki received 14 votes, just one short of the required majority. Von Frenckell secured the one missing vote during the interval, from whom and by what means has remained a secret. On the second ballot Helsinki received 15 votes, Los Angeles 5, Minneapolis 5 and Amsterdam 3. The news from Stockholm was greeted with rapturous joy all over Finland.

Finland was a country of only four million inhabitants. The population of Helsinki was about 380,000. Over 90 percent of national income was derived from forestry and two-thirds of the people lived in rural areas. The wars had badly crippled the Finnish economy. There was lack of adequate housing, and many basic foodstuffs and consumer items were strictly rationed. To cap it all, Finland had to pay to the Soviet Union $300 million in war reparations of industrial products. Olympic preparations would be a heavy economic burden in these circumstances. One of the few advantages was that most of the venues were already in place in Helsinki as a legacy of the cancelled 1940 Games, although mostly in bad repair.

On September 8, 1947, the Finnish state, the city of Helsinki, the Finnish NOC, and 26 leading sports organizations created a society called XV Olympia Helsinki. The board of the society was to act as the Organizing Committee of the Olympic Games. Its self-evident chairman was Erik von Frenckell. Political balance was upheld by co-opting high representatives of both the SVUL and the TUL as vice-chairmen in the persons of Akseli Kaskela and Olavi Suvanto, respectively. Practical issues were eventually entrusted to a professional in military organization, Major General A. E. Martola, as director of the Games.

The organizing committee acquired its operating capital by borrowing a total of 330 million Finnish marks from the national betting pools office; this sum was repaid from the gate receipts after the Games. The city and the state agreed to shoulder the costs for such works and procurements that would be of lasting benefit to society. Luckily for the organizers, construction and repair works of most Olympic venues fell into that category. The city committee put up to supervise Olympic construction was chaired by von Frenckell, which was also quite helpful. Olympic spending was justified with the argument that it would speed up necessary improvements. As the Olympic Village of the 1940 Games had been converted to family apartments, a new one was built next to it at Käpylä. Consisting of 13 buildings and designed for 4,800 athletes, it was also converted to housing after the Games. The city of Helsinki was given an uplift: an amusement park was created next to the Olympic Stadium, two new hotels were built, and the first set of traffic lights was installed. The state built a new airport for Helsinki, improved roads and railways, and laid a new sub-marine cable between Finland and Sweden, which brought a substantial improvement in telephone and telegraph connections to the West.

The Olympic Stadium, inaugurated in 1938, was renovated and furnished with temporary wooden stands, which enlarged the seating capacity from 50,000 to 70,000. The nearby Swimming Stadium had been left unfinished by the outbreak of the war, and its pools had been used as potato cellars during the war. The works were now finished and up-to-date filtering machinery was installed. Other venues to be restored and enlarged were the Velodrome and the Exhibition Hall, the arena for many indoor sports. The Rowing Stadium at Meilahti Bay was renovated, but the International Rowing Federation considered the location too exposed to sea winds. New facilities were built at the more sheltered Taivallahti Bay nearby, and the Meilahti venue was left to canoeists. Helsinki shared some of its responsibilities with other Finnish towns. The modern pentathlon competition was held at Hämeenlinna, and Tampere, Lahti, Turku, and Kotka all hosted matches in the Olympic football (soccer) tournament.

The year 1952 saw Finland ready to welcome the world. The situation of the country had improved considerably during the five years since the Olympic Games were awarded to Helsinki. Rationing was ended for most consumer items. The war reparations bill proved to be a blessing in disguise, as Finnish industry was diversified to keep up with Soviet demands. The last reparations delivery train was set to leave for the USSR later in 1952, marking the formal end of Finland's dependent position after the war. The domestic political scene was stabilized after the defeat of the communists in the elections of 1948 and their subsequent removal from the government. Finland was thereafter governed by a coalition of Social Democrats and centrist parties. Foreign policy was still in the strong hands of President Paasikivi, but Finland was clearly considered to belong to the Soviet orbit of influence: in 1947 Finland had to refuse American aid under the Marshall Plan. However, it had also become clear that Finland was not subjected to the kind of pressure that Eastern European countries had to endure. The Treaty of Friendship, Cooperation and Mutual Assistance signed by Finland and the USSR in 1948 did not include binding military stipulations, and it allowed Finland at least some leeway in its dealings with Moscow and the outside world.

The domestic sports scene was stabilized as well, at least for the time being. TUL athletes took part in the London Olympic Games in 1948 and a new cooperation treaty between the SVUL and the TUL was forged in 1950 after much wrangling. Communists' bid for control in the TUL had meanwhile failed in 1948. The Olympic truce was upheld for the duration of the Games, although it did not last long. The two federations were to continue their separate and tortuous existence until 1993.

All these positive developments notwithstanding, the fact remained that Helsinki was the smallest city ever to be entrusted with hosting Olympic Summer Games, and arranging a full range of Olympic events would stretch its resources to the utmost. Von Frenckell, having elbowed his way into the IOC in 1948, hoped to bring about a reduction in the size of the Games, or at least to limit their growth. At the IOC Session in Rome in 1949 it was proposed that the number of medal events in Helsinki should not be higher than in London in 1948. In this context von Frenckell declared that he would also be happy to cut most or all team sports from the Olympic program, as well as many women's track and field events. The international sports federations would have none of it, of course. At its Copenhagen Session in 1950 the IOC set the number of medal events to be contested in Helsinki to 148, as opposed to 136 in London. The most significant addition was in women's gymnastics, where medals would hereafter be decided in five individual categories as well as in two team events. After a further addition of one more weightlifting weight class, the final number of Olympic events in Helsinki was 149. The only relief to the organizers was the demise of the Olympic art competitions, cut from the Olympic program in 1950 and replaced by an art exhibition.

Helsinki 1952—1912 Olympic star Jim Thorpe (left) and Avery Brundage at a 1952 U.S. Olympic Committee fundraiser. Courtesy of University of Illinois Archives, Avery Brundage Collection.

When the IOC awarded the 1952 Games to Helsinki in 1947, the cold war was just beginning. In the following five years things only seemed to go from bad to worse. The partition of Germany was formalized in 1949, when both the Federal Republic of Germany and the German Democratic Republic (GDR) were founded. In the same year Mao Zedong's army chased the Guomingdang regime to Taiwan, and the People's Republic of China was established on the mainland. The Korean War broke out in 1950, resulting in millions of deaths and bringing the world close to nuclear war. The cold war presented the IOC several thorny problems ahead of the 1952 Games, the most pressing of which was the entry of the Soviet Union to the Olympic Games.

Having won The Great Patriotic War at horrendous cost, the Soviet Union was regimented for ideological warfare against the West. Sport was found to be an excellent weapon in this, a way to demonstrate the superiority of socialist culture over that of the decadent West. Because of this, it was of paramount importance that Soviet athletes must not lose to their Western competitors. Consequently, they tended to compete abroad only when success was guaranteed. Stalin himself was known to take an active interest in the performances of Soviet athletes abroad. The chairman of the All-Union Sports Committee, Nikolai Romanov, was duly demoted after bad results at the world speed skating championships in Helsinki in February 1948. The Soviet decision not to enter the London Olympic Games becomes understandable in this light.

The objectives of the Soviet leadership were clearly stated in a Communist Party Central Committee resolution dated December 27, 1948: all interested state and party organs were called to "help Soviet sportsmen win world supremacy in the major sports in the immediate future." In order to enter competitions abroad, it was necessary to acquire membership in the international federation of the respective sport. The Soviet Union had achieved this in most Olympic sports by 1952. The Soviets usually added three demands to their applications: Russian should be accepted as another official language of the federation, a permanent seat in the executive organs should be reserved to the USSR, and Francoist Spain should be excluded from membership. These demands were always rejected and subsequently dropped. The delicate question of amateurism was circumvented in a way that had profound consequences for Olympic sports. In 1945 the USSR had adopted a policy to pay cash prizes to athletes for breaking records. This decision was reversed in July 1947 as a gesture of goodwill to the guardians of amateur ethics in world sports organizations: from now on, there were to be no money prizes and no professional athletes in Soviet sports. Instead, athletes were given day jobs at the various supporting organizations and went on training full-time. The credibility of this arrangement was questioned from the start, but it was accepted by the international federations. State amateurism became a fact of life for 40 years or more.

As far as the International Olympic Committee was concerned, the question of Soviet membership was complicated by deep-rooted suspicions on both sides. Several leading members of the IOC, including President J. Sigfrid Edström and his heir apparent, Avery Brundage, had staunch anti-communist credentials and made their personal opinions of the Soviet system known in no uncertain terms. The feeling was reciprocated in full, as attested by an internal memorandum written in 1950 by P. Sobolev, head of international relations at the Soviet state sports committee.

[Edstrom] . . . is a reactionary and was a supporter of the Nazi regime in Germany, and opposes all motions to democratize international sports organisations. The Vice-President of the Executive Council is Avery Brundage, . . . a powerful Chicago businessman who decides on all things in American amateur sports and has introduced criminal habits in them. A. Brundage is known for his pro-Fascist views. Up until the Japanese attack on Pearl Harbor he used to declare his sympathies with Hitler quite openly.

Despite these misgivings, a party central committee approved a Soviet application for membership in the IOC and the formation of a Soviet Olympic Committee on April 18, 1951. This decision is partly explained by an overall *détente* offensive launched by the USSR in order to break its diplomatic isolation due to the Korean crisis. The application was approved at the IOC Session in Vienna on May 7, 1951: there were 31 votes for Soviet membership, none against, and three abstentions. Sports bureaucrat Constantin Andrianov, handpicked by Soviet sports authorities, became the first IOC member from the USSR. Though the IOC had always chosen its representative from each country rather than simply accept a government appointee, IOC members knew they had no choice in this instance and admitted Andrianov to their ranks. As the Soviet Union failed to attend the Olympic Winter Games in Oslo 1952, due at least partly to the appraisal at a high level that Soviet winter sports teams were not yet competitive enough, the grand entry was to take place in Helsinki.

The IOC Session in Vienna in May 1951 also had to reach a decision on the German Question. A new National Olympic Committee (NOC) had been founded in the Federal Republic of Germany in 1949. The IOC Session in Copenhagen in 1950 gave it a provisional recognition but did not promise that Germany could enter the 1952 Games. In August 1950 the West German NOC made the following declaration to the IOC Executive Board: "The German sporting youth most deeply condemns the atrocities committed by the representatives of the Nazi regime that have caused so much suffering in almost the whole world. It hereby expresses its profound regret for these" (Quoted by Otto Mayer, *Á travers les anneaux olympiques* [1960], 200). Moved by this, the Executive Board decided to recommend that the next IOC Session in Vienna sanction German entry to the Helsinki Games. In April 1951, matters were complicated by the founding of the Olympic Committee of the German Democratic Republic (GDR). The East German Committee called for equal recognition by the IOC, which rejected it on the principle that there could be only one NOC for any one country—as Germany was still considered by all parties concerned.

The IOC hosted a meeting between representatives of Eastern and Western NOC's in Lausanne on May 22, 1951. An agreement was signed according to which the sole leadership of the German team at the 1952 Games was vested in the West German NOC. A unified team would be selected from the best athletes of East and West according to results of common trial competitions. GDR sports officials had second thoughts, however, and called for equal representation in a new united German NOC. This was unacceptable to the West Germans, and new rounds of talks led to no result. Not helpful in reconciling the two Germanies was the fact that Karl Ritter von Halt, the last *Reichssportführer* of the Third Reich, had assumed the presidency of the West German NOC—and resumed his seat in the IOC—in 1951 soon after his release from a Soviet prisoner-of-war camp. IOC President Edström called representatives of both German NOC's to last-minute talks in Copenhagen on February 8, 1952. What followed was a curious episode. The meeting was to begin at 10 A.M. but the East German delegation did not arrive in Copenhagen until 2 P.M., delayed by travel and passport problems. Pleading tiredness, the East Germans failed to emerge from their hotel by the end of the day, and as the IOC representatives had a morning plane to catch for the Winter Games in Oslo, the meeting was called off. No more negotiations were held. Athletes from the GDR did not participate in Olympic trials, and Germany was represented by a team that included only West German athletes at the Helsinki Games. This was not the only German team in Helsinki, however. The Saar, separated from the rest of Germany after the war and created as a semi-independent state under French control, entered an Olympic team of its own for the first and only time. By the time of the next Olympic Games the Saar had been safely reunited with West Germany.

Even more intractable was the Chinese question. Most members of the Chinese Olympic Committee had followed the Guomingdang government to Taiwan (or Formosa, as the island was usually called in the West at the time) and two out of three Chinese IOC members were living in exile. In February 1952 a diplomatic (or rather undiplomatic) envoy of the People's Republic of China appeared at the IOC Session in Oslo and demanded that the IOC grant recognition to the All-China Athletic Federation that had been established in Beijing. President Edström dismissed the man unceremoniously, but the issue resurfaced at the next session, held in Helsinki on the eve of the Olympic Games. The IOC heard delegates from both Taiwan and the mainland demand sole recognition to their own NOC (one had also been founded in Beijing) and total exclusion of the other. The Taiwan Chinese based their case on legalistic arguments, the mainland Chinese on the claim that they were now the actual representatives of 600 million people. Tired of the political invective hurled from both sides, the IOC looked for a compromise solution.

The executive board proposed at the session that both Chinas be excluded from the Helsinki Games. To general surprise, this was defeated by a vote of 29 to 22. Another motion that both teams be allowed to compete passed. Next the session decided to leave the matter in the hands of the international sports federations: in any given sport, the entrant would be that Chinese team that was recognized by the federation for that sport. President-elect Avery Brundage finally announced that neither of the two Chinas would be recognized by the IOC for the time being, but "out of sympathy" all those Chinese athletes who were already in Helsinki or on their way there would be allowed to compete, even if this was against the rules of the IOC. This was not acceptable to the Taiwanese, who withdrew altogether from the Games. The People's Republic sent a team of 40 athletes to Helsinki, but it arrived on July 29, too late for all but one athlete to compete. Wu Chuan-yu took part in the heats of men's 100-meter backstroke swimming. He was to remain the only Olympic athlete of the People's Republic of China for the next 28 years.

The Games of the Fifteenth Olympiad were opened in the Helsinki Olympic Stadium on July 19, 1952. The Olympic flame was flown from Greece to Denmark and carried in the torch relay through Sweden to the Finnish border. Erik von Frenckell, ever the conciliator, had proposed an alternative route through the Soviet Union, but the Soviets had not shown much interest. A local touch was provided by an additional flame lit from the rays of the midnight sun on top of Pallastunturi fell in Lapland. How exactly this was done on an overcast night was a question no one cared to ask: only years later were rumors heard of another plan involving a hidden gas pipe and a match. The two flames were united and relayed to Helsinki. The enthusiasm of the Finnish people was unwavering. It was estimated that one million people came to see the torch relay along its route—a quarter of the whole population. The torch was brought to the stadium by the man who personified Finland's past athletic glory. The 55-year-old Paavo Nurmi was reluctant to play the part at first but it must have been gratifying for him to appear in front of some of the same IOC leaders who had banned him as a professional back in 1932. There were two uninvited guests at the opening ceremony. One was Barbara Rotbraut-Pleyer, a young German peace activist who tried to mount the podium to deliver her message to the world but was courteously ushered away. The other was incessant rain, which could not be helped.

The cold war made its presence felt through the housing arrangements during the Helsinki Games. The Soviet Union demanded that their athletes and those of their allies be housed separately from other teams. The organizers acquiesced and placed the athletes of the socialist countries into an Olympic village of their own at the newly-built campus area of the Technological University at Otaniemi, separated from the city by a bay. Contacts between Eastern and Western athletes outside the sporting arenas were limited to chaperoned "friendship meetings" of selected representatives. The organizers and the Finnish government were nervous about possible defections or provocations. A Union of Free Eastern European Sportsmen, based in New York, had applied for a right to send its athletes to compete at the Games, but the IOC rejected the claim on the basis that the organization did not represent any single geographical entity. Exiles did try to make contact with athletes from their homelands, but in the end there was only one recorded case of defection, involving the Romanian pistol shooter Panait Calcai. Of course, communist sports officials had left home those athletes deemed most unreliable, such as the great Estonian shot putter and decathlete Heino Lipp.

Direct athletic confrontations between East and West, and between Soviet and American athletes in particular, were laden with political symbolism. There were heated contests in weightlifting, and the American press had a field day when FBI agent Horace Ashenfelter beat the Soviet runner Vladimir Kazantsev in the 3,000-meter steeplechase final. However, the most politically charged contest took place between the Soviet and Yugoslav soccer teams. The teams met in the second round of the elimination tournament, and it was made clear to the Soviet players that defeat against Tito's clique was out of the question. The Yugoslavs led the match 5 to 1, but the Soviets managed an incredible comeback to draw 5 to 5 and force a replay. Before the second match the Soviet team received a telegram of encouragement from Stalin himself. When they lost, 3 to 1, team officials were immediately sent to Moscow to receive their punishment, which luckily affected only their careers in sports. The Soviet press reported extensively on the successes of Soviet athletes and minimally on their defeats. Victories of the smaller Eastern bloc countries were also highlighted. The magnificent Hungarian team led by Ferenc Puskás defeated the Yugoslavs in the soccer final, and the most celebrated athlete of the Games was Emil Zátopek of Czechoslovakia, the Human Locomotive, who won three gold medals in long-distance running and became an adoptive son of the Finnish public, short of heroes of its own in its most beloved sport. Zátopek's wife Dana won gold in women's javelin throw on the day of her husband's victory in the 5,000 meters, and their "golden kiss" became the leading human-interest story of the Games.

As had become customary over the years, various scoring schemes were applied during the Games to keep track of the success of nations. The IOC strongly condemned this, and its newly-elected President Avery Brundage, in particular, maintained the principle that the Olympic Games were for individual athletes only, not for national teams. In Helsinki medal counts and point scores became serious business, as the Soviet Union was trying to topple the hitherto unchallenged Americans from their throne and replace them as the leading sports nation in the world. In the final analysis, the United States won on the count of gold medals (40 to 29) and overall medals (76 to 71), but many different calculations were circulated in the world press. The Soviets declared themselves winners on overall points, but their numbers were hotly denied by the American sports press and strongly doubted by most neutral observers.

For the host nation, the Helsinki Games were a resounding success. A country of only four million people organized the largest sports gathering of the world in the middle of the cold war and received almost unanimous praise for the work—the only serious cause of anyone's complaint was the unseasonably cold weather. The Games brought huge improvements in national and urban infrastructure. Most of all, after years spent in isolation and uncertainty, the Olympic Games gave Finland a chance to be seen and counted among the nations on the western side of the Iron Curtain. Finland found recognition for its international role as a neutral country providing its good services to others.

Finns like to call their Helsinki Games "the last real Olympic Games." This refers to the familial atmosphere at the Games, due to the skill of the organizers to make a virtue out of necessity and turn the small scope of the host city to their favor. However, this conceals the fact that the 1952 Games marked a return to expansion after the war and the austerity of the London Games. There were more participating nations (69) and athletes (4,925) than ever before in Olympic history. Germany and Japan were readmitted to the Olympic movement, and with the entry of the Soviet Union the Games became for the first time ever a true world wide event. This expansion came at a price, as the Olympic Games became irredeemably a platform of political expression: success, participation, and non-participation in them became political statements. No longer could the Games be only about sports.

BIBLIOGRAPHICAL ESSAY

The archives of the Organizing Committee of the Games of the Fifteenth Olympiad are kept at the Helsinki City Archives, Eläintarhantie 3 F, 00530 Helsinki. Other primary source material can be found at the Sports Archives of Finland, located at the Sports Museum of Finland in the Olympic Stadium in Helsinki. The adjacent Sports Library has a good collection of literature relating to the Olympic movement in general and the 1952 Games in particular. The personal archives of Erik von Frenckell, IOC member and chairman of the Organizing Committee, are in the possession of his family and not currently available for research except by special permission. Material relating to the 1952 Games is also available at the Olympic Studies Centre in Lausanne and at the Avery Brundage Collection at the University of Illinois Archives, Urbana, Illinois.

The Official Report of the Organizing Committee for the Games of the XVth Olympiad Helsinki 1952 (Porvoo, Finland, 1955) was edited by Sulo Kolkka, chief of the press department during the Games, and published in Finnish, English, and French. The Organizing Committee published a bulletin in 16 issues from November 1949 to August 1952 (*XV Olympiad Official News Service*) in English and French, which contains valuable information on the preparations, invitations, and entrants; the final issue gives the full results of the competitions. Other official publications included an *Official Guide* for Olympic visitors in seven languages, a press guide, and daily programs.

Among the official publications of the Olympic Committees of major nations competing at the Helsinki Games are: Asa Bushnell, ed., *United States 1952 Olympic Book: Quadrennial Report of the United States Olympic Committee* (New York, 1953); Cecil Bear, ed., *The Official Report of the XVth Olympic Games, Helsinki, July 19–August 3, 1952* (London, 1952); *Die Olympischen Spiele 1952. Das offizielle Stan-*

dardwerk des Nationalen Olympischen Komitees (Stuttgart, 1952) and *L'Italia alla XV Olimpiade. Giochi di Helsinki, giochi invernali di Oslo* (Rome, 1953).

As for secondary literature, not to be missed by those with knowledge of German is Kristina Exner-Carl, *Sport und Politik in den Beziehungen Finnlands zur Sowjetunion 1940–1952* (Wiesbaden, 1997). While focusing on the political aspects of sports relations between Finland and the USSR on a longer time span, this academic dissertation contains valuable information based on Russian archival sources on the entry of the Soviet Union to the Olympic movement in general and on the Soviet response to the Helsinki Games in particular. For Soviet sport in general, see also James Riordan, ed., *Sport under Communism (USSR, Czechoslovakia, China, Cuba)* (London, 1981); and *Sport, Politics and Communism* (Manchester, 1991) and Robert Edelman, *Serious Fun. A History of Spectator Sports in the USSR* (Oxford, 1993). The German and Chinese questions are well covered in the standard works of Olympic history, as in Richard Espy, *The Politics of the Olympic Games* (Berkeley, 1979). The return of West Germany to the Olympic Games is thoroughly documented in the official history of the German NOC: *Rückkehr nach Olympia. Nationales Olympisches Komitee für Deutschland. Vorgeschichte, Gründung, Erste Jahre* (Munich, 1989).

Unfortunately, not much has been written in English about Finnish sports history. The preparations for the 1952 Games are described in Mika Wickström, *Helsinki 1952* (Helsinki, 2002), which contains a summary in English. *Sports and Physical Education in Finland* (Helsinki, 1987), a study published by the Finnish Society for Research in Sport and Physical Education, contains information on the historical development of Finnish sports organizations. Political divisions in Finnish sports between the world wars are discussed by Leena Laine in her article "TUL: The Finnish Worker Sport Movement," in Arnd Kruger and James Riorden, eds., *The Story of Worker Sport* (Champaign, IL, 1996). As for things purely Olympic, finally, Finland's past athletic glories are evoked in Matti Hannus, *Flying Finns. Story of the Great Tradition of Finnish Distance Running and Cross Country Skiing* (Jyväskylä, Finland, 1990).

MELBOURNE 1956

Ian Jobling

THE GAMES OF THE SIXTEENTH OLYMPIAD

Only one year after the end of World War II, a group of Australians from Victoria banded together to bring the 1956 Olympic Games to Melbourne. The Victorian Olympic Council (VOC) had reserves of just 6 pounds, 7 shillings, and 10 pence (i.e., fewer than 13 Australian dollars) when it reconvened in June 1946, its first meeting in seven years. It is not surprising then that there was much laughter when Ronald Aitken moved a motion for the VOC to apply for Melbourne to host an Olympic Games. However, the motion was accepted unanimously.

Several Australian cities had previously put forward proposals to host the Olympics. Soon after the inaugural modern Olympic Games in 1896, Melbourne's *Argus* proposed that "these new Games might offer themselves to the delighted gaze of Melbourne." In 1906, Richard Coombes, IOC member from Australasia, wrote in a letter to Baron Pierre de Coubertin that "it is certainly hoped and expected that in due course the Olympic Games will be allotted to this part of the world." There were suggestions that Perth host the Olympics of 1916, then 1920. Sydney was proposed for 1930, the expected year of completion of the Sydney Harbour Bridge. Of course, the celebration of the Olympiad did not fall in that year; it is a pity that it could not have been foreseen that the completion of the bridge would be delayed until 1932.

Edgar Tanner, secretary-treasurer of the VOC, forwarded the VOC's proposal to the Australian Olympic Federation (AOF) in July 1946 and asked the IOC how to proceed with the bid. He gained support from the Lord Mayor of Melbourne, Sir James Connelly, and a former Lord Mayor (1940–1942), Sir Frank Beaurepaire. Beaurepaire's public profile in Australia and in the international Olympic Movement was a key factor in the success of Melbourne's bid. He had won three silver and three bronze medals in three Olympic Games (1908, 1920, and 1924) and had been an official at the 1932 Olympics. Following his return from Los Angeles in 1932, he developed automobile tires using the brand name "Olympic." Beaurepaire assumed the presidency of the VOC in May 1947 and was instrumental in urging the Melbourne City Council to establish an invitation committee composed of influential media figures and businessmen. Friction arose because, apart from Beaurepaire, no member of the VOC or any sports organization was represented on this committee.

An extravagant invitation book, with additional copies bound in either suede or merino lamb's wool, was sent to all IOC members and other international sports administrators and public figures. The book provided reasons why Melbourne should become an Olympic Games host: Australia was only one of four nations to have been at every Summer Olympic Games, and because of that it was more senior in the Olympic movement than any other competitor in the Southern Hemisphere; there was a concept of the Olympics being world games, and thus it was time for them to be in the Southern Hemisphere; and, with the development of pressurized aircraft, it would take at most 30 hours to reach Melbourne, a time comparable to traveling to many other venues. The invitation book also claimed that Melbourne's bid had the "active interests of all athletic organizations, government and the people."

Melbourne 1956—Cultural competitions or exhibitions have always been a part of each Olympic celebration. This photo shows the architectural design exhibit held in conjunction with the 1956 Summer Games in Melbourne. Courtesy of University of Illinois Archives, Avery Brundage Collection.

Although it was expected that the IOC would decide which city would host the 1956 Olympic Games at the London Olympics of 1948, the decision was postponed until the following year in Rome. Australians lobbied extensively during the 1948 Olympic Games; Beaurepaire and Connelly were in London and Europe for almost three months. In Rome in April 1949, Beaurepaire, respected among the IOC as an athlete-businessmen, and the rest of the Melbourne delegation were the last to present their city's case to the IOC. Six U.S. cities were bidding, the main contenders being Detroit and Los Angeles. Other cities bidding were Buenos Aires, Mexico City, and London. Despite the competition, Melbourne won by a vote of 21–20 in the fourth round of balloting.

One would have thought that the magnificent Melbourne Cricket Ground (MCG) would have been the most appropriate choice for the main venue for the Olympic Games, but this was not an automatic selection. The Organizing Committee (OC), formed in October 1949, vacillated over six other sites. The OC and the trustees of the MCG negotiated from late 1949 to early 1952. A major contention was whether this major cricket and football arena should be remodeled and resurfaced for an Olympic Games of a mere seventeen days duration at the expense of one football and two cricket seasons. Over that period, three sites were successively designated as the main stadium. Originally it was Olympic Park. Then the Royal Agricultural Showgrounds (RAS), despite their location among sheep and cattle yards, abattoirs and tanneries, had state and local government support. However, in 1951, alarmed at the cost of redevelopment of the RAS in a period of inflation and with a shortage of building materials, the state government indicated that it might have to withdraw its support for the Games unless the commonwealth government made a substantial financial contribution. In contrast to the earlier vision that the Games would boost development in Victoria, they were now seen as a burden on the economy. At the IOC meeting in Vienna in May 1951, Hugh Weir (IOC member from Australia) gave an ambiguous report of progress because at that time the site of the main stadium venue had not been settled, and some felt that Victoria should forgo the right to stage the Games.

At the next meeting of the IOC in Helsinki in July 1952, it was reported that Princes Park in Carlton was to be the main venue, but in 1953, Victorian premier John Cain, again alarmed at renovation costs of £2 million for a second stadium and in favor of utilizing the MCG, vetoed the proposal.

After a three-day meeting, which included Prime Minister Robert Menzies, it was finally resolved that the commonwealth government would pay half the costs of construction for the Games, which included modifications to the MCG, the swimming pool, and the velodrome, and for administration and promotion. The balance would be financed by the Victorian government and the Melbourne city council. There was an agreement to share profits and losses, and the State Savings Bank of Victoria guaranteed £1 million to cover operating costs. Financing the athletes' village was resolved when Victoria received an advance of Commonwealth State Housing Agreement funds to erect a cheap public housing project in the suburb of Heidelberg.

Another issue of concern to the OC and the IOC related to Australia's strict quarantine laws, which prevented foreign horses from entering the country. As a consequence, the equestrian events were held in Stockholm, June 10–17.

On the day IOC president Avery Brundage visited the MCG in April 1955, there were only six workers on the site because of a labor dispute. The irate Brundage administered a severe scolding to the MCG organizers (he later termed it "a mild atomic explosion" [Guttmann, *The Games Must Go On*, p. 159]), accusing them of incompetence and intimating that, even at that late stage, several other cities (he seemed to favor Philadelphia) would be prepared to stage the 1956 Games. Although the Australians did not receive Brundage's anger well, the lambast seemed to work; there was much more cohesion among the individuals, committees, and agencies during those final eighteen months of preparation, as well as a positive mood of anticipation and diligence—only global war could jeopardize the success of these first Olympic Games to be held in the Southern Hemisphere.

On October 29, 1956, a mere twenty-four days prior to the opening ceremony on November 22, war broke out between Egypt and Israel. Britain and France joined. On November 4, following attempts to liberalize the communist regime of Hungary, Soviet troops launched an attack on Budapest. Antagonism toward the Soviet Union and especially its Olympic athletes seemed inevitable.

The United States and the Soviet Union had emerged from World War II as dueling superpowers, and many thought the supremacy of their ideologies would be tested in the international sporting arenas. These world tensions affected the final preparation for the 1956 Olympic Games in several ways. The traditional torch relay bearing the Olympic flame from the *altis* at Olympia, Greece, was delayed a day because the conflict in the Suez Canal had affected flight schedules at the Athens airport. Fortunately, time was made up along the route. Cruise ships en route to Melbourne were forced to sail around the Cape of Good Hope. The Hungarian revolution caused the Hungarian Olympic team and officials to arrive in Australia one week later than scheduled.

The OC had anticipated a record number of teams and countries in Melbourne, but several countries threatened boycotts. Egypt, protesting against the "cowardly aggression" of certain nations, was the first country to withdraw from the Games. Iraq and Lebanon also withdrew. Several nations boycotted to protest against the actions of the USSR in Hungary. The Netherlands Olympic Committee sent a gift of 100,000 guilders—the amount of money saved by not competing in Melbourne—to aid victims in war-torn Hungary. Dutch athletes, already in Melbourne, were recalled. Spain also withdrew. The Swiss Olympic Committee decided to send a team only if there was unanimity among the seven participating Swiss national sports federations; there was not. Otto Mayer, the chancellor of the IOC and a Swiss citizen, was appalled at the decision; he was reported as stating that "it is a disgrace that Switzerland, a neutral nation and the very country where the IOC has its headquarters should set such a shameful example of political interference with the Olympic ideal." The Swiss Olympic Committee changed its mind and decided to send a team, but unfortunately, their indecisiveness meant that there was not enough time for the entire team to travel to Melbourne, so it withdrew. As late as November 13, five Scandinavian countries (Denmark, Finland, Iceland, Norway, and Sweden) had not made a firm decision to compete, despite collectively having more than 200 athletes in Australia. At a meeting of the Scandinavian Federation in Melbourne it was decided that all countries would compete. Both the People's Republic of China and the island nation of Taiwan (Formosa) had been recognized by the IOC in 1954, but tension between these two Chinas was so great that mainland China withdrew from the Games.

Throughout the period of these conflicts and vacillations, the OC and other Australian officials worked hard to encourage nations to compete. In the weeks leading up to the Games, the chair of the OC, Kent Hughes, and the chief executive officer of the Games, Sir William Bridgeford, appealed to athletes and spectators to ensure that the true spirit of the Olympic Games would triumph. Internationally, Otto Mayer and Avery Brundage exhorted athletes and governments not to prevent the Olympic Movement from fulfilling its humanitarian role in the interests of world peace and to keep politics out of the Olympic Games.

The withdrawals in October and early November caused some organizational problems. The number of athletes was reduced considerably. In the final analysis, 91 member nations of the IOC were sent invitations to participate—eighty initially accepted, and eleven subsequently withdrew (People's Republic of China, Egypt, Gold Coast, Guatemala, Holland, Iraq, Lebanon, Malta, Panama, Spain, and Switzerland). Ultimately, sixty-seven nations participated, bringing 2,813 male and 371 female competitors.

At the IOC Congress in Athens in May 1954, the IOC endorsed the holding of an arts festival instead of an arts competition; it was also decided that the festival be national rather than international in character. The festival was divided into sections—Visual Arts, Literature, and Music and Drama. Visual arts included exhibitions of architecture and sculpture, painting and drawing, and graphic arts. The literature exhibition included early Australian examples of historical interest, books by Australian authors, and exceptional examples of book production in Australia. Music and Drama was divided into three sections: theatre, orchestral music, and chamber music. The OC contributed £4,000 to the civic committee toward the expenses of the Arts Festival. In addition, a World Congress on Physical Education, held during the week prior to the Games, attracted 350 delegates from more than thirty countries.

It was not until the mid-1950s that the IOC began to recognize the potential financial windfall to the Olympic Movement that would flow from the sale of television rights. At this time, even IOC president Avery Brundage was wary of such an initiative, uncertain of its impact on the spirit of the Olympic Games. Four overseas companies made bids to the OC for exclusive newsreel and television rights in December 1955, with one London broadcaster offering £25,000. There was considerable opposition to this development. By April 1956, all television companies refused to pay for television rights to cover the Games because of a conflict over what was a news item and what was an entertainment package.

The chairman of the OC, Kent Hughes, met with people representing newsreel interests in New York in July 1956, and, aware that an average of 2 minutes of newsreel per day of the Helsinki Games of 1952 had been used, offered 3 minutes per day. However, American television newsreel interests requested 9 minutes daily—3 minutes for each of three news broadcasts. It became clear, however, that no television entertainment departments and no film entrepreneurs would be interested in Olympic coverage if more than 3 minutes per day were granted to the newsreels. Eventually, newsreel companies and international television networks boycotted the Melbourne Olympics. The OC decided on the production of a 16-mm color film and a black-and-white film, thereby satisfying the requirements of the IOC, and a French film unit also undertook to make a feature-length, widescreen color film.

Regular television transmission in Australia from stations in Melbourne and Sydney began in October 1956. The question of Australian television coverage of the Games was revived only a few days before the opening ceremony on November 22. Arrangements had been made with the local television stations to televise from any site where seating had been fully sold, and since this was the case with the main stadium (the MCG), as well as many other venues, the television companies were given the rights to televise daily. The charge for this live coverage, the first for a host nation, was a nominal payment to the OC because there were so few television sets—approximately 5,000—in operation.

In a unique arrangement, GTV9, a television station, and Ampol Petroleum joined forces to turn Ampol petrol stations into "television theatres" for people with no access to television sets in their homes. Community halls were also utilized, and many charity organizations contacted GTV9 and Ampol for permission to charge admission fees. For ten of the fifteen days of the Games, the three television stations (Channel 9, plus HSV7 and ABV2) provided more than 20 hours of coverage per day to Victorian viewers. A 16-mm film was flown to Sydney, allowing New South Wales to receive coverage each night.

A most significant change in format from previous Olympic Games was a part of the Closing Ceremony that symbolized the Olympic philosophy of internationalism and goodwill. Throughout the Games, athletes, particularly medalists, were identified by nation. But the closing ceremony in Melbourne would be different. The idea was generated in a letter from John Ian Wing, which Kent Hughes received on the Wednesday of the final week of the Games. Wing, a 17 year-old Chinese-Australian, wrote:

> The march I have in mind is different than the one during the Opening Ceremony and will make these games even greater, during the march there will only be 1 NATION. War, politics and nationality will be all forgotten, what more could anybody want, if the whole world could be made as one nation. Well, you can do it in a small way . . . no team is to keep together and there should be no more than 2 team mates together, they must be spread out evenly, THEY MUST NOT MARCH but walk freely and wave to the public, let them walk around twice on the cinder, when they stop the public will give them three cheers. . . . It will show the whole world how friendly Australia is. (John Ian Wing to Kent Hughes, December 4, 1956, Australian Gallery of Sport and Olympic Museum)

It was not until lunchtime on the day before the Closing Ceremony that, with permission from the IOC president, arrangements were endorsed. It was a splendid Closing Ceremony. There was, as stated in the official report,

> a prophetic image of a new future for mankind—the athletes of the world not now sharply divided, but . . . marching as one in a hotchpotch of sheer humanity, a fiesta of friendship, . . . A wave of emotion swept over the crowd, the Olympic Flame was engulfed in it and died; the Olympic flag went out in tears, not cheers, and a great silence. This, more than any remembered laurel of the Games, was something no-one had ever experienced before—not anywhere in the world, not anywhere in time.

Wing's vision of Olympism has become a tradition of the Closing Ceremony of every Olympics since 1956.

At the Opening Ceremony, athletes from Greece entered the stadium to the cheers of over 100,000 spectators. The Australian junior mile record holder, Ron Clarke, was the last of 3,500 torch bearers; the first relay runner on the host nation's soil was an Australian-born Greek, the second an Australian aborigine. When John Landy, the great sub-4-minute miler, pronounced the Olympic oath, spectators had difficulty following his version because he had been supplied with a different one from that printed in the program.

Australian athletes won a total of thirteen gold medals—their best ever performance. Overall, thirty-six Olympic and eleven world records were broken. The United States was dominant on the track with Bobby Morrow a triple gold medalist by winning the 100- and 200-meter sprints and anchoring the 4×100-meter relay; Ira Murchison, Leamon King, Thane Baker, and Morrow broke the world record. In the 110-meter hurdles both Lee Calhoun and Jack Davis recorded the same time of 13.5 seconds; Calhoun was awarded the gold and Joel Shankl came third, giving the United States a medal sweep. Americans won the gold and silver medals after a great struggle in the decathlon between the world-record holder, Rafer Johnson, and Milton Campbell.

Like Morrow, Australia's golden girl, Betty Cuthbert, won three gold medals in the 100- and 200-meters and the record-breaking 4×100-meter relay. Ireland's Ron Delany shattered the hopes of many Australians by beating John Landy in the glamour track event, the 1,500 meters. Landy, who had become the second person to break the 4-minute mile two years earlier, won a bronze medal. A strategy of varying pace was successful for Soviet distance runner Vladimir Kuts in both the 5,000 and 10,000 meters. After finishing second to Emil Zatopek in the marathons of 1948 and 1952, Algerian Alain Mimoun, wearing number 13 on his French team singlet, won in 2 hours and 25 minutes.

Australians "scooped the pool" in swimming. Dawn Fraser made her Olympic debut at these Olympics and went on to win the 100-meter freestyle in Rome and Tokyo in 1960 and 1964, respectively. Murray Rose won three gold medals and Jon Henricks two. Their race against the United States in the 800-meter relay final, with John Devitt and Kevin O'Halloran as teammates, resulted in a world record time of 8 minutes, 23.6 seconds. Diving in the first enclosed diving pool ever used at an Olympic Games, America's Pat McCormick became the first ever to win consecutive gold medals in both the springboard and tower events.

Although there is much more known now about the Cold War, those present at the Olympic Games in Melbourne seemed to embody the spirit of an Olympic "truce," especially in relation to the athletes from the U.S.S.R. It was clear from their cheers and encouragement that the huge crowds in the main stadium appreciated the efforts of Kuts and the many successful Soviet women athletes in the field events. The magnificence of the male and female gymnasts from the Soviet Union, who won eight individual and two team gold medals, also enthralled the many spectators at the West Melbourne Stadium. There was, however, an infamous incident in the semifinal of the men's water polo match between Hungary and the Soviet Union. The Hungarians were leading 4–0 in the second half when two members of the Soviet team taunted the Hungarians by repeatedly calling them "fascists." At one stage the referee ordered five players out of the water for punching, kicking, and scratching. Although clearly an exaggeration, a newspaper reported that the pool was like a "bloodbath" after Valentine Prokopov swam to Ervin Zador of Hungary and punched him the eye while the ball was at the other end of the pool. As Zador clambered from the pool with blood streaming from his eye, the Swedish referee called off the match, declaring Hungary the winner. The crowd was incensed at the behavior of the Soviet team and only the appearance of police, who had been waiting out of sight, prevented a riot from developing.

On the other hand, not even the notorious 10-foot-high barbed-wire fence separating the men's and women's residences could prevent the blossoming romance of a Czechoslovakian and an American; discus thrower Olga Fikotova and hammer thrower Harold Connolly, gold medalists in their respective events, later married in Prague.

For many Australians, as well as visitors to the first Olympic Games in the Southern Hemisphere, the 1956 Melbourne Games were an opportunity to comprehend the dictum, "it's not the winning but the taking part." These Games truly deserve to be known as the "Friendly Games."

BIBLIOGRAPHICAL ESSAY

The Australian Gallery of Sport and Olympic Museum (AGOS&OM), located at the Melbourne Cricket Ground, the site of the main stadium for the 1956 Olympic Games, has a permanent exhibition pertaining to the Melbourne Games. Many of the documents, the final *Official Report of the Organising Committee for the Games of the*

XVIth Olympiad Melbourne, 1956 (1958) and other reports and press releases (many uncatalogued), are located in the storage areas of AGOS&OM, along with an outstanding collection of memorabilia and artifacts, including albums, letters, magazines, maps, charts, identity cards, certificates, diplomas, invitations, stamps and first day covers, postcards, posters, programs, and other assorted publications. The most useful of the many donated collections are those of Doris Carter, Julius ('Judy') Patching, and George Moir. Many of the personal papers of Sir Frank Beaurepaire are also located in the AGOS&OM; the University of Melbourne archives contains other papers of Beaurepaire and material relating to the Invitation Committee. The National Library of Australia holds the Kent Hughes papers, which contain correspondence to and from the International Olympic Committee, and the E. A. Doyle papers, which include many Games-related correspondence, clippings, and documents. The library and the museum of the International Olympic Committee in Lausanne, Switzerland, and the library of the International Olympic Academy in Olympia, Greece, house information about the Melbourne Olympics from countries other than the host nation.

The Victorian Olympic Council and the Australian Olympic Federation (both now known as Committees) also hold extensive archival records and materials, including the official final report and Bill Uren's *Olympic Games, Melbourne 1956: Australian Team Reports* (1956).

Excellent sources in North America are contained in the Avery Brundage Collection, which is on microfilm and housed in several locations, including the University of Illinois at Urbana-Champaign, the Centre for Olympic Studies at the University of Western Ontario, and the Fred Ziffren Resource Center at the Los Angeles Amateur Athletic Foundation. The Ziffren Center also has a collection of the weekly syndicated newspaper columns from February to December 1956 by American journalist and Olympic athlete Ralph C. Craig.

In addition to the organizing committee's official report, the U.S. Olympic Committee's report is Asa Bushnell, ed., *United States 1956 Olympic Book. Quadrennial Report of the United States Olympic Committee* (New York, 1957); the British report is Cecil Bear, ed., *The Official Report of the XVIth Olympic Games Melbourne 1956* (London, 1957); and the Canadian report is K. P. Farmer, et al, eds., *Canada Competes at the Olympic Games 1956* (Montreal 1956). See also G. F. James, ed., *The Art Festival of the Olympic Games, Melbourne* (Melbourne, 1956).

Several books have been published recently about Australia at the Olympic Games, especially Australian gold medalists; Gary Lester, *Australians at the Olympics—A Definitive History* (Melbourne, 1984) and Max and Reet Howell's *Aussie Gold: The Story of Australia at the Olympic Games* (Albion, Queensland, 1988) are most useful. A more recent and encompassing volume, which includes a substantive section on the Melbourne Olympics, is Harry Gordon's *Australia and the Olympic Games* (St. Lucia, Queensland, 1994). Other useful books are Keith Donald and Don Selth, *Olympic Saga: the Track and Field Story, Melbourne, 1956* (Sydney, 1957); Graham Lomas, *The Will To Win: The Story of Sir Frank Beaurepaire* (London, 1960); and Keith Dunstan, *The Paddock That Grew: The Story of the Melbourne Cricket Club* (Surry, New South Wales, 1988), which includes a fascinating chapter ("Olympic Year") about the effect of the 1956 Olympics on this very conservative cricket club. Finally, the life of Kent Hughes, chairman of the Melbourne Olympic Games Organizing Committee, has been chronicled in Frederick Ward, *Kent*

Hughes: A Biography of Colonel The Hon. Wilfred Kent Hughes (South Melbourne, 1972).

The story of how Melbourne became the first city in the Southern Hemisphere to stage an Olympic Games is described by Ian Jobling, "Proposals and Bids by Australian Cities to Host the Olympic Games, *Sporting Traditions*, 11, 1 (November 1994): 47–56. Another recent article is Graeme Davison, "Welcoming the World: The 1956 Olympic Games and the Representation of Melbourne," *Australian Historical Studies*, 28, 109 (October 1997): 64–73. Australian relations with Avery Brundage are detailed in Allan Guttmann, *The Games Must Go On* (New York, 1984). The first major use of television in an Olympic Games and the foreboding of what was to come has been told by Stephen Wenn in "Lights! Camera! Little Action: Television, Avery Brundage, and the 1956 Melbourne Olympics," *Sporting Traditions*, 10, 1 (November 1993): 38–53. Sasha Soldatow, *Politics of the Olympics* (North Ryde, New South Wales, 1980) and Hilary Kent and John Merritt's "The Cold War and the Melbourne Olympic Games" in Ann Curthoys and John Merritt, *Better Dead than Red* (Sydney, 1992) provide some background to the politics of the era. Shane Cahill's thesis, "'The Friendly Games'?: The Melbourne Olympic Games in Australian Culture" (master's thesis, University of Melbourne, 1989) is also useful. See Dawn Fraser and Lesley H. Murdoch, *Our Dawn: A Pictorial Biography* (Birchgrove, New South Wales, 1991), Dawn Fraser and Harry Gordon, *Gold Medal Girl: Confessions of an Olympic Champion* (Birchgrove, New South Wales, 1965), and Harry Gordon, *Dawn Fraser* (Melbourne, 1979), for information on Australia's most celebrated gold medalist.

The three morning newspapers (the *Age*, the *Argus*, and the *Sun*) and one evening newspaper (the *Herald*) provided excellent coverage of the preparations for the Olympics and proudly portrayed Melbourne as a progressive, international city that had successfully staged what was to become known as "the Friendly Games." In 1983, James Murray produced a video on the Melbourne Games, *Olympic Glory: The Golden Years–The Melbourne Games*, in association with Up Video Sports.

ROME 1960

Floris J. G. van der Merwe

THE GAMES OF THE SEVENTEENTH OLYMPIAD

The year 1960 was a remarkable year for matters of international interest: John F. Kennedy was elected president of the United States at the age of 43; the death of remarkable figures such as Clark Gable, Boris Pasternak, and Albert Camus left the world poorer; the first laser (an acronym for "light amplification by the stimulated emission of radiation") device was demonstrated; the anti-Apartheid movement was founded in London; Adolf Eichmann was caught in Argentina; the British Prime Minister, Harold Macmillan, heralded the end of colonialism and, last, but not least, many African countries, then known as Somalia, Togo, Chad, Upper Volta, Benin, Mali, Gabon, Ivory Coast, Cameroon, Madagascar, Congo, Mauritania, Niger, Nigeria, and Senegal, gained their independence.

But, the most relevant event started on August 25 and lasted until September 11, 1960. Of the 95 countries recognized by the IOC, 83 attended the Games of the XVII Olympiad in Rome, Italy. This was the largest number of attending nations to date. During the opening ceremony, Italy's 1948 discus champion, Adolfo Consolini, took the oath on behalf of the 5,348 competitors (of whom 610 were women). Rome, or the Eternal City as it is often called, was an earlier contender for the Olympics of 1904, 1908, and 1944. Other candidates for 1960 were Lausanne, Detroit, Budapest, Brussels, Mexico City, and Tokyo.

Morocco, Tunisia, Sudan, and San Marino made their debuts at these Olympic Games. It was also the first Olympics that was free of political issues, with the two Germanys marching under one flag and the Republic of China marching as the territory of Taiwan, and called Formosa, albeit under protest.

It is ironic to note that Rome had actually been the city that had killed the ancient Olympic Games in 394 C.E. For the Games of the XVII Olympiad, the new and old worlds were interwoven to present a spectacular atmosphere, aided from time to time by an ancient Roman custom of waving flaming torches. This, for example, gave the closing ceremony a special touch. About 100,000 spectators lit rolls of newspapers, magazines, or programs, when darkness enfolded the stadium after the Olympic flame had been extinguished.

Some of the ancient venues created an unparalleled backdrop for modern day sporting spectacles. The wrestling, for instance, took place in the Basilica of Maxentius. Two thousand years before, similar contests had taken place there, and, in what is left of Caracalla's baths, gymnastics were performed. Again a thread could be drawn from the present to the past.

Instead of using the main stadium for the start and finish of the marathon as was customary, it started in front of the Capitol and finished almost under the Arch of Constantine, next to the Colosseum. As it was run at night, the marathon was one of the most colorful ever staged. The whole route meandered through ancient Roman history and was lit by spectators waving torches. Apart from this, the 1960 marathon signalled a new era in world sport—that of the dominance of African runners.

Some of the newly built facilities had been erected with funds from the weekly professional soccer lottery—a historical fact of great significance, since these were still the days of a puritanical International Olympic Committee. The organizers had more than $30 million to spend on a brand new stadium that could seat 100,000 spectators, as well as on the renovation of the Baths of Caracalla, the Basilica of Maxentius, the Arch of Constantine, and the Appian Way.

Apparently they made good use of the available funding, as the marble stairs to the press box in the Stadio Olimpico, a lift in the diving tower leading to the platform, and an excellent Olympic Village proved. This village was connected to the stadium by a large new bridge over the River Tiber. Besides the Olympic Village, new highways and tunnels had also been built, as well as a new water supply system. The *Villaggio Olimpico* was a good excuse as any to get rid of a once swampy, slum-ridden area of the city. It was described as a city-within-a-city and was a fully self-contained unit, with a bank, post office, shopping center, and hospital. Everything the officials and athletes would need was catered to. After the Games it became a low-cost housing project for thousands of government workers. In his managerial report, Frank Braun, the South African IOC member, wrote that he "cannot proceed without congratulating the Italian Organising Committee upon its splendid training venues."

During these Games the Albano system in rowing was first used and has been used ever since. Before the Rome Games, overhead steering markers had been used, but this was not feasible on Lake Albano; therefore the racing lanes were individually buoyed out. In the process, a new word was created in rowing circles.

The heat that Rome often experiences in July and August compelled the organizers to move the opening of the Games to August 25—a record late date for a northern country. Habitually the track-and-field events followed the opening Olympic ceremony, but the organizers of these Games had realized that the Italian public would simply skip the more boring second half of the program and head for their summer holiday venues if the schedule of events was not slightly altered. The most popular track-and-field events were therefore offered in the latter half of the program. This ruse worked and the public stayed to watch.

There was no escaping Rome's intense summer heat, however, and it duly took its toll when a cyclist collapsed and died during the 100-kilometer time trial. At first the heat was blamed for his death, but it was later discovered that drugs had largely been responsible.

One of the most fascinating success stories of the Rome Games was the achievement of the black American sprinter Wilma Rudolph. She won three gold medals in the sprints and relay. One of 19 children, Rudolph had survived double pneumonia and scarlet fever in early childhood and had been crippled by polio at eight years of age. During the two years that the little girl had been confined to a bed and chair, her family had massaged her paralyzed leg daily. She had used braces for walking until she was 11, but at 16 she won her first Olympic medal when she received a bronze in Melbourne (third in the 4 × 100-meter relay event). Four years later she became the first American woman to win the sprint double as well as gold in the relay. All these factors won her the admiration of the sports-loving world.

Among the male runners, Herb Elliott showed his class when he beat his opponents by 20 yards in the 1,500 meters. This Australian eventually retired as the unbeaten champion in the 1,500-meter run or metric mile.

The American boxer Cassius Clay was another superstar who first stepped into the limelight at Rome. He was so proud of his gold medal in the light-heavyweight (81 kilogram) class, that he kept it on for two days. Clay, later called Muhammad Ali, had his first professional boxing contest within two months after winning the gold medal at the Rome Olympics, and four years later he became the youngest world heavyweight champion ever at 22 years of age.

There were other achievements worth mentioning: A Soviet Union gymnast, Boris Shakhlin, won four gold, two silver, and one bronze medal and was the overall winner of the most medals; Aladár Gerevich of Hungary—50 years and 178 days old—won his sixth team saber gold medal in as many Olympic Games, apart from being the oldest participant in Rome; Edoardo Mangiarotti of Italy reached a milestone when he brought his total number of fencing medals to 13 (six gold, five silver, and two bronze) in five Games; in the high jump seven feet (2.13 meters) was cleared for the first time; and, finally, the 800-meter event for women was run for the first time since 1928.

For the South Africans a huge disappointment awaited. Their hopes for a gold medal had rested on Gert Potgieter, who held three world records in the 440-yard hurdles. Potgieter's 400-meter hurdles challenge to Glenn Davis of the United States faded when he was injured in a serious car accident in Germany just two weeks before the Games.

More countries than ever before won medals in the Rome Olympiad, while 17 world and 43 Olympic records were broken. This was only one of the reasons why IOC President Avery Brundage called it the finest Games in history. The 17 sports resulted in the Soviet Union finishing at the top of the log with 103 medals, against the 71 of the United States. There were also those who did not perform as expected. The poor and humiliating performances of the French at the Rome Olympics led to Charles de Gaulle's subsequent ambitious program of reform.

The Games of 1960 was the first in which a number of independent black African nations were represented in the Olympic movement. It was therefore the beginning of Africa's Olympic history in the broader sense. In subsequent Olympic Games, this continent's black sports people distinguished themselves as a world force in track and field and in boxing in particular.

Clement "Ike" Quartey of Ghana was the first black African to win an Olympic medal—a silver in boxing. But it was the marathon victory of 28-year-old Abebe Bikila that opened the floodgates of black African talent that has seen athletes from this continent virtually dominate world distance running ever since. Bikila, a member of the palace guard of Emperor Haile Selassie of Ethiopia; was an unknown running his third marathon. Refusing refreshments along the way, he broke Emil Zátopek's 1952 Olympic record by nearly eight minutes.

This first Olympic marathon to be run by moonlight was a fittingly dramatic setting for the arrival of Black Africa as the new power in world distance running. Not only Bikila's was victory in the marathon an Olympic record, but this was also the first gold medal for a black athlete from Africa. The fact that he had run barefooted added to his fame. When he returned home after the Games he was promoted from private to corporal in the Imperial Guard (and promoted again to captain after the Mexico Olympics). White South Africans had finished first and second in the 1912 marathon, but this was the first time that two black athletes from Africa finished in the first and second places, as Abdesiem Rhadi ben Abdesselem of Morocco won the silver medal.

Four years later Abebe Bikila won the 1964 marathon in Tokyo—only five weeks after having his appendix removed. Again the Ethiopian won the race in record time, almost five minutes ahead of his nearest rival, and this time it was also a new world record. Bikila's victory in 1960 had far-reaching effects. He became a hero overnight and inspired many a young African athlete to similar performances. African athletes and their coaches discovered that their own training methods were not inferior, just different. In other words, they could continue with what they were doing without trying to imitate successful Western nations.

The Olympics of 1960 was the last in which the old South Africa participated. In 1952, the Soviet Union rejoined the Olympic Games movement and it quickly became clear that political pressure on South Africa would increase. Opposition to South Africa's racist sports policy developed in the Olympic ranks in 1955 when Dr. Herman Santa Cruz of Chile headed a United Nations fact-finding committee on South Africa's racial policies. His finding was that in applying apartheid in sport, South Africa was contravening the Olympic rules. The situation gained momentum when in May 1959 General Stortschev, the Russian delegate to the IOC, requested that this body suspend South Africa's membership. It would, however, take a further 11 years for the IOC to take such a drastic step.

Despite the South African government's 1956 sports policy (formally espousing racial segregation in sport), the S.A. Olympic and National Games Association (SANOC) nevertheless encouraged all affiliated sport associations in South Africa to allow non-white sport associations to become affiliated with the National Games Association in 1959. This would allow suitable nonwhite candidates to be considered for participation in future Olympic Games.

Following discussions relating to South Africa's proposed expulsion from the IOC at the 55th sitting of the IOC in Munich (between May 25 and 28) in 1959, South Africa's representative on the IOC, Reginald Honey, gave the assurance that nonwhite athletes who could meet the required Olympic standard would be considered for Olympic participation. Honey's exact words at this IOC meeting were:

> . . . while it [SANOC] does not control all South African bodies and therefore cannot dictate their policy, it is taking active steps to endure them to compete in international sport and particularly in the Olympic Games. It has made a public statement that if any non-white amateur athlete proves through tests that he is of international or

Olympic standard, no objection will be raised to his being sent to take part in these over-sea competitions.

It seems that Honey prematurely told the IOC that the South African government would raise no objection to this problem. The SANOC also informed the IOC that it would provide training and coaching facilities and organizational leadership to nonwhite athletes.

This only temporarily lifted the pressure on South Africa. At the 59th session of the IOC in Moscow in June 1962, the S.A. Olympic Committee was warned that unless this body publicly distanced itself from government policy before the next sitting in 1963, it would be expelled because it was not functioning in accordance with Olympic protocol. South Africa was accused of contravening the rule that

... no discrimination is allowed against any country or person on grounds of race, religion or politics.

The SANOC did indeed make efforts to comply with the wishes of the IOC but could not persuade the government to amend its sports policy in order to eliminate racial discrimination in sport. Despite the S.A. Olympic Committee's assurances that it would send a mixed team to Tokyo, the African and Asian delegates insisted on expulsion. On the grounds that the S.A. Olympic Games Association had not made satisfactory efforts to eliminate racial discrimination in sport, the IOC decided to withdraw South Africa's invitation to take part in the Tokyo Games.

South Africa was, however, invited to the Mexico City Games of 1968 after the government had made five concessions. These were that whites and nonwhites would form a single team for the Games, would travel from South Africa as one contingent, would live together, be dressed the same. and march together under the South African flag, would compete against one another, and would be selected by a multiracial selection committee under the chairmanship of the president of the S.A. Olympic Games Association.

Major pressure on the IOC—between 40 and 50 nations threatened to boycott the Games if South Africa was allowed to participate—and in light of circumstances, which varied from the uproar following the murder of Martin Luther King, Jr. on April 4, 1968, to threats that could jeopardize the safety of white South Africans in Mexico, Avery Brundage was forced to announce in late April that South Africa's invitation to the Mexico City Games had been withdrawn.

The IOC, however, remained interested in the removal of racial discrimination from South African amateur sport and stated its intention to discuss progress in this regard again in 1970. South Africa's status was thus again the subject of discussion at the 69th sitting of the IOC in Amsterdam in May 1970. An item to expel South Africa from the IOC passed by a vote of 35 for, 28 against, and 3 abstentions. From May 1970 South Africa was therefore no longer a member of the International Olympic Committee. This was the end of a process that had had its origin a decade earlier just before and after the Rome Olympics.

It was only when President F. W. de Klerk lifted the ban on the ANC (African National Congress), the SACP (South African Communist Party) and the PAC (Pan-African Congress) on February 2, 1990, that the beginning of the end of South African sports isolation was heralded. Many developments following this action led to the readmission of South Africa to the IOC on July 9, 1991, opening the doors of international sport to the country. An invitation to participate in the 1992 Olympic Games in Barcelona was issued to SANOC on July 25, 1991.

The IOC had always been a relatively poor organization, but matters started to change after the Rome Olympics when the IOC began to realize the enormous financial potential of television rights.

In 1956 Brundage had said that the IOC had survived for 60 years without television, and that it was willing to wait another 60 years, but in Rome a different ball game awaited him. The Italian National Olympic Committee opened the eyes of the IOC in terms of the money that could be generated from television rights. Live television coverage via Eurovision came to a total of 93 hours and 40 minutes. CBS-TV paid $394,000 for these rights and the total global revenue was about $1.2 million. No wonder the Games were such a financial success—with the puritan IOC receiving five percent of the profit. By 1968 the American television rights were selling for $4.5 million.

The growth of media coverage after the Rome Games was astronomical and had far reaching effects. In 1936, 1948, and 1956, only one country had television coverage of the Games. In 1952 there were two. In 1960 there were 21 with the figure growing and exceeding 200 during the Sydney Games. No less than 18 European countries would follow the Rome Olympics live on television, and it was available in North America only hours later.

Currently the broadcasting rights of the Olympic Games are owned by the IOC, not the local Games organizers, as was the case in 1960. The reason for this is that in 1958, after the Melbourne incident, the IOC altered its Rule 49 that had allowed television rights to be negotiated by each organizing committee. In 1966, after a tug-of-war between various recipients, Brundage came up with the Rome Formula for distribution of the money earned through television rights. But by 1968 the IOC had decided to keep the revenue for itself and to distribute the profits to the international federations and the local organizing committee.

It is this rather recent income from television rights that has been primarily responsible for the phenomenal growth of the Olympic Movement. The positive aspects are that more funds are channelled to the Olympic Movement, more people can share in the spectacle worldwide, and there are more sponsors available for athletes. On the other hand the income from television rights has led to gigantism of the Olympic movement with overcommercialization as its by-product.

BIBLIOGRAPHICAL ESSAY

Primary sources of official Olympic materials are maintained at the International Olympic Committee library and archives in Lausanne, Switzerland. Much of the material relating to the period of Avery Brundage's tenure as IOC president, including the 1960 Rome Games, is housed in the Brundage Papers at the University of Illinois archives, Champaign-Urbana, Illinois.

The organizing committee's official report, edited by Romolo Giacomini and translated by Edwin Byatt, is *The Games of the XVII Olympiad, Rome, 1960: Official Report* (Rome, 1960). Other publications prepared by the organizing committee include *Games of the XVII Olympiad: Official Souvenir, Rome 1960* (Rome, 1960);

Olympic Rules and Sport Regulations/Regoli olimpiche e regloamenti sportivi (Rome, 1960); and a catalog of an exhibition of sport photography, *Esposizione Olimpica di Fotografica Sportiva-Palazzo della Sport* (Rome, 1960).

National Olympic committee reports on the Rome Games include Arthur G. Lentz and Asa S. Bushnell, eds., *United States 1960 Olympic Book: Quadrennial Report of the United States Olympic Committee* (New York, 1961); *Australia at the XVII Olympic Games, VII Olympic Winter Games* (Melbourne, 1960); Phil Pilley, ed., *The Official Report of the Olympic Games, XVIIth Olympiad, Rome, August 25–September 11, 1960* (London, 1960); *Die Olympischen Spiele 1960, Rome-Squaw Valley: Das Offizielle Standardwerk des Nationalen Olympischen Komitees* (Stuttgart, 1960); and *Canada Competes at the Olympic Games 1960* (Montreal, 1961).

Other, nonofficial publications include Harold Lechenperg, ed., *Olympic Games 1960: Squaw Valley, Rome* (New York, 1960), which treats each event separately and contains many excellent photographs, color illustrations, and tables of results; Harold N. Abrahams, *XVII Olympiad, Rome 1960* (London, 1960), an account by the 1934 British sprint medalist and Olympic administrator; Neil Allen, *Olympic Diary: Rome 1960* (London, 1960); John A. Talbot-Ponsonby, *The Equestrian Olympic Games, Rome 1960* (n.p., 1960); and Province of Naples, *Olympic Events: Events at Naples, XVIIth Olympiad Rome 1960* (n.p., 1960).

A fresh approach was followed by Kristine Toohey and A. J. Veal, *The Olympic Games: A Social Perspective* (Oxford, United Kingdom, 2000). Here one finds more information on the influence of economics, politics, drugging, and mass media on the Olympic movement, including the Rome Games.

For information on South Africa's role in this history, the following are helpful: Floris Van der Merwe, *Sport History: A Textbook for South African Students* (Stellenbosch, South Africa, 2001), and the General Manager's Report, *South African Olympic Games Team* (Rome, 1960), as well as the minutes of the meetings of the executive and council of the South African Olympic and Commonwealth Games Association, 1959.

James M. Tanner, in his study of 137 track-and-field athletes and his comparison with weight lifters and wrestlers at the Games, has made a huge contribution to sport science. This classic work in anthropometrics includes statements of those days that are still valid, even in this postmodern age. The full reference is James M. Tanner, *The Physique of the Olympic Athlete* (London, 1964).

Some articles on relevant issues are as follows: Mark Will-Weber, "Victory Lap," *Runner's World* 34, 4 (April 1999): 106, which profiles Herb Elliott; Mark Will-Weber, "Abebe Bikila," *Runner's World* 31, 8 (August 1998): 100, on Bikila's victory in the marathon at Rome, his paralysis due to a car crash, and his state funeral in Addis Ababa; and Doug Mills, "An Olympian Odyssey," *Life* 19, 10 (September 1996): 16, which looks at Muhammad Ali's changing attitudes towards the Olympic Games.

Other useful articles include Judith P. Josephson and Robert Jordan, "Wilma Rudolph," *Children's Digest* 45, 4 (June 1995): 24, which contains biographical information, as well as details of her post-Olympic activities, as well as the creation of the Wilma Rudolph Foundation in Indianapolis, Indiana, for underprivileged children, and her death due to brain cancer in 1994. For further information on Rudolph, see also Evelyn Ashford, "In Her Tracks," *New York Times Magazine* (January 1, 1995). Ira Berkow, "Forever the Regal Champion," *New York Times* (November 13, 1994) is a tribute to Rudolph upon her death.

A documentary film version of the Rome Games is *The Grand Olympics* (1961), directed by Romolo Marcellini. It focuses on the strong performances of Soviet athletes.

TOKYO 1964

John Slater

THE GAMES OF THE XVIII OLYMPIAD

The 1964 Tokyo Olympic Games were among the best organized and the best executed in the history of the Olympic Games. *Life* magazine said that in terms of excitement, achievement, and the preparations made by the Japanese, they were the greatest Olympics ever held, an assessment shared by many observers. The Tokyo Games have become known by many names—"the happy Games," "the technology Games," "the television Games," even "the science fiction Games."

The onset of World War II forced the abandonment of the first Tokyo Olympic Games in 1940. The war also thwarted the hopes of the Tokyo Organizing Committee to hold the 1944 Games. And long after V-J Day, Japan's need to put the war behind it dictated that country's approach to hosting the 1964 Games. At war's end Japan lay in ruins, its cities devastated, its economy nonexistent, its standing among the nations of the world destroyed. Some 80 percent of the buildings in Tokyo had been leveled by bombs. In suffering defeat, Japan had lost face. The nation was occupied by foreign troops. Yet, less than 20 years after the war, following an astonishing recovery, Japan was ready to make a comeback. It did so by staging the most expensive and arguably the most successful Olympic Games ever. The 1964 Games symbolized Japan's return to the civilized world.

The 1951 Treaty of San Francisco brought an end to the occupation of Japan by the United States and restored full sovereignty to the island nation. Just one year earlier Japan's National Olympic Committee had been recognized by the International Olympic Committee (IOC). In 1950 the IOC named Ryotaro Azuma, president of both the Japanese Olympic Committee and the Japan Amateur Sports Federation, as the second IOC member from Japan. Japanese athletes were allowed to take part in the Helsinki Summer Games in 1952, a return to Olympic competition for the first time since 1936. In May 1952 the Tokyo Municipal Assembly boldly approved a resolution authorizing the city to place a bid to host the 1960 Summer Olympic Games. The official invitation to host the Games in Tokyo was submitted on July 2, and preliminary preparations were begun. On May 15, 1955, the International Olympic Committee voted to determine the site of the 1960 Games. The Tokyo candidacy gleaned only four votes. Tokyo was eliminated in the first round of voting, placing last in a field of seven cities, but the Japanese were undeterred.

In October 1955 the Tokyo Municipal Assembly again authorized a bid, this time for the 1964 Games. And this time the Japanese lobbied hard. The mayor of Tokyo attended the IOC's 1956 general session and personally invited the group to hold its 1958 general session in Tokyo, in conjunction with the Third Asian Games. The IOC accepted. On October 4, 1957, the Japanese cabinet endorsed Tokyo's candidacy, giving the city the backing of the nation. At its 1958 meeting in Tokyo, the IOC was impressed with the Japanese organization and handling of the Asian Games. The Emperor of Japan personally welcomed the IOC members at the meeting's opening session, an elaborate ceremony that included performances by a full orchestra and chorus. The lobbying strategy paid off. It also did not hurt Tokyo's cause when Azuma was elected Governor of Tokyo in April 1959, on a platform to rebuild the city for the Olympic Games. When the vote finally came, at the IOC's meeting in Munich on May 26, 1959, Tokyo received 34 of 58 votes cast, winning out over Detroit with 10 votes, Vienna with 9, and Brussels with 5.

Tokyo 1964—Opening Ceremonies at the Tokyo Games, 1964. Courtesy of University of Illinois Archives, Avery Brundage Collection.

The moment the decision to place the Games in Tokyo was reached, Japanese officials raised the five-ring Olympic flag over the city, and preparations began in earnest. Azuma, as a member of the IOC, was in an ideal position to coordinate those preparations. At the time, Tokyo was the world's largest city and one of the most densely populated metropolitan areas in the world. Tokyo was regarded as a city planner's nightmare, a hodgepodge of buildings and narrow lanes best suited to oxcarts and rickshaws. In the 1960 census its population numbered nearly 10 million people in an area of 501,920 acres, and the city was growing at the rate of 400,000 people per year. Traffic was a nightmare, water was becoming a scarce resource, and the housing market was very tight. In order to host the Games and the 2 million visitors the Games were expected to attract, Tokyo would need more than stadiums and sport facilities. It also needed new roads, better mass transit, improvements to water and sewer infrastructure, and more accommodations for visitors.

Azuma headed up one of the most ambitious urban construction projects of the twentieth century, a five-year, 24-hour-a-day effort. His plan to rebuild Tokyo for the Olympic Games won the backing of all levels of government. A state minister in charge of Olympic affairs was appointed, with the power to convene a cabinet ministers' conference to solve Olympic problems. Laws were passed, fund-raising committees established, and special taxes levied. Having won the right to host the Games, the Japanese spared no expense to make them a showcase. The Ministry of Transportation built the Tokaido Line, a Tokyo-to-Osaka bullet train, at a cost of just over $1 billion. It spent another $500 million building two new subway lines and a monorail from Tokyo International Airport at Haneda to the heart of Tokyo. The Construction Ministry spent $500 million building a metropolitan highway network that included 18 miles of new expressways with double and triple elevated crossings, 4 city roads, and 22 other highways designated *Olympic roads*. Three sewage disposal plants were constructed, and miles of sewer pipe laid. Water works were improved. Tokyo International Airport was refurbished. Some $87 million in subsidies were made available to construct a half-dozen new hotels and to make existing hotels and inns acceptable to foreign visitors. The new hotels included Japan's largest hotel and the tallest building in Tokyo, the 17-story Hotel New Otani, with accommodations for more than 1,000 guests. The harbor facilities at Tokyo and Yokohama were remodeled so visitors could arrive in and stay aboard "hotel" ships during the Games. The Postal Services Ministry spent $50 million on communication facilities, and NHK, the Japan Broadcasting Corporation, paid $33 million to establish a broadcasting center near the Olympic Village.

The total expenditure on the Games and related improvements came to some $2.8 billion, six times more than any previous Olympic host city had spent to stage the Games. There were human costs, as well. More than 100 workers were killed and 2,000 injured in construction accidents on Olympics-related projects.

Some $56 million was spent to build or renovate athletic facilities. The Games were spread over 30 different venues, but 13 of the sites were grouped at three locations: Meiji Olympic Park, Komazawa Sports Park, and Yoyogi Sports Center. Meiji Olympic Park, in the outer gardens of the Meiji Shrine, was the site of the National Stadium, which had been built in 1958, prior to the Third Asian Games. For the Olympics, the stadium was expanded by 25,000 seats, increasing its capacity to 72,000. The stadium was used for the opening and closing ceremonies, track and field events, and the final equestrian events. The park also housed the Tokyo Metropolitan Gymnasium, built in 1954 for the World Wrestling Championships and used in 1964 for gymnastics events; Tokyo Metropolitan Indoor Swimming Pool, built for the Third Asian Games and used for water polo matches; and Tokyo Metropolitan Track and Field.

Komazawa Sports Park was created for the Olympic Games. Its facilities included a 20,000-seat stadium used for football (soccer) games, a gymnasium used for wrestling events, an indoor volleyball court, hockey grounds, and a hall used for fencing events.

The centerpiece of the Tokyo Olympic Games was the Yoyogi Sports Center, situated near the Olympic Village at Yoyogi. Olympic authorities constructed a stunning, 11,000-seat National Gymnasium to house the swimming events and a 4,000-seat National Gymnasium Annex for basketball competition. The structures were designed by world-renowned architect Tange Kenzo of Tokyo University. The National Gymnasium utilized a high-tensile cable-and-steel suspension roof—the world's largest suspension roof—over a base of reinforced concrete. The facility, which re-creates the sweep of a Japanese temple, is an important contribution to modern international architecture.

Most of the 5,558 athletes who took part in the Games—4,826 men and 732 women—were housed in the main Olympic Village at Yoyogi, in an area known as Washington Heights. Washington Heights was a compound of nearly 600 houses and apartment buildings built by the U.S. military for married personnel and their families. The facility was turned over to Japan specifically for use in the Olympics. The Olympic Village furnished dormitory space, dining halls, clinics, post offices, shops, and a recreation center. Secondary Olympic villages were located at some of the more distant venues. Among these were cycling, held at Hachioji city; yachting, at Enoshima; canoeing, at Lake Sagami; and the preliminary equestrian events, held at Karuizawa.

Credentials were issued to some 1,153 journalists, 179 photographers, 115 news agencies, and 60 photo agencies. In addition, 2,548 domestic and 656 foreign television personnel were accredited. The main Press Center was located about a hundred yards from the National Stadium. It provided writing and communication facilities for journalists and featured eight giant IBM computers that received and displayed results from all the games sites. NHK built a seven-story Olympic Broadcasting Center in the Yoyogi area that contained radio and television studios; editing, dubbing, and recording equipment; booths for announcers and other broadcast necessities for both national and international audiences. Many of the media people stayed at the seven-story Press House, built specially for the Olympics, just 170 yards from the Press Centre. After the Games, the building was converted into 169 apartments.

Most of the athletic facilities were ready for use during Tokyo International Sports Week, held in October 1963 as a kind of dress rehearsal for the Olympic Games. The entire construction project was completed before the Games began on October 10, 1964. The unusual autumn date was a compromise that took into consideration Japan's midsummer heat, the rainy season, students' schedules, and the likelihood of typhoons.

Initially, all 20 of the then prevalent Olympic sports—athletics (track-and-field events), archery, rowing, basketball, boxing, cycling, canoeing, fencing, football, gymnastics, handball, hockey, modern pentathlon, swimming and diving, equestrian sports, shooting, water polo, weight lifting, wrestling, and yachting—were to be included. Volleyball also was to be included for the first time at an Olympic Games. At its 1960 session in Rome, the IOC approved the addition of judo. Olympic officials later deleted archery and handball, leaving a total of 20 sports. Demonstration sports included baseball and budo, a traditional form of Japanese martial arts.

The 1964 Games included a number of firsts. They were the first Olympic Games to be held in Asia. They were the first to include judo, a Japanese sport, and volleyball for both men and women. They were the first to exclude participation by South African athletes because of that country's practice of apartheid. And they were the first to be boycotted because of Cold War politics.

When Jakarta hosted the Fourth Asian Games in 1962, the Indonesian government denied visas to athletes from Israel and Taiwan. The IOC responded by suspending the Indonesian Olympic Committee. Incensed, Indonesian President Sukarno announced his country's withdrawal from the Olympic movement. He then organized his own "Games of the New Emerging Forces" (GANEFO). Forty-eight nations attended GANEFO, which was held in November 1963. Because GANEFO was not sanctioned by the international sport federations, many federations suspended the athletes who took part. Although most of the suspensions were later withdrawn, those of the International Amateur Athletic Federation and the International Swimming Federation remained in force at the time of the Tokyo Olympic Games. They applied to a total of 17 would-be Olympians—11 from Indonesia and 6 from North Korea. When the disqualified athletes arrived in Japan with their national teams, the Tokyo organizing committee denied them admission to the Olympic Village. The impasse was resolved only on the eve of the Games' Opening Ceremony, when the entire Indonesian and North Korean teams left the country.

The Tokyo Games also attracted a call for another boycott that did not materialize. Writing in the March 1964 issue of *Ebony* magazine, runner Mal Whitfield urged black American athletes to boycott the Games "if Negro Americans by that time have not been guaranteed full and equal rights as first-class citizens." Whitfield, a gold medalist in the 1948 and 1952 Olympic Games, estimated that blacks would make up about 25 percent of the U.S. contingent. His proposal may have foreshadowed events at the 1968 Mexico City Games.

Many of the other firsts registered by the 1964 Olympic Games fell within the area of technology. The Games built on Innsbruck's use of computers to relay results and other information among Olympic sites and were the first to use computers to maintain databases of participants and to compile athletic records. The 1964 Games were the first to utilize an electronic "judge," rather than a human eye, to take finishing times to one one-hundredth of a second and to determine automatically the order of finish in swimming events. They also were the first to use electronic music, composed for the Opening Ceremony by Toshio Mayuzumi, which combined the recorded tones of Japanese temple bells at Nara, Kyoto, and Nikko with pure electronic sounds produced in the studios of NHK. A Japanese firm, Seiko, overcame the virtual Swiss timekeeping monopoly to become the provider of official timing devices for the Games. Seiko furnished stopwatches, digital stopclocks, photoelectric timing devices, and large spectator clocks. A Seiko subsidiary, Epson, developed crystal chronometers and printing timers used for official timekeeping. Later, Epson would use the same technology to produce some of the world's most successful printers for calculators and computers. For all of these reasons, some observers referred to the 1964 Games as "a festival of science and technology."

Others called the Games "the television Olympics," since they became a showcase of Japanese broadcasting technology. The Tokyo Games were the first to be televised in color, prompting an enormous surge in sales of color television sets. They were the first Games to feature slow-motion instant replay, since NHK had built video recorders that could both replay highlights in slow motion and freeze a single frame of the action. And they were the first to utilize satellite transmission of television coverage.

Television was the principal means the Japanese had chosen to tell their story to the world. Two full years before the Games began, the newsletter of the Games, *Tokyo Olympic News*, observed that while an estimated 600 million viewers worldwide would watch the televised Olympics, only about 30,000 spectators from overseas would attend Olympic events each day. The Japanese planned to promulgate television programming by airlifting videotapes to the home country. In addition, they hoped to use some form of simultaneous relay broadcasting. As early as 1959 NHK had explored the possibility of creating relay stations between Tokyo and

Europe on the one hand and Tokyo and the United States on the other. The scheme proved unworkable, but in 1962 the Soviet Union was said to be building a microwave television relaying system across Siberia, and if it were to become usable by 1964, it could provide a link to Western Europe. Another possibility would be to use space satellites as relay stations.

U.S. telecommunication satellites had successfully relayed television broadcasts between Europe and America in 1962, but since the low-level satellites used in that experiment orbited the earth, a satellite could relay a signal between any two points for only about 15 minutes before it passed out of range. About 30 such satellites would be needed to allow constant worldwide relaying. The science fiction writer Arthur Clarke had suggested in a 1945 magazine article that just three satellites, positioned high above the equator in stationary, geosynchronous orbit—that is, orbiting the earth at the same speed as the earth's rotation—could theoretically provide fulltime, worldwide communication. But it wasn't until 1963, with the launch of the first of the Syncom series of satellites designed by the Hughes Corporation, that U.S. scientists could achieve geosynchronous orbit. Tests showed that a full-time communications satellite relay was indeed possible.

The Japanese immediately asked if the United States could provide a satellite to relay Olympic television signals. U.S. officials were receptive to the idea, and the U.S. Department of State asked the Communication Satellite Corporation (COMSAT) to look for a possible ground receiving station on the West Coast. COMSAT reported that a Navy antenna at Point Mugu, California, could be modified to receive television signals from a satellite for less than $500,000.

On July 23, 1964, the White House announced that the Games would be televised by satellite in "an outstanding demonstration of technological partnership by the United States and Japan." The Japanese were finishing a new $2 million space communication station at Kishima, 50 miles northeast of Tokyo. The signal would be sent from there to Syncom III and then through Point Mugu to a Bell System switchboard in Los Angeles. From there the pictures would be distributed to U.S. and foreign participants. They would be relayed via microwave to Buffalo, New York, and on to Montreal for Canadian viewing. A chartered jet would ferry videotapes from Montreal to Hamburg for use by the European Broadcasting Union, beating a flight from Japan by 12 hours. It was the first live coverage of a Summer Olympics in the United States, although in the end only the Opening Ceremony was televised live in the U.S. The plan fell victim to a COMSAT requirement that all experimental space-relay signals be made available equally to anyone who wanted them. Since NBC had paid $1.5 million for the exclusive U.S. television rights to the Games, the network was not interested in sharing the signal with its competitors. And NBC even created a controversy with its broadcast of the Opening Ceremony, by choosing to air it on tape-delay on the West Coast, rather than cancelling the Johnny Carson show. Canada and many European countries got much more coverage from the satellite transmission than did the United States.

The 1964 Games were also the first to conduct a large-scale survey of the television audience. The survey found that during the two-week period of the Games, life in Japan was centered on the Olympics. More than 98 percent of the respondents to the survey had watched Olympic events on television, and 61 percent of them watched frequently. No event in postwar Japan had united the Japanese people in the same way.

The Tokyo region suffered a severe three-month drought in 1964, and during parts of August much of the city had water available only nine hours a day. The problem was ameliorated during the Games by importing water from Kanagawa Prefecture and across Saitama Prefecture from the Tone River. A typhoon also threatened Honshu the week before the Games began, but it caused no damage.

The Olympic torch relay began in Olympia, Greece, and visited Athens, Istanbul, Beirut, Teheran, Lahore, New Delhi, Rangoon, Bangkok, Kuala Lumpur, Manila, Hong Kong, and Taipei before arriving in Okinawa and splitting into four segments for an extensive tour of Japan. The runner who carried the torch into the stadium for the lighting of the cauldron was Yoshinori Sakai, a young man who had been born near Hiroshima on the day in 1945 that the first atomic bomb was dropped.

A record 94 nations took part in the Tokyo Games, 16 of them participating in the Olympics for the first time. The Opening Ceremony was held in afternoon sunlight, under cloudless skies. Twelve thousand brightly colored balloons and 8,000 pigeons were released, and five jet planes of the Japanese Air Self-Defense Force drew gigantic colored rings—the Olympic emblem—in the sky above the stadium. During the Games themselves, 41 world records were established—15 in athletics, 19 in swimming, 6 in weight lifting, and 1 in shooting. Eighty-six men's Olympic records and 62 women's records were shattered. Among the memorable performances were those of the Japanese women's volleyball team, which overcame a significant height disadvantage to defeat the Soviet women in the final match; Ethiopia's Abebe Bikila, who repeated his Rome victory to become the first two-time Olympic marathon winner; and U.S. swimmer Don Schollander, who became the first American to win four gold medals in an Olympics since Jesse Owens in 1936.

Art displays accompanied the Games. Some 400,000 visitors saw an exhibition of ancient art treasures in the Tokyo National Museum. Other exhibitions were mounted at the National Museum of Modern Art, the Matsuya Department Store, Ueno Park, and the Communications Museum. There also were performances of traditional Japanese arts, including Kabuki and Noh theatre, Bunraku puppet shows, court music, traditional dance and Japanese music, and folklore.

The official documentary film, *Tokyo Olympiad*, was directed by Kon Ichikawa, the doyen of the Japanese film industry. It was the first Olympic film to be shot in Cinemascope. In its original, 170-minute version it is sometimes compared to *Olympia*, Leni Riefenstahl's portrayal of the 1936 Berlin Olympics. Making the film required more than 100 cameras, including high-speed and underwater cameras; 400,000 feet of film; 164 cameramen; and a staff of more than 500 helpers. Ichikawa said of the film that he was attempting to emphasize the idea of One World and mankind's persistent striving for peace.

The excellent organization and perseverance of the organizing committee has been credited with much of the success of the Tokyo Games, but the involvement of the Japanese people, who threw themselves into the Games, also counted for much. At the close of the Games the London newspaper *The Times* said, "The organization and the industry of the hosts has been massive." IOC President Avery Brundage commented, "The entire nation from newsboy to industrial tycoon adopted the Games as his own project and went out of his way to please the visitors."

After the Tokyo Games, a grateful IOC presented five awards. The Olympic Cup was presented to the City of Tokyo for its "perfect" organization of the Games.

The only other city to be so honored was Helsinki, for the 1952 Olympic Games. The Olympic Diploma of Merit was presented to Tange Kenzo for his creative design for the National Gymnasium and to Kon Ichikawa for his production of *Tokyo Olympiad*. The Count Bonacossa Trophy, awarded annually to the National Olympic Committee that shows "the greatest initiative in the cause of advancing the Olympic Ideal," was presented to the Japanese Olympic Committee for its endeavors during the five years before the Games. The fifth award, the Tokyo Trophy, was established in 1964 by the Tokyo Metropolitan Government, to be awarded to those who displayed the highest qualities of sportsmanship. It was presented to two Swedish yachtsmen in the Flying Dutchman class who rescued an Australian team that had capsized and then continued the race in which they were competing.

BIBLIOGRAPHICAL ESSAY

The fullest book-length treatments of the Tokyo Games are found in Harald Lechenperg, ed. *Olympic Games 1964: Innsbruck, Tokyo*, translated by Bert Koetter (New York, 1964), and Carl A. Posey, *The Olympic Century: The Official 1st Century History of the Modern Olympic Movement*, Vol. 16, *The XVIII Olympiad: Tokyo 1964, Grenoble 1968* (Los Angeles, 1996). The organizing committee's official report is *The Games of the XVIII Olympiad, Tokyo, 1964: The Official Report of the Organizing Committee*, 2 vols. (Tokyo, 1964). The committee also issued other publications, including *Tokyo Games Facilities/Les Installations des jeux de Tokyo* (Tokyo, 1964) and the serial *Tokyo Olympic News*, the official foreign language bulletin issued in English and French from May 1961 through October 1964, first bimonthly and then monthly. Other publications prepared for the organizing committee include *Tokyo Olympics Official Souvenir Book 1964* (Tokyo, 1964).

The pages of the official IOC periodical, *Olympic Review*, provide an excellent resource. The complete run of the periodical, which has had a number of name changes over the years, may be consulted at the library of the Amateur Athletic Foundation of Los Angeles, or on-line at the AAFLA Web site, http://www.aafla.org. For matters touching on IOC deliberations, the minutes of their meetings are preserved in the archives of the Olympic Studies Centre at the Olympic Museum in Lausanne, Switzerland.

The Avery Brundage Collection at the University of Illinois Archives at Champaign-Urbana contains several boxes of IOC correspondence, newspaper clippings, and other material bearing on the Tokyo Games, which took place when Brundage was president of the IOC. Another source of information about Brundage's presidency is Allen Guttmann, *The Games Must Go On: Avery Brundage and the Olympic Movement* (New York, 1984).

Information about Tokyo in the 1960s is available in many places, including *Japan: The Official Guide*, 9th ed. (Tokyo, 1962); *Japan: The Pocket Guide*, 10th ed. (Tokyo, 1959); and Walt Sheldon, *Enjoy Japan: A Personal and Highly Unofficial Guide* (Rutland, VT, 1961). Edwin O. Reischauer, *My Life Between Japan and America* (New York, 1986), reveals much about Japan and the Tokyo Olympics from the viewpoint of the man who served as U.S. Ambassador to Japan from 1961 to 1966. Any of Reischauer's many other books about the Japanese can provide valuable insights into the Japanese character.

Autobiographies of participants and observers constitute another useful source of information. Among these are Neil Allen, *Olympic Diary: Tokyo 1964* (London, 1964); Christopher Brasher, *Tokyo 1964: A Diary of the XVIIIth Olympiad* (Tokyo, 1964); Dawn Fraser and Harry Gordon, *Below the Surface* (New York, 1965); Dorothy Hyman, *Sprint to Fame* (London, 1964); and Edward Seidensticker, *Tokyo Rising: The City Since the Great Earthquake* (New York, 1990). The GANEFO controversy is discussed in many books about politics in the Olympics, and in Ewa T. Parker, *GANEFO: Sports and Politics in Djakarta* (Santa Monica, CA, 1964).

The development of satellite television transmission was well covered in the pages of the *New York Times*, which also provided useful daily coverage of the Games.

MEXICO CITY 1968

Joseph L. Arbena

THE GAMES OF THE NINETEENTH OLYMPIAD

The 1960s was a decade of controversy and conflict, of ferment and protest: the Vietnam War escalated; international condemnation of South African apartheid intensified; the rapid move toward independence altered the political map of Africa; civil war in the former Belgian Congo led to the death of United Nations Secretary-General Dag Hammarskjöld; the Cuban missile crisis carried the world to the brink of nuclear war; student unrest shook France, Germany, Japan, and the United States; rebellious popular behavior provoked often brutal responses in such places as Brazil and Uruguay; and the black civil rights movement in the United States brought change along with serious white resistance. In 1968 alone, assassins in the United States ended the lives of Martin Luther King, Jr. and Robert Kennedy, and violent confrontations marred the Democratic national convention in Chicago, while in both France and the United States university students raised their protests to new levels, and in China the Cultural Revolution raged on. Also that year the Soviet Union invaded Czechoslovakia to suppress a nationalistic and ideologically deviant movement.

Host Mexico City and the Summer Olympics scheduled for October 12–27 could not avoid those forces. Perceived as most dangerous was a predominantly student protest and demand for change that began as a meaningless fistfight between two secondary school students but triggered an armed intervention by police and riot-control troops. University students, particularly at the National University (UNAM), began to organize for action, eventually directing demonstrations, some quite impressive, and calling a general strike that only partially, yet noticeably, materialized. In turn, the army occupied the UNAM campus and continued to harass student leaders. The climax came on October 2 when troops surrounded a group of students and sympathizers in the Plaza of the Three Cultures, or Tlatelolco, as the surrounding area was known in the fifteenth-century Aztec capital of Tenochtitlán. Without cause or warning the troops fired into the crowd, killing between 100 and 500 persons and wounding perhaps a thousand more. Following that massacre, more protesters and suspected dissidents were arrested, tortured, and/or killed. Others were pursued for several years.

Well before that confrontation, at its 60th General Session in Baden-Baden, Germany, on October 18, 1963, the International Olympic Committee (IOC) accepted Mexico's City's bid, initially submitted on December 7, 1962, to host the 1968 Summer Olympics, rejecting similar invitations from Detroit, Lyons, and Buenos Aires. In anticipation of this victory, in May 1963, then President Adolfo López Mateos (1958–1964) had decreed the establishment of the organizing committee for the Games of the XIX Olympiad, though it was not formally constituted until after the IOC decision. Following the Baden-Baden meeting, the government created an executive commission directed by the longtime sports promoter General José A. Jesús Clark Flores; vice chairmanships were filled by Augustín Legorreta, for finance, and Pedro Ramírez Vázquez, for building, who were to be aided by eighteen special sections.

Mexico City 1968—The Olympic torch relay has been a standard part of the Games since 1936. Here a runner carries the torch through the streets of Mexico City prior to the start of the 1968 Summer Games. Courtesy of University of Illinois Archives, Avery Brundage Collection.

In June 1965 President Gustavo Díaz Ordaz (1964–1970) chose López Mateos to fill the still-vacant chairmanship of the organizing committee, but due to declining health, the former president stepped down after one year and was replaced by the architect Ramírez Vázquez. In October 1966, the committee created seven departments to carry out its functions: administration, sports technique, public relations, courtesies to visitors, control of installations, control of programs, and artistic and cultural activities. Now, with advanced computer assistance and the aid of numerous government agencies and private companies, the serious work began. The organizing committee also initiated a sophisticated campaign of publicity and public relations.

As the new structure commenced its labors, many Mexicans viewed it as a means to advance their country's long attempt to raise its global prestige and thereby earn greater acceptance as a place safe for tourists and foreign investors. The student movement of July–October 1968 seemed to threaten those dreams, which explains, without excusing, the government's harsh reaction, especially at Tlatelolco. In addition to the 1968 Olympics, Mexican officials no doubt considered the impact of any social uprising on their obligation to host the 1970 soccer World Cup, another step in that long process of Mexican efforts to overcome its status as a Third World country and five decades of foreign memory of its Revolution (1910–1920). Overlapping this concern was the perception that any prolonged instability would bring into question the hegemony of the ruling Partido Revolucionario Institucional

(PRI) {Institutional Revolutionary Party} and the authority of President Díaz Ordaz. Therefore, security for the Games was increased, whether necessary or not.

Meanwhile, within the IOC, a potentially disruptive debate arose over the role of South Africa, which had been banned from Tokyo in 1964 because of racial policies offensive to the expanding body of black African states and to the increasing number of more sensitive people in other world communities. Some eight months before the XIX Olympiad, the IOC, based on a pledge from South African whites that they would modify their selection process to permit blacks to qualify, lifted the ban. In response, African nations announced plans to boycott the Games and soon had the support of countries in the Caribbean, the Islamic world, and Eastern Europe, bringing to around forty the number of countries expressing their willingness to be absent from Mexico City. Finally the Soviet Union threatened to stay home. Attempts to negotiate a compromise failed, so a divided and reluctant IOC voted to withdraw the invitation sent to Pretoria. The Mexicans also chose to deny entry to all Rhodesian athletes, despite their country's promise to send an integrated team, because of perceptions that the governing regime was composed of white racists and that black Africans would again be offended.

Less directly political were several other issues facing the IOC before and during the Games. Performance-enhancing drugs were not yet a source of intense preoccupation, and irregular testing and observation brought only one expulsion: for alcohol abuse. Of greater importance to Olympic leaders was the suspicion that not all female athletes were truly female, either because of genetic irregularities or medical treatments. Therefore, at least 640 females scheduled to compete were subjected to gender tests, but none of them were disqualified.

As at the 1968 Winter Games in Grenoble, the IOC struggled to abort the spread of commercialism, at least among athletes, and thus the decline of amateurism as defined by the IOC. But the IOC was virtually powerless to stop the trend, and the Games, both winter and summer, generated a spate of stories about athletes who received gifts or kickbacks for their participation. A major source of income came from the makers of sports equipment, who paid athletes to wear their products and to display conspicuously their brand names. Pressure to do this increased as television became more intrusive. Mexico City represented the first serious attempt at live broadcasting for a major market, the success of which would generate a television explosion at future Games. At Mexico City, the scheduling of the Games and of some of the events was to a degree influenced by this desire to maximize the North American television audience. The IOC wanted the revenue, the manufacturers wanted the exposure, and the athletes wanted pay for their cooperation. This alliance would eventually bring openly professional athletes to virtually all Olympic sports, as fans and sponsors sought the best athletes, and the IOC could not disrupt the Games by banning so many obvious violators.

If Mexico's historic reputation and recent domestic unrest raised doubts about its ability to fulfill its Olympic responsibilities, even greater concern among some participant countries arose because of Mexico City's relatively high altitude of 7,400 feet. Critics predicted that this site, by far the highest in Summer Olympic history, would physically harm the athletes and distort the competition. To equalize the competitors, the British proposed that athletes be limited in the amount of time they could train above a certain altitude, an idea that received only mild support and was impossible to enforce. Mexican officials tried to reduce the nervousness by citing the number of local residents and foreign tourists who frequented the capital each year without obvious difficulty and by staging three pre-Olympic international sports competitions that experienced minimal problems; in the end, no nation withdrew from the Games because of the altitude issue. Of less concern were the growing congestion and pollution caused by the city's nearly ten million inhabitants living and working in an environment with too little air movement; a few alarmists did call attention to the intestinal discomfort often cited as a problem among foreigners visiting Mexico.

Ultimately, 113 countries sent 5,531 athletes (4,750 males, 781 females) to participate in 182 competitive events involving eighteen official and two demonstration sports. In the end, by whatever means, athletes from forty-four countries carried home 174 gold, 170 silver, and 183 bronze medals. Track and field, with 780 males and 239 females representing ninety-two countries, was the leading category of athletic performance. All sporting events were held in and around Mexico City, except the sailing competitions, which were assigned to Acapulco and its yacht club, 250 miles south on the Pacific coast. To house so many visiting athletes and conduct so many events, the Mexicans needed to prepare adequate physical facilities. The decision was made to take advantage of space all over the sprawling city, to maximize intercultural contacts, and to organize local services to meet the need: it was decentralized planning at its practical limits.

The Olympic Village for athletes was newly constructed south of the capital. The 5,000-unit complex combined large, urban apartment blocks with varied open spaces; it provided facilities to entertain the residents, aid in their training, and encourage them to mix across national lines. To the northeast of the village was the new 22,000-seat Sports Palace, with its masonry base capped by a copper-covered dome. Another new facility was the Olympic pool and gymnasium, a compound structure with both an aquatic center for swimming and diving and a small arena for volleyball. To the southeast, at the famous tourist site of Xochimilco, home of the floating gardens that dated back to the fifteenth-century Aztecs, the Mexicans created a fine basin that served both rowing and canoeing. Other new structures included a prefabricated fencing arena, a velodrome next to the Sports Palace, and the partially roofed Aztec Stadium, which was privately financed, used in 1968 for Olympic soccer, and then fully exploited during the 1970 World Cup.

Among the several renovated structures, the most used was the University City Stadium, renamed the Olympic Stadium, with its modernistic design and its art work based on indigenous motifs. This was the site of the Opening and Closing Ceremonies and most of the track and field competitions. The refurbished National Auditorium in Chapultepec, with 12,800 seats, served successfully as the gymnastics venue. Weight lifting was held in the Insurgentes Theater, water polo in the UNAM pool, and target shooting on a military base.

Expanding on the Games' athletic content, Mexican officials, with encouragement from the IOC, sponsored cultural and academic activities equal to the number of Olympic sports and often integrated with them. Thus the year-long Cultural Olympiad, in which 97 countries participated, offered such programs as international festivals of the arts, folk arts, sculptors, and poets; exhibitions of Olympic philately and of the history and art of the Olympic Games; exhibitions on space research and nuclear energy; ballet; an international youth film festival; an international meeting of young architects; an Olympic camp for world youth; and a presentation of the XIX Olympiad in motion pictures and television. These events were held in museums and auditoriums, along busy thoroughfares, and in the city's green and spacious Chapultepec Park. One example of this cultural cooperation, still visible in the city, was the group of nineteen abstract, monumental concrete sculptures crafted by an international team and erected along a seventeen-kilometer stretch of the southern Periferico (the circumferential highway around the capital) named the "Route of Friendship"; these sculptures straddled both sides of the Olympic Village. IOC President Avery Brundage expressed hope that Mexico's expansive cultural program would mark a return to "the purity, beauty and simplicity" of the Olympic tradition.

Perhaps observers realized that this would be a special Olympic event when, at the opening ceremony, Norma Enriqueta Basilio, a twenty-year-old hurdler, became the first woman in Olympic history to bring the Olympic torch into the stadium and carry it up ninety-two steps to light the Olympic flame, a feminist prize even Avery Brundage applauded.

Across the Games themselves, almost certainly the altitude did enhance performance, especially at the shorter racing distances and in field events, as well as among athletes who had trained extensively far enough above sea level; it often hampered those who had not. The sport that seemed to suffer most from the thin air was rowing, in which oxygen resuscitations were required on at least sixteen occasions. Still, uneven performances by athletes regardless of where they trained suggests a psychological dimension as well. For whatever combination of factors, these Games witnessed some remarkable feats, as 252 competitors surpassed previous Olympic records in those sports that can meaningfully be measured precisely in time, weight, or points. In total, competitors matched or surpassed twenty-four world and fifty-six Olympic records.

It was in track and field that so many records fell; only twelve of thirty-eight track-and-field events failed to tie an old record or produce a new one. Besides the altitude, track performances were surely improved by the new, all-weather synthetic track, called Tartan by the 3M Company that developed and manufactured it. Its surface maintained uniform toughness and even resiliency, did not rut, and was impervious to weather. Competing mainly at the Olympic Stadium, male and female track-and-field participants combined to equal or exceed seventeen world and twenty-six Olympic records. In the five long-distance running events (1,500 meters and up) athletes from Ethiopia, Kenya, and Tunisia swept the gold medals, demonstrating both the benefit of their longtime high-altitude training and the increasing importance of their continent in the global sports arena. Highly acclaimed was Kipchoge "Kip" Keino of Kenya, whose time of 3:34.9 in the 1,500 meters easily beat the Olympic record of Herb Elliot of Australia; in this race, Keino defeated his closest competitor, Jim Ryun of the United States, by almost three seconds and twenty yards.

Surely the most spectacular of the records was set in the long jump. First, the United States's Ralph Boston reached the world record in a qualifying leap on his way to a bronze medal. The next day he watched in amazement as the erratic but recently very successful Bob Beamon, who had won twenty of his last twenty-one meet competitions, reached the incredible distance of 29 feet 2 1/2 inches, almost two feet over the existing record of 27 feet 4 3/4 inches, setting a mark that lasted some twenty-five years. It was a humid, overcast day, ideal for the long jump, yet only Beamon put together the moves for so impressive a performance.

Although aided some by the thinner air and lower gravitational force, U.S. high jumper Dick Fosbury and numerous pole-vaulters, such as U.S. gold medal winner

Bob Seagren, likewise benefited from new technologies and revised techniques. Gold medalist Fosbury forever changed high jumping with his headfirst, stomach-up, flat-body leap, the "Fosbury flop," made less dangerous with the placement of a thick, foam-filled landing pad instead of the traditional sand or sawdust pit; he won with a height of 7 feet 4 1/2 inches. The vaulters at last learned to take advantage of the fiber glass poles introduced a few years earlier to rise to new standards. Nine men cleared the historic Olympic barrier of 17 feet; Seagren won at 17 feet 8 1/2 inches. Less heralded but equally admirable was Al Oerter's fourth consecutive Olympic record and gold medal in the discus throw, a result of hard work and concentration.

In addition to the official Mexican desire to promote the host country and its willingness to spend for that purpose, the larger political atmosphere encroached on the Games in several ways, though local student activists who had generated such emotions over the previous two-and-a-half months were absent, due perhaps to a lack of organization, a fear of government brutality, or a sense of nationalistic interest in seeing the Games succeed; it will probably never be known for certain which determined the lack of further protest. What is certain is that spectators vigorously welcomed the Czechoslovakian delegation and adopted as one of their special heroines Vera Cáslavská, its highly talented gymnast, who became the symbol of suffering under communist aggression and, perhaps more generally, of small-country resistance to great power domination. While Cáslavská could never drive the Soviets from her homeland, she, her fans, and the people of her country could take pride in her outstanding performance: four gold and two silver medals and the individual title, topping three Soviet stars and two East Germans. Even some other communist athletes cheered her on. After competing in three Olympics (1960, 1964, 1968), Cáslavská had earned seven gold and four silver medals.

Perhaps the most controversial and memorable political statement was that made by Tommie Smith and John Carlos of the United States. Teammates from San Jose State College, they had considered the suggestion of activist sociologist Harry Edwards to boycott the Games to protest mistreatment of blacks and denial of their human and civil rights and had helped him organize in 1967 the Olympic Project for Human Rights (OPHR). Eventually they chose to attend, though basketball great Lew Alcindor (later Kareem Abdul-Jabbar) did not, but they still sought a way to express their deep convictions. Smith and Carlos got their chance when they won gold and bronze medals, respectively, in the 200-meter sprint. On the victory stand, during the national anthem, the two bowed their heads, closed their eyes, and raised their arms straight up, Smith's right and Carlos's left fist covered by black gloves, in the well-known Black Power salute; their shoeless feet showed only long black socks, a symbol of black poverty. For this act they were suspended from their national team and expelled from the Olympic Village. During the awards ceremony, silver medalist Peter Norman of Australia wore a badge supporting the OPHR that he had received in advance from Smith and Carlos, in sympathy with their movement.

As the two militants were preparing to depart Mexico, three of their black teammates, medal winners in the 400-meter final, expressed their sympathy by donning black berets when entering the stadium to receive their medals. After winning the 4×400-meter relay, those three and a fourth runner mounted the victory stand, left hands under their jackets, saluted, and assumed the military at-ease position during the playing of "The Star-Spangled Banner." Bob Beamon later demonstrated his solidarity by wearing black socks while trying another jump following his record leap.

Whether the appeal of 1936 Olympic hero Jesse Owens for black moderation mattered or not, not all U.S. blacks at the Games chose to protest. Wyomia Tyus impressively won the 100-meter sprint, becoming the first woman to win consecutive Olympic sprint titles, and later helped the 400-meter relay team to a gold medal, yet took no political action. Houston's George Foreman not only opposed the protest effort but marched around the ring waving a small U.S. flag after winning the gold medal in heavyweight boxing. Others may just have remained silent out of fear of retaliation or because of money offers from sports agents or manufacturers.

After the Games had ended and the foreign athletes and media had departed, Mexicans assessed the impact of that unique spectacle. Official reports indicate that expenditures were higher than those of Rome in 1960 but well below those of Tokyo in 1964. The total outlay in U.S. dollars was $175,840,000 (93.9 percent spent within Mexico): $53.6 million for sports installations, $16.56 million for city works, $16.08 million for athlete housing in the Miguel Hidalgo Olympic Village, $12.72 million for accommodations for the cultural delegations in the Narciso Mendoza Village, and $76.88 million for organizing committee direct expenditures. All but the last item represented investments in permanent constructions to benefit the city and country in the future and were spent in conjunction with various government agencies such as the Ministry of Public Works and the Department of the Federal District.

To cover these costs the organizing committee derived income from a range of sources: the Mexican government provided a subsidy equivalent to $56,816,000; committee activities, including ticket sales, brought in an additional $20,064,000. Of the latter, $6.41 million derived from international television rights—ABC alone paid $4.5 million for the U.S. market and sent a staff of 450 to handle production and transmission. Another $3.89 million came from foreign services and royalty payments, while an additional $9.76 million was derived from local television rights, concessions, royalties, services, and contributions of in-kind goods and services by various private companies. To carry out its work, the organizing committee for a brief period in October 1968 employed as many as 14,000 people, though the number was generally much less before September and dropped rapidly afterward. Independent of the committee, expenditures of the participating nations were estimated at more than $2 million.

For this price, Mexicans received not just the pleasure and profit of the Games themselves. In theory they indirectly benefited from the increased spending by visiting teams and tourists and an increase in tax collections. They also inherited a technologically superior television and communications system, a few pre-Hispanic archeological ruins exposed during construction, housing units in the two Olympic Villages, numerous works of art created especially for the occasion and left for public enjoyment, an improved athletic infrastructure, vast experience in organizing and conducting an elaborate global festival, and a sense of national achievement and pride.

Simultaneously, Mexicans cheered their largest Olympic squad ever, 300 athletes in eighteen events, who gave their country its best results ever: three each of gold, silver, and bronze medals. Mexicans hoped thereby that the Games did in fact improve their country's international image and stimulate long-term tourism and economic activity. Surely they paid a price, at Tlatelolco and in government spending. But for many, apparently it was a price worth paying. Unfortunately, Mexico has not since matched its athletic performance of 1968, winning infrequently at later Games; even with extensive help from Cuban coaches and advisers, they won only four medals total in the 1988, 1992, and 1996 Summer Games. At Sydney in 2000, they improved to six: one gold (in women's weightlifting; the first gold since 1984), two silver, three bronze. Tied to this athletic stagnation has been apparent incompetent administration of the national sports system and a deterioration of the facilities built or upgraded in the 1960s.

Despite the alarming warnings, threatening outside forces, and obstacles within Mexico City, in the words of Bob Phillips, writing in the British report on the Games: "The ultimate winners of the Games were the Mexicans themselves, and their organisation at every venue was virtually beyond criticism." These Games were, in short, "the biggest and the best" since the Olympics were revived in the modern era. It is hard to disagree.

BIBLIOGRAPHICAL ESSAY

Considerable primary source material and selected printed materials related to the Mexico City Games is contained in the research center of the International Olympic Committee in Lausanne, Switzerland, and in the Avery Brundage Papers in the archives at the University of Illinois, Urbana-Champaign, Illinois. Material related to the work of the organizing committee, the cultural events, the Rhodesian problem, and the Smith and Carlos dismissal may be found, as well as a large collection of newspaper clippings, press releases, and five scrapbooks of material on the South African readmission question. In Mexico, the archives of the organizing committee are in the Archivo General de la Nacion. Additional materials may be consulted at the Centre for Olympic Studies, University of Western Ontario, London, Ontario, Canada.

Among the published sources, the place to begin is Beatrice Trueblood, ed., *Mexico 1968*, 4 vols. (Mexico City, 1968). This is the official report of the organizing committee, and the four volumes cover the country, the organization, the Games, and the cultural Olympiad. Before and during the Games, the committee published *Noticiero Olimpico* to communicate to the public its plans and scheduled events. Beginning in 1966, the committee also published *Mexico 68*, a series of forty newsletters in English, containing promotional material and background information on the Games.

Useful descriptions and analyses by foreign observers come from Bob Phillips, ed., *Official Report of the Olympic Games* (London, 1969), the official British Olympic Committee report; Francisco Echeverria and Jose Maria Mugica, eds., *Juegos Olimpicos— Mexico 68* (Zallia, Spain, 1968), a Spanish summary; and Caetano Carlos Paioli, *Brasil Olimpico* (Sao Paulo, 1985), a Brazilian outlook. The official U.S. Olympic Committee report is Arthur G. Lentz and Frederick Fliegner, eds., *1968 United States Olympic Book* (Lausanne, 1968), while the Canadian version is E. H. Radford and Francis J. Shaughnessy, eds., *Canada Competes at the Olympic Games 1968* (Montreal, 1969).

Additional insights into the construction projects completed for the Games are found in Barclay F. Gordon, *Olympic Architecture: Building for the Summer Games* (New York, 1983). Brazilian experts look at the construction and other technical and scientific aspects of sports performance in Mexico in Arthur Orlando da Costa Ferreira, et al., *Olimpiada-Mexico 68* (Brasilia, 1969). A critical British perspective of the altitude and facilities at these "unfair" Games is found in Christopher Brasher, *Mexico 68. A Diary of the XIXth Olympiad* (London, 1968).

For discussions of the contemporary political atmosphere in Mexico, especially the student protests of 1968 and the government excesses at Tlatelolco, consult Barry Carr, *Marxism and Communism in Twentieth-Century Mexico* (Lincoln, NE, 1992) and Elena Poniatowska, *Massacre in Mexico* (New York, 1975). More on the Mexican context of the 1960s is found in Ariel Rodriguez Kurl, "El otro '68: politica y estilo en la organizacion de los Juegos Olimpicos de la Ciudad de Mexico," *Relaciones* 76, XIX (Autumn 1998): 109–129.

A consideration of how the 1968 Olympics fit into Mexico's long-term sports policy and its connection to larger domestic and foreign affairs is offered by Joseph L. Arbena, "Sport, Development, and Mexican Nationalism, 1920–1970," *Journal of Sport History* 18 (Winter 1991): 350–64. Armandow Satow traces the expanding role of Mexico in the Summer Olympics in a series of twelve articles published in July 1980 in the Mexican newspaper *Uno Mas Uno*. Mexico's long-term failure to build on its medal success of 1968 is highlighted in Francisco Ponce, "Despues de los Juegos Olimpicos el gobierno no ha hecho nada," *Proceso* 1244 (September 3, 2000): 90–91, and Mauricio Mejia, "Mexico nunca aprovecho el entusiasmo de los Juegos de 1968," *Proceso* 1244 (September 3, 2000): 92.

For an understanding of the meaning of the U.S. black protests in relation to the Games, consult Arthur R. Ashe, Jr., *A Hard Road to Glory: A History of the African-American Athlete since 1946* (New York, 1988), the series of introspective pieces contained in *Sports Illustrated* 75 (August 5, 1991), and David K. Wiggins, "'The Year of Awakening': Black Athletes, Racial Unrest and the Civil Rights Movement of 1968," *The International Journal of the History of Sport* 9 (August 1992): 188–208.

An excellent illustrated history of the Games is Antonio Lavin, *Mexico en los Juegos Olimpicos MCMLXVIII* (Tacubaya, Mexico, 1968), which also contains a survey of Mexican participation in the Olympics since 1928. A set of reminiscences of knowledgeable spectators is *Tafnot 68* (Los Altos, CA, 1969), a *Track & Field News* publication based on a tour to the Games sponsored by the magazine.

MUNICH 1972

Maynard Brichford

THE GAMES OF THE TWENTIETH OLYMPIAD

With a long tradition of public interest in athletics and sports, German proponents of Olympism overcame the initial opposition of their national gymnastics societies to the international Olympic Games. By 1896, under the leadership of Dr. Willibald Gebhardt, Germany had joined the modern Olympic Movement. The International Olympic Committee (IOC) awarded the 1916 Games to Berlin, but they were canceled due to World War I. The German team returned to Olympic competition in 1928 and finished second to the United States in total medals. In the summer of 1932, the IOC awarded the 1936 Olympic Games to Berlin. Adolf Hitler's Nazi Party came to power in 1933. Under Hitler, the Olympics became a priority event to showcase the new regime's program to restore the shattered German economy. The racist ideology of the Nazis, however, created many problems and inspired groups in other countries to join a movement to boycott the games. By the effective use of promises and some moderation of official policies, the German hosts avoided the boycott, staged the games, and reaped a propagandistic harvest in worldwide press coverage and Leni Riefenstahl's film *Olympia*. After 1936, the policies of the Nazi dictatorship were a major factor in polarizing the fascist-communist conflict in Europe, which led to World War II in 1939. The Holocaust and the destruction of the German economy during the war prevented German participation in the postwar Olympics until 1952. In 1960, International Olympic Committee president Avery Brundage succeeded in persuading the Federal Republic (West Germany) and the Democratic Republic (East Germany) to send a united team to the Rome games. Though the German states were still occupied by NATO and Warsaw Pact troops respectively, economic aid programs helped restore the West German economy, and the national devotion to sports brought both Germanys back into the Olympic Movement. Meeting in Rome on April 22, 1966, the IOC awarded the 1972 games to the German cities of Munich, Augsburg, and Kiel.

The German Federal Republic hailed the 1972 games as an opportunity to demonstrate the stability of the new federal government, the restoration of the economy, and German dedication to the ideal of peaceful competition in international athletics. In welcoming the athletes of the world, German president Gustav Heinemann acknowledged that the games alone would not "be able to banish disputes and discord, violence and war from the world, even for a short time," but he welcomed them as "a milestone on the road to a new way of life with the aim of realizing peaceful coexistence among peoples." Under the leadership of Organizing Committee chairman Willi Daume, the entire program was planned in meticulous detail. An astute German industrialist, Daume had been chosen for IOC membership in 1957. In April 1969, the Organizing Committee concluded a contract with the American Broadcasting Company (ABC) television network for $7.5 million for television rights and $6 million for the technical costs of producing the broadcasts. The Munich committee combined massive support from governmental agencies with television revenues and promotional fundraising to build a futuristic stadium, Olympic village, sports arenas, and water sports sites. A new subway system connected these facilities with the center of the city. The principal Munich site was built upon piles of rubble dumped after the postwar reconstruction of the bombed city. Under the direction of Otl Aichers, a graphic artist, coordinated colors and a series of sport pictographs were employed to negate the memory of the nationalistic propagandistic themes of the Berlin Olympics.

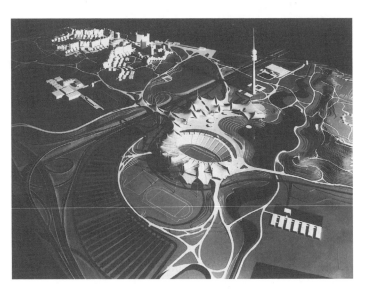

Munich 1972—Architectural model of facilities of the 1972 Summer Games in Munich. Courtesy of University of Illinois Archives, Avery Brundage Collection.

At the IOC meeting before the Games, President Avery Brundage recalled the Olympic controversies of the 1956, 1960, 1964, and 1968 Games and proclaimed that the Olympic Movement was "strong, healthy and flourishing." He conceded that success brought greater "commercial and political intrusion" and urged that the rules relating to amateurism "should be made stronger and enforced more rigorously" (*Olympic Review*, 59 [Oct. 1972]: 346–47, 379). German president Gustav Heinemann acknowledged that the Olympic Games "have at no time been capable of bringing the peoples to refrain from violence." In deploring nationalism, he regretted that the 1936 Berlin games "were abused by the then rulers in Germany for their purposes" (Wallburg-Zgoll, *Die Spiele der XX Olympiade Munchen*, 1972, p. 3).

By 1972, global television coverage had made the Olympics a venue for political protests as well as international athletic competition. Millions of viewers could remember the 1968 riots, boycotts, and black-power protests in Mexico City. Before the Munich Games began, the IOC was faced with a widespread boycott by

African nations and voted to bar the Rhodesian team. With an Olympic team from the German Democratic Republic (East Germany) competing for the first time, the stage was set for competition between the communist East and the capitalist West. Press officer Hans Klein provided luxurious quarters for 7,000 print, radio, and television journalists and technicians, while the athletes were housed in a new Olympic Village, consisting of a series of high-rise apartments interspersed with lower, four-story buildings. Shops and transit facilities were nearby, and care was taken to insure a park-like setting that would make the complex attractive as private housing after the Games.

The Opening Ceremonies occurred before 80,000 spectators on August 26 in the new Olympic stadium. Competition began the following day and lasted until September 11. The United States and the Soviet Union men's track-and-field teams each won six gold medals. Four additional gold medals were evenly divided between the West and East German teams. Finland's Lasse Viren won the 5,000-meter and 10,000-meter races, becoming only the fourth Olympian to do so in the same Games. The U.S. runner Frank Shorter won the marathon.

The East German women won 6 of 14 women's track-and-field events, while the West German women won 4 events. In swimming, Mark Spitz of the United States won seven gold medals, four in individual events and three in team relays. Freestyle specialist Shane Gould of Australia won three gold medals as well as a silver and a bronze in the women's competition. But U.S. swimmer Rick DeMont was disqualified after winning the 400-meter freestyle when traces of an illegal drug were found in his system during routine testing after the race. DeMont had taken asthma medicine the night before the race; team doctors were unaware that it contained a banned drug.

While the track-and-field and swimming events were well covered by the international television networks, the Munich games marked the emergence of women's gymnastics with television coverage of Olga Korbut of the Soviet Union. The diminutive Soviet gymnast, who had made her team only as an alternate, captivated television audiences while winning two gold medals and a silver medal in individual competition. East Europeans dominated the weight lifting and wrestling events. American television viewers were dismayed when only one American won a gold medal in boxing.

In one of the greatest controversies of the Munich Games, the American basketball team lost to the Soviet Union in the finals, ending a 62-game Olympic winning streak for the United States. The disputed 51-50 Soviet victory came after the game was twice resumed after the final horn had apparently sounded. The first resumption was on the order of the head of the International Basketball Federation; the second, amidst great confusion, occurred because of a claim that the clock had not been properly adjusted after the first resumption of play. Impassioned appeals from the Americans, who had been leading 50-49 when the game ended for the first time, were unsuccessful, and members of the U.S. team refused to attend the victory ceremony to accept their silver medals.

In retrospect, the meticulous preparations by the German hosts, the political boycott threats, and the thrilling performances by the athletes were overshadowed by an act of political terrorism. Early on the morning of September 5, eight Palestinians seized eleven members of the Israeli team in a raid on their apartments in the Olympic Village. Two Israelis were killed during the capture. After a day of siege and unsuccessful negotiations in which the terrorists demanded the release of more than 200 Palestinians jailed in Israel and 2 well-known German terrorists, the German police allowed the terrorists to move the hostages to the airport in anticipation of a flight to a Middle Eastern destination. As the terrorists and hostages made their way toward a waiting airplane, the police opened fire. In the ensuing gun battle, all of the remaining hostages and three of the Palestinians were killed.

After stormy meetings of the IOC's executive board and then the full executive committee during the afternoon and evening of September 5, the committee voted to continue the Games. At a memorial service on September 6, German president Heinemann spoke of his grief and sorrow. IOC President Brundage mourned the loss of "our Israeli friends" and observed that "the greater and more important the Olympic Games become, the more they are open to commercial, political, and now criminal pressure." He expressed confidence that the public would agree that the Committee could not "allow a handful of terrorists to destroy this nucleus of international cooperation and good will [which] we have in the Olympic Movement." He declared a day of mourning and announced that "the Games must go on" (Guttman, *The Games Must Go On*, pp. 253–54). Amid continuing criticism from Arab spokesmen and western sport figures and columnists, the Munich Games ended on September 11.

The Munich Games had been a huge success for the television networks, and the resulting bonanza speeded the commercialization and professionalization of the modern Games. The Mexico City Games of 1968 had opened the American market. The efficient German arrangements at Munich facilitated worldwide coverage and produced over $12 million for the IOC and the international athletic federations. The tangible and intangible publicity benefits to Munich and Bavaria have continued. The superb facilities allowed the athletes to compete under favorable conditions and establish many new world records.

On the other hand, these Games are most often remembered for the media coverage of terrorism and security problems at the Olympic venue. The murders by terrorists of members of the Israeli team provided both journalists and academics with new opportunities to condemn Germany, the host committee, the IOC, and the Olympic Movement. The September 5 events at Munich's Olympic Village have a continuing presence in the media of the global village. The August 26, 2002, issue of *Sports Illustrated* contained an article on the shortcomings of the German security efforts, activities of the Black September plotters, and Israeli vengeance missions.

Terrorism, or the intimidation, threatening, or frightening of athletes and spectators by acts of violence at sport spectacles, has trumped the Olympic goals of brotherhood and international understanding. Electronic and print media have devoted increasing attention to threats and acts of terrorism. Security expenditures have escalated at each succeeding Olympic Games. The Games are staged amid global concerns about terrorism and violence. Media spokespersons continue to criticize and second guess officials for a lack of foresight in preventing criminal acts of terrorism and a lack of sensitivity concerning the victims. Media accounts (and sometimes those of government representatives) often confuse the problem by defining terrorism as instances where "freedom fighters," "defenders of a faith," or patriotic, political, and religious zealots justify their violent actions to secure worldwide coverage of another "evil" government or system. In these times, the peacekeeping efforts of the United Nations and the global fraternization occasioned by the Olympic Games seem like feeble gestures compared with the continuous reports of terroristic violence and death. Despite Munich and what has come after, the idealism expressed in the concept of the Olympic Games has survived, and the Games do go on.

BIBLIOGRAPHICAL ESSAY

For primary source material, the Avery Brundage Collection at the University of Illinois Archives, Urbana-Champaign, Illinois, contains about 5,000 documents on the plans, preparations, and events of the games. Of particular interest are three folders of material on the Israeli tragedy and two folders on the Rhodesian problem.

English, French, and German accounts in a pre-Games bulletin, *Olympia in München* (Munich, 1970–72) document the progress of Olympic plans and building construction. A. Louis Wallburg-Zgoll, *Die Spiele der XX. Olympiade Munchen 1972: Hymne an den Sport* (Frankfurt, 1972) is an illustrated, multilingual tribute to the Olympic movement with photographs of facilities and an account of the "German Excavations at Olympia" exhibition in Munich. The organizing committee's official report is *Die Spiele: Der offizielle Bericht . . . der XX. Olympiade München 1972*, edited by Liselott Diem and Ernest Knoesel, 3 vols. (Munich, 1974). American participation is documented in the illustrated *1972 United States Olympic Book* (Lausanne, 1972), edited by C. Robert Paul, Jr. Two pictorial histories with German text, Harry Valérien, *Olympia 1972* (Munich, 1972) and Werner Schneider, *Die Olympischen Spiele 1972* (Stuttgart, Germany, 1974), cover the results of all major events. Werner Trockau, *München Olympia '72* (Alsdorf, Germany, 1972) is a paperback account of the games. Plans for the yachting competition at Kiel are covered in Werner Istel, ed., *Olympic Yachting Kiel '72* (Bielefeld, Germany, 1972). The results are printed in *Kiel '72* (Bielefeld, Germany, 1972). Arnd Krüger, *Sport und Politik* (Hannover, Germany, 1975) discusses the Munich games in the context of the German sports tradition.

For the architecture of the Olympic facilities, see W. D. Thiem, "XX Olympic Games, Munich," *Progressive Architecture* 53 (August 1972): 58–63, which discusses the stadium, sports and swimming arenas, velodrome, media center, and Olympic Village. Also of interest are R. Middleton, "Munich 1972," *Architectural Design* 42 (August 1972): 477–89; A. Best and D. Rowlands, "Munich Olympics," *Design* 285 (September 1972): 29–53; and V. Mahler, *Olympiastadion* 137 (October 1972): 26–33.

The first interpretive account in English after the Games was Hans Lenk's chapter, "The 1972 Munich Olympic Games: A Dilemma?" in Peter J. Graham and Horst Ueberhorst, eds., *The Modern Olympics* (West Point, NY, 1976): 199–208. Allen Guttmann discusses the Munich games at length in his biography of Brundage, *The Games Must Go On* (New York, 1984). The title of Guttmann's book is taken from Brundage's remarks following the Israeli tragedy. Richard Mandell, *The Olympics of 1972, a Munich Diary* (Chapel Hill, NC, 1991) provides an egocentric, aesthetic appreciation of the Olympics embedded in involuted prose and sociological hostility. Nevertheless, it is one of the best accounts of an Olympic spectacle. Mandell's view is that the games were a financial success for Munich and Bavaria but were an ideological and political failure for the IOC and the German government. For the Israeli tragedy, see Serge Groussard, *The Blood of Israel: The Massacre of the Israeli Athletes, the Olympics, 1972* (New York, 1975). Jim McKay, *My*

Wide World (New York, 1973) recalls the Munich Games from his position as ABC's television host; it was McKay who kept millions of viewers informed as the tragedy unfolded. Finally, for a contemporary pictorial review and reaction, see *Life* magazine, September 15 and September 22, 1972.

The Munich terrorist tragedy has inspired two films: *21 Hours at Munich* (1982), directed by William A. Graham, and *Triumph and Tragedy: The 1972 Munich Olympics* (1992), directed by Bud Greenspan. The Graham film is a made-for-television production that utilized the actual Munich locations, while the Greenspan film puts the director's very personal touch on the subject.

MONTREAL 1976

Bruce Kidd

THE GAMES OF THE TWENTY-FIRST OLYMPIAD

The 1976 Olympics were experienced and have been remembered as a kaleidoscope of contradictory narratives and outcomes. Promised as modest, self-financing Games, they ended up with such monumental facilities, constructed with such little regard for their cost, that the Montreal Games have become the byword for gargantuan extravagances. Yet the venues proved to be admirably suited for athletes and spectators, and the events were extremely well organized, enabling superb performances in virtually every sport. The heavy military security, the clumsy censoring of the Arts and Culture Program, and a last-minute walkout by African nations had little effect upon the mood of the participants; an international, carnivalesque atmosphere reigned throughout. The Games provided a heady stimulus to the development of Canadian and Quebec sport and fitness and pioneered the development of new sources of Olympic revenues.

Montreal was a fitting site for Canada's first Games. Standing at the junction of the St. Lawrence and Ottawa Rivers, it was founded in 1643 near a long-established Iroquois village as the jumping-off point for French exploration of the interior. It quickly became the center of the North American fur trade. By the nineteenth century, the Scottish and English merchants who emigrated after the French and Indian War ended in 1763 had made it the leading economic, political, and cultural center of the new Dominion of Canada and the cradle of Canadian sports. The male, middle-class Anglo-Montreal citizens who codified and publicized the first sports rules started an Olympic Club in 1842, and held a Montreal Olympics in 1844. Pierre de Coubertin visited their successors during his North American field trip in 1889–90 and they took an early interest in his Games. A Montreal police constable, Etienne DesMarteau, won Canada's first official Olympic gold medal in 1904, and Montreal citizens helped create the Canadian Olympic Committee (now Association) two years later. They bid for the 1932, 1956 (Winter and Summer), and 1972 Olympics, before beating Los Angeles and Moscow to win the right to stage them in 1976 at the IOC's 70th session in Amsterdam in 1970.

But the politics of language, nationalism, and regionalism were to confound organizers' hopes for a smooth preparation of facilities and programs. During the 1960s, Quebec society was transformed by a broad state-led secularization and modernization often referred to as the "quiet revolution." Seeking to be *maîtres chez nous* (masters of our house), French-speaking Quebecois, the descendants of the original European settlers, aggressively challenged the Anglo-Canadian elite's economic and cultural hegemony, particularly the expectation that everyone speak English in the workplace and commerce. Though united in the desire for language rights, French-Canadians were divided about the best strategy to advance their interests within the Canadian federation. Quebec nationalists sought French unilingualism and ever greater powers for the provincial legislature— their national government. Federalists like Pierre Trudeau, who became prime minister in 1968, championed a bilingual pan-Canadianism.

Montreal 1976—The Olympic Games foster friendships that transcend racial and ethnic barriers, as shown in this photo of Canadian and Asian athletes shaking hands. Courtesy of the International Centre for Olympic Studies, University of Western Ontario.

The largest and most visible English-Canadian presence was in Montreal, where they made up just 16 percent of the population. (French speakers comprised 64 percent, and those from other backgrounds 20 percent.) The city was the site of the fiercest debates about the national question, the most volatile demonstrations for and against language laws, and a small but growing number of bombing attacks by Quebec revolutionaries against English corporations and federal institutions. Nationalism also fueled a growing militancy among the working class. These tensions evoked a deep resentment in the English-speaking majority in other parts of Canada. In the western provinces, many opposed federal bilingualism and felt Montreal and Quebec were unfairly favored, while western economic problems were ignored. On this unpropitious terrain, the Trudeau government decided against financial assistance for Montreal's bid (though it promised full support for Vancouver's simultaneous bid for the 1976 Winter Games).

Charismatic Montreal mayor Jean Drapeau made oratorical virtue out of necessity in his presentation to the IOC, promising low-cost Games. But his real ambition was to create a lasting symbol of *la survivance*, the will of French Canada to survive two centuries of English-Canadian attempts at assimilation. (After Paris, Montreal is the largest French-speaking city in the world.) But he still needed federal funding for the necessary facilities. A succession of political crises hardened the federal government against Drapeau's increasingly more urgent appeals. In October 1970, the revolutionary Front de Libération de Québec (FLQ) kidnapped a British consul and a Quebec cabinet minister, provoking Trudeau to declare martial law. In 1972, a general strike led by nationalist trade unions rekindled the anxieties in and about Quebec. In the federal election of that year, Western alienation reduced Trudeau's Liberal Party to minority government status. It was only in 1973, when the Province of Quebec reluctantly accepted responsibility for any deficit, that the Trudeau government agreed to create a lottery and a coin and stamp program to provide revenue for the Games. The organizers could finally budget with confidence. But the clash of nationalisms had cost them 34 months of precious time.

Preparations were further complicated by the ambitious design Drapeau had encouraged French architect Roger Taillibert to devise for the main facilities in Olympic Park. Olympic Stadium was to include a 50-story tower and a retractable roof. The engineering for the velodrome, a "giant arc of a roof sweeping over glass walls, rising higher and higher with no visible means of support, then sloping back to earth," was among the most complex in the world. Construction was frequently disrupted by Taillibert's penchant for last-minute changes, the incompetence of contractors hired because of political connections, strikes and stoppages in the context of continuing federalist-separatist and English-French tensions, and rapid inflation. Most of the key decisions were made in secret by Mayor Drapeau. There was virtually no accountability to anyone else. It was only when the province assumed full responsibility for construction in November 1975 that significant progress began to be made. Uncertainly about whether enough would be completed in time kept the IOC and everyone else on tenterhooks until a few weeks before the Opening Ceremony. (As it was, Olympic Stadium was not finally completed until 1987.)

There was no end to the controversy. First came the China question. In 1970, as part of the bid, the Trudeau government undertook to honor the fundamental IOC requirement that it grant entry to all IOC-recognized participants, "pursuant to the normal regulations." Few at the time realized that this nebulous phrase bore any substance. But several months prior to the Games, the government indicated that the usual regulations would be used to bar athletes and coaches from the Republic of China (Taiwan), in accordance with the one-China policy it had adopted in 1970. A compromise was reached only 48 hours before the opening ceremony: the delegation would be allowed to enter Canada on condition that they be designated as being from Taiwan at the Games. At that point, the Taiwanese withdrew.

During the same week, while African runners were turning in record performances on the practice track at Olympic Park, African sport leaders sought some gesture of condemnation for the New Zealand rugby tour of South Africa then taking place in the aftermath of the apartheid regime's brutal suppression of the children's revolt in Soweto. The IOC chose to do nothing, arguing that rugby was not an Olympic sport. This seeming insensitivity, at a time when there were only 5 black IOC Members in the 41 NOCs from Africa, so enraged the African political leadership that it ordered its athletes home. Twenty-two teams (including Iraq and Guyana) sadly but proudly departed, some after participating in the preliminary events. (Seven other African NOCs did not send teams to Montreal.) The walkout had a sobering effect upon the international community. Within days, the two largest federations—International Amateur Athletic Federation and la Fédération Internationale de Football Association—expelled white South Africa from their memberships. The IOC soon became a strong ally of the international campaign against apartheid sports.

The final embarrassment occurred four days before the opening ceremony. Shortly after midnight, work crews dismantled and destroyed an outdoor art and photographic exhibit along the marathon route that was mildly critical of the city's wholesale demolition of single-family housing, including a number of grand nineteenth-century mansions, to clear the way for high-rise apartments and commercial offices. (A provincial court compensated the artists five years later.) It underscored the mayor's dictatorial style and the antagonism among the Olympics, conservationists, environmentalists, and community advocates of alternative public investments, which had also plagued the Games from the beginning.

When the Olympics finally opened on July 17, 4,834 male and 1,251 female athletes from 88 nations remained in the lists. The turmoil and conflict of the preparation period were quickly, if temporarily, forgotten.

In the first full day of competition, a tiny, seemingly fearless 14-year-old Romanian gymnast captured the public imagination. Nadia Comaneci scored an unprecedented perfect 10 on the uneven parallel bars, then immediately followed that feat with another perfect 10 on the balance beam. During the rest of the competition, she earned another five 10s and won the all-round title, the bars and the beam, and the hearts of the live and television audience. The Soviet women were equally breathtaking. Nelli Kim also recorded two 10s, and with the graceful Ludmilla Tourischeva and ebullient Olga Korbut, extended their country's unbeaten record in Olympic team competition to seven straight championships. Though overlooked in the media frenzy around Comaneci and her rivals, the men's competition was just as exciting, with the team title decided by the final routine on the horizontal bars. Mituso Tsukahara scored a 9.9 to bring Japan its fifth straight crown. The individual champion was Soviet Nikolai Andrianov who took home four gold, two silver, and one bronze medals.

Performances were also electrifying at the Olympic pool. World records were smashed or equaled in all but 3 of the 26 events. The United States dominated the men's competition, winning 12 of 13 events, while women from the German Democratic Republic (GDR) won 11 of 13 events, often in times once thought unattainable. Petra Thümer's new record of 4:09.89 in the 400-meter freestyle would have taken the silver medal in the men's event in Mexico just eight years earlier. The GDR's 17-year-old Kornelia Ender was the overall star, winning an unprecedented four gold medals (and a silver in the medley relay), including two in world-record times within 27 minutes of each other.

In rowing, relative novice Pertti Karppinen of Finland took the men's single sculls in a masterfully paced race, overtaking the favorites in the last few meters. The GDR won five of the men's and four of the women's races, placing in every event.

Despite the absence of the Africans from the running events, track and field produced some stirring contests. Caribbean runners Hasely Crawford of Trinidad in the 100 meters, Don Quarrie of Jamaica in the 200 meters, and Alberto Juantorena of Cuba in the 400 and 800 meters were popular winners of the men's sprints. Though favored in the 400, the tall, explosively striding Juantorena was not expected to have either the stamina or the tactical experience for the longer race. But in the final, he led from the break, fought off all challengers, and won convincingly in a new world-record time. Four days later he was equally impressive in the

400, winning in the fastest time ever recorded at sea level. Finland's imperturbable Lasse Viren achieved another remarkable double in the 5,000 and 10,000 meters (repeating his victories at Munich), outdistancing his rivals with brazenly gradual—but powerfully sustained—accelerations over the final laps. World records were achieved by America's Edwin Moses (400-meter hurdles), Sweden's Anders Garderud (steeplechase), America's Bruce Jenner (decathlon), and Hungary's Miklos Nemeth (javelin).

Among the women, the GDR was in a class by itself, winning 9 events and 19 medals overall. In the pentathlon, the three GDR competitors—Siegrun Siegl, Christine Laser, and Burglinde Pollak—finished just five points apart. The most popular victor was Poland's 30-year-old Irene Szewinska (Kirszenstein), already a six-time Olympic medallist, who pulled away from 18-year-old rival Christina Brehmer of the GDR in the last 100 meters of the 400 meters to win handily and set a new world record. The Soviet Tatanya Kazankina not only won her specialty, the 1,500 meters, but captured a hotly contested 800 meters, in which she had just been entered on the final day, in world-record time.

Montreal was an excellent Games for spectators. The spacious Olympic Park, with four main venues and two practice tracks, handy eating establishments, souvenir kiosks, and picnic areas immediately adjacent to the Olympic Village; the efficient Metro and bus system; and several open, gregarious entertainment quarters facilitated a continuous, convivial festival. Olympic veterans say Montreal was the most spirited Games of the post-World War II period. But the Games did not give tourism the expected boost. Despite 3,250,000 paid admissions, few hotels were completely full, and during the Games taxi drivers staged a one-day tie-up of downtown traffic to protest the loss of business to the organizing committee's 1,035-car fleet. Many visitors were athletes and coaches themselves, who came to watch, trade pins, and talk—not to spend money. They camped, rode their bicycles, and ate packed sandwich lunches. Those who relied on television enjoyed greater and more sophisticated coverage than ever before. In Canada, the Canadian Broadcasting Corporation telecast 175 hours, five times what it had shown from Munich.

More than half the entered teams took medals home from Montreal, but few Games have been so dominated by the athletic superpowers. Taken together, the U.S.S.R., the United States, the two Germanys, and Japan captured 60 percent of the medals. The Soviet model of sports development, cloned in its European satellites and Cuba, claimed half of all medal winners. The most noteworthy results were achieved by the GDR. With athletes drawn from a relatively closed population of just 17 million, it won 40 gold medals, just seven less than the Soviet Union and six more than the United States (although the Americans won more medals overall). While it is now evident that many of those victories were enabled by performance-enhancing drugs, as was alleged at the time, they were also achieved by the dogged application of sports science to the material conditions of performance, the development of an extensive school sports system, and a regime of hard training. In the wake of the Games, a growing number of sport leaders beat a path to the German College of Physical Culture in Leipzig, where the GDR coaches were trained.

Competition for women in three sports—basketball, handball, and rowing—and four events were added to the program in Montreal. The example of so many strong, healthy, athletically talented women helped demolish the myths of female biological frailty, which frustrated the growing demands of western women for sporting opportunities. But the messages were not unambiguously enabling. The celebrated success of Comaneci accelerated the infantalization of women's gymnastics and body image begun by Olga Korbut, the International Gymnastics Federation, and the American Broadcasting Company in Munich. The statuesque Ludmilla Tourischeva, the champion Comaneci dethroned, was the last physically mature female gymnastic star to win an Olympic gold medal.

The Games provided an important stimulus to both Quebec and Canadian sport and fitness. In Montreal, they left behind an impressive array of training halls, administrative offices, and skilled and confident Francophone leaders. It was the beginning of a proud new age for Quebec sports. Although some of the new facilities proved too expensive to maintain for sports, the much-criticized Olympic Park has become a successful tourist attraction. At the same time, the stimulus of the Games persuaded federal decision makers to replace the inefficient, volunteer administration of the Olympic sports in Canada with a state-designed and financed professional infrastructure. The resulting Canadian sport system has significantly improved opportunities for high performance athletes. Federal spending on the Olympic sports increased five times between 1970 and 1976. The Games also contributed to the growing popularity of physical fitness. Although measurement is admittedly imprecise, national surveys indicate a 41 percent increase in participation between 1976 and 1981.

Montreal also stimulated new sources of revenue for Olympic Games and the Olympic Movement. The Organizing Committee's innovative approach to sponsorships, inviting competitive bidding for two-year agreements (compared with the three-month contracts in Munich), and granting exclusivity in product categories, paved the way for the heady commercialization of the 1980s. Its success in obtaining separate contracts with the television networks for technical services, revenue that was not fully shared with the IOC, eventually drew the IOC into negotiations in the interest of maximizing joint revenues. The Olympic lottery generated $235 million for the Games, seven times the $32 million expected, thereby opening a new source of revenue for cash-starved governments.

Total revenue for the 1976 Olympics was $430 million, against operating expenses of $207 million. If staging the Games alone is considered, the 1976 Games generated a surplus of $223 million. It is only when the capital cost of building the facilities is entered that the shortfall became $1.2 billion. All three levels of government have contributed to the reduction of this debt. Montreal citizens finally paid off the city's share, raised through an annual property tax surcharge, in 1993. Consumers of tobacco in Quebec are still paying a special provincial Olympic levy. While the original obligations have been paid off, the funds are now used to maintain and upgrade the facilities. The staggering burden of the Montreal facilities has led the IOC to revise the rules for Olympic financing, so that only facility rentals can be charged to a Games budget. The architect of this approach, Vice President Richard Pound of Montreal, contends that the host communities get the benefit of facility after-use, so they should be expected to pay the lion's share of their cost. The nightmare of debt, during a period when the expectations for public services and the fiscal difficulties of governments are both increasing, has forced other Olympic boosters to be much more careful and accountable in their proposals for Games. In Calgary, the lessons of Montreal contributed to a much more open approach to planning the XV Olympic Winter Games and a genuine attempt to involve citizens in staging them. In Toronto, they persuaded the city council to develop a social contract, including public and private sector obligations to share in any debt, to govern its 1996 bid. Ironically, as the cost and complexity of staging the Olympics continue to rise, the necessity for a democratic discussion and decision on whether to and how to stage the Games might well be Montreal's most important legacy.

BIBLIOGRAPHICAL ESSAY

The Canadian Olympic Collection in the Rare Books and Special Collections Division of McGill University contains the published documents from the city of Montreal and the Comité d'Oganizateur des Jeux Olympiques (COJO). The Web site is http://digital.library.mcgiull.ca/olympics/frames.php. The collection was recently transferred to McGill after the Canadian Olympic Committee closed its archives in Montreal. Information about the collection is still being transferred to the McGill database. The remaining records are accessible but uncataloged in the Archives Nationales du Quebec in Montreal.

The National Archives of Canada (NAC) in Ottawa contains files on the federal government's responsibilities for Olympic security and the Olympic lottery, and the personal papers of COJO commissioner general and Loto Canada president Roger Rousseau. The NAC also has a complete set of the videotapes of the television coverage, and an extensive photo collection of the Games. The relevant Web sites are http://www.archives.ca and http://www.nlc-bnc.ca/olympiens.

The three-volume *Report of the Commission of Inquiry into the Cost of the 21st Olympiad*, by Albert A. Malouf (n.p., 1980) documents mistakes, but Nick auf der Maur's muckraking *The Billion Dollar Game* (1975) is much more illuminating. There are also useful chapters on the Games and the Quebec political background in Brian McKenna and Susan Purcell, *Drapeau* (Markham, Ont., 1981). The annual reports of the Olympic Installation Board in Montreal detail the special Olympic taxes on the Games debt.

A useful window on the pan-Canadian politics of the Games is provided by the Parliamentary Debates on Bills C-196 (1973) and C-63 (1975), which provided federal financing for the Games, and Bill C-85 (1975), which gave the government temporary arbitrary powers to strengthen security for the Games. See also Rick Baka, "Canadian Federal Government Policy and the 1976 Olympics," *Journal of the Canadian Association of Health, Physical Education, and Recreation* 42, 4 (1976): 52–60; C. E. S. Franks et al., "Sport and Canadian Diplomacy," *International Journal* 43, 4 (1988): 665–82; and Bruce Kidd, "The Culture Wars of the Montreal Olympics," *International Review for the Sociology of Sport* 27 (1992): 151–64.

Doug Gilbert's almost daily reports and columns in the *Gazette* (Montreal) from 1970 to 1977 constitute an extremely comprehensive source for the developments, controversies, events, and evaluations of the Games. In July 1991, the *Gazette* published David Stubbs's 17-part follow-up series on the stars of the Games.

Novelist Jack Ludwig's *Five Ring Circus* (Toronto, 1976) and John MacAloon's "Festival, Ritual, and Television," in Roger Jackson and Tom McPhail, eds., *The Olympic Movement and the Mass Media* (Calgary, 1989) provide the best accounts of the street life and festival.

Robert Barney, et al., *Selling the Five Rings: The International Olympic Committee and the Rise of Olympic Commercialism* (Salt Lake City, UT, 2002), ably analyzes the television negotiations. Other media analyses include Leon Chorbajian and Vince

Mosco, "1976 and 1980 Olympic Boycott Coverage," *Arena Review* 5,3 (1981): 3–28; R. H. McCollum and D. F. McCollum, "Analysis of ABC TV Coverage of the 21st Olympiad Games," in Jeffrey Segrave and Donald Chu, eds., *Olympism* (Champaign, IL, 1981); and Yakov Rabkin and David Franklin, "Soviet/Canadian Press Perspectives on the Montreal Olympics," in *The Olympic Movement and the Mass Media* (Calgary, 1989). The CBC's five-volume commentators' guide, *From Athens to Montreal* (Toronto, 1976), was prepared by Jack Sullivan.

MOSCOW 1980

James Riordan

THE GAMES OF THE TWENTY-SECOND OLYMPIAD

The Moscow Summer Olympic Games of 1980 were remarkable in many ways. For a start, this was the first time in the history of the modern Olympics that a Communist country had been selected to host the Games. As subsequent events were to show, the choice proved controversial. The entry of Soviet troops into Afghanistan in December 1979, just over six months before the Games were to open, provided "the peg on which to hang the boycott coat," as one anti-Moscow campaigner put it. The Moscow boycott campaign was launched by U.S. president Jimmy Carter and supported by the British, West German, Norwegian, Canadian, and Japanese governments.

Moscow also witnessed the change of the International Olympic Committee (IOC) presidency from Lord Killanin to Juan Antonio Samaranch, the entry of new nations into the Olympic arena—Angola, Mozambique, Vietnam, and Zimbabwe (whose all-white women's field hockey team won a gold medal)—and the first black woman to win a gold medal in a field event (Maria Colon, javelin). It was also the first Olympics in two decades that was not followed by a Paralympics—not through boycott, but because the Soviet authorities refused to host Games for the disabled (since no disabled sport existed in the Soviet Union).

The IOC selected Moscow as the 1980 Olympic site at its 75th Session on October 23, 1974, in Vienna; Moscow won the vote comfortably over its sole competitor, Los Angeles. At the time many felt the USSR worthy of the honor: not only was it the most successful and versatile nation in Olympic history in sporting performance, but it was considered to have done much in Olympic forums to enhance the preeminent role of sport and the Olympic Movement. It was a popular choice with both East European states (but not with all communist nations—China turned down its invitation) and many Third World countries, whose political and sports causes had gained Soviet support in such matters as the banning of South Africa from the Olympic Movement.

As for Western governments, despite their distaste for communism and the Soviet human rights record, it was generally thought that the appointment of Moscow as Olympic host might somehow make a contribution to the process of détente then underway. At the very least, it might encourage some liberalization within the country or even expose it to the world as a cynical violator of the Helsinki Accords.

Inasmuch as sport was, in effect, a political institution in the USSR, it was a relatively straightforward task to prioritize, within the centrally planned system, the building of Olympic amenities by July 1980. In the five-year breathing space between 1975 and 1980, *Gosplan*, the state planning agency, constructed or reconstructed the necessary facilities in the five Soviet cities scheduled for Olympic events: Moscow as central venue; Tallinn, Estonia's capital on the Baltic, for yachting events; and the three cities in which preliminary soccer matches were to be played: St. Petersburg (then Leningrad); Kiev, capital of the Ukraine; and Minsk, capital of Belorussia. The choice of five cities representing different Soviet republics (subsequently to become capitals of independent states after 1991) was a novel attempt to share Olympic kudos over a wide geographical area. By the summer of 1979, virtually all preparations were complete and a dress rehearsal was held at the Seventh USSR Spartakaid Finals, involving 10,000 athletes, including over 2,000 invited from 84 foreign nations.

Moscow had adopted the motto of the Roman architect Vitruvius—"Utility, Durability, and Beauty"—in developing its Olympic construction plan. It was claimed that all the new facilities had been envisaged in the Master Plan for the Development and Reconstruction of Moscow; the sports complexes were therefore distributed widely about the city so as to ensure their future use by all Muscovites.

Major events, including the Opening and Closing Ceremonies, were held in the Lenin Central Stadium, which had been built in 1956 (on the site of the prerevolutionary Moscow River Yacht Club) but had been refurbished with new floodlights, electronic scoreboards, a Tartan track surface, and seating for 103,000 people. Swimming, diving, boxing, and basketball events were held in the new Olympic Palace of Sport, on Peace Avenue (*Prospect miria*), covering nearly 16 acres. The swimming area, with its 50-meter pool, accommodated 7,500 spectators, and the diving area held 4,500, while the partitioned boxing and basketball halls seated 18,000 and 16,000 fans, respectively.

The rowing, kayaking, and canoeing events took place on the Krylatskoe Rowing Canal built seven years previously for the 1973 European Rowing Championships; it had a basin 2,300 meters long and 125 meters wide, enabling eight sculls (or, as the official handout put it, "8 skulls") or 11 kayaks or canoes to race simultaneously. Cycling was held on a newly constructed wooden track (unhappily, of Siberian larch, which subsequently warped badly) in a velodrome at the same venue, with seating for 6,000.

Also new was the trade-union-run Bitsa Park Equestrian Center, covering more than 110 acres. Since equestrianism was a sport unknown to the great bulk of Muscovites (apart from thoroughbred racing at the Hippodrome Racetrack), it is hard to believe that the facility was one that actually fitted in with the Master Plan for Moscow.

Other sports planned for various parts of Moscow included wrestling and fencing at the Central Army Sports Club; handball at the Dinamo and Sokoloniki stadiums; gymnastics, volleyball, and judo at the Central Stadium's Palace of Sport;

shooting at the Dinamo Club's Mytishchi base; field hockey at Dinamo's smaller arena; weight lifting at the Izmailova Palace of Sport; and soccer at various venues (the Lenin and Dinamo stadiums in Moscow, Dinamo stadiums in Kiev and Minsk, and the Kirov Stadium in St. Petersburg).

The Olympic Village in southwest Moscow, which subsequently became a housing estate, was a 15-minute ride from the Lenin Stadium and housed 12,000 athletes and officials in 18 16-story apartment blocks covering 263 acres. Two athletes were officially allocated to each room in the two- and three-room apartments, but owing to the boycott, many people did not have to share a room. Other amenities in the village included a 1,200-seat theater and a concert hall, two 250-seat cinemas, a dance hall, a disco, a library and—novel to Moscow—amusement arcades. Sports facilities included tennis courts, swimming pools, saunas, and a training track. Another dent in Soviet mores was the Center for Religious Ceremonies, containing separate rooms for the various religions. Security measures were rigorously implemented on entry into the village, which perhaps was just as well (in keeping Soviets out), for the food supplied by the cafes and restaurants (catering 4,000 diners simultaneously) was far superior to what most Soviet people had ever seen.

The distaste in some Western circles for communism and the USSR found expression in a spate of anti-Moscow articles in the press that appeared as soon as the 1980 venue became known. Reports said that the authorities were planning to remove all schoolchildren, prostitutes, and dissidents from the capital in time for the Games, a claim that was to be proved correct in the case of the last two categories. In Great Britain, British Olympic Association (BOA) officials struggled against what they perceived as a political campaign led by the right wing, supported by certain religious and human rights groups, and exploited by some MPs (members of Parliament), who took advantage of the publicity an anti-Olympic issue generated.

A new period in the anti-Moscow Games campaign began with the entry of Soviet troops into Afghanistan on December 27, 1979. It provided the campaigners with precisely the ammunition they needed. As Richard Palmer testified, "It was the most intensive pressure that had even been applied to sport." Following President Carter's lead, the British prime minister, Margaret Thatcher, called on the BOA on February 17, 1980, to "approach the IOC urgently and propose that the Summer Games be moved from the Soviet Union." A few days later, she appealed to British athletes, over the heads of their national federations and the BOA, to boycott the Games, declaring that athletes had the same responsibility for the defense and preservation of freedom as other citizens. President Carter's special envoy on the boycott campaign, Lloyd Cutler, began his peregrinations around the world to urge other nations to join the U.S. boycott.

The pressure now became intense. In Britain, Dr. Robert Runcie, the new archbishop of Canterbury, published a strong statement against athletes taking part in the Moscow Olympics, as did other church leaders—although the Methodists and Baptists left the decision up to the consciences of individuals. Big business began to withdraw offers of financial aid. The television networks, which had already spent millions of dollars on broadcast rights, announced that coverage of the Games would be drastically cut and not be shown during peak viewing hours.

Where Olympic associations did not join the boycott, governments put every obstacle in the way of athletes intending to participate in the Games. For example, the British government announced that special leave would not be granted to civil servants and army personnel hoping to compete in the Games. The foreign office withdrew the liaison services of the senior diplomat at the British Embassy in Moscow who had been expected to act as British Olympic attaché, a post that traditionally went to a security forces person. The House of Commons approved of the boycott by a 315–117 vote, although a public-opinion poll showed 70 percent of the public in favor of British athletes going to Moscow. It was virtually impossible to have a dissenting voice heard in the media. Such was the hysteria that the British government prevented the review in the press of books with a contrary view, such as James Riordan's *Soviet Sport: Background to the Olympics.*

Despite all this pressure, the BOA decided by a 19–1 vote, with four abstentions, "for immediate acceptance of the invitation to Moscow." Subsequently, the yachting, field hockey, and equestrian federations voted against going to Moscow.

Like other Olympic associations that defied the U.S. boycott call, the BOA had to overcome enormous difficulties. Given the lack of funds, the troubled domestic atmosphere, and the government's refusal to allow the British state airline, British Airways, to fly anyone or anything involved in the Olympics to Moscow, British athletes and officials had to be ferried out to Moscow and back home only for the duration of their events, not for the whole Games. As a concession to the boycott campaign, it was decided that only the British *chef de mission* would take part in the opening ceremony and that the Union Jack would not be raised nor the national anthem played in any ceremonies.

On May 27, 1980, the IOC announced that 85 countries had accepted invitations to compete in Moscow. Of the twenty-two nations that had won two or more gold medals in the 1972 and 1976 Olympics, only five had decided not to compete in Moscow: the United States, West Germany, Norway, Kenya, and Japan. The most conspicuous break in the boycott was paradoxically made by Western Europe, nations closely allied to the United States. In fact, the British team, consisting of 326 persons, was the fourth largest at the Games. Of course, in Britain there was no official government welcome home for the athletes and no recognition for gold medalists.

Like its quid pro quo, the Communist boycott at the 1984 Los Angeles Games, the Moscow boycott was an abject failure. The Games went on, scarcely diminished, and Olympism gained in moral stature, while the boycott's protagonists soon disappeared from the historical stage.

All through the Games the Soviet organizers arranged cultural events featuring major orchestras, ballet and opera companies, folk troupes, and theater companies. Concerts were held both in traditional venues, such as the Bolshoi and the Tchaikovsky Concert Hall, as well as in the concert hall of the Olympic Village. Most athletes and team officials stayed away from many of the events, and the halls were more than half empty, especially in the Olympic Village. This was due not only to pressures of sports preparation and athletic tastes, but also to the fact that many delegations were forced to fly in and out owing to lack of funds because of the boycott. Nevertheless, the aim to inject a much-needed cultural ingredient into the Olympics was appreciated by those who took advantage of the cultural feast.

The cultural tone of the Olympics was set at the opening ceremony. At 4:00 P.M. on Saturday, July 19, the Games were opened by Soviet President Leonid Brezhnev, accompanied in the VIP delegation by Lord Killanin, IOC president; Juan Antonio Samaranch, the president-elect; and Ignaty Novikov, chairman of the organizing committee. Dmitri Shostakovich's *Festive Overture* had been chosen as the Olympic fanfare, heralding the entry into the Lenin Stadium of Greek chariots and young men and women wearing white Greek tunics, scattering rose petals along the track. They were followed by the parade of participants—most marching under their nation's flag, but some marching beneath the Olympic flag and represented by a single token member or a Soviet substitute. A special welcome was given to new members of the Olympic family: Mozambique, Angola, Vietnam, Laos, and Zimbabwe.

At the end of the parade, eight athletes carried out the unfurled Olympic flag and it was hoisted up the flagpole, with 22 snow-white doves released into the air. The Olympic torch bearer now appeared: the three-time Olympic triple-jump champion, Victor Saneyev. He handed it over to the lofty basketball captain, Sergei Belov, who climbed up a pathway formed by white boards held on the heads of spectators sitting in the east stands. Once the flame was lit, the gymnast Nikolai Andrianov pronounced the Olympic oath on behalf of the athletes, and the former wrestling champion Alexander Medved spoke the Olympic oath on behalf of the judges and officials. A unique feature of this ceremony was the "Greetings from Space": a television picture of two Soviet cosmonauts that appeared on the electronic screen as they conveyed greetings from outer space to all athletes. Then began the colorful, beautiful, and multi-ethnic folklore display by over 16,000 artists from all over the country—so rich and moving that one hardly dared blink for fear of missing something.

The closing ceremony was almost as exhilarating, culminating with the launching of a giant inflated Misha Bear, the Games' symbol, into the Moscow night air (he came down in the grounds of nearby Moscow University).

For Western nations, the Moscow Olympics and the boycott controversy brought to a head some of the tensions that had long been latent in the Olympic movement and in society generally. The first was the action of traditionalist, anti-communist groups who wished to see the abandonment of the Olympic Games as they were constituted. As long as the West was winning and could dictate sports policy, there was never a suggestion that the Olympics were too big, too political, too nationalistic, or unworthy of a particular country, even including Nazi Germany in 1936. The loss of this supremacy in sports forums caused such groups to conclude that the time had come to sever links with the Olympic movement and to form a West-oriented grouping of sports nations. Although these groups were defeated, the danger still exists of them seizing other international incidents to destroy the Olympic Games and fragment the structure of world sport.

The second tension that the boycott controversy made manifest in the West was that between the traditional amateur-elitist and the ascendant commercial-professional ethos. In those Western states attending the Moscow Games, it was the former that won the day. For traditional (and conservative) figures like British Olympic president Sir Dennis Follows, the marquis of Exeter, and Lord Killanin, the dominant credo in regard to sport had always been that it should be divorced from politics, government interference, and commercialism and should also represent a firm commitment to the Olympic ideal. British and French governments tended to espouse that philosophy too, particularly as it absolved them of any financial commitment to sport. The year 1980 changed all that. The Moscow Olympics marked the first time in which the democracies of the West became deeply involved in the government of sport. The notion that Avery Brundage had perpetuated for years, that international sport competition, like the Olympics, could flourish separately from governmental activity, was finally laid to rest.

If the consequences of the Moscow Olympics were dramatic for Western states, they were resounding for the states of Eastern Europe, particularly the host country, the USSR. After its moment of sporting glory, the Soviet Union rapidly began to fall apart. Two years after the Games, Brezhnev died; five years after the Games, Mikhail Gorbachev came to power with his radically new policies of perestroika and glasnost. Nine years after the Games, the communist edifice crumbled throughout the eight nations of Eastern Europe; the Soviet Union followed suit and ceased to exist as a unitary state in late 1991.

It would be a bit extravagant to blame the Moscow Olympics for the demise of communism. And yet for many citizens of communist states in Eastern Europe and the Soviet Union, the 1980 Olympics brought tensions to a head, especially as the public was able to see the tensions in its own backyard. It is noteworthy that when the revolutions swept across Eastern Europe in late 1989, there was an intense debate about sport. Far from being at the periphery of politics, sport was right at the center. In Romania, athletes manned the barricades, with Dinamo Club members defending their patron, the Securitate, in opposition to army athletes of Steaua, whose gold medalists in shooting were among those firing on the secret police. Romanian rugby captain Florica Marariu and teammate Radu Dadac were just two of the sports heroes who fell in battle. In East Germany, sports stars such as Katarina Witt, Roland Matthes, and Kornelia Ender all complained of having their homes and cars vandalized by erstwhile fans angry at the privileges of the stars and their close identification with the communist regime.

The events of 1989 and afterward in the one-time communist states demonstrated that to many people, sport, and particularly elite Olympic sport, was identified in the popular consciousness with privilege, paramilitary coercion (the two largest and best-endowed sports clubs in all communist states were the armed forces clubs and Dinamo, the sports club sponsored and financed by the Security Forces), hypocrisy (having to pretend that communist athletes were amateur when everyone knew they were paid by the state and given either army officer sinecures or fictitious employment at industrial plants), and distorted priorities (the enormous sums of money that were lavished on sports stars and the Moscow Olympics, while sports facilities for the masses—not to mention hospitals, schools, housing, and consumer goods for the public generally—were poor and minimal). In the case of the non-Soviet nations, the Soviet sports structure was regarded as an alien, government-imposed institution.

The principal reason for the Soviet targeting of the Olympics to achieve world supremacy would seem to have been an attempt to gain recognition and prestige for the communist states and their brand of communism, and thereby to advertise that brand, especially in the Third World, as being superior to the capitalist system. However, to many people in Eastern Europe and the USSR, the Olympic achievements and the Moscow Olympics diverted attention from the realities of living under communism. It is hardly surprising, then, that leaders in the post-perestroika period radically changed their scale of priorities. No longer seeing the need to demonstrate the advantages of socialism, they have tried to distance themselves from the state-directed economy and the totalitarian political system that had failed so badly.

Therefore, to the majority of the public in the communist states, especially the Soviet Union, the Moscow Olympics brought home the vast gap between elite sport and the rest of society, the manipulation of sport for political ends, and the profligacy of pouring funds into a sporting spectacle for propaganda purposes when the economy was teetering on the brink of bankruptcy.

Notwithstanding the political shenanigans around the Games, the venues in the 21 sports were full, as always, of excitement, heroism, pathos, and memorable moments. In the absence of top rivals in some events, the Games presented opportunities for older athletes to grab the limelight unexpectedly one last time. The great Cuban heavyweight boxer Teofilo Stevenson won a record third gold, to add to Cuba's 6 boxing gold medals out of 11 gold medals in all. The East German runner Waldemar Cierpinski took his second marathon gold. Another veteran star was Ethiopia's 42-year-old Miruts Yifter, who won gold medals in both the 5,000-meter and 10,000-meter races. Other veteran winners were Britain's Alan Wells and Italy's Pietro Mennea, who took gold medals in the 100-meter and 200-meter sprints, respectively; and Britain's Daley Thompson, who won his second Olympic decathlon. In her last Olympic appearance, the great Romanian gymnast Nadia Comaneci won one more gold. However, as if to emphasize the thin line between success and tragedy, the Soviet Union's Yelena Mukhina broke her neck in gymnastics training just before the Olympics, paralyzing her from the neck down.

To sum up, whatever happened elsewhere in the world in July 1980, and whatever momentous events were to come in the Soviet Union, for those who attended the Moscow Olympic Games the overriding memory is of a magnificent sporting and cultural spectacle, an efficient if sometimes rigid organization, and an extremely joyful Games. And it did not rain once.

BIBLIOGRAPHICAL ESSAY

The Moscow organizing committee's official report on the Games is *Games of the XXIInd Olympiad*, 3 vols. (Moscow, 1981), published also in French and Russian editions. The British report, British Olympic Association, *The Official British Olympic Association Report of the 1980 Games* (London, 1981) includes a review of the boycott campaign in Great Britain. The U.S. version is *United States Olympic Book 1980* (Colorado Springs, CO, 1980), although the U.S. boycott limits its coverage of the Moscow Games. The German Democratic Republic (East Germany) Olympic Committee, whose team did participate, published *Spiele der XXII. Olympiade Moskau 1980* (Berlin, 1980), while the Federal Republic of Germany (West Germany), which joined the boycott, published *Moscow 80. Das Offizielle Standardwerk des Nationalen Olympischen Komitees für Deutschland* (Munich, 1980).

A glossy Soviet publication on the Games, with many pictures as well as detailed information on preparations and events, is *Moscow '80* (Moscow, 1980), with text in English, Russian, French, and German. In addition to the official report, the organizing committee published a number of other books, including *Olympiada 80* (Moscow, 1980); *The Moscow Olympic Program of Cultural Events* (Moscow, 1980); and various others with compilations of participants, rules, event schedules, and results.

A number of Congressional documents on the U.S. boycott have been published. The House of Representatives Committee on Foreign Affairs hearing on the question is *U.S. Participation in the 1980 Summer Olympic Games*, 96th Cong., 2nd sess., Jan. 23 and Feb. 4, 1980, while the Senate hearings are Committee on Foreign Relations, *1980 Olympics Boycott*, 96th Cong., 2d sess. Another House of Representatives document of interest is *Alternatives to the Moscow Olympics*, a hearing before the Subcommittee on Transportation and Commerce of the Committee of Interstate and Foreign Commerce, 9th Cong., 2d sess., Jan. 30, 1980.

A substantial number of secondary works exist on the boycott question. One of the first was James Riordan, *Soviet Sport: Background to the Olympics* (London, 1980), which argued against British participation in the boycott. Christopher Booker, *The Games War: A Moscow Journal* (London, 1981), attempts to place the Games in a political context dating back to 1974. James Riordan, "Great Britain and the 1980 Olympics: Victory for Olympism," in Maaret Ilmarinen, ed., *Sport and International Understanding* (Berlin, 1984), 138–44, emphasizes the failure of the boycott, while Hartford Cantelon, "The Canadian Absence from the XXIInd Olympiad—Some Plausible Explanations," in the same volume (pp. 145–51), discusses the Canadian position. See also Barukh Hazan, *Olympic Sports and Propaganda Games: Moscow 1980* (New Brunswick, NJ, 1982). A more recent analysis is Derick L. Hulme, *The Political Olympics: Moscow, Afghanistan, and the 1980 U.S. Boycott* (New York, 1990).

LOS ANGELES 1984

Wayne Wilson

THE GAMES OF THE TWENTY-THIRD OLYMPIAD

The decision of the International Olympic Committee (IOC) awarding the 1984 Olympic Games to Los Angeles culminated decades of effort by the Southern California Committee for the Olympic Games (SCCOG) to bring the Games to Los Angeles a second time. Formed in 1939, seven years after Los Angeles hosted the X Olympic Games, SCCOG participated in every Olympic bid competition for the next 39 years before achieving success.

The successful bid for the 1984 Games was a cooperative effort. SCCOG, headed by Los Angeles attorney John Argue, worked with the city of Los Angeles to develop the bid, with strong backing from Mayor Tom Bradley. Despite the city's involvement, SCCOG and other private sources funded the entire bid.

Winning the bid was a two step process. First, Los Angeles had to convince the United States Olympic Committee (USOC) to select Los Angeles as the American candidate city. Second, the city had to make a presentation to the IOC. Promising a Spartan Games, Los Angeles successfully cleared the first hurdle in September 1977 when the USOC selected it over New York.

In the wake of the financially troubled Montreal Games, there were few cities eager to host the Olympic Games. In fact, the only other serious competitor seeking to host the 1984 Games was Teheran, whose bid was withdrawn voluntarily in 1977. Thus, Los Angeles was unopposed. On May 18, 1978, the IOC at its Eightieth Session in Athens provisionally awarded the Games to Los Angeles.

Final approval of Los Angeles's bid was subject to the city signing a contract stating that Los Angeles would abide by all IOC rules. One of the IOC's rules called for the host city to assume financial responsibility for staging the Games. Los Angeles officials, concerned about Montreal's experience and public opinion polls that indicated only 35 percent of Los Angeles voters favored public funding of the Games, balked at the IOC's terms.

Soon after the IOC awarded provisional host status to Los Angeles, Mayor Bradley, at the urging of private backers of the bid, created a committee of seven community leaders to continue negotiations with the IOC. The group named itself the Los Angeles Olympic Organizing Committee (LAOOC). The impasse between the IOC and Los Angeles was resolved after weeks of negotiations when in October 1978 the IOC withdrew its demand that the city agree to assume financial liability. The IOC instead agreed to a plan whereby the privately financed LAOOC and the USOC would assume the financial risk. The USOC's willingness to become involved in the arrangement was motivated, in part, by the organizing committee's promise to share a portion of any surplus funds generated by the Games. The city of Los Angeles, LAOOC, IOC, and USOC signed a series of agreements based on these principles that concluded with a final contract executed on March 1, 1979.

The LAOOC incorporated formally on June 15, 1978. A 22-person executive committee was formed in January 1979. Paul Ziffren became LAOOC chairman and Peter Ueberroth was appointed president in late March. Ziffren was a prominent Los Angeles attorney who had been involved in state and national Democratic Party politics for many years. The appointment of Ziffren, a pillar of the Los Angeles establishment, was not surprising. The selection of Ueberroth was another matter.

A graduate of San Jose State University, who had tried out unsuccessfully for the 1956 Olympic water polo team, the 41-year-old Ueberroth was virtually unknown to the general public. While still in his twenties, Ueberroth had founded a company called First Travel and developed it into one of the nation's largest travel agencies. His entrepreneurial spirit, business experience, and international negotiating ability gained in the travel industry impressed his early backers on the board of directors such as Argue and David Wolper.

Throughout the planning and staging of the Games, Ueberroth was the central figure. The second-in-command on the LAOOC staff was the executive vice president and general manager, Harry Usher. Usher, who joined the organizing committee in early 1980, earned his B.A. at Brown University and a law degree at Stanford University, where he was an editor of the *Stanford Law Review*. Prior to his appointment, Usher had been an attorney in Los Angeles for many years, specializing in entertainment law.

The organizational structure of the LAOOC was fluid. The LAOOC staff grew from a nucleus of eleven employees in 1979 to more than 1,700 by late May 1984. During the Games, the number of paid staff swelled to about 12,000. They were joined by 29,000 volunteers. Another 36,000 people worked for companies hired by the LAOOC to provide various services.

Because the LAOOC had no public funding, Ueberroth and the board had to devise ways to limit costs and maximize revenues. Central to their strategy was the use of existing sports facilities in Southern California. Most major venues existed already. Although the committee spent millions of dollars refurbishing existing facilities, only three new venues—cycling, swimming, and shooting—had to be built from scratch. Corporate sponsors funded the swimming and cycling facilities.

Another way in which the organizing committee held down costs was to rely heavily on volunteers. Some volunteers worked for the LAOOC throughout the entire planning and staging of the Games. Most, however, worked during the sixteen days of sports competition and the period immediately preceding and following the Games.

The LAOOC derived revenue from four major sources: sponsorships, television broadcast rights, ticket sales, and the sale of Olympic commemorative coins. Olympic sponsorship, giving companies the right to have their names associated with the Olympic Games in exchange for cash, goods, or services, was not a new concept. Ueberroth, however, refined the practice by reducing the number of available sponsorships and giving companies exclusive marketing rights in specified product categories while charging higher fees than ever before. The LAOOC offered three levels of corporate participation: official sponsor, official supplier, and official licensee. A total of 164 companies joined the program and contributed $126.7 million in cash, services and products. This figure is somewhat misleading, though. The LAOOC structured the payment schedule so that it received much of the money up front, thus enabling the committee to invest the payments. The committee earned more than $76.3 million from such investments.

The sale of television broadcast rights was an even bigger revenue source. ABC Sports and foreign broadcasters paid $286.8 million for the rights to broadcast the Games.

Ticket sales brought in $139.9 million. The sale of Olympic coins accounted for an additional $36 million.

The LAOOC's strategy of controlling costs and generating revenue proved to be more effective than virtually anyone had anticipated. The LAOOC, several weeks after the Games, announced an estimated surplus of $150 million. That estimate grew to $195 million by year's end and to $225 million in a 1985 audit. When the LAOOC liquidating trust closed in 1988, the final valuation of the surplus was $230 million.

Los Angeles 1984—This photo shows the entrance to the Los Angeles Coliseum, main venue for the 1984 Summer Games. Robert Graham's sculpture "Gateway," featuring two headless athletes, caused a stir at the Games, but Graham maintains that the sculpture embodies traits common to all athletes, regardless of race. Courtesy of Larry Maloney.

The announcement of the unexpectedly large surplus created considerable controversy. Many vendors who had done business with the LAOOC complained that they had provided products and services at reduced prices to support the cause of the Olympic Movement. A few volunteers argued that they should receive part of the surplus. And, there were proposals to share the funds with Third World

National Olympic Committees. In the end, though, the surplus was divided among the USOC, the national governing bodies (NGBs) of Olympic sports in the United States, and a newly formed youth sports foundation in Southern California.

Organizers of the 1984 Games were responsible for staging competitions in twenty-one medal sports (the LAOOC counted diving, synchronized swimming, and water polo as part of swimming) and two demonstration sports, featuring a record 221 events.

The LAOOC in its earliest days concentrated on raising revenue. Once that was accomplished by the sale of television rights to ABC Sports in September 1979, identifying and securing sports venues became a top priority. The LAOOC acquired almost all of the necessary venues by early 1983.

During the summer and fall of 1983, the committee sponsored international competitions in archery, water polo, shooting, swimming, synchronized swimming, diving, cycling, rowing, canoeing, and gymnastics. These competitions, known collectively as LA83, were a dress rehearsal for the Olympic competitions in 1984. They provided an opportunity to test planning assumptions and served as the basis of final preparations for the following summer.

As the date of opening ceremonies drew nearer, the LAOOC underwent a process that it called venuization. The purpose of venuization was to develop venue teams at each competition site comprised of people from functional areas such as security, protocol, press operations, and food services. At each venue a commissioner was responsible for on-site management. All the sports commissioners were influential civic or business leaders. Their role was to serve as the liaison to the relevant international sports federation, while exercising some political clout at the local level. Many commissioners had little, if any, experience in the sport for which they were responsible. Technical expertise at each venue was supplied by a sports manager who reported directly to the commissioner.

The geographic scope of the 1984 Games was enormous. In addition to widely dispersed sports venues, there were three Olympic villages at the University of California at Los Angeles, the University of Southern California, and the University of California, Santa Barbara. The Games encompassed approximately 4,500 square miles of Southern California. Furthermore, early rounds of the soccer tournament took place in Maryland, Massachusetts, and northern California.

Olympic architecture in most Olympic cities has focused on the creation of new stadiums and arenas. Los Angeles, however, already had most of the necessary facilities. The task of architects and designers in Los Angeles, therefore, was not to design sports facilities, but rather to decorate them and the surrounding communities. In doing so, they hoped to create "a sense of place in a city without a center" and to persuade Southern Californians to rally around the Games by creating a spirit of celebration and pageantry.

The LAOOC succeeded on both counts with a design scheme it dubbed "Festive Federalism." Festive Federalism, or the Look as it also was called, featured pastel colors and unusual geometric shapes, presented through the use of banners, sonotubes, and fabrics mounted on bailing wire, chain link fences, and scaffolding.

A year after the Games, an official LAOOC publication referred to the Look as the "single outstanding feature" of the Games. While that may have been true, the road to Festival Federalism was a convoluted one. Between 1979 and 1982 the organizing committee considered and rejected the work of several designers. There was tension throughout the process between a majority on the LAOOC who wanted a patriotic "Red, White and Blue" theme and Executive Vice President/ General Manager Harry Usher, who wanted a less chauvinistic approach. Usher, despite pressure from other senior managers, held firm and selected the design concept of the Los Angeles design firm, Sussman/Prejza, which worked closely with architect Jon Jerde to make the Look a reality. The design plan was implemented at a cost of $12 million and 100,000 hours of labor devoted to installation.

The LAOOC, like any organizing committee, was beset by a variety of obstacles and controversies. The committee's most serious problem, the Soviet-led boycott, reached a climax less than three months before opening ceremonies.

From the day that the IOC awarded the Games to Los Angeles, there existed the possibility of a Soviet-led boycott of the 1984 Games in retaliation against the American-led boycott of the 1980 Moscow Games. Sensitive to the problem, LAOOC representatives met several times with members of the Soviet Union's NOC over a five-year period, beginning with Ueberroth's visit to Moscow in 1979 to attend the All-People's Spartakiade. In December 1983 a fourteen-person Soviet delegation made an eight-day visit to Los Angeles that concluded with the signing of a protocol agreement in which the Soviet NOC put forward several requests related to the entry of the Soviet Olympic delegation into the United States and housing arrangements for them in the Los Angeles area.

Contacts between the LAOOC and the Soviet Union's NOC took place against a backdrop of anti-Soviet political activity in California and the presidency of Ronald Reagan, who in 1983 called the Soviet Union the Evil Empire. Relations took a turn for the worse in September 1983 after a Soviet aircraft shot down a Korean Air Lines plane, killing 269 passengers. The California legislature responded with a unanimous resolution of condemnation that included a clause demanding that athletes from the Soviet Union be banned from competing in the Los Angeles Games. Most legislators had not realized when they voted that the resolution contained the anti-Soviet clause. And, although the legislature eventually rescinded the call for a ban, the USSR reacted by pulling athletes out of the remaining LA83 events.

Meanwhile, a Southern California citizens' group called the Ban the Soviets Coalition demanded that the Soviet Union be barred from the Games. The group announced plans to gather a million signatures on petitions calling for the ban, but only about 10,000 people actually signed. Recognizing that the attempted ban would fail, the coalition also proposed protest demonstrations against the Soviet team in Los Angeles and the use of freeway billboards advising Soviet athletes how to defect.

The Reagan administration made no effort to deny entry to athletes from the Soviet Union. However, in March 1984 the administration did deny a visa to attaché Oleg Yermishkin, who had planned to accompany the Soviet team to Los Angeles. An anonymous administration source claimed that Yermishkin was a senior KGB operative.

In early April several stories appeared in the Soviet press criticizing preparations for the Games in stronger than usual terms. A particular concern, according to these articles, was the security of athletes from the USSR. The Soviet NOC issued a statement on April 9 charging that a campaign characterized by open threats of physical violence and harassment had been mounted in the United States against the Soviet Union's participation in the Olympic Games. The statement also complained about entry procedures for the Soviet Olympic delegation, which, according to the statement, violated the Olympic Charter. It demanded an emergency meeting of the IOC executive board to ensure United States compliance with the charter.

Responding to the escalating rhetoric, Ueberroth met with Soviet NOC representatives and top IOC officials in Lausanne, Switzerland. The Soviet representatives repeated their complaints. The meeting ended without resolution of the issues. The situation did not improve in the days that followed. On May 8, 1984, just hours after the start of the torch relay, the Soviet NOC announced officially that it would not participate in the 1984 Games.

Faced with the prospect of a Soviet boycott, the LAOOC responded by attempting to obtain commitments to attend the Games from more nations than had competed in Munich in 1972, thereby establishing a new record for participating nations. Toward this end, the committee established a twenty-four hour phone bank to call and cajole NOCs. The committee also sent envoys abroad, cabled and called embassies in Washington, D.C., and worked through American embassies in foreign countries in an attempt to contain the boycott.

The effort received a boost on May 12 when the People's Republic of China announced it would send a team. Several days later Romania also declared its intention to defy the boycott. On June 2, the deadline by which NOCs had to accept the invitation to send a team to the Games, the LAOOC was able to announce that 142 nations had accepted. A record number of 140 nations eventually did participate; fourteen others took part in the boycott led by the USSR.

The question of whether the boycott was inevitable or caused by events in the United States remains a matter of debate. Opinions among the principals within the U.S. government, LAOOC, and Soviet NOC were not unanimous in 1984 and remained divided in subsequent years. Although the prevailing opinion among Americans involved in the negotiations with Soviet representatives was that the boycott was unavoidable, there were some who believed that Soviet officials were sincere in their expressed concerns about athlete entry and security and that the American State Department undermined the LAOOC with its dogmatic Cold War behavior.

Another major obstacle facing Ueberroth and the organizing committee was the Greek reaction to the LAOOC's plan for the torch relay. As a way of raising money for charities, the LAOOC decided to sell kilometers along the relay route. Companies or individuals could run in the relay only if they paid a $3,000 participation fee.

Many Greek citizens, sports officials, and politicians, including the leftist mayor of Olympia, site of the eternal Olympic flame, objected to what they termed a defilement of a sacred Greek symbol. The Greek reaction was a reflection both of genuine opposition to the plan and political opportunism on the part of those who wished to capitalize on anti-American sentiment in Greek politics. The mayor of Olympia threatened to prevent the lighting ceremony from taking place in his city. Ueberroth countered by threatening to use a flame that already had been lit at Olympia and transported to IOC headquarters in Switzerland. The issue was resolved when the LAOOC agreed to halt remaining sales of kilometers and the Greek government permitted the lighting ceremony to take place at Olympia. Fearing demonstrations, however, the Greeks cancelled the traditional relay from Olympia to Athens. Before halting sales, the LAOOC raised nearly $11 million from the torch relay. The committee distributed the proceeds to several organizations including the YMCA, Boys Clubs, Girls Clubs, and Special Olympics. The relay, which began on the same day that the Soviet Union announced its boycott, covered 15,000 kilometers in thirty-three states and the District of Columbia and proved to be a major factor in galvanizing public enthusiasm for the Games.

The Olympic Arts Festival took place from June 1 to August 12 under the direction of Robert Fitzpatrick, president of the California Institute of the Arts. The festival featured nearly 900 presentations of dance, theater, music, film, and visual arts by American and international artists. The Times Mirror Company contributed $5 million to stage the festival; the LAOOC budgeted $3 million for the festival. Attendance at the festival totaled 1.3 million spectators.

Opening ceremonies took place on July 28 at the Los Angeles Memorial Coliseum before a live audience of 92,655 and 2.5 billion television viewers in the United States and abroad. Planned and staged by film producer and LAOOC board member David Wolper, the ceremonies were well-received by the American public and American media. Highlights included a card trick in which the audience created the flags of the world, the flight of a man using a jet pack strapped to his back, and the flame lighting atop the stadium by the 1960 decathlon gold medalist, Rafer Johnson.

More than 7,000 athletes competed in Los Angeles. Yet, the quality of competition clearly suffered from the boycott, especially in boxing, wrestling, gymnastics, weightlifting, and track and field. Still, athletes broke or tied thirteen world records and more than eighty Olympic records.

Among the memorable moments of the competitive program were the running of the first Olympic women's marathon, the on-track collision between runners Mary Decker and Zola Budd in the women's 3,000-meter final, Carl Lewis's four gold medals, Greg Louganis's superb diving performance, and the controversial disqualification of American boxer Evander Holyfield.

American athletes won 174 medals, far ahead of their closest rivals the West Germans, who won 59, and the Romanians, who took 53. The boycott of Soviet and Eastern European athletes gave Americans an opportunity to win medals in sports, such as gymnastics and cycling, in which traditionally they had not been top performers. That these victories were achieved in the absence of athletes from the boycotting nations did not seem to dampen the fervor of American spectators or the American media. In fact, before the Games ended, several athletes from other countries complained about the pro-American bias of ABC's television coverage, which was shown in the Olympic Villages.

Two potential problems that worried the LAOOC staff as they planned for the Games, smog and traffic jams, never developed during the 16 days of competition. Air quality, at least by Los Angeles standards, remained good throughout the Games. Freeway traffic actually moved faster than normal because of the LAOOC's mobilization of public and private buses to carry spectators, and the reduced number of vehicles on the roads during rush hours due to companies voluntarily changing their regular business schedules.

The Games ended on August 12 with closing ceremonies at the Coliseum again directed by Wolper.

The Games of the Twenty-third Olympiad live on in the collective memory of Angelenos as a shining moment in the city's history when people cooperated with each other, institutions functioned well, and the traffic flowed. The pageantry, logistical efficiency, and financial success of the 1984 Games so enhanced Ueber-roth's reputation as an effective leader that Mayor Bradley turned to him following the 1992 civil disturbances in Los Angeles that resulted in fifty-five deaths and more than $1 billion in property damage. Bradley appointed Ueberroth to lead Rebuild L.A., a private group charged with stimulating economic development in poor Los Angeles neighborhoods. Ueberroth resigned as president after one year but remained on the board of directors.

The 1984 Games' financial success also contributed to the perception that the Olympic Games could create financial benefits for host cities, corporate sponsors, and broadcasters. The financial lure of the Olympic Games was readily evident in the host city bid process that followed the 1984 Games. Whereas only Los Angeles had bid to host the 1984 Olympics, six cities presented bids to the IOC in 1986 with the hope of hosting the 1993 Games. The LAOOC's corporate sponsorship system, in which companies paid high fees in exchange for exclusive rights in specific product categories, was adopted by all subsequent organizing committees and provided the blueprint for the IOC's worldwide TOP sponsorship program launched in 1985.

In physical terms, the Games left behind a swim stadium, velodrome, shooting range, many refurbished sports facilities, and an administrative building on the UCLA campus. Most of the sports venues used in the Los Angeles Games, though, existed before 1984.

The local economic impact was substantial. Economics Research Associates, a Chicago research firm, estimated in a 1986 report that the Olympics brought $2.4 billion into the Southern California economy.

The most tangible legacy of the Games was the Olympic surplus, calculated in 1985 at about $225 million. The USOC received 40 percent of the surplus. The NGBs of Olympic sports in the United States got 20 percent. The rest was set aside for use in Southern California and became the endowment of the Amateur Athletic Foundation of Los Angeles (AAF). The AAF began operations in 1985 with an endowment of $91 million. In the eighteen years following 1984, the foundation invested $100 million in youth sport programs in Southern California, while simultaneously increasing its assets to more than $130 million to ensure future funding in the community.

BIBLIOGRAPHICAL ESSAY

The Amateur Athletic Foundation of Los Angeles (AAF) sports library and the Special Collections Department of UCLA's University Research Library have excellent collections on the 1984 Games. The AAF materials are part of a larger Olympic collection that includes the official report, or what passes for the official report, of each modern Olympic Games. The 1984 materials include the official report; LAOOC brochures, guides, and programs; national team media guides; videos; photographs; musical works; posters; Harry Usher's office files; audiotapes and transcripts of interviews with more than 100 LAOOC staff, including Paul Ziffren, Peter Ueberroth, and Usher, conducted by *Los Angeles Times* reporter, Kenneth Reich; the seven-volume ABC Sports 1984 Olympic research manual; U.S. Information Agency documents on the boycott; extensive newspaper clippings files; and numerous artifacts. The UCLA collection is equally impressive. It contains nearly 1,700 archival boxes on the 1984 Games. Included are the official report, LAOOC publications, videos, and 130,000 photographs. More important for serious researchers, UCLA has thousands of pages of internal LAOOC documents and press releases. Special Collections has developed an index to the Olympic collection and the staff is knowledgeable about the holdings.

The AAF and UCLA Special Collections maintain a good working relationship and will work together to assist researchers. Both collections are open to the public. An advance telephone call or letter will facilitate the use of either collection.

Official Report of the Games of the XXIIIrd Olympiad Los Angeles, 1984 (Los Angeles, 1984) is most the complete information source. A fully searchable full-text online version of the official report is available at http://www.aafla.org/search/search.htm. *Olympic Retrospective: The Games of Los Angeles* (Los Angeles, 1985), published by the LAOOC, is a 596-page paperback that repeats, in condensed form, much of the information from the report while also presenting a myriad of new statistics and details.

Peter Ueberroth, *Made in America: His Own Story* (New York, 1985), written with Peter Levin and Amy Quinn, presents the LAOOC point of view in a readable style enlivened by Ueberroth's observations of his contemporaries in sport and government. Kenneth Reich, *Making It Happen: Peter Ueberroth and the 1984 Olympic Games* (Santa Barbara, CA, 1986) is a thoughtful, more critical examination of Ueberroth and the LAOOC corporate culture.

Economic Research Associates, *Executive Summary, Community Impact of the 1984 Olympic Games in Los Angeles and Southern California* (Chicago, 1986) analyzes the economic impact of the Games.

Olympic Dreams: The Impact of Mega-Events on Local Politics (Boulder, CO, 2001), by Matthew J. Birbank, Gregory D. Andranovich, and Charles H. Heying, offers a theoretical analysis of urban politics to explain the bid and organizing efforts that led to the 1984 Games. The authors also discuss the impact of the Los Angeles Games on other American cities, particularly Atlanta and Salt Lake City.

Several excellent articles on the Olympic design appear in *Design Quarterly*, 127 (1985) which was devoted entirely to the 1984 spectacle.

Bud Greenspan's official film of the Games, *16 Days of Glory* (video, 1986) presents evocative portraits of athletes who competed in Los Angeles.

Doctoral dissertations on the Los Angeles Games include Harold Wilson, "The Golden Opportunity: a Study of the Romanian Manipulation of the Olympic Movement during the Boycott of the 1984 Los Angeles Olympic Games" (Ohio State, 1993) and Susanna Levitt, "1984 Olympic Arts Festival: Theatre" (University of California, Davis, 1990).

In the popular press, *Sports Illustrated*'s articles were consistently reliable. The *Los Angeles Times* provided the most comprehensive journalistic coverage.

SEOUL 1988

Ron Palenski

THE GAMES OF THE TWENTY-FOURTH OLYMPIAD

Throughout the 1980s, the international Olympic Movement underwent such a profound change that even the semiofficial biography of the International Olympic Committee (IOC) president Juan Antonio Samaranch was titled *Olympic Revolution*. But rather than calling for a new order with a banging of drums and the clarion call of trumpets, the movement evolved, led by the Swiss-based IOC and driven by Samaranch, moving and swaying to the beat of world politics, and sometimes calling the tune itself, and plunged into global marketing, altering not just its own financial structure but the monetary basis of all international sport. The 1980s left behind forever the notion that sports, through such self-generating incomes as gate receipts, could be self-supporting.

Central to the evolution were the 1988 Games, the twenty-fourth in the modern era, as the IOC likes to term them, in Seoul, an improbable venue when the IOC chose it in the Rhineland spa town of Baden-Baden in 1981. South Korea had scant tradition of Olympic involvement, was of little standing in international sport, was not high on the world's consciousness of Asia and, most significant, was not recognized politically by any of the communist states. In 1981, a year after Samaranch had taken over from the affable Irish peer Lord Killanin as IOC president, the Olympic Movement was in a period of high political uncertainty. It was a time of boycott. African, Asian, and West Indian states had either left or stayed away from the Montreal Games in 1976 because of their abhorrence of South Africa's apartheid system of separate racial development. In 1980, there had been the American-led Western boycott of the Moscow Games because of the Soviet presence in Afghanistan, and in 1984, there was the tit-for-tat boycott of the Los Angeles Games by communist states, with the notable exceptions of Romania and China (the latter dramatically thumbing its nose at Moscow by choosing the Games Moscow spurned to make its reappearance at the Olympics).

The selection of Seoul to host the 1988 Games immediately raised the prospect of a fourth consecutive boycott, a prospect that could have crippled the Olympic Movement and grossly devalued the Games' insistence that it was a vehicle for international understanding, peace, and goodwill. Seoul's candidacy was fortunate in that, because of the risks of boycotts (and because of the financial risks), few cities were then lining up to host the Games; its only serious opposition was the Japanese city of Nagoya, the overwhelming favorite when the IOC members met in Baden-Baden. No one knows, then or now, what really influenced the ninety-odd IOC members who decided where the 1988 Games should be held; they were not delegates from their countries, and they need explain their decisions to no one. A noisy protest in Baden-Baden by environmentalists against Nagoya's candidacy may have influenced some members to go for Seoul; a desire to spread the Games more widely (Japan had already hosted a Summer and a Winter Games) may have influenced others. The intense politicking within international sports and the role played by the chairman of Adidas, Horst Dassler, a man of great persuasion and monetary influence, may also have changed some minds. (An expert in what was then the fledgling world of sports marketing, Dassler was something of a Father Christmas to financially strapped organizations, which then included the IOC.) Whatever the influences, Seoul prevailed over Nagoya 52–27.

The outcome of the vote in Baden-Baden set Samaranch on a seven-year course of diplomatic shuttling rivaled in its air miles only by former U.S. Secretary of State Henry Kissinger, as he sought to avert yet another boycott or any other event that could disrupt or demean the first of his Games (Los Angeles had been chosen when Killanin was president, and so Samaranch saw Seoul as the first of his era). Samaranch, unlike Killanin or Avery Brundage, was not worried by the potential eventual size of the Olympic Games and was open with his ambition for the Games to be a truly international sporting extravaganza for all sports and all countries.

The South Koreans were equally open about their motives for wanting to stage the Games. They were not the first country to see the Games as a window on their world as they sought, sometimes painfully and violently, to make the transition from military government to democratic rule and attempted, like their neighbor, longtime antagonists and one-time occupiers Japan, to muscle their way into international trade. South Korea selected a decorative motif known as a *Sam Taegeuk* as the Games emblem and said it symbolized the blending of traditional values and ideals with the much more pragmatic goal of making their way in the larger world.

Opposing that goal was their neighbor to the north, the communist state of North Korea, created by the Soviet Union in the area occupied by the Soviet army when Japan surrendered to end World War II. Under Kim Il Sung, the North Koreans coveted the South, which they had failed to gain by military means during the Korean War, and they looked to their communist allies for fraternal opposition to the Seoul Games. But as the South Koreans entered into a massive building and economic reconstruction program for the Games, and as Samaranch flew around the world charming, persuading, and cajoling countries into committing themselves to the Games, the leaders in Moscow were both more liberal and more pragmatic than their predecessors. By the mid-1980s, Mikhail Gorbachev was in power, and the mood of boycott was fading as countries realized that there was more to be gained by being at the Games than there was by staying away from them. It was revealed that East Germany, then a powerful sporting nation, if through questionable means, had been desperate to go to Los Angeles in defiance of Moscow but was forced to fall into line. Those days were gone; Samaranch knew most of the Communist states would be in Seoul.

The focus had turned to North Korea, which had demanded that if the Games were going to go ahead in Seoul (and there was never any serious suggestion that they would not), Pyongyang should have its share of Olympic sports. In the interest of stability, Samaranch went along with the idea and organized a series of historic meetings between the two Koreas with the IOC as the broker, although there was no precedent for sharing the Games that are awarded to a city, not a country, and certainly not to a combination of countries. The North insisted on simultaneous opening ceremonies in Seoul and Pyongyang, and a share of sports, notably the whole soccer tournament. There was a practical reason for this. Soccer's world governing body, Fédération Internationale de Football Association (FIFA), had suspended North Korea for refusing to play in an Olympic qualifying match, and Pyongyang saw the staging of the Olympic soccer tournament as an ideal way of gaining reinstatement.

The negotiations between North and South were almost as protracted as the negotiations thirty years earlier that eventually led to the end of the Korean War. Underlying the proposition of shared Games was the knowledge that Olympic events are not played out in a vacuum. The quest for Olympic medals is accompanied by the electronic eye of television and thousands of journalists and commentators, and North Korea had to face the unpalatable fact that if some sports were on its hitherto closed territory, so would be the inquisitive hordes. This was something that could not be countenanced, and eventually the sharing plans foundered but on the rocks of practicality, with Samaranch telling them that planning required certain deadlines to be met. The North Koreans withdrew but left behind a suspicion rather than a threat that the Seoul Games might still somehow be disrupted, although it became evident as the Games approached that Pyongyang would risk losing much more than it could possibly gain if it attempted some form of disruption in a city that would be crowded with athletes and officials from communist states.

Just in case, security was stepped up along the border at the 38th parallel and at the bizarre meeting point of Panmunjom, where North and South Korean soldiers—the latter backed by United Nations forces—daily stare each other down. And the United States found the need to conduct military exercises in the region at the time of the Games, greatly increasing its naval presence in the Yellow Sea and the Sea of Japan.

Samaranch kept the door open to North Korea to compete in the Games until the last, knowing Kim Il Sung could not afford the loss of face at home that participation would entail. The Soviet Union made clear its view of the relative importance of the Olympics vis-à-vis North Korea on the occasion of the fortieth anniversary of the founding of North Korea a few days before the Games. Premier Mikhail Gorbachev and Foreign Minister Andrei Gromyko had been invited by Kim to the celebrations, but they sent instead a relatively low-level official. At the same time, a full Soviet delegation went to Seoul for the Games.

Even once the Games began, the international politicking continued. During the opening ceremony, there was an inadvertent reference to Jerusalem being the capital of Israel. This deeply offended the Arab states and they threatened to walk out. An apology from the organizing committee cooled things down.

South Korea's problems were not just with geopolitics. There was also television. The world's most pervasive information medium—before the Internet—made its tentative Olympic beginnings at Berlin in 1936, and between 1960 and 1980 it underpinned the IOC's finances. Fees for the rights to exclusive coverage of the Olympics were dominated by the three American networks. For the 1960 Games in Rome, CBS paid $394,000 for its exclusivity, and by 1980, NBC paid $87 million—and lost heavily, because of the boycott. Rights fees took off in the early 1980s at two Games with real-time coverage of the Games, Los Angeles in 1984 (ABC, $225 million) and the Winter Games in Calgary in 1988 (ABC, $309 million). Since the Games were in North America, finals in high-interest events were scheduled for prime time, and the scheduling of events was more or less what it would have been without television. The situation in Seoul, however, was different. Initially, the sports federations planned their Games programs without regard for television. In viewer interest terms, this primarily meant the International Amateur Athletic Federation (IAAF), controller of all track-and-field events. On the advice of International Management Group, one of the world's most successful sports marketing companies, Seoul sought a U.S. rights fee from television of something in the region of $750 million—an enormous sum in the best of times, but for the American networks, Seoul was not providing the best of times. Given the time difference, high-interest finals such as the 100-meter track clash—billed as a showdown between American Carl Lewis and Canadian Ben Johnson—would be late at night or early in the morning U.S. time. No American network would pay such an amount for dead-time viewing or, worse, delayed coverage.

NBC, which talked the Koreans down to $300 million for the rights, appealed to Samaranch, and he and other IOC officials gave the Koreans guidance. At the same time, the Koreans and television executives leaned on the IAAF to alter competition times to better suit peak viewing in the United States. Eventually the times were changed (the 100-meter final was run late in the morning, Seoul time, exceptionally early for such a prestigious race), and NBC was happy. So too was the IAAF, which, according to journalists Vyv Simson and Andrew Jennings in *The Lord of the Rings* (1992), gained an extra $20 million from the Seoul organizers for changing the event times. Primo Nebiolo, an Italian who was then president of the IAAF and one of the power players in international sports, denied that this payment was made.

When most people think of the Olympics, they may recall some of the athletic greats of past Games, such as Paavo Nurmi, Emil Zatopek, Vera Čáslavská, or Nadia Comaneci, or if they think of Seoul, they may think of Ben Johnson and the doping scandal or the athletic feats of swimmers Matt Biondi or Kristin Otto. It is most unlikely they would think of, or even know of, the people who make the Games happen—those, often in appointed positions, who work behind the scenes to get the Games in the first place and then ensure their smooth running. People such as Samaranch and Nebiolo were world figures with as much political influence as any head of state, and sometimes more than many. Kim Un-Yong was not a name that was on many lips when Seoul won the Games or even when it staged them, yet he was almost a sixth Olympic ring. David Miller, the English journalist who wrote Samaranch's biography, described Kim as the second most influential man in the Olympic Movement during Samaranch's tenure as president. He had been assistant to the prime minister; a diplomatic envoy in the United Nations, Washington and London; and deputy director-general to the South Korean president; and he had moved in circles of tremendous power and influence. He led South Korea's bid for the Games, and thereafter no significant decision was made without his advice or input.

The world of politics in sport can be as byzantine and corrupt as the real political world, with a credo that the ends justify the means. For most of the world, the shadowy maneuverings behind the scenes, the power of the dollar, and the lust for real power are irrelevant when it comes to the Games themselves. The Games are judged on the quality of the sports events and the type of show the host city puts on. Seoul surpassed all its predecessors. It helped, of course, that the Olympic world was united for the first time since Munich in 1972, with just six national Olympic committees choosing not to attend. North Korea (officially, the Democratic People's Republic of Korea) and Cuba would not compete unless the Games were held in both Koreas, Nicaragua stayed away because of difficulties at home, and Albania, Ethiopia, and the Seychelles did not respond to the invitations the IOC sent them. Normally it is the host city that issues the invitations, but the IOC took over to minimize the risk of offending those countries that did not recognize South Korea. Cuban President Fidel Castro was reported to be "very, very sad" that failure to stage the Games in both Koreas meant Cuba could not attend. The sadness did not stop Castro, however, from criticizing the other socialist countries that were in Seoul.

Reveling at being under the gaze of the world, the South Koreans described staging the Games as a "fantastic journey" on which they were guided by five themes they called the Quintessence of the Seoul Olympics and to which they gave the acronym CLUE. "C" was for the Games of total *culture* (the biggest arts festival staged in conjunction with a Games) and for the Olympics of *compassion* (events for the disabled and the funding of the Paralympics that followed the Games). "L" was for the Olympics of a future *legacy*. "U" was for the Games of *unity*. And "E" was for the Olympics of a new *era*.

Much of the Olympic-speak centers on the themes of international understanding and peace and goodwill, phrases that can sound like empty rhetoric more in keeping with the United Nations than the real world of sporting endeavor that crosses all racial and socioeconomic boundaries. But events at an Olympics can give real meaning to the words, and this time, in the case of Seoul, truly the sporting world was united and the Olympics showed that no other force could so bring humanity together into harmony.

The Seoul Games were the largest in history—in size, technology, and publicity—and they were an exceptional success. Samaranch described them as the best Games there have been (a phrase devalued by repetition). Kim, the power behind the Seoul throne, afterward pointed to the success of the Olympics in areas where other international efforts have been dismal failures. He noted that the Olympics had led to South Korea's establishing diplomatic relations with many socialist countries and a trade office in China. For South Koreans, the 1988 Olympics brought about a significant change in the country's international understanding.

The press chief at Seoul was Jae-won Lee, who in 1994 was invited to the Olympic Congress in Paris that marked the centenary of the Olympic movement. The Games, he said, provided a channel of communication for South Korea that previously had not existed, enabling it to have sporting relations as a prelude to diplomatic relations.

This was the case at the Seoul Asian Games of 1986 and the Seoul Olympics in 1988. These two Games made it possible for Korea to open dialogues, compete together and to succeed in diplomatic relations with China and most Eastern European countries. In Korea, we are always mindful and grateful for the courage of sports leaders in China and Eastern Europe, and the inspiration we drew from the IOC. The Olympic movement changed our world forever and for the better. (Jae-won Lee, "The Olympic Movement and International Understanding," paper presented at the Centenary Olympic Congress, Paris, August 1994).

The world was not entirely in peace and harmony at Seoul. One who was out of kilter was the Canadian sprinter Ben Johnson, who clearly had not heeded—or whose advisers had not heeded—a growing clamor within sport that the misuse of drugs had gone far enough. There have been reasons to suppose that some sports authorities have not pursued drug abusers as diligently as they should, or as thoroughly as they said they were, but there was no denying the growing international mood against drug abuse in sport. Johnson served to intensify that mood. Samaranch had warned as recently as Calgary, the Games before Seoul, that the IOC would do whatever it could in its power to rid the sports world of drugs.

There could have been no better public example of cheating than Johnson's. Before the Seoul Games, he and Carl Lewis were the most publicized Olympic athletes, and their meeting in the 100-meter final was the most anticipated event; the defending champion an American against the world champion and world record-holder. The final has been called the most watched footrace in history, and perhaps it was, Johnson winning relatively easily with his right arm raised in a gesture of victory. But two days later it was revealed that he had tested positive for anabolic steroids, and his title was stripped from him. Subsequently, his world record was removed from the record books, and Canada began a series of investigations into how it could have happened.

The sensational disqualification focused attention on drugs in sports like no other occurrence before it—and there had been plenty of them—but the only reputation to be sullied was Johnson's—not Seoul's and not the Olympics'. His exposure led to greater efforts around the world to stop the illicit use of drugs in sport and also to the realization that in modern sport the vast sums of money on offer were, to some, worth the price. Exposing those who use or misuse drugs is one step. The next problem confronting sports was exposing and eliminating those who supplied and prescribed them. Johnson did not act on his own.

The outstanding woman sprinter of the Games, Florence Griffith-Joyner, had been drug tested with negative results, but she too became, both during the Games and later, a suspect figure. Some newspapers reported in plain English that she abused drugs while others merely hinted. Nothing was ever proven. The flamboyant "Flo-Jo," as she was known, died in 2001 from a heart condition.

The legacy of a united sporting world was not all that Seoul left the Olympic Movement. It also gave it a new flag. The original Olympic flag, the five Olympic rings on a white background, was based on a design by Baron Pierre de Coubertin himself and made in the Au Bon Marché store near Coubertin's birthplace in Paris. It was first flown in 1914 on the occasion of the twentieth anniversary of the creation of the IOC but did not serve as a standard for the Games until 1920 in Antwerp. It had become worn with the years, and the IOC asked the Seoul organizers to come up with a new one. The Antwerp flag, as it had become known, was retired to the Olympic Museum in Lausanne, and Rohr Tae Woo presented its replacement to Samaranch in 1985. Fittingly, it was wholly Korean made—from pure Korean raw silk and the needlework by the deft hands of women skilled in Korea's traditional methods. The impact of Seoul, both literally and figuratively, continues to hang over subsequent Games.

BIBLIOGRAPHICAL ESSAY

Two widely contrasting books, David Miller, *Olympic Revolution, the Olympic Biography of Juan Antonio Samaranch* (London, 1992) and Vyv Simson and Andrew Jennings, *The Lord of the Rings: Power, Money and Drugs in the Modern Olympics* (London, 1992), form the basis of contemporary research of the Seoul Games. Miller provides the orthodox, authorized, and almost sanitized version of Olympic history under Samaranch's presidency. Simson and Jennings provide almost the opposite: a study of the politicking and wheeling and dealing that are endemic to any multinational organization. The balance, as always, is somewhere in between.

The U.S. Olympic Committee's official report is *Seoul Calgary 1988* (Sandy, Utah, 1988); the Canadian version is David W. Ellis, *Canada at the Olympics, 1988* (St. Albert, Alberta, 1989). Various issues of the IOC's *Olympic Review* from the time of the awarding of the Games until their completion provided commentary and reportage on Seoul's organizational progress, as does *Seoul Flame*, the official newsletter of the Seoul organizing committee. Richard Pound's *Five Rings Over Korea* (Toronto, 1994) gives an official view of the protracted series of meetings between South and North. (Pound was an IOC member in Canada and member of the IOC's Executive Board.)

A useful view from within Seoul of the Olympics and their impact on Korean society comes from Jae-won Lee, who was the press chief during the Games. He wrote *Seoul Olympics and the Global Community* (Seoul, 1992) and "The Olympic Movement and International Understanding" (paper presented at the Centenary Olympic Congress, Paris, August and September 1994). For other inside views, consult Park She-jik, *The Seoul Olympics: The Inside Story* (London, 1991); Kim Un-yong, *The Greatest Olympics: From Baden-Baden to Seoul* (Seoul, 1990); and Vincent J. Ricquant and C. S. Smith, *The Games Within the Games: the Story Behind the 1988 Seoul Olympics* (Seoul, 1988). Two other books that may prove useful are James T. Larson, *Global Television and the Politics of the Seoul Olympics* (Boulder, CO,1993) and Bill Toomey, *The Olympic Challenge*, 1988 (Costa Mesa, CA, 1988).

Documentary film sources on the Seoul Games include Bud Greenspan, *16 Days of Glory: Seoul '88* (1989), a highlights film produced by NBC, which provided television coverage of the Games: *Seoul Summer Olympics* (1988), and a celebratory film, *The World Comes to Seoul* (1989), produced by the Seoul Olympic Organizing Committee.

Simon Winchester, *Korea* (New York, 1988) and Bevin Alexander, *Korea, The Lost War* (London, 1989) provide insightful background on Korean politics and people. Daily coverage during the Games in the *Korean Herald* complemented my own personal observations.

BARCELONA 1992

Miquel de Moragas

THE GAMES OF THE TWENTY-FIFTH OLYMPIAD

Barcelona, as the capital of Catalonia, had already given an impulse to its modernizing drives and its expression of Catalan national identity in the Universal Exhibition of 1888 and the International Exhibition of 1929. Both of these events were in many respects precursors of what would later occur with the Olympic Games: renovation and freeing up of large swaths of the city, new ways of relating to the Spanish national government, pacts hammered out among rival political groups to achieve a common objective, an opening up of the city to international relations, expression of Catalan cultural and political identity, economic and tourist development, and innovation in design and architecture.

Barcelona had already been a candidate to host the Games on several occasions (1924, 1936, 1948, 1972). The city came closest to success in 1936, when the Games were finally awarded to Berlin.

The political circumstances in Spain in the years following 1936 and the advent of the Francisco Franco dictatorship ruled out any further bids until the 1980s, with the restoration of democracy after Franco's death in 1975. Furthermore, in July 1980, Barcelona-born Juan Antonio Samaranch was elected president of the International Olympic Committee (IOC), and the then mayor of Barcelona, Narcís Serra, sent him a congratulatory telegram, reminding him that they had once had a conversation about Barcelona's chances of hosting the Games.

The nomination of Barcelona as a candidate to host the 1992 Games took place in a politically favorable context and in a climate of consensus among the three principal levels of government involved: the Spanish national government, the Catalan state government, and Barcelona's city government.

The context was also favorable within the Olympic Movement itself, in which the president, Juan Antonio Samaranch, was to exercise a positive influence on behalf of the city. However, this influence was diplomatically exercised and took the form of public neutrality, right up to the final moments in Lausanne when he announced that the host city for the 1992 Games would be "the city of . . . 'Barsa-lona'" (using the Catalan rather than the Spanish pronunciation). On October 17, 1986, at the 91st IOC Session, Barcelona triumphed over the rival candidates of Amsterdam, Belgrade, Birmingham, Brisbane and, especially, Paris. On the third ballot, Barcelona received 47 votes (an overall majority), against 27 for Paris.

The first organizational challenge was to decide on a city–Games relationship model, which would include not only economic and urban planning considerations, but also political and cultural factors; also needed was an organizational structure that would serve to coordinate all later actions.

Barcelona 1992—The Palace on Montjuïc served as a magnificent backdrop for the events of the 1992 Summer Games in Barcelona. Courtesy of Larry Maloney.

The 1992 Games were organized within a still incomplete and weak framework on the part of the IOC. Indeed, it was to be experience gained in Barcelona that would make a notable contribution to the development of IOC regulations on such important considerations as the number of athletes participating, accreditation, distribution of sponsorship and television resources, and follow-up committees.

Barcelona's organizational model was essentially public, with participation by a private sector group. The fact that the organization was public in nature had a bearing on the final model of the Games themselves, in that it eliminated speculation and channeled investment into long-term public interest objectives. As Josep Miquel Abad, chief executive of the Barcelona Organizing Committee (COOB'92), put it:

> I believe the great strength of the Barcelona Games, and in general of the cities that have followed this same model, was to put the immense energy of the Games at the service of the city, and not the other way around. That was the great strategy. Because the cities that did not apply this approach came up against many problems, among other reasons because they made investments not in response to the city's logic or for permanent ongoing use, but rather in response to a major yet once-off demand, and as a result use of the facilities was limited. (Quoted in Moragas, et al., *Barcelona: l'herencia dels Jocs [1992–2002]* [Barcelona, 2002], 15–16)

The final model for the 1992 Games was the outcome of a series of tensions and consensus between the various players: the Spanish and Catalan governments, the Barcelona city government, the Olympic Committees, the media, sponsors, and others. Each of these participants was to achieve at least part of its main objective in the final outcome. For the Spanish government, the Games were part of an overall España '92 program, which included the 500th anniversary of the discovery of

America and the Universal Exhibition in Seville. The overall aim was to offer a new image of Spain and its parliamentary monarchy—modern, competitive, and governed effectively by the socialists.

For the Catalan government (the *Generalitat*), the main priorities were the Catalanization of the Games and ensuring that Barcelona '92 would not be overshadowed within the overall España '92 program; it was also keen to limit expenditures and not overspend the budgeted sum of 4 billion pesetas.

The main objective of Barcelona was more varied and perhaps more practical in emphasis: first, the aim was to complete an urban reform program that had already been designed but not executed; the city also wished to promote itself as a great business center and a first-class tourist destination. To achieve these objectives the city government had to secure the necessary funding and also maintain its autonomy and leadership of the process. For this purpose, Pascual Maragall i Mira, Barcelona's mayor, became president of the organizing committee.

The Spanish Olympic Committee played an advisory role in the organization of the athletic aspects of the Games. Its main achievement—and also its priority—was to assure the success of Spanish athletes, who won an unprecedented 22 medals (13 gold, 7 silver, and 2 bronze), placing them in sixth place in the medal standings. Until then, Spain's entire history of participation in the Olympics had resulted in a total of only 26 medals, only 4 of which were gold.

This same balance of satisfaction was found in public opinion. The widespread institutional and popular satisfaction in Catalonia with the presence of symbols of Catalan identity (thousands of Catalan flags, some Olympic flags, and very few Spanish flags on the city's balconies and in the stadiums) was balanced by satisfaction throughout Spain with the success of the Spanish team and the prominent role afforded the king of Spain in the media.

The historical image of the Barcelona Games was formed around the concept of "the Games of Urban Transformation." The first great planning decision was to create four Olympic areas interconnected by the new *rondas* (city ring roads): Montjuïc, Diagonal, Vall d'Hebron, and Parc de Mar, along with other facilities in outlying towns and cities within Barcelona's metropolitan area.

This process coincided with what was known as the democratization of local government in the 1980s and the consequent struggle to undo the damage caused by the urban speculation inherited from the Franco regime.

There were four main objectives: to provide the city with a new roadway network, to establish new public sport and leisure facilities, to open up the city to the sea, and finally, to restore balance to the city by ensuring that the development work took place in all neighborhoods.

A total of 169 National Olympic Committees participated in Barcelona '92, and a total of 9,368 athletes (6,660 men and 2,708 women) took part in 284 competitions (25 official Olympic sports and three demonstration sports). Adding in judges, referees, and official staff members brings the total number of participants to 16,000. In addition, an unprecedented number of accredited journalists and media personnel covered the Games: 4,880 journalists from a total of 1,700 different publications and 7,951 television and radio staff.

In comparison with previous Games, there was very little opposition to Barcelona '92 or support for any type of boycott, either at the international level or within the city itself. The tensions that did exist concerned the presence of the symbols of Catalan identity, and they were resolved positively with high levels of community participation, as seen on the streets and at the stadiums.

All recent Summer Games have also seen criticism of social aspects of the associated urban planning schemes. In Barcelona, in contrast, the only criticisms were of the poor quality of some of the buildings due to tight deadlines. From the perspective of the year 2004, and so-called antiglobalization protests, it may seem surprising that so few critical voices were raised to protest against the presence of multinationals and the commercialization of the Barcelona Games.

Between Seoul 1988 and Barcelona 1992, events of transcendental international importance occurred: the collapse of the Berlin Wall and the reunification of Germany, the collapse of communism and the Soviet Union, and the abolition of apartheid in South Africa. Barcelona was therefore able to host the Games in excellent conditions for full international participation. For the first time in 20 years, all the countries with a National Olympic Committee participated. Cuba and North Korea, absent from Los Angeles and Seoul, returned; South Africa (excluded since 1960 because of apartheid) was also present. Estonia, Latvia, and Lithuania all participated with their own teams, while the other former Soviet republics paraded in a "unified team," although the winners were hon-

Barcelona 1992—Santaigo Calatrava's telecommunications tower was an integral part of an $8 billion infrastructure improvements campaign for the 1992 Barcelona Games. Courtesy of Larry Maloney.

ored with the flags of their own republics. Slovenia, Croatia, and Bosnia-Herzegovina also had their own Olympic Committees, while Serbian, Montenegrin, and Macedonian athletes were present on an individual basis, due to the United Nations ban on Serbia and its allies because of the war in Bosnia-Herzegovina.

The European Union was present at the 1992 Games (Barcelona and Albertville) with promotional activities for its institutions (ceremonies, banners on the street) and technologies (high-definition television). For the first time, at least visibly, the European Union had to accept the contradiction between the new European model of a community of nations and the markedly individual nation-state focus of Olympic ceremony and ritual.

It can be seen, therefore, that Barcelona was host city at one of the best periods in the history of the Olympic Games; the dimensions of the Games on a global scale had been confirmed, as had their funding systems with stable sponsorship programs and payment of television rights. The Cold War and the days of international boycotts were over, and later upheavals concerning globalization, new forms of international terrorism, and the Olympic crisis of 1999 were all in the future.

Organizational expenditure for Barcelona '92 totaled $1.36 billion, while total investment reached $8.01 billion. Also, 85 percent of expenditures were profitable long-term investments. For its part, the organizing committee (COOB '92) closed its accounts in July 1993, with a surplus of $3 million out of a total budget of $1.64 billion. The surplus was used to set up the Fundació Barcelona Olímpica.

Of note here are the wide variety of investors, the majority being public sector (67 percent), as opposed to private sector (33 percent); the scale of the investments in transport infrastructure (42 percent); and the limited investment in sports facilities (9 percent). By the year 2004, the public sector will have received a more than adequate return for their investment in Barcelona '92, leaving the city in an improved strategic position. In 1990, Barcelona occupied eleventh place in one ranking of desirable European cities, whereas by the year 2001 it was in sixth position.

One of the best indexes of the effects of the Olympic Games is its impact on tourism. In 1990 Barcelona had 118 hotels with 10,265 beds. By 1992, this capacity

Table 1
COOB '92 budget

Income		Expenditure	
Sponsorship	62 %	Security and others	14%
Television rights	33 %	Olympic family	19 %
Others	5 %	Competitions	12 %
		Technology	19 %
		Media	19 %
		Investments	17%

Source: Brunet, 2002.

Table 2
Funding for Olympic investments in Barcelona '92

COOB'92	3 %
European Union	1 %
Spanish state	12 %
Generalitat of Catalonia	15 %
Barcelona City Hall	2 %
Spanish private sector	22 %
International private sector	11 %
Other Spanish public sector companies	14 %
HOLSA (Spanish state and Barcelona City Hall)	16 %

Source: Brunet, 2002.

Table 3
Olympic investments in Barcelona '92

Sports facilities	9 %
Hotels	13 %
Housing and offices	15 %
Costs, cleaning and parks	6 %
Cultural/leisure facilities	2 %
Roads and transport	42 %
Telecommunications	19 %

Source: Brunet, 2002.

had risen slightly to 148 hotels and 13,352 beds. However, by 2002, these figures had risen dramatically to 223 hotels and 36,901 beds, with projected figures of 253 hotels and 46,391 beds by the year 2004. In 2001, tourism in Barcelona rose by 7.6 percent, whereas worldwide tourism fell by 1.3 percent. Average hotel occupation rates in the city have been at 80 percent in recent years. These figures represent a major increase in the number of overnight stays, with a jump from 3,795,522 in 1990 to 7,969,496 in 2001. Barcelona is the European city with the greatest increase in overnight stays (an increase of 104.9 percent), although it is still far behind the figures for total number of stays for London (120,400,000 overnight stays; 31 percent increase for the same period), and Paris (31,633,273 overnight stays; 1.5 percent increase).

Public participation was most notable in the organization of the Olympic Volunteers. A total of 110,000 volunteers signed up, of whom some 35,000 were finally selected and trained for various organizational support tasks. The participation of the Barcelona public must also be mentioned. The first sign of this popular support occurred on the night the city was awarded the Games, but the first real explosion of public enthusiasm came, as it does in all host cities, with the arrival of the Olympic torch and the beginning of its journey. Finally, during the Games themselves, there were many spontaneous demonstrations of support and enthusiasm on the streets and in the stadiums. This festive public atmosphere quickly spread to the athletes, officials, and press, and was a key factor in the overall success of the Games.

The Barcelona Games consolidated the model, initiated in Seoul 1988, of organizing the Special Olympics in the same city as the Olympics themselves and using the same facilities, organizational framework, and more importantly, harnessing the same spirit of public participation in the Games. The Barcelona '92 Paralympics, "yet unbeaten for their exceptional organization" in the words of the IOC, hosted a total of 3,020 athletes from 82 countries, a figure later exceeded in Atlanta with 3,195 athletes from 103 countries, and Sydney with 3,843 athletes from 123 countries.

However, the value here does not lie in growth alone but rather in the convergence of the two movements in a renewed philosophy of Olympism. The 1992 Games have been referred to as the "The Communication Games," and not only in terms of the symbolic and cultural aspects, but also for the important role played by television transmission rights in their funding. COOB '92 benefited from a sponsorship program initiated in the 1984–1988 period that operated at three different levels: TOP (The Olympic Programme) Sponsors, reserved for multinational sponsors; Olympic Games Sponsorship, for local sponsors of the Organizing Committee; and National Sponsorship, for sponsors of the National Olympic Committees. This represented a major source of income not only for the International Olympic Committee ($95 million for TOP 1 in Seoul and Calgary 1988 and $175 million for TOP 2 in Barcelona and Albertville 1992), but also for the Organizing Committee, which, as has been seen, obtains close to 40 percent of its income via this channel. Income from sponsorship must also be seen in the light of the income deriving from television rights, even higher than income from sponsorship and, undoubtedly, a motivating factor in the latter.

The final negotiation of television rights between COOB'92, the IOC, and NBC was another of the keys to the success of the organizing committee.

As these figures suggest, Barcelona '92 saw the creation of an audiovisual production industry, with 2,700 hours of Olympic television broadcasting, a figure which was to rise slightly in the following Games: Atlanta (3,000 hours) and Sydney (3,400 hours).

This new link between the Games and the visual media was also reflected in the cooperation program between the U.S. network, NBC, and Cablevisión, which marked the beginning of experimentation with pay-per-view television. The Barcelona Games were, in fact, the last Games of the "broadcasting era." Four years later, the "Internet era" was to begin in Atlanta. Barcelona '92 made

Barcelona 1992—Water polo competition at the Barcelona Games. Courtesy of Larry Maloney.

cautious use of new computer and communication technology, taking no significant risks and thus ensuring maximum effectiveness. The approach was one without innovations but also without error. The technological setting was thus also favorable to the success of the Barcelona Games. As the last Games of the "broadcasting era," they avoided the risks of using an innovation (Internet) that was not yet sufficiently sure-footed and instead achieved an unprecedented television audience, calculated at between 700 million and 1 billion viewers for the opening ceremony.

The design of the host city symbols (logotype and mascot) was the first major challenge for Barcelona '92's artistic policy. From the outset, the design of these symbols was seen as a test of the organizers: would they prove sensitive to the modern in art and Catalan design or would they opt for the conservative tradition of design in commercial sport? The logo, designed by Josep Maria Trías, was rapidly accepted by art critics and the public, which appreciated its connotations of the Mediterranean, Spanish artist Joan Miró, the dynamism of the human body, and modernity. Acceptance of the mascot Cobi, designed by Javier Mariscal, was more difficult, both for aesthetic reasons and questions of identity. However, Cobi was finally accepted and accomplished a difficult mission: receiving recognition as a

Table 4
Evolution of Olympic television rights

(in million US $)	
1988: Seoul	407,133
1992: Barcelona	635,560
1996: Atlanta	882,000

Source: International Olympic Committee.

Table 5
Television rights for the Olympic Games Comparison between NBC (USA) and the European Broadcasting Union (EBU)

(in million US $)	NBC (USA)	Increase between consecutive Games	EBU (European television stations)	Increase between consecutive Games
Seoul'88	300	33 %	28	41 %
Barcelona'92	401	34 %	90	221 %

Source: International Olympic Committee.

high-quality design and also being commercial, while breaking away from the conformity and bad taste prevailing in sports and Olympic design at the time.

The ceremonies are the main embodiment of the artistic dimension of the Olympic Games, complemented by the design of the symbols (logo and mascot) and the route of the Olympic torch relay. The Barcelona organizers were often praised on the crucial role played by the ceremonies in the overall success of the 1992 Games. Research on television coverage of the ceremonies shows that the response was unanimously positive. There was a general recognition that Barcelona had taken viewers to a new frontier, a new kind of spectacle, well suited to the conditions of space and time of modern ceremonies. The Barcelona model did, of course, have an influence on the Atlanta and Sydney ceremonies; however, we must also consider the influence of the ceremonies of previous Games, especially Los Angeles and Seoul, on the Barcelona model. The ceremonies, the importance of which has not been fully comprehended by the press or indeed by the Olympic Movement itself, are a synthesis of the Olympic values and the host city or nation's identity in just a few images and motifs.

The Barcelona Games witnessed impressive performances by Australian swimmer Kieren Perkins, British cyclist Chris Boardman, and the American 4×400-meter relay team, all of whom set world records. The gymnast Vitaly Scherbo of the Unified Team (the former Soviet republics) won six gold medals, and the partisan Spanish crowds hailed Spain's best performance ever with twenty-two medals, only four fewer than its combined total at all previous Games.

Professional basketball players were permitted to compete for the first time, and the American "Dream Team" dominated the event. Controversies in judging again marred the boxing competition, and five participants were sent home for drug violations. It was noted that for the first time, all three medal winners in the shot put had endured previous drug suspensions.

Many nations provided their medal winners with cash awards, among them Spain, which gave its medal winners each a pension worth $1 million; China, whose gold-medal athletes received $50,000 and a solid gold soda can; and Taiwan, which awarded each member of its team $400,000.

As part of its candidacy, Barcelona had proposed a comprehensive four-year cultural and artistic program known as the Cultural Olympiad (1989–1992). This model was also followed by Atlanta and Sydney. However, rather than incorporate new content, these schemes merely took advantage of the Olympic Games to revitalize the city's existing art and cultural programs. Time and experience have also highlighted the difficulties of sustaining a four-year program, and they have also highlighted the strong demand for cultural activities during the period of the Games themselves. Moreover, time has also shown that the concept of the Cultural Olympiad suffers from an underlying contradiction: the Games themselves are not adequately showcased as a cultural event. The lack of references to the Olympic phenomenon and to sport in general in the Cultural Olympiads is surprising.

More than a decade after the Games, Barcelona and its citizens are increasingly convinced of the success of the 1992 Games. After all, the international press and television said so, and the IOC President Samaranch said so in his closing address: "You have achieved it. These have been, without any doubt, the best Games in Olympic history." The final assessment will have to await historical perspective. Now, it can be said that Barcelona left a worthy legacy to the Olympic Movement, from which later host cities would benefit. However, it must also be said that Barcelona played host to the Games at one of the best possible periods in the one hundred years of history of the Olympic Movement.

BIBLIOGRAPHICAL ESSAY

The organizing committee's report of the Barcelona Games is *Official Report of the Games of the XXV Olympiad* (Barcelona, 1993), a four-volume set that thoroughly covers all aspects of the committee's work. The Games archives, now mostly recorded on laser discs and cross-referenced in a data base, are located, along with a small museum, at the Olympic Stadium on Montjuïc. The official report of the U.S. Olympic Committee, *Barcelona Albertville 1992* (Salt Lake City, 1992) is heavily pictorial but also contains the results along with some commentary on the United States at the Games. Larry Maloney's essay on these Games in the 1996 edition of this book puts a somewhat different spin on Barcelona 1992 and is worth consulting. Newspapers that covered the Games extensively include the *New York Times*, the *Washington Post*, and the *Atlanta Journal/Constitution*, but the most complete coverage is found in *La Vanguardia*, a Barcelona paper.

A number of important studies of the Barcelona Games have been published under the auspices of the Centre d'Estudis Olimpics, located at the Universitat

Autonoma de Barcelona. These include Miquel de Moragas and Miquel Botella (eds.), *The Keys to Success: The Social, Sporting, Economic and Communication Impact of Barcelona '92* (Barcelona, 1995) and *Barcelona: L'herencia dels Jocs (1992–2002)* (Barcelona, 2002). In the first volume, see especially Joan Botella, "The Political Games: Agents and Strategies in the 1992 Barcelona Olympic Games," 139–148; Miquel Botella, "The Keys to Success of the Barcelona Games," 18–42; and Ferran Brunet, "An Economic Analysis of the Barcelona '92 Olympic Games: Resources, Financing and Impact," 203–237. In the second volume, which deals more with the long-term legacy of the Games, see Ferran Brunet, "Analisi de l'impacte economic dels Jocs Olimpics de Barcelona, 1986–2004," 245–274; Pere Duran, "Turisme: impactes dels Jocs i de la seva image sobre el turisme," 275–294; and Lluis Millet, "Els Jocs de la ciutat," 295–308. Although these three articles are written in Catalan, readers familiar with Spanish should be able to get through them profitably.

On the political issues between Spain and its restive northeastern province, Catalonia, see John Hargreaves, *Freedom for Catalonia: Catalan Nationalism, Spanish Identity, and the Barcelona Olympic Games* (Cambridge, England, 2002). The impact of televising the Barcelona Games is discussed in Miquel de Moragas, et al., "The Worldwide Audience for the Olympics," in Miquel de Moragas, et al., *Television in the Olympics* (London, 1995).

The opening and closing ceremonies of the Olympics are covered in Miquel de Moragas, John MacAloon, and Montserrat Llines (eds.), *Olympic Ceremonies: Historical Continuity and Cultural Exchange* (Lausanne, 1996), a book that resulted from an international symposium on Olympic ceremonies that the Centre d'Estudis Olimpics sponsored in November 1995.

Finally, the noted Olympic filmmaker, Bud Greenspan, chronicled the Games in *Barcelona '92: 16 Days of Glory* (1993), and NBC, the network that telecast the Games, produced a highlights film, *Barcelona '92 Olympic Games* (1992).

ATLANTA 1996
Larry Maloney

THE GAMES OF THE TWENTY-SIXTH OLYMPIAD

Atlanta has striven to claim status as a competent world-class city ever since Union General William T. Sherman torched the city during the American Civil War. Today, Atlanta is a sprawling metropolis of 3 million people and arguably the most progressive city in the American South. Yet, more than a century after the flames of war, residents of Atlanta continued to search for validation that they lived in an international city. Some of Atlanta's visionaries saw a bid for the 1996 Olympic Games as the vehicle to make that dream a reality, even though few in the Olympic Movement believed this first-time candidate was ready to host the Summer Games. To the surprise of its critics, however, the Olympic flame engulfed the heart of Atlantans in 1996, the Centennial Games of the modern Olympic Movement.

Early in the contest to host the 1996 Games, many Olympic watchers considered the birthplace of the ancient and modern Olympics, Athens, as the natural choice; regardless, its chronic pollution and Greece's political instability precluded a *fait accompli* in the host city selection process. Of the five remaining competitors—Atlanta; Belgrade, Yugoslavia; Manchester, England; Melbourne, Australia; and Toronto, Canada—three produced bids strong enough to challenge Athens's claim. Melbourne last hosted the Olympic Games in 1956 and used a compelling "Time for Another Continent" slogan. The Melbourne committee thoughtfully recognized the financial burden of an Australian Games on national Olympic committees (NOCs) by budgeting $40 million to subsidize athlete travel and accommodation costs. Toronto's media and communications facilities had few rivals in North America, and the city carried the United Nations' designation of the most multicultural city on earth.

Atlanta's strengths, however, exceeded those of its competitors. The International Olympic Committee (IOC) Evaluation Commission ranked Atlanta highest for its infrastructure and facilities. More IOC representatives visited Atlanta than any other bid city, and Billy Payne, a local lawyer and president of the organizing committee, circled the globe for two years meeting with IOC members. Atlanta surpassed the competition's international credibility through the diplomatic negotiations of Andrew Young, former mayor of Atlanta and former U.S. ambassador to the United Nations.

Two components of Atlanta's bid swayed IOC members. First, Young assured African IOC delegates that Atlanta's civil rights history and reputation for racial harmony proved the city could host a successful multicultural Olympics. Second, Atlanta's organizing committee proposed a substantial revenue-sharing package. Like Barcelona's financial package for the 1992 Olympics, the Atlanta committee planned to distribute 10 percent of excess revenue to the IOC, with an additional 10 percent targeted for the national organization, the U.S. Olympic Committee (USOC). Atlanta surpassed Barcelona's generosity by offering to disburse half of the remaining surplus to the NOCs.

The fierce competition for the 1996 Games culminated at the IOC session in Tokyo in September 1990. The campaign to host these Olympics had cost the bidding cities more than $100 million, of which Atlanta spent an estimated $7.3 million. In fact, candidate financial expenditures reached such exorbitant heights that the IOC later enacted new regulations to curb excessive and unnecessary bidding costs, which included a $200 limit on gifts to voting members.

The decision on the 1996 Olympic city required five rounds of voting. Athens won the first two rounds of voting but began to lose ground, finally succumbing to Atlanta on the fifth ballot, 51–35. Even before the celebration of victory began, the expectations inherent in hosting the Centennial Games saddled Atlanta with a task as daunting as its postwar reconstruction. Along with these heightened expectations, Atlanta had to endure criticism from the cities that lost, as well as from those who supported their campaigns. Athens led the unsuccessful competitors in suggesting that Atlanta won because of a conspiracy organized by Atlanta-based Coca-Cola, the oldest corporate supporter of the Olympic movement. The Greek newspaper *Eleftherostypos* declared, "The Olympic flame will not be lit with oil, but with Coca-Cola." Spyros Metaxas, the outspoken president of the Athens committee, went further, emphatically stating that Athens would never again bid to host the Olympic Games.

The depth of Athens's and Melbourne's bitterness toward Atlanta resurfaced a year later when they informed the German periodical *Der Spiegel* that some bid cities had bribed IOC members. In its article, *Der Spiegel* alleged that Atlanta bought the votes of eighteen IOC members with promises of free heart surgery in the United States, gold credit cards, up to $120,000 in cash, and college scholarships for their children. Isolated incidents occurred during the selection process that coincided with the allegations of bribery. For example, one IOC official suffered a heart attack while visiting Atlanta, and the bid committee and the hospital covered the medical expenses as a professional courtesy. No evidence existed prior to the Games that substantiated the claims that Atlanta willfully attempted to undermine the bidding process with this or other acts. However, as a result of the myriad investigations following the Salt Lake City bidding scandal, information came to light that Atlanta offered IOC members extravagant gifts that exceeded IOC guidelines.

Atlanta's troubles extended beyond international headlines and the bruised egos of competitors. U.S. newspapers criticized Atlanta as a second-tier city with a plethora of fast food restaurants and a dearth of culture. Charges of nepotism were leveled against the Atlanta Committee for the Olympic Games (ACOG) as relatives of city officials and ACOG board members received paid staff positions. City leaders questioned the committee's ethics when former staff members, as well as city officials, received contracts for Olympic goods and services. Critics likened the computer-generated mascot, Izzy, to a large blue sperm. Even the state flag's confederate battle insignia fueled editorial criticism. Georgia Governor Zell Miller felt the flag's historical links to slavery and segregation conveyed the wrong message about the new American South, but his attempt to have the flag redesigned prior to the Olympics derailed when political extremists mobilized on both sides of the issue and polls indicated that 59 percent of the state's citizens opposed its redesign.

ACOG unwittingly fueled national criticism by selecting controversial communities to host Olympic events. The committee chose Atlanta's neighbor to the north, Cobb County, to host preliminary volleyball competitions. Soon thereafter, the county's conservative government passed a resolution stating that homosexual lifestyles were not compatible with the community's values. The resolution created a firestorm extending beyond

Atlanta 1996—Performers at the Opening Ceremonies for the 1996 Olympic Games in Atlanta celebrate the centennial of the Olympic Movement. Courtesy of Larry Maloney.

Cobb County's borders. Gay rights groups challenged ACOG, stating that the committee's pledge "to reunite the family of man in the profound bond of the Olympic spirit" was a farce if gay athletes and visitors felt unwelcome at venues. Gay activists demanded that Cobb County be dropped as a site, or they would "shut Atlanta down" during the Games. Four-time gold medallist Greg Louganis, an openly gay athlete, appealed to ACOG to change the venue to another county. After the Cobb County commission refused to alter its stance on the resolution, ACOG moved the preliminary volleyball competition to downtown Atlanta.

In addition to the Cobb County debacle, ACOG's efforts to include golf on the 1996 program proved controversial. Although IOC members informed ACOG there was insufficient time to approve golf for 1996 and openly questioned the sport's elitist image, the committee continued to lobby for the sport and made the fatal mistake of choosing the Augusta National Golf club as the proposed venue. Augusta National's reputation for excluding women and minorities caused residents of Atlanta to question ACOG's judgment. The Atlanta City Council shared the community's misgivings and wrote to Juan Antonio Samaranch, the IOC president, asking that he oppose the Augusta golf course. ACOG finally dropped its campaign after Samaranch publicly stated that the proposal had only a "slim possibility of being approved."

Previous Olympic cities endured similar bouts of unfavorable publicity and persevered to host successful Games, but claims of discrimination raised against ACOG had explosive potential. Atlantans expected ACOG to cure the city's social ills by building new roads, providing housing for the homeless, and creating good jobs for the unemployed. As these improvements failed to materialize, citizen groups attacked ACOG for failing to address the city's most pressing problems, and city council members suggested that Games officials were unwilling to work with a predominantly black council. The location of Olympic venues fueled calls of racism when ACOG moved the planned tennis facility from an unsupportive white suburb, while black neighborhoods near the proposed Olympic Stadium felt helpless in their fight to change that venue's location. Community wrath toward ACOG culminated with a speech by Martin Luther King III, a county commissioner and the son of the slain civil rights leader, who declared, "Greed, exclusivity and elitism have become the symbols of Atlanta's Olympic movement, all things that my father fought against—and they are all reflected in the [stadium] deal before us, the rich and affluent on one side, the poor and hopeless on the other side" (*Atlanta Journal/Constitution*, March 6, 1993). It began to appear that international sporting events were exempt from the city's tradition of racial harmony.

Atlanta 1996—U.S. gold medalist Amy Van Dyken won the 50-meter freestyle and the 100-meter butterfly at the Atlanta Games of 1996. She was also a member of the 4 × 100-meter medley relay and 4 × 100-meter freestyle relay teams that won gold medals. Courtesy of Ed Goldstein.

Unfortunately, Atlantans expected far more than the organizing committee was able to provide. ACOG's contract with the IOC contained no requirement to improve the city's infrastructure nor the plight of the poor. Moreover, as a private entity, the committee had no legal obligation to the city's disadvantaged residents. However, the organizations' leadership felt a civic obligation that all the city's residents should benefit from the Games and therefore made substantial commitments to assist Atlanta's poor and minorities. First, ACOG adopted strict equal opportunity standards. Minority- and female-owned companies received more than 32 percent of all Olympic contracts, a significant milestone. The committee also established a policy that favored bids including minority subcontracting. ACOG set similar standards in its hiring practices: 32 percent of the committee's management consisted of minorities, and women represented 35 percent of the committee's managers.

ACOG's minority enrichment strategy encompassed the entire state with the development of a program to assist the state's underprivileged. The committee stated repeatedly that the 40,000 Olympic volunteers would be chosen based on their history of volunteer service. The warning proved successful, and the largest training program for volunteers in the history of the Olympic movement was born. More than 540,000 volunteers joined the Olympic Force, a multiyear volunteer training program designed to improve impoverished communities and to assist the state's youth before the Olympic Games.

No less important was the committee's and the city's efforts to improve dilapidated Olympic neighborhoods. More than 50 percent of Atlanta's impoverished families resided in the downtown area, where the majority of Olympic activities took place. The proliferation of inner-city neighborhoods scarred by urban decay led one city planner to state, "It doesn't take a genius to figure out what the story's going to be in 1996. The splendor of the Olympics amid the squalor of Southern poverty. Boy, that's written all over every tabloid in the world" (*Atlanta Journal/Constitution*, April 5, 1992). When the city faced an avalanche of necessary projects to complete by 1996,

ACOG and the business community stepped forward to assist Atlanta's poorer neighborhoods. Atlanta-based foundations funded redevelopment projects, and a consortium of banks loaned $120 million to build or refurbish homes and apartments in Olympic neighborhoods. ACOG worked with nonprofit groups to build homes near the Olympic stadium. The committee even funded construction of two of the stadium houses, and more than 200 ACOG employee volunteers assisted with construction.

Atlanta 1996—U.S. sprinter Michael Johnson, shown after he broke the world record in the 200-meter dash. Courtesy of Ed Goldstein.

Additionally, ACOG worked with the city to lessen the impact of Olympic construction. Neighborhood groups surrounding the Olympic stadium were adamant in their opposition to its construction. Already living in the shadow of Fulton County Stadium, residents felt a second sports structure nearby would lead to further deterioration of the neighborhood and result in lower property values. With support from the Urban Land Institute in Washington, D.C., residents persuaded the city to demolish the older facility after the Games. As part of the package in which ACOG agreed to cover the costs of demolishing the existing stadium, the committee further appeased residents with a package of minority employment and training programs.

ACOG's laudable steps to ensure a role for the city's minority community received less recognition than deserved, partly due to national circumstances beyond ACOG's control. For instance, funding for the Olympic spectacle soared as each new Olympic city schemed to improve upon the success of its predecessors. Atlanta planned to surpass Barcelona's extravaganza, but revenues failed to keep pace with burgeoning expectations. Lackluster economic performance in the United States increased the burden of convincing corporations of the 1996 Games' worth, and IOC financial requirements dampened ACOG's ability to finance the

Olympics. The IOC sought to avoid a situation in which both the USOC and ACOG competed for funds from the core group of U.S. Olympic supporters, and asked that both organizations join forces to finance their programs. Consequently, individual corporate sponsorships for the 1996 Olympics reached an unprecedented $40 million, only $28 million of which supported staging of the Games.

Companies initially balked at paying the sponsorship fee, principally due to the downturn in the U.S. economy. The auction for television rights proved equally difficult. Payne predicted in 1990 that U.S. television rights would sell for an extraordinary $600 million, a $199 million increase over the rights for Barcelona. In the midst of a recession, ACOG quickly lowered its projection to $500 million, and the IOC delayed negotiations, hoping the economy would improve. The National Broadcasting Company (NBC) eventually purchased U.S. television rights for $456 million, only $6 million above the figure ACOG needed to meet its budget projections.

Atlanta 1996—The men's backstroke competition. Courtesy of Ed Goldstein.

Meanwhile, costs continued to soar. The original estimate to host the Games for $1.01 billion climbed to $1.7 billion. Projections for surplus revenue of $132 million dwindled to $19 million due to higher costs and promises to the city's minority community. For example, estimates for the Olympic stadium jumped from $145 million to $209 million after ACOG agreed to cover post-Olympic demolition costs for Fulton County Stadium. Escalating costs caused a certain degree of anxiety among IOC members. ACOG's organizational structure and charter ensured that Atlanta and state residents would be shielded from any Olympic deficit. If the committee failed to raise sufficient funds, plans for an extravagant Centennial Games would have to be curtailed. The prospect of trimming Olympic luxury to meet a restricted budget prompted IOC member Dick Pound to announce, "We will never award the Games in the future to a city in the United States or elsewhere, which has no significant public sector commitment, either in the form of a financial contribution or at the very least, in the form of a guarantee to meet the necessary costs of organizing the Games" (*Atlanta Journal/Constitution*, May 18, 1994).

Although ACOG vowed to host the Games without taxpayer assistance, the city of Atlanta made no similar claim. Atlanta needed up to $500 million to complete necessary infrastructure improvements by the time of the opening ceremonies. Half the needed funds were provided by the federal government, but the Georgia state legislature offered no state funding and blocked attempts by the city to raise revenue through a 1 percent increase in the city's sales tax and a surcharge on tickets to sporting and cultural events. The financial logjam left a sour taste in the mouths of Atlanta's taxpayers; polls indicated that half the city's residents were resigned to paying higher taxes to support Olympic-related development. Ultimately, voters accepted the grim reality and approved $149 million for critical infrastructure improvements, far short of the revenue needed. Eventually, the city sold vendor licenses in an attempt to cover some of the municipality's costs of staging the Games. By opening ceremonies, downtown streets were lined with hawkers of everything from Olympic T-shirts to generic goods from India, which gave these Games the feel of a county fair.

In spite of budget woes and hyper-inflated expectations, Atlanta's Games began with great fanfare with opening ceremonies that highlighted the best of southern heritage, as well as, unfortunately, pickup trucks and cheerleaders. These Games opened with a contingent of 10,750 athletes from 197 countries, the largest participation at any Olympic Games. The joy of the evening gave no hint of the trouble to come.

Within days of the opening ceremonies, problems began to mount on two critical fronts—information retrieval and transportation. IBM designed an information system, Info 96, to provide athletes with web access and journalists with statistics, up-to-the-minute results from events, and detailed information on each of the athletes involved in the Games. The media began referring to the system as Info 97 due to sluggish delivery times. In addition to late results, information on athletes and events often contained inaccurate information. The system generated so many complaints from the world's media that ACOG decided to forgo the fees for use of Info 96.

ACOG's transportation system fared just as poorly. Cities across the country loaned the committee buses to transport athletes and spectators to events. The committee needed 3,600 drivers for the fleet of 1,650 buses, not all of whom could be recruited locally. Approximately 10 percent of the drivers came from outside the Atlanta metro area, and the training provided to those drivers proved insufficient. Consequently, athletes and spectators alike fumed on buses lost somewhere in Atlanta. The most devastating example of this incompetence involved David Khakhaleishvili, a Georgian judo athlete preparing to defend the gold medal he had won at Barcelona. He was disqualified when he missed his weigh-in because his bus driver could not navigate the one-mile stretch of streets from the Olympic Village to the judo venue.

Bungled information and direction-challenged bus drivers paled in comparison, however, to the tragedy that unfolded at Centennial Olympic Park on the morning of July 27. The park, envisioned three short years earlier by Billy Payne as the $50 million answer to urban decay, became the most popular gathering place for the Atlanta Games. Everyone, regardless of credentials or tickets, reveled in the spirit of the Games in this park, and thousands of athletes and spectators alike crowded into the park at night for evening concerts.

During one of these concerts, Richard Jewell, a park security guard, spotted a suspicious satchel and immediately began to clear people from the area. At 1:25 A.M., the satchel exploded, hurtling nails and screws through the concert crowd. Within moments, two were dead and 110 injured. Jewell initially received a hero's welcome for his actions that potentially saved many lives. Within days, however, Jewell became the FBI's prime suspect in the bombing, and word leaked to the media. After three months of investigation and public scrutiny that ripped Jewell's life apart, the FBI cleared him as a suspect and continued the hunt for a terrorist. More than two years after the bombing, the Department of Justice issued a warrant for the arrest of Eric Rudolph for the Olympic Park bombing and several other bombings in the Atlanta area; however, Rudolph remained at large until May 2003, when he was arrested in Murphy, North Carolina.

Every Olympic city since Munich has dreaded the prospect of terrorism being imbedded in its Olympic legacy, and Atlanta was no different. The difference in Atlanta, however, was the defiance the public showed toward such an act. Although the initial shock prevented most from venturing downtown, a sea of Olympic spectators soon clogged the streets in a matter of hours, and attendance at Olympic events remained high. When the park reopened on July 30, 350,000 people passed through to pay their respects to those killed and injured, and to reclaim what the bomber tried to deny them—their right to celebrate the Olympic spirit.

In spite of tragedy and technical problems, the athletes of the world provided spectacular performances for the Olympic Movement's centennial celebration. The "Pocket Hercules," Naim Suleymanoglu of Turkey, managed to win a third consecutive gold medal at these Olympic Games, the only weightlifter ever to do so. For the first time ever, the U.S. women's gymnastics team won the gold medal, a feat made all the more incredible given that the team's golden fate rested on the final vault of an injured but courageous Kerry Strug.

Carl Lewis won his fourth consecutive gold medal in the long jump, capping a 12-year Olympic career in which he won nine gold medals overall, while Michael Johnson became the first man ever to win gold in both the 200-meter and 400-meter events. Additionally, U.S. women ruled the team events by winning gold in softball, soccer, and basketball, as well as the 4×100-relay.

At these Games, the United States proved once again that the host country has a home field advantage by winning 101 medals, compared with Germany, who won the next highest total of medals, with sixty-five. However, seventy-eight nations shared in the wealth of gold, silver and bronze, more than at any previous Olympic Games, while athletes from Costa Rica, Ecuador, Syria, and Hong Kong won the first gold medals for their countries.

Closing ceremonies brought collective relief to the organizers and the city's residents, even if they failed to reach the much-hoped-for mark of the best Games ever. This failure, however, seems fitting to the history that is the Atlanta Olympics. The athletes provided the world with seventeen days of sporting miracles, but the tragedy of the bombing, combined with the committee's missteps in technology and transportation, tarnished a legacy that could have been golden. City and state leaders share in this blame, as they failed to see the Olympic enterprise as Barcelona had envisioned, as the city's catalyst into the twenty-first century. Instead, they focused on keeping the costs to a minimum for this once-in-a-lifetime opportunity. It is this lack of vision to dream on a grand scale when the opportunity presents itself that will keep this great southern city searching for validation of its international stature.

BIBLIOGRAPHICAL ESSAY

The official report of the Atlanta Games is ACOG, *The Official Report of the Centennial Olympic Games* (Atlanta, 1997). Its three sections deal respectively with planning and organization, events during the Games, and results. In addition, ACOG published many other works before and during the Games, ranging from media guides to a daily bulletin (the *Daily Olympian*) to after-action reports; many of these are on file at the library of the Amateur Athletic Foundation of Los Angeles (AAFLA), whose website is http://www.aafla.org. C. Richard Yarbrough, *And They Call Them Games* (Macon, GA, 2000) is an insider's account of ACOG's work by its director of communications. Harvey K. Newman, *Southern Hospitality: Tourism and the Growth of Atlanta* (Tuscaloosa, AL, 1999) devotes a chapter to the impact of the Atlanta Olympics on the city. The Paralympics are described in *The Triumph of the Human Spirit: The Atlanta Paralympic Experience* (Oakville, ON, Canada, 1997). No specific author is credited with writing this book.

For pictorial works on the Atlanta Games, see the IOC, *Official Commemorative Book of the Centennial Olympic Games: Atlanta 1996* (San Francisco, 1996), and Glenn Hannigan, *One Glorious Summer: A Photographic History of the 1996 Atlanta Olympics* (Marietta, GA, 1996). Skip Rosen looks at the business interests behind the Games in *Empowering the Olympic Movement* (Atlanta?, 1996), a reprint of a *Fortune* magazine feature article. The IOC published *1996 Centennial Olympic Games Television Report* (Lausanne, 1997), a summary of the television experience at the Games.

Contemporary magazine and newspaper sources include *Sports Illustrated*, which, in addition to regular coverage in the magazine, produced the *Olympic Daily*, providing in-depth coverage of the previous day's significant moments. Other sources for coverage of Atlanta prior to and during the Games include the *Atlanta Journal/Constitution*, the *New York Times*, the *Washington Post*, the *Wall Street Journal*, and *Business Week*.

Olympic filmmaker Bud Greenspan produced *Atlanta's Olympic Glory* (1996), the official film version of the Games, as well as *70 Meters to Olympic Glory* (1996), which deals with the archery competition at the Games.

SYDNEY 2000

Richard Cashman

THE GAMES OF THE TWENTY-SEVENTH OLYMPIAD

The Sydney Games took place at a problematic time for the International Olympic Committee (IOC), which was engulfed by scandals, primarily relating to revelations about the Salt Lake City Bid Committee, from November 1998 through much of 1999. After an IOC Commission, set up to investigate improper behavior, recommended that seven IOC members be expelled and another 10 members be warned, 10 members either resigned or were expelled. The Games were also important for the reputation of President Juan Antonio Samaranch, who bore the brunt of the criticism resulting from the scandals. They were also his last Games as president.

The success of the Games—from the point of view of an athletic event, in terms of the efficiency and smoothness of the organization and the level of community support—provided Sydney and Australia with much good publicity. The positive media reporting of the Games was even more important for the reputation of the soon-to-retire president and the International Olympic Committee. It provided a much-needed breathing space for the implementation of reform measures.

Sydney Olympic 2000 Bid Limited was created in May 1991, as an incorporated public company, headed by a prominent solicitor, Rod McGeoch, though the bid was underwritten by the New South Wales government, which accepted the responsibility for the construction of the venues. The Sydney bid for the 2000 Olympic Games benefited from the international contacts established and the knowledge gained from the failed bids of two Australian cities: Brisbane in 1992 and Melbourne in 1996. The bid also gained bipartisan political support at all levels of government and strong community support. In *Australia and the Olympic Games*, Harry Gordon claims that Australia and Greece are the only two nations to have attended every Summer Games, although this statement has been contested by the Olympic historians of three other nations—France, Great Britain, and

Switzerland. However, there is no question of the Australian passion for the Olympic Games and its long tradition of Olympic success, particularly in swimming.

The Australian bid was judged technically superior and highly marketable. Central to the bid strategy was the location of the majority of venues and the athletes' village at Homebush Bay, about 9 miles west of the city center. The establishment of this Olympic precinct meant that the athletes as well as officials and the media had minimal amount of travelling to most Olympic venues. Staging of the Games during the first month of spring, rather than in the heat and humidity of summer, was also beneficial for athletes. Darling Harbour, located in the city, was a subsidiary Olympic precinct. At the time of the bid, the site of the Games had been fully identified and the International Aquatic and Athletic Centers—the latter became the Olympic warm-up track—had been commissioned and construction had begun. Both centers were opened in 1994. The State Sports Center, which contained facilities for hockey and indoor sports, also became part of the bid.

Homebush Bay consists of about 1,900 acres of land in the demographic heartland of Sydney—west of the city and the focus of population growth in recent decades—where world-class sporting facilities were considered most needed given that the existing major sport grounds and indoor facilities were in the city and its eastern suburbs. Sydney, it was claimed, needed larger facilities because the capacity of Sydney Football Stadium was just 45,000 and the largest indoor stadium in the city, Sydney Entertainment Center, had seating for only 10,000.

Homebush Bay includes some remnant eucalyptus and casuarina woodlands and extensive wetlands, with a good covering of mangroves. The area is the home of a variety of mammals, reptiles, amphibians, and birds. It had been the location of an armaments depot, abattoir, brickworks—the remnant quarry remains a feature of Millennium Park—and various recreational operations. Over some decades Homebush Bay had been the site of unrecorded and unregulated dumping of household and industrial garbage, including toxic waste, so that it had become degraded. After the potential of the site had been identified for urban renewal in the 1970s, the State Sports Centre, Bicentennial Park, and a privately developed business complex, the Australia Centre, were opened in the 1980s. The winning of the Olympic bid accelerated this development that had been planned to occur gradually over a period of years up to 2010.

Homebush Bay consists of three major areas: Bicentennial Park (opened in 1988), Sydney Olympic Park, which was ready for the 2000 Olympic Games, and Millennium Park, which was partly completed by 2000 but will undergo further redevelopment. The remediation of Homebush Bay and the related concept of a green Games were attractive features of the bid because the environmental measures proposed were more ambitious than at any previous Olympic Games, and the idea anticipated the IOC's adoption of the environment as the third strand of Olympism in 1994. There had been some environmental initiatives at the 1994 Lillehammer Winter Olympic Games, but Sydney's green promises were more ambitious than those of any previous Games in that they related to six key areas—energy and water conservation, waste disposal, recycling of water, transportation, the improvement of air, and the protection of significant cultural and physical environments. Greenpeace Australia was involved in the bid from its planning stages. Environmental issues also shaped the contours of Sydney Olympic Park: treated and capped waste formed the basis of the man-made hills of the Olympic Park since it was considered best to deal with the past problems of Homebush on the site rather than exporting them elsewhere.

The Sydney bid team adopted a clever and professional political campaign that exploited the existing bid system to the limits by offering indirect benefits—such as scholarships, employment, travel assistance, and sport programs—to the families of IOC members from some less affluent countries. The bid team maximized Sydney's strengths and minimized its weaknesses. The Games were marketed as the athletes' Games, held in a safe country with minimal security problems and a strong sporting reputation. The bid committee countered a potential criticism of the bid—the cost of transportation—by offering to pay the travel costs of all visiting teams.

Despite all these advantages, Sydney won the vote only narrowly, defeating Beijing by two votes—45 to 43—after Beijing had led Sydney in the first three rounds. The issue of human rights, which had been publicized dramatically when many dissidents were killed in the 1989 crackdown at Tiananmen Square, probably swayed enough IOC members to support Sydney because there were many in the IOC who were attracted by the lure of taking the Olympic Games to a new

Sydney 2000—By 2000, commercialism was becoming ever more visible at the Olympic Games, as seen in this photo of a McDonald's booth at the Sydney Games. Courtesy of the International Centre for Olympic Studies, University of Western Ontario.

frontier and the biggest country in the world. No one campaigned against Sydney, whereas there were members of the U.S. Congress who spoke out against human rights abuses in Beijing.

Although the bid contract was signed by the city of Sydney, it was the New South Wales Government that played a central role in organizing and financing the Games. It underwrote the 1992 estimated cost of running the Games at $1.7 million, though this figure had escalated to $3.75 million by 1996. These costs, however, did not include large-scale infrastructure costs such as the cost of remediation of Homebush Bay, the railway link to Olympic Park, and other large ticket items such as the eastern suburbs subway extension. To ease the burden on the taxpayer, the government sought private sector funding to build and run major venues, such as Stadium Australia, the SuperDome, and the Olympic Village. The city-airport motorway and railway also used private sector funding, although the government provided most of the capital for the rail line. One result of private involvement was that the capacity of the Olympic Stadium was increased from 80,000 to 110,000, enabling Stadium Australia to offer a larger number of units that were part of the public bond issue that helped finance the Stadium. The Sydney Olympic Games was also financed by the city and federal governments: the former contributed money for civic improvements, and the federal government made contributions in areas such as security and customs.

The Games organizations setup reflected this structure. Initially there was a clear division between the Organizing Committee (SOCOG), the body set up to stage the

Games—with members nominated by the city and state government and the Australian Olympic Committee—and the state government, which controlled the Olympic Coordination Authority (OCA), the institution responsible for building the venues. OCA was directly responsible to the Minister for the Olympics, Michael Knight. However, the relations between SOCOG and other Olympic-related bodies—OCA, the Australian Olympic Committee, and the New South Wales Government—were often strained in the initial years, and there were a number of changes in the key personnel of SOCOG. The friction of an independent SOCOG was shelved and Michael Knight became President of the SOCOG Board in 1996. While some critics regarded this move as an unfortunate politicization of SOCOG, it resulted in a less troubled relationship between SOCOG and the New South Wales Government.

Sydney, like any Olympic city, had its share of political controversies from the time it won the bid until it staged the Games. After the euphoria of winning the bid waned, there was frequent media and public criticism of SOCOG and the New South Wales Government about their excessive high-handedness and secretiveness in matters relating to the Games—the details of the bid contract were made public shortly before the Games. The ticketing fiasco of 1999 was one of the more damaging controversies when it was revealed that only a fraction of tickets for some prime events were available for sale to the public. Before that there was equal rancor about the marching bands when it became known that a majority of the members of the marching bands, who performed at the Opening Ceremony, had been recruited from overseas. The

Sydney 2000—Beach volleyball, a popular sport around the world, has recently been added to the schedule of the Summer Games events. Here Eric Fonoimoana of the United States defends the U.S. title in the gold medal match against Brazil at the Sydney Games, 2000. Courtesy of Larry Maloney.

problems of SOCOG were the subject of a long-running and clever television comedy, *The Games*, which satirized the organizing committee as bumbling and inefficient. This program demonstrated how Australians appropriated the Games, using humor to poke fun of those who took the Games too seriously. However, the integration of the Games into Australian popular culture demonstrated just how seriously Australians took the Games.

The question of Australia's indigenous communities was the most sensitive and problematic political issue for the local Olympic organizers. This human rights issue was also of great interest to the international media. There was the issue, first of all, of how Australia's indigenous communities should be represented in the Games. There was also the possibility that there would be demonstrations by indigenous peoples and arrests during the Games, which had occurred at the time of the Brisbane Commonwealth Games in 1982. While all Australian political parties recognized that Aborigines were worse off materially, educationally, and health-wise than the rest of the community, there was disagreement among politicians and the community more generally about what policies were appropriate to deal with this situation. While some favored an official apology to Aborigines, reconciliation, and a commitment to land rights—which had been the matter of two High Court decisions in the 1990s—others did not. Aboriginal communities were divided about whether to use the Games to highlight their predicament to the world or whether to support the Games, particularly because the Australian Olympic team included some high profile Aboriginal athletes, including Cathy Freeman.

The only Aboriginal demonstration to occur during the Games was a peaceful one, with a small tent embassy of 150 persons set up in Victoria Park near the University of Sydney. That an Aboriginal protest did not occur was in part because SOCOG adopted an inclusive attitude towards Aborigines and in this respect adopted a more progressive attitude than the community at large. Realizing the sensitivity of indigenous issues, SOCOG recruited Aboriginal athletes and established a special Aboriginal unit to deal directly with Aboriginal leaders and communities. Indigenous issues also featured prominently in the cultural presentation of Australia. An ambitious four-year Cultural Olympiad opened in 1997 with a festival of indigenous cultures, *The Festival of the Dreaming*. However, the budget for arts festivals in the next years was slashed and the rest of the arts festival was largely marginal to the Olympic Games.

The Olympic torch first arrived in Australia at the sacred site of Uluru where it was presented first to the elders, the traditional owners of the land. Aborigines were also highlighted in the Opening Ceremony with the Aboriginal musician Djakapurra Munyarryan instructing young Australia, portrayed by a 14-year-old white girl, Nikki Webster, on the land and its ancient culture. The climax of the Opening Ceremony occurred when Cathy Freeman lit the cauldron.

While the ideal of the green Games was an attractive one, it proved difficult to deliver in its various dimensions to the satisfaction of environmental groups, such as Greenpeace Australia and Green Games Watch 2000, a watchdog group set up by the state government to monitor the delivery of environmental initiatives. While there was some praise for the athletes' village, which was an environmental showcase, additional costs and the Olympic time frame made it difficult to fulfill what were wide-ranging and ambitious promises. By 1997 SOCOG was retreating from the concept of the green Games when it referred to the Sydney Games as more green than any previous Olympic Games. However, the ultimate assessment of the success of the green Games will not be evident for decades when it will be known whether the remediation of Homebush Bay was properly done or whether, as one green critic suggested, it was a "shoddy" undertaking.

There were few anti-Games protests before or during the Games although there was some community opposition to particular facilities. The Bondi Beach Volleyball

Stadium was a controversial development because it closed off a substantial section of a popular surfing beach for some six months, and some feared that it would cause environmental damage to the beach. The development of the Ryde Pool, the venue for some of the preliminary Olympic water polo competitions, closed a public pool for two years and converted part of a public park into a privately-owned leisure facility. Auburn Council, one of the poorer municipalities in Sydney, believed that its taxpayers had to bear an unfair burden for the creation of Sydney Olympic Park, which lay within its boundaries. Whereas the abattoir had paid taxes to the Auburn Council, no taxes were forthcoming from Sydney Olympic Park.

The impact of the IOC scandals made the final lead-up years of the Sydney Olympic Games problematic. Until June 2000 there were some fears that tickets would not sell, that the support of sponsors would fall short of targets, and that the negative international atmosphere would tarnish the Games. They made it difficult for SOCOG to raise sponsorship money in the crucial lead-up years. Because of a shortfall of $200 million in sponsorship, SOCOG introduced cuts of $75 million in May 1999. Australia did not fully escape the fallout from the Salt Lake City corruption scandal, and there were questions about some of the tactics employed by the Sydney bid team. An Australian IOC member, Phil Coles, faced accusations of impropriety but was eventually exonerated.

The torch relay proved the circuit breaker that changed the atmosphere in the Olympic city from one of criticism and negativity to one of community involvement and support. It allowed greater public ownership of the Games that many Australians had regarded up to this point as SOCOG's or the state government's. The Australian torch relay was the longest and most ambitious undertaken: after the torch was lit in Olympia and conveyed to Athens, there were brief stopovers in 12 countries of Oceania before the torch relay traveled around Australia for 100 days. The torch relay was carefully organized to maximize community involvement: half the 11,000 torch-bearers were chosen by community committees, and the torch made frequent lunch-time and evening stops where community cauldrons were lit.

There was a remarkable contrast between the Olympic torch relay and the massive and well organized protests of some 10,000 demonstrators against globalization that took place when the Asia-Pacific Summit of the World Economic Forum was in Melbourne from September 11 to 13, 2000. On the second day of the forum, the police charged the protesters, injuring 200. Meanwhile there was an outpouring of public enthusiasm for the other form of globalization as the torch relay finally reached Sydney before the opening of the Olympic Games on September 15.

The Sydney Opening Ceremony followed the Seoul and Barcelona models of the cultural presentation of the nation: the presentation of the land and its traditional inhabitants, the importance of fire and water to the island continent, the coming of immigrants, and the making of a vibrant and technologically advanced nation. The initial segment, "Deep Sea Dreaming," introduced the Aboriginal notion of the dreamtime and the importance of the ocean to the island inhabitants of Australia. Water was again featured when the cauldron was lit in a pool of water before it ascended to its pinnacle framed by a waterfall. In the parade of athletes, North and South Korea marched as one team, and four athletes representing the newly-independent East Timor marched under the Olympic banner.

The final seven torch-bearers were all women, celebrating 100 years of women in the Olympic Games. They also highlighted the impressive contribution of Australian women to Australia's Olympic tradition.

Although some preliminary football matches had been played before the Opening Ceremony, the triathlon, a new event, was the first competition of the Sydney Games. With the athletes diving into Sydney Harbour, adjacent to the Harbour Bridge, and completing the event at the Opera House, the triathlon provided the world audience with a picture postcard of Sydney.

The Games proceeded smoothly and successfully over 16 days. The weather was mostly warm and sunny, even though it was the first month of spring, the transport infrastructure and Sydney Olympic Park coped well with vast crowds, and there were no problems of security or criticism of excessive commercialism. Sydney also learned from the problems Atlanta had faced that led disgruntled journalists to write negative stories, and the Main Press and Broadcasting Centres were carefully planned. The many volunteers, who had been trained by TAFE (Technical and Further Education) were praised as helpful and cheerful. Most of the specialist volunteers were university trained.

Although Australians took great pride in the performance of the Australian swimming team, led by Ian Thorpe, who won three gold medals, the performance of Cathy Freeman in the 400-meter race was the Australian highlight of the Games. Having won a silver medal in 1996 and having lit the cauldron, Freeman was expected to win a gold medal in this event. Much was made of her success. During her victory lap Freeman draped the Australian and Aboriginal flags on her back, and the leader of the opposition, Kim Beazley, declared that she had run 400 meters towards reconciliation.

Comedians Roy Slavin and H. G. Nelson, known simply as Roy and H. G. (their real names were Greg Pickover and John Doyle) produced a popular comedy program, *The Dream*, screened each evening of the Games. In addition to satirizing Olympic pomposity, Roy and H. G. helped incorporate the Olympic Games into everyday life, and with their humorous comments on lesser-known sports, they helped the less knowledgeable sports fans gain greater access to the Games.

The relationship between SOCOG and SPOC (Sydney Paralympic Organizing Committee) was a close one and as a result the transition from the Olympic to the Paralympic Games was relatively smooth and trouble free.

The positive publicity generated by the Sydney 2000 Olympic Games boosted the local economy, with Sydney becoming the most popular international convention destination by 1999. Many have claimed an increase in international tourism since the Games, though it is not easy to isolate Olympic tourism from other forms of tourism. The economy of New South Wales was boosted in the lead-up to the Games with the state boasting the lowest unemployment in the country in the 1990s. However, the education and health budgets suffered in the years before the Games when money was shifted to pay for the cost of Olympic construction.

Some wondered if the Olympic image of Australia as a tolerant and multicultural society was not diminished by the controversial treatment of Asian refugees in 2001. If Australians took more pride in indigenous history and culture, there was no evident improvement in race relationships after the Olympic Games. However, the symbolic highlighting of Aborigines in the most important staged event in Australia may have some lasting impact.

While the expansive Sydney Olympic Park proved a wonderful and atmospheric place during the Olympic Games, there were doubts after the Games of the wisdom of investing so much of the city's reputation in such a large sporting district. Sydney Olympic Park was often a lonely and desolate place in 2001 and many in the local media branded it a white elephant. The two largest venues, Stadium Australia (downsized to 80,000) and the SuperDome (with a capacity of 21,000), operated at a loss in the years after the Games because there was insufficient demand for venues of that size and there were alternative venues in the city and its eastern suburbs.

By 2002 there was the promise of more elite sports being staged at Olympic Park, and the Olympic Stadium was chosen as the venue for the principal matches of the 2003 Rugby World Cup. The post-Games Master Plan of the Sydney Olympic Park Authority, set up in 2001, proposed the construction of residential properties (apartments housing a permanent population of 5,000) and proposed attracting commercial tenants as well to the center of Sydney Olympic Park. Most of the other Olympic venues, such as the velodrome and the shooting and tennis centers, also suffered from insufficient use to cover the post-construction costs of operation.

It is likely that the long-term assessment of the Sydney Olympic Games will be affected by the viability of Sydney Olympic Park and whether it will become a burden on the state's resources as an under utilized luxury item. If the vision of Sydney Olympic Park is not realized, it is likely that the longer-term assessment of the Games will be less positive than the closing remarks of President Samaranch that the Sydney Games were the "best ever" Olympic Games, accolades that had been delivered after the Seoul (1988) and the Barcelona (1992) Olympic Games.

BIBLIOGRAPHICAL ESSAY

After the Games the archives were located at the New South Wales State Archives, though the State Library of New South Wales (Sydney) and the National Library of Australia (Canberra) have significant collections of books and other records. The Centre for Olympic Studies at the University of New South Wales is the holder of some supplementary material, including some 20,000 slides that cover the public activities of SOCOG from 1994 to 2000. Much of the memorabilia of the Games, including objects used in the Opening Ceremony, is now in the possession of the Power House Museum. A unique feature of the *Official Post-Games Report of the XXVII Olympiad* (2001) was that it was edited by an Olympic scholar, Kristine Toohey, who recruited 13 scholars to contribute material for volume 2. The Bud Greenspan film of the Sydney 2000 Olympic Games was released on the 2001 anniversary of the Games.

Material published on the bid and the pre-Games period includes Douglas Booth and Colin Tatz, "Swimming with the Big Boys? The Politics of Sydney's 2000 Olympic Bid," *Sporting Traditions* 11, 1 (Nov. 1994): 3–23; Janet Cahill, *Running Towards Sydney 2000: The Olympic Flame and Torch* (Sydney, 1999); Richard Cashman, *Olympic Countdown: Diary of the Sydney Olympics* (Sydney, 1999); Richard Cashman and Anthony Hughes, eds., *Staging the Olympics* (Sydney, 1999); Harry Gordon, *Australia and the Olympic Games* (Brisbane, 1994); Ian Jobling, "Bidding for the Olympics: Site Selection and Sydney 2000," in Kay Schaffer and Sidonie Smith, eds., *The Olympics at the Millennium* (New Brunswick, NJ, 2000): 258–71; Helen J. Lenskyj, "When Winners Are Losers: Toronto and Sydney Bids for the

Summer Olympics," *Journal of Sport and Social Issues* 24 (Nov. 1996): 392–418; Rod McGeoch, with Glenda Korporaal, *The Bid: How Australia Won the 2000 Games* (Melbourne, 1994); Dennis H. Phillips, *Australian Women at the Olympic Games*, 3d ed. (Sydney, 2000); and Alan Thompson, ed., *Terrorism and the 2000 Olympics* (Canberra, 1996).

With regard to the impact of the Games in Sydney, see Richard Cashman and Anthony Hughes, eds., *Auburn Council: Home of the 2000 Olympics* (Sydney, 1999); Richard Cashman and Anthony Hughes, eds., *Mosman Council: Forum on the Impacts of the Olympics* (Sydney, 1998); Helen Lenskyj, *The Best Olympics Ever: Social Impacts of Sydney 2000* (New York, 2002); and Kristy Ann Owen, *The Local Impacts of the Sydney 2000 Olympic Games: Processes and Politics of Venue Preparation* (Sydney, 2001).

Environment: Sharon Beder, "Sydney's Toxic Green Olympics," *Current Affairs Bulletin* 70, 6 (2000): 12–18; Richard Cashman and Anthony Hughes, eds., *The Green Games: A Golden Opportunity* (Sydney, 1998).

Indigenous issues: Genevieve and Richard Cashman, eds., *Red, Black, and Gold: Sydney Aboriginal People and the Olympics* (Sydney, 2000); Darren Godwell, "The Olympic Branding of Aborigines: The 2000 Olympic Games and Australia's Indigenous Peoples," in Kay Schaffer and Sidonie Smith, *The Olympics at the Millennium* (New Brunswick, NJ, 2000): 234–57; Michelle Hanna, *Reconciliation in Olympism: Indigenous Culture in the Sydney Olympiad* (Sydney, 1999).

Media: Australian Broadcasting Corporation, *The Games* (n.p.); Philip Bell, Channel 7, Roy and H. G., *The Dream* (n.p.); Helen Wilson, "What is an Olympic City? Visions of Sydney 2000," *Media Culture and Society* 18 (1996): 603–18.

Sydney Olympic Park: Richard Cashman, "What is Legacy?" unpublished paper (Lausanne, 2002); Glen H. Searle, "Uncertain Legacy: Sydney's Olympic Stadiums," *European Planning Studies* 10, 7 (2002): 845–60; Sydney Olympic Park, *Master Plan*, SOPA (Sydney, 2002); James Weirick, "A Non-Event? Sydney's Olympics," *Architecture Australia* 85, 2 (Mar./Apr. 1996): 80–83.

Universities and volunteers: Richard Cashman and Kristine Toohey, *The Contribution of the Higher Education Sector to the Sydney 2000 Olympic Games* (Sydney, 2002).

ATHENS 2004

Christine Sell

THE GAMES OF THE TWENTY-EIGHTH OLYMPIAD

Athens last hosted an Olympic Games in 1896. The city was chosen as the first host of the modern Games, in deference to Greece as the birthplace of the Olympic Games. Greece had hoped to be the host city for the Centennial Games in 1996. However, severe and constant pollution, as well as uneasiness about Greece's chronic political troubles, blocked the selection. Since Greece had participated in every Games of the modern Olympic movement, the loss of the Centennial Games was a bitter defeat that toughened the nation's resolve to bring the Games back to Athens.

In 1994 the International Olympic Committee (IOC) refined the bid process for host city selection during its 102nd session. The IOC announced that henceforth the process, conducted by the IOC Evaluation Commission, would have two stages. The first stage included the preparation and public release of a report that would examine selected cities. The commission formed a selection college, its members drawn from the various bodies with obvious interests in and connections to the Olympic Games (including the international federations, national Olympic committees, various IOC members, and the chairman of the IOC Evaluation Commission). This college then selected several candidate cities, based on the evaluation commission's report. The second phase began with visits to the various candidate cities. These visits, which provided the voting body an opportunity for firsthand evaluation of the finalists, were critical to the process of host city selection.

In 1997, at the 106th session of the IOC, the host city was chosen from among five finalists, drawn from 11 candidates. The finalists were Cape Town, Buenos Aires, Stockholm, Rome, and Athens. On September 5, after five rounds of secret voting, Athens was chosen over Rome by a 66-41 vote to host the XXVIII Olympic Games. Greece rejoiced in the choice. Athens, its premier city, would host the first Olympic Games of the 21st century and of the third millennium.

Athens's bid included the dates of the Olympic Games (August 13–29, 2004) and a budget of $1.6 billion. The IOC believed the bid to be well constructed and well reasoned. Of the 39 necessary venues, 29 were already in place, including the Olympic Stadium. In addition, the city had installed a high quality technological infrastructure and had made plans to include vestiges of the Ancient Games in the 2004 Games. A major drawback was Athens's perennial air pollution, which was exacerbated during the high temperatures of summer.

Greece, or the Hellenic Republic as it is sometimes called, is among the least populated nations ever to host the Summer Olympiad. It is the most southeastern country in Europe, at the southern end of the Balkan peninsula. Greece's 51,000 square miles include more than 400 islands, which account for about one-fifth of its territory. A 1997 population estimate reveals a citizenry of almost 10.6 million. About 63 percent of the population is urban, with a majority centered around Athens, Thessaloníki, Macedonia, and on the islands. Athens itself has a population of about 772,000 and the surrounding region of Attica has about 3.52 million.

Following the award, the Greek government established a corporation, the Organizing Committee for the Olympic Games—Athens 2004 S.A., or ATHOC. Conducting the daily business and the financial arrangements for the Games placed an enormous burden on ATHOC and the government itself. In order to meet the needs of the Olympics and to accommodate the honor of selection as host, ATHOC, the city of Athens, and the Greek government initiated a vigorous and ambitious campaign to ensure the success of the Athens Games. The committee would deal with the creation of the Games (the Olympic program, the Cultural Olympiad, and the Paralympic Games), venue construction, and security, while the government would support these efforts, work to ameliorate the problem of pollution, and work to solve the quandaries caused by shortages in accommodations and inadequacies in transportation and other tourist amenities. To accomplish its goals, ATHOC worked (and is working) with the IOC Coordination Commissions, local governments, the Interministerial Committee, and the Special Secretariat for the Olympic Games of the Greek government, the international sport federations, and various national sport federations.

In July 2001, the IOC appointed IOC member Denis Oswald as the chairman of the Coordination Commission for the Games, with responsibility for the strict oversight of ATHOC's preparations for the Games.

In 1998–99, ATHOC developed a master plan (approved by the IOC in May 1999), that calls not only for the completion of all arrangements for the Games but also for the adherence to a timetable. The entire plan encompasses 27 different programs, each with its own time frame, and each program's various sub-programs (for a total of 250 sub-programs). The corporation is responsible for the Olympic Works (venues), accommodations, security, transportation, technology, broadcasting, sports (the Games program), marketing and public relations, cultural programming, financial management, the Paralympic events, management of image and identity of the XXVIII Games, and human resources (officials, employees, and volunteers). While ATHOC has suffered some upheaval—loss and replacement of members and structural reorganization—the corporation has survived. Forced by the IOC to restructure from the unwieldy 15-member board to a streamlined executive committee of 5, ATHOC has continued diligently to pursue its goals.

The government of Greece is closely involved with the 2004 Athens Games. The prime minister, Costas Simitis, appoints all members to ATHOC's board. The executive committee, which exercises ATHOC's authority, is required to meet at least three times each month. The president and the managing director are empowered directly by the prime minister and he alone determines the powers and limitations of these two ATHOC positions. The full board meets only once per month to ratify the work of the executive committee and approve budgets and financial statements.

According to the committee, the total budget for the Games will be 1.962 billion euros. By January 2001, ATHOC had raised 448.1 million euros. The committee received 213.3 million euros from the first of its seven Grand National Sponsors and 234.7 million euros from other programs. ATHOC projected that 183 million euros will be generated by ticket sales, that 235 million will come from the Greek government, that 736 million will come from broadcasting rights, and that 544 million will be raised through marketing of sponsorships and licensing agreements. Other resources, such as funds from the European Union, would account for 264 million euros.

From August 25 through September 29, the XXVIII Olympic Games will present 28 sports encompassing 37 disciplines from aquatics to table tennis to tae kwon do to sailing. The Athens Games will host archery events, canoeing events, a triathlon, gymnastics, weight lifting, a modern pentathlon, hockey, handball, beach volleyball, and badminton, among others. These events will certainly be focused in Athens, but some sports, such as soccer, will have venues in other cities such as Thessaloníki.

ATHOC's mission statement promises that the Athens Games will strive to present the Olympics "on a human scale." This coincides with current thinking on the Games. IOC president Jacques Rogge has said that the Olympic Games cannot sustain the kind of expense and breadth of activity that marked the Olympic Games of the 1980s and the 1990s—particularly those staged in the United States. The committee intends to control the commercial aspects of the Games while providing its participants and spectators with a unique and memorable experience. Through its venues and its programming—including the Cultural Olympiad—ATHOC hopes to showcase not only the Games, but also the achievements of the modern Greek society, while using traditional symbols and events to focus attention on the Ancient Games as well. In all its aspects, the Athens Olympic Games are informed by Olympism—that philosophical construct invented by Baron Pierre de Coubertin to explain his concept of the modern Olympic Movement.

The committee is well on its way to completing the construction or refurbishment of most of the venues. New construction includes a broadcasting center, a press center, three indoor sport halls, an equestrian center, a shooting center, two stadia, a rowing venue for canoe and kayak, a canoe slalom venue, a beach volleyball center, a sailing venue, and the Hellinikon Olympic Complex, an Olympic baseball center. Venues that have been or will be upgraded include the Olympic Stadium, the aquatic center, an indoor sport hall, the velodrome, the Peace and Friendship Stadium, the tennis center, the Kaftantzoglio Stadium in Thessaloníki, and the Patras National Stadium. In addition, ATHOC is working to complete temporary installations for the mountain bike venue, the triathlon and its cycling venue, and the course for the cycling road race.

The Olympic Village, a 310-acre complex, is sited in northern Athens, about 7 miles (11 kilometers) from the Olympic Stadium. ATHOC has budgeted $300 million for the site, which will house about 18,000 athletes in 2,292 homes. After the Games, the village will become a housing development for 10,000 Greek citizens.

The Cultural Olympiad takes as its theme "Sport is Culture." Its mission is to give to the world a demonstration of the eternal links between Olympism and culture by placing the human being at the center of all its undertakings; to solidify the natural relationship of Olympism with the history of Greece; and to demonstrate the principles and ideals of Olympism through the presentation of Athens 2004—Culture (the official name of the Cultural Olympiad in Athens). The Cultural Olympiad, loosely adhering to one of the rules of the older Olympic *Concours d'Art*, and initiating its "Sport is Culture" theme, began presenting artistic works in October 2001 when Marton Simitsek of the ATHOC executive committee and Roula Vavalea, the manager for culture and ceremonies, announced the opening of *Triptyk—the Dance of the Centaurs*, a presentation staged by the Zingaro Theatre group.

The committee envisions the succession of cultural events as a kind of relay wherein the baton is passed from artist to artist. The cultural committee has challenged its participants "to go beyond the limits of human ability through artistic expression." Its objectives are threefold: (1) to encourage new artists, (2) to promote the essential message of the Olympic Games, and (3) to facilitate international cooperation between artistic creators from Greece and other nations. The committee has stated that it intends to "bridge word (*logos*), time (*chronos*), and place (*topos*) by bringing the most important cultural events to historical, archaeological, and timeless places."

The cultural events will continue through the end of the Games and will include music, dance, theater performances, fine art exhibits, and other events. Conferences, cinema, architecture, literature, digital culture, archaeological exhibits, and special *Kouros/Kori* awards to young creators will bring culture and art to the athletes, spectators, Greek citizens, and viewing audiences around the world. Ancient Greek tragedies as well as modern theatrical and performance art events will comprise segments of the entire program, which will take place in Athens and throughout the country. For those Olympic scholars and devotees who are familiar with Baron Pierre de Coubertin's original concept of Olympism and the role of the arts in the Olympics, ATHOC, through its Cultural Olympiad, is bringing that vision into focus. As a gesture and perhaps a challenge to future host cities, the Athens 2004 Cultural Olympiad Committee has extended to Beijing the invitation to grasp the baton and to continue the Greek initiative, through China's presentation of the Olympic Games, both athletic and cultural, in 2008.

Athens is the first host city which, by operating under a unified management structure, will be responsible for presenting both the Olympic and the Paralympic Games. Two weeks after the completion of the Olympic Games, from September 17 to 28, Athens will host 4,000 Paralympic athletes from 130 countries, along with 2,000 team officials. These Games feature 18 events, 14 of which correspond to Olympic events (archery, athletics, basketball, cycling, equestrian, fencing, football, judo, sailing, shooting, swimming, table tennis, tennis, volleyball) and 4 that are unique to the Paralympic Games (boccia, goalball, powerlifting, and wheelchair rugby.) Both the Olympic and the Paralympic Games will be held at the same venues, which are being equipped with the facilities necessary for the accommodation of disabled athletes and spectators. Moreover, Greece is attempting to upgrade disability structures in all its cities to make them accessible to all.

All participants will be accommodated in the Paralympic Village, which is being built within the Olympic Village. ATHOC intends that disability requirements for the Paralympic Village will be generally incorporated into the design of the Olympic Village.

Preparations for the Paralympic Games have gone forward, although not without some problems and delays. In April 2002, the International Paralympic Committee (IPC) visited Athens ostensibly to view the various competition sites. However, the IPC elected to discuss transportation issues and infrastructure designs in order to anticipate and identify any shortcomings. The meeting concluded that ATHOC will need to provide about 300 buses equipped to carry at least four (but preferably six) wheelchairs. While other transportation modes such as light rail, Metro, and suburban rail appear able to accommodate the needs of disabled riders, the meeting did uncover the need to provide taxis and other conveyances that are equipped to service disabled people.

Environmental issues present a particularly difficult challenge for the organizing committee and the Greek government. The nation's economy experienced accelerated industrialization, primarily during the 1970's. A serious byproduct has been severe air pollution. In Athens, air pollution is caused not only by industrial pollution, but also by exhaust from gasoline and diesel engines. Poor air quality threatens the health of breathing-impaired citizens and has caused noticeable erosion of historic stone and marble buildings and sculptures, prompting the government to install (prior to the Olympic bid) various air quality monitoring stations in Athens and other cities. Most recently the focus has been placed on reducing the pollution caused by heating systems and industries. While the problem of automobile, truck, and bus exhaust is still a cause for concern, the government has made great strides in readying Athens for the Games and continues its efforts to reduce toxic emissions.

Water pollution in general has also been a vexation for Greece, especially municipal wastewater, sewage, and industrial waste in and around the gulfs of Saronikos and Thermaïkos. Greece has made it a part of the Olympic mission to produce an Olympic Games that focuses not just on the competition but also on the improvement of its environment. Despite all efforts to date, however, environmentalists are still concerned that some of the Olympic venues are wreaking permanent damage on species, water systems, and land. They have expressed particular concern about the rowing center at Schinias, near the tomb of Marathon. Environmentalists charge that the construction necessary to prepare this venue for the Games will cause permanent damage to the ecosystems in the area. ATHOC and the government have countered most of the charges with statistics and reports by their own experts, but the real environmental effects of the Games probably will not be apparent for several years.

Early on, Greece and Athens faced a problem with accommodations for spectators and Games officials. The IOC anticipated that nearly 1.5 million spectators would be coming to the Games, yet Athens, by January 2002, had only 15,200 rooms (by contrast Atlanta made 60,000 rooms available and Sydney 29,000). Athens's organizers had reserved 13,000 hotel rooms and nearly 3,000 rooms on cruise ships docked near Piraeus. The shortfall, according to Olympic officials, was over 2,800 rooms.

Recent reports seem to indicate that through extraordinary efforts to upgrade existing facilities, and to construct some new ones, the accommodations problem is nearly solved. In April 2002, the IOC reported through its international marketing director, Michael Payne, that the Athens Olympic Organizing Committee had made tremendous efforts, and accommodations were no longer a concern. Greece coped with the creation of new living spaces by forming a government-owned real estate corporation, approved by the Greek parliament, to acquire and manage hotels, the Olympic venues, and other real estate projects built for the 2004 Olympic Games.

Security, as at every Olympic Games, has been a concern for ATHOC. In the past, Athens had been thought to be a potential gathering point for international terrorists, and the city has been criticized for its seeming inability to contain domestic terrorists. Two days before Athens was awarded the 2004 Games, a car bomb exploded in the city, destroying the automobile but causing no injuries or deaths. The group claiming responsibility for the bombing announced the incident as being a protest against staging the Olympics in Athens. While the international community was alarmed by the event, local and national officials downplayed the bombing, calling it "a game by some youngsters throwing gas canisters to attract attention."

In January 2002 Athens held discussions with Interpol to review the general security arrangements for the Games. Because of the events of September 2001, security at any major gathering is a serious concern for all nations. Athens is no exception. Ronald Noble, head of Interpol, and Gianna Angelopoulos-Daskalaki, head of ATHOC, have held meetings to explore the needs and concerns of both the international community and the organizing committee. To date, no substantive details have been released about these meetings, but ATHOC has released press statements that highlight the role of the government in the overall planning.

A related concern, not just for Athens, but for future Olympic Games as well, is the cost of security. Athens projects that it will need about 50,000 security officers. The government has formed the Central Security Office of the Olympics Games (DOAO). The office will train new security officers and establish plans for emergency evacuations and other disaster relief arrangements. The projected budget for security now stands at around 700 million euros, with most of the expenses projected for personnel and surveillance equipment. Should Athens decide to incorporate plans like those implemented at Salt Lake City, the cost will be significantly higher. The Salt Lake City Games included flyovers by military planes, the presence of the National Guard, and sophisticated machinery for metal, chemical, and biological materials and weapons detection. Because the rising costs of security measures also includes liability costs, security for an Olympic or any other international event has become a topic of discussion and debate. The arguments center on who should bear the costs of security for the Games—the host nation or all the participating nations? A settlement to this argument may have to await the end of the Athens Games and the presentation of the final bill for preventing both disastrous occurrences and security breaches.

The increased concern about terrorism has brought about greater international cooperation on security matters. Greece is receiving assistance by way of training and information from France, Israel, Great Britain, Australia, Spain, Germany, and the United States about methods for countering terrorism. Sydney has made special efforts to assist Athens, as the security measures for the Sydney Games were quite complex and sophisticated. Athens is aware that the security technology at Sydney far outpaced anything currently within its existing capabilities. Yet the concern of the international community is for the safety of the athletes and the spectators, as well as the citizens of Greece. Thus many nations are offering Athens the benefit of their experience and technology. The Greek government understandably has taken an active interest in the security provisions for the Games and, under the auspices of the public order minister, Mihalis Chrisohoidis, Greece is taking advice from Great Britain and other nations.

The 2004 Games have not yet happened. What may be the outcome of these Games is open for speculation. The country and the committee are rushing to finish the necessary work to present the Games, and observers believe that Athens will host a very fine Games. As with all recent host cities and nations, Athens and Greece anticipate a significant legacy from these Games. ATHOC expects that the Games will provide to all nations a vivid and lasting understanding of Greece and its natural and cultural heritage. A good Olympic Games fosters continuing tourism and increased economic investment, so the organizers intend to highlight the achievements of modern Greece and demonstrate its potential for such investment. The protection and enhancement of the natural environment is expected to be an enduring legacy of these Games. Attention to the reduction of pollution in major urban centers, the preservation of wildlife and natural areas, as well as the restoration of irreplaceable monuments will be a gift of the Games to the peoples of Greece and the world.

The presentation of an Olympic Games may have effects on the host city and nation that extend beyond the traditional and obvious by-products of tourism, convention business, and new recreational facilities. The people of Greece will benefit from the number of jobs created to stage the Games and from increased revenues from visitors during the Games. Beyond the short-term gains of a boost in employment directly linked to the Olympic presentation, host cities and nations may find that some of the jobs created for the Games sustain themselves in new industries, such as those related to transportation and security.

While many of the economic benefits are confined to the areas near the venues, rather than throughout the country, the improvements are still important to the country. For example, the improvements to communications and other electronic infrastructures benefit the country, so long as careful planning and future maintenance strategies have been included in the Olympic plan. New communications and electronic technologies and new telephone systems can be used for years beyond the two weeks of the Games.

Not as apparent perhaps but equally as important are the legacies of the cultural Olympiad. The possible collaborations of artists and artistic companies, the construction of new venues for performance and presentation, as well as the introduction of cultural and artistic events to underexposed audiences bode well for the creation of a cultural industry in the host city and nation.

Moreover, the venues that are constructed for disabled athletes remain a part of the landscape and translate into new and needed services for citizens, as well as a selling point for future events for disabled participants and for tourism locales for disabled visitors.

Improvement to infrastructures such as airports, trains, urban transportation systems, and outlying rail and road systems are among the legacies that remain with a host nation. In Athens, the development of a subway system, the purchase of buses equipped to carry disabled athletes, and the creation of new (or refurbishment of old) rail systems will bring to Athens and Greece the benefits of quicker, safer travel. For a small nation like Greece, this major investment makes it an attractive partner for future economic development with the European Union and other partners. For Greece and Athens, all the potential for a brighter future rests in the successful planning and staging of the XXVIII Olympic Games.

BIBLIOGRAPHICAL ESSAY

The Athens Games will take place nearly two years after the writing of this article. Necessarily, the information during the final two years of preparation is not found here. However from the time that Athens was awarded the bid for 2004, a wealth of information about the preparations for these Games has been made available through the Athens Organizing Committee, the Greek Ministry for Culture, the Greek Ministry for Sport, and the Greek Olympic Committee.

The Internet provides access to information about the organizing committee, the progress of the Games as the committee nears its goal, and controversies surrounding sports, venues, environments, and costs. Official reports, annual reports, IOC news releases, ATHOC news releases, the *Athens 2004* magazine, and indeed hundreds of pages of information, are all available through the Athens Organizing Committee's Web site (http://www.athens.olympic.org). Still other Web sites have sprung up to inform the public about the bid process and the financial issues surrounding the mounting of an Olympic Games (for example, http://www.gamesbids.com). Information on the venue construction, security problems and systems, and on the Greek political, geographical, environmental, and social landscapes are available (http://www.sports-venu-technology.com, http://www.joneslanglasalle. com.hk/Press/2001/160401.htm, and http://alexandros.com/Greece/). The International Olympic Academy Web site (http://www. ioa.org.gr) provides much background on the Ancient Games, as well as the current events surrounding the Athens Games.

Newspapers such as the *South Africa Sunday Times* (Business Times), the *Times* (London), the *New York Times*, the *Chicago Tribune*, *Athens News*, as well as the Associated Press wire service, Reuters information service, and many others have carried various articles about development plans, controversies surrounding the Games, and environmental and political crises, in addition to reports of bombings, threatened boycotts, and international efforts to ensure the safety of the Games.

Upon the close of the Athens 2004 Games, the official documents and papers of the organizing committee as well as all other associated documents will be archived. The Athens 2004 Committee intends that all the records, objects, and memorabilia from both the Olympic Games and the Paralympic Games will be held in the archives. The collection itself will be governed by a foundation and housed in a research center dedicated to Olympism. To date, no final decision has been made on the location of the center.

BEIJING 2008

Ying Wushanley

THE GAMES OF THE TWENTY-NINTH OLYMPIAD

On July 13, 2001, at the 112th International Olympic Committee (IOC) session in Moscow, the IOC members elected Beijing to be the host city for the Games of the XXIX Olympiad in 2008. With Beijing's victory, the People's Republic of China (PRC) became the third Asian country chosen to host a Summer Olympic Games after Japan (Tokyo, 1964) and Korea (Seoul, 1988).

Beijing's success came eight years after a heartbreaking loss to Sydney for its bid to host the 2000 Games. At the 1993 IOC session in Monte Carlo, the capital of China led Sydney in each of the first three rounds of the election, only to lose by two votes in the final round. There was speculation that Beijing's loss and Sydney's victory was the result of European and United Kingdom-aligned votes after Manchester, England, was eliminated in the third round. There was certainly more political opposition against China from the West. The 1989 Tiananmen crackdown on Chinese student protests was still in the recent memory of world events. The U.S. Congress formally campaigned against Beijing's bid to host the Games, citing human rights violations, Tibet issues, and religious repression in China.

The choice of Beijing symbolized a new era for China in the Olympic Movement. China's rise to Olympic prominence was, however, by no means a smooth journey. In the half century since its acceptance into the Olympic Movement, the PRC remained controversial and its relationship with the IOC was often strained. For three decades, the two China (the PRC and the Republic of China, or Taiwan) issue haunted the Olympic Games as well as China's presence in the Olympic Movement. In the 1980s and 1990s, however, China's image in the Games changed significantly from a radical left-wing political rebel to more of a rule-abiding athletic competitor. Chinese athletes not only took part in more and more Olympic events but also became a real threat to the traditional U.S.-Soviet Union Olympic dominance. Yet controversy never seemed to stay away from the Asian giant. Along with China's improving performance in the Games, there came the growing suspicion about the means that led to its improvement. When some Chinese athletes were caught using performance-enhancing drugs at international sports competitions, China's image was again damaged, and the integrity of its sports system was challenged. Public suspicion of the purity of Chinese athletes remains today. Outside the domain of the Olympics, accusations of widespread human rights violations by the Chinese government, especially since Tiananmen, cast dark clouds over the moral qualification of the communist regime to hold the Olympic Games—a symbol of world peace and human dignity.

Beijing's loss in 1993 was disappointing to the Chinese, but the experience of going through the complete bidding process proved to be invaluable for Beijing's second attempt. On September 6, 1999, Beijing officially launched its campaign with the formation of the Beijing 2008 Olympic Games Bid Committee (BOBICO). The full-fledged BOBICO consisted of 10 departments ranging from research and analysis to press and publicity, external relations, sports and venues, construction and project planning, technology, finance and marketing, and environment and ecosystem. Headed by Liu Qi, mayor of Beijing, the committee was composed of a large entourage of administrators and a staff of 70 members. BOBICO also recruited a team of goodwill envoys including two of the world's most popular movie stars, Jackie Chan and Gong Li. The goodwill team expanded worldwide with renowned international artists joining its list, bringing not only great publicity but also huge financial resources to Beijing's bid. Three of the world's greatest tenors, Luciano Pavarotti, José Carreras, and Plácido Domingo, for example, gave a joint performance for Beijing's campaign at the Forbidden City just three weeks before the IOC's Moscow session, attracting 30,000 people, each of whom paid between $280 and $1,700 for the event.

In January 2001, BOBICO released the Beijing 2008 Candidate City's logo, motto, and Web site. The logo, resembling both a traditional Chinese artifact known as the China Heart Unit and a person performing the martial art tai chi, symbolizes unity, cooperation, exchange, and development as well as gracefulness, harmony, vitality, and mobility. The motto "New Beijing, Great Olympics" represents the modern image of Beijing, a city with a 3,000-year history and a dynamic present brought about by reform and China's opening up to the rest of the world.

Beijing's application package made a very positive impression on the IOC's first evaluation team—the IOC Candidature Acceptance Working Group. In its August 2000 report of the initial 10 applicant cities to the IOC Executive Board, the working group gave high praise to Beijing's bid, especially in the areas of government support and public opinion, Olympic Village plan, accommodations, and general concept of the proposal. A Gallup poll in early 2000 showed that more than 94 percent of Beijing's 12.5 million citizens supported Beijing's bid. The IOC commissioned an independent poll in early 2001 that produced a similar result. In November 2000, Chinese President Jiang Zemin and Premier Zhu Rongji wrote IOC president Juan Antonio Samaranch and IOC members, guaranteeing their personal and the Chinese government's full support for Beijing's bid and pledging respect to the Olympic Charter and the regulations of the international federations related to the Olympic Games. The Chinese government and Beijing municipal government also agreed to cover any shortfalls from the Games. Despite its understanding that most of Beijing's infrastructure and sport arenas were still in the computer-graphics stage, the IOC Working Group wholeheartedly endorsed the city's bid and recommended it to the IOC Executive Board along with the bids of

Osaka, Paris, and Toronto. It did not endorse the other bids by Bangkok (Thailand), Cairo (Egypt), Havana (Cuba), Istanbul (Turkey), Kuala Lumpur (Malaysia), and Seville (Spain).

The working group's evaluation of applicant cities was part of the new host city election procedure that the 110th IOC Session in 1999 established. Following this new procedure, cities must pass an initial selection phase during which a team of experts examine the basic technical requirements. The cities are then put forward to the IOC Executive Board. Once approved by the executive board, the cities become official candidate cities and are authorized to go forward into the full bid process. The full bid process includes the submission of a candidature file to the IOC, followed by a visit of the IOC Evaluation Commission to each of the candidate cities. The evaluation commission studies the candidatures of each candidate city, inspects the sites, and submits a written report on all candidatures to the IOC two months before the IOC session at which the host city will be chosen.

With the recommendation of the IOC Working Group, the IOC Executive Board in August 2000 chose to accept five cities—Beijing, Osaka, Paris, Toronto, and Istanbul—as final candidate cities to host the 2008 Games. The IOC Evaluation Commission was soon formed to conduct the second phase of the candidature procedure. Headed by Hein Verbruggen, an IOC member from the Netherlands and president of the International Cycling Union, the commission was composed of 17 representatives of all components of the Olympic Movement: the IOC, the international federations, the national Olympic committees, the International Paralympic Committee, athletes, former organizers of Olympic Games, and experts in various fields. Between February 21, 2001, and March 29, 2001, the commission paid a four-day visit to each of the candidate cities and conducted evaluations of each city on the basis of 18 factors within an overall risk assessment framework. The factors were: 1) National, Regional, and Candidate City Characteristics; 2) Legal Aspects; 3) Customs and Immigrations Formalities; 4) Environmental Protection and Meteorology; 5) Finance; 6) Marketing; 7) Sports and Concept; 8) Paralympic Games; 9) Olympic Village; 10) Medical/Health Services; 11) Security; 12) Accommodations; 13) Transport; 14) Technology; 15) Communications and Media Services, 16) Olympism and Culture; and 17) Guarantees. The mission of the commission was to verify the information in a city's candidature file, determine whether the plans are feasible, and make an overall risk assessment. The commission held its final meeting in Lausanne between March 31 and April 3, 2001 and produced the "Report of the IOC Evaluation Commission for the Games of the XXIX Olympiad in 2008."

The report rated the bids by Paris, Toronto, and Beijing as excellent and believed that any of the three cities would be able to organize an excellent Olympic Games in 2008. It nevertheless hinted that the Commission was less satisfied with Paris's Olympic Village planning and with Toronto's promise of some of its planned sport venues and the Village developments. In contrast, it praised Beijing's "high quality bid" as the result of "the combination of a good sports concept with complete Government support." The commission's subtle yet favorable stance toward Beijing's bid was evident in the conclusion of the report: "It is the Commission's belief that a Beijing Games would leave a unique legacy to China and to sport and the Commission is confident that Beijing could organize an excellent Games."

On the eve of the 112th IOC Session in Moscow, the IOC members were poised to elect the host city of the 2008 Games. According to the IOC procedure, voting takes place in successive rounds until one candidate receives a majority of the votes. Non-votes, spoiled votes, and abstentions do not count toward the calculation of the majority. If two or more cities are tied for the lowest number of votes, a runoff election is held between them, with the winner going on to the next round. The members vote electronically and individual votes are not recorded to shield the member from external pressures. All members present can vote except those from a country that has a city vying for election. Once a city drops out of the race, the members from that country are allowed to vote in the next round. The election took place on July 13, 2001, with 105 IOC members eligible for voting in the first round. Thirteen members from Canada (4), China (3), France (3), Japan (2), and Turkey (1) could not vote in the first round.

There was hardly any competition. After the first round of voting, Osaka dropped out of the race, having received the fewest votes. After the second round, the election was over. In front of a live audience including all five candidate city delegations and the world's media via closed circuit television, IOC president Juan Antonio Samaranch announced Beijing the winner of the election.

The final vote was:

First round: Beijing, 44; Toronto, 20; Istanbul 17; Paris, 15; Osaka 6 (eliminated)

Second round: Beijing, 56; Toronto, 22; Paris, 18; Istanbul, 9

Beijing was never challenged. Its victory, as many Olympic experts and insiders had predicted, had been a foregone conclusion.

Why was Beijing's bid such an overwhelming success? Critics have attempted to provide answers, but none seemed simple. Nevertheless, one can gain great insight into the issue by examining the event from various perspectives.

Ideologically, there seemed no better host city than Beijing for spreading the Olympic ideal and promoting world peace. After the Games in Barcelona (1992), Atlanta (1996), and Sydney (2000), Beijing became the most logical choice because of its geographic location and cultural uniqueness. The simple and most powerful factor in Beijing's bid was China's population of 1.2 billion. If the goal of the Olympic movement is truly to "contribute to building a peaceful and better world by educating youth through sport practiced without discrimination of any kind and in the Olympic spirit," Beijing, the capital of the world's most populous nation, was certainly the most ideal place for the 2008 Games.

Beijing's bid offered distinctive cultural features and proposed an extensive program promoting Olympism by blending sport with culture and education. This cultural program would be spread over four years from 2005 to 2008 and include festivals celebrating one of four major themes each year: 1) Sport and Humanity-—from Olympia to the Great Wall, 2) Environment and Humanity—from exploitation to adaptation to harmony, 3) Culture and Humanity—from individual inspiration to common achievement, and 4) Olympism and Humanity—celebrating our diversity. It is no doubt a powerful proposition that if China can commit itself to the preservation of human dignity, the world is assured a much greater chance for mutual understanding, respect, and peace.

Awarding the 2008 Games to Beijing makes economic sense for both the success of the Games and the financial stability of the IOC and the Olympic Movement. No other candidate cities offered a monetary guarantee as satisfactory as that of Beijing. With China's newfound wealth following its market reform in the 1980s and a continuing economic growth rate of approximately 10 percent annually, Beijing was by far the strongest candidate financially. To host the 2008 Games, the Chinese government pledged a seven-year $10 billion budget for Olympic sports facility construction between 2001 and 2008 and a ten-year $12 billion budget for improving Beijing's environment beginning in 1998. An estimated $150 billion will be spent on the Games' related infrastructure and city improvement. With a Beijing Games, the IOC is guaranteed a financial success. As China's Vice Premier Li Langqing, the head of the Beijing delegation, made clear in Moscow, "If there is a surplus in the Games revenue, we will use it to set up an Olympic Friendship and Co-operation Fund for financing sports undertakings in developing countries. If there is a deficit, the difference will be covered by the Chinese Government." As an advocate for and contributor to the advancement of developing countries including the building of their sports infrastructures, China's promise had conceivably a broad international appeal as well as among the IOC members. Choosing Beijing also makes economic sense for the Games, where the Olympic symbol is traded as a commercial commodity. With a larger consumer market, a greater number of corporations would be willing to sponsor the Games in exchange for selling their products. What better market than China with a population of 1.2 billion people, a fast-growing economy, and the emergence of an unprecedented massive consumer culture?

Beijing's major obstacle was politics. Those issues that may have contributed to Beijing's defeat eight years earlier still remained—the widespread accusations of the Chinese government's violation of human rights, suppression of religious freedom, and Chinese athletes' use of performance-enhancing drugs in international competitions. But times had changed, and so had the perceptions of the issues. In 1993, the U.S. Congress passed a resolution opposing Beijing's bid for the 2000 Games, accusing the Chinese government of the widespread violation of human rights, systematic suppression of the Tibetan people, and greater repression of religion. In 2001, the U.S. opposition was downgraded to a nonbinding congressional subcommittee resolution calling on the IOC to deny Beijing's bid for the 2008 Games because of China's human rights record. No less significant was the shift of the Dalai Lama's view on the issue. In 1993, Tibet's exiled spiritual leader insisted that the Olympic Games must not take place in China "as long as a totalitarian regime is in power." The Dalai Lama softened his position eight years later when he stated that he would support Beijing's bid if it would promote human rights in China. For some, the IOC's choice of Beijing symbolized the world's capitulation to the communist regime and the condoning of human-rights violations in China. For others, awarding the Games to Beijing created a strong incentive for China to be on its best behavior, which consequently would promote China's economic and social progress, stimulate its development of democracy, and improve its condition for human rights. For many, at least among the IOC members, Beijing was simply the best choice for hosting the Olympic Games in 2008.

BIBLIOGRAPHICAL ESSAY

Official records related to the evaluation of candidate cities and election of the Host City for the Games of the XXIX Olympiad in 2008 are available at the IOC Olympic Studies Center in Lausanne, Switzerland, as well as through the Olympic Museum and Olympic Studies Center's Web site (http://museum.olympic.org).

The two documents that provide the most detailed information regarding procedures, methods of analysis, areas of assessment, and conclusion of the evaluation are *Report by the IOC Candidature Acceptance Working Group to the Executive Board of the International Olympic Committee* (Lausanne, Switzerland, 2000) and *Report of the IOC Evaluation Commission for the Games of the XXIX Olympiad in 2008* (Lausanne, Switzerland, 2001). The IOC also maintains a Moscow 2001 Web site (http://moscow2001.olympic.org/en/session/index.asp) with all official records of IOC activities during its 112th Session including the election of the host city for the 2008 Games.

Both official Web sites of the Beijing 2008 Olympic Games Bid Committee (BOBICO) (http://beijing-2008.org/eolympic/eindex.shtm) and the Beijing Organizing Committee for the Games of the XXIX Olympiad (BOCOG) (http://beijing-2008.org/new_olympic/eolympic/eindex.shtm) contain comprehensive information regarding Beijing's bid for the 2008 Games including the complete candidature files and transcripts of the Beijing Candidate City delegation's presentation at the IOC Moscow session. The BOCOG Web site is run in English, French, and Chinese. The BOBICO also has a Spanish translation. Major English language newspapers and popular magazines in North America and Europe devoted significant amounts of space to analyzing the bidding for the 2008 Games and the election of the host city. Four major English language Chinese magazines and newspapers, *Beijing Review*, *China Today*, *People's Daily*, and *China Daily*, also had extensive coverage of the events. A monograph authored by the U.S. Congress, *Human Rights Policy under the New Administration: Hearing and Markup of H. Res. 188 and H. Con. Res. 106 before the Subcommittee on International Security, International Organizations, and Human Rights of the Committee on Foreign Affairs and the Commission on Security and Cooperation in Europe, House of Representatives, One Hundred Third Congress, First Session, June 10, 1993* (Washington, D.C., 1993) details the charges against the Chinese government on human rights violations, Tibetan issues, and repression of religious freedom prior to the election of the host city for the 2000 Games. The periodical *Congressional Records*, also published by the U.S. Government Printing Office, is one of the most reliable and insightful sources regarding the U.S. government's view on China in general and on Beijing's bids for the Olympic Games in particular.

II THE WINTER GAMES

PRE-OLYMPIC WINTER GAMES

Yves Morales
Translated by Johanna Hackney

The modern Summer Olympic Games was created in 1896, but not until 1924 did the International Olympic Committee (IOC) organize an International Week in Chamonix consecrated to winter sports corresponding with the Olympic Games of Paris. More precisely, it is a matter of studying the homogenization of the Olympic culture in the realm of winter sports while observing the conflicts generated at the international athletic proceedings level. We consider the Olympic ideal and the thoughts of Coubertin as more than a philosophy. They represent a vast system of ideas that are an expression of history, that is, an ideology that evolves while adapting to the awareness of the era and connecting with historical contexts. When observed constantly, the ideas continually present themselves.

In the Nordic countries with their regions of snow and ice, the history of skiing and skating dates back to prehistory. Skiing and skating, which the Scandinavians linked at the beginning of the twentieth century with other winter sports such as bobsledding, curling, and ice-yachting, are perfectly adapted to the climatic conditions of these northern regions. These activities are also utilitarian and are an integral part of Scandinavian cultural traditions. From the end of the nineteenth century, these sports developed in most of the industrialized countries that had snow cover during the winter, but winter sport competitions proposed before 1914 in central Europe and on the American continent were isolated demonstrations that failed to win international recognition.

Ice skating was something of an exception. Skating had been widely practiced in central Europe since the sixteenth century, and it was also popular in North America. It was elevated to an international sport with the creation of the International Skating Union in 1892. The union was founded with the goal of standardizing the rules to allow international speed and figure skating competitions and of organizing those competitions. Ice skating, which was practiced in most of the countries of the International Olympic Committee at the time of its creation in 1894, was to be included in the Athens Olympic Games of 1896, but the organizers did not have an ice rink. It wasn't until the London Games in 1908 that ice-skating was included in the Olympic program. Sweden played an important role in this matter through its IOC representative, Viktor Balck, who headed the International Skating Union from 1893 to 1925. Balck, also the founder of the Swedish Olympic Committee, was a member of the IOC from 1894 to 1920 and was a close friend of Pierre de Coubertin.

Skiing races and competitions were organized as early as 1843 in Norway, and the *Grand Prix* of Skiing was held on February 12, 1879, beginning a long series of prestigious skiing competitions. The first luge and tobogganing races debuted at the end of the nineteenth century in the Swiss Alps and in Canada before relatively small numbers of spectators.

Balck organized the first international winter sport competition in 1901 in Sweden and Norway. After 1901, these competitions regularly took place in Stockholm or in Christiania, Norway, every two years, and later, every four years, until 1926. Balck's influence also brought the world skating championships into the program of the Nordic Games, which helped give them a much more international character. In this endeavor, C. de Rosen and Thorsten Nordenfelt, two active members of the Scandinavian Olympic movement, gave much help to Balck. The Nordic Games took place seven times: in 1901, 1905, 1909, 1913, 1917, 1922, and 1926. Skiing was the principal sport, with arduous races of 30, 60, and even 210 kilometers, which testified to the practical utility of the equipment, as well as the endurance of the competitors. There were also competitions in ski jumping, skijoring, skating (speed and figure), curling, and ice hockey. Some nonwinter events, such as equestrian races, fencing, and swimming were also contested at the Nordic Games.

Pierre de Coubertin's enthusiastic report in *Revue Olympique* in 1901 about the first Nordic Games showed his interest in incorporating these games into the Olympics because they represented what Coubertin considered a universal constant, "the culture of effort which is not the feature of any other race." But even though Coubertin recognized them as the Northern Olympics, these games remained totally independent of the Olympic Movement. Winter sports were still too foreign to central Europeans to have included them in international competitions, such as the Olympic Games. Nevertheless, the idea was not totally forgotten; it was simply put on hold as long as the competition conditions were judged too unequal. As Coubertin affirmed, "This will always be one of the drawbacks of the Nordic Games; England, Germany, Holland, and Russia, as well as southern regions, will have great difficulty furnishing capable champions to fight victoriously against Sweden, Norway, and Finland. This is not, however, a sufficient motive for not accepting the battle" (Coubertin, "Olympiades boreales . . . ," *Revue Olympique* [April 1901]: 17–24). The inclusion of winter sports into the Olympic Movement also had to wait until advances in transportation and communication in the early twentieth century facilitated the spread of an international athletic culture. With respect to skiing, however, no one could envision a rival to the Scandinavian specialists because so few people outside Scandinavia skied. Even in the 1920s, the Scandinavian countries monopolized winter sports, most notably skiing.

The first concrete problem in integrating winter sports into the Olympic Games was related to the athletic equipment and the snow. Because of this, most felt that the competitions would have to be separated according to the seasons. Skating was the exception again, because the technology of making artificial ice was available. But for the snow sports, no one knew how to create artificial snow. As Coubertin indicated, "Modern industry managed to create artificial ice, but it is hardly reasonable to rely on the moment where a perfected chemistry will be able to spread resistant and durable snow on the side of hills." Consequently, the IOC was content to "[gather] these particular sports elsewhere in winter under the name of the Nordic Games" (Coubertin, "III. Le programme des Jeux," *Revue Olympique* [December 1909]: 184–87).

The idea that the Olympic Games included all sports for all was contradicted by this exception for winter sports, but this was justified by the few member countries of the IOC that practiced these sports because of their particular geographic and climatic conditions, and the transportation and communication difficulties that these sports involved. Winter sports did not constitute part of the cultural landscape of central Europe. Similarly, winter tourism was hardly developed except for a few ski resorts situated in the Swiss Alps (in Davos and Holy-Moritz). Although the original Olympics admitted some models of differentiated cultural practices according to the countries, and even according to the races and sexes, winter sports were still considered too exotic or too different to become part of the Olympics.

Since the development and institutionalization of winter sports began in the United States, Canada, Japan, and the countries of central Europe between the end of the nineteenth century and the beginning of the twentieth century, the popularity of skiing, skating, and other winter sports began to increase. Enthusiasts created clubs and national federations to bring together the followers of these sports, and some ski resorts began effective publicity campaigns to draw tourists. As John B. Allen has indicated, the grouping together of skiers in American athletic clubs owed much to the Norwegians and the Swedish. As immigrants to America, they participated in the formation of the first snowshoe clubs in January 1861 in Onion Valley and La Porte, California. One purpose of these clubs was to organize speed skiing competitions which were the objects of much wagering. From a less lucrative perspective, the Kristiania Ski Club organized skiing in Norway in 1867, and on January 4, 1883, the Society for the Development of Skiing (Foreningen til Ski Fremme Idraettens) was founded in Norway.

The formation of winter sport organizations spread across Europe. In Germany, skiers started the Todtnau Ski Clubs in the Black Forest and in Munich in 1891. In Austria, the ski clubs of Mürzzuschlag and of Vienna were also created in 1891. In Switzerland, the members of the Tödi section of the Swiss Alpine Club founded the first ski club in Glarus on November 19, 1893. According to Paul Schnaidt, former director of the Swiss School of Skiing, the Norwegian influence at this time was particularly important, as countries began to follow the Norwegian example and form national skiing federations. In 1896, Russia organized a skiing federation, and Bohemia followed suit in 1903. On November 24, 1904, the Swiss Association of Ski Clubs was founded, and in 1905, a Ski Federation of Central Europe was formed which included the German, Austrian, and Swiss organizations. The year 1905 saw the establishment of the National Association of Skiing in the United States. In France, federations did not exist at this time, but the French Alpine Club assumed this role after 1906. The organizational movement rapidly spread in these countries, and the numerous winter sport championships and competitions that were organized testified to the vitality of these sports outside of Scandinavia.

Organizational conditions were divided among three interest groups of varying influence according to the country. First, nationalist leaders favored the popularization of skiing and noted its military usefulness. In Italy, Austria, and France, Alpine battalion skiers played a very active role in the propagation of skiing.

Second, commercial interests saw advantages in marketing winter sports. Winter sport development in Europe was closely related to the development of ski resorts. As early as the end of the nineteenth century, the Swiss resorts of Davos and Holy-Moritz were quite successful and attracted many English tourists. Many other ski resorts in the Alps, the Pyrenees, the Jura, the Vosges, and on most of the snow-covered mountains of other western countries soon followed. As tourist spots, these resorts appeared as elitist, designed for rich people who were more or less snobs. This elitist context next to spectacular competitions led to situations where athletic merit was not necessarily respected and where cash prizes were proposed to the participants. Coubertin thought it decadent, and the moral context that developed around these sports was not immediately conducive to their integration in the Olympic family.

Third, those who wanted to stage competitions often found themselves in conflict with proponents of battalions and tourism, although their own position is somewhat difficult to define. Before World War I, international competitions organized in central Europe were not championships in the strict sense of the word and appeared more as a means of popularization and of skiing propaganda than as athletic contests. The privileged practitioners were the Scandinavian, Norwegian, Swedish, or Finnish skiers, and when they participated in the organized international competitions in central Europe, they generally were declared ineligible because there was such a significant difference in their level of skill compared to that of the other competitors. Their supremacy was incontestable and justified the envy of their methods and techniques. Moreover, the Nordic Games were otherwise seen as a reference point with regard to athletic prowess in skiing. In other words, organized winter sport competitions in the Alps were pale copies of the Nordic Games. The splendor and the charm of the Alpine winter athletic demonstrations did not compensate for the authenticity of the Nordic Games. This position did not favor the popularization of winter sports until the creation of equal practice conditions.

Certain winter sports, in which the Scandinavians did not exercise the same supremacy, developed in non-Scandinavian countries. In ice skating the worldwide winners' list showed that the English, the Americans, the Russians, and the Canadians became true specialists. An International Ice Hockey League was even created in 1908 at France's initiative. It first grouped together England, Belgium, Switzerland, and France, then Germany, Czechoslovakia, Austria, Sweden, Spain, Italy, and lastly, the United States and Canada, which produced the best hockey teams during this period. In curling, Scotland was an invaluable reference. Tobogganing, luging, and bobsledding didn't really exist in the Nordic countries, and it was in the Alps and in Canada that the biggest number of experts in these sports could be found. In Switzerland, alpine skiing emerged in 1911 under the influence of English Arnold Lunn, but the sport again was too isolated to be incorporated into the proceedings of this period.

The rise of winter sports in western Europe and on the North American continent explained the first wave of desire to integrate the winter sports into the Olympic program since their universal character began progressively to assert itself. As early as 1906, the Olympic Review echoed this change by underlining that "the winter strength is located within reach of a bigger portion of the European territory that one did not imagine until now." In 1910, during a session of the IOC, the Englishman De Courcy-Laffan asked the Swedish Colonel Viktor Balck, who was in charge of organizing the Olympic Games in Stockholm, to consider integrating the Nordic Games into the program of the Olympic Games. Balck quickly protested, and then after consultation with his Swedish colleagues, he indicated that he was ready to prepare a program of winter sports for 1912 that he would present at the Budapest session in 1911. In May 1911, at the 13th session of the IOC in Budapest, the Italian delegate, Count Eugène Brunetta d'Usseaux, asked if the Swedish committee, which was in charge of the 5th Olympic Games in Stockholm, had ensured the integration of the winter sports into the Olympic program. The Swedish replied that this was not possible because the Nordic Games must take place during the winter of 1913. The Count Brunetta d'Usseaux then renewed the notion of the annexation of the Nordic Games of 1913 to the 5th Olympics in 1912, but Balck firmly opposed this idea, and after a long discussion, it was decided not to integrate the Nordic Games (and consequently winter sports) into the program of the 5th Olympics. In the Stockholm Olympic Games, the organizers used inaccessibility to a covered artificial ice rink as an excuse for not including ice skating in the Games.

To better understand these resistances, it is necessary to see winter sports as cultural possessions that were submissive to social, political, and economic stakes. According to this point of view, winter sports were perceived by the Scandinavians and a majority of the members of the IOC, such as Pierre de Coubertin, as a means of expression that were specific to the northern regions and were hence justified to a cultural protection reflex. In conclusion, the stated question was one of the definition of a legitimate international athletic culture. Now, the Nordic countries were not ready to lose their hegemony or hand over to the IOC a domain where their position of leadership appeared to them completely legitimate. It is plausible that this position equally expressed a nationalistic attitude that traced the limits of the universalist ideology that emerged before World War I.

The situation nevertheless can seem paradoxical. On the one hand, the Scandinavian opposition was evident in regards to the integration of winter sports into the Olympics Games and was in contradiction with the Olympic internationalization of sports. From this perspective, it is the very legitimacy of the Olympic Movement, and its universalist principle that was called into question. On the other hand, one must underline the strong implication of Scandinavian countries in the development of the Summer Olympic Games. Viktor Balck was a personal friend of Pierre de Coubertin and worked actively for the propagation of the Olympic Movement. The success of the Stockholm Games in 1912 testified to the successful integration of the sports in these regions. In comparison with the Olympic nature, and as far as the success of winter sports was confirmed all over the world, it is difficult to see with which argument the Scandinavians were able to maintain their conservative attitude. It is this paradox that persuaded the IOC session held in Paris in June 1914 to add ice hockey, skating, and skiing to the list of optional sports in future Games. In anticipation of the Berlin Olympic Games that would be held in 1916, German organizers had the same idea of holding ski competitions (distance and jumping) in Feldberg (Black Forest). The Scandinavian members strongly opposed this, but the Berlin Olympic Games never occurred because of World War I.

As Pierre de Coubertin said in one of his last writings, the Olympic works were never isolated from the historical circumstances into which they integrated. The particular postwar context confirmed this line of conduct. The internationalization of the sport movement was just started before the war and accelerated in the 1920s with the increase of large competitions. One could witness a general phenomenon of cultural homogenization around the athletic nature. Similarly, political factors were carried over into athletic rivalries, which encouraged the diversification of competition methods and strongly encouraged favoring the advent of a Winter Olympics. It is in this sense that one can understand the importance of integrating winter sports into the Olympic Movement, to encourage the competitiveness of all the countries newly concerned by these activities, and the ultimate reluctance of the Scandinavian countries, which saw their monopolistic domain eroding where the competition henceforth asserted itself, and where cultural traditions became diluted. Of course, the position can seem confusing since one must concede that the Olympics facilitate jointly and in a manner that may seem contradictory the internationalization of practices and a new form of nationalism.

According to one point of view, the integration of winter sports into the Olympic Movement eventually occurred but not soon enough. In accordance with decisions made before the war, the IOC modified the program of the Olympic Games. In 1920, in Antwerp, artistic figure skating appeared for the second time in the Olympic program, while ice hockey appeared there for the first time in the form of a world championship. In 1921, Pierre de Coubertin proposed a series of meetings and Olympic lectures in order to answer certain questions and to facilitate the position of the meeting of the IOC Congress. He also proposed a consultative lecture on winter sports on May 26 and 27, then a lecture about mountain climbing on May 28, and finally a lecture on equestrian sports on May 29 and 30. The IOC Congress took place in Lausanne, Switzerland, from the 2nd to the 7th of June 1921. Coubertin appointed the presidency to the Swede Sigfrid Edström, who replaced Viktor Balck as the head of the Swedish delegation.

This Congress unfolded in an unstable atmosphere exasperated by the question of nationalism. As Coubertin indicated in his Olympic memoirs, he had to scheme in order to obtain the organization of the 1924 Olympic Games in France. As early as June 2, the IOC granted his request to award the eighth Olympics to the city of Paris. On Sunday, June 5, 1921, the question of the integration of winter sports into the Olympic program was presented to the IOC Congress especially as the report made by M. Megroz in the name of the consultative lecture was for him favorable. One can note here the influence of the French delegation composed of Frantz Reichel, M. Albert Glandaz, Marquis de Polignac, and Count Clary, but also the insistence of the representative of Canada, James Merrick, and of Switzerland, Godefroy de Blonay. It is necessary to emphasize that in 1920, Coubertin announced his strong opposition to the integration of winter sports into the Olympic program, but the arguments held by the advisory committee in favor of the Winter Games were clearly justified, as much as from a technical point of view as from a geographical one: "Outside of northern countries, certain nations in central and western Europe are henceforth themselves in a position of organizing a competition of winter sports, which by their rough and splendid demonstration of modern physical activity are worthy to take place in the program of Olympic games."

According to the collection of testimonies, and notably that of Coubertin, Scandinavian hostility remained strong and discussions became heated in light of what appeared to the Scandinavians to be a takeover by force. For them, the only legitimate organizational framework for winter sports remained the Nordic Games and they maintained that they must preserve this monopoly. According to the report written by the president of the French Alpine Club in 1923, this opposition was perceived by the other members of the IOC as a retrograde reaction of Nordic nations that "consider winter sports as national sports being reserved for them by the right of mastery and seniority."

The interpretations are various on what facilitated the resolution. Was it the concession of the Congress to the Scandinavians? Or was it the goodwill of the Swedish, and notably the president of the Congress, Sigfrid Edström, who wished to avoid the discord? Be that as it may, the vote would eventually be a compromise. The assembly of the IOC accepted that France would organize an International Winter Sports Week under the patronage of the International Olympic Committee but refused to grant it the statute of first Winter Olympic Games. Thus, the winter week preceded the Summer Olympic Games organized in Paris in 1924, but the champions of the winter sport events did not have the right to a medal.

The International Winter Sports Week was proposed under an experimental title, but the position taken was judged disappointing for everyone, including the president of the French Alpine Club, who thought that the IOC must open more widely the Olympic doors to winter sports, in the very interest of those sports. As Pierre de Coubertin indicated in his Olympic memoirs, it was a first comparatively small step but was nevertheless decisive: "Winter sports were widespread in several countries, . . . there they present an amateur character, with athletic dignity so frank and so pure, that their total exclusion from the Olympic program removes a lot of value."

Given that the success of the 1924 International Winter Sports Week was far from assured, it was necessary to regulate the problem of its organization. One had to determine the location of the International Winter Sports Week and the committee's organization. On these subjects most of the decisions would be delayed. According to Arnaud Pierre and Terret Thierry, the decision of organizing these events in Chamonix took place under curious conditions. In fact, if the idea of granting this event to Chamonix was proposed as early as November 11, 1921, by Jules Couttet, the president of the Winter Sports Committee in Chamonix, it would be necessary to wait until February 6, 1923, a year before the winter week, for an agreement to be signed between the French Olympic Committee and the municipality of Chamonix. But it is necessary to recognize that in this period, Chamonix was probably the only French ski resort truly capable of organizing this type of demonstration. It was one of the rare cities to possess a hotel infrastructure, some access by railway, and a geographic position allowing it to accommodate this event. Furthermore, Chamonix was the preferred ski resort by the French Alpine Club for its international ski competitions.

As for the concerns of the organizational committee, they were equally confusing. The French Ski Federation did not yet exist, and it was the Commission of Winter Sports of the French Alpine Club that had been assuming that role since 1906. In 1922, the IOC therefore required the French Alpine Club to prepare the organization of skiing events that would be included in the Olympic framework. It is also from this date that the French Alpine Club would, in accordance with the athletic rules, look to organize a French Federation of Skiing after the Games. In regard to the skating and bobsledding events, the responsibility for organizing the events resided with the French Federation of Winter Sports, which was founded in 1921 in response to a request from the IOC.

But in order to assure an optimal cohesion of the Olympic device, the IOC had to contend with the concerns of the international federations. In fact, since the

Lausanne Congress in 1921, the IOC had granted them the right of technical direction of the international competitions and games. Now the problem in the realm of winter sports was that few of the international federations were organized. Only the International Skating Union and the International Ice Hockey League existed at that point in time. This implies that some institutional upheavals would accompany the genesis of the Winter Olympics.

As for bobsledding and curling, the creation of international federations would be directly due to the initiative of the Olympic movement, which was a matter of affirming the change of monopoly in the realm of winter sports. Frantz Reichel, the General Secretary of the National French Athletic Olympic Committee, was in charge of founding these federal structures. He summoned international congresses of bobsledding and curling on November 23 and 24, 1923, to the Sporting Club of Paris and thus provoked the creation of an International Bobsledding and Tobogganing Federation as well as an International Curling Federation.

The position was somewhat different in the world of skiing. From 1910 to 1914, there only existed a single international authority in this athletic domain, which was the International Commission of Skiing, which assembled the Norwegian, Swiss, Swedish, and Bohemian federations, the Great Britain ski club, Germany, Italy, Spain, and the Commission of Winter Sports of the French Alpine Club. The rare meetings aimed essentially at establishing uniform athletic regulations and largely revolved around Scandinavian suggestions. In recess because of the war, this Commission was restored by the initiative of the Nordic countries after a congress was held in Stockholm in February 1922 (at the Nordic Games). The subsequent congress was held in Prague in 1923 and proposed a new compilation of the athletic rules, which had a definition of amateurism produced according to the Olympic standard, but the International Skiing Federation did not always exist. That is why the Congress made this question the order of the day at the next meeting in 1924 on the issue of the winter week in Chamonix.

It is necessary to emphasize that at this point the Scandinavians (Swedish, Norwegian, and Finnish) had the largest number of athletes scheduled to participate in the International Winter Sports Week. In this period of political turbulence, the participation of foreign delegations was an important detail to regulate in order to guarantee the success of the games. Although it was necessary to qualify the political repercussions of the winter week in Chamonix, in the case of a demonstration that remained somewhat confidential, its organization was dependant on French foreign policies as well as the Summer Olympics Games, which constituted a sort of premise.

As Pierre Arnaud perfectly showed in various articles and Fabrice Auger in his excellent thesis on the Olympics, Olympic humanism was composed of the general feeling of a phobia of Germany that touched all of the Allied countries and drove the defeated countries to boycott. Before the Games, certain members of the IOC, and notably Coubertin, were in favor of the German reintegration into the Olympic Movement, in strict application of humanist principles and a nonpolitical stance. But under the simultaneous pressure of federal structures (for example, the French Alpine Club) and political strengths (notably the Service of French Foreign Workers), the IOC changed its position.

Quite obviously, from one political view, the Olympic Games represented a powerful lever of foreign policy. Thus in 1924, the IOC definitively adopted the French position that only authorized countries in the League of Nations would participate in the Games. In fact, Germany was excluded. This decision tore apart the member countries of the League of Nations. Since 1922, the Scandinavian countries, neutral during the conflict, clearly indicated they were in favor of Germany participating in the Olympic Games. They had a much more important reason for not participating in the Chamonix Games. It underscored their disapproval of the political ostracism of which Germans were the victims. In 1922, the Scandinavians invited Germany and Austria to participate in the Nordic Games in Stockholm, against the recommendation of the Allied countries. At the same time, the German press widely urged the Nordic nations to massively boycott the 1924 Olympic Games.

Various diplomatic visits were then engaged, notably by the French ambassador to Norway, and it was only on the eve of the Games, the closing day of registration, December 13, 1923, that the situation was resolved. Sweden and Norway officially announced that they would participate in the Chamonix events (as well as Switzerland, England, and Yugoslavia). Meanwhile, it is necessary to point out that Austria was invited to the Games, on the basis of its admission to the League of Nations in April 1923. The International Winter Sports Week in Chamonix suddenly found a certain audience on the international plain.

The International Winter Sports Week in Chamonix took place from January 24, 1924, to February 4, 1924. We will not dwell on the difficulties of the organization of the events, on the somewhat handcrafted character of this first Winter Olympics, or on the exploits of engaged competitors. These aspects were widely discussed up to here. The athletic and institutional consequences of these Games interest us above all else.

Sixteen nations engaged in what was considered a winter prelude to the Summer Games: Austria, Belgium, Canada, United States, Finland, France, Great Britain, Hungary, Italy, Latvia, Norway, Poland, Sweden, Switzerland, Czechoslovakia, and Yugoslavia (Luxembourg and Japan withdrew). It was a lot less than the 44 nations that participated in the Summer Games in Paris.

Two hundred and ninety-three competitors were registered in the events of the Winter Games, of which only 13 women competed since the figure skating events were the only events offered to them. The competitors faced off in 16 tests: 7 skating tests (four distance races: 500 meters, 1,500 meters, 5,000 meters, 10,000 meters; male figure skating; female figure skating; and couples figure skating); an ice hockey event; a bobsledding event consisting of teams of four, 4 skiing events (distances of 50 kilometers and 18 kilometers, ski jump, combined events of jump and distance); and finally, a military patrol event; and an event in which curling was proposed as the title demonstration.

It is necessary to underline that skiing was heavily influenced by nationalism. Thus, skiing events were strongly marked by the consequences of the war. In certain respects, the winter week took on the appearance of a warlike Olympics. The military character of the ceremonies served to reinforce the international prestige of France. The fanfare of the 3rd Alpine Battalion accompanied the parade of athletes. The newspapers and periodicals such as *l'Auto* or *Sports de Neige et de Glace* widely used the warlike metaphor and spoke of an "international Olympic army that will deliver itself to an unrelenting fight." The press insisted relentlessly on the fact that protocol demanded that the parade be organized by alphabetical order of teams and therefore Austria opened the procession followed by 15 other nations, which was hardly appreciated by the French as a symbolic view. The procession was completed by mountain guides, skiing instructors, firemen, hotel unions, school-children, and former war combatants, many of whom were wounded from the war thus recalling the dramatic effects of the then recent conflict.

To give a more solemn character to the event, Count Clary (President of the National Olympic Committee and a French athlete) got the Olympic oath to be pronounced at the beginning of the winter week. Symbolically, France chose the alpine racer Camille Mandrillon as the flag carrier for the French delegation, and it was therefore a military skier that pronounced the Olympic oath. The French Minister of War and Pensions insisted that the military patrol event be part of the program of games, even if it only appeared in the titles of the demonstration. It was a 30-kilometer event, with teams of four, consisting of the shooting of 18 bullets at a target representing a human outline. Six teams competed, and to the surprise of all, it was a neutral country, Switzerland, that won this event instead of the favored team, Finland, while France finished third.

With all events counted, including the demonstration events, the results of the Chamonix Winter Week were as follows:

1. Norway with 134.5 points
2. Finland with 76.5 points
3. Great Britain with 30 points
4. United States with 29 points
5. Sweden with 26 points
6. Austria with 25 points
7. Switzerland with 24 points
8. France with 19.5 points
9. Canada with 11 points
10. Czechoslovakia with 8.5 points
11. Belgium with 6.5 points
12. Italy with 1 point

The big winners of these games were the Norwegians and the Finnish. Their success persuaded them of the need for international Olympic events. They had total supremacy in the two main disciplines: skiing and speed skating. This superiority was predictable as evidenced by the physical preparation of their racers and their technical mastery. Additionally, these events seemed to have evoked respect. Archives indicate that although the spectator population was not impressive from a sheer numbers perspective, the notoriety of the Olympic Winter Week was amplified by the press, which widely popularized the event through the mass media. Winter Games eventually took place in the final manner of the Olympic demonstrations.

The entrance of skiing in large international competitions thus brought a new dimension to this sport. This event strongly contributed to the neglect of the utilitarian, ludic, civic, or hygienic justifications in order to give it a more prestigious athletic orientation. Its character was exclusively Nordic, a benefit to the popularization that would be confirmed by the creation of the International Federation of Skiing. In fact, the Congress of the International Commission of Skiing, called together in Chamonix in 1924, decided at last on its creation. Nevertheless, the

Scandinavians imposed certain conditions. The statutes of the new International Federation of Skiing, notably article 17, included the role of the committee and the selection of a president, a vice president, a secretary-treasurer, and seven members, of which three would be from Norway, Finland, and Sweden. The posts of president and of secretary-treasurer were reserved for one of these countries. The Swedish Major Ivar Holmquist became the first president of the International Federation of Skiing while the Norwegian, Finnish, and Swedish members of the direction committee formed the executive committee. The Scandinavians strove to preserve their monopoly over the ski organizations of the world. In this sense, they benefited from the organization of the games in Chamonix and nothing could oppose the official integration of the winter sports into the Olympic program.

The 24th session of the IOC, held in Prague in May 1925, decided to group the Winter Olympic Games in a special cycle distinct from the Summer Games. The Swede Sigfrid Edström declared that after having been the adversary, he had clearly joined forces. A charter of Winter Games then was proposed by the executive committee of the IOC. It would be voted on as to whether or not to definitively institute the cycle of Winter Olympic Games. Among the anxiously awaited decisions made by the technical Olympic Congress, one of the most notable was that the IOC granted the International Winter Sports Week in Chamonix the title of the "first Winter Olympic Games in history." Therefore, the Winter Games were only recognized retroactively. At the same time, political tensions between Sweden and Norway contributed to the disappearance of the Nordic Games.

CONCLUSION

The 1920s represented a turning point in the history of the Olympics wherein the governments acutely seized upon the propagandist character of sports as a symbolic means of judging their national power in the world. It was the moment where the champions and the Olympic victories became prestigious instruments in a context where free competition took on a universal character. The early resistance of Scandinavian countries to the integration of skiing into the Olympic program was able to fade behind the symbolic benefits of affirming their national identity in comparison to that of other athletic nations. The central theme of the Olympic notion was that it leaned on universality while nationalism was simultaneously denied, preserved, and surpassed. However, patriotism was not denied; quite the opposite. In the peaceful manner of competition, the games translated a certain sense of internationalization that transcended feelings to give them a new sense.

Humanism was at the heart of the matter, but it is necessary to remember that the Olympics were both a system of competitions and a system of ideas submissive to political, economical, and cultural contexts. The contribution of the Olympic Movement in the domain of winter sports proved to be crucial. The official organizational symbol was formed by five rings signifying the universal character of the games, which had tremendous repercussions on the development of winter sport competitions. Thanks to the Winter Games in Chamonix, skiing has obtained the status of a universal sport, in its Nordic disciplines first of all. The subsequent years would open upon a new cultural conflict between the Nordic countries and the Alpine nations involving the integration of downhill skiing events into the International Skiing Federation.

BIBLIOGRAPHICAL ESSAY

E. John B. Allen, *From Skisport to Skiing* (Amherst, MA, 1993) is the basic history of the sport and includes a good deal of information on the Nordic Games and the origins of the Winter Olympic Games. Other works on skiing include Yves Morales, "La diffusion du ski en France et les influences etrangeres, fin XIXe siecle–milieu du Xxe siecle," part of a special issue of *Stadion* (2001) devoted to the history of sport in France. See also Serge Lang, *Le Ski et autres sports d'hiver* (Paris, 1967) and Arnold Lunn, *A History of Skiing* (Oxford, 1927). Yves Morales carries the history of French skiing past 1924 in "Le virage sportif du Ski Francais dans l'entre-deux-guerres," in Serge Fauche, et al., eds., *Sport et demtites* (Paris, 2000): 271–287.

For the Nordic Games, Leif Yttegren, "Nordic Games: Visions of a Winter Olympics or a National Festival?" *International Journal of the History of Sport* 11, 3 (December 1994): 496–505, and Ron Edgeworth, "The Nordic Games and the Origins of the Olympic Winter Games," *Citiusm Altius, Fortuis* 2, 3 (May 1994): 29–37, are good places to start. Kristen Mo, "Norwegian Resistance against the Winter Olympics of the 1920s," in Roland Renson, et al., eds., *The Olympic Games through the Ages: Greek Antiquity and Its Impact on Modern Sport* (Athens, 1991) is also useful. Peirre Arnaud, "Des jeux de al guerre aux jeux de la paix: Sports et relations internationales (1920–1924)" in Pierre Arnaud, et al., eds., *Education et politique sportive XIXe et Xxe siecles* (Paris, 1995): 315–48, details the difficult transition period in international sport immediately after World War I. The changing views of the IOC on winter sports in the Olympics may be mined from Norbert Muller, *Cent ans de congres olympiques 1894–1994* (Lausanne, 1994).

Works dealing with the Winter Sport Week in Chamonix (the first Winter Olympics) are discussed in the bibliography following that entry.

CHAMONIX 1924

Paula D. Welch

FIRST OLYMPIC WINTER GAMES

When plans for reviving the modern Olympic Games were underway in 1894, figure skating was among the disciplines proposed for the competitive program. However, nearly three decades passed until winter sports were officially sanctioned. Opposition from Scandinavian countries prevented the introduction of winter sports until 1908, when figure skating was included in the London Olympics. Resistance to winter sports centered on the inability to conduct competition at the same time and in the same venues as the Summer Games. Another obvious problem for some countries was the lack of mountainous regions suitable for skiing. The 1912 Stockholm Olympic Organizing Committee refused to conduct winter competition because of a lack of facilities. Eventually, Olympic organizing committees were persuaded to divide the program into separate entities because of the growing interest in winter sports.

Baron Pierre de Coubertin, founder of the modern Olympics, viewed winter sports as truly amateur endeavors and especially valuable because they were "so pure in their sporting dignity." The popularity of winter sports, particularly in Europe, and the organization of winter sports federations established the foundation for international competition. While the appearance of figure skating in the 1908 London Olympic Games was overshadowed by more established Summer Olympic sports, the occasion did acknowledge winter sports as legitimate competitive events at the Games.

In 1920, additional impetus to winter sports competition occurred prior to most of the events at the Antwerp Games. A modest program of winter sports, including ice hockey and figure skating, attracted athletes from nine countries. Although the International Olympic Committee (IOC) did not sanction the competition, the success of the experiment could be measured by the level of competition and the enthusiasm of the competitors. Like most other athletic events that have reached worldwide prominence, the winter sports in Antwerp and their unofficial association with the Olympic movement began inconspicuously. The success of the competition provided winter sports enthusiasts with sufficient evidence to convince the IOC that a quadrennial program of winter sports could develop into an international event.

At its meeting in Paris on March 22, 1922, the IOC announced that skating events would initiate the 1924 Olympic competition, as part of a separate program of winter sports. Because the sports at Chamonix were not designated Olympic by the IOC in 1924, some journalists referred to them as the "winter sports at Chamonix." The French Olympic Committee called the competition an International Winter Sports Week in Chamonix. In anticipation of future competition, some reporters incorporated the term "Olympic" in 1924 newspaper accounts when they wrote about the "Olympic Games at Chamonix." In 1925 at the IOC Congress in Prague, the IOC officially sanctioned the Olympic Winter Games and retroactively declared the competition at Chamonix the I Olympic Winter Games. The 1925 Congress also determined that summer and winter competition would take place in the same year and, if desired by a national Olympic committee, in the same country. The 1924 Games coincided with the thirtieth anniversary of the revival of the Games and were an important milestone for Coubertin, who wished to conclude his term of office after the Games were held in his native France. He successfully negotiated his wishes, and the town of Chamonix was chosen to inaugurate the events of the anniversary year.

Chamonix 1924—The 4-man bobsled team from Switzerland, gold medalists at Chamonix. Courtesy of the International Olympic Committee, IOC Museum Collections.

France had largely recovered from the devastating effects of World War I. Hosting the Winter and Summer Olympic Games was an additional indication that the country had overcome the destruction left by the invading German army and four years of trench warfare. Most of the railroad lines destroyed during the war had been rebuilt by 1921. Although the national debt had reached nearly 40 million francs in 1924, there were signs of economic recovery. Unemployment was nearly nonexistent, with the reconstruction of 22,000 factories boasting modern equipment.

At Chamonix, French officials had to overcome hotel shortages for an influx of visitors. The population of the winter resort was 3,000, and fewer than 2,000 visitors could be accommodated. French Olympic Games officials worked with local citizens to find space for another 1,000 visitors by placing beds in the corridors, ballrooms, and billiard parlors of hotels and inviting private citizens to open their homes. But this was still woefully inadequate, since between 20,000 and 30,000 visitors were anticipated. By November 1923, about 65 percent of the hotel rooms in Chamonix had been reserved for Olympic committee members, athletes, trainers, officials, and newspaper correspondents. In order to accommodate the majority of the spectators, the French Olympic Committee referred guests to hotels in Aix-les-Bains and Annecy and provided twice daily excursion trains to and from Chamonix. In addition, special bus service was made available to Olympic visitors. French officials boasted of a new aerial railway line built to carry passengers from Chamonix to the L'Alguille du Midi. While not built specifically for the Chamonix Games, the railway was scheduled to be completed before the competition began. The special mountain rail line consisted of two 18-passenger cars, designed so that one car ascended while the other descended.

Athletes from 16 nations entered the first Olympic Winter Games. The program included ice hockey, bobsledding, figure skating, skiing, and speed skating, but women could compete only in figure skating. Not until 1948 were skiing events organized for women, and not until 1960 was speed skating sanctioned for women. In 1998, women debuted in ice hockey, and four years later, women first competed in bobsledding. The staid members of the IOC were reluctant to approve endurance events or traditionally masculine sports for women, since medical experts questioned the effect of such events on a woman's childbearing ability until well into the twentieth century.

The first Olympic Winter Games athletes assembled at the city hall in Chamonix on January 25, 1924. After four days of slushy thaw, the precedent-setting Opening Ceremonies were enhanced by cold weather and blue skies, and thousands of spectators gathered in the small Alpine town to view the festivities. A total of 408 men and women, nearly all of the athletes and officials, took part in the festivities. The procession, led by the French Blue Devil band and the Austrian team, paraded through the streets of the village to the Olympic skating rink, where they were reviewed by Count de Clary, president of the French Olympic Games Committee, and Marquis de Polignac, vice president of the committee. Gaston Vidal, undersecretary of state for physical education, presided over the opening ceremonies. Skier Camille Mandrillon recited the Olympic oath. This newly launched event lacked some of the ceremonial features to which contemporary Olympic devotees have grown accustomed. However, the absence of a head of state opening the Games, an Olympic flame ceremony, and an oath on behalf of the officials apparently did not detract from the I Olympic Winter Games.

The 500-meter speed-skating race was the inaugural event of the first Olympic Winter Games, and Charles Jewtraw of the United States became the first gold medalist of the Olympic competition, beating his personal best by two seconds and winning over twenty-six other skaters from ten countries. The first gold medal in women's Olympic winter competition went to an Austrian figure skater, Herma Planck-Szabo. In that same event, 11-year-old Sonja Henie, who would become one of the most famous and successful Olympic champions, finished last among the eight skaters from six nations. In an era before indoor rinks, skaters formulated their strategy by considering not only their opponents but also the weather conditions. The women's school figures were skated in nearly ideal outdoor conditions, but during the free-skating phase of competition, the ice was hard and brittle and the weather unusually windy and cold. The outstanding Olympian in these Games was Thorlief Haug of Norway, who won gold medals in the 18-kilometer and 50-kilometer cross-country skiing races and in the Nordic combined event.

The 12 days of competition culminated at the collective medal presentation during the closing ceremonies on February 5, 1924. Coubertin presided over the festivities in the same outdoor rink where eager athletes had awaited the start of the Games. He was assisted by Count de Clary, the Marquis de Polignac, and Franz Reichel, General Secretary of the French Olympic Games Committee. Unfortunately many athletes had departed Chamonix, and other members of their teams accepted the medals. Although press coverage of the I Olympic Winter Games was not as extensive as it was for the Summer Games, leading American and European newspapers sent correspondents to chronicle the event.

The Games were successful in many respects, but financial losses detracted somewhat from the overall celebration. Costs ran to 3 million francs, but gate receipts totaled only 250,000 francs. Attendance was estimated at no fewer than 3,000 each day, but many entered on free passes. Perhaps to ensure larger crowds than the poorly attended Antwerp Games, officials had offered free passes not only to the Olympic family but also to others in an attempt to increase attendance. Financial backing came from the city of Chamonix, the department of Haute Savoie, and the French government. There were reports that French officials had anticipated a financial shortfall. Apparently the French Olympic Committee members were guided more by their enthusiastic support for the Olympic Games and the prestige of hosting the event than by their desire to make the Olympics a financial success.

Success was measured by the enthusiastic crowds and the apparent high level of athletic performances in the individual events and the exciting ice hockey competition. Canada and the United States had each scored four victories when they met in the gold medal game. The main topic of conversation among sports enthusiasts on the eve of the championship centered on which style of play would dominate: the smooth Canadian teamwork or the stellar individual effort by the Americans. The largest crowd of the Games filled the stands, purchased standing room space on roofs of nearby houses, and even perched atop chimneys to watch the Canadians dominate the game 6–1 and claim the Olympic championship.

For the first time, the death of a former head of state cast a shadow over the Olympic competition. Just as the hockey match ended, the announcement of former U.S. president Woodrow Wilson's death transformed the upbeat Olympic mood to a somber homage. After a moment of silence, the Olympic and U.S. flags were lowered to half staff while the band played "The Star-Spangled Banner." Athletes and spectators paid tribute to the wartime leader; some linked Chamonix's gathering of the peoples of the world to Wilson's League of Nations.

Perhaps feeling secure in knowing that the Winter and Summer Olympic Games could stand alone as truly distinct international events, Coubertin announced his retirement as president of the IOC on November 16, 1924, revealing his intentions to relinquish his official position while continuing his ardent support of the Olympic movement.

The legacy of those first Olympic Winter Games rises from the successes of stellar athletes and the large number of spectators drawn to international competition. Indeed, the winter competition has endured as evidenced by the continued interest in the Olympic Winter Games that began in an atmosphere of limited media exposure. The IOC's official designation of the winter sports as the Olympic Winter Games separates them from the Games of the Olympiad, the Summer Olympic Games. The numbering of the Olympic Winter Games begins with Chamonix, the I Olympic Winter Games. When the Olympic Winter Games were interrupted during World War II, they resumed as the V Olympic Winter Games in 1948 rather than the VII Olympic Winter Games. In contrast, each four year interval of the Summer Olympic Games is assigned a Roman numeral even though the Games were not held during World Wars I and II.

BIBLIOGRAPHICAL ESSAY

Because the Chamonix Olympic Winter Games were the first official Olympic program of winter sports, there are only limited sources and brief references to the event. Although there was no official report prepared, the French Olympic Committee published *Resultats des concours des jeux d'hiver organizes par le comite Olympique francais* (Paris, 1925), which is a listing of the official results.

Newspapers provide the most detailed descriptions of the Games. Don Skene of the *Chicago Tribune* wrote a series of articles chronicling the Games from start to finish. His description of the opening ceremonies on January 26, 1924, provides some insight into the protocol of early Olympic Winter Games. *New York Times* reporters covered other aspects of the Games, including problems encountered by small resort towns unaccustomed to dealing with large numbers of visitors. Additionally, articles in the *Times* of London describe the daily events and athletes of the leading nations. Although the IOC does not support the concept of awarding points and declaring national winners, newspaper correspondents devised point systems and identified the dominant nations.

Secondary literature on the Chamonix Games is also limited. John Lucas, *Saga of the Modern Olympic Games* (New Brunswick, N.J., 1980) includes some interesting facts about the Olympic Winter Games. Paula Welch, *History of American Physical Education and Sport*, 2d. ed. (Springfield, Ill., 1996) includes a chapter on the Olympic Winter Games. Robert Hunt Lyman, ed., *The World Almanac* and *Book of Facts* (New York, 1925) includes background information about postwar France, including rail and building reconstruction, industrial power, government, and general economic status.

Readers should consult the general bibliography for other relevant secondary sources on the Chamonix Games.

ST. MORITZ 1928

Susan Saint-Sing

SECOND OLYMPIC WINTER GAMES

The Second Olympic Winter Games, held in St. Moritz, Switzerland in 1928, were unique for several reasons, not the least of which were the erratic weather and the spectacular gold medal performance of Norwegian figure skater Sonja Henie. The Second Winter Games were the first to enjoy official inclusion in the Olympic program from the outset. The inaugural Olympic winter sports carnival, held at Chamonix, France in 1924, had originally been labeled as International Sports Week before the International Olympic Committee (IOC) decided a year later that they were a successful experiment that should be repeated and rechristened them the First Olympic Winter Games.

The shifting dynamics of post–World War I international politics also shaped the unique nature of the St. Moritz Games. The Second Winter Games were the first postwar Olympics held outside of territory of the victorious Allied nations. In fact, the IOC deliberately selected neutral Switzerland for the 1928 Winter Games, and neutral Holland for the 1928 summer Olympics, to counter criticisms that after three successive Olympic celebrations in Belgium and France the Olympics had become the exclusive province of the Great War's victors. To underscore the IOC's new commitment to internationalism, the Second Winter Games also witnessed the return of Germany to the Olympic fold.

In addition to its political capital as a neutral site, St. Mortiz offered the IOC several other attractive qualities. The town was one of the oldest and most exclusive Alpine winter resorts. Nestled in the Alpine region known as the Engadine, St. Mortiz had been a tourist destination for Europeans for more than five hundred years. Originally, pilgrims made the trek to the town to bathe in its renowned mineral springs. By the nineteenth century St. Mortiz had become the leading tuberculosis sanitarium in Europe for wealthy consumptives seeking fresh air and winter sunshine. British patients at St. Moritz started the modern winter sports industry in the region, staging sledding and skating races as therapeutic leisure. In the 1880s wealthy winter visitors built one of Europe's first and most famous bobsled runs, the Cresta, at St. Moritz. By the 1920s the town had become one of Europe's leading destination resorts, famed for its winter sporting opportunities. St. Mortiz's upscale clientele and reputation for glamour were precisely what the IOC desired in a Winter Games site in this era. The elegant resort also provided a spotlight on women athletes breaking into the male preserves of winter sports. The female skaters' hemlines threw the press corps into a *paparazzi* frenzy. These features made the Second Olympic Winter Games a fascinating combination of controversy and spectacle.

In an era when the public understood that the true Olympic Games were the summer Games, St. Moritz was the second effort by the IOC to open a new franchise. The idea of winter sports as part of the greater Olympic celebration year began officially in 1924 at Chamonix. Scandinavia's existing Nordic Games already attracted the finest winter athletes in the world. The IOC overcame opposition from the Scandinavian nations, the U.S., and even Baron Pierre de Coubertin to inaugurate the Olympic Winter Games. Initially, Coubertin insisted that one host city stage both winter and summer games. His idea was formalized as part of the official Polignac Charter of 1921. This put many cities into a quandary as they realized they could not host winter and summer due to climatic conditions. Amsterdam, selected in 1921 by the IOC to host the summer 1928 Games, could not offer suitable climate or terrain for a Winter Olympics. In 1925 the Olympic Congress provided the option of allowing separate sites for summer and winter Games. St. Moritz beat out two other Swiss resorts, Davos and Engelberg, to win the honor of hosting the Second Olympic Winter Games.

St. Moritz won the bid in part because it was Europe's leading winter resort and had many facilities in place. Bobsled originated in Switzerland and St. Moritz's Cresta run was the most famous course in the world. The site of the first bobsled event ever raced, the naturally cooled (unrefrigerated) track still stands today. The renowned Kulm Hotel provided its spectacular ice rink for skating and hockey. Sitting at 6,066 feet above sea level, St. Moritz provided idyllic alpine terrain, high society glitz, and a tradition of elite winter sports competition. After winning the Games the Swiss quickly made the few preparations not already in place, including the construction of a pavilion for 400 dignitaries and a grandstand for 5,000 spectators.

On the eve of the opening of the Second Olympic Winter Games jolly festivities lit the snowscape around St. Moritz. Athletes, officials, and fans readied for an exuberant winter sports carnival. On February 11, 1928, the Second Winter Games opened in the midst of a blinding snowstorm. Competition ran from February 11 to February 19. The number of competitors nearly doubled from Chamonix, with 464 athletes (438 men and 26 women) taking part in 14 events. The number of nations also expanded from 16 to 25, including the first appearance by Japan at a Winter Olympics as well as the return of Germany to the Olympic fold. Germany's return was opposed by Belgium but to no avail. The Weimar regime was reinstated by the IOC. The Swiss crowd gave a warm reception to the Germans and the Austrians—the Great War's losers and Switzerland's next-door neighbors.

In their infancy, the Olympic Winter Games struggled with the logistics of staging consistent, fair, world-class competitions. The infrastructure necessary for meeting unexpected problems and conditions were not yet in place. International standards for winter sports, from the height of ski jump hills to the quality of ice conditions, had not yet been established. Unfortunate weather extremes and nationalistic fervor quickly exposed these flaws. The *Föhn*, the warm Mediterranean wind that can cause the normally crisp snow and ice to turn into slush in the Swiss Alps, wreaked havoc on the St. Moritz Games. Swiss ice, as witnessed by the popularity of its winter resorts, was generally known as the world's finest. Though the Games opened in blizzard conditions, the *Föhn* quickly made its unwelcome arrival. The wind ravaged ice and snow conditions.

In the opening days of the Second Olympic Winter Games Nordic skiers faced ski wax nightmares in the face of the warm winds. They tried homemade concoctions to overcome the rapidly changing snow conditions. The grueling 50-kilometer cross-country ski race started with temperatures near zero degrees Fahrenheit. In a matter of hours temperatures soared as high as seventy-seven degrees Fahrenheit. Puddles of slush dotted the course. Picking the right ski wax, normally a key to victory in cross country skiing, became all important for this race. The right wax could mean the difference between the wooden skis of the era sticking like water clogged tree branches or gliding over the treacherous conditions. Sweden's Per Erik Hedlund did the best job of selecting wax and overcoming the deteriorating conditions to get the gold in 4:52:03. Hedlund wore a white uniform, perhaps to repel the heat, with a red cap rather than the official blue team uniform usually worn by the Swedes. From 1928 until 1976, the Swedish team wore Hedlund's uniform—white winter gear and red hats—to honor his feat. Hedlund's triumph proved an exception. Norway dominated all the remaining Nordic skiing events. The Norwegians swept the 18-kilometer race. They also took three medals in the Nordic combined (a ski jump and an 18-kilometer race) and the gold and silver in the ski jump.

Setting early trends in being bigger and better than the previous Olympic host, the St. Moritz's ski jump hill overshadowed Chamonix's incline. At a towering 310 feet in elevation, it was the highest ski jump in the world, but not the safest. The height of the takeoff as well as the design of the downhill run-out below the jump raised safety concerns among the competitors. Critics complained that the Swiss had manufactured a jump to favor their own jumpers. When Norway's Jacob Tullin Thams, the defending Olympic champion, was taunted by Swiss accusations that the Norwegians were afraid of the hill, he jumped to a world record 73 meters. He lost his balance at the finish line and crashed beyond the slope of the hill's run-out. Tullin Thams was rushed to the hospital where he spent the rest of the Olympics recuperating. Since ski jumping was scored on a combination of distance and style points, Tullin Thams record-setting leap earned him only twenty-eighth place after deductions from his fall were made to his tally. Tullin Thams eventually turned winter defeat into summer victory. At the 1936 Berlin Olympics he won a silver medal in yachting. The poorly designed ski jump hill at St. Mortiz led the International Ski Federation to restrict jump height to protect both the jumpers and the sport's reputation.

Bad weather and questionable officiating also plagued skating. One of the most exciting competitions, strewn with controversy, came in the 10,000-meter speed skating race. Irving Jaffee of New York City beat Norway's favored champion Bernt Evenson by three seconds in a heat and seemingly won the gold medal. Near the end of the event with every top-ranked skater having finished their heats, the unusual thaw deteriorated ice conditions and the Swiss official in charge canceled the 10,000-meter event. U.S. officials protested the cancellation. Initially the IOC sided with the Americans and determined that if the event could not be rescheduled then Jaffe would be the winner. The thaw as well as the departure of the Norwegians for an important competition in Oslo, made a restart impossible. The International Skating Federation overruled the IOC and upheld the cancellation of the 10,000-meters. American officials and newspapers cried foul and blamed nefarious European interests for discriminating against U.S. athletes.

The American speed skating team, speed skating athletes from other nations, Norwegian, Swiss, and other European correspondents, and even the French IOC demanded that Jaffee be awarded the gold, but to no avail. Swiss skaters declared their support for Jaffee by carrying a banner that read "Long Live America." They paraded the banner in front of the hotel where the Swiss official who canceled the race was staying. The protests went unheeded. For the record books the race was officially entered as no contest. In 1932 at the Lake Placid Olympic Winter Games, Jaffee won the 10,000-meter speed skating race and finally received a gold medal.

The Jaffee affair was one of several controversies that plagued the U.S. skating team. Infighting between American Olympic Committee Chairman General Douglas MacArthur, the International Skating Union, and the Amateur Skating Union for the right to select the skating team before the Games began created much anxiety among American athletes. An official U.S. Olympic skating team was not finalized until the athletes were crossing the Atlantic on their way to Switzerland. The internal struggles also destroyed efforts to send an American ice hockey team to St. Mortiz.

The U.S. fared better in the bobsled than in speed skating, even though the *Föhn* took its toll here as well. Bad weather required two of the four sled events to be canceled. Rumors of heavy wagering on the races raised the specter of sabotage to the sleds. Swiss officials responded by heightening security. The drivers of USA I and USA II, William Fiske and Jennison Heaton dubbed their sleds Hell and Satan. Their machismo paid off as Fiske's team won gold and Heaton's squad won silver in the five-man race. The 1928 Olympics were the only one in which teams had a choice to field either a four- or a five-man team. All of the competitors chose the five-man option for the pushing and weight advantage in the downhill run. The U.S. sleds were piloted by American expatriates who wintered in Alpine resorts and had considerable experience on the Cresta run. The pushers were recruited by an advertisement placed in the Paris edition of the *New York Herald Tribune* to attract wealthy Americans vacationing in Europe.

Jennison Heaton did even better in the skeleton than in the bobsled, winning the gold medal in the one-man skeleton, a head first version of the luge. His brother John took the silver. The Heatons, natives of New Haven, Connecticut, summered in Paris and wintered at St. Moritz. They upset the favored St. Moritz winter resident, Britain's Earl of Northesk who finished third behind the American siblings. Clearly, sledding was largely the pastime of the wealthy leisure classes in Europe and North America who had the money and time to devote to their outdoor passions. Indeed, most of the winter sports in that era were the provinces of affluent dilettantes. After their 1928 triumphs, the Heatons remained fixtures at the St. Moritz Tobogganing Society. They donated the Heaton Cup as a token of their love for the Cresta. At the age of forty, John Heaton returned to his beloved St. Moritz for the 1948 Olympic Winter Games. He hurled himself down the Cresta once again. In another remarkable performance he earned his second Olympic silver medal in the skeleton.

North Americans also dominated ice hockey even though the U.S., beset by internal problems, failed to field a team. The Canadian team so outclassed all of its competitors in pre-Olympic practices that in an unprecedented move the judges gave the Canadians a bye to the medal round. The Canadians proved that they merited the special treatment. Made up of University of Toronto alumni who dubbed their squad the Toronto Graduates, the reigning Canadian amateur champions annihilated the Swedes, Swiss, and British by scores of 11 to 0, 14 to 0 and 13 to 0 to win the gold medal. The Graduates scored thirty-eight goals in the tournament and allowed none.

As the St. Moritz Games came to a close, the *Föhn* finally dissipated and frigid conditions and firm ice returned for figure skating. In the pairs skating France won its only medal as Andrée Joly and Pierre Brunet danced to victory. In the men's figure skating Sweden's Gillis Grafström won his third straight Olympic gold medal (in addition to Chamonix in 1924 he won in Antwerp in 1920 when the event was included in the summer Games). The most luminous star of the 1928 Olympic Winter Games emerged in women's figure skating. On the ice rink in front of the Kulm Hotel Norway's Sonja Henie began her ascent to international fame. After finishing last—as an eleven-year-old—in 1924 at Chamonix, Henie dazzled the world in St. Moritz, winning her first of her three consecutive gold medals in Olympic figure skating. "It can be stated without fear of contradiction, that the chances are that the world has never seen a more finished, graceful and dexterous skater than little Miss Sonja Henie of Norway," wrote Gustavus T. Kirby, representative for the American Olympic Committee for the St. Moritz Games.

In 1928, figure skating was the only Olympic sport that permitted women to compete. Henie starred in the events that the international media proclaimed as the epitome of feminine athleticism. The press featured the sexuality of the female figure skaters, focusing on the revealing costumes, particularly the daring hemlines and tight sweaters. The media served up the women Olympians in a cheesecake-style to sell the women to global audiences more as objects of desire than as world-class athletes. Sonja Henie epitomized the mixture of sex appeal and athletic skill used by a patriarchal press to promote women's sport to a patriarchal society.

Henie's grace and strength made women figure skaters into the winter Olympic counterparts to the sexy, swimsuit-clad naiads of the summer Games. Henie retired from competition after the 1936 Games and went on to Hollywood movie stardom. In a society that valued women more for their beauty than their prowess, Henie's sex appeal rather than her athletic skill proved to be her most enduring asset.

Lost in the global rapture with Henie, Fritzi Burger of Austria finished second and Beatrix Loughran of the U.S. finished third. Then, as now, figure skating judging proved controversial. The U.S. judge put Loughran ahead of Henie in the standings. The Norwegian judge then voted the U.S. skater seventh. Throughout her career rumors of vote buying and other irregularities swirled around Henie, whose father was suspected of using his wealth to influence judges. Henie's amateur standing was also frequently under fire from those who claimed that she received large fees to appear in competitions. Critics accused her of being one of the highest paid amateurs in the world of sport.

As part of the Olympic Charter for the Winter Games, host countries showcased various other winter sports and activities. At St. Moritz there were several exhibition events including skijöring (races in which skiers were pulled along by horses), barrel jumping by ice skaters, and curling. Curling had been included as a medal sport in the First Olympic Winter Games. The British won that competition while the Swiss withdrew—perhaps explaining why curling was relegated to an exhibition event at St. Moritz. The resort was a continental curling center where Scottish and English winter vacationers flocked to enjoy the normally exceptional ice and blue sunny skies. The Swiss curling clubs were, however, dominated by the British. There was little native Swiss interest in curling. Curling disappeared from the official Olympic program as a medal sport until 1998 at Nagano.

Nationalism also played a role in another demonstration event. The Swiss scheduled a 28-kilometer military ski patrol race as a demonstration sport. The event, which resembles what is now known as biathlon, consisted of teams of four soldiers skiing through mountain terrain while carrying rifles and full field packs. The Swiss were certain they would dominate the race but the Norwegians proved once again the superior skiers. The Swiss team finished third behind Norway and Finland.

As in 1924, Norway dominated the 1928 Olympic Winter Games. Although the IOC tried to discourage national ranking systems and medal counts, the world press ignored the wishes of the Olympic potentates and merrily tabulated national standings. Norway won 6 gold, 4 silver, and 5 bronze medals. The United States won 2 gold, 2 silver, and 2 bronze medals. Sweden won 2 gold, 2 silver, and 1 bronze medal. Finland won 2 gold, 1 silver, and 1 bronze medal. Host Switzerland managed only a single bronze medal. In the charts of national superiority constructed in American newspapers, Norway led the scoring with 90.5 points. Surprisingly, the United States finished second overall with 50.5 points. The American press noted that the U.S. would have scored 61.5 had the 10,000-meter speed skating results been included in the count. Sweden finished third with 40 points, followed by Finland with 39.5 points, Austria with 22 points, and Canada with 13.5 points.

In the summer of 1928, winter athletes again appeared at the Olympics. They were featured in Canadian sculptor R. Tait McKenzie's entries in the Olympic arts festival. The presence of bronze winter athletes in Amsterdam symbolized that the Winter Games had become a part of the Olympic movement. No longer were the Winter Games merely an experimental sideshow. Although not as popular as their summer counterparts, St. Moritz's successful staging of an Olympic Winter Games wed the new festival to the established modern Olympic calendar.

The 1928 St. Moritz Olympic Winter Games revealed that the same problems that created conflicts in summer Olympics would cause controversy in the winter versions. Problems with judging and rule-making, internecine warfare between the IOC, National Olympic Committees, and sport federations, battles over definitions of amateurism, criticisms of the weather and hospitality of host sites, struggles to control media relations, and rampant nationalism plagued both the winter and summer Olympics. St. Mortiz delivered one media star—Sonja Henie—to the world. It also placed women's figure skating at the center of public consciousness of winter sports. Norway continued its domination of Nordic sports. The U.S. finished a surprising second—although much of the American press treated the Winter Games as comic opera.

In the end, in spite of the weather, newly elected IOC president Henri Baillet-Latour declared the Games a success. The glorious facilities, the striking setting, the warm hospitality, the efficiency of Swiss and the unexpectedly large attendance proved to the IOC that St. Moritz was indeed an Olympic site of the highest caliber. No doubt the memories helped St. Moritz win the Winter Games again in 1948.

BIBLIOGRAPHICAL ESSAY

Scholars have not yet thoroughly explored the 1928 Olympic Winter Games. Most American newspapers provided some coverage of the events through wire service reports. Big city dailies provided fairly extensive coverage, in particular the *New York Times* and *New York Herald Tribune*. The daily press in the rest of the English-speaking world, particularly in Great Britain and Canada, also reported on the Games. *The Times* of London and other major British papers ran stories from St. Moritz. English-language magazines included little coverage of the second Winter Games.

Official Olympic documents can be found at the IOC Archives in Lausanne. They include the *Rapport general du comité executif des IImes jeux olympiques d'hiver et documents officiels divers* (Lausanne, 1928) the *Resultats des Concours des IImes jeux olympiques d'hiver organises à St. Moritz* (Lausanne, 1928) and the *General Rules and Programs of the 2nd Olympic Winter Games* (Lausanne, 1928). The Swiss Olympic Committee's official bulletin for St. Moritz Games is *Bulletin offciel du Comité Olympique Suisse*. Swiss organizing committee reports, written in German, include *Olympische Winterspiele St. Moritz, 1928* (Lausanne, 1928) *Olympische Winterspiele St. Moritz, 1928: Allgemeine Bestimmungen und Programme* (Lausanne, 1928) and F. J. J. Buytendijk, and Willi Knoll, eds., *Die sportarztlichen Ergebnisse der II. Olympschen Winterspiele in St. Moritz, 1928* (Bern, 1928).

NOC reports on St. Moritz in English include the American Olympic Committee, *Report of the American Olympic Committee: Ninth Olympic Games, Amsterdam, 1928; Second Olympic Winter Sports, St. Moritz, 1928* (New York, 1928). The French report is Comité Olympique Française, *La Participation française auz jeux de la axe olympiade: Saint-Moritz, Amsterdam, 1928* (Paris, 1929). In German see Julius Wagner, Fritz Klipstein, and Franz Messerli, *Die Olympischen Winterspeile 1928 in St. Mortiz* (Zurich 1928). Photographs of the Winter Games can be found in Carl J. Luther, *Olympische Wintersport* (Zurich, 1929).

Ellen Phillips, *The VIII Olympiad: Paris, 1924; St. Moritz, 1928* (Los Angeles, 1996) a volume in the United States Olympic Committee's official history of the modern Olympic movement provides a reliable overview. E. John B. Allen, *From Skisport to Skiing: One Hundred Years of an American Sport, 1840–1940* (Amherst, 1993) contains a section on the American view of cross country skiing at St. Moritz as well as material on what Lake Placid organizers learned in Switzerland for the 1932 Winter Games. Lisa H. Albertson, ed., *Chamonix to Lillehammer: The Glory of the Olympic Winter Games* (Salt Lake City, 1994) includes material on St. Moritz as does Bud Greenspan, *Frozen in Time: The Greatest Moments at the Winter Olympics* (Santa Monica, 1997).

A secondary source on the evolution of St. Moritz into winter sports center is Stuart Stevens "The Chuting Party." *Ultra Sport* 3 (December 1986): 42–49. Michael Seth-Smith, *The Cresta Run: History of the St. Moritz Tobagganing Club* (London, 1976) covers the history of sledding at the resort. For information on curling see David B. Smith, *Curling: An Illustrated History* (Edinburgh, 1981). Sonja Henie's autobiography is *Wings on My Feet* (New York, 1940). Raymond Strait and Leif Henie offer a longer view of Sonja Henie's life in *Queen of Ice, Queen of Shad-*

ows: The Unsuspected Life of Sonja Henie (New York, 1985). Benjamin T. Wright, *Skating Around the World, 1892- 1992* (Davos, Switzerland, 1992) is the International Skating Union's official history. Interesting insights into Scandinavian uses of the Winter Games for nationalistic purposes can be found in Per Jørgensen, "From Balck to Nurmi: The Olympic Movement in the Nordic Nations," *International Journal of the History of Sport* 14 (December 1997): 69–99; and Matti Goksøyr, "The Popular Sounding Board: Nationalism, 'the People' and Sport in Norway in the Inter-War Years," *International Journal of the History of Sport* 14 (December 1997): 100–114.

English language dissertations which cover some aspects of the St. Moritz Games include Donald E. Fuoss, "An Analysis of the Incidents in the Olympic Games from 1924 to 1948, with Reference to the Contribution of the Games to International Good Will and Understanding" (Ph.D. diss., Columbia University, 1951); and Mark Dyreson, "'America's Athletic Missionaries': The Olympic Games and the Creation of a National Culture, 1896–1936" (Ph.D. diss., University of Arizona, 1989). Fuoss concentrates on the international political climate surrounding the Olympics in the 1920s while Dyreson focuses on the role of the Olympics in shaping American culture.

LAKE PLACID 1932

John Fea

THIRD OLYMPIC WINTER GAMES

Prior to 1932, the village of Lake Placid, New York, located in the heart of the famed Adirondack forest preserve, was little more than a regional summer and winter vacation haven. Much of the activity in the tiny community centered around Melvil Dewey's Lake Placid Club, a summer resort catering to New York vacationers. In 1905 Dewey decided to keep the club open for the winter, thus setting the stage for the development of winter sports in Lake Placid. Such development proceeded rapidly. By 1921 Lake Placid had its own ski jump, speed-skating facility, and ski association and was emerging as one of America's premier winter sports facilities. From February 4 to 13, 1932, this small community would play host to a relatively new venture in the Olympic movement, the Winter Games.

Bringing the Olympics to Lake Placid was not easy. Probably the biggest obstacle organizers faced in securing the Winter Games was proving to the International Olympic Committee (IOC) that Lake Placid was an Olympic-caliber winter sports center and thus a legitimate potential host. While Lake Placid had adequate facilities, it was not as well known in the winter sports world as were European resorts like St. Moritz, the host of the 1928 Winter Games. One advantage for Lake Placid was that the 1932 Summer Olympic Games had been awarded to Los Angeles, and the recent practice of the IOC was to give the host country of the Summer Games the opportunity to host the Winter Games that same year. While this custom made Lake Placid's chances more promising, other American locales such as Lake Tahoe, Yosemite Valley, and Denver, sites closer to Southern California, also were interested in hosting the games. Furthermore, the IOC was considering Montreal, Canada, and Oslo, Norway, just in case the Americans were unable to provide the necessary funding and facilities for the Games.

The responsibility for securing the Games for Lake Placid rested on one man, the secretary and eventual president of the Lake Placid Club, Dr. Godfrey Dewey, the son of the club's founder, Melvil Dewey. Dewey convinced both local and state officials of the possibility of hosting the Winter Games. In March 1928 the town of Lake Placid formed a committee to prepare a bid for the games. Franklin D. Roosevelt, governor of New York, convinced the state legislature to back the Lake Placid bid and to authorize partial funding. Early in 1929 Dewey and his Lake Placid delegation traveled to Lausanne to present the advantages of their venue. By the time of this trip, the prime competition Lake Placid faced came from a group of Californians intent upon keeping the Winter and Summer Games together in the Los Angeles area. While none of the American sites completely satisfied the IOC as far as the development of their facilities was concerned, Dewey was able to convince the committee that Lake Placid was the best-equipped American site available. On April 10, 1929, despite an angry protest from the California group, the 1932 Winter Olympic Games were awarded to Lake Placid.

The village of Lake Placid and the state of New York quickly rallied to provide leadership for the development and preparation of their Olympic venue. Governor Roosevelt provided funding to establish a temporary state commission, which included representatives from the Lake Placid Olympic Committee (LPOC), the New York state assembly, and the state conservation department. Dewey became president of the LPOC and was the most influential person in the organization of the Games. Avery Brundage, who had just succeeded Graeme Hammond as president of the American Olympic Committee (AOC), was involved in publicizing the Games and providing equipment and training facilities for the American athletes.

Yet it was the LPOC, led by Dewey, that confronted the biggest task: preparing the community to host this international event. The committee estimated that it needed to prepare for 600 contestants from 25 nations (65 nations were invited, but not all were expected to accept the invitations) as well as for 8,000 daily spectators. The bulk of the site development centered around the construction of a bobsled run and a stadium that could be used for the Opening and Closing Ceremonies, speed skating, and ice hockey. Shortly after the IOC chose Lake Placid, the New York legislature approved a bill that provided $125,000 for the construction of the bobsled run. The committee hired Berlin bobsled designer Stanislaus Zentzytsky to build the structure, which turned out to please both the competitors and the IOC.

The only major problem the Lake Placid developers faced in their preparation for the Games was that a New York law forbade the removal of trees from Adirondack forests. The construction of the bobsled run directly violated this "forever wild" ordinance, since it required that approximately 2,500 trees be cut down. Protests from local environmentalists caused Dewey and his committee to appeal to Governor Roosevelt for a constitutional amendment. After heated debate in the state assembly, the environmental faction was appeased, and construction of the bobsled run went forward.

Mother Nature also provided a scare for Lake Placid organizers. The village received virtually no snowfall during the two months prior to the Games. Worse, New York was hit with an unusual heat wave in mid-January. Temperatures jumped to 50 degrees, ice rinks thawed, and the U.S. bobsled team was forced to cancel practice because the bobsled run was unusable. Fortunately for the organizers, the temperature dropped a few days later, and a winter storm dumped six inches of snow on the village.

Aside from the local debates over environmental issues regarding individual sporting events, there were no serious political controversies surrounding the

Games. President Herbert Hoover was invited to open the Games, but unable to attend, he paved the way for his prospective election opponent, Governor Roosevelt, to handle the task. Using the Opening Ceremonies as another political campaign stop on his way to the presidency, Roosevelt called for world peace in his brief remarks, broadcast nationwide over the National Broadcasting Company (NBC) and Columbia radio networks (the two networks that covered all of the athletic events). During the festivities Eleanor Roosevelt took a ride down the new bobsled run, delighting the crowds. The importance of Roosevelt's role in convincing the New York legislature of the viability of the Games in Lake Placid cannot be overstated.

The Lake Placid Games brought some new ventures in Olympic winter sports. A controversy centered around the style of the speed-skating competition. Traditionally, competitors skated against the clock in these events, with those skating the three fastest times receiving medals. Dewey proposed an American *pack-style* of skating, especially for the distance events, which meant that athletes skated against each other rather than against the stopwatch. Dewey believed that not only was pack skating more entertaining; but since it allowed all competitors to participate at once, it provided the same ice conditions for all the skaters. The IOC approved Dewey's suggestion; but after American victories in some of the early events, European skaters protested to the International Skating Union (ISU). The ISU upheld the protest, forcing the races to be rerun; unfortunately for the Europeans, the Americans won those races too. Lake Placid also saw the emergence of women's speed skating as an Olympic sport and of dog-sled racing and curling as demonstration sports.

The Lake Placid organizers were forced to stage these Games amid a worldwide economic depression. During the two months before the Games, nation after nation withdrew their teams from competition because they could not finance their athletes; other nations greatly reduced the size of their teams. The number of withdrawals caused Sweden and other nations to propose a postponement of the Games until better economic conditions prevailed. Moreover, Canada, France, and Sweden complained that the Americans were not providing a high enough exchange rate on their respective currencies. The AOC under Avery Brundage worked with state and federal government agencies to do everything possible to enable European teams to attend the Games. The North Atlantic Passenger Agreement reduced ship fares up to 20 percent for athletes traveling to the Games, and President Hoover exempted foreign participants from usual passport and visa fees.

Hoover's gesture was particularly welcome in light of the strict immigration requirements imposed on those coming to America. The United States even offered to finance the German hockey team's trip to America, an offer that the Germans eventually accepted. Even with these measures, a smaller-than-expected number of athletes competed in the Games. When the closing date (December 24, 1931) for applications arrived, 17 nations, accounting for 364 athletes, had accepted invitations. Participating nations included Austria, Belgium, Canada, Czechoslovakia, Finland, France, Germany, Great Britain, Italy, Japan, Hungary, Norway, Poland, Romania, Sweden, Switzerland, and the United States.

The host country provided most of the excitement in the competition. Twenty-one-year-old Jack Shea, a Lake Placid native, won the first gold medal of the Games in the 500-meter speed-skating event and later went on to win the 1,500-meter event as well. Irving Jaffee of the United States captured both distance speed-skating races, winning the 5,000- and 10,000-meter events. Sonja Henie of Norway, who had won the gold medal in women's figure skating at St. Moritz, charmed spectators by winning her second gold medal at Lake Placid. Edward Eagan, a member of the victorious U.S. four-man bobsled team, became the first man to win gold medals in both the Winter and Summer Games. Eagan had won the light-heavyweight boxing title in the 1920 Games at Antwerp.

The total cost of the Lake Placid Olympics was $1.05 million, most of which was spent on the construction of the bobsled run and the Olympic stadium. Funding came from a variety of sources. The town of North Elba (in which Lake Placid village is located) passed a $200,000 bond issue in 1929 with the hope that the money would cover all the expenses of the Games. The community was promised that their costs would eventually be reimbursed through ticket sales. Unfortunately for the citizens of North Elba, the $200,000 fell well short of the expenses required to stage the Games, and proceeds from ticket sales did not exceed the amount of the bond. The bulk of financial assistance came from the New York state legislature. The state appropriated $500,000 for the construction of facilities, $125,000 for the bobsled run, and $375,000 for the completion of the Olympic stadium. Perhaps Dewey's greatest accomplishment was in convincing the state to allocate such funds during the Great Depression.

Overall, the 1932 Lake Placid Olympics were small and simple compared to present day Olympic extravaganzas. The small size of the Games created an atmosphere that was not conducive to any major controversies or political issues. In 1932 the Winter Olympic Games had yet to achieve the prestige and popularity that the Summer Games enjoyed; the quiet simplicity of Lake Placid did not further enhance the worldwide image of the Winter Games. Yet for those Lake Placid organizers who sought to establish their community as one of the world's leading centers for winter sports and provide an event centered around the athletes rather than the venues, the Games proved a success.

BIBLIOGRAPHICAL ESSAY

Historical material on the Winter Olympic Games, especially secondary sources, is very limited. It is especially scarce for the 1932 Games because the Great Depression caused such limited participation.

For historians willing to take the challenge of providing new interpretations of the Lake Placid Games, the official records of the games are held by the Olympic Regional Development Authority (ORDA) located on Main Street in Lake Placid, New York (http://www.orda.org). The ORDA also operates the 1932 and 1980 Olympic Museum. The bulk of the material is accessible to researchers. The records include minutes of all meetings of the organizing committee and records of the committee's lobbying of state and federal officials, including the International Olympic Committee. The Lake Placid village library (http://www.lakplacid library.org/collections.html) also contains primary collections, including back issues of the *Lake Placid News*, the Lake Placid Club archives, and other collections related to the history of North Elba, Lake Placid, and the Winter Olympic Games.

An official report of the Lake Placid Games does exist, edited by the director of the Olympic Publicity Committee: George M. Lattimer, ed., *Official Report: III Olympic Winter Games: Lake Placid 1932* (Lake Placid, NY, 1932). It provides statistics chronicling the finances, events, and development of the Olympic movement in

Lake Placid. The organizing committee also published *Setting the Stage for the III Olympic Winter Games* (New York, 1932) and *Official Souvenir Book of the III Olympic Winter Games* (New York, 1932), and a *News Bulletin*, issued between October 1930 and early 1932. The official Canadian report is W. A. Fry, ed., *Canada at the Xth Olympiad 1932* (Dunnville, Ontario, 1932).

Without a doubt, the most complete journalistic coverage of the local, developmental, and political issues surrounding the Lake Placid Games is the *New York Times*. The *Times*'s in-depth reporting makes it the most useful source of information on the Games. The national scope of the *Times*, coupled with the local interest of the Games in New York, provide for quite thorough coverage. The *Lake Placid News* also provides insight to local issues affecting the Games.

The most thorough historical monograph on the Lake Placid Games is a local history written by Lake Placid residents George Christian Ortloff and Stephen C. Ortloff, *Lake Placid, The Olympic Years, 1932–1980: A Portrait of America's Premier Winter Resort* (Lake Placid, 1976). The work, while quite popular in nature, does provide information on the history, politics, and preparations surrounding the Games. It is also helpful in placing the Games in their local context. Another useful piece that places the Games in a historical context with other Winter Games is Marc Onigman, "Discontent in the Olympic Winter Games, 1908–1980." In *The Modern Olympics*, eds. Peter J. Graham and Horst Ueberhorst (West Point, N.Y., 1976). Onigman provides one of the few scholarly treatments of the 1932 Lake Placid Games, with much of his research stemming from *New York Times* accounts.

Historians and other researchers interested in the Games should contact either Barbara Reid, the North Elba town historian, or the archivist of the Olympic Regional Development Authority for further information.

GARMISCH-PARTENKIRCHEN 1936

Jon W. Stauff, updated by the editors

FOURTH OLYMPIC WINTER GAMES

When German Olympic officials, eager to erase the disappointment of the canceled 1916 Berlin Games, won the right to organize the XI Olympic Games of 1936, they also became hosts to the IV Winter Olympic Games. While these Winter Games may have been treated initially as a mere sideshow to the summer event, they assumed greater importance after the seizure of power by Adolf Hitler and the National Socialist Party in January 1933. As an opposition party, the Nazis had been predisposed against the modern Olympic Movement for political and ideological reasons, but they revised their position once the minister for popular enlightenment, Joseph Goebbels, and others recognized the international propaganda potential inherent in the Olympics, particularly the Summer Games in Berlin. Senior Nazi officials would work alongside leading non-Nazi Olympic functionaries to insure that the Garmisch-Partenkirchen Games would be the grandest in history, not only to glorify the Olympic movement and to show German athletic prowess, but also to convince the world that Berlin, despite Germany's oppressive political culture, was a suitable venue for the summer Games later that year. This desire to collect international prestige for Germany would often overshadow mere sporting ambitions to cast doubt upon the true intentions of the organizers of the Garmisch-Partenkirchen Games.

Three vacation areas submitted bids in 1933 to host the 1936 Winter Games: Schreiberhau, Braunlage-Schierke, and Garmisch-Partenkirchen. A combination of factors favored the candidacy of the neighboring Upper Bavarian resorts of Garmisch and Partenkirchen. The two towns had the necessary infrastructure and experienced personnel to host such a large competition. There was a tested ski-jumping facility in Partenkirchen, good cross-country trails, excellent ice surfaces, and a challenging bobsled run already in operation. The presence nearby of the Zugspitze, Germany's tallest mountain, provided insurance against a lack of snow that had plagued previous Winter Olympics. Local sports officials from the

Garmisch and Partenkirchen ski clubs and the Riessersee sport club had organized multisport competitions, including the annual Winter Sport Week, for years. And the proximity of Garmisch and Partenkirchen to the large cities of Munich and Innsbruck, combined with plenty of accommodations for German and international spectators, created the possibility of attracting large crowds to the contests that would bolster both short- and long-term economic prospects. These advantages of the Bavarian site were enough to convince IOC officials to select Garmisch and Partenkirchen in May 1933.

The Nazi leadership also favored the Garmisch-Partenkirchen bid. Bavaria was home to the National Socialist Party, with Munich serving as party headquarters and

Nuremberg playing host to the annual party conventions. The natural Alpine beauty of the Werdenfelserland region, with its impressive landscapes, mountain peaks, and blue Bavarian sky, provided the perfect backdrop for the awe-inspiring ceremonies favored by the Nazis. The national government would spare no expense in preparing the area for the Games, as such a grand spectacle required magnificent facilities to match the beautiful scenery and international fanfare of an Olympic Games.

Garmisch-Partenkirchen 1936—A summer view of the ski jump at Garmisch-Partenkirchen, Germany, site of the 1936 Winter Games. Courtesy University of Illinois Archives, Avery Brundage Collection.

Karl Ritter von Halt, a German IOC member since 1929, presided over the organizing committee (OC). He served as a member on the Berlin organizing committee as well as president of the International Handball Federation. Ritter von Halt appointed Peter von Le Fort, an officer of the Partenkirchen ski club, as executive secretary. Other notables, including the mayors of Munich, Garmisch, and Partenkirchen; a military officer; a duke; and several government officials took places as OC members. Also present were Reich Sport Leader Hans von Tschammer und Osten, who would become president of the German Olympic Commission, and Munich banker Friedrich Döhlemann, who served as the OC's vice president/treasurer. The committee began its work on June 1, 1933, and received its charter in August of that year. Le Fort's appointment exacerbated tensions between Garmisch and Partenkirchen officials, and Nazi town councillors in Garmisch fought for the dismissal of Le Fort from the OC. The Reich Sport Office deemed this action to be a "violation of leadership principle" (*Fuhrerprinzip*), and Garmisch officials later paid for their indiscretion when the two towns were merged in 1935, with Partenkirchen benefiting from the administrative consolidation.

Despite this local friction, the planning of the Games proceeded relatively smoothly, with organizers conducting their business on a small-scale, personal level. A general secretariat coordinated the financial advisory committee, the legal counsel, the venue construction office, and the various event committees (in addition to those offices responsible for media relations, ticket sales and advertising, and traffic coordination). Separate subcommittees for ice, bobsled, and skiing events operated in both construction and event areas. A total of 2.6 million Reichmarks (RM), including a RM 1.1 million grant from the Berlin government, covered the costs of facilities construction and other organizing expenses. Despite the existence of functioning venues in the area, organizers planned the construction of a new ski stadium, an ice arena with an artificial ice surface, new cross-country trails, and a state-of-the-art bob run. All facilities, with the exception of the ice arena, were finished by the winter of 1934–1935, thus allowing them to be tested in competition before the Olympic Games in 1936.

Organizers incorporated the existing ski jump on the Gudiberg into a new ski stadium. Workers renovated the old jump in the style of the famed Holmenkollen facility in Norway for use in the Nordic Combined event and built a new, bigger jumping facility adjacent to the old jump for the special jumping event. The Partenkirchen municipal construction officer, supported with technical assistance by the International Ski Federation (FIS), oversaw this construction. The stadium, designed to accommodate 40,000 spectators in the stands and 60,000 in total, would serve as the site of the Opening and Closing Ceremonies and, eventually, 80,000 fans would squeeze into the facility to watch Birger Ruud win the special jumping competition. (Officials turned away 50,000 more spectators and set up loudspeakers outside the stadium to allow them to follow the activities inside.)

The frozen Riessersee, one of Germany's oldest winter sport venues, was the site for ice hockey, speed skating, and the German national winter sport of *Eisschiessen*, an indigenous form of curling. Two hockey rinks were located in the infield of the speed-skating oval, and the *Eisschiessen* rinks stood adjacent to the south side of the oval. To the east of the lake was the new bob course, designed by Stanislaus Zentzytsky, the same Polish engineer who had designed the 1932 Olympic bobsled run at Lake Placid. Organizers also built a new ice arena, with seating for over 2,000 and room for 10,000 spectators in all, to host the artistic skating events. The open-air arena, featuring an artificial ice surface of 10,000 square feet, was completed in 1934, but adjustments to the facilities were made through the end of 1935.

New events in addition to the national folk sport of *Eisschiessen* made their way onto the Olympic program in Garmisch-Partenkirchen. Alpine countries finally succeeded in overcoming the resistance of the Scandinavian bloc to have Alpine skiing competition included in the winter Olympic Games. A combined event, consisting of a downhill race and two slalom runs, was scheduled for both men and women. After 1936, Alpine skiing would find a permanent place in the winter Olympics. Another program addition as a demonstration sport was military ski patrol, a forerunner of the present-day biathlon. While many countries in Europe and the United States participated in military ski-patrol competitions, the inclusion of the sport may also be interpreted as a gesture to appease Nazi officials, who looked favorably upon any sporting activity that could be combined with military training. These additional contests boosted the number of competing athletes over the 1,000 mark for the first time in the history of the Winter Games.

As important as making a positive sporting impression was to the organizers, enhancing Germany's international prestige also ranked high on the OC's list of priorities. Olympic officials, whether out of a sense of ideological conviction or based on a simple strategy of survival, had resigned themselves to working together with the Nazis to make the Winter and Summer Games powerful political statements of the reborn German nation. Leading functionaries, including Carl Diem, organizer of the XI Summer Games, knew that just one incident might be enough to endanger the Berlin event, especially in light of a boycott movement in the United States. Diem expressed his concerns to Ritter von Halt and urged that any evidence of institutionalized anti-Semitism be removed from the roads between Munich and Garmisch-Partenkirchen as well as from the host towns themselves. Efforts were made to prevent any public demonstrations of anti-Semitic behavior in order to preserve a hospitable climate that would win favorable world opinion regarding Berlin's summer festival. While Diem has been honored by the Olympic Movement for his painstaking efforts to promote international sport, he has also been vilified for his collaboration with Nazi leaders in preparing the 1936 Berlin Games. Historians claim that the exchange with Ritter von Halt shows that Diem did not oppose anti-Semitism from an ethical standpoint but from a practical one: bad international press would fuel the fires of the boycott movement and prevent Germany from gaining international prestige from the Olympics. While the debate over Diem's motives may continue in the future, what cannot be argued is the test-run nature of the Garmisch-Partenkirchen event in relation to the XI Summer Games. The experience acquired in Garmisch-Partenkirchen would help German Olympic leaders with their planning for Berlin.

Over 6,000 SS and SA troops performed bodyguard functions for Adolf Hitler when he opened the Games on February 6. Ritter von Halt, in his opening address, stated, "We Germans want [also] to show the world that, faithful to the order of our Fuhrer and federal Chancellor [i.e. Hitler], we can put on an Olympic Games [that will be] a true festival of peace and sincere understanding among peoples." Organizers took great pains to control the image of the Games in the international press; foreign photographers did not receive credentials to work in Garmisch-Partenkirchen, thus forcing the international press corps to rely upon German photos that had received official approval for distribution. The OC wrote newsletters and arranged briefings for foreign journalists to further control the message. Organizers achieved some measure of success in this enterprise; most American newspapers sent their Berlin political correspondents (who had no expertise in sports) to cover the Games, and these journalists reported mostly favorable stories about the organization of the Games and the events themselves. Sonja Henie's third gold medal in figure skating, the ski jumping of Birger Ruud, and the American victory in the two-man bobsled competition provided enough positive material to relegate the only major sporting controversy of the Games, the gold medal-winning British ice-hockey team and the questionable citizenship of some of its Anglo-Canadian members, to a supporting role in press coverage. The media did nothing to fuel movements to boycott the Berlin Games that summer.

For all their efforts to awe an audience of foreign spectators, German organizers need not have made such a fuss. There were only 2,000 foreign athletes and spectators in the area for the Games. Still, the 1936 Garmisch-Partenkirchen games proved to be impressive enough to merit the award of the V Winter Olympic Games to be held in 1940. In the postwar era, Garmisch- Partenkirchen has served as a popular ski resort and winter sport competition site. The 1978 World Alpine

Skiing Championships took place in Garmisch-Partenkirchen, and town officials continue to bid for major competitions as a means of boosting the local economy. Garmisch-Partenkirchen may be reached easily by train from Munich, and the Olympic ski and ice stadiums may be visited all year long.

BIBLIOGRAPHICAL ESSAY

The official repository of the records of the 1936 Winter Games Organization Committee is the German Federal Archives, Potsdam Branch (former German Central Archives, Division I, of the German Democratic Republic), Berliner Str. 98–101, Potsdam, Germany. Once thought to be lost, these records are once again available, thanks to German unification. There are twenty boxes of material listed in the archive's catalog, but a significant portion of the documents, including some that may shed light on the relationship between the Nazis and the OC, are not available. The records are cataloged under "70 Or 1," and the archive will promptly photocopy its catalog upon request for a small fee. Although Garmisch-Partenkirchen officials will happily refer people to Potsdam, the town archive retains some documentation pertaining to the Games as well as other memorabilia.

The official report on the Games, prepared by the Garmisch-Partenkirchen organizing committee, is *Amtlicher Bericht hrsg. vom Organisationskomitee die IV. Olympischen Winterspiele 1936, Garmisch-Partenkirchen e.V.* (Berlin, 1936). The committee also published a number of other works, some of which are in German, French, and English. See *Offizielle Ergebnisse der IV. Olympischen Winterspiele 1936 in Garmisch-Partenkirchen* (Berlin, 1936) and *Bericht des Präsidenten des Organisations-Komitees der IV. Olympischen Winterspiele 1936 Dr. Ritter von Halt* (Garmisch-Partenkirchen, 1935). The report published by the American Olympic Committee is Frederick W. Rubien, ed., *Games of the XIth Olympiad, Berlin, Germany and the IVth Winter Games, Garmisch-Partenkirchen* (New York, 1937). The French Olympic Committee's report is *La participation francaise aux jeux de la XIme Olympiade Garmisch-Partenkirchen—Berlin 1936* (Paris, 1937).

There has been little written about the Garmisch-Partenkirchen Games in English, as most works have focused on the Berlin Summer Games. However, Arnd Kruger and William Murray (eds.), *The Nazi Olympics: Sport, Politics, and Appeasement in the 1930s* (Urbana, Ill., 2003) contains articles on both the 1936 Winter and Summer Games, written from the perspectives of ten different participating nations. William Shirer devotes several entries of his *Berlin Diary* (New York, 1941) to the Games, paying attention to news coverage of the event by foreign newspapers and criticizing the naïveté of several of the American correspondents. A short article about the skiing events by Nicholas Howe, "1936: Garmisch-Partenkirchen," is in *Skiing* 40 (September 1987): 56.

The availability of secondary material in German is not much better. Arnd Kruger's *Die Olympischen Spiele 1936 und die Weltmeinung* (Berlin, 1972) is the most complete analysis of the organization of the 1936 Winter Games from a scholarly standpoint, yet this analysis is a sidelight to Kruger's excellent investigation into world public opinion and the Summer Games. The community of Garmisch-Partenkirchen published a fiftieth-anniversary retrospective of the Games, *50 Jahre Olympiasport—Garmisch-Partenkirchen 1936–1986* (Garmisch-Partenkirchen, 1986), which contains reprinted material from contemporary accounts written by organizers, in addition to results, pictures, and details about facility construction. Garmisch-Partenkirchen's continued prominence as a winter sport competition site has kept the town in the media spotlight. Students should survey German newspapers and periodicals (particularly the Munich-based *Suddeutsche Zeitung*) for coverage of the town and its history.

SAPPORO/ ST. MORITZ/ GARMISCH-PARTENKIRCHEN 1940

Swantje Scharenberg

OLYMPIC WINTER GAMES (NEVER HELD)

During the 36th Session of the International Olympic Committee (IOC) in Warsaw in 1937, Japan received the honor of hosting the V Olympic Winter Games in Sapporo, one year after Tokyo had been awarded the 1940 Summer Games. According to an IOC decision in 1926, the country hosting the Summer Games had priority for the site of the Winter Games.

Werner Klingeberg, a sports consultant paid by the German government, worked as a technical adviser to the IOC. At the 37th Session of the IOC, held in Cairo in 1938, Klingeberg reported that the financial and organizational requirements for Sapporo were assured, with Hokkaido's government providing a budget of 1.25 million yen ($356,426). During the Cairo session, the IOC member from China, Chen-ting Wang, pleaded via telegram for a change of the Games site because of the Japanese invasion of China the preceding year. Despite concerns over the increasing politicization of sport and evidence of Japan's militarism and expansionism, the IOC remained committed to the Japanese site for the 1940 Games.

The IOC encountered problems with the International Ski Federation (FIS) almost immediately after the Cairo session, resulting in drastic changes to the Olympic program. According to FIS regulations, ski instructors were allowed to compete in the Olympics; according to the IOC amateur code, they were not. The FIS rejected the IOC's demands to exclude "professional" skiers and insisted upon its own right to determine the amateur status of its members. As a compromise between the FIS and the IOC could not be reached, the IOC canceled the Alpine ski competition for the 1940 Winter Games. Meanwhile, the external and internal political pressures upon Fuminaro Konoe's government in 1938 caused a reduction of the financial commitment to the Games. Initially, the Japanese Olympic Committee (JOC) tried to cope with the setbacks, but on July 15, 1938, one year after the beginning of the war with China, the committee informed the Japanese public that both the Summer and Winter Games of 1940 were canceled.

The choice of Helsinki on July 18, 1938, as the new location for the Summer Games gave hope to Oslo's bid for the Winter Games. On September 3, however, the executive committee of the IOC, meeting in Brussels, decided to award the Games to St. Moritz, the host of the 1928 Winter Olympics. St. Moritz had the necessary sporting facilities and in 1928 had demonstrated its ability to organize an impressive Olympic Games. By October 1938, the program for the Games, scheduled to begin in February 1940, had been completed, with competition in figure skating, speed skating, ice hockey, bobsled, and military patrol, with ski jumping and slalom as demonstration sports. The Swiss Organizing Committee (SOC) intended to circumvent the dispute with the FIS by making ski jumping a demonstration sport, but after further consideration of the position of the FIS, the committee canceled the event. The IOC was notified of this decision during its 38th Session in London in June 1939; it gave the Swiss a week to reconsider, but the Swiss refused to put ski jumping back on the program. In a secret vote, the IOC, seeing no alternative, took the Games away from St. Moritz and awarded them to Garmisch-Partenkirchen in the German Alps. Never before had the IOC removed a city as a Games host.

Garmisch-Partenkirchen's selection as a substitute site for the 1940 Winter Games had been facilitated by the appointment of Karl Ritter von Halt to the IOC executive committee in 1937; at the same time, Theodor Lewald had been forced to resign his IOC membership because of his Jewish ancestry and was replaced by the politically reliable General Walter von Reichenau. These moves increased German influence within the Olympic movement, so that in May 1939, a month before St. Moritz was replaced, IOC president Henri Baillet-Latour confidentially asked Ritter von Halt whether Garmisch-Partenkirchen could host the Winter Olympics again. Sports officials around the world had been impressed by the Berlin Games of 1936 and were not particularly concerned by the politics of the National Socialist regime, although many regarded it as inhumane and monstrous. By 1938, the Jewish pogroms had begun, and in March 1939, German troops occupied all of Czechoslovakia in violation of the Munich agreement. By this time, sport had become officially a part of the state apparatus with the foundation of the Nationalsozialistische Reichsbund fur Leibesubungen on December 21, 1938. Among other things, this party-affiliated organization was responsible for international sport exchange.

The German government agreed to host the Winter Olympics in Garmisch-Partenkirchen but refused to recognize an independent Czech national Olympic committee. To keep the IOC happy, however, the Germans did not require Czech athletes to compete under the German flag, even though they did not acknowledge Czech sovereignty. Official IOC statements have always emphasized the political neutrality of sport, but many saw the decision to award the 1940 Winter Games to Garmisch-Partenkirchen (and therefore to Nazi Germany) as acceptance of and even support of the German political situation and thus a political victory for National Socialism. Sport as an effective international symbol of peace became a propaganda tool and reflected one aspect of Nazi Germany's foreign policy.

A day of skiing with more than 12,000 participants, an impressive display of mass sport, had been planned for the Games. The event would feature Hitler, who, at the end of his speech, would donate skiing huts to Germany and other nations. Following a military demonstration, the three-hour event would end, as it had in Berlin in 1936, with Richard Strauss's "Olympic Hymn." Invitations coupled with the generous promise to pay for all internal travel costs and to reduce the accommodation fee to only three Reichsmarks (RM) per person per day was meant to sidetrack any international boycott movement before it could start.

Eighteen nations quickly accepted the invitation to Garmisch-Partenkirchen: Argentina, Belgium, Bohemia, Bulgaria, Estonia, Finland, France, Greece, Great Britain, Hungary, Italy, Latvia, Liechtenstein, the Netherlands, Norway, Slovakia, the United States, and Yugoslavia. On July 1, 1939, the initial meeting of the German Organizing Committee (GOC) was held. In addition to agreeing to finance extensions to the skating rink and ski stadium, Hitler provided six million RM for the construction of a 50-meter indoor swimming pool. A torch relay from the site of the first winter Games in Chamonix, France, via St. Moritz, to Garmisch-Partenkirchen, an innovation designed to appeal to the public, was planned.

The GOC intended to have an extraordinary meeting to clarify the amateur status dispute with the FIS. This meeting, however, never took place. Instead, the question of the justification of the Winter Olympics arose as a result of the public conflict with the FIS over amateurism. Opponents of the Winter Olympics regarded the Games as competition to the FIS-sponsored world championships. In the summer of 1939, the Scandinavian countries, Poland, France, the Netherlands, and Switzerland spoke in favor of a rejection of the Winter Olympics. After reports of this controversy reached foreign newspapers, the GOC, to save the Games, invited 1,235 foreign athletes and promised to assume full travel and accommodation costs. Travel to Oslo after the Games would be facilitated so that athletes could still take part in the FIS world championships.

World War II began with the German invasion of Poland on September 1, 1939, only twelve weeks after the IOC's decision to award the Games to Garmisch-Partenkirchen. On September 9, a progress report on site construction for the Games was published; it was impossible to halt construction without returning the Games to the IOC. Hitler demanded the continuation of site work for another three weeks. On September 26, one day before the surrender of Warsaw, Hitler again insisted upon an accelerated completion of the Olympic facilities. Shortly afterward, all work on the site was halted as the workers were needed elsewhere. It was only in November, however, that the Reichsportfuhrer informed the IOC that the Ministry of the Interior, which was responsible for sport, had decided to return the Games to the IOC. According to an IOC resolution of 1938, the Olympic Games could not be held in a war zone. Officially, this decision was based on the refusal of the British and French governments to restore world peace.

Despite the cancellation of the Games, Hitler tried to safeguard the chances of organizing his massive winter spectacle. On December 27, 1939, Hitler ordered the finance minister to continue the construction of facilities at Garmisch-Partenkirchen, using local workers. The Fourth Winter Sport Week, intended to be a substitute for the Winter Olympics, inaugurated the newly built sport complex at Garmisch-Partenkirchen. This international event, important for Nazi foreign policy, was to be honored with the presence of 15 IOC members as well as representatives of the various sport federations from those European nations not yet participating in the war. The significance of the event was dimmed when the important neutral skiing nations—Switzerland, Sweden, Norway, Finland, and the Netherlands—declined to participate. Those 182 athletes who did participate all came from nations linked to or dependent on Germany—Italy, Yugoslavia, Hungary, Romania, and Bulgaria.

BIBLIOGRAPHICAL ESSAY

The German Organizing Committee published an official report about its preparations for the Games, *Vorbereitung zu den V. Olympischen Winterspiele 1940 Garmisch-Partenkirchen* (Munich, 1939), edited by Carl Diem. No similar reports appear to have been prepared by committees representing Sapporo or St. Moritz, although each did publish other works. The Sapporo committee published a program and book of regulations in German and French editions in 1938, and the St. Moritz committee published *Projet de Programme* (Geneva, 1939).

The sport historian Hajo Bernett has published several works bearing on the 1940 Games. His article, "Das Scheitern der Olympischen Spiele von 1940," *Stadion* 6 (1980): 251–90, examines the impact of the Sino-Japanese and Russo-Finnish wars on the 1940 Games. Two books, *Nationalsozialistische Leibeserziehung. Eine Dokumentation ihrer Theorie und Organisation* (Schorndorf, Germany, 1966) and *Sportpolitik im Dritten Reich* (Schorndorf, Germany, 1971) take a broader look at sport in Hitler's Germany, as does Carl Diem, *Der deutsche Sport in der Zeit der Nationalsozialismus* (Cologne, 1980), a publication of the Carl-Diem-Institut. See also Dieter Steinhofer, *Hans von Tschammer und Osten: Reichssportfuhrer im Dritten Reich* (Berlin, 1973) and Hans-Joachim Teicher, *Internationale Sportpolitik im Dritten Reich* (Schorndorf, Germany, 1991) for other perspectives. Arnd Kruger also comments on the 1940 Games in "Deutschland und die Olympische Bewegung (1918–1945)," in Horst Ueberhorst, ed., *Geschichte der Leibesubungen* (Berlin, 1982), vol. 3/2, pp. 1026–47.

For information on the Sapporo effort, consult Kunihiko Karaki, "Die Aufgegebenen Olympischen Spiele in Tokio 1940," *Hitotsubashi Journal of Arts and Sciences* 23 (December 1982): 60–70.

CORTINA D'AMPEZZO 1944

Astrid Engelbrecht
Translated by Jamey J. Findling

OLYMPIC WINTER GAMES (NEVER HELD)

After the members of the International Olympic Committee (IOC), in the 34th Session at Warsaw in 1937, had, with the exception of Sigfrid Edström, unanimously supported the continuance of the Winter Games and had reached an agreement to stage the V Winter Games in Sapporo, the representatives from Oslo, Cortina d'Ampezzo, Montreal, and St. Moritz advanced their cases for hosting the V Winter Games in 1944. St. Moritz, citing its successful experience with the 1928 Games, had submitted its application as early as March 1935; Montreal, which did not submit its formal application until July 1938, emphasized its existing infrastructure. The application from the national Olympic committee of Italy, promoting Cortina, did not arrive until shortly before the 36th Session in London in September 1939. At that session, after the representatives had reported on the progress of their plans to host the 1944 Games, a majority of the 35 members present voted for the Italian winter resort of Cortina d'Ampezzo. St. Moritz finished second in the voting, its chances ruined by a conflict between the International Ski Federation (FIS) and the Swiss Olympic Committee over the program of competition and the eligibility of ski instructors.

Shortly before the London session, World War II began with Adolf Hitler's invasion of Poland. The Soviet invasion of Finland on November 30, 1939, forced the Finnish organizing committee to abandon its plans to host the XII Summer Games in Helsinki in 1940. Meanwhile, on November 25, 1939, the president of the IOC, Henri Baillet-Latour, informed the national Olympic committees that the 1940 Winter Games, originally scheduled for Sapporo and then moved to Garmisch-Partenkirchen, were cancelled and that prospects for the 1944 Winter Games were uncertain. By 1943, the fate of the Cortina Games was clear: "Even if the war should end this year, as some optimistic people believe, it would still be too late to hold the 1944 Games," wrote James F. Simms, an official of the United States of

America Sports Federation, to Avery Brundage, the head of the U.S. Olympic Committee.

By order of Baillet-Latour, neither IOC Executive Committee meetings nor sessions were held during the war, nor was the admission of new IOC members or national Olympic committees decided upon. Once again, war had put the future of the Olympic Games in doubt. For Brundage, the virtual suspension of IOC activity was frustrating; many longtime members of the IOC were dead, and others had not been heard from since the beginning of the war. "We will have our hands full in getting the Olympic machine operating after the war," he wrote Edström. In the Western Hemisphere, an alternative appeared to be the Pan-American Games, planned for 1942, but the entry of the United States into the war in 1941 delayed the inauguration of those games until 1951.

In general, there was a stagnation of Olympic activity during the war, although at the beginning of 1944, more frequent correspondence among IOC members indicated a gradual reactivation of the organization. In 1944, the 50th anniversary of the founding of the IOC was solemnly celebrated on a modest scale in Lausanne. With the slogan "Revival of the Olympic Games," the continuation of the Olympic ideal was recaptured. By the first postwar session of the executive committee in August 1945 in London, IOC leaders, including Edström and Brundage, had already agreed that the 1948 Olympic Games would take place in any case.

BIBLIOGRAPHICAL ESSAY

There is a good deal of correspondence dealing with the question of the 1944 Winter Games in the Avery Brundage Collection at the University of Illinois Archives, Urbana, Illinois. As president of the U.S. Olympic Committee, Brundage carried on a steady correspondence with Baillet-Latour, Edström, and other significant figures in the IOC. Information on the various IOC sessions at which the wartime Games were considered may be found in the session minutes and reports; these can be found at a number of repositories, including the IOC archives in Lausanne; the Centre for Olympic Studies at the University of Western Ontario, London, Ontario; and the Brundage Collection.

ST. MORITZ 1948

Janice Forsyth

FIFTH OLYMPIC WINTER GAMES

The V Winter Olympic Games took place in St. Moritz, Switzerland, from January 30 to February 8, 1948. It marked the second time St. Moritz had hosted the winter event, the first being in 1928. As such, St. Moritz has the distinction of being one of the few cities in Olympic history to host the Games twice. At the 1948 Games, 713 athletes representing 28 countries competed in eight medal events, including Alpine skiing, bobsled, figure skating, ice hockey, Nordic skiing, skeleton, ski jumping, and speed skating.

Twelve years had passed since the last Olympic Games. This interruption was due to the outbreak of World War II, which forced the IOC to cancel the events planned for 1940 and 1944. After the war, only two hosts stepped forward for 1948—Lake Placid, United States, and St. Moritz, Switzerland. In an effort to alleviate political posturing among the competing nations, the IOC decided to award the games to Switzerland, a neutral country in the war. In spite of this arrangement, postwar politics inevitably shaped affairs in St. Moritz.

Similar to the 1920 Summer Games in Antwerp, following the close of World War I, the 1948 Winter Games were a celebration of the victorious nations of war. For 1948, neither Germany nor Japan was invited to take part in the Games in St. Moritz. The exclusion of these two countries did not last long as both Germany and Japan returned to Olympic competition in the early 1950s. New countries in the Winter Olympic Games included Chile, Denmark, Iceland, Korea, and Lebanon.

While Germany and Japan were conspicuously absent, the U.S.S.R. was noticeably present, having sent ten observers to St. Moritz to determine where the U.S.S.R. would have finished in the final medal standings had it actually sent athletes to the Games. Though Russia had been one of the founding members of the modern Olympic Movement, it had long since rejected the imperialist aims of the Olympic Games. As a result, Russia had not participated in any Olympic events, winter or summer, since Antwerp in 1920. By the end of World War II, the Soviet Union had renewed its interest in the Olympic Movement and began to develop its domestic sport program with the ideological goal of utilizing the international stage of the Olympic Games to celebrate and promote communism. Having developed their own system for counting medals, the Soviet observers determined that their athletes would indeed have dominated most events and that Russia would have emerged as the nation with the most medals. Based on these preliminary results, in 1951 the Soviet Union applied for and received full membership to the IOC and participated in the Summer Games in 1952 after a forty-year absence from Olympic competition.

While Soviet observers were busy determining how their nation would fare at future Olympic events, participating nations were struggling with the lack of financial and human resources brought about by the prolonged war effort. The effects of the war had a significant impact on the athletes, some of whom arrived in St. Moritz with little or no equipment. In one notable case, skiers from Norway had to borrow skis from American athletes in order to compete. Furthermore, the average age for athletes in St. Moritz was higher than in previous Winter Olympic Games, a sign that the war years had severely hampered training schedules among competing nations.

Despite its celebrated status as being one of the most fashionable resorts in the world, the arrangements in St. Moritz received mixed reviews from the participants. The Americans in particular found ample reason to complain. Specific grievances were noted about cold hotel rooms, the lack of American-style food, and the inability of most hotels to accommodate entire teams. Due to the limited infrastructure in St. Moritz, all of the contestants had to be dressed for competition before arriving at their particular venue since there were no dressing rooms at the event sites. A few American hockey players lamented this situation, as they had to walk to the outdoor rink located a short distance from their hotel.

In spite of the perceived shortfalls, the 1948 Winter Olympic Games included an expanded program of events for female athletes. In addition to figure skating, women were now permitted to compete in Alpine skiing, featuring the downhill, slalom, and combined events. Despite the increased number of competitive opportunities for women at the Winter Olympic Games, the number of female athletes competing in St. Moritz had decreased slightly from 80 competitors in the 1936 Winter Games to 77 athletes in 1948. In typical IOC fashion, female competitors were still limited to feminine-appropriate sports, a trend that was maintained in Alpine skiing where the downhill and slalom courses selected for the women were less challenging than those chosen for the men. At the end of competition, five countries dominated the women's events—Austria, Switzerland, United States, Canada, and Great Britain. Interestingly, in the final tally, the Austrian team won a total of eight medals (men and women combined), of which the female athletes won six. The female skier, Trude Beiser, won Austria's only gold medal in the combined event.

In terms of disputes, the most controversial issue was the presence of two American hockey teams in St. Moritz. One of the central issues in this debate was amateurism; another was jurisdictional authority over Olympic participation. On one side of the struggle was the team selected by the Amateur Athletic Union (AAU) and supported by the United States Olympic Committee (USOC), the body responsible for determining American participation in Olympic Games, and its president, Avery Brundage. On the other side was the team selected by the Amateur Hockey Association (AHA) and supported by the Ligue Internationale de Hockey sur Glace (LIHG), the body responsible for endorsing the participation of national ice hockey teams in Olympic competition. Whereas the AAU claimed amateur status, the AHA made no apologies for its professional links. What began as a domestic struggle between two American hockey teams for the right to compete in the Olympic Games soon evolved into a showdown between Brundage, the LIHG, the Swiss Organizing Committee, and the IOC.

Relations between the competing organizations had been strained for several years but exploded on the eve of Olympic competition. In an effort to resolve the dispute equitably, the IOC Executive Committee prohibited both teams from playing, citing irregularities in their entries. For one thing, the AAU team did not have the support of the LIHG; nor did the AHA team have the support of the USOC. In a move that surprised the IOC, the Swiss Organizing Committee, fearing the LIHG would boycott the Games if the AHA team were not allowed to participate, ignored the IOC ruling and permitted the AHA team to play and the AAU team to march in the Opening Ceremony. The reason for this decision was practical—without the support of the LIHG, the Swiss would lose the financial support gained through hockey ticket sales, a major source of revenue for the Games. In the first game played by the AHA, disgruntled AAU players cheered for the opposing Swiss team. The ongoing struggle strained relations between members of the two American hockey teams, many of whom were friends and played for the same collegiate teams back home. In retaliation, the IOC moved to eliminate hockey as an official Olympic event. Eventually, the IOC and the Swiss Organizing Committee reached an agreement to keep hockey as part of the official program, but the results of the games in which the AHA team played would not count in the final standings. As it turned out, the AHA team placed fourth, losing the bronze medal to Switzerland.

After the 1948 Winter Games, the IOC suspended the LIHG from IOC membership, thereby eliminating hockey from future Winter Olympic Games. This suspension was reversed in 1949 when the IOC welcomed the LIHG back into the Olympic family amid assurances from the hockey federation that its policy on amateurism conformed to IOC rules. In the end, the controversy resulted in a struggle for control over amateur hockey in the United States, as well as between the IOC and the LIHG. Within the United States, the struggle led the acknowledgement and acceptance of commercial interests in hockey. Within the IOC, the entire struggle demonstrated that economic concerns took precedent over amateur ideals.

Intrigue and debates about amateurism also surrounded another sport—women's figure skating. In the 1940s, the IOC, especially Brundage, became increasingly concerned about female figure skaters using the Olympic Games as a stepping-stone to professional skating careers. Of course, Brundage was referring to Norway's Sonja Henie, who signed a $1 million Hollywood movie contract after winning the gold medal at the 1936 Games in Garmisch-Partenkirchen. In order to curb this trend, Brundage had inserted himself squarely in the middle of the controversy surrounding the eligibility of Barbara Ann Scott, Canada's sporting heroine in the post-World War II era.

The story began in 1947 when Scott won the world championship in women's figure skating. Upon her arrival home in Ottawa, the mayor presented her with the keys to a new yellow convertible car. News of this gift quickly reached Brundage, who alerted the IOC of the situation. He claimed that Scott was no longer eligible for the 1948 Winter Olympic Games since she had relinquished her amateur status when she accepted the gift. Right away Canadian media and sport authorities severely criticized Brundage for his involvement. In the Canadian press, reporters positioned him as the villain and circulated the story that he had timed his accusations to eliminate Scott from Olympic competition so as to provide her American rival, Gretchen Merrill, with a clear competitive advantage. The Canadian Olympic Association (COA) and the Amateur Athletic Union of Canada (AAU of C) argued that Brundage, as a member of the USOC, had no right to be intruding on Canadian sporting affairs. The AAU of C, the parent organization responsible for Canadian participation in Olympic Games, took responsibility for the entire affair, claiming it had guaranteed Scott that her amateur status would not be affected if she accepted the car. Even Canadian Prime Minister William Lyon Mackenzie King rallied on Scott's behalf, asking Canadian IOC representative J. C. Patteson to protect her amateur standing. In the end, Scott returned the car, competed in the 1948 Winter Games and won the gold medal with little challenge from the other competitors. Gretchen Merrill, the American skater, placed a distant eighth. When a reporter asked Scott if she would turn professional if she won the gold medal, she replied that she enjoyed competing and that there were no world championships in professional figure skating. Soon after she won the gold medal, Scott turned professional and accepted the offer of a new car from the mayor of Ottawa.

Beyond the politics surrounding issues of amateurism, weather played havoc with the events, especially since most took place outdoors. The weather had a notable impact on ice hockey where, on clear sunny days, players had to wear eye black and occasionally lost sight of the puck in the glare of the ice. On snowy days, they sometimes lost the puck in the snow and had to suspend play until the puck was found. When the snowfall was particularly heavy, play was suspended every fifteen minutes in order to shovel the rink. On warm days, when the wind called the Föhn blew in from the south, the hockey players and figure skaters had to contend with a slow, slushy surface. Though the weather caused delays in ice hockey, as well as the 10,000-m event in speed skating, none of the events was cancelled. The Föhn also affected the bobsled events by slowing the finishing times.

Havoc of another sort made news in St. Moritz. In this case, the media focused on the alleged sabotage of a two-man American bobsled. The story that unfolded in the press reported that an unidentified culprit had damaged the bobsled in order to eliminate the American team from competition. Amid these allegations, it was discovered that the sabotage was actually an accident. The shed that was used to store the bobsleds was also a garage. In the night, a driver had accidentally backed into the American bobsled, damaging its structure. The driver came forward when accusations of foul play were reported in the press. The incident had no serious consequences for the American bobsled team since the broken sled was used only for practice runs. The American team placed third in the final medal standings.

A winter version of the summer pentathlon was devised as a demonstration event for the 1948 Games—it was the first and last time this event was held. A total of 14 athletes participated in the winter pentathlon, which was a combination of five winter and summer Olympic events, including fencing, shooting, equestrian riding, downhill skiing, and cross-country skiing. A number of unfortunate circumstances turned this event into a comic and, at times, painful experience. In downhill skiing, two athletes sustained broken legs. In the equestrian event, muddy conditions on the track caused many of the horses to slip and fall, resulting in further injuries, this time to both horses and athletes. Sweden finished in the top three spots, and William Grut, the second-place finisher, went on to win the gold medal in the pentathlon at the Summer Olympic Games in London in 1948.

The choice of sports for the Games demonstrated the uneven level of competitive development among the participating nations. This was most evident in ice hockey where the Italians sustained an epic defeat, losing 31–1 to the Americans. Although the Italian athletes were ridiculed for their poor athletic performance in hockey, their behavior was held up as an example of the true Olympic spirit. Despite the lopsided victory, the Italians maintained their composure and civility towards the Americans and always apologized for heavy body checks. In one notable instance, when an Italian player cut the face of an American competitor, the entire Italian team rushed out onto the ice, carried the victim to the bench and helped tend to his injury.

On the whole, the 1948 Winter Olympic Games were a relatively quiet affair. In retrospect, this tranquility was really the calm before the storm. In the following years, issues related to amateurism, nationalism, and doping would eclipse the intentions of the IOC to promote the Olympic Games as a place for peaceful intercultural contact and learning.

BIBLIOGRAPHICAL ESSAY

A comprehensive list of official reports from the IOC, Swiss Organizing Committee, and USOC on the 1948 Winter Olympic Games was published in the first edition of the *Historical Dictionary of the Modern Olympic Movement* (1996) and will not be reiterated here. Nor does this essay include the short list of secondary sources identified in the 1996 text. This information was omitted to avoid repetition. As such, readers are encouraged to accept this list as a supplement to the original text, with important contributions to the field noted below.

At present, several sets of the Avery Brundage Collection are located in North America. The original collection is housed at the University of Illinois Archives in Urbana, Illinois. Two microfiche collections are located at the University of Western Ontario (UWO) in London, Ontario. Of the two sets at UWO, one set is housed at the International Centre for Olympic Studies; the other is located at Weldon Library. All of the sets are identical and offer an excellent selection of primary source documents related to Brundage's involvement in the 1948 Olympic Games in St. Moritz.

Few secondary sources have been published since 1996—all focus on the hockey controversy. For a thorough analysis of this dispute, see the published articles by Gordon MacDonald, including "American Organizational Struggles Surrounding Ice Hockey at the 1948 Olympic Games," *Fourth International Symposium for Olympic Research* (October 1998): 99–106 and "A Colossal Embroglio: Control of Amateur Ice Hockey in the United States and the 1948 Olympic Winter Games," *Olympika: The International Journal of Olympic Studies* VII (1998): 43–60. A detailed study of the issues related to amateurism and jurisdictional conflict between national and international sport bodies, and the impact of these relationships on the 1948 Winter Games, can be found in Gordon MacDonald, "A History of Relations between the IOC and IFs, 1894–1968" (Ph.D. diss., University of Western Ontario, 1998).

Secondary sources on Barbara Ann Scott and her participation in the 1948 Winter Games that were not included in the first edition of this text are worth mentioning here. For a analysis of the politics surrounding her participation the Winter Games, see Stephen Wenn, "Give Me the Key Please: Avery Brundage, Canadian Journalists, and the Barbara Ann Scott Phaeton Affair," *Journal of Sport History* 18, 2 (Summer 1991): 241–254. Researchers interested in the feminization of Barbara Ann Scott are referred to Don Morrow, "Sweetheart Sport: Barbara Ann Scott and the Post World War II Image of the Female Athlete in Canada," *Canadian Journal of History of Sport* XVIII, 1 (May 1987), 36–54.

A good introduction to the events and issues surrounding the 1948 Winter Games can be found in George Constable, *The XI, XII, & XIII Olympiads, Berlin 1936, St. Moritz, 1948* (Los Angeles, 1996).

OSLO 1952

Gordon MacDonald and Douglas Brown

SIXTH OLYMPIC WINTER GAMES

At its annual session in 1947 (held in Stockholm, Sweden), the International Olympic Committee (IOC) voted to award the Olympic Winter Games of 1952 to the city of Oslo, Norway. The Oslo bid successfully defeated those of Cortina d'Ampezzo, Italy, and Lake Placid, United States, on the first ballot. In doing so, it became both the first capital city and the first Scandinavian city to host the Olympic Winter Games.

The IOC's rationale for choosing Oslo seems to have been based on several factors. First, Oslo had expressed its desire to host the Winter Games as early as 1936, when it offered to stage the 1940 Games. However, in 1936, the IOC's tradition of allowing the city awarded the Summer Games the privilege also of organizing the Winter Games dictated that the 1940 Winter Olympics would be hosted by Japan. They were scheduled to be held in Sapporo. Of course, neither the Summer nor the Olympic Winter Games of 1940 were held due to World War II.

Second, after the War, when London agreed to host the 1948 Olympic Games, it declined to exercise its option of organizing the Winter Games and suggested that Oslo stage them instead. However, Oslo also refused because of the Norwegians' wish to focus their attentions and resources on rebuilding their war-torn country. Rather, the Norwegians decided to wait and bid for the 1952 Olympic Winter Games. Thus, on August 22, 1946, the Oslo city council voted to submit its bid. At this early stage the municipality of Oslo agreed to finance the construction and maintenance of the various venues. This pledge of support boosted the strength of the bid. When the time came for the IOC to make its decision, the city of Oslo commanded a positive profile due to previous national and international interest in staging the Games in Norway. In addition, Oslo's strong technical bid influenced the IOC's choice.

In addition, the IOC likely had reasons to reject the other two bids. For example, Lake Placid had already hosted the 1932 Olympic Winter Games, and the United

States had proven to be a long distance to travel for the European teams that made up the majority of competitors. Second, Cortina d'Ampezzo's bid, coming as it did from a German ally in World War II, might not have been seen by IOC members (in 1947) as a prudent choice.

Once granted the Winter Games, the Norwegians promptly created an organizing committee composed of four municipal and four sport organization representatives. It functioned at this size for approximately one year, until 1948, when a second Norwegian, Olav Ditlev-Simonsen, Jr., joined Thomas Fearnley as a member of the IOC. Ditlev-Simonsen was made chair of Oslo's organizing committee and took over the responsibilities of guiding its work as well as delivering various progress reports to the IOC at its annual meetings.

The most important municipal representative on the committee was arguably Brynjulf Bull, mayor of Oslo. Because of the municipality's heavy financial investment in the Games, the mayor had a vested interest in staging them successfully and economically. The city of Oslo granted a total of 10.7 million Norwegian kroner (about $1.5 million) over a five-year period to pay for the cost of the Games.

Though Oslo had many good winter sport facilities at the time of its bid, an enterprise of this magnitude required the renovation of existing facilities and the construction of new ones. Oslo's most famous facility was (and still is) the world-renowned Holmenkollen ski jump. This facility was renovated to accommodate a restaurant and shops underneath the jump's take-off ramp. While spectator seating was quite limited, there was room for more than 130,000 in the immediate area of the jump. Reports from the 1952 Winter Games indicated that this number of people did, in fact, attend the jumping competitions. As the *New York Times* noted, such a large attendance was even more impressive if one considered that it represented nearly five percent of Norway's population in 1952.

Other facilities for skiing were constructed at Norefjell, 75 miles from Oslo, and Rodkleiva. It was at these venues that the Alpine skiing events were held. Because of Norefjell's distance from Oslo, accommodations were built at the site for the competitors. Access to Norefjell was also enhanced by improving roads and bridges. Unfortunately for the organizing committee, an unusually small snowfall occurred in February 1952, and the downhill courses were made race-worthy only through the efforts of a large number of volunteers and the military in moving snow from nearby areas. Even so, the scarcity of snow forced organizers to reschedule some events and limit the amount of training time for the competitors. Despite these inconveniences, all the scheduled races were held.

For the opening and closing ceremonies and the skating events, Bislett Stadium in Oslo was chosen. When renovations were completed, it accommodated 27,000 spectators, but there were only 3,000 seats. Apparently this was not a problem for the Norwegians, who were accustomed to standing at sport competitions.

Controversy surrounded construction of the ice hockey facilities. Although the IOC had removed ice hockey from the Winter Games program after the fiasco in 1948 at St. Moritz, the Oslo organizing committee hoped that hockey would be returned to the program. Nonetheless, the Norwegians decided to propose several arenas for ice hockey matches in the hope that the ongoing dispute between the IOC and the International Ice Hockey Federation would be resolved before the Games.

The International Ice Hockey Federation demanded that the main arena for the competition, Jordal Amfi, have an artificial ice surface to ensure the best possible conditions for the matches. The Norwegians were extremely reluctant to go ahead with such an expensive project as late as 1949, especially when it was not clear whether the competitions would definitely take place. Even the official report of the Games notes that the topic of the stadium was one of the favorites of the press during this period. However, the Norwegians finally capitulated and began renovating the stadium to provide an artificial ice surface. Ultimately, in 1950, the dispute between the IOC and the International Ice Hockey Federation was resolved and hockey was placed on the program.

The venue for the bobsled competition was also the cause of some discussion. The cost of constructing a permanent course was deemed to be prohibitive, especially since the sport had little popularity in Norway. Hence, the organizing committee decided to go ahead with the construction of a temporary bobsled run built entirely of snow and ice. Under the direction of Swiss experts, a temporary course was constructed in 1951. It worked well enough for the process to be repeated in 1952.

Besides the competition venues, accommodations for competitors, coaches, and foreign spectators, as well as communications facilities for the influx of journalists, had to be constructed or renovated. Three Olympic Villages were constructed for competitors and coaches in the Oslo area. International sport federations personnel and IOC members occupied most of the hotels in Oslo. To accommodate tourists, the organizing committee created a system of billeting Olympic visitors in private homes in Oslo. This strategy provided space for 6,000 people.

While the VI Olympic Winter Games were not beset with the politically motivated difficulties of other Olympic competitions, there were several contentious issues. Most notable was the question of inviting German athletes to participate in the Games. Anti-German feelings, underscored by memories of the hated Nazi occupation forces, were still prevalent in Norway during preparations for the Games. As the official report noted dryly, public discussions on this particular topic "were rather lively."

The case of a Norwegian speed skater, Finn Hodt, provides a good example of the feelings of some Norwegians at that time. The Norwegian Skating Union had proposed Hodt as a member of the speed-skating team, but the Norwegian Olympic Committee rejected him because he had been a Nazi collaborator during the Second World War.

A similar situation developed within the IOC during this period. Some of its members were opposed to retaining German members who had joined the IOC before the war. The greatest controversy revolved around Karl Ritter von Halt, a former Nazi and the organizer of the 1936 Games in Berlin. Despite the protests of some IOC members, President J. Sigfrid Edström did not allow a vote to be taken and the Germans remained members of the IOC. However, it is significant to note that Olav Ditlev-Simonsen, Jr., claimed in a 1951 letter to Avery Brundage that Ritter von Halt had promised him that he would not attend the 1952 Games.

Interestingly, the IOC Executive Board also recommended in 1950 that the Germans not participate in Norway. However, this recommendation was never acted upon by the general session of the IOC, and the West Germans, whose Olympic Committee had been recognized by the IOC, took part in the Games at the invitation of the Norwegians. The Norwegians also informed the IOC that the royal family would not participate in the Opening Ceremonies if the Germans were invited to the Winter Games. With the lessening of hostility toward the Germans and their subsequent inclusion in the Games, the royal family relented and took part in the opening of the Games. Indeed, the Germans were well received by the Norwegian people as representatives of a new and democratic West Germany. This was not the case for East Germans. Although the East Germans also had a national Olympic committee, the IOC had not resolved its status, and, as a consequence, the East Germans were not invited to attend.

In 1951, the Soviet Union, also on the fringe of international sport, indicated that it wished to become involved in the Olympics. Its national Olympic committee had been recognized by the IOC, and there was considerable speculation as to whether the Russians would send a hockey team to the Winter Games. However, because the Soviet application to join the International Ice Hockey Federation was not made in time, they were denied participation. (In order to participate in the Olympic Games a country must have its national federations controlling the various sports recognized by the corresponding international federations.)

As with earlier Summer Games, a torch run was incorporated into the ceremonies surrounding the Winter Games. However, instead of starting in Olympia, Greece, the 1952 winter torch run commenced in Morgedal, Norway, and was carried out entirely on skis. The reasons for this unusual format were twofold. First, Morgedal was the birthplace of one of Norway's most famous skiers and, second, skiing had long been an integral part of Norway's history and culture. Much like previous torch runs, the flame entered the stadium shortly after the parade of athletes from the 30 nations represented at the Games.

While Olympic competitions are normally declared open by the head of state of the country in which they are held, the Oslo Games were officially opened on February 15, 1952, by Princess Ragnhild, granddaughter of the head of state. She was given this honor because her grandfather, Haakon VII, and her father, Crown Prince Olav, were in London attending the funeral of King George VI of England.

The program of the VI Olympic Winter Games was similar to that of the 1948 Games in St. Moritz, with the addition of the giant slalom event for both women and men and the 10-kilometer Nordic (cross-country) event for women, and the dropping of the Alpine combined event for men and women. The women's giant slalom was won on February 14 (it was held one day before the official opening because of scheduling requirements) by Andrea Mead Lawrence of the United States, who also won a gold in the slalom event. To the delight of the home-town fans, a Norwegian, Stein Erikson, won the men's event. Finnish skiers swept the medals in the women's 10-kilometer Nordic event.

In keeping with most previous Winter Games, a demonstration sport was placed on the program. While there had been suggestions within the IOC for displays of curling and military patrol on skis, the Norwegians opted for the sport of bandy, a sport similar to soccer but played on ice. It is primarily a Scandinavian sport; only Norway, Sweden, and Finland fielded teams.

The Winter Games, as usual, saw certain persons achieve star status. As expected, the Scandinavian countries dominated the Nordic ski events. The Norwegians were delighted by the fact that one of their speed skaters, Hjalmar Andersen, won three gold medals. Of note also was Germany's successful return to the Winter Games. They won both the two- and four-man bobsled events. Making good use of the laws of momentum in their victories, the combined weight of their four-man team was an astounding 1041.5 pounds (approx. 472 kg). (Because of the spiraling weights of the teams, the international federation for bobsled and tobogganing decided just prior to the Games to limit the weight of future teams to 880 pounds.)

Ice hockey was reinstated into the program of the Games, and eight teams eventually took part. As in 1948 some controversies occurred, although this time it concerned the conduct of several teams and players. The rough play of the U.S. team offended many Norwegian spectators. In fact, after the Games had concluded, an editorial in an Oslo paper suggested that the behavior of the U.S. players lowered the Norwegian opinion of the United States so much that Norway's opinion of the Soviets might improve.

While this seems hardly serious, it was one example of burgeoning Cold War attitudes in the early 1950s. A more blatant example of Cold War attitudes may be seen in the Soviet press reaction to the silver medal won by the U.S. hockey team. By tying the Canadian team 3-3 in their final game, the U.S. team vaulted into second place in the standings, forcing Sweden and Czechoslovakia to play for third (communist Czechoslovakia lost). The Soviet press immediately accused the Canadians and Americans of conspiring to produce the tie, a typical example of bourgeois capitalist cheating. Naturally, both accused teams denied the charge.

The political and economic consequences of the VI Olympic Winter Games for the city of Oslo were perhaps not so pronounced as they were for other cities that have hosted the Olympic Games. However, the Norwegians did benefit from the construction of new facilities and the renovation of old ones. For a country in which a large segment of the population was physically active, these improvements were welcomed. With regard to the Olympic Villages, one was turned into a hospital's staff residence, while another provided homes for senior citizens and old-age pensioners.

Economically, the Games were a major expense for Oslo's citizens, particularly since the municipality provided the bulk of the funding, which would come from local residents. Of course, the Games drew a large number of foreign visitors to Oslo, helping to offset the costs. Furthermore, the publicity created by the Games enhanced tourism in ensuing years. Finally, more intangibly, it may be argued that the Games helped provide a psychological boost to most Norwegians recovering, as they were, from the effects of the war.

In summary, the VI Olympic Winter Games were relatively uneventful compared to many other Olympic festivals. The organizing committee was congratulated on its effectiveness, particularly in light of the sometimes difficult weather conditions. The IOC members, at least, were impressed with the Games. They proceeded to award the Olympic Cup of 1952 to Oslo for its excellent job of organizing the Winter Games. The VI Olympic Winter Games saw the issue of Nazi Germany put to rest, and provided a preview of the Cold War attitudes between East and West that were to become so apparent several months later during the Summer Olympics of 1952.

BIBLIOGRAPHICAL ESSAY

The most comprehensive source of information on the VI Olympic Winter Games is unquestionably the official report of the organizing committee. The English version, Rolf Petersen, ed., Margaret Wold and Ragnar Wold, trans., *Olympic Winter Games Oslo 1952* (Oslo, 1952), contains a wealth of information on the preparations for the Games as well as a report on the athletic competitions.

This report is not easily obtainable due to the limited number printed. Besides the one held by the IOC, there is another located at the International Olympic Academy at Olympia, Greece

A similar report, P. Chr. Andersen, *The Olympic Winter Games Oslo 1952* (Oslo, 1952) contains much of the same information as the official report but in an abbreviated form and with a greater focus on the competitions. The International Centre for Olympic Studies at the University of Western Ontario, London, Ontario, Canada, has a copy of this work. The official U.S. report is Asa Bushnell, *United States 1952 Olympic Book: Quadrennial Report of the United States Olympic Committee* (New York, 1953), and the Canadian report is James Worrall, et al., eds., *Canada Competes at the Olympic Games 1952: Official Report of the Canadian Olympic Association, 1948–1952* (Montreal, 1952). The West German version is *Die Olympische Spiele 1952, Oslo und Helsinki, das Offizielle Standardwerk des Nationalen Olympische Komitees* (Frankfurt/Main, 1952).

The papers of Avery Brundage, IOC president from 1952 to 1972, provide a comprehensive source of information on the IOC's involvement with the Oslo Winter Games. This includes several letters to Brundage from the chair of the organizing committee, Olav Ditlev-Simonsen, Jr., as well as newspaper clippings, press releases, and programs. The Brundage Papers are held at the University of Illinois archives, and a printed guide is available.

Several IOC publications mention the Oslo Games. The *Bulletin du Comité International Olympique* 27 (1951): 35–36 has a report on the preparations for the Games. *Bulletin du Comité Internationale Olympique* 1, (1952): 4, also contains information on the Oslo Winter Games.

The National Olympic Committee of Norway also published several news bulletins prior to the Games. These were entitled the *Olympic Winter Games News Bulletin* 1–4 (1951–1952) and copies may be found in the Brundage Papers. They also contain information about the preparations for the Games as well as general facts about Norway.

CORTINA D'AMPEZZO 1956

Jim Nendel

SEVENTH OLYMPIC WINTER GAMES

On January 26, 1956, more than 12,000 spectators in the Cortina Ice Stadium anxiously awaited the official opening of the VII Olympic Winter Games that would run for the next eleven days. Finally the moment, which the 6,000 residents of the idyllic mountain village and millions around the world watching for the first time on live television had anticipated, arrived. The Olympic flame, which had been carried all the way from the Temple of Jupiter in Rome, entered the stadium. As a record setting 818 athletes from 32 nations watched, the flame was passed into the capable hands of Italian speed skating champion Guido Caroli. Caroli carried the torch onto the rink. As his eyes rose to salute the presidential box he tripped over a loose public address system wire and sprawled headfirst onto the ice in full view of all watching. Was this an omen of doom to befall these Games, which were being staged in the midst of intense regional and global political tension? The flame did not go out when Caroli fell, and he proceeded to carry on and fulfill his duty. The same may be said for the people of Cortina. They carried on in the midst of world tension, and staged one of the most spectacular Olympic festivals of the post-war period.

The natural amphitheater that was the venue for the 1956 Winter Olympic Games in Cortina d'Ampezzo was an apt setting, which mirrored the political environment surrounding these games. This village, situated in the lovely Ampezzo Valley, sat amidst the jagged peaks of the Dolomites that dominated the horizon. The mountains served as a reminder of the powerful forces of nature and of the awesome splendor of this area. Although a lack of snowfall in the mild winter of 1956 created logistical problems for the organizers, the pleasant sunny weather allowed visitors to enjoy the spectacular mountain vistas, and the exciting competition. The storms that can wreak havoc upon these mountain regions did not appear during this athletic spectacle.

Similarly, the political storms of the Cold War which were to exact their toll on later Olympic contests did not rage during these Games. That is not to say that the specter of such events was not present. The Cortina Games took place at the height of the Cold War, shadowed by the rhetoric of that contentious battle in much the same way that the Dolomites shadowed Cortina with their powerful presence. Cortina witnessed the Soviet Union's entrance into the Winter Olympics. As first time participants, the Soviets would dominate the contests. The political conflicts beneath these Winter Games were not limited to the classic East/West battle of the United States and the Soviet Union; they also included a regional battle rooted in Cortina's rich history.

Cortina had long been a pawn in European power struggles. Known as the "*Regina delle Dolomiti*" (Queen of the Dolomites) due to its location in the heart of this mountain range, Cortina was first known for its grazing pastures. Long a battleground of the Holy Roman Empire, it was governed under feudal control until it was granted a type of federal republic status by Prince Charles of Luxembourg in 1337, with authority for signing treaties and limited self rule. Later in the fourteenth century it fell under Venetian control, and then in 1515 it was annexed to Tyrol. This region was handed over to Austria during the Napoleonic Wars as a result of the treaty of Campo Formio in 1797. In 1815 the Congress of Vienna reaffirmed this treaty, and Cortina remained under Austrian control until World War I when the front line cut across the Dolomite peaks during some of the coldest winters of the century. Austrian and German soldiers lined up on one side and faced the Italian alpine troops across the trenches. From May 1915 to November 1917, this front line was the scene of bloody battles fought in these high mountains. The rugged mountain terrain and weather was an enemy to both sides and exacted an awesome toll of its own. At the conclusion of the war, Italy, which had occupied Cortina during the battle, was given authority over the region. Thirty-seven years later Italy hosted its first Olympic Games in the village, which had been in its possession for less than a half-century and which still had strong linguistic and cultural bonds with Austria.

Italy had been scheduled to host the 1908 Games in Rome, but these Games were given instead to London. Italians, eager to showcase their nation and its athleticism, had to wait nearly fifty years for their next Olympic opportunity. During this period Italy transformed itself into a sporting nation, chiefly through the influence of its fascist dictator, Benito Mussolini. In the seven years from 1928 to 1935, the number of sports installations including gymnasiums, sports fields, and academies for physical education, grew from 502 to 5,198. One of these installations was Campo Mussolini, named after the Italian dictator, which was located near Cortina in the Dolomites.

In fact, this was Cortina's second selection as a host city for the Winter Games. In 1939 it had been awarded the 1944 Winter Games, but World War II forced the cancellation of those Games. Immediately after the war, the International Olympic Committee (IOC) member and Italian Games promoter Count Alberto Bonacossa, who had spearheaded the bid for the 1944 Games, set to work to regain host privileges for Cortina. The count, who was the Italian national champion in figure skating from 1914 to 1928, and his wife Marisa, an Italian figure skating champion from 1920 to 1928, cooperated with the *Comitato Olimpico Italiano* (CONI) to prepare a bid for the 1952 Games. The final vote went against Cortina as Oslo won the bid. Undeterred, the committee tried again for the 1956 games. The IOC met in

Rome from April 24 to 29, 1949, to select the host city for 1956. Cortina easily won over Montreal, Colorado Springs/Aspen, and Lake Placid.

With the awarding of the Games, Italy became the first of the World War II Axis powers fully welcomed back into the Olympic fold and given the charge of hosting this grand world event. Nationalistic tensions still existed in the area, however, especially in the German speaking sector of the community. The region included a large majority of former Austrians who suddenly found themselves in what had become part of Italy after World War I. Some communities in the region in 1956 were still 70 percent German-speaking. During the 1950s protests erupted throughout the region as the German-speaking segment of the region demanded more autonomy from the Italian government. The fact that Italy was awarded the games in a former Austrian territory must also have infuriated the Austrians. However, CONI did an excellent job of organizing these Games and built spectacular facilities, thus diffusing the ire of the Austrians for the duration of Cortina's Olympic festival.

Austria, however, would not allow the IOC to forget the fact that Italy was hosting what many Austrians believed to be their Games and pushed hard to land a bid for Innsbruck. This feat was nearly accomplished for the 1960 Games when the Austrians attempted to discredit the U.S. bid site of Squaw Valley, California. Even after Squaw Valley had been awarded the bid in Paris in 1955, the Austrians continued to challenge the U.S. resort's ability to host the 1960 games. At the IOC meeting at Cortina the Austrians once again led the charge to damage the reputation of Squaw Valley and rescind the bid awarded to the California area. The Austrians even hosted IOC President Avery Brundage after the Cortina Games were over and convinced him to make a statement that there was still the potential to take the games away from his American homeland and give them to Innsbruck. Austria's subtle pressure was eventually overcome by the Squaw Valley organizing committee to retain its bid, but enough force was exerted to assure Innsbruck of the 1964 bid. Throughout the Cortina Games Brundage praised Austria for its successes. In numerous press releases he elaborated on his claim that Austria could be considered the true champions of the Games due to the number of medals it had won in relation to the small size of the country. The Austrians indeed did well at Cortina, winning eleven medals, second only to the Soviet Union, but the amount of support from Brundage was seemingly excessive, especially coming from a man who preached that winning was not the essential object of the Olympics.

This regional dispute, though significant, was overshadowed by the rhetoric of the Cold War battle between the U.S.S.R. and the United States. Although Cortina did not have to deal with the political struggles erupting in Olympic venues that future games did, the underlying tension was still present. The Soviet team came to Cortina prepared to compete, and proved that they were extremely capable, garnering sixteen medals, seven gold, three silver, and six bronze. In the next 38 years, until the breakup of the Soviet Union, the Soviets would finish in first place in the medal counts in every winter Olympic Game except for 1968, when Norway defeated them and 1984 when they lost to the East Germans. At Cortina, Austria was the closest of any other country with four gold, three silver and four bronze medals for a total of eleven. Sweden, Finland, and Switzerland followed with ten, seven, and six medals respectively, while the United States won seven medals, only two of which were gold. Notably, the Norwegian team, which had dominated the Winter Olympic Games since their inception in 1924 at Chamonix, fell to seventh place in the medal count, winning only four medals. The only other time Norway had not won the medal count was in 1932 at Lake Placid when they elected to send a smaller team than usual.

The American media response to the Soviet prowess was reflective of the time period. A cursory reading of any major U.S. newspaper of the time shows how prevalent was the mistrust of the Soviet Union and its political system. Every day there were articles detailing Soviet policies and actions. These attitudes found their way to the sports sections of newspapers and magazines in attributing success of the Soviet team to its machine-like quality. *Sports Illustrated* described the Russians as having "cased Cortina like bank heisters planning a caper." The magazine claimed that the Soviets sent a "posse" to measure the speed skating track at Lake Misurina to insure that its distance was accurate and used a "mechanized skater" to test the glide potential of the ice. *Life* ran a headline which read, "Russians Smother All But Li'l Abner Of The Alps," referring to the individual achievements of Austrian skier Toni Sailer, who, they noted, was the only athlete not to crack under Soviet domination. These negative portrayals of the Russian team inferred that the Soviet presence was a threat to the future of the Olympic movement because of its intense focus on nationalism. The president of the German National Olympic Committee, Dr. Karl Ritter von Halt, blasted the communist nation's athletes as "sham amateurs" and charged that they "were damaging to the spirit of the Olympic Games." He condemned the "win at all costs attitude" of the "newcomer sports nations." In the United States, Senator John Marshall Butler (R., Md.) stated that the Soviet Union was "polluting the Olympic Games with professionalism." He further noted that Moscow had "12,000,000 professional athletes who have their sinister eyes fixed on the 1956 Olympic Games." Butler felt that the ulterior motive of the U.S.S.R. was "not to advance the ideals of fair play and sportsmanship but International Communist domination."

The amazing irony to all of these charges is that they are the same accusations which had been leveled against U.S. Olympic teams since the beginning of the modern games in Athens in 1896. Nevertheless, the verbal battle raged on. When Soviet athletes failed, it was hailed as proof of communism's failure, whereas when they succeeded, it was met with responses such as that of *Newsweek's* summation that it was "hardly surprising." *Newsweek* quoted a Tel Aviv fan as saying "They ought to be good at it. They've got snow on their boots all year round." Longtime Olympic correspondent Arthur Daley of the *New York Times* supported this view in his article, "Why The Surprise?" In his column, Daley, in addition to elaborating on the Soviet system, also pointed to the geographical location of dominant countries in past Winter Games and showed that the only true surprise of the games was Russia's defeat of Canada in the ice hockey competition. Hockey was Canada's national game and the Canadians had only lost once, in 1936 to Great Britain. Daley equated this incredible feat to the possibility of the Russians beating Americans in baseball, something seemingly "inconceivable." In another article Daley subtly attacked the Russians by comparing their rise in prominence in international sport with that of two former U.S. enemies, Germany and Japan. Daley noted how the Russians had risen to dominance immediately whereas the other two had done it over a prolonged period of international competition. Once again, the hints of a sinister Soviet threat were clearly articulated. This Western attitude of giving the Russians their due while focusing on the covert professionalism in their athletic system, and therefore the unfair playing field which it created, would continue for decades until the IOC began to allow professionals into the Games in 1992, shortly after the collapse of the U.S.S.R.

Economically, these Games were profitable although not as profitable as they could have been. Because of pre-Olympic publicity in the media about how difficult it would be to get accommodations and tickets, many people did not attempt to make the trip to Cortina and watched the Games on television instead. As a result, there were an estimated 1,000 hotel rooms available in the valley daily throughout the Games.

What those who did not make the effort missed was an incredible display staged by Cortina's organizers. Amidst all of the political rhetoric surrounding the 1956 Games was a magnificent show of athletic ability, organization, and sportsmanship. Cortina had spent $5 million to build an amazing Olympic complex. The Italian government had raised the money through the football pool *Toto Calcio*. Twenty percent of the revenue from this form of betting on Italian soccer matches went directly to the Italian Olympic Committee for the "support of sport." Ironically, IOC President Avery Brundage's pure amateur festival was financed through gambling on professional sports.

Two million dollars of this money was spent to build a beautiful outdoor stadium that held 12,000 spectators. This was the venue for the opening and closing ceremonies as well as for the ice hockey and figure skating events. This was the last time that these events would be held outdoors at an Olympic Winter Games. The playing surface was large enough for two hockey rinks and the ice was frozen by 175,000 feet of ammonia tubes. A complex of thirty dressing rooms for figure skaters, locker rooms for four hockey teams, and an array of training rooms, showers, steam baths, and massage rooms were situated beneath the ice. The stadium itself was designed in a Tyrolean architectural style to resemble an alpine chalet, that aesthetically blended in with the surroundings. In addition, a magnificent ski jump named *Italia* was constructed at a cost of $350,000. The venue had modern lines and was a striking architectural gem.

The bobsled track was updated and the turns reconfigured to meet the current standards of the sport; it proved to be a very fast course. A 6,000-seat snow stadium was built for the cross-country events with its south-facing grandstands ideally situated for lighting for television and movie cameras. For the alpine skiing events the downhill course was extended to meet international standards. The only problem that Cortina faced was a lack of snow. Italian alpine troops were called in to move snow from higher elevations for the skiing events, thus saving the organizing committee from having to send those events to a backup location.

The Italians built an outdoor speed skating rink at nearby Lake Misurina. Initially, there was much consternation about this venue choice from the International Skating Union (ISU). These concerns focused on three issues. First, its distance from Cortina; second, the choice of a natural lake for an event due to the lack of consistency of the ice; and third, the altitude. In fact, Sven Laftman the president of the ISU, threatened to withdraw speed skating from the Games if the events were held at Lake Misurina. At the St. Moritz Games in 1948 a number of accidents occurred that were blamed on the altitude of the venue. Skaters allegedly became dizzy in the light air. Information had gotten to the ISU that Misurina was one hundred meters higher than St. Moritz. Fortunately, the organizers at Cortina were able to correct the misconceptions about their venue and informed the IOC that Misurina was actually one hundred meters lower than St. Moritz. They also pointed out that a strong precedent had been set for events on natural lakes at Garmisch-Partenkirchen in 1936, as well as the fact that Lake Misurina is only 8.4 miles from Cortina, much less than any of the distances traveled at Oslo four years earlier. As it turned out, the ice at Lake Misurina was extremely fast. The location contributed to the setting of one world record, the equaling of another, and the eclipsing of every Olympic record. In all, 77 skaters bested previous Olympic marks during the competition.

Along with the presence of the Soviet team for the first time and Italy's first ever role as hosts, there were other innovations and accomplishments at the Cortina Games. They were the first to be televised live, reaching millions of viewers throughout the world and showcasing the potential relationship between television and the Olympic Games. They also were the first to have a woman athlete, Italian skiing champion Signora Giuliana Chenal Minuzzo, recite the athlete's oath at the opening ceremony. Austria's Toni Sailer became the first alpine skier to sweep the gold medals in alpine skiing, winning all three events. A Finnish ski jumper, Antti Hyvarinen, became the first man outside of Norway to win the gold medal in the ski jumping event. His teammate, Aulis Kallakorpi, won the silver medal. Japan won its first winter Olympic medal when Chiharu Igaya, a Dartmouth college student, took second place in the special slalom event. For the first time since 1908, when figure skating was part of the summer games, one nation swept the figure skating competition as the U.S. men took the three top places led by gold medalist Hayes Alan Jenkins. Ronald Robertson won the silver medal while Jenkins' younger brother and future gold medalist at Squaw Valley, David Jenkins, took the bronze. These Games also included the first men's 30-kilometer Nordic skiing race as well as the first women's Nordic 3 × 5-kilometer relay race. These were the only additions to the program from the Oslo Games of 1952. The Soviets had petitioned to have women's speed skating added but were rebuffed.

Along with these innovations and achievements the Cortina Games produced several great champions who became global sport heroes. Along with the three medalists in the men's figure skating, the United States won gold and silver in women's figure skating. The Olympic champion of the 1956 Games was Tenley Albright. She overcame a severe cut on her ankle, inflicted by her own skate in a practice session before the Games began, to win the competition. Her father, a surgeon, flew to Cortina to sew her up and she was able to withstand a strong performance from American rival Carol Heiss to win. The sixteen-year-old Heiss would win the gold medal at the 1960 Games at Squaw Valley and later marry gold medalist Hayes Jenkins. Both Albright and Heiss would go on to become American media darlings due to their Olympic success.

A rivalry developed at Cortina in Nordic skiing where, for the first time, two men who would dominate the world scene in the sport for years to come competed on the Olympic stage. The defending Olympic champion in the 50-kilometer race, Veikko Hakulinen of Finland, and Sixten Jernberg of Sweden competed in all four events in Cortina. Hakulinen won one gold and two silver medals while Jernberg garnered one gold, two silvers, and a bronze medal, in the process dethroning Hakulinen in the 50-kilometer race. In speed skating the Russians dominated. Evgeny Grishin led the way with two gold medals. In the Western media Grishin's feats were not celebrated as individual achievements in the way that those of athletes from other nations were, but rather were viewed as wins for a nameless, faceless Soviet sports machine. This was the beginning of a Cold War tactic used to discount Soviet triumphs by condemning their mechanistic and totalitarian approach to the Olympics.

In terms of pure domination, the alpine skiing events witnessed performers who completely outclassed their rivals. Often forgotten in the focus on the men's races was the decisive victory of Switzerland's Madeleine Berthod who crushed the field by 4.7 seconds in the downhill. On the men's side, Japan's skiing hero Chiharu Igaya was a fan favorite who hoped to bring honor back to his country, which had been so demoralized since World War II. Igaya did just that by finishing in second place amidst a protest by other competitors that he straddled a gate. The protest was denied and Igaya became a hero in his home country. However, Toni Sailer's decimation of the competition on the men's side left no doubt as to who the true star was of these games. In light of his sweep of the alpine events, the media put him in a special category of Olympic champions alongside Jesse Owens and Emil Zatopek.

Sailer won the giant slalom by 6.2 seconds, the special slalom (the term in Cortina for what today is the slalom) by 4.0 seconds over Igaya, and the downhill by 3.5 seconds. To understand the magnitude of his victories it should be noted that in the giant slalom event, no other Olympic champion has ever had a victory margin of more than 2.3 seconds, yet Sailer won by nearly three times that margin. Especially sweet for Austria was the vindication that Sailer provided through his victories, in light of the political history of the region. The Austrians no longer possessed Cortina but they had Toni Sailer. This twenty-year-old was awarded a true hero's welcome after the Games and showered with gifts and honors including the Golden Cross of Merit, Austria's most distinguished medal. Once again, one of the ironies of the Cortina Games was that Sailer's victory in the downhill would have been jeopardized if not for a helping hand from Italy. This time it came in the form of the Italian ski team trainer, Hansl Senger, who saw that the strap on Sailer's ski had broken and gave him the strap from his own ski so that Sailer could make his run and complete the sweep. Nationalistic pride and regional animosity had been put aside, at least temporarily, and the spirit of sportsmanship had prevailed in Cortina.

In remarkable fashion, these Games did mirror the ideals of sportsmanship and fair play that the Olympics embodied. Even amidst the pending storms of political conflict, the sun shone on Cortina d'Ampezzo, and the young men and women who competed did so in friendship and goodwill. The achievements of great athletes were remembered rather than the rancor of rival political ideologies. In the same way that Guido Caroli was able to carry on with dignity after the opening ceremony fall with the Olympic torch, the crowd's appreciation of the Winter Olympic Games of Cortina carried on in the spirit of *citius, altius, fortius*. The focus of the Cortina Games was squarely on the athletes' efforts and accomplishments.

BIBLIOGRAPHICAL ESSAY

The CONI organizing committee's official report to the IOC is *VII Giochi Olimpici Invernali/VII Olympic Winter Games* (Cortina d'Ampezzo, 1956) in Italian and English; there is also a French edition: *VII Jeux olympiques d'hiver Cortina d'Ampezzo* (Cortina d'Ampezzo, 1956). The committee published daily programs, rules booklets, site descriptions as well as a travel planner and guide. The U.S. Olympic Committee report is Asa S. Bushnell and Arthur G. Lentz, eds., *United States 1956 Olympic Book: Quadrennial Report of the United States Olympic Committee* (New York, 1957). The Canadian report is K. P. Farmer et al., eds., Canada *Competes at the Olympic Games 1956* (Montreal, 1956), and the German version is *Die VII. Olymischen Winterspiele 1956 Cortina d'Ampezzo, das Offizielle Standardwerk des Nationalen Olymischen Komitees* (Stuttgart, 1956). The Italian Olympic Committee (CONI) prepared a report, *VII Giochi Olimpici Internali/VII Olympia Games Cortina d'Ampezzo* (Rome, 1956) in English as well as Italian, and a pre-games publication intended to attract spectators to the games, *Olimpiade nelle Dolomiti, dale Tofane all tre cime di Lavaredo. Edita in occasione dei VII Giochi olimpici invernali, Cortina d'Ampezzo 26 Gennaio-5 Febbraio 1956* (Milan, 1955).

The *Avery Brundage Collection* is a wonderful source of information due to Brundage's position as the president of the IOC at the time of these games. His papers are available at the University of Illinois Archives, and also at The Pennsylvania State University at University Park special collections on microfilm. Programs, clippings, organizing committee reports, letters and correspondence can be found in these collections including a competitor's questionnaire given to athletes during the Cortina games.

For background on Cortina and the surrounding region, consult Charles A. Gulick, *Austria from Hapsburg to Hitler, vol. 1* (Berkeley, 1948); Karl R. Standler, *Austria* (New York, 1971); and Z. A. B. Zeman, *The Break up of the Hapsburg Empire, 1914–1918* (London, 1961).

Primary sources which give good accounts of the Cortina Games include most major U.S. newspapers including the *New York Times*, the *Chicago Sun-Times*, the *Chicago Tribune*, and the *Los Angeles Times*. *The Times* of London also had daily coverage. U.S. magazines which covered the games included *Sports Illustrated, Time, Newsweek,* and *Life*.

Many secondary works on the 1956 Winter Games are in German and many of those are uncritical works focusing on the beauty of the area and the heroes of the competition. Researchers may want to look at Carl Diem, *Die Olypischen Spiele 1956. Cortina d'Ampezzo, Stockholm, Melbourne* (Stuttgart, 1957). Also see Werner Eberhardt, *Olympische Winterspiele, Cortina d'Ampezzo 1956* (Berlin, 1956); Harald Lechtenperg, *Olympische Spiele, 1956: Cortina, Stockholm, Melbourne* (Munich, 1957); and Martin Maier, *So war es in Cortina* (Vienna, 1956). Books in English with some valuable resources are Bud Greenspan, *Frozen in Time: the Greatest Moments at the Winter Olympics* (Los Angeles, 1997), Gale D. Benn, *Olympic Gold: Summer and Winter Games; The Official Record of Championship Performances Since 1896* (New York, 1972), Frank Litsky, *The Winter Olympics* (New York, 1979), and Julian May, *The Winter Olympics* (Mankato, 1976).

For the Soviet influence in the Olympics, some works can be helpful including Yuri Brokhin, *The Big Red Machine: The Rise and Fall of Soviet Olympic Champions* (New York, 1978); James Riordan *Soviet Sport: Background To the Olympics,* (Oxford, 1980); Marat Vasil'evich Shishgin, *Scaling The Olympus* (Moscow, 1967); Norman Shneidman, *The Soviet Road To Olympus: Theory and Practice of Soviet Physical Culture and Sport* (Toronto, 1978); and Valeri Shteinbakh *The Soviet Contribution to the Olympics*, (Moscow, 1980).

The Journal of Sport History and the *International Journal of Sport* as well as *Olympika* have published articles that focus on some aspects of the Cortina games. Examples are G. A. Carr, "The Involvement of Politics in the Sporting Relationships of East and West Germany, 1945–1972," *Journal of Sport History*, 7 (Spring 1980): 40–51; Gigliola Gori, "Model of Masculinity: Mussolini, the 'New Italian' of the Fascist Era," *The International Journal of the History of Sport*, 6 (September 1999): 27–61.

SQUAW VALLEY 1960

Tim Ashwell

EIGHTH OLYMPIC WINTER GAMES

Squaw Valley was the Brigadoon of Winter Games, a community that magically appeared out of the windblown snow of California's Sierra Nevada range and then disappeared. Most of the man-made evidence of the games is gone, including the ice arena that witnessed the U.S. hockey team's miraculous gold medal performance. What remains, however, is the land itself: a natural bowl 1/2 mile wide and 2 miles long carved into the eastern face of the Sierras at 6,200 feet above sea level. Towering above are three alpine peaks, the tallest, Squaw Peak at the western end, rising steeply to 8,885 feet. The valley is located nearly astride the California-Nevada state line, overlooking Lake Tahoe, 40 miles southwest of Reno and 200 miles northeast of San Francisco. Add to the terrain the copious snows that blanket the Tahoe Basin each year and Squaw Valley becomes the ideal location for the world's finest athletes to celebrate their skills.

That, at least, was the dream of Alexander C. Cushing, a socially prominent New York attorney and avid skier who first visited the valley in 1947. Cushing was so taken by the land that he purchased 574 acres, raised $400,000 from friends back east, among them Laurance Rockefeller, and moved his family west to start a ski resort. When Cushing learned in December 1954 that the United States Olympic Committee (USOC) would entertain bids from communities hoping to host the 1960 Winter Games, he saw an opportunity to promote California tourism in general and his properties in particular. He quickly won expressions of support from the state's publicity-conscious governor, Goodwin Knight, and the state's two U.S. senators. State senator Harold Johnson, whose district included Squaw Valley, agreed to file legislation in Sacramento guaranteeing $1 million in site development funds if Cushing managed to win the USOC's endorsement. "None of them thought I had a chance," Cushing recalled, "but they naturally couldn't go on record saying they were against the Winter Olympics coming to California."

(Melvin Dursing, "The Great Winter-Olympics Fight," *Saturday Evening Post*, February 22, 1960, 35, 73).

The chances of that actually happening, all agreed, were slim. When Cushing arrived at the USOC meeting in New York in January, 1955, Squaw Valley's facilities included one chair lift, two rope tows, and a modest lodge. His rivals included such well-established winter sports centers as Aspen, Colorado; Sun Valley, Idaho; and Lake Placid, New York, host of the 1932 Winter Games. Extolling Squaw Valley's natural beauty and California hospitality, as well as his pledges of support from the state's establishment, Cushing persuaded the USOC to back his bid for the 1960 Games.

Rushing back to California, Cushing hurriedly raised a $50,000 campaign fund to sell Squaw Valley to the International Olympic Committee (IOC), which would meet in Paris in June. Most of the money came from investors in the Squaw Valley Development Company, who saw an opportunity to garner badly needed publicity for their struggling resort. The possibility that Squaw Valley would actually be chosen still appeared remote. Squaw's rivals for the bid included St. Moritz, which had successfully hosted the games in 1928 and 1948, Garmisch-Partenkirchen, the 1936 site, and Innsbruck, the acknowledged favorite.

Clearly unable to compete with the European candidates in terms of facilities, Cushing chose to make the valley's unspoiled environment his selling point. He would offer the IOC an ideal Olympic venue built from the ground up. "Psychologically," he recalled, "this was our knockout punch. Ours would be a healthy, unadorned games, in a clean, simple atmosphere, free from commercial pressure and public interference" ("The Great Winter-Olympics Fight," 73).

Squaw Valley's presentation was dedicated to "Restoring the Olympic Ideal to the Winter Games." An Olympic Village with a common dining room would be constructed to feed and house the world's athletes, a first for the Winter Games. Venues would be clustered within walking distance of the village, not scattered across the countryside. Costs, he promised, would be reasonable. Transportation and living accommodations would not exceed $500 per athlete. Finally, Cushing argued, it was time for the IOC to acknowledge geopolitical realities of the postwar world. The time had come for a member of what he described as the Pacific family of nations to host the event.

On June 15, 1955, on the second ballot, IOC members cast 32 votes for Squaw Valley and 30 for Innsbruck. By the narrowest of margins, the 1960 Winter Games had been awarded to the obscure California ski area. Squaw Valley's obscurity was underscored at the Closing Ceremonies of the 1956 Games at Cortina d'Ampezzo. The mayor of the host city of the next Games traditionally takes part in the festivities, but Squaw Valley was an unincorporated village with no local government. IOC member John J. Garland of Los Angeles was drafted to fill in on behalf of his home state.

That Squaw Valley was awarded the Winter Games is, if not magical, a testimony to the promotional skill of a politically savvy resort owner from a state synonymous with self-promotion. Cushing had arrived in Paris with a plaster scale model of the valley and glossy brochures depicting unbuilt facilities. Delivering on the promises made to the IOC would prove a formidable task.

Financing the games was an immediate problem. The original $1 million appropriation was inadequate. The centerpiece of the games, 8,500-seat Blyth Memorial Arena, which would be the scene of the Opening and Closing Ceremonies as well as figure skating and hockey, was budgeted at $4 million. Infrastructure for the Olympic Village, including a sewage treatment plant, had to be constructed. The state's share of the cost quickly escalated to $2.4 million, then $4 million and eventually $8 million. Reluctant legislators balked. Although much of the site would revert to state park land after the Olympics, Cushing and other private developers would reap the profits.

Governor Knight and his successor, Edmund "Pat" Brown, however, remained firmly behind the project. California was the fastest-growing state in the union but still suffered from a nagging inferiority complex. The Olympics represented an unparalleled opportunity to promote the state on the world stage. The possibility that California might botch its opportunity and forfeit the games was unthinkable. A new state agency, the California Olympic Commission, was created to coordinate development at Squaw Valley and administer the games. H. D. Thoreau, great-grandnephew of the famous writer, was appointed managing director of the games.

Cushing had expected to chair the organizing committee himself but was eased out of the process in 1956 as the budget soared. San Francisco businessman Prentis Cobb Hale, Jr., headed the Olympic Organizing Committee and rallied private support for the Games. The committee provided Cushing two free tickets to the Games and continued to consult him as a technical advisor, but he had no official connection with the project he had made possible.

At some point between the IOC's vote in 1955 and the Opening Ceremonies, the idea of a rustic, intimate Games was forgotten. This was, after all, California. Walt Disney was enlisted as Pageant Director and promised a spectacle no one would soon forget. The Olympic Village would be decorated with giant snow sculptures made of plaster, which, Disney insisted, looked like actual snow. The athletes would be treated to nightly entertainments hosted by television personality Art Linkletter, including a "western night" featuring a frontier-saloon motif and highlighted by a mock gunfight featuring movie cowboys. Such Hollywood touches, as well as the proximity of Nevada's glittering gambling casinos, caused several European delegates to worry that the combination of western informality and show business would taint the Games, one expressing the fear that Squaw Valley would be "another Disneyland." Addressing the IOC in San Francisco five days before the Games began, IOC president Avery Brundage also seemed to have Disney in mind. "Sport," he warned, "must be amateur or it is not sport at all, but a branch of the entertainment business."

The Olympic facilities themselves were, if not exactly rustic, tightly bunched in the valley, and athletes could, as Cushing had promised, walk from their rooms to most of the events. The only venue outside of Squaw Valley was the Nordic skiing course, located twelve miles away at McKinney Creek. Several Scandinavian nations noted the course was more than 6,000 feet above sea level and worried the thin air would ruin the races. While the cross-country racers worried about the altitude, they at least knew they would have races to run. Citing a lack of potential entrants and the high cost, the organizing committee announced it would not build a bobsled course. The sport had been a fixture since the 1924 Games, but the bobsledders' protests were ignored. They held their own world championships in Cortina d'Ampezzo two weeks before the Squaw Valley Games.

New technologies were introduced. For the first time, both the indoor and outdoor skating rinks were artificially refrigerated and maintained by a fleet of six Zamboni ice resurfacing machines. Electronic timing and scoring devices were installed to determine medalists and flash results to the press. Organizers hoped to reduce traffic congestion by directing spectators to outlying parking lots paved with packed snow and sand and delivering them to the valley by bus.

As costs climbed, Congress and the state of Nevada pitched in to fund construction. By 1960, the cost of turning Squaw Valley into an Olympic site totaled $15 million. The final bill, including indirect expenses such as the accelerated completion of the interstate highway linking San Francisco and Reno and expansion of Reno's municipal airport, eventually reached an estimated $20 million.

As the organizers rushed to complete construction, Cold War rivalries threatened to disrupt the Games. The China question posed the most serious danger. The United States refused to recognize the People's Republic of China, insisting that the Nationalist regime on Taiwan represented China. The People's Republic had withdrawn from the IOC in 1958, but the Nationalists remained a problem. The IOC voted that the Taiwan government could not represent China either, triggering threats of reprisals from Congress and pro-Nationalist groups in the United States. As a compromise, the IOC allowed Taiwanese officials, who had no Winter Games athletes in any case, to attend because they had been invited prior to the decertification vote. India, fearful of offending the People's Republic, withdrew. East and West Germany were willing to field a joint squad, but the State Department refused to issue visas to the full complement of East German officials and journalists, claiming the delegation included spies and propagandists. Again, a compromise was reached.

As the Opening Ceremonies approached, the Games faced another threat, one that no amount of diplomacy could avert. A warm front swept over the mountains from the Pacific and torrential rains drenched the valley. The snow-and-sand parking lots began to melt away and Cushing feared "the whole mountain was going to come down in a flash flood." Then, on the morning of the Opening Ceremonies, the temperature dropped and the rain turned into a blizzard. Organizers considered postponing or curtailing the ceremonies, but after four hours, the snow slackened and the sun emerged. It took several hours to clear the roads and plow the snow away from the arena, but the Games would go on.

Squaw Valley welcomed the world on February 18, 1960. Nearly 800 athletes from thirty nations were on hand, along with 12,500 paying spectators. For the first time, a national television audience watched the ceremonies live across the United States. Disney came through in lavish style: a chorus of 2,500 accompanied by a 1,200 piece band performed as 1952 gold medalist Andrea Mead Lawrence skied down Papoose Peak bearing the Olympic torch. She passed the flame to speed skater Ken Henry, who circled the outdoor rink before lighting the ceremonial torch atop the Tower of Nations. As he did, 2,000 pigeons, feathered stand-ins for doves of peace, were released from inside the arena and swirled overhead. A few stragglers stayed behind and roosted in the eaves, making encore appearances from time to time throughout the Games.

The blizzard that nearly disrupted the ceremonies forced a one-day delay in the downhill skiing events and reminded organizers that too much snow could prove as disastrous as too little. French ski official Robert Faure noted Squaw's proximity to Donner Pass. "The history of America's march westward," he observed, "is full of tragic adventures of pioneers perishing in the snow" (*Time*, February 8, 1960, p. 50). Once the remains of the blizzard were cleared away, however, neither the weather nor the altitude played a significant role. Attendance picked up, and the athletes provided several memorable performances with a surprising number coming from members of the host squad.

Figure skaters Carol Heiss and David Jenkins captured gold medals, while Americans also claimed silver medals in the women's and pairs events. Penny Pitou, the leading United States hope for a skiing medal, captured two silvers, trailing Germany's Heidi Biebl in the downhill and Switzerland's Yvonne Ruegg in the giant slalom. Teammate Betsey Snite finished second to Canada's Anne Heggtveit in the slalom.

The most astounding United States victory, and one of the most unlikely triumphs during the Games, came in ice hockey. The underdog Americans upset Canada 2–1 and the Soviet Union 3–2, thanks to the acrobatic play of goalie Jack McCartan and the goal scoring of brothers Bill and Roger Christian. The United States clinched the gold medal with a come-from-behind 9–4 victory over Czechoslovakia. Reporters eager to detect signs of a thaw in the Cold War made much of the fact that Soviet hockey captain Nikolai Sologubov visited the U.S. locker room before the final period of the gold-medal game and urged the weary Americans to rejuvenate themselves with oxygen. "The big joke," McCartan later admitted, "was that the guys who didn't take the oxygen were the ones who scored the goals."

Sweden's Kars Lestander captured the biathlon, a shooting and skiing event contested for the first time at Squaw Valley. Lestander logged the fifteenth-fastest time over the 20-kilometer course but was perfect on each of his twenty rifle shots. Veikko Hakulinen of Finland, the 1952 gold medalist in the 50-kilometer cross-country race, narrowly missed recapturing his title as he finished behind teammate Kalevi Kamalainen, but he helped his nation capture the 40-kilometer relay by overtaking the leader in the final 50 yards.

Women's speed skating was also contested for the first time at Squaw Valley, and the Soviet Union's Lidia Skoblikova won gold at both 1,500 and 3,000 meters. The Soviet men also dominated their events as the U.S.S.R. claimed six gold medals in speed skating. Overall, the Soviet Union claimed twenty-one medals, including seven golds, more than any other nation. The combined German team took four gold medals home. The United States, Norway, and Sweden each won three.

The Games closed with another Disney-produced ceremony on February 28. Total paid attendance for the eleven days was 240,904, fewer than the 300,000 organizers had hoped for, but still a record. Visitors to the valley, however, were only a fraction of the total audience.

CBS purchased exclusive U.S. television rights to the Games for $50,000 and found it difficult to sell enough advertising before the Games to cover its investment. As the Games went on, however, and American athletes encountered unexpected success, audiences for the network's nightly coverage increased steadily. The medium was still testing its wings in 1960, but as *Sports Illustrated* marveled after the Games, "it soared triumphantly over Squaw and bore a whole nation of sports fans into new heights of excitement."

The Olympic site was turned over to California's State Division of Beaches and Parks two days after the Closing Ceremonies. As critics feared, it became a white elephant requiring continuing subsidies. In the early 1970s, the state sold most of the Olympic property to a commercial development firm that quickly declared bankruptcy because it could not generate enough revenue to maintain the facility. Alexander Cushing repurchased much of the property and resumed building the resort of his dreams. The Squaw Valley Games, which Cushing had promised would be "unadorned, clean and simple" and a throwback to simpler days, were in fact symbolic of modern times.

Frankly conceived to yield private profit, the Squaw Valley Games became a heavily subsidized public project. Government funding was rationalized on the grounds that the Olympic site would become a recreation area for the people, albeit one operated by private corporations. The intermingling of state and corporate interests fueled the U.S. postwar economic boom, a boom which was most explosive in California where the defense and aerospace industries, utterly reliant on government support, led the economy.

The organizers also consciously turned their back on the elitism of posh European resorts and embraced American popular culture. Squaw Valley was, in fact, another Disneyland, an artfully created artificial environment. After Squaw Valley, network television cameras and the viewers at home, not spectators at the site, would become the primary Olympic audience. The unexpected success of the 1960 Winter Games as television entertainment presaged the vast audiences and multi-million-dollar television contracts that would radically alter the Games.

BIBLIOGRAPHICAL ESSAY

The California State Archives in Sacramento hold the records of both the California Olympic Commission and the State Division of Beaches and Parks, as well as legislative documents concerning state appropriations both before and after the Games. Among the holdings are design blueprints for Squaw Valley's buildings. No specific user's guide is available, but the archives are indexed in a topical card catalogue. Since the valley lies within the boundaries of the Tahoe National Forest, more information on the development of Squaw Valley may be found in the files of the U.S. Forest Service, Department of Agriculture, held by the National Archives and Records Administration, Washington, D.C.

Los Angeles Times columnist and Olympic Games historian Bill Henry served as official public address announcer for the Squaw Valley games. His papers, including Olympic memorabilia, are in the Occidental College Library, Los Angeles. The Avery Brundage Papers at the University of Illinois Archives contain material from the organizing committee, newspaper clippings, photographs, programs, and press releases, as well as information on the Disney pageants and some newsreel footage of the Games.

Official reports include Robert Rubin, ed., *VIII Olympic Winter Games, Squaw Valley, California 1960: Final Report* (Sacramento, Calif., 1960), the organizing committee's report to the IOC; Arthur G. Lentz and Asa S. Bushnell, eds., *United States 1960 Olympic Book: Quadrennial Report of the United States Olympic Committee* (New York, 1961); and K. P. Farmer and E. H. Radford, eds., *Canada Competes at the Olympic Games 1960* (Montreal, 1961). See also the German report, *Die Olympische Spiele 1960: Rom–Squaw Valley: Das Offizielle Standardwerk des Nationen Olympischen Komittees* (Stuttgart, Germany, 1960).

Secondary literature on the Squaw Valley games is limited. Aside from the standard general histories of the Olympic Games, see Harald Lechenperg, ed., *Olympic Games 1960: Squaw Valley, Rome*, trans. by Benjamin B. Lacy, Jr. (New York, 1960) for a detailed if plodding chronicle of the event. The Disney contribution is described in John Ormond, ed., *The Pageantry Story* (Burbank, Calif., 1960).

The most thorough contemporary newspaper coverage of the games may be found in San Francisco's dailies, the *Chronicle* and the *Examiner*. The *Los Angeles Times*, under sports editor Paul Zimmerman, offered fewer column inches but better writing. The tone of the California dailies can best be described as euphoric, testimony to the state's psychological as well as material investment in the Games' success. *Sports Illustrated*'s coverage of the Games, spearheaded by Roy Terrell, was exemplary. Among general-interest periodicals in the period leading up to the Games, the *Saturday Evening Post* and *Life* provided some coverage, while *Time* and *The Nation* occasionally examined the mushrooming cost of the Games with a jaundiced eye.

The best evidence of the Squaw Valley Games would be kinescopes of CBS-TV's eleven days of coverage, anchored by Walter Cronkite. Some footage survives in scattered form at the network and in the hands of private collectors, but neither the Museum of Television and Radio in New York nor the UCLA Film and Television Archives in Los Angeles, the most accessible sources for such things, holds a copy.

Newsreels were still alive in 1960 and present an alternate source of visual evidence that should not be ignored. The Brundage Collection and the UCLA Archives, for instance, both hold the Hearst Movietone footage of the Games, and excerpts are available at audio-visual centers across the country.

INNSBRUCK 1964

Carly Adams

NINTH OLYMPIC WINTER GAMES

For the Austrian people, the selection of Innsbruck as the host city for the 1964 IX Winter Olympic Games represented the progress that their nation had made since the end of World War II. In 1945, Austria gained autonomy from the German Reich and a decade later, with the signing of the Austrian State Treaty, the four-power occupation of the country ended, and Austria was recognized as an sovereign nation. On October 26, 1955, the Austrian Parliament implemented a constitutional law establishing the nation's foreign policy of permanent neutrality. In the 1950s in an attempt to improve its social, political, and economic structures, Austria adopted the Social Partnership (*sozialpartnerschaft*) system. This system was a cooperation between industry, agriculture, and government that allowed corporatism, state intervention, and compromise as a method of resolving controversial issues. This new Austrian Model aided in placing the country on a similar technological and economic level with other Western European nations.

Innsbruck first entered the bidding process to host the Winter Olympics in the mid-1950s with an attempt to secure the 1960 Games. However, in a close vote, the IOC awarded the Games to Squaw Valley, the first time since 1932 that the Winter Olympic Games had been awarded to a non-European city. Fortunately, Austrian organizers did not succumb to their defeat but renewed their efforts, which, in May 1959, resulted in the awarding of the 1964 Games to Innsbruck in a landslide vote over Calgary, Canada, and Lahti, Finland, in the first round.

Innsbruck, the capital of the Tyrol province, was home to approximately 100,000 people. By 1964, Austria was the world's leading exporter of ski equipment and the second largest producer behind West Germany. Austrian officials had contributed approximately $20 million from Marshall Plan funds toward the development of ski resorts in the western provinces. Because of the fame of Austrian skier Toni Sailer, who won three Alpine gold medals at the 1956 Cortina d'Ampezzo Winter Games in Italy, the country was in a prime position to capitalize on this investment. Tyrol,

Salzburg, and Cathinia, the western provinces of Austria, succeeded in attracting the most foreign visitors. By 1963, tourism accounted for 9 percent of the nation's per capita national income, with revenues from foreign tourists reaching $362.4 million.

The Innsbruck Organizing Committee spent almost $40 million preparing for the Games. To accommodate the Alpine skiing events, a new ski area was created in the mountains at Axamer Lizum, 12 miles outside of Innsbruck. A new bobsled and luge course and two ski jumping hills overlooking the city were built. Inside the city, a new ice stadium was constructed, along with eight 11-story apartment buildings to house the more than 1,300 athletes who would participate in the Games. Private businesses also built several new hotels, restaurants, and ski lifts, and improved area roads and bridges to handle the expected onslaught of 150,000 daily visitors. To move spectators between athletic venues, organizers planned to use buses and ban automobiles from the different venues.

Throughout the duration of the Games, the physical arrangement of the site drew extensive criticism. The events were dispersed among venues outside of the city, with only the ice hockey and skating events taking place within the city limits. The inaccessibility of the Olympic Village was another area of contention. The athletes were housed 10 miles from the city and were rarely seen on the streets of Innsbruck. The invisibility of the competitors detracted from the festive-like atmosphere that typically characterized the Olympic Games.

The success of the 1964 Games was threatened by the unpredictability of the weather. Obviously, snow and cold conditions are critical for constructing Winter Olympic venues such as the luge and the bobsled runs. However, this was one aspect of the Games the organizers could not control. In the weeks leading up to the Games, temperatures persistently rose to above freezing, and rain caused the snow to disappear from the slopes and the other snow-dependent venues. With no significant snowfall for more than seven weeks, this was the mildest first week of February in Austria for nearly 60 years. Officials called in 3,000 Austrian soldiers to deliver 40,000 cubic meters of snow to the ski courses, luge, and bobsled runs. Snow was trucked from distant places and then hauled up the slopes on wooden sleds; workers worked around the clock hand-packing snow to reconstruct the courses. An additional 20,000 cubic meters of snow was held in reserve and six artificial snowmaking machines were imported from the United States. The warm weather threatened to cancel the Austrian national bobsled championships in the week prior to the opening of the Games. Lugers, bobsledders, and skiers all had to contend with uncertain practice schedules and the uncertain quality of their courses.

According to local folklore, the cause of this weather was the Föhn, the warm, dry, downslope wind blowing from the south that caused both the temperature and anxiety to soar. Local lore said the Föhn induced melancholy, confused people's thinking, and encouraged suicides. Some schools even cancelled examinations when the Föhn blew, and many considered it a bad omen to begin new ventures under its influence.

On January 23, the day of the full-scale dress rehearsal of the Opening Ceremony, disaster struck. British bobsledder Kazimirez Kay-Skrzypeski was killed while completing a training run, and two German lugers and an American bobsledder also suffered serious injuries while practicing. The following day, after a British luger was seriously hurt, International Federation officials agreed to construct wooden lips at the top of the steepest curves to decrease the chance of injury.

Unfortunately, this was not the end of the tragedies. Two days later, on January 26, 19-year-old Australian skier Ross Milne died after he collided with a tree while training on the Patscherkofel ski course. On the same day, two Liechtenstein skiers crashed, resulting in a fractured arm for one and a broken leg for the other, and Prince Karim, the aga khan of Iran, had a near miss. Persuaded by the multitude of incidents, officials decided to cancel the following day's practice sessions to inspect the ski trails. The inspections resulted in the addition of extra safety precautions. Two extra gates were introduced to the men's downhill run at Patscherkofel, a trail known to the European press as the Course of Fear, and straw was added to pad the hundreds of tree trunks that lined the courses. Also, the women's downhill course at Lizum was shortened because of a lack of snow at the top, and three compulsory gates were added to control skiers' speed. As a further safety precaution, three doctors stood at each finish line, trails were patrolled by rescue squads, and helicopters were ready to evacuate seriously injured athletes and to reach inaccessible areas. Despite all of this, a female British spectator suffered a fractured skull when a toboggan careened off the course during the women's event. The death and injuries of these individuals cast a shadow over what should have been a time of celebration. As a tribute to the deaths, all flags were flown at half-staff throughout the Games, and a black mourning ribbon was attached to the Olympic banner.

Under this cloud of death and injury, the Opening Ceremonies were held on January 29, 1964, at the base of the Bergisel ski jump. This was the first time in the history of the Winter Olympic Games that the Opening Ceremonies were not held at the ice arena. Dr. Adolf Schaerf, president of Austria, and Heinrich Drimmel, chair of the Innsbruck organizing committee and Austria's minister of education, welcomed over 1,300 athletes from 36 different nations who were prepared to compete for 34 gold medals over the following two weeks. Some 50,000 spectators attended the event.. On behalf of all the athletes, Paul Aste took the oath, but injected a significant change. Traditionally, the oath had ended with the words "for the glory of the sports and the honor of our countries." In an attempt to rid the oath of nationalistic elements, Aste eliminated the word "countries," replacing it with "teams."

In addition to the modification of the athletes' oath, the 1964 Innsbruck Games were notable for several significant innovations and format changes. For the first time, the sport of luge was included on the Olympic program, and the ski jumping competition was divided into two events: 70 meters and 90 meters. Also, bobsledding returned after a four-year hiatus. In 1960 at Squaw Valley, the cost of building a complete run had been too high. Therefore, bobsledding had been temporarily excluded from the program. During the Innsbruck Games, the American press also dropped its practice of keeping daily point scores of the Games, a procedure that never had official IOC recognition. Also, timing to a hundredth of a second was introduced in Alpine skiing.

However, the most significant advance came in figure skating, where computers were used for the first time as judging aids. Seven months prior to the Games an immense electronic data processing system, provided by the International Business Machines (IBM) company was installed in Innsbruck. The $2.5 million worth of equipment proved to be a major improvement, speeding up events by making scores instantly available. Along with figure skating, 11 other data-feeding points at competition sites relayed information to a processing center at Innsbruck University.

For the first time in the Winter Games, the Olympic flame was lit in Olympia, Greece. Organizers borrowed this tradition of lighting the flame in front of the Temple of Hera in Olympia from the Summer Games and through an extended torch relay of individuals of different nationalities, genders, races, and creeds across continents, the flame was carried to Innsbruck. Since 1964, the flame has always been lit in Olympia for the Winter Games, creating another connection between the Ancient Greek Olympics and the modern Olympic Movement.

During the Games, athletes from all over the world succeeded in breaking records and showcasing outstanding performances. The Innsbruck Games marked the first time sisters won gold. French skiers Christine and Marielle Goitschel finished first and second respectively, in the women's slalom and then traded medal places in the giant slalom. However, the most notable athlete was Lidia Skoblikova, a Soviet speed skater. The 24-year-old Chelyabinsk physiology teacher triumphed in the 500-meter, 1,000-meter, 1,500-meter, and 3,000-meter events, setting three new records. She was consequently recognized as the first competitor to win four individual gold medals in a single Olympic Games. When she returned home, the Soviet Union made Skoblikova a member of the Communist Party, and a panel of media sports experts named her 1964 Soviet Athlete of the Year. This was the first time a woman had won the award.

Eugenio Monti of Italy is also worthy of mention for his act of sportsmanship at the Innsbruck Games. Monti had been a competitive skier, but after injuring his knee in 1952, he joined the Italian bobsled team. Throughout his athletic career, he had won world championships, but Olympic gold had eluded him. In 1964, as he awaited his last run, a call for help came over the loudspeaker. Tony Nash of Great Britain had broken a bolt supporting the runners on his sled just prior to his last run. Not wanting to win the event through the default of one of the favored competitors, Monti gave Nash the same bolt from his own sled, and Nash and his teammate Robin Dixon went on to win the two-men bobsled event. Monti and his teammate Gergio Siopaes placed third, a respectable position, but not the gold medal for which Monti had been striving. After the Games, Nash nominated Monti to receive the Pierre de Coubertin Fair Play Trophy, which the UNESCO council and International Sportswriters Association awarded. For his unselfish act of sportsmanship, Monti was the first recipient of the Coubertin award.

During the 1960s, the issue of apartheid plagued the Olympic movement. At the 1964 Games, IOC President Avery Brundage announced that South Africa would be barred from the upcoming Tokyo Summer Games because of its policy of racial segregation in sports. In order to be included in the Games, the South Africa National Olympic Committee (SANOC) had to publicly and formally disassociate itself from the policy of apartheid. SANOC, however, failed to meet the IOC's deadline. During the IOC session in Innsbruck, the national Olympic committees from Algeria, Nigeria, Congo Brazzaville, and Sierra Leone, all newly independent countries, were granted full recognition, bringing the number of member nations in the Olympic Movement to 114.

Like most other Olympic Games celebrations, Innsbruck endured its share of controversy. Issues that are still prevalent concerns in the twenty-first century Olympic Movement—biased judging, professionalism, and protests using the

Olympic Games as a platform—all played a role in the controversial events of 1964. Both the men and women's figure skating finals were marked with protests concerning biased judging. The U.S. hockey coach complained that his squad was unfairly matched against European professionals, and the Canadian hockey team boycotted the medal ceremony. They were one of three teams to finish with identical 5-2 records behind the unbeaten Soviets but lost out on a medal because the tie-breaking system was based on goals allowed in all seven games. The Canadians demanded that a tie-breaking system based on goals scored in the final four games of the event be used, but this was not allowed, and Sweden and Czechoslovakia won the silver and bronze medals. Also, Brundage, a staunch believer in amateurism, saw that two German athletes were stripped of their silver medals when it was determined that they were professionals. Outside of the Olympic arena, U.S. officials denounced the harsh treatment three American athletes received at the hands of the Innsbruck police after they were charged with stealing a car and resisting arrest. The charges were later reduced, but Judge Franz Obholzer refused any court discussion of the alleged brutality. Highlighting the connection between politics and the Olympic Games, 5 Iranian students were arrested for parading with anti-Shah banners, and another 25 were detained after demonstrating for the release of imprisoned countrymen. The Olympic Games have always been and will continue to be the largest stage and the best way to achieve the most attention for a political protest.

After the conclusion of the Games, controversial and disastrous events continued to occur. One week after the Closing Ceremony, three Missoula, Montana, students were given suspended sentences for stealing flags used at the Games and told to avoid Austria in their future travels. Most unfortunate was the freak accident resulting in the death of two competitors after the Closing Ceremonies. German Barbi Henneberger and American Wallace "Bud" Werner were buried under a Swiss avalanche while filming a skiing movie.

After an eventful and emotionally trying two weeks, the festivities at Innsbruck came to a close on February 9, 1964. The Games overcame tragedy, controversy, and uncooperative weather. Despite these difficulties, organizers succeeded in creating an atmosphere of athletic spirit and Olympic celebration.

BIBLIOGRAPHICAL ESSAY

Primary resource material concerning the 1964 Innsbruck Winter Olympics may be found in the Avery Brundage Collection at the University of Illinois Archives in the United States. A microfilm copy can also be found at the International Centre for Olympic Studies at the University of Western Ontario, Canada. Brundage was president of the IOC from 1952 to 1972.

The official report of the Innsbruck Organizing Committee is Friedl Wolfgang and Bertl Neumann, *Official Report of the IXth Olympic Winter Games Innsbruck 1964* (Vienna, 1967). The report was also published in German and French editions. Apart from this report, the committee published souvenir books, daily programs, and reports of the results, often in multilingual editions, as well as *IX. Olympische Winterspiele Bulletin*, a multilingual newsletter published intermittently between September 1961 and May 1964.

The U.S. Olympic Committee report is Arthur G. Lentz and Asa S. Bushnell, eds., *1964 United States Olympic Book* (New York, 1965), which examines both the

Winter Games in Innsbruck and the Summer Games in Tokyo. The British Olympic Committee report is Doug Gardner, ed., *The British Olympic Association Official Report of the Olympic Games 1964: 18th Olympiad, Tokyo, October 10–October 24; 9th Winter Olympic Games, Innsbruck, January 29–February 9* (London, 1965). The Canadian Olympic Association report is Francis J. Shaughnessy, J. H. Bowden, and E. H. Radford, eds., *Canada Competes at the Olympic Games 1964* (Montreal, 1965). Although the Games have been numbered incorrectly, *Die VIII. Olympischen Komitees fur Deutschland* (Stuttgart, Germany, 1964), is the German interpretation of the Games.

Secondary literature regarding the Innsbruck Games is sparse, especially in English. Sources include Harald Lechenperg, *Olympic Games 1964: Innsbruck-Tokyo* (New York, 1965); Christopher Ondaatge and Gordon Currie, *Olympic Victory* (Toronto, 1967), which recounts the victory of the Canadian bobsled team; and Kurt Bernegger, et al., *Olympia Innsbruck 1964* (Innsbruck, Austria, 1964), which chronicles all aspects of the Games. The *New York Times*, *Sports Illustrated*, and the Canadian *Maclean's* magazine, provide good coverage of the competition during the Games, although with little academic substance.

For an understanding of the nation of Austria see Peter Thaler, *The Ambivalence of Identity: The Austrian Experience of Nation-building in a Modern Society* (West Lafayette, IN, 2001) for an examination of Austria's socioeconomic environment, intellectual foundations, and national identity since World War II. See also Kurt Steiner, ed., *Modern Austria* (Palo Alto, CA, 1981), which presents an excellent summary of the political, cultural, and social forces at work in the nation. Also, John Fitzmaurice, *Austrian Politics and Society Today: In Defense of Austria* (Basingstroke, England, 1990) deals with the provincialism, pragmatism, and absence of open debate on key issues that have marked postwar Austria, arguing that these factors have produced a weak ethical climate in politics.

GRENOBLE 1968
Douglas Brown and Gordon MacDonald

TENTH OLYMPIC WINTER GAMES

When French President Charles de Gaulle officially opened the X Olympic Winter Games in Grenoble, France, on February 8, 1968, the future of the Olympic Winter Games had rarely looked more bleak from the perspective of the International Olympic Committee (IOC). With President Avery Brundage at the lead, the IOC and the Olympic movement seemed to be completely at odds with the Winter Games. Almost every aspect of the Games in Grenoble came under criticism for one reason or another. Excessive political intervention, commercialism, organizational headaches, and even the attitudes of the athletes were regarded as contradictory to the true spirit of the Olympic Games. Despite the shadow of criticism and controversy, the Olympic Winter Games of Grenoble saw the emergence of several Olympic heroes and the beginning of some enduring Olympic traditions. In all, 1,065 male and 228 female athletes from 37 countries participated in these first broadly televised Olympic Winter Games. There were also 1,545 accredited members of the press in Grenoble. The competitions ran for an unprecedented thirteen days, February 6–18, 1968.

The Dauphine city of Grenoble began its effort to host the X Olympic Winter Games in 1960. The bid became official on December 30, 1960, when the mayor of Grenoble, Albert Michallon, officially informed Brundage of the city's application to host the games. The prefect of the Isere, Francois Raoul, and president of the Dauphine Ski Committee, Raoul Arduin, are recognized in official reports as the initiators of the bid. Even at this early date, Brundage was notorious for his antagonistic attitude towards the Winter Games movement. At the IOC Executive Committee meeting in Rome in 1960, he asked the IOC to reconsider its support of the Winter Games beyond its commitment to Innsbruck in 1964. For Brundage, the Winter Games did not reflect the high standard of amateurism befitting Olympic endorsement. He pointed his finger at the international sport federations and the national Olympic committees for not strictly applying the amateur rules to the athletes under their jurisdiction.

Grenoble began the preparations required of any bidding city immediately. By the end of 1962 the organizing committee had received several important local government and commercial subsidies amounting to 170,000 francs. These efforts helped Grenoble to be chosen as the host city for the X Olympic Winter Games during the IOC General Session in Innsbruck, Austria, on January 28, 1964. After three ballots, Grenoble finally won the bid over Calgary, Canada, by a vote of 27–24. There was some suggestion that the IOC selected Grenoble for the Winter Games as a consolation prize to France, since Lyon had been unsuccessful in its bid to host the 1968 Summer Olympic Games. Just two days before Grenoble was selected to host the Games, the life of the Winter Games had been given a temporary reprieve at an IOC Executive Committee meeting in Innsbruck. The IOC decided it would commit itself to the Winter Games until the close of the 1972 Games. Once again, the IOC stressed that the national Olympic committees (NOCs) had to enforce the amateur code more stringently.

Grenoble marked the beginning of a new era in Olympic Winter Games. The Games had become a huge media event and hosting them meant extensive capital investments. It is difficult to determine the actual cost of any Olympic Games because of the immense capital involved and the many indirect expenses that the hosting region incurs. The official report from Grenoble indicates a total expenditure of $240 million, or just over one billion French francs. *Gigantism* was the descriptive word used by Brundage and other critics when referring to the phenomenon that appeared to be enveloping these Games.

Not long after Grenoble won the bid, issues that would become synonymous with the Games began to surface. In 1965, the IOC began questioning the host committee's decision to hold events at six distant venues throughout the Dauphine region. Only the skating events (speed and figure) and ice hockey events would be held in Grenoble itself. The other events were scheduled for Autrans (cross-country skiing), St. Nizer (90-meter ski jumping), Villard de Lans (luge), Chamrousse (Alpine skiing) and Alpe D'Huex (bobsled). The long distances between venues forced the organizers to plan for three separate Olympic Villages. The main village was in Grenoble, and the other two villages were in Chamrousse and Autran. Early on, the IOC was concerned that this arrangement would be detrimental to the spirit of the Games. At the end of the Games, most observers maintained that a single athletes' village is most desirable and most in keeping with the intended experience of the Olympic Games. The Grenoble organizing committee justified the three separate Olympic Villages by explaining that it was necessary to accommodate the technological advances that were becoming part of the Games. Critics claimed that the strategy was really intended to accommodate the technology of television. The organizing committee recouped $2 million from the sale of television rights, a significant increase over the $936,667 that the Innsbruck organizers received in 1964. According to the director of technical services for the Organizing Committee, Jean-Paul Courant, the number of athletes did not increase from the previous games in Innsbruck, but the number of press representatives increased at a "rate which can almost be described as disturbing" (Courant, "Tenth Winter Olympic Games," *IOC Academy Proceedings*, 1969). Compromising the athletes' experience at the Olympic Games in favor of creating larger and more spectacular media events has, of course, become an ongoing theme for Olympic Games organizers.

Not only were there concerns about the athletes' village, but the selection of the competition venues was also severely criticized. The bobsled and luge tracks were the most controversial. The installations were extremely expensive and received too much direct sunlight, which continually melted the ice and made them unsuitable for racing except in the very early morning. The schedules for bobsled and luge competitions were continually altered, and in one instance the number of runs used to determine the championship had to be reduced because of deteriorating track conditions.

The logistical and economic feasibility of hosting bobsled and luge events at the Olympic Winter Games has become persistent theme for the IOC and host organizing committees. Costs, environmental damage, and the esoteric nature of the sport are issues that contribute to this ongoing debate. The exclusivity of participation in these sports is often used to criticize the Olympic Winter Games within the context of a truly universal sport movement. There may be some truth to the argument that the Winter Games are simply an event for the wealthy nations of the Northern Hemisphere.

The Grenoble Games held a political significance for France that brought national government personalities into the picture. With the competition sites at distant corners of the Dauphine region, safe and efficient travel between venues was an important consideration. Schemes for road development became the primary responsibility of the national government. Eventually, a national government committee headed by Prime Minister Georges Pompidou was established. Consequently, President Charles de Gaulle and Prime Minister Pompidou projected prominent images of French nationalism during the Games. With de Gaulle, the symbol of French nationalism, and Brundage, the staunch symbol of Olympism, both vying for a platform in Grenoble, it is surprising that the athletes received any media attention.

There is evidence from a 1965 IOC Executive Committee meeting that French government interference with the French NOC and the Grenoble Organizing Committee was exceeding the IOC's level of tolerance. While Brundage was openly critical, the French became defensive. In the official report of the Games, Count Jean de Beaumont, an IOC member in France and president of France's NOC, offered a lengthy defense of the French government's role in the Games. The grateful recognition offered by Beaumont stands in defiant contrast to Brundage's report. This dispute evidently stemmed from an earlier disagreement, with Cold War overtones, between Brundage and the Soviet representative on the IOC, Konstantin Andrianov, over government involvement in the staging of Olympic Games.

A Cold War issue of much greater significance involved the recognition of an independent team from East Germany. The IOC had already recognized the NOC of East Germany (GDR). At this time, the North Atlantic Treaty Organization (NATO) had blocked East German delegations from travelling to NATO countries by forcing its members to deny them entrance visas. The NATO initiative was a protest against the international travel restrictions that the GDR imposed on its private citizens, seen as a basic human-rights violation. As a NATO member, France was obligated to uphold the organization's policy. While the IOC was prepared to recognize a separate team from East Germany, the French government was in a position to bar the East German Olympic delegation from entering the country. The question of their participation was answered, however, in 1967, when the president of the Grenoble Organizing Committee, Albert Michallon, received confirmation from Prime Minister Georges Pompidou that the French government would take no action to block the entrance into France of the East German Olympic team. Consequently, the Olympic Winter Games in Grenoble saw the beginning of a new era in international sport. Although the East German performances in Grenoble were unremarkable, their presence made an impact. Ironically, the East Germans' debut was marred by a scandal in the women's luge event. After the East German women had recorded three of the four fastest times in the women's single event, they were disqualified when it was revealed that they had heated the runners of their sleds.

While South African participation in the Olympic Winter Games in Grenoble was not an issue, the debate over their reinstatement into the Olympic Movement was raised at the IOC General Session held on February 1–5, 1968, just before the Games. Beginning in 1961, the South African issue had become a permanent agenda item at IOC meetings. Once the IOC members had voted (by mail ballot for those who could not attend the Grenoble session), the announcement came that South Africa had been accepted back into the Olympic family. The results of the vote were 37 in favor of reinstatement, 28 opposed, and 1 abstention. The possibility of a South African team's participating in the summer Olympic Games in Mexico City was the obvious consequence, but the accompanying significance of this message was repugnant to many members of the international sport community. Without hesitation, countries threatened to boycott the Summer Games. In the *New York Times*, stories of athletes boycotting indoor track-and-field meets in New York City nearly eclipsed the final coverage of competition from Grenoble. With the African nations encouraging a broad Soviet-led boycott of the Mexico City Games, the IOC eventually reconsidered its decision and backed down from its proposal to readmit South Africa.

Of all the peripheral events and issues surrounding the Olympic Winter Games in Grenoble, Avery Brundage's crusade against commercialism was the most memorable and one of the most embarrassing for the Olympic movement. Although he was critical of the commercialism that pervaded every winter sport, his primary target was Alpine skiing. Brundage's attack on the ski industry and individual athletes was truly exceptional, even by his standards. By allowing their images to be used in advertising and receiving under-the-table payments, the Alpine skiers, in Brundage's opinion, had gone too far. Brundage refused to participate in any of the medal ceremonies for the Alpine events. A year after the Games, he spearheaded an unsuccessful campaign to have the medals won by these skiers returned to the IOC.

The most notable effort to rid the Games of rampant advertising was a proposal to have the trademarks removed from the athletes' skis. The IOC negotiated with the Fédération Internationale de Ski (FIS) prior to the games to assure Brundage that this would in fact occur. At the last minute, the FIS informed the IOC that this was not a feasible solution. The skiers, coaches, and manufacturers protested that tampering with their cosmetics would alter the balance of the skis and create technical difficulties for the skiers. As an alternative solution, the FIS proposed that skis be confiscated from the athlete immediately after their descent. This would prevent them from displaying trademarks while posing for photographs. The IOC seemed reasonably content with this solution until a newspaper photograph showed Jean-Claude Killy, an outstanding French skier, accepting congratulations from a friend and prominently, but probably accidentally, exposing his Rossignol ski gloves to the photographer. A significant personality at the center of the FIS/IOC negotiations was the Austrian Marc Hodler, who was both the IOC treasurer and the president of FIS. In its history, the IOC has never lacked for examples of conflicting interests within its membership.

When the effort to rid the Olympics of commercialism was juxtaposed with the IOC decision to welcome South Africa back into the Olympic Movement, the media recognized the opportunity to scrutinize the values of the movement and, in particular, those of Avery Brundage. When the IOC made its official statement about South Africa's reinstatement on February 17, the press had already covered Brundage's outspoken criticism over the Games' commercialism. The media characterizations were most unflattering, particularly in France. Following the IOC vote to reinstate South Africa into the Olympic Movement, for example, a French journalist working for *Le Monde* described the IOC and Brundage as racist. Indeed, when the Olympic flame was extinguished on February 18, it would have been difficult to find many supporters for Brundage outside of the IOC membership. The media played a key role in questioning the social and cultural priorities established by the IOC.

Placing the political and administrative controversies aside, two true sport stories emerged from the 1968 Olympic Winter Games in Grenoble. Rightly so, these are the stories of athletes who, despite being targeted in the IOC's crusade against commercialization, established themselves as icons in Olympic history by virtue of their athletic talents. The dashing Alpine star from France, Jean-Claude Killy, and the elegant figure skating ingenue from the United States, Peggy Fleming, are still synonymous with the athletic excellence that is often overlooked in analytical Olympic history. Killy carried France's expectations for Olympic greatness long before the Games were officially opened. He had been the leading international skier the year preceding the Olympic Games. A lengthy profile of Killy in the *New York Times Magazine* speculated that he could win everything. By the end of the Games, the forecasts were proven correct, and Killy duplicated the 1956 feat of Austria's Toni Sailer by winning gold medals in all three Alpine events. While it is important to note that Killy's medals did not all come without controversy themselves, the combination of circumstances, good and bad, that surrounded his victory at these Games is what has made an indelible mark in the Olympic history books.

To list and discuss the many events that have contributed to the Killy legend would take an entire book. Regardless, it is worth mentioning one matter that is illustrative of the discussion on commercialization. Brundage's threats to purge the Olympic Games of Alpine skiing and its growing commercialism were likely a factor that ultimately contributed positively to Killy's image at the Games. Brundage naturally implicated Killy in the issue of commercialism. The direct and public criticism for accepting endorsements from ski manufacturers (whether true or false) really became trivialized or regarded as just another adversity for Killy, the athlete, to conquer in his quest for Olympic triple gold. Clearly, the Olympic audience was far less critical of the athletes' forays into the marketplace of sport than the IOC.

How ironic that Killy, the demon of commercialism in Brundage's eyes, has sustained his prominent role in the international Olympic Movement even after a period of some thirty-five years. Jean-Claude Killy retired from amateur skiing shortly after the Grenoble Olympics but remained a prominent sport figure in

France. As a very important footnote to the X Olympic Winter Games, Killy became the co-president of the Olympic Winter Games Organizing Committee in Albertville, France, for the 1992 Games and later a member of the IOC itself. In two of the three Winter Games hosted by France, Killy has been the most prominent and popular French personality involved. In the greater scope of Olympic history, Killy is not remembered as an athletic hero embroiled in controversy, but rather for his athletic accomplishments at the 1968 Olympic Winter Games in Grenoble and his long involvement with the Olympic Movement.

Peggy Fleming's fame as an elegant sport heroine has also lasted to the present day. She demonstrated that her presence in the Olympic movement was more than just a sparkle. As the world figure-skating champion of 1967, she was clearly favored to win the gold medal at Grenoble, which she did with relative ease. Despite the lack of suspense in the competition itself, Fleming's personality captured the media's affection. The Fleming image fit into the stereotype of the Olympic Games ice princess that probably began in earnest with Barbara Ann Scott in 1948 and persists even today, in large part because of the attractiveness of the sport on television. Although the Grenoble Games took place in the era of racial and gender equal-rights awareness, it is clear that women's issues had not infiltrated the thinking of the sports press. While the coverage on Fleming rarely described her athletic attributes, her personality and the nature of figure skating reinforced the media's ideal of a female Olympian. According to the American press, the future of women's events in the Olympic Games looked promising because there were also some "good lookers" among the female cross-country skiers. The *New York Times* described how female Nordic skiers in Grenoble were slimmer and prettier than the "burly and buxom" athletes from the Innsbruck Games (*New York Times*, February 6, 1968). The stereotyping of Killy and Fleming, the dashing Alpine playboy and the demure skating princess, are parallel media images that seem to be repeated at each Olympic Winter Games.

The Austrian equivalent of Jean Claude Killy, Karl Schranz, deserves a brief mention in this history of the Grenoble Olympic Winter Games. For Schranz, the 1968 Games may be considered the beginning of an Olympic nightmare for Austria. Many enthusiastic fans of Alpine skiing during this era felt that Schranz was unjustly disqualified after marking the fastest time in a rerun during the slalom event. The dispute gave Killy his third gold medal of the Games. This was only the beginning of Schranz's frustration with the Olympic movement. The clear favorite for gold medals in 1972 Games in Sapporo, Schranz was singled out by the IOC for alleged violations of amateurism and banned from amateur competition. This was the climax of Brundage's crusade against commercialism.

In conclusion, controversy dominated the Olympic Winter Games of Grenoble. As host, the Grenoble Organizing Committee was in a difficult position because of the inevitable problems associated with hosting an event of an unprecedented scale. At the same time, the IOC was attempting to resolve problems that confronted the future of the Olympic Movement and looked to the Games in Grenoble for ways in which its position could be supported. It is difficult to say if these Games represent a turning point in the history of the Winter Olympics, but certainly specific issues came to the forefront in Grenoble. This is evident by the establishment of an IOC commission to examine and report on the future of the Olympic Winter Games. As the Games in Grenoble closed, the IOC, and specifically Brundage, were predicting a showdown between the Olympic Movement and the forces of nationalism and commercialism at the Sapporo Games in 1972. The Karl Schranz episode is evidence that this showdown did, in fact, materialize.

BIBLIOGRAPHICAL ESSAY

Regrettably, there are few scholarly books that examine the Olympic Winter Games from a true social or cultural perspective. While there are some excellent academic books that study the modern Olympic Games and the associated Olympic Movement, the Winter Games phenomenon is usually eclipsed in the overall analysis.

The preceding essay relies most extensively on the official report, *Xes Jeux Olympiques d'hiver: Grenoble 1968* (Grenoble, 1968), published by the organizing committee in Grenoble. This two-volume lists the results, describes the investments and venues in the Dauphine region, lists expenses, explains the administrative structures needed to host the games, and includes reports from key individuals. Prior to the Games, the organizing committee also published a series of sophisticated bulletins under different titles. See, for example, *Xes jeux Olympiques d'Hiver: Rapporte Preliminaire* (Grenoble, 1967) and *Grenoble—Dauphine—Ville Olympique - France* (Grenoble, 1965). These hardcover volumes resemble promotional books for the Dauphine region, although occasionally there is some interesting information on the committees and the construction details of the venues. Neither the official report nor the bulletins are easily obtainable.

National Olympic committee reports may be useful. The United States report is Arthur G. Lentz and Frederick Fliegner, eds., *1968 United States Olympic Book* (Lausanne, 1968). For Great Britain, consult Bob Phillips, ed., *The Official Report of the Olympic Games, 1968: XIXth Olympiad, Mexico City, October 12–27: Xth Winter Olympics, Grenoble, February 6–18* (London, 1969). E. H. Radford and Francis J. Shaughnessy edited Canada's report, *Canada Competes at the Olympic Games 1968* (Montreal, 1969), while the West German version is Walter Umminger, ed., *Die X. Olympischen Winterspiele, Grenoble 1968. Das Offizielle Standardwerke des Nationalen Olympischen Komitees* (Dortmund, Germany, 1968). Competing in their first Winter Games, the East Germans published *X. Olympische Winterspiele Grenoble 1968* (Berlin, 1968) and *Olympiamannschaft der DDR, Olympische Winterspiele 1968* (Dresden, 1968) to chronicle their effort. It appears that during this era, the team leaders who wrote the final Olympic Games reports for the NOCs were given some liberty to interpret and describe the team's experience. One is not likely to find recent NOC reports displaying the same candor as those from the 1968 Games. Contemporary NOC reports are generally much more formal and written in a guarded, diplomatic tone.

The Avery Brundage Collection, at the University of Illinois Archives, is a valuable source for researchers in virtually any area of Olympic studies, including the 1968 Winter Olympics. In these archives, one finds personal correspondence between Brundage, IOC members, leaders of the International Sport Federations, national Olympic committees, and Olympic Games organizing committees. Information pertaining to the Grenoble Olympics Games is located in several sections of the collection, but there is a useful printed guide. There are microfilm copies of the Brundage papers in other libraries and archives around the world.

Newspapers are excellent primary sources for analyzing the media's interpretation of the Olympic Winter Games in Grenoble. A cursory survey of the *New York Times*, the *Times* (London), and *Le Monde* (Paris) provides a valuable glimpse at the media's response to the athletes, the competitions, and the persistent issues of commercialism and nationalism.

Wolf Lyberg's translation and annotations of minutes from the IOC's General Sessions and Executive Committee meetings are an important source for tracing the history of IOC debates regarding South Africa, commercialism, and East Germany's entrance into the Olympic movement. These translations also describe the IOC's monitoring of the preparations and progress of Olympic Games organizing committees. Copies of these minutes are available at the IOC archives in Lausanne and at the Centre for Olympic Studies at the University of Western Ontario, London, Ontario, Canada.

Finally, a journalistic account, in the book *Olympic Report—1968* by James Cootes (Bristol, England, 1968), provides an interesting and thorough account of the competitions in Grenoble and Mexico City. Although there is a British bias, this book is an objective and concise description of the X Olympic Winter Games. Another firsthand account is L. R. Hesler, *The Winter Olympics: Scrapbook of the 1968 Winter Olympic Games* (Knoxville, Tenn., 1968).

SAPPORO 1972

Junko Tahara

ELEVENTH OLYMPIC WINTER GAMES

The history of the Winter Olympic Games in Sapporo can be traced back to the fifth Olympic Winter Games in 1940. According to the then Olympic Charter, the host country of the Summer Games also had the right to hold the Winter Games in the same year if the country could guarantee to organize all sports of the Winter Games successfully. Japan was preparing to hold the 5th Winter Games in Sapporo, where skiing was very popular, in addition to the 12th Olympic Games in Tokyo in 1940.

Though Japan considered it an honor to hold the first Olympic Games in Asia, the tragedy of war with China attacked the dream of the Olympics. To make matters worse, the IOC had opposed the International Ski Federation (FIS) in the issue of the amateur eligibility of ski instructors. In the IOC session in Cairo in March 1938, the IOC resolved that no skiing events would be held in the V Winter Olympic Games in 1940. The V Winter Games was awarded to Sapporo, but four months later, in July 1938, Japan regrettably relinquished hosting the Games in 1940 by both Tokyo and Sapporo, because there was little prospect of an end to the war.

Sapporo stood as a candidate to be the host city of the 10th Olympic Winter Games in 1968, but gathered only six votes, making it fourth among six cities in the voting results of the IOC session in Innsbruck in 1964. The people in Sapporo, however, did not lose their enthusiasm for the Olympics. Sixty-two organizations, including the federation of physical education in Sapporo, sent a succession of petitions for re-candidacy to host the Winter Olympic Games to the mayor of Sapporo and the municipal assembly. In accordance with their zeal, Sapporo launched activities for bidding to host the Winter Olympic Games again.

The ballot for the site of the 1972 Winter Olympic Games was held at the IOC session in Rome in April 1966. The IOC President, Avery Brundage, mentioned that IFs (International Federations) had made a secret vote on the candidates of the

1972 Winter Games but he had told the IFs that the IOC strictly reserved the right to choose Games organizers by itself. Marc Hodler, who was also the president of FIS, spoke of a possibility to divide the Games but was told that the IFs considered Sapporo to be the best of the sites.

Banff, Canada, one of the leading proposed sites, was strongly opposed by the Canadian Wildlife Association (CWA), as well as by activist bird-watchers because they feared that the invasion of the Lake Louise area near Banff would be a disruptive influence on the wildlife. Many IOC members had received vehement protest letters from environmentalists. The IOC could not ignore these voices and the Banff candidature was especially discussed before the vote. It was Brundage's opinion that the IOC in principle should not be the cause of controversy within a country. The result of the ballot was that Sapporo won 32 votes in the first ballot, Banff won 16, and Lahti (Finland) and Salt Lake City (United States) won 7.

Sapporo was uniquely situated for hosting the Winter Games. The city had the largest population (one million) of any Winter Games host city. The capital city of Hokkaido, located on the northernmost main island of Japan (longitude 143°12′ east and latitude 43°4′ north) was ideal for outdoor sports. The average temperature in February is –4.55°C, the daytime average is –2°C, and the humidity is around 74 percent. To the foreign journalists' surprise, the altitudes of the mountains at the sites for the Games were very low. The sites for the Alpine events in Europe usually had altitudes of 2,000 m to 3,000 m, but Mt. Eniwa was the highest in Sapporo at only 1,320 m. This meant athletes were hardly affected by the altitude. New and harmonious facilities, including ultramodern arenas, press centers, living quarters, and other Olympic structures, were arranged within 40 km of the city center and connected by a new rapid transit system.

The controversy on amateurism has continued from the beginning of Olympic history. However, Karl Schranz, an Austrian skiing star, was one of the most memorable names because he characterized the issue of amateurism. Three days before the Opening Ceremony, the IOC decided to exclude Schranz, a favorite in the men's Alpine events, from the competition. Leading skiers were compensated by manufacturers in return for exposure of their products in international competition. It was rumored that Schranz had earned upward of $60,000 a year. Brundage was an autocratic protector of amateurism. He was determined to put an end to "shamateurism" and commercialization by skiers when he arrived in Sapporo. Brundage had a blacklist of 40 names of skiers, but Schranz was the only skier to be punished by exclusion. Schranz's name and photograph had been used in commercial advertising, which made him the most serious offender. Schranz said, when asked about Brundage's threats, "This thing of amateur purity is something that dates back to the nineteenth century when amateur sportsmen were regarded as gentlemen and everyone else was an outcast. The Olympics should be a competition of skill and strength and speed— and no more." Karl Heinz Klee, president of the Austrian Ski Federation, threatened to withdraw his team from the Olympic Games. However, at Schranz's urging, the other Austrians remained in the competition.

Another controversy occurred in ice hockey. In the 1968 Olympics, Canada was a bronze medallist and a six-time winner of the competition. This time, however, Canada refused to send its team to Sapporo. In 1970 the Canadians had withdrawn from international amateur tournaments in a dispute about the use of professional players. They considered the USSR to be of dubious amateur status, and they thought it was unfair to compete against the USSR without playing professionals.

Still another political incident happened between North Korean and Japan. The organizing committee wanted to use both English and Japanese designations for each delegation in order to make it easier for Japanese people to understand them. However, the North Koreans were outraged and refused to enter the Olympic Village unless only the English name for North Korea was used. There was no acceptable Japanese translation for this nation, because North Korea was not recognized diplomatically by Japan. Japanese officials imposed an English-only rule for designnations of all official countries.

The 11th Olympic Winter Games in Sapporo opened on February 3 and closed on February 13, 1972. The prospective participants during the preparatory stage were 2,300 athletes and officials from 42 countries. The actual participants were 1,128 athletes (911 males and 217 females) and 527 officials from 35 countries. It is said that the causes of the shortfall in expectations were the high traveling expenses to Sapporo and a strong yen and a weak dollar, which had been caused by the introduction of a floating exchange rate system.

The athletes competed in 6 sports (biathlon, bobsled, skating, ice hockey, luge, and skiing) and 35 events, which was the same number as in the previous Games in Grenoble in 1968. The programs were carried out as scheduled in good weather.

The most successful athletes were Ard Schenk (the Netherlands) in men's speed skating and Galina Kulakova (USSR) in women's Nordic skiing, who won three gold medals. The absence of Schranz of Austria may have influenced the order of medalists of Alpine skiing. Francisco Fernandez-Ochoa won the slalom for Spain's first-ever Winter Olympics gold medal, and Marie-Thérèse Nadig (Switzerland), a 17-year-old, won two gold medals.

The highlight of the Olympic Games for the Japanese spectators was the 70-meter ski jumping. Three of the Japanese ski jumpers, led by Yukio Kasaya, swept the medals and three Japanese national flags fluttered in the blue sky. In the 90-meter ski jumping, Wojciech Fortuna won Poland's first gold medal. In the Nordic combined, the gold medal went to Ulrich Wehling of East Germany.

Controversy on scoring the figure skating occurred in Sapporo. The compulsory figures and the free skating program each counted 50 percent toward the total score. The men's figure skating champion was Ondrej Nepela (Czechoslovakia) and the women's champion was Beatrix Schuba (Austria). Janet Lynn (United States) performed like a pixie dancing on ice, and captivated the people with her technical skill and grace. She placed first in the freestyle despite a fall, but ended up with the bronze medal.

For the first time in Olympic history, the progress of the Games was telecast by satellite over a worldwide hookup with color pictures every day. Sapporo was known as the Television Olympics. Data communications equipment transacted all sorts of records rapidly. The original research by Japanese technical experts, who measured a ski jump with an electrical device accurately and instantaneously, was highlighted. Though the measuring instrument was not introduced officially in these Games, there was hope for its practical use in the near future.

A total of 13 cultural events were held over three weeks in connection with the Olympic Games. In addition to the Snow Festival and folk entertainment, various programs, such as the traditional arts of Japan, and the Munich Philharmonic Orchestra were featured.

In order to provide the people in Sapporo and Japan with a better understanding of the Olympics, the organizing committee, government, administrative bodies of

Hokkaido and Sapporo, and related organizations conducted various Olympic activities in conjunction with one another. They endeavored to advertise the Sapporo Winter Olympic Games at every opportunity, in particular at the Snow Festival, at a commemorative event to celebrate the decision to have Sapporo host the Olympics, commemorative events every 100 days before the Games, commemorative events of Olympic Days, the national sport festivals, school festivals, various sporting meetings, and exhibitions of tourism and the products of Hokkaido. Furthermore, 22 kinds of printed matter, including leaflets and brochures in English and French, were published. Other activities included a public competition to find slogans, the production of a film, a photographic contest for international goodwill, lecture meetings, a special showing of Olympic films, and tours of the Olympic sites.

There were two stages in the promotion of the Sapporo Winter Olympic Games. In the first stage the media reported on the plans for preparations and the construction of the stadium and related facilities for the Olympics, giving priority to asking people for their understanding and cooperation. In the second stage the media emphasized progress made in the preparations, knowledge of the Olympics, ways in which citizens could cooperate, and knowledge of public morality. For children, the Olympic Games of Sapporo Children Societies (Sapporo no Kodomokai Olympic Taikai) was held as part of the commemorative events taking place 500 days before the Games. On this occasion, children's societies of the city of Sapporo met together and a program connected with the Olympic Games was held.

The realization and success of the Sapporo Olympics could not have occurred without citizens' enthusiasm and activities. As mentioned above, after the failure of the bid for the 10th Olympic Winter Games, nongovernmental agencies were the prime movers for re-candidacy. On March 3, 1967, after the successful bid for the 11th Winter Games, the Sapporo Olympics Cooperative Association (Sapporo Olympic Kyoryoku Kai) was established. This body comprised representatives of local economic organizations, organizations of sport and physical education, women's associations, and all neighborhood associations. Furthermore, in order to draw the varying activities of each group together, the Sapporo Olympics Citizens' Movement Promotion Liaison Council (Sapporo Olympic Shimin Undo Suisin Renraku Kaigi) was established on December 8, 1970, and it developed concrete action. The objectives of the movement were 1) to understand the Olympics, 2) to welcome people from all over the world kindly, 3) to have a clean environment in the winter, 4) to do winter sport, and 5) to improve morality in commerce.

In schools, an Olympic Education was developed actively as a central point for international understanding, making good use of the opportunity to host the Olympic Games. Guidebooks and material for the Olympic Education were distributed to every school and used in social studies, physical education, foreign language (English), morality, special activities, and school events. Students of primary and secondary schools within the Sapporo city limits were invited to enter an essay contest on the theme of Winter Olympics, and 726 essays from 32 schools were entered in the contest. In the Olympic Games in Sapporo, 2,429 students of primary and secondary schools participated in the Opening and Closing Ceremonies and in the torch relay. There were 34,840 spectators from 189 schools who enjoyed the Games in the many Olympic venues.

The Olympic Games was an epoch-making international event for Sapporo and contributed greatly to the economics of Sapporo city and also to Hokkaido. The total amount of direct and indirect expenditure was estimated at $10.5 billion. The expenditure breaks down into approximately $1 billion for investment, approximately $43 million for provisional expenditure of business expenses for preparations and operating expenses for the Games by the government and public organizations, and approximately $4.8 million for the strengthening of athletes and events. The breakdown of investment is approximately $48 million (a little less than 5 percent) for the construction of sport facilities, $467 million (46 percent) for roadworks, approximately $217 million (21 percent) for providing transportation such as underground railways, and $190 million (19 percent) for providing the Olympic Village, Olympic Hall, and hotels among other facilities. The $1 billion of investment had a considerable ripple effect as it doubled to a $2 billion profit.

During the Games, many athletes, officials, and spectators traveled to the sport facilities and tourist attractions of Sapporo. The total number of people involved in the Games was estimated at approximately 1,270,000 during the Games and the amount of consumption by them was estimated at approximately $157 million.

The population of Sapporo city was approximately 760,000 in May 1965 when Sapporo was a candidate. It increased to 1,057,000 in May 1972 after the Olympic Games, becoming the seventh largest city in Japan. The cause of the increase in population was considered to be the employment opportunities and economic activities associated with the Olympic Games. Sapporo increased its population through the redevelopment of the urban environment from hosting the Games.

Sapporo was awarded the Olympic Cup in the IOC Session on August 24, 1972, just before the Olympic Games in Munich. Sapporo was the fourth winner of this prize as a host city of the Olympic Games, following Oslo (Norway) for the 6th Winter Games in 1952, Helsinki (Finland) for the Games of 16th Olympiad in 1952, and Tokyo (Japan) for the Games of 18th Olympiad in 1964. Hosting the Olympic Games in 1972 aligned Sapporo with a sister city, Munich, which held the Summer Games in the same year. Both cities were connected by the Olympics and vowed to promote friendship between its citizens, develop intercity relationships, and contribute to world peace and goodwill.

It is said that the redevelopment of Sapporo city was brought forward as many as 10 to 15 years by investments in relation to the Olympic Games. The Sapporo Winter Olympic Games brought immeasurable benefits, both moral and material, for the people of Sapporo and Hokkaido, and formed the basis for an improvement in their living conditions and also in the development of the city. The greatest fruits of the Games, were not only the organizing committee and administrative bodies, but also the citizens who were involved in the Olympic Movement to successfully develop and stage the Olympic Games. The population of Sapporo welcomed people from all over the world with the word *Yokoso*, meaning welcome. A warm friendship across international borders sprang up between them in the sport facilities, the Olympic Village, and on the streets. The Olympic Games, a symbol of peace, was finally in Sapporo 32 years after its first bid in 1940.

BIBLIOGRAPHICAL ESSAY

The Sapporo Winter Sports Museum, located at the site of Okurayama Ski Jump for the Sapporo Olympics, opened in 2000 and replaced the old Sapporo Winter Sports Museum in Nakajima Park in Sapporo. This museum houses a collection of much memorabilia, artifacts, documents, and literature on the XI Olympic Winter Games in Sapporo 1972.

The Prince Chichibu Memorial Sports Museum and the Prince Chichibu Memorial Sports Library, located at the site of the National Stadium for the 1964 Tokyo Olympics in Tokyo, houses approximately 1,800 items of memorabilia, artifacts, documentary records, and literature on the Sapporo Olympics of 1972. It is the only museum in Japan that shows various sport exhibits at one site and includes the history of sports in Japan and the Olympic Games.

The Avery Brundage Collection contains a variety of organizing committee documents, clippings, and a cassette recording related to the Games that is on microfilm and housed in several locations, including at the University of Illinois at Urbana-Champaign, the Centre for Olympic Studies at the University of Western Ontario, and the Library of the University of Queensland, Brisbane in Australia.

The Japanese Olympic Organizing Committee published in French, English, and Japanese the following: *The 11th Olympic Winter Games: Sapporo 1972. Official Report* (Sapporo, Japan, 1972); *Sapporo Olympic Winter Games. Official Programme* (Sapporo, Japan, 1972); *Program for the Opening Ceremony* (Sapporo, Japan, 1972); *Program for the Closing Ceremony* (Sapporo, Japan, 1972); and *Preparations for XI Olympic Winter Games, Sapporo 1972* (Sapporo, Japan, 1971). The organizing committee also published, in a variety of languages, guidebooks, press guides, and an edition of sport regulations.

Various participating nations published their own official reports: Austrian Olympic Committee, *München 72—Sapporo 72. Das offizielle Werk des Österreichischen Olympischen Komitees* (n.p., 1972); British Olympic Association, *The Official Report of the Olympic Games, 1972: XXth Olympiad, Munich, August 26–September 11: XIth Winter Olympics, Sapporo, February 3–13* (London, 1973); and Doug Gardner, ed., *The British Olympic Association Official Report of the Olympic Games 1972, XXth Olympiad Munich, August 26–September 11, XIth Winter Olympics Sapporo, February 3–13* (London, 1972); the Sport Canada Directorate—Department of National Health and Welfare in cooperation with the Canadian Olympic Association, *The XI Olympic Winter Games Sapporo, Japan, February 3–13, 1972* (n.p., 1972); *Canada at the XI Olympic Winter Games, Sapporo, Japan, February 3–13,1972* (Ottawa, 1972); Canadian Olympic Association, *Canada at the Olympics Sapporo/Munich 1972* (Montreal, 1972); Czechoslovak Olympic Committee, *Czechoslovak Sportsmen at the 11th Olympic Winter Games at Sapporo 1972* (Prague, 1971); Federal Republic of Germany Olympic Committee, *Die Spiele der XX Olympiade Winterspiele Sapporo 1972, das Offizielle Standardwerk des Nationalen Olympischen Komitees für Deutschland* (Freiburg, Germany, 1972); and *Die Olympiamannschaft der Bundesrepublik Deutschland. Sapporo 1972* (Düsseldorf, 1972); German Democratic Republic, *XI. Olympische Winterspiele Sapporo 1972* (Berlin, 1972); Swiss Olympic Committee, *Sapporo/München 1972. Rapports sur la participation Suisse aux jeux de la 20e Olympiade* (Lausanne, 1972); United States Olympic Committee, *United States Olympic Winter Sports Teams, XIth Olympic Winter Games: February 3–13, 1972, Sapporo, Japan* (n.p., 1972); and C. Robert Paul and Frederick Fliegner, eds., *1972 United States Olympic Book* (Lausanne, 1972).

The U.S. Olympic Committee published an excellent book series on the Olympics: *The Olympic Century, The Official First Century History of the Modern*

Olympic Movement. In this series Volume 17 is useful: George G. Daniels, *The XIX Olympiad Mexico City 1968/Sapporo 1972.* (Los Angeles, 1996).

Two *Sports Illustrated* articles are William Johnson, "The Big Man Lowers His Olympic Boom" (January 17, 1972): 18–19, and William Johnson, "As Smooth as Silk in Sapporo" (February 22, 1971): 17–19.

The success of German, Austrian, and Swiss athletes at Sapporo produced several celebratory books in German. See Karl Erb, *Die goldenen Tage von Sapporo. Olympicshen Winterspiele 1972. Die Schweizer Erfolge* (Derendinger/Solothurn, West Germany, 1972); *Erwin Flieger, Sapporo 1972. Das Olympiawerk der Stiftung Deutsche Sporthilfe* (Zürich, 1972); Ferdi Huber and Armin Och, *Schweizer siegten in Sapporo. Dank an unsere Madaillen-Gewinner* (Zürich, 1972); and Kurt Lavall, *Die Sieger von Sapporo* (Düsseldorf, 1972).

INNSBRUCK 1976

John J. Kennedy, Jr., updated by Morgan Patrick

TWELFTH WINTER OLYMPIC GAMES

In 1972, International Olympic Committee (IOC) President Avery Brundage expressed his hope that "the Winter Olympics receive a decent burial in Denver." Brundage had long hated the Winter Games because of increasing pressure for professional participation, growing commercialism, and the lack of worldwide attraction to winter sports. His wish almost came true.

In May 1970, Denver, Colorado, was awarded the honor of hosting the 1976 Winter Olympic Games. The city had spent more than $750,000 since 1963 in order to get the Games. One of the reasons that the IOC awarded the Games to Denver was the organizers' promise that the cost of the festival would be around $14 million. The IOC was attracted to this proposition, since a low-cost Games had worked in Squaw Valley, California, in 1960. The organizers also claimed that 80 percent of the needed facilities were already in place, mainly due to the popularity of winter sports in the local area. Finally, the fact that the Winter Olympics in 1976 would coincide with the centennial of Colorado's statehood and the bicentennial of the founding of the United States made the event seem like a fitting celebration.

Vancouver, Canada, had also been campaigning for the Games, but two factors hampered its chances. First, the organizers estimated it would cost $65 million to stage the Games. Second, the 1976 Summer Games had already been awarded to Montreal, and the IOC was reluctant to award the same country both Olympics. Sion, Switzerland, and Tampere, Finland, had also bid for the Games, but Denver remained the favorite and was selected.

However, after Denver had been selected, certain problems still remained. The organizers had been adept at wooing the IOC but not the voters of Colorado, who soon discovered that the estimated cost of the Games was based on faulty data. In addition, the organizing committee made other mistakes in its public relations, with the result that the awarding of the Games to Denver seemed more troublesome then blissful. The state's economic problems needed more attention and funding than a ten-day sports festival. Citizens were also concerned about the fragile environment of the nearby Rocky Mountains and the condition of the athletic facilities. All of this led voters to reject a $5 million appropriation to fund the Games in a referendum on November 7, 1972. With this defeat, Denver organizers could not continue to prepare for the Olympics, and the city forfeited its right to hold the Games.

By this time, the IOC had a new president, Michael Morris, Lord Killanin. Already burdened with a difficult task following the terrorist attack at 1972 Munich Olympics, Killanin remarked that Denver's rejection threatened to end the Winter Games permanently. In fact, Avery Brundage was so glad about the Denver debacle that he stated that he would have used the opportunity to terminate the Winter Olympics if he had still been in office. Killanin, on the other hand, did not share Brundage's viewpoint and stated that the Winter Olympics would continue despite the setback.

As a matter of fact, many other cities were very eager to bid for the Winter Games once it became clear that Denver would be unable to stage the event. The list of cities included Lake Placid, New York (site of the 1932 Games); Squaw Valley, California (site of the 1960 Games); Salt Lake City, Utah; St. Moritz, Switzerland (site of the 1928 and 1948 Games); Cortina d'Ampezzo (site of the 1956 Games) and Trentino, Italy; Chamonix and Grenoble, France (sites of the 1924 and 1968 Games, respectively); Oslo, Norway (site of the 1952 Games); and Innsbruck, Austria (site of the 1964 Games). Also, previous bid cities Vancouver, Canada; Sion, Switzerland; and Tampere, Finland, expressed interest.

Since so many of these cites had already hosted previous Winter Olympics, it appeared that the existing venues and other facilities would help keep costs down. This led Sion and Tampere to drop out due to lack of time to build facilities. Lake Placid was viewed as a favorite but the city depended on state and federal funding, and this made it an unattractive choice after Denver's withdrawal. Chamonix was also a favorite, but its bid failed to include the bobsled/luge events due to high cost of track construction.

The IOC met in Lausanne, Switzerland on February 4, 1973, and chose Innsbruck as the 1976 site. No announcement of either the vote or why Innsbruck was chosen was made. However, Killanin stated that the IOC was rethinking ways to select sites for the Winter Olympics, since few cities could stage such a large event and only one-fourth of the countries with national Olympic committees participated in the Winter Games. One improvement that did come out of the Denver withdrawal was a policy requiring all future Olympic host cites to post a surety bond and sign a contract guaranteeing that they would uphold their obligation to stage the Games.

In all likelihood, Innsbruck was chosen because of the efficiency of the 1964 Games, the available funds from Austrian skiing and tourism, and respect for Mayor Alois Lugger. Also, the IOC's relations with Austria had been chilly since national hero and skiing champion Karl Schranz had been disqualified from the 1972 Sapporo Games because Brundage thought he was too closely linked with professionalism. The awarding of the Games to Innsbruck was seen as a way to reestablish good relations.

One of the IOC's main concerns at the time was gigantism. Innsbruck spent only $148 million for the Games, since it was using many of the 1964 facilities. However, the 1968 Games in Grenoble had cost $250 million, while the 1972 Games in Sapporo had cost more than $1 billion. Meanwhile, the Summer Games scheduled for Montreal later that year were struggling with cost overruns, faulty planning, and labor difficulties. All of this led Killanin to warn ambitious cities to plan and budget carefully before bidding for the Olympics. Cutting costs and forcing cities to carry out their responsibilities as a host city for the Olympics were Killanin's solutions to the problem. Others felt that reducing the number of sports and events was the better solution to gigantism, but Killanin felt it would rob athletes of their dreams and take away some of the charm of the Olympics.

A more important issue was that of security. Innsbruck would be the first Games since the Munich terrorist massacre. Just six weeks before the Games, terrorists assaulted the Organization of Petroleum Exporting Countries (OPEC) headquarters in Vienna, resulting in three deaths and 80 persons taken hostage. International tensions ran very high. In fact, the Shah of Iran canceled plans to attend the Games even though an entire hotel in Igls (site of the bobsled and luge run) had been rented for him and his entourage. To counteract any threat, 5,000 police and specially trained soldiers were assigned to security duty. Although some were offended, the government declared that the highest measure of security demanded a visible presence and that therefore steel-helmeted police with machine guns would be a normal sight during the Games. Although the organizing committee never revealed how much was spent for security, one estimate was that it ran over 30 million Austrian schillings ($1.7 million), not including military personnel costs. In fact, the soldiers patrolled so diligently that photographers complained that they could not get good angles for their pictures.

At the Olympic Village, security measures were even more stringent. Photo-identification cards were needed for entry into the village, and 2-meter cyclone fencing with electronic sensors surrounded the entire complex. Armed police with dogs patrolled the grounds, which were illuminated by floodlights at night. The village housed 1,650 athletes and officials, segregated by sex. Security personnel outnumbered athletes two to one and seemed to diminish the charm of the festival. However, the Munich tragedy made the thwarting of any future attacks a top priority.

Austrian President Rudolf Kirchschlaeger received the 89-member Austrian team at the Baroque, a former royal palace. There they gave pledges of good sportsmanship while he urged them to compete fairly and to give their best.

As had been the case in 1964, there was a severe snow shortage by January 1976, forcing the organizers to implement what was called "Operation Snowlift." More than a thousand truckloads of snow were brought to the Tyrol from the Brenner Pass on the border with Italy. Also, Austrian army troops packed down the ski runs by hand. Fortunately, the weather turned favorable when a storm dropped 3 feet of fresh snow a week before the Opening Ceremony.

The Olympic Village opened January 27. The weather was agreeable, and the ski runs were deemed perfect after many record-breaking practice runs. On February 4, the Opening Ceremony was held at the Bergisol Stadium before a crowd of 60,000. Since Innsbruck was the first city to host two Winter Olympics, two flames were lit to mark the occasion. The first was lit by 1964 luge gold medalist Josef Feistmantl and the other by the 1964 women's downhill champion Christl Hass. Alpine skier Franz Klammer recited the athlete's oath. Policemen conducted random bag and pack searches throughout the ceremony. This Opening Ceremony was noted for being more muted rather than spectacular. Indeed, the entire Games was more of a low-key, human-scale festival instead of larger-than-life like previous Olympics. This was because Innsbruck had gone through the spectacle 12 years before. Traffic flowed smoothly most of the time, and seats were readily available for nearly all events. Altogether, the participants numbered 1,128 (900 men and 228 women), from 37 nations. The number of participating nations equaled the record set in 1968, but the total number of athletes was the lowest since 1964.

The most memorable image from the Games was Franz Klammer wildly racing down the mountain to win the Olympic downhill. This was a genuine triumph for the local spectators, the home team, and the entire Austrian winter tourism industry, and it also helped erase the disappointment of the Karl Schranz controversy of 1972. Not until the last event of the Games did an Austrian win another gold medal; this was Karl Schnabl's victory in the 90-meter ski jump. Ski coach Toni Sailer (winner of all three Alpine events in 1956) half-jokingly said that the police presence was there to guarantee his personal safety should Austria perform poorly.

The star of the ski slopes was Rosi Mittermaier, a 25-year-old German waitress. She won the downhill and the slalom but lost in the giant slalom by 0.12 seconds. The winner in this event was Kathy Kreiner of Canada. However, Mittermaier's performance was the best for a female Alpine skier in Olympic history. The other men's Alpine events were won by Peiro Gros of Italy (slalom) and Heini Hemmi of Switzerland (giant slalom).

In men's Nordic skiing, Soviets Nikolai Bazhukov and Sergei Savelyev won the 15- and 30-kilometer races, respectively, while Ivar Formo of Norway won the 50-kilometer race. East Germans Hans-Georg Aschenbach and Ulrich Wehling won the 70-meter ski jump and Nordic combined events, respectively, while Finland won the relay. In the women's events, Helena Takalo of Finland won the 5-kilometer race and Raisa Smetanina of the Soviet Union won the 10-kilometer race. The Soviet Union also won the women's relay. In addition, Soviet Nikolai Kruglov won the 20-kilometer individual biathlon event, and the biathlon relay was won by the Soviet Union as well. On a side note, American William Koch won a silver medal in the 30-kilometer race. No other American has won a Nordic skiing medal in the Winter Olympics since.

At the bobsled course in Igls, the East Germans swept all the gold medals in the bobsled and luge events. The West Germans took three silver and two bronze medals in bobsled and luge, while the Austrians won only one bronze medal, in the luge doubles.

The Soviet Union continued their domination of ice hockey, winning the tournament ahead of Czechoslovakia and West Germany. In figure skating, Irina Rodnina successfully defended her figure-skating pairs title, with her husband and new partner Aleksandr Zaitsev. Englishman John Curry and American Dorothy Hamill, both coached by Carlo Fassi, won the men's and women's singles titles. Hamill's victory also started a fashion trend in the United States for short wedge-style haircuts modeled on hers.

In speed skating, Soviets dominated: Yevgeny Kulikov won the men's 500-meters, Tatyana Averina the women's 1,000- and 3,000-meters, and Galina Stepanskaya the women's 1,500-meters. Norwegian winners included Jan Egil Storholt (1,500-meters) and Sten Stensen (5,000-meters), while Dutchman Piet Kleine took the 10,000-meters title and American Sheila Young the women's 500-meters. A total of seven Olympic records were set at Innsbruck during the speed-skating competition.

Two new events were added to the Olympic program during these Games. The men's 1000-meter speed-skating event was first contested, with American Peter Mueller, Norwegian Jorn Didriksen, and Soviet Valery Muratov taking first, second, and third, respectively. More noticeable was the addition of an ice-dancing competition to figure skating. Soviet pairs dominated the contest, with Lyudmila Pakhomova and Aleksandr Gorshkov winning and Irina Moiseyeva and Andrei Minenkov taking second. The American pair, Colleen O'Connor and James Millns, took third.

There were two positive drug tests during these Games. Soviet cross-country skier Galina Kulakova, who won four gold medals in Nordic events, lost her bronze medal in the women's 5-kilometer race after a positive test for ephedrine, a nonprescription decongestant that she had used merely to clear up a case of the sniffles. Czech hockey team doctor Otto Trefny was banned for life after giving his team captain, Frantisek Pospisil, codeine to combat the flu. Although the Czech team had to forfeit one of their victories, they still won the silver medal.

Another controversy involved Radio Free Europe (RFE) and Radio Liberty. RFE had first been accredited to cover the Olympic Games in 1952, but the IOC withdrew the authorization after Communist states alleged that RFE was broadcasting propaganda. These nations claimed that RFE's application had not been formally channeled through a national Olympic committee. The IOC would stand by its decision despite a protest from U.S. Secretary of State Henry Kissinger, who termed the IOC's action a "craven capitulation."

Two other problems arose during these Games. The first was an epidemic of influenza that spread throughout Innsbruck. In fact, this was the flu that Czech hockey captain Frantisek Pospisil had. Defending 1972 women's downhill champion Marie-Therese Nadig of Switzerland came down with this flu and had to withdraw from the event. The second was that fact that the medal ceremonies were held at the ice arena after the day's competitions. This was not well received by spectators, who preferred to see the ceremonies held at competition venues instead.

On a humorous note, Mayor Lugger took a ceremonial ride down the bobsled run at Igls, in the hope that it would become a tourist attraction. The mayor unbuttoned his trousers to ease his girth before getting into the sled. At the ride's end, he clambered out of the sled, waved to the crowd, and his pants fell to the ground.

The good weather continued throughout the festival, and even security became more relaxed. In the medal count, the Soviet Union won 27 medals, followed by East Germany (19), the United States (10), West Germany (10), and Norway (7). The home team of Austria won a total of 6 medals.

On February 15, the Closing Ceremony was held, again with tight security. Killanin, who was relieved that these Games had no major disturbances, gave thanks to the Austrian organizers and also addressed the issue of professional participation in the Olympics. He maintained that open competition was a possibility for the future but that it was still too soon for the Olympic Movement to embrace professional athletes.

After the Denver fiasco, Innsbruck was a blessing for the IOC and the Winter Olympics in general. Facing a possible demise of the Winter Games, Austria had hosted a peaceful, efficient Games right when they were badly needed for the

Olympic Movement. Innsbruck, a city of medieval walls, narrow alleys, and baroque churches, shined brightly among Olympic cities.

BIBLIOGRAPHICAL ESSAY

The principal official report on the 1976 Innsbruck Winter Games is *Endbericht/Rapport Final/Final Report/Zakdyuchitedbnuii Otchet. XII Olympische Winterspiele Innsbruck 1976* (Innsbruck, 1976), which is available in several languages. The U.S. Olympic Committee's Report is *1976 United States Olympic Book* (Munich, 1976), while the British Olympic Association's is *Olympics '76: British Olympic Association Official Report* (London, 1976). The Austrian official report is Thaddaus Podgorski ed., *Olympische Winterspiele Innsbruck '76* (Vienna, 1976).

Pictorial works of the 1976 Winter Olympics include *Innsbruck-Montreal 1976: The Pictorial Record of the 1976 Games* (Montreal, 1976); Graham Fulton-Smith, *Olympics 1976: Montreal, Innsbruck* (New York City, 1976); Kurt Bernegger, *Innsbruck '76-Tirol, Austria-4.2- 15.2 Olympische Winterspiele 1976* (Vienna, 1976); and Teddy Podgorski and Helga Zoglmann, *Olympische Winterspiele Innsbruck 1976: Daten, Fakten, Berichte* (Vienna, 1976). See also *Olympische Winterspiele '76 Innsbruck* (Salzburg, 1976), nominally written by Karl Schranz, the Austrian ski hero whom Avery Brundage banned from the 1972 Sapporo Games.

Denver's withdrawal as host city is admirably explained in Mark S. Foster's, "Coloradoans Reject the 1976 Winter Olympic Games: A Look Behind the Ballots," *Colorado Magazine*, 53:2 (Spring 1976), 163–86. Foster shows how the convergence of numerous political and social trends brought about the referendum's defeat.

An interesting inside perspective on the machinations surrounding the Denver abdication and the Innsbruck selection is found in Lord Killanin (Michael Morris), *My Olympic Years* (New York, 1983). Killanin's books illustrates the clublike atmosphere in which IOC dealings took place, although his version of the story should be taken with some skepticism. A more balanced look at the broader political context is available in Richard Espy, *The Politics of the Olympic Games* (Berkeley, Calif., 1979) and Allen Guttmann, *The Olympics: A History of the Modern Games* (Champaign, Ill., 2002).

For those wishing to know more about Austria and its political and social conditions at the time of the Games, consult Kurt Steiner, ed., *Modern Austria* (Palo Alto, Calif., 1981) and John Fitzmaurice, *Austrian Politics and Society Today: In Defence of Austria* (Basingstoke, England, 1990).

LAKE PLACID 1980

Harold E. Wilson, Jr.

THIRTEENTH OLYMPIC WINTER GAMES

Lake Placid's quest for the Olympic Games to return to the small Adirondack community began not long after the Third Olympic Winter Games held there in 1932. Lake Placid bid five times for the Winter Games (1948, 1952, 1956, 1968, and 1976) before it was successful in 1980. However, the 1980 Lake Placid Olympic Winter Games were born out of controversy and pursued by controversy even after the Games had ended. As one Olympic historian succinctly said, they "were an organizational disaster."

On November 7, 1972, the citizens of Colorado voted against public funding for the XII Olympic Winter Games in Denver in 1976, thus forcing Denver to relinquish its right to host the Games. Almost immediately Lake Placid, the only city in the United States with enough international winter sports facilities to host an Olympic Games, moved to host the 1976 Winter Games. But on January 4, 1973, the U.S. Olympic Committee (USOC) chose Salt Lake City, despite unsecured financial backing and discontent among Utah residents, as its candidate city to take over the organizing of the 1976 Winter Games. Three weeks later, on January 26, when funding for the Salt Lake City bid fell through, the USOC switched its support to Lake Placid. But on February 4 the International Olympic Committee (IOC) chose Innsbruck, Austria, to host the XII Olympic Winter Games over Chamonix, France; Tampere, Finland; and Lake Placid, New York. Despite a strong presentation, Lake Placid was fighting against intangibles beyond its control.

"I was frightened that Lake Placid was going to be successful with a very plausible bid but there were members of the Executive, sufficient as it turned out, who felt that the Movement behaved tactlessly over the Karl Schranz affair in 1972 at the Winter Games in Sapporo, and here was an opportunity to make peace with the people of Austria, who were staunch supporters of the Olympic Games, particularly those of the winter, which they organized well in 1964," said IOC President Lord Killanin.

Lake Placid immediately submitted a bid for the 1980 Winter Games to the USOC, which gave its support on November 20, 1973. Lake Placid's plan was to present a simpler Olympic Winter Games that would return to the basic principles of the Olympic movement. "They are just games," said the Rev. Bernard Fell, executive director of the Lake Placid Olympic Organizing Committee (LPOOC) and later president of the committee. "We think they should be low key, as they were in 1932."

Competition was sparse for the XIII Olympic Winter Games. Initially the bid cities were Lahti, Finland; Chamonix, France; Lake Placid, New York; and Vancouver, British Columbia. When Lahti and Chamonix dropped out early, only Lake Placid and Vancouver remained as serious contenders. After Vancouver withdrew its candidacy on October 4, and Quebec City, Canada, expressed a brief interest, Lake Placid stood alone. On October 23, 1974, the IOC, meeting in Vienna, awarded the XIII Olympic Winter Games to Lake Placid.

Immediately after winning the right to host the Games, the LPOOC got an inkling of coming difficulties when environmentalists protested about the damage that commercialization of the Games would bring to one of the last unspoiled areas of New York state. Similar protests had caused Denver to surrender the 1976 Olympic Winter Games. The difficulties would only grow.

Lake Placid, a village of just 3,000 people, is located in a remote part of the Adirondack mountains, and early on the LPOOC was concerned about how to get some 50,000 Olympic visitors in and out of the town on three two-lane highways. Since most of the hotel accommodations in the region were reserved for Games officials and other members of the Olympic family, spectators would have to commute daily from as far away as 90 miles. In order to avoid traffic jams, organizers banned private cars from the village, instead using a network of buses and shuttles to move people from remote parking facilities into the village and to the venues. Within Lake Placid, transportation priority would be given to athletes, coaches, and security officials, followed by Olympic officials, VIPs, and, finally, spectators. These transportation plans did not sit well with the IOC, and at the 1976 IOC session in Montreal, the LPOOC was sternly questioned about the viability of their transportation program. These concerns were prophetic as the major organizational problem during the Games was transportation. A preview of what was to come happened at a pre-Olympic ski jumping competition in February 1979, when spectators caused an 11-mile traffic jam. During the opening ceremonies, the two largest delegations, the Soviet Union and the United States, arrived late due to transportation problems. Spectators were often stranded and missed the events that they had bought tickets for. Some bus drivers, not familiar with either the area or winter driving conditions, simply got lost. The traffic situation in the Lake Placid area during the Games caused New York governor Hugh Carey to declare a limited state of emergency five days into the Games.

From the beginning, financial troubles beset the LPOOC. The initial budget prediction of $30 million increased by almost 500 percent before the Games with projections of up to $200 million by the time of the Games. Initial estimates of the costs of construction doubled by the time of the Games, and administrative costs, once estimated at $12 million, rose to $60 million. The federal government supplied $57 million and added another $11 million to help offset rising costs. Construction cost overruns, strikes, and supplier bankruptcies added to the financial woes of the LPOOC. After charges of nepotism and mismanagement, federal auditors investigated the LPOOC. The marketing director was replaced in light of questions of improprieties in accounting practices and in the awarding of contracts. Another director was asked to resign when it was learned that he had not filed income tax returns for a number of years. The company that had been awarded the food management contract fell under federal investigation after allegations were made about its associations with organized crime. Finally, the crime rate rose dramatically during the years leading up to the Games.

While some athletic facilities remained from 1932, more had to be constructed. The Mt. Van Hoevenberg bobsled run required reconstruction as a refrigerated bobsled and luge run. Twin ski jumping towers built at Intervale were met with protests from environmentalists and preservationists when it was discovered that they would be the most visible objects on the mountain range and that they would abut the site of abolitionist John Brown's farm and burial site.

In addition, a new ice arena and speed skating oval had to be constructed. Almost all of these sites were beset with strikes, construction problems, building code conflicts, and a lack of funds. During the reconstruction of the bobsled/luge run a boulder, sent flying through the air during excavations, damaged the run and set back progress. A $25,000 fire raged through the ski jump facilities and delayed completion. Until the beginning of the Games, observers questioned the safety and stability of the new 8,500 seat Olympic Ice Arena. Despite the problems, the venues were all finished in time for the Games and received high praise. But no facility brought as much consternation as the proposed Olympic Village.

Located in Ray Brook, seven miles west of Lake Placid, the Olympic Village had been planned to be converted to a federal prison following the Games. The $49 million facility was paid for by the Federal Bureau of Prisons. Appalled by the cramped living conditions, where two to four people were assigned a 10×10 foot room (later to be a prison cell), most delegations sought private accommodations for their athletes. According to IOC rules, all countries were required to pay the requisite room charge of $27.50 per athlete per day whether their athletes stayed in the Olympic Village or not. However, the IOC was so dissatisfied with the living conditions that it waived this obligation for delegations that found other accommodations.

Shortly after Lake Placid was named as host city, the LPOOC began negotiations with television networks for broadcast rights. By fall 1975, the LPOOC and the USOC, its partner in the negotiations, had concluded that ABC was the network of choice. Up to the beginning of the Innsbruck Winter Games, and against IOC rules, the LPOOC, USOC and ABC were secretly negotiating. When these talks were made public, NBC and CBS protested that they were not allowed to bid on equal footing with ABC. As a result the IOC eliminated the LPOOC from the final negotiations and concluded broadcast rights negotiations with the networks on its own. The IOC was also dissatisfied with the involvement of the USOC in the negotiations, calling some of its tactics "blackmail." On June 11, 1976, ABC won the broadcasting rights for over $15 million. A month later, during the IOC Session in Montreal, the IOC Executive Board chastised the LPOOC for negotiating with ABC without its approval. And at its 1977 Session in Prague, the IOC decided that all future television negotiations, beginning with those for the 1984 Games, would involve the IOC.

To say that IOC/LPOOC relations were rocky is an understatement. The stresses led many to believe that the future of the Winter Games was in serious trouble. On December 23, 1978, at the dedication of the 70-meter ski-jump facility in Lake Placid, LPOOC president Ronald MacKenzie died of a heart attack and many believed that the stress he was under as head of the LPOOC led to his death. Art Devlin, Olympic ski jumper and member of the LPOOC, agreed to be interim president. A month later Rev. Bernard Fell, executive director of the LPOOC, was named the new president, but relations with the IOC did not improve.

Besides the administrative problems that plagued the LPOOC, international problems added extra pressures on the Lake Placid Olympic Winter Games. On November 4,1979, Iranian militants seized the U.S. Embassy in Teheran, Iran, taking sixty-two Americans hostage. Just over a month later, on December 25, the Soviet Union moved 40,000 troops into Afghanistan, supposedly at the invitation of its pro-Marxist government, to put down a revolt. In actuality the Soviets supported a coup to impose more dependable pro-Soviet leadership. In the United States, the Jimmy Carter administration, frustrated by its lack of early success in resolving the Iranian hostage crisis, sought ways to force the Soviet Union out of Afghanistan. Choosing a high profile response, the administration decided to call for a boycott of the 1980 Summer Games, scheduled to be held in Moscow, a move that directly influenced the Lake Placid Olympic Winter Games. From January 4, 1980, when Carter first stated the possibility of an Olympic boycott, the government pursued an intense effort at consensus building to convince its allies to join in a boycott of the Moscow Games.

With tensions mounting as the Lake Placid Games approached, President Carter dispatched Secretary of State Cyrus Vance to Lake Placid to discuss the situation with representatives of other national Olympic committees and the IOC. He was also to open the Eighty-second IOC Session to be held in Lake Placid just prior to the start of the Games. Breaking with protocol, which called for a simple address opening the session, Vance made a blatantly political speech denouncing the Soviet actions and calling for a boycott of Moscow. So engrossed in his topic, he failed to open formally the IOC session, which IOC president Lord Killanin did the next day. Many present thought the speech was inappropriate and hurt relations between the IOC and the United States. Cyrus Vance defended his viewpoint a few years later: "The [IOC] committee itself is really quite divorced from the real world. It's its own little group that picks its own successors. I think it really has pretty much lost touch with reality, and really doesn't realize the political consequences of the issues involved."

Another international situation that caused havoc at Lake Placid was the China question which reared its head one more time. As in 1976 at Montreal, the Nationalist government of Taiwan wanted to participate as the Republic of China, but the People's Republic of China (PRC) threatened to pull out if this was allowed. On January 15, 1980, a Swiss court upheld the October 1979 IOC decision to bar Taiwan from using the name Republic of China, its flag, and its national anthem. A week later Taiwan filed suit in a Lake Placid court attempting to halt the Winter Games pending a solution to the name question. On January 30, the PRC delegation reported to the Olympic Village to participate in Olympic competition for the first time since 1952. Taiwanese athletes were refused entry to the Olympic Village on February 6, and a week later they asked the IOC to be excused from the Games. If they had withdrawn after accepting the invitation to compete they would have faced possible IOC sanctions. Since they felt they had done nothing to warrant such a penalty, they requested an excused absence.

Anti-Soviet feeling reached a climax at the Games when the United States ice hockey team, which had lost to the Soviets 10 to 3 in a practice game only weeks earlier, upset them 4 to 3 in the hockey semi-finals. They then followed with a victory over Finland (4 to 2) to win the gold medal. Besides the U.S. hockey victory, Americans responded with national pride to Eric Heiden's five speed skating gold medals.

The Americans were not the only people to enjoy significant performances by their countrymen. Liechtenstein's skiier Hanni Wenzel became that country's first Olympic gold medalist, winning both the women's slalom and the giant slalom. In the men's slalom, the legendary Ingemar Stenmark of Sweden also took gold. Soviet figure skater Irina Rodnina took her third consecutive gold medal in the pairs competition, as did East Germany's Ulrich Wehling in the Nordic combined.

Lake Placid organizers also planned a cultural program that they hoped would make their area more attractive for future tourism. With a $1.5 million federal appropriation, director Carol Hopkins created and oversaw a festival that included exhibitions in sculpture, photography, film, and music. The Los Angeles Chamber Orchestra and the Cantelina Chamber Players performed in concert, and a large, children's art program brought in artwork from 135 countries under the aegis of the United Nations Children's Fund. However, since Plattsburg, New York, 47 miles from Lake Placid, hosted most of the cultural program, crowds were small and the impact on the area was minimal.

Economically the village of Lake Placid went through a number of drastic changes. Major hotel chains built new facilities, sometimes to the detriment of long established hotels and inns. Small privately-owned businesses were forced to compete with large chains and corporations. In addition, many citizens and businesses were displaced to make room for Olympic visitors, both official and unofficial. The transportation problems not only inconvenienced the spectators, but also harmed local businesses which complained that spectators came into the village, went to the events, and then were bussed out of town again. However once the Games ended, most looked forward to the tourist boon that they expected would follow.

At Squaw Valley, host of the 1960 Olympic Winter Games, most of the facilities were destroyed or fell into disrepair due to lack of use, but Lake Placid became the unofficial winter sports capital of the United States. Following the Winter Games, the USOC established a winter sports training center at Lake Placid, ensuring year-round use of the facilities. The tourist season, which usually lasted only through the summer months, now extended into the winter. One year after the Winter Games, there were more than 700 ice hockey games and four ice shows scheduled for the Olympic Arena, which was open to the public twenty hours a day. The bobsled and luge runs and ski jumps were also used year round. Over 60,000 tourists per year paid $1.00 per person to tour the facilities, and lift-ticket revenues increased from $860,000 during the Olympic year to $1.5 million in 1981. With all the post-Games success, many residents still worried that the $8.5 million debt that the Lake Placid Winter Games had incurred would result in increased sales and property taxes.

On May 15, 1981, the New York state legislature appropriated $6 million to buy and operate the Olympic facilities, establishing the Olympic Regional Development Authority (ORDA) to manage the sites. The state budgeted $3.5 million annually, and Lake Placid chipped in $300,000 a year, for ORDA's budget. In addition, the Olympic Lottery, held in 1979 to help fund the Games, generated another $4 million. By March 1982 the LPOOC was able to pay off $8.2 million of the $8.5 million debt. Today Lake Placid still hosts many international competitions and remains the premier winter sports training center in the United States.

Lake Placid's legacy has also been seen in subsequent Olympic Winter Games. The IOC made three decisions based on its experiences in Lake Placid. First, it decided that it would never again award the Games to a small village, opting instead for larger cities that would have the financial and physical infrastructure to handle such a large spectacle. Second, the Winter Games were expanded from 10 to 12 days in length. Third, the IOC continued to be intricately involved in all future television negotiations.

BIBLIOGRAPHICAL ESSAY

Records on the 1980 Lake Placid Winter Games are available in the archives of the 1932/1980 Lake Placid Olympic Museum in Lake Placid, New York. Other research centers that have information concerning all facets of the Olympic Movement include the Amateur Athletic Foundation of Los Angeles Library (AAFLA), Los Angeles, California, (http://www.aafla.com), and the Centre for Olympic Studies (http://www.uwo.ca/olympic) at the University of Western Ontario, London, Ontario, Canada. The AAFLA site contains full copies of most of the official reports and issues of the IOC's *Olympic Review*, *Olympika*, and the *Journal of Sport History*.

The official report published by the Lake Placid Olympic Organizing Committee, *Final Report/Rapport final* (Lake Placid, 1981) is not very useful, but it does contain some interesting information. The committee also published *Official Results of the XIII Olympic Winter Games–Lake Placid 1980* (Lake Placid, 1980). The USOC's report, *United States Olympic Book 1980* (Colorado Springs, 1980), provides insights by various authors on the Lake Placid Games and the competitions. The Canadian official report is Pierre Labelle, ed., *L'Equipe olympique canadienne/The Canadian Olympic Team: XIII. Winter Olympic Games/XIIIe jeux olympique d'hiver* (Montreal, 1980), and the British Olympic Association's report is *Sport: Official British Olympic Association Report of the 1980 Games* (London, 1981). See also the West German report, *Lake Placid 80. Das Offizielle Standardwerk des Nationalen Olympische Komittees fur Deutschland* (Munich, 1980), and the East German report, *XIII. Olympische Winterspiele Lake Placid 1980* (Berlin, 1980).

The coverage of the Lake Placid Winter Games provided by *The New York Times* is comprehensive, very useful, and easily accessible in most major libraries. *The New York Times Index* by itself is a wealth of information. In addition to *The New York Times* coverage, one should not overlook the reporting of news magazines such as *Newsweek*, *Time*, *U.S. News and World Report* and *Sports Illustrated*.

The most thorough historical monograph on the Lake Placid Games is a local history written by Lake Placid residents George Christian Ortloff and Stephen C. Ortloff, *Lake Placid, The Olympic Years, 1932–1980: A Portrait of America's Premier Winter Resort* (Lake Placid, 1976). The work is quite popular in nature, but it does provide information on the politics and preparations surrounding the Games and is helpful in placing the Games in their local context. Unfortunately, the book covers only the site development to 1976. The best analysis of the environmental debates surrounding the Adirondacks and the Games is Jane Eblen Keller, "Olympics Illuminate the Long War over the Future of the Adirondacks," *Smithsonian* 10 (February 1980): 42–51. Another useful piece that places the Games in their historical relationship with other Winter Games is Marc Onigman, edited by Peter J. Graham and Horst Ueberhorst, "Discontent in the Olympic Winter Games, 1908–1980," in *The Modern Olympics* (West Point, NY, 1976). The work was published prior to the Lake Placid Games but is valuable for understanding the role Lake Placid played in the bidding for previous Winter Olympics.

Many books are available on aspects of the Lake Placid Games, though none deals exclusively with the history of the Games. Considering the historical nature of the Lake Placid Games, such a study would be valuable not only to historians but also to managers and those interested in sports marketing. The Associated Press, *Pursuit of Excellence: The Olympic Story 1980* (Danbury, CT, 1980) comes closest to providing a comprehensive history of the 1980 Lake Placid Games. Tim Wendel, *Going for the Gold* (Westport, CT, 1980), John Powers and Arthur C. Kaminsky, *One Goal: A Chronicle of the 1980 US Olympic Hockey Team* (New York, 1984), and the New York Times, comp., *Miracle On Ice* (New York, 1980) cover the U.S. team's hockey victory over the Soviets, and their subsequent gold medal victory. In 1981 *Miracle on Ice* aired as a made-for-television movie.

For an in-depth analysis of the television negotiations for the Lake Placid Winter Games see Robert K. Barney, Stephen R. Wenn, and Scott G. Martyn, *Selling The Five Rings: The International Olympic Committee and the Rise of Olympic Commercialism* (Salt Lake City, UT, 2002) See also the memoirs of former IOC president Lord Killanin, *My Olympic Years* (London and New York, 1983); the British version is more critical of the United States. For insight into the IOC's operations see Wolf Lyberg, *The IOC Sessions*, Vol. 2 (Lausanne, 2002), which provides summaries of all IOC sessions, which are closed to the public.

A number of books address the political aspects of the Olympic Games, and more specifically, the U.S. boycott of the Moscow Olympic Games. While they do not deal specifically with the Lake Placid Winter Games, they provide important historical context for them. Among these are Derick L. Hume, Jr., *The Political Olympics: Moscow, Afghanistan, and the 1980 U.S. Boycott* (New York, 1990); Baruch Hazen, *Olympic Sports and Propaganda Games: Moscow, 1980* (New Brunswick, NJ, 1982); John Hoberman, *The Olympic Crisis: Sport, Politics and the Moral Order* (New Rochelle, 1986); and Richard Espy, *The Politics of the Olympic Games: With an Epilogue 1976–1980* (Berkeley, CA, 1981). Allen Guttmann, "The Cold War and the Olympics," *International Journal* 43 (1988): 554–68, is helpful for the political background of the Olympics and the Cold War.

SARAJEVO 1984

Robert Dunkelberger

FOURTEENTH OLYMPIC WINTER GAMES

The 1984 Winter Olympic Games were the crowning achievement for both the city of Sarajevo and the country of Yugoslavia. It was a statement made by an entire nation that had reached the point where it was able to organize and host an Olympic Games. The 1984 Olympics demonstrated the promise of Yugoslavia and Sarajevo, seventy years after the one event that left the city's name indelibly etched on the pages of history, the June 1914 assassination of the Archduke Franz Ferdinand that contributed to the onset of World War I. What could be considered an even greater tragedy is how the promise the Olympics showed for Yugoslavia was lost; only nine years after the completion of the Games many of the competition sites lay in ruin, just some of the many victims of a terrible civil war. But for two weeks in February 1984, the world looked to Sarajevo as the center of athletic competition, where all nations could meet and set aside their animosities. The XIV Winter Olympics gave Sarajevo the chance to shine as never before.

Sarajevo was first mentioned in the late 1960s as a potential site for the Winter Olympics. An international study completed in 1968 concluded that Yugoslavia, and the Sarajevo area in particular, would be a suitable location for a Winter Olympics if the proper facilities could be developed. The Organization for Economic Cooperation and Development (OECD), based in Paris, prepared a report recommending the creation of a winter sports industry in Yugoslavia that would help the nation's economy. Officials in Sarajevo decided to combine these ideas and use the Olympics to turn the area into a center for winter tourism that would continue to draw people long after the Games had ended. That Sarajevo should compete for the Winter Olympics was first proposed in the early 1970s, and cooperation with the International Olympic Committee (IOC) was established in 1971. In 1977 the city set up committees to prepare a bid for the 1984 Games, which were awarded at the 80th Session of the IOC on May 18, 1978, in Athens, Greece. In January of that year a group of French cities withdrew from the competition, leaving Sapporo, Japan, and Göteborg, Sweden, along with Sarajevo, as the three candidates for the Olympics. In the second round of voting, by a count of 39–36 over Sapporo, Sarajevo was awarded the XIV Olympic Winter Games.

Although the entry of Sarajevo into the competition for the Winter Olympics was initially a surprise, the city had several advantages over the other contenders. The scheduled events were to be located in a compact area, with no site more than 15 miles from the city. It also had long been an area for winter sports, and Yugoslavia had hosted the world and European figure-skating championships, ice-hockey tournaments, and World Cup Alpine ski races. The two other sites had major disadvantages that made them less attractive as host city for the Games. Göteborg's plan was to have the events at widely scattered locations that would require the use of air transport, which was not a practical method for the movement of thousands of spectators. The original budget for the Swedish Olympics was very expensive, and the proposed cost continued to escalate. Sapporo also was not looked on as favorably as Sarajevo for a potential Olympic site. The Winter Games had been there just six years before, and areas of the world that had never hosted an Olympics were considered more desirable. The Sapporo area in northern Japan had the same problem as Göteborg, with long distances between sites that would require the construction of miles of access roads and a four-lane highway.

Another major reason the IOC awarded Sarajevo the XIV Winter Olympics was that the Games would help an area that needed the boost an Olympic connection would provide, especially in terms of tourism. A second reason was that the Olympic spirit and influence would move into a new territory, that of Eastern Europe and the Communist bloc, and help bring that area closer to the rest of the world. This was the first time a Winter Olympics was held in a developing country, and it was a chance for a Communist nation to prove that it was up to the challenge.

Sarajevo city officials were extremely proud of the award and intended to use the Olympics as a means of stimulating the city's growth as a winter sports resort and tourist attraction. The original budget for the Games was $160 million, and the level of popular support for them was shown when a referendum for higher taxes to pay for construction was approved by 96 percent of the voters. This occurred despite difficult economic times in Yugoslavia, with an inflation rate of 50 percent, a large trade deficit, a $20 billion foreign debt, and high unemployment. It did not seem possible that the weak economy could handle the cost, but after the death of Marshal Josip Broz (Tito), the leaders of Yugoslavia were determined to host the Games as a matter of national pride and to prove they were worthy successors of Tito's legacy. It was also an opportunity for the Yugoslavian athletes to perform in front of their fellow citizens.

The most important Yugoslav officials for the XIV Olympic Winter Games were Branko Mikulić, president of the organizing committee; Ahmed Karabegović, the secretary-general; and Anto Sučić, then mayor of Sarajevo, who became president of the executive committee. They kept a tight reign on all aspects of planning and funding for the Games, which contributed to their success. The full organizing committee, appointed in April 1980, made the decisions on the program of activities and construction of facilities necessary for the competition. The sports facilities were constructed in consultation with the appropriate international sports federations to ensure they conformed to all regulations. The majority of the sports venues were completed by the end of 1981 and were ready for competition in December 1982, more than a year before the start of the Olympics.

The finances needed to support construction in the first few years after the Games were awarded came from the Yugoslavian government and funds borrowed from banks and the IOC. Money later came from foreign market revenues, which was the largest single source of income. The marketing of the Winter Olympics was a great success for Yugoslavia and the main reason the Games ultimately showed a profit. The money from the sale of television rights, sponsorships, licensing agreements, donations, advertising, tickets, and other sources totaled over $100 million. The largest part of this funding came from ABC Television, which bid $91.5 million for the U.S. broadcast rights. Two-thirds of the total, or $61 million, went to the organizing committee, and the other third, $30.5 million, went to the IOC. Yugoslav Television also produced extensive coverage of the Games, which amounted to over 200 hours for worldwide transmission to an audience of more than two billion people. Although a socialist country was the host of these Olympics, there was no hesitation on its part to associate with capitalist institutions and corporations in order to raise money. The justification was that athletics were supposed to be above political influences, so it was not hypocritical to accept capitalist money to support the Olympics. The organizers of the Olympic Games were realists as well as socialists and knew they had to have the cooperation of corporate sponsors in order to acquire the necessary funding. There was no other way to host the Winter Olympics successfully.

That the Games were well-organized financially was shown by the fact that the original budget of $160 million was reduced to $135 million by finishing construction projects ahead of schedule and canceling the construction of some roads, ski lifts, and parking lots. This contrasted sharply with the 1980 Winter Olympics, held in Lake Placid, New York, which was originally budgeted at less than $100 million but ended up costing $185 million and leaving a large deficit. Olympic money transformed Sarajevo into a respectable winter resort that became a source of pride for Yugoslavia.

All the existing sports facilities in the Sarajevo area had been built after World War II. In 1978, these consisted of one sports arena with artificial ice, cross-country and biathlon tracks on Mt. Igman, and downhill and slalom courses on Mt. Jahornia. Sports facilities that needed to be constructed were Alpine skiing runs, 70- and 90-meter ski jumps, two indoor ice rinks and an outdoor one for speed skating, and a combined bobsled/luge run. In addition to this work, construction and remodeling had to be carried out for facilities to accommodate athletes, officials, other members of the Olympic delegations, and the press. The Olympic Village built for the athletes housed over 2,200, and the village for the press had room for 8,500 people. Both were begun in 1982 and completed the following year. Construction work on the competition venues began during the summer of 1979, when skiing trails were laid out on the three mountains around Sarajevo used for the Games. Mount Bjelašnica was the site of the men's downhill race course, which in order to match international ski-racing rules had to have an 800-meter vertical drop but was discovered to be nine meters short. The problem was solved when a four-story lodge was built on top of the mountain, with a restaurant on the third floor where the starting gate was located. This raised the course to the required height. It was also necessary to remodel the 55,000-seat Koševo stadium, which would be used for the Opening Ceremonies, as well as the Zetra Arena for ice hockey and figure skating, which seated over 8,500 people and would be the site of the Closing Ceremonies.

Extensive work had to be done with the infrastructure in the Sarajevo area, including the construction of a new road network nearly 100 miles in length. The railway station and airport were remodeled and expanded, water and sewage networks and power lines were improved, and fifteen hotels were built or remodeled. The Olympics raised the standard of living in Sarajevo with improvements that would not have been carried out otherwise. This construction greatly increased the tourism capabilities of the area; local leaders hoped these facilities would establish Sarajevo as a thriving ski center and lead to greater numbers of tourists bearing hard currency from the West.

Numerous publications and five films informed people of the progress of work on the XIV Winter Olympic Games and highlighted the tourist and recreational potential of the Sarajevo region and all of Yugoslavia. The promotion of the Olympics in Yugoslavia included an exhibition entitled "Sarajevo—Olympic City," which discussed the economic possibilities of the Games and the development of tourism. Two of the Olympic films, *Welcome to Sarajevo* and *Sarajevo Is Building*, were involved in the promotion, along with the mascot for the Games, Vučko the Wolf. Eighty thousand visitors saw the exhibition in Sarajevo. An international exhibit, "One Thousand Olympic Exhibitions in the World," was a thematic poster exhibition presented in over 1,000 cities on six continents. It was shown in Yugoslavian diplomatic and business sites and in cultural and information centers.

The IOC continued its defense of amateurism in the Sarajevo Olympics by upholding the International Ski Federation's ban on champion skiers Ingemar Stenmark of Sweden and Hanni Wenzel of Liechtenstein from the Games for having accepted appearance money. More controversy surfaced just before competition began when the United States alleged that the Canadian hockey team had players who had signed professional contracts and were therefore ineligible. A compromise was eventually worked out with the IOC whereby five men from three Olympic teams who had competed in the professional National Hockey League (NHL) were withdrawn by their countries before the start of hockey competition, while any players who signed professional contracts but had not yet played were still eligible. The only other eligibility issue occurred when a member of the Mongolian cross-country ski team was found to have used banned drugs and was subsequently disqualified from the 50-kilometer race. With the exception of these relatively minor problems, the Games proceeded with a minimum of controversy.

The XIV Olympic Winter Games were the largest yet staged, with 49 nations represented, an increase of 12 over 1980, and the most athletes ever in competition—over 1,500. Thirty-nine medal events were held, including one new event, the women's 20-kilometer cross-country ski race. Spectators filled all of the hotels in a 100-mile radius around Sarajevo, forcing 25,000 tourists to stay in private homes in the city. One thousand buses were used to transport athletes, officials, and the press between competition sites, hotels, and the Olympic Village. This was one area of concern for the organizing committee, since they did not want a repeat of the nightmare at the 1980 Winter Olympics in Lake Placid, where transportation was undependable at best.

The Winter Olympic Games officially began on February 8, 1984, with a 90-minute Opening Ceremony staged at a cost of nearly $250,000 and featuring 7,000 young ballet dancers. Yugoslav figure skater Sanda Dubravčić lit the Olympic flame. Although the ceremony was a success, problems with the weather began almost immediately. The pre-Olympic competitions held in Sarajevo the year before had been affected by a lack of snow on the mountain ski runs. There was some concern this might happen again, and as a precaution, snowmaking machines were made available. The problem during the Olympics, however, was too much snow and blizzard-like conditions. The men's downhill race, originally scheduled for the first full day of competition, was postponed three times before it was finally run one week late. The delays ensued when a storm hit the afternoon of February 9 and lasted four days. The violent snowstorms on Mount Bjelašnica featured steady winds of 90 miles per hour, with gusts up to 130, and deposited almost three feet of new snow on the mountain, producing conditions with visibility of less than 100 feet. All Alpine events were called off for the first four days but were rescheduled and eventually made up with little trouble. Air transport for visitors was also hurt by the storms, with the Sarajevo airport shut down for two days. But excellent work by the Yugoslav snow removal crews, including hundreds of students, kept the roads passable and the ski runs in good condition. The delays caused by the weather were the only real interruptions in an otherwise trouble-free Olympic Games.

The 1984 Winter Olympics featured a number of fine performances. Katarina Witt of East Germany won the first of her two gold medals in women's figure skating, and her teammate Karin Enke set a world's record in the women's 1,500-meter speed skating race. Women speed skaters recorded the finest efforts of the competition, with the only Olympic records of the Games being set in all four events. The highlight of the Olympics for Yugoslavia was when Jurij Franko won the host country's first-ever Winter Olympic medal by earning a silver in the men's giant slalom. Although this might have been the high point for the people of Sarajevo and Yugoslavia, the Games themselves represented the culmination of years of hard effort and showed what the country was capable of accomplishing. The XIV Olympic Winter Games closed with an impressive ceremony attended by 8,500 people in the Zetra Arena on February 19. The promise of national cooperation unfortunately turned out to be short-lived; Yugoslavia was torn apart only seven years later in a bloody and destructive civil war.

The Winter Olympics was a great success for the organizing committee, which realized a profit of 2 billion Yugoslav dinars, or $10 million, based on the exchange rate in September 1984. The rapid rate of inflation in the country during this time caused the value of the Yugoslav currency to fall dramatically, making it very difficult to determine at any one time the accuracy of the finances for the Games. The surplus was used to develop sports and tourism in the Sarajevo area. The Olympic Games provided the city with a debt-free winter resort to attract foreign tourists who previously had been familiar only with the summer beaches along the Adriatic coast. The success Sarajevo enjoyed with the Winter Olympics, however, was not shared by all. ABC Television had much lower than expected ratings for the Games, which affected the amount networks bid for television rights in the future. This was a serious concern because it limited the amount of money Olympic committees could expect to receive from this most important of revenue sources. A major cause of the low ratings was a lack of live coverage in the United States due to the six-hour time difference between Sarajevo and New York City and the fact that all of the winners were known by the time the broadcasts began each evening.

The Winter Olympics had a positive effect on the culture and economy of Sarajevo, exactly what the organizers had intended. It promoted the development of winter sports in Yugoslavia with the establishment of new sports clubs and an increased interest among young athletes. Many of the facilities built for the Games were adapted for use afterwards as business establishments—shops, warehouses, catering facilities, department stores, and parking garages. The computer center was utilized as a commercial and banking center, and the Olympic Village became a housing development. The new airport, hotels, post offices, restaurants, and remodeled railroad station improved the quality of life in Sarajevo. The Winter Olympics also created 9,000 jobs, supplied training for personnel who worked during the Games, and gave them new skills for future employment.

The glow of Olympic success lasted for a time, with a continuation of cultural programs including ballet, drama, and music, and a brief upsurge in economic conditions. But by the end of 1985, Yugoslavia was still beset with severe economic problems, with yearly inflation of 80 percent and a national unemployment rate of 13 percent. The real disaster began in 1992 with the civil war that engulfed Bosnia and Sarajevo. The city was under siege for over three years, a situation no one could have foreseen after the glory of 1984, until it was finally lifted in 1995. The mountains around Sarajevo that formerly hosted skiing events held artillery raining down death and destruction. The Zetra and Skenderija arenas, as well as the Olympic stadium and museum, were all reduced to burned-out ruins. Yet even after such carnage, hope remained. In 1999 the Zetra Arena reopened as an Olympic sports complex, and in 2002 Sarajevo made an official bid to host the 2010 Olympic Winter Games—an attempt to recapture the magic of the past and to rebuild a shattered city. Although the siege of Sarajevo represented the worst in a people, the 1984 Olympics proved that it was possible for the different ethnic groups comprising Yugoslavia to put aside their age-old animosities and accomplish what had not been thought possible: to host a successful and memorable XIV Olympic Winter Games.

BIBLIOGRAPHICAL ESSAY

Official records of the organizing committee of the XIV Olympic Winter Games were part of the archives located in the Olympic Museum established after the Games in an old Sarajevo villa. In 1992, when the siege of the city began, one of the first targets of the artillery was the museum, which was subsequently gutted by fire, destroying all records. The one remaining source for official records on the games is the IOC's Olympic Research and Studies Center in Lausanne, Switzerland.

An archival collection that contains important material on the 1984 Olympics is the Olympic Collection, 1976–97 (Record Series 26/20/137) in the University Archives at the University of Illinois at Urbana-Champaign. It is a collection of publications on the Summer and Winter Olympics, with items on the Sarajevo Olympics including promotional brochures, the organizing committee's final report, and the Yugoslav Olympic newsletter *Sarajevo '84* (1984–1987).

Several published works on the 1984 Winter Olympics provide excellent accounts. Two previews of the Olympics are Slobodan Stajić, et al., *Sarajevo '84: All on the Games* (Sarajevo, 1984), which describes in detail Sarajevo's architecture, its cultural and historical heritage, and the athletic facilities and courses built for the competition, and Phyllis and Zander Hollander, eds., *The Complete Handbook of the Olympic Winter Games: 1984, Sarajevo, Yugoslavia* (New York, 1983), a U.S. television viewers' guide to the Olympics that contains articles on Sarajevo, ABC Sports television coverage, and a section on each of the events, with a history of its origin and a preview of the leading medal candidates.

A comprehensive summary is Organizing Committee of the XIV Winter Olympic Games 1984 at Sarajevo, *Sarajevo '84: Final Report* (Sarajevo, 1984), the authoritative source on the planning of the Games, including information on finances, the Olympic officials and organizational structure, and the construction of athletic and accommodation facilities. Dick Schaap, *The 1984 Olympic Games: Sarajevo/Los Angeles* (New York, 1984) is a fine documentation of the 1984 Olympics published by ABC Sports. It is a day-by-day review of the competition with a human interest look at the athletes.

Several journal articles provide a view of the 1984 Winter Olympics at various stages in its history. An article that examines the cities in competition for the Games is "Candidate Cities for 1984," *Olympic Review* 127 (May 1978): 276–84. Helmut Koenig, "Sarajevo: A Miracle in the Balkans," *Physician and Sportsmedicine* 11 (September 1983): 146–48, 153 describes the preparations Yugoslavia made for the Olympics, and an excellent summary of the Winter Olympics is Milomir Niketić, "XIV Olympic Winter Games, Sarajevo 1984," *Yugoslav Survey* 25 (November 1984): 3–22. Finally, the *Yugoslavian Tourist Review*, a publication of the Yugoslavian Tourist Board, contains considerable information on the Games in its 1984 (vol. 1, no. 1) and February 1985 (vol. 1, no. 3) issues.

Three newspapers that gave in-depth coverage of the Sarajevo Olympics are the *Times* (London), *New York Times*, and *USA Today*. The *Times* (London) provided a view of the Olympics from a perspective different from that of newspapers in the United States, with interesting commentary on the use of professionals in Olympic competition and the manner in which Yugoslavia conducted the Games. The *New York Times* coverage of the Olympics was thorough, with a number of articles on the disappointing performance of U.S. athletes, especially the hockey team's attempt to defend its 1980 gold medal. Probably the most expanded look at the 1984 Winter Olympics was provided by *USA Today*. This was the first Olympics the newspaper covered after its inception in 1982, and each issue dealt extensively with the U.S. team and events surrounding the Games. The journalistic style is more popular than that of the other newspapers, but it does provide some information on the Winter Olympics not found elsewhere.

There are two videos available on the Sarajevo Olympics: *1984 Winter Olympics Highlights* by ABC Video Enterprises, which is 60 minutes in length and covers the highlights of each event, and *A Turning Point: The Official Film of the XIV Winter Olympics* (1984), a 40-minute IOC production.

CALGARY 1988

Kevin B. Wamsley

FIFTEENTH OLYMPIC WINTER GAMES

Calgary's fourth bid to host the Winter Olympic Games was granted on September 30, 1981, at the XI Olympic Congress in Baden-Baden. Under the auspices of the Canadian Olympic Development Organization (CODA), formed in 1957 and reorganized in 1978, a select group of local economic and political elites lobbied at home and abroad, spending $2.5 million to persuade International Olympic Committee (IOC) delegates to select Canada as host of the 1988 Winter Games. What followed was a massive and elaborate campaign by a newly formed organizing committee, Olympiques Calgary Olympics (OCO'88), to guarantee the support and enthusiasm of Calgarians in hosting the highly valued Olympic caravan. Olympic ideologies, constantly reshaped and articulated by the IOC according to the crosscurrents of particular global relations, had long ago permeated Canadian society; so much so that any resistance to hosting the festival was rapidly submerged and the integrity of Olympic discourse, with a history of contradictions in practice, was never questioned.

OCO'88 successfully translated the Olympic aura with its attendant ideologies into a cultural happening of volunteerism, spectatorship, and celebration, whose residual substance is still visible in the city of Calgary. Facilities, venues, and the idea of hospitality were defined as symbols of identity for Calgarians. Citizens were mobilized on a massive scale to donate time and money as the responsibility for the image of the city, the province of Alberta, and all of Canada was linked inextricably to the success of the Games. Funding for what became known as the billion dollar games was provided by the most lucrative television contract ever signed for an Olympic Games, support from all levels of government, sponsorships from international, national, and local corporations, and other monies raised by OCO'88. An important part of global image construction during the festival was a weakly-contrived, government and OCO'88-sponsored program of Native American involvement in some of the ritual aspects of the Games and Native American arti-facts removed from Canada during the European invasions of past centuries.

The building of elaborate Olympic facilities, frequently cited as a "legacy" to be left behind for the benefit of Calgarians, and the idea of showcasing the city to the whole world were well established practices and articulated to delineate measures of success prior to the Games. OCO'88 was able to achieve its prescribed goals while attracting little damaging public criticism in the process. IOC president Juan Antonio Samaranch called the festival "the best organized Olympic Winter Games ever" (*Olympic Review* 243 [1988]: 4).

Calgary, once an outpost for the Northwest Mounted Police, a Canadian Pacific Railway town, home since 1912 to different forms of the internationally renowned Calgary Stampede, and oil capital of Canada since its discovery in nearby Turner Valley in 1914 has projected varying, sometimes contradictory images.

The capitalist work ethic dominates the oil-driven economy and, furthermore, the ways of thinking in Calgary, with an emphasis on a trickle-down distribution of wealth and resistance to any form of federal control in economic matters. The tourism programs of the local and provincial governments emphasize the mountain playgrounds, surrounding wilderness, and the western character of the Stampede; yet, the contradictory images of Calgary as a modern, dynamic, business-minded city are promoted just as fervently. The bid committee for the 1988 Winter Olympic Games emphasized these cultural and geographical elements as assets in their extensive lobbying program for hosting privileges. But when the status of host city was granted to Calgary over Falun and Cortina d'Ampezzo, the organizing committee adopted a vigorous, resilient, and impersonal corporate business strat-egy in operating all aspects of the Olympic building and staging process.

The board of directors of the organizing committee was male-dominated, even-tually consisting of 29 members, including lawyers, justices, businessmen, and politicians; former premier Peter Lougheed was appointed the 29th member. From the successful bid to the Closing Ceremonies, the individuals exerting the most influence on all aspects of the Games, including media and political relations, sig-nature facilities, and official ceremonies, were Frank King, chemical engineer, oil-man, and chief executive officer of OCO'88; Bill Pratt, former manager of the Calgary Stampede and president of OCO'88; Ralph Klein, mayor of Calgary; and Dr. Roger Jackson, former Olympic gold medalist, president of the Canadian Olympic Association (COA), dean of the Faculty of Physical Education at the Uni-versity of Calgary, and member of the OCO'88 board of directors. As part of the bid to the IOC and throughout the establishment of venues and construction of facilities, OCO'88 emphasized that Calgary would not experience the same finan-cial problems as Montreal had in 1976. In the final few years leading up to the Games, it was evident that a profit was forthcoming and that endowment funds, secured in financial contracts with funding sources for post-Games maintenance of facilities, would be considerable. The domineering approach that the OCO'88 adopted was borrowed in part from Peter Ueberroth's method of management of the 1984 Games in Los Angeles. In the midst of many firings and resignations within OCO'88, Ueberroth gave an inspirational speech suggesting that such things were just part of the process. King maintained that OCO'88 would not be remembered for its methods in the accomplishment of tasks, and Pratt was known for his intolerance of "bullshit and wimps" (*Maclean's*, February 1988). Men and women who were at odds with upper level management were fired or forced to resign and abuse of volunteers, philosophical differences, or a restructuring of responsibilities were most commonly cited as reasons for leaving or dismissal.

David Leighton was hired as president of OCO'88 in 1982 at a salary of $100,000 but resigned under pressure five months later, citing differences in management philosophy. It was suggested that he was not a team player, wanted to use paid employees, and had lost the confidence of the board of directors. Bill Pratt was chosen to replace Leighton and, immediately, a volunteer labor strategy similar to that used during the Stampede became fundamental to the Olympic project. The let's get it done philosophy of Pratt, at the expense of cordial interpersonal relations, was often cited as a manifestation of administrative efficiency. Conflicts were defined as miscommunications in public and media relations; challenges and criticism were thus structured so as not to interfere with administrative methods and the completion of physical or ideological projects. A three-man committee of OCO'88 members was selected to review the management of the organization following Mayor Klein's threat of a public inquiry. As a result of the report, Frank King was promoted from his volunteer leadership position within OCO'88 to the $150,000 chief executive officer's post in 1986.

Under a reorganized OCO'88, more full-time staff were hired and 75 volunteer committees were formed along with over 200 subcommittees. By the end of the Games, OCO'88 had mobilized 9,000 volunteers, who worked countless hours. The unveiling of cultural programs, an arts festival, a nationwide torch relay, and increased national and international media attention as the Games drew closer served to create local enthusiasm. Record levels of unemployment, empty office and warehouse space, and housing vacancies in the years prior to the Games helped to legitimize the massive amounts of construction taking place, under the auspices of job creation, global attention for business investment and tourism, and the legacy of facilities to be left for Calgarians.

ABC television bid an unprecedented $309 million for the broadcast rights to the Olympics. International official sponsors, licensees, distributors, and corporate donations principally in goods and services provided funds as well. OCO'88 distributed television income toward facilities and services, while the federal, provincial, and local governments contributed $506 million toward construction and the upgrading of existing sites. OCO'88 guarded the official symbols vehemently, investigating some 300 businesses and individuals and launching 52 lawsuits related to the protection of over 200 Olympic-related symbols and words. The Miss Nude Olympics at a local bar, for example, was changed to the Miss Nude O-Word.

After Calgary was chosen as host city for the XV Winter Games, resistance to staging the Games was related to financial concerns, administrative conflicts, and site controversies. All sites for events, with the exception of the speed-skating oval, which had not been chosen, were changed after the presentation of the original bid in Baden-Baden. The most controversial site change involved the development of Mount Allan for downhill skiing events, rather than the original plan of utilizing Mount Sparrowhawk and Mount Shark. Many groups argued that Allan was a poor selection because of possible environmental damage and its incapacity to sustain an adequate ski slope during and after the Olympics. Fifteen years of research on Allan, conducted by the Canadian Forestry Service, suggested that average snowfall was far below the standard required for a ski resort. Dr. John Read resigned from OCO'88 over the decision, charging that Alberta Premier Peter Lougheed had personally ordered the organization to select Allan for development, providing a winter complement to the provincially funded $140 million golf facility at Kananaskis. The $27 million development, funded for the most part by the provincial government, was called *Nakiska*, the Cree word for meeting place. A $5 million computerized snowmaking apparatus was installed at Nakiska to offset possible problems due to lack of snowfall or Chinook winds.

The Olympic Saddledome, a civic symbol and home to the National Hockey League Calgary Flames, was under construction before the bid was secured. Bill Pratt served as project manager for the $98 million dollar facility, funded eventually by the three levels of government and OCO'88. Unlike other venues, the Saddledome cost exceeded the budget by $16.5 million.

Ski-jumping, luge, and bobsled venues were originally planned for the nearby town of Bragg Creek. After some local resistance and the sentiment that the facility should be located closer to Calgary, OCO'88 decided to purchase land on the Paskapoo slopes just outside of the city limits. The federal government handled the design and construction of the $72 million Olympic Park. Practice and competition ski jumps were constructed, facing northward, along with an artificially cooled, combined bobsled and luge track despite warnings that westerly Chinook winds could prove dangerous to ski jumpers. A first-class training center and athletes' accommodations were also constructed on the site. A private donation matched by the federal government funded the building of an Olympic Hall of Fame.

The town of Canmore hosted the biathlon, cross-country skiing, Nordic combined, and disabled Nordic skiing events at the $17 million Nordic Centre. Construction was justified as a tourism venture to support the town's economy, which had long depended upon mining. Some thought, however, that such a facility was too distant from Calgary to be maintained as a training center and was both too challenging and not scenic enough for recreational skiers.

Some competitors resided at an athletes' village in Canmore, but the main athletes' village consisted of seven residence halls at the University of Calgary. The federal government, provincial government, OCO'88, and the university combined interests in conjunction with a previously planned expansion of the Faculty of Physical Education. As a result, $103 million worth of new facilities were constructed including a $40 million speed-skating oval. For the first time at the Winter Games, speed-skating events were held in a fully enclosed structure. University students were forced to relocate to accommodate athletes, and classes were cancelled during the Games.

Canadians were initiated into the Olympic experience through a cross-country, 18,000-kilometer (11,160 miles) torch relay sponsored by Petro Canada, involving some celebrities and 6,520 public participants selected from 6.5 million applications. The $50 million excursion lasted 88 days, with the torch leaving Signal Hill in Newfoundland and travelling by runner, boat, snowmobile, airplane, and helicopter to the Opening Ceremonies at McMahon Stadium in Calgary. The base of the torch resembled the Calgary Tower, a city structure transformed during the Olympics into a giant torch visible for 15 kilometers. Affiliation with the Olympic Games proved to be profitable for Petro Canada as it was reported that, during the torch relay, gasoline sales increased by $23 million per month.

Another component of OCO'88's elaborate program of mobilizing support for the Games was the distribution of Olympic Education Resource Kits to 13,500 elementary schools across the country. Children were educated on the value of the Olympic Movement and were encouraged to be excited about the festival. Almost a half million students in Alberta were involved in Olympics-related curriculum projects leading up to the Games, a significant element in generating contrived excitement in a structured cultural context.

OCO'88's operations were slighted somewhat by a ticket scandal engineered by the ticketing manager, James McGregor. Known as Jiminy Tickets, McGregor had required U.S. customers to pay face value in their currency to his company, World Tickets. He was later charged with fraud, theft, and mischief. Further controversies unfolded when ticketing supervisor Kenneth Melnyk revealed that Olympic insiders such as the IOC, international sport federations, and national Olympic committee members, along with Games sponsors and suppliers, would receive 50 percent of the allotted tickets for Olympic events. Complimentary ticket distribution to the so-called Olympic Family and its guests was an IOC policy. OCO'88 was forced to redistribute some tickets when it was charged with providing preferential treatment to staff members. To satisfy the public anger over ticket distribution, additional seating was added to some venues.

The IOC demanded the usual luxury treatment for its members, families, and guests. For each member of the Olympic retinue, a luxury sedan and driver was provided. Over 700,000 kilometers was logged by the 216 automobiles. These dignitaries joined 60,000 spectators for the colorful, elaborate Opening Ceremonies at the newly expanded McMahon Stadium. Over 8,000 performers participated, with costumes made by 1,600 volunteers. For the first time, seating was provided for the athletes to watch the spectacle after their entrance.

The Olympic program was expanded to 16 days to allow for an extra weekend of prime-time television viewing. Warm Chinook winds gusting to almost 60 miles per hour forced the rescheduling of 30 events. With the performances of Matti Nykanen of Finland, Yvonne Van Gennip of Holland, skaters Katarine Witt and Debi Thomas, and skaters Brian Boitano and Brian Orsor, whose competitions were translated into epic proportions, and the accomplishments of Raisa Smetanina of the Soviet Union, winning her ninth medal in her fourth Olympics, the Games unfolded as had been promised in pre-Olympic publicity. For the Calgarians and visitors, individual characters, rather than elite Olympic athletes, received the most public attention. Ski jumper Michael Edwards of Great Britain, nicknamed Eddie the Eagle, and the Jamaican bobsled team became the focus of controversy for officials, satirical heroes for the spectators, and saleable commodities for small-scale profiteers. The celebrating and competitive anomalies were a break from contrived experiences but were absorbed readily by the powerful Olympic culture.

OCO'88 billed the Olympic Arts Festival as the most comprehensive and longest-running event ever held in association with the Winter Games. Over 600 exhibitions and performances in the visual, literary, film, and performing arts were presented over a period of five weeks at a cost of almost $13 million. The most intense resistance to the Games was conducted against The Spirit Sings exhibition, sponsored by Shell Canada and the federal government and hosted by the Glenbow Museum. In organizing the exhibition, six curators spent five years examining over 6,000 displaced native and non-native artifacts from collections around the world. The Lubicon Cree called on museums to boycott the exhibition in protest of the many years of abusive treatment of the Cree by the federal government. A land settlement had been promised in 1940 and, in the meantime, many Native Americans had been arbitrarily removed from lists officially recognizing their status; trapping lands within a 10-mile radius of their communities were destroyed by oil development. Alberta's Native Affairs minister suggested in 1984 that the Lubicon Cree did not even exist. The United Council of Churches and United Nations Human Rights Committee reported, however, that oil companies and the government had taken actions with serious consequences for the tribe. As a result of Chief Bernard Ominyak's lobbying, 29 museums refused to participate in the exhibition and 700 Mohawks in Quebec voiced their support of the Lubicons along the route of the torch relay. In general, the federal government promoted Native American involvement in official ceremonies, medal insignias, and cultural activities to avoid criticism during the Games; OCO'88 was accommodating in order to secure its financial partnership with the government and to suit the usual Olympic requirements for spectacle.

OCO'88 successfully delivered its legacy of facilities, carrying the signature of prominent Games organizers; furthermore, profits of over $30 million were registered and endowments for the operation of facilities and staging of sporting events were established. The University of Calgary houses some of the best facilities in North America. Indeed, the Olympic Oval is perhaps one of the most impressive success stories related to the legacy of Olympic facilities. The oval facility and competitive programs have boosted Canada's speed-skating performances significantly. Other facilities such as the ski jumps and sliding venues remain useful only to elite athletes. Hence, venues tend to promote sport spectatorship rather than participation. Since the dismantling of OCO'88, assets and endowments under the administration of CODA have given that organization considerable power in controlling facilities and distributing funds to sport-related endeavors. Partnerships established with government and corporate sponsors were crucial sources of revenue and aided in the absorption of cultural resistance, while bringing the business of corporations closer to the daily lives and cultural experiences of Canadians. Thousands of Canadians were mobilized and animated through this event, particular images were portrayed to the world, and Calgary continues to bear the physical and ideological residue of an Winter Olympics city. In the post-Games era, Calgary has extensively and successfully promoted its tourist image around the Winter Games and, without question, is in many respects an Olympics city.

BIBLIOGRAPHICAL ESSAY

For an overview of sources pertaining to the Calgary Olympics see Gretchen Ghent, "Bibliographical Notes and Sources of Information," in John Tewnion, *The University of Calgary and the XV Olympic Winter Games* (Calgary, 1993). A comprehensive and accessible collection of materials exists in the University of Calgary Libraries including OCO'88, *Rapport officiel des XVes Jeux Olympiques d'hiver—XV Olympic Winter Games: Official Report* (Calgary, 1988), progress reports, newsletters, press releases, curriculum resource kits *(Come Together: The Olympics and You)*, media guides, regulations, terms related to the XV Olympic Winter Games, facts, and information. Gretchen Ghent and her research assistant, Hillary Munroe, abstracted all records and publications from the Games. Lists of holdings may be obtained through the Internet and over 1,200 citations to periodicals can be located through the CD-ROM, *SPORT discus*. The University Library Special Collections has copies of all public and semi-public documents. The official repository for records of the Games is the city archives of Calgary. The records consist of documents, contracts, agreements, correspondence, photographs, posters, artifacts, audiotapes, and broadcast videotapes from OCO'88, city, individuals, and private agencies. Public accessibility is excellent.

For other collections, see the Amateur Athletic Foundation of Los Angeles Library; Canadian Olympic Association, Montreal; and the Olympic Hall of Fame at Canada Olympic Park, J. Thomas West, director. The communications media department at the University of Calgary holds the *Official 1988 Calgary Winter Olympics* video by ABC Sports, a highlight production. Also in the film library are 500 hours of video highlights from the Games. An extensive collection of photographs is housed at the Glenbow Museum in Calgary. An attractive pictorial version of the Games is found in Lloyd Robertson and Brian D. James, *XV Olympic Winter Games: The Official Commemorative Book* (n.p., 1988).

For an anecdotal autobiographical diary of the Games, see Frank W. King, *It's How You Play the Game* (Calgary, 1991). A critical assessment of the Games and their implications for the city is provided in Chuck Reasons, ed., *Stampede City* (Calgary, 1984), particularly "It's Just a Game? The 1988 Winter Olympics." Dominique Nguyen, ed., *Les jeux Olympiques: Calgary 1988* (Bordeaux, France, 1988), contains a series of articles on the Games dealing principally with its urban impact in such areas as tourism and the city's image. J. R. Brent Ritchie analyzes marketing in "Promoting Calgary through the Olympics" in Seymour H. Fine, ed., *Social Marketing* (Boston, 1990). For a good analysis of particular issues see Harry H. Hiller, "The Urban Transformation of a Landmark Event: The 1988 Calgary Winter Olympics," *Urban Affairs Quarterly* 26 (September 1990): 118–37, and "Impact and Image: The Convergence of Urban Factors in Preparing for the 1988 Calgary Winter Olympics," in Geoffrey J. Syme, *The Planning and Evaluation of Hallmark Events* (Aldershot, England, 1989): 119–31; Valerius Geist, "Bighorn Sheep and the Calgary Winter Olympics," *Probe Post* 9 (February 1987): 20–24; Herbert and Patricia Kariel, "Tourist Developments in the Kananaskis Valley Area, Alberta, Canada and the Impact of the 1988 Winter Olympic Games," *Mountain Research and Development* 8 (1988): 1–10; C. F. Feest, "Glenbow Incident: The Spirit Sinks," *European Review of Native American Studies* 1 (1987): 61–63; and M. Myers, "Glenbow Affair," *Inuit Art Quarterly* 3 (winter 1988): 12–16. The following periodicals provide extensive additional information on various aspects of the Games: *Alberta Report*, *Maclean's*, *Windspeaker*, and to a lesser extent, *Olympic Review*, *Time*, and *Saturday Night*.

ALBERTVILLE AND SAVOIE 1992

Michelle Lellouche

SIXTEENTH OLYMPIC WINTER GAMES

Michel Barnier was a 17-year-old spectator at the 1968 Grenoble Winter Olympics when fellow Frenchman Jean-Claude Killy won his gold medals. Barnier became a young political star as a deputy in the National Assembly representing the Savoie department, while Killy became an entrepreneur in Savoie's L'Espace Killy resort. Killy and Barnier became friends and met at one of the many Savoie resorts, Val d'Isère, on December 5, 1981. Both were interested in expanding the Savoie department's tourist economy, which was hampered by the area's outdated transportation system. They agreed that the way to showcase the Savoie as a winter resort area and therefore get the much needed improvements quickly was to host a Winter Olympics.

However, a state or region could not sponsor a Games; a city was needed. If one of the ski resorts was chosen as the lead city, the others might refuse to participate. In addition, the Savoie resorts were all small and hard to reach. Hence, the obvious choice became the slightly larger, easily accessible town of Albertville, although Barnier knew that even most French people had no idea just where Albertville was located.

On June 11, 1982, Barnier and Killy presented their idea to Albertville's mayor Henri Dujol and the town council. Barnier, now head of the department's regional council, Killy, and Dujol announced the bid on December 11, 1982. The race to the Olympics was on.

Thirteen cities were bidding for the Games of 1992, spending more than $100 million in the process. For the Winter Games, Albertville was joined in the bidding by Cortina d'Ampezzo, Italy; Falun, Sweden; Sofia, Bulgaria; Berchtesgaden, West Germany; Lillehammer, Norway; and Anchorage, the United States. It was the first bid for Albertville, Anchorage, and Berchtesgaden, which had been the winter playground of the Nazi elite. Cortina had hosted the Games in 1956 but had lost in its bid in 1988. Falun and Sofia represented countries that had never hosted Winter

Games, although Falun had bid four times before, withdrawing twice and failing in 1984 and 1988. Berchtesgaden had more facilities in place than any of the other cities, all within a 25-mile radius. By contrast, Albertville offered snow venues spread over a 650-square-mile area and nothing but promises to build ice venues.

The 91st International Olympic Committee (IOC) session was held in Lausanne, Switzerland, in October 1986. Albertville's winning hinged on Paris's bid for the Summer Games failing, which was almost certain. IOC president Juan Antonio Samaranch had engineered Paris' entry to compete with his hometown of Barcelona, and IOC members knew their president wanted Barcelona to win. If Albertville won, the strong Paris bid would necessarily fail, since the last time the same country had hosted both the Summer and Winter Olympics was 1936.

Albertville's bid was presented October 15, beginning with a film by Robert Enrico. Then Barnier, Killy, and French Prime Minister Jacques Chirac spoke. Chirac spoke for both Paris and Albertville and spoke so persuasively that it looked as if Paris would win. Instead, to preserve Barcelona's bid, the groundswell for the French bid was switched to Albertville. Voting for the Winter Games was conducted on October 17, before that for the Summer Games, and in the longest election in Olympic history, Albertville won on the sixth ballot, with 51 votes to Sofia's 25.

Once the bid was won, the real work began. Killy became committee president on January 13, 1987. A skeleton staff had been in place since 1983, and venues had been selected in October of that year. However, the IOC wanted a streamlined Games, which meant eliminating several resorts as venues. The former hero, Killy, now had to be the villain, angering the owners of the resorts left off the revised list. There were calls for him to resign, including one from his fellow 1968 gold medalist, Marielle Goitschel, who managed one of the excluded resorts. Disenchanted with the lack of unity, Killy resigned on January 29, 1987.

The organizing committee, officially titled the Comité d'organization de jeux olympics d'Albertville et de la Savoie and known as COJO, was formally created on February 24, 1987, with Barnier as president. Samaranch, however, wanted Killy back; Killy relented and became copresident of COJO in April 1988.

Even scaled down, the Albertville Games were still the most decentralized in history, with 10 venues spread over 650 square miles of the French Alps. There were several athletes' villages instead of a central Olympic Village as in past Games, but this feature was unpopular with the athletes. The host city of Albertville staged the Opening and Closing Ceremonies as well as the speed and figure skating events. Various villages and resorts served as sites for other events: the Val d'Isère resort hosted all of the men's Alpine events except the slalom; Tignes hosted the freestyle skiing events; Les Trois Vallées staged the ski jumping and Nordic combined events at Courchevel; hockey and the women's Alpine events were at Méribel; the men's slalom was at Les Menuires; speed skiing took place at Les Arcs; bobsled and luge at La Plagne; cross-country skiing and biathlon at Les Saisies; and curling at Pralognan-la-Vanoise. Tignes and Albertville also hosted the Paralympic Games for the disabled.

The organizing committee took pride in the fact that for the first time, the question of environmental protection was considered in the planning for the Games. However, protestors outside the stadium prior to the Opening Ceremonies recited a litany of environmental horrors that the Games had brought. For a gondola lift between Méribel's ski run and the Brides-les-Bains' main athletes' village, the French government removed protection on a forest preserve, allowing 100 acres of trees to be cut down. Thirty-five million cubic feet of earth were removed from various mountainsides to build ski runs and parking lots. The ski jumps had to be anchored in place as they were built on unstable ground caused by a high water table.

Perhaps the largest environmental (and economic) disaster was the bobsled and luge run, the white elephant of every Winter Games. Located at La Plagne, it had to be propped up several times because it was built over an old mine and kept sinking into the ground. It was also in direct sunlight and would not naturally freeze. The budget skyrocketed from $12 million to $37 million as 40 tons of ammonia were brought in to freeze the track. In December 1990, the run was closed due to an ammonia leak. Sirens were put in place and gas masks were given to the residents of nearby La Roche because of the leak and the fact that the track was built in an avalanche zone.

Despite those environmental problems, Albertville was in the forefront of green Europe in its use of facilities—most structures built for the Games were reused, dismantled, or sold. The 33,000-seat stadium at Albertville was built on temporary scaffolding and sold to Barcelona for the Summer Games. The speed-skating track was converted into a running track with a rubberized surface. The figure skating rink's 9,000 seats were reduced to 1,200 and most of the space became offices. The COJO offices were in a technical college, which converted them to their original use upon COJO's dissolution. The Méribel hockey rink had only 1,750 permanent seats out of 6,000, with the rest of the building being converted into shops, restaurants, offices, and housing. The press center at La Léchère became a conference center. The finish stadiums for spectators at the ski events were sold, along with 450 other prefabricated buildings.

To provide for the ice events, five skating rinks were built in the area. Pralognan-la-Vanoise, with a population of just 650, contributed to the building of an ice rink (reportedly $3,400 per inhabitant), hoping for a glamour event. Instead, Pralognan received the decidedly unglamorous demonstration sport of curling, with a $400 per day maintenance cost, and the residents voted the village administration out of office. Four villages were on the verge of bankruptcy by the eve of the Games; Brides-les-Bains had a $10 million deficit, incurred in building a casino, town hall, and the main athletes' village.

While the resorts were going into debt, COJO created several sponsorship categories to lure corporations into joining the worldwide Olympic program. In honor of Pierre de Coubertin, there was the Club Coubertin, consisting of some of the largest companies in France: Crédit Lyonnais (banking), Renault, Bis (temporary personnel), AGF (insurance), Evian, Candia-Yoplait, Alcatel (telecommunications equipment), France-Télécom (television), Thomson SNCF (French railway), La Poste (post office), and IBM.

In addition to Club Coubertin, there was the Club des Quinze, composed of 15 companies including Club Med, whose Val d'Isère resort was the skiers' village, and Arthur Andersen Consulting, which had helped prepare the Albertville bid. There were also 24 official suppliers and 12 authorized dealers.

Another major source of funding for the Games was $289 million from the sale of television coverage to the European Broadcasting Union, Australia's Nine Network, Japan's NHK, Canada's CBC, and America's CBS (which accounted for $243 million). CBS won the Games on May 25, 1988, with a bid that was $68 million more than that of NBC, $43 million above the IOC minimum, and part of an astounding $3.6 billion CBS spent on sports in an ultimately successful attempt to boost ratings. CBS had not carried an Olympics since it pioneered U.S. Olympic coverage in 1960 at Squaw Valley and Rome and finished selling advertising time only two days before the Games began. However, despite the mostly taped, commercial-heavy coverage, the network attracted a large audience and won 15 of 16 nights of prime-time coverage, the most ever for a Winter Olympics.

The American telecast was revolutionary in many respects. In addition to 116 hours on CBS, 45 hours were carried by cable network TNT (Turner Network Television), which paid $50 million to CBS for the rights to cover Albertville and Lillehammer. CBS's on-air talent was a mix of sports and news personalities, as it had been in Squaw Valley and Rome, with no single prime-time anchor as ABC and NBC had used in their Olympic broadcasts. Paula Zahn of the news department and Tim McCarver of the sports department shared the duties.

For the first time, coverage was edited at the remote site and transmitted via fiber optic cable, microwave, and Eutelsat (European domestic satellite) to the International Broadcast Center at Moutiers for either further editing or broadcasting. CBS did not want to rely on on-site recording and having to carry the tape back to Moutiers to do the broadcast, due to unpredictable weather and road conditions. Instead of building a master control room at Moutiers, CBS shipped two remote trucks to the Games. Even the anchors' studio sets were preassembled and tested in the United States before being sent to France. In keeping with the recyclable nature of the Games, all the broadcasting materials were packed up and shipped to Lillehammer for the next Games.

Albertville was known as the First Games of the New World Order, the first Olympics since the collapse of Communism. While Calgary had been dominated by the Soviet Union and East Germany, these countries did not exist any more. The remains of the Soviet Union became the Unified Team on January 24, 1992, consisting of athletes from Russia, Ukraine, Belarus, Kazakhstan, and Uzbekistan. The team wore matching CCCP uniforms ordered from Yugoslav manufacturers prior to the dissolution; the left sleeve bore the athlete's home republic name, the right, its flag. They marched under the Olympic flag and used the Olympic anthem. While the Unified team did get an Adidas sponsorship, the athletes were busy selling USSR souvenirs in the athletes' villages to obtain hard currency.

The former Soviet republics of Latvia, Estonia, and Lithuania fielded teams for the first time in 56 years. In fact, Latvian bobsledders Janis Kipurs and Zintis Ekmanis, former medal winners for the Soviet Union, had manned barricades in the May 1990 independence movement. The Latvians bartered use of the only luge run in the former Soviet Union for airline tickets and hotel rooms at foreign competitions.

Germany fielded a joint team for the first time since 1964, and the former East Germans had to adjust to the loss of state subsidies. Bobsled driver Harald Czudaj admitted he had informed on teammates to the East German secret police, the Stasi, but those same teammates supported him. Yugoslavia split into Yugoslavia, Croatia, and Slovenia. Almost all the Yugoslavian winter sport athletes and all medal winners in prior Games had been Slovenians. Slovenia team officials gave their previous year's uniforms and advice to the Yugoslavian team, but the Slovenian skiers refused to share lockers with the Yugoslavs.

In an interview with *Europe* magazine (January–February 1992), Killy stated his goal for Albertville on the eve of the Games: "I would like them to go home with the feeling that they spent time on another planet, the planet of the French

Olympics." The spectacle surrounding the Games was designed to accomplish this. The torch relay began on December 14, 1991, when a special Concorde flight brought the flame from Athens to Paris. The flame was carried by 5,598 runners, all young people born between 1971 and 1976, on a 57-day course across the 22 regions and 60 departments of France, including the island of Corsica. Every night when the flame stopped, there was a special Olympics light and sound show by Jean-Michel Jarre in the most historic part of the city or town in which the procession found itself.

The world was welcomed to the "Planet of the French Olympics" on February 8. To the sounds of otherworldly percussion, the 1,808 athletes marched in behind women costumed as snow globes, labeled with the French names of the 63 countries fielding teams. The elaborate Opening Ceremony continued with a vengeance as 300 professional dancers and 1,500 local performers acted out a bizarre futuristic tribute to winter sports. The "Marseillaise" was sung a capella by a 12-year-old girl; on hearing the bloody lyrics from such an innocent voice, many French citizens added their voices to the call for the song's alteration. French figure skater Surya Bonaly, who is black and at the time claimed to be from Reunion Island off Africa (she was actually from Nice), gave the athlete's oath, which led to racist phone protests to COJO.

Then the Games began. Over 900,000 tickets were sold, 20 percent over the estimates. The weather, which had dumped too much snow in previous weeks, precipitating an avalanche at Christmas, cooperated, postponing only one event (women's giant slalom) for only one day. Otherwise, the 57 events produced 330 medals in 12 sports: Alpine skiing; bobsled/luge; biathlon (with women competitors and electronic targets for the first time); cross-country skiing; figure skating (without compulsory figures for the first time); hockey; Nordic combined; ski jumping; speed skating; short track speed skating (becoming a full medal sport); freestyle skiing (moguls, a first time full medal event); demonstration events such as aerial, ballet, and speed skiing; and the demonstration sport of curling. Participating in these 12 sports were 1,318 men representing all competing countries and 490 women representing 49 countries. Most of the women had to take a new femininity test, the *sry* gene test, which replaced the Barr body count test. The French medical ethics committee protested as the test was often inaccurate, but the French government refused to carry the protest to the IOC.

Germany led the medal count with 26, followed by the Unified Team (23), and Austria (21). The United States finished sixth, leading once again to criticism over its poor showing. Actually, Albertville marked the best performance by a U.S. team overseas since 1952, with 9 of the 11 medals (and all the golds) won by women, but 4 of the medals were won in events not even contested at Calgary.

The medals were the traditional gold, silver, and bronze with a distinctive engraved center of Lalique crystal, which caused problems. Austrian bronze medalist Stefan Kreiner dropped his medal while packing and it shattered. Killy himself replaced it, admonishing Kreiner to be careful; there would not be another one.

Italian Alberto Tomba became the first Alpine skier to defend his gold (in the giant slalom); American Bonnie Blair became the first woman speed skater to defend her gold (in the 500-meter race). The Unified Team's cross-country skier Lyubov Egorova was the most decorated athlete of the Games, with three golds and two silvers. Fellow cross-country skier Raisa Smetanina became the oldest medal winner (at age 40) and most decorated athlete in Winter Olympics history—

the first to win in five consecutive Games and winner of the most medals (four golds, five silvers, one bronze) in a career. Slalom skier Annelise Coberger of New Zealand won Oceania's first Winter Olympics medal; speed skater Qiaobo Ye won the People's Republic of China's first medals (in the 500-meter and 1,000-meter races). Finland's ski jump sensation Toni Nieminen became the youngest gold medalist ever by one day at 16 years and 259 days.

For all the superlatives, some simply competed for their country's honor and, with their hopeless performances, once again there came calls to limit the Games to the best, especially after a Moroccan skier was so slow in giant slalom that the next skier passed him, and after the Puerto Rican bobsled team was flipped over for a mile of its run. The British team limited its membership to those ranked in the top 50 of a particular sport, leaving at home the hero of Calgary, ski jumper Eddie "The Eagle" Edwards. But in rebuttal to those calls, there was surprise silver medalist Paul Wylie, an American figure skater who had never finished in the top five at a world championship and had made the American team by one-tenth of a point. He gave the performance of his career and won the Olympic Spirit Award.

The Closing Ceremonies on February 23 were yet another bizarre musical spectacle accompanied by drums, including a tribute to Lillehammer featuring a Viking ship and a giant polar bear float. The ceremonies were overshadowed by the absence of the Swiss team, which was mourning the Games' only fatality, speed skier Nicholas Bochatay, who died in a training accident.

The Games did accomplish some of Savoie's objectives. The high-speed TGV trains began running to Albertville. A four-lane highway was built linking Albertville to Lyons, France, and Geneva, Switzerland. Albertville built a new hospital, cultural center, and five new hotels. Tourism rose during the summer of 1992 and, by the winter, area hotels reported record occupancy, with ski lift receipts up 60 percent in Les Trois Vallées. A quarter of the visitors had never been to the area before but had seen the Games on television. But Brides-les-Bains' famous waters were mortgaged for the next 30 years. Taxes were up 15 percent in Méribel. La Plagne's bobsled track must remain open for at least three years to pay its debt. Regional unemployment rose from 7.5 percent to 10 percent. The Games ended with a deficit, because of a greater number of athletes (400 more than at Calgary) and journalists (7,000 from 120 countries) than anticipated, and the costs of the ski jump and luge run. The final cost estimates varied from $692 million to $800 million. In the end, the French government and the Savoie department paid the $52 million deficit, split 75 percent to 25 percent.

Killy and Barnier received the Olympic Order in Gold at the conclusion of the Games. Barnier won reelection in March 1993 and Killy was named the president of Amaury Sports. Overall, Albertville had been a rousing success—no disasters, no delays, no scandals.

BIBLIOGRAPHICAL ESSAY

The archives of the Albertville Games probably reside with the Comité National Olympique et Sportif Français in Paris; the published record is *The Official Report of the XVI Olympic Winter Games of Albertville and Savoie* (Paris, 1992); a copy is at the Amateur Athletic Foundation in Los Angeles. The foundation also possesses research materials and other information from CBS related to the television coverage of the Games.

Books previewing the Games include Daniel and Susan Cohen, *Going for the Gold* (New York, 1992) on the Winter Games, aimed at younger readers, and the more in-depth Martin Connors, Diane L. Dupis, and Brad Morgan, *The Olympic Factbook* (Detroit, 1992), which covers both Albertville and the Summer Games in Barcelona. The U.S. Olympic Committee's *Barcelona/Albertville 1992* (Salt Lake City, UT, 1992) provides an overview of each event, with U.S. finishes, and lists all U.S. team members.

Journalistic sources provide the most information on Albertville. The April and May 1992 issues of *Olympic Review* provide an overview of the Games. Sally Jenkins, "New Allegiances," *Sports Illustrated* 76 (February 24, 1992): 38–41, discusses the Eastern European competitors' problems, as does Mark McDonald, "Tough Sledding," *Dallas Morning News* (February 7, 1992) and Jere Longman, "New World Order," *Sporting News* (January 13, 1992): 47. The *Anchorage Daily News*'s series on that city's bid called "Reaching for the Rings," beginning October 9, 1986, is worth pursuing as is William Oscar Johnson and Anita Verschoth, "Olympic Circus Maximus," *Sports Illustrated* 65 (October 27, 1986): 39–43, also on the bidding process. Ken Stephens, "Disposable Olympics," *Dallas Morning News* (November 24, 1991) provides an excellent account of the building of the Games' facilities. For information on Jean-Claude Killy see Randy Harvey, "Can the French Re-Enlist Killy?" *Los Angeles Times* (March 1, 1988), and Olivier Margot, "Killy Réve Encore du 'Petit Prince,'" *L'Equipe* (February 8, 1992) and "Je n'ai peut-être pas d'avenir," *L'Equipe* (February 29, 1992).

The environmental impact of the Games is thoroughly discussed in Margaret Schilling, "Will the Olympics Kill the Alps?" *World Press Review* 39 (February 1992): 47. The impact of the Olympics one year later is detailed in Christopher Clarey, "Albertville Learning to Turn Gold, Silver, and Bronze into Green," *New York Times* (February 13, 1993). For a preview of the Games and an English language interview with Killy, see Ester Laushway, "Spreading the Olympic Spirit," *Europe* (January/February 1992). For CBS ratings, see Steve McClellan, "Olympic-Size Ratings for CBS," *Broadcasting* (February 17, 1992): 6–7. The Olympics from a U.S. perspective is analyzed in John Powers, "US Fails to Scale Olympic Heights," *Boston Globe* (February 23, 1992).

CBS produced two videos: *1992 Winter Olympics Highlights* and *1992 Winter Olympics Figure Skating* (1992). One feature film, *The Cutting Edge* (1992), recreates inaccurately the Calgary and Albertville figure skating competitions; the skating was choreographed by 1980 men's gold medalist Robin Cousins.

LILLEHAMMER 1994

Larry Maloney

SEVENTEENTH OLYMPIC WINTER GAMES

When Norway's Crown Prince Harald first heard of Lillehammer's intentions to bid for the Winter Olympics, he declared, "You must be kidding" (Matti Mathisen, "The Road to the Olympic Games," *Destination Lillehammer* [1989]: 5) Herein lies the beginning of a tale as rich as Norwegian folklore, in which a small community set its sights on hosting a premier sporting event and succeeds not only in preparing one of the greatest Winter Olympic Games in history but also in presenting the Olympic movement with a variety of innovative programs that will affect future host cities for years to come.

By the early 1980s, the tiny community of 23,000 and the surrounding region had fallen under the shadow of the west coast's booming oil trade; the prospect of better livelihoods lured Lillehammer's young residents, particularly its women, away from Norway's listless interior. City leaders considered a bid for the 1992 Winter Games as a panacea for the region's declining fortunes. Skepticism from across the country did not deter the bid committee from pursuing the Games with vigor, stating that "Lillehammer was born for the Winter Olympic Games." (Matti Mathisen, "The Road to the Olympic Games," *Destination Lillehammer* [1989]: 8). The International Olympic Committee (IOC) considered such a claim premature, especially since some IOC members consistently misidentified the city as Hammerville. The Games eventually went to Albertville as France's consolation prize for Paris' impending loss of the 1992 Summer Games to Barcelona. However, the IOC decision to alternate the Winter and Summer Games every two years, starting in 1994, prevented Lillehammer's organizing committee from brooding long over its loss.

The committee quickly formulated plans to bid for the XVII Winter Olympic Games. Lillehammer orchestrated a campaign that presented the city as the winter sports capital of the world, due to the fact that Norway's athletes owned more Winter Olympic medals than any nation other than the Soviet Union. Organizers proudly boasted that Lillehammer was the only city in the world with a skier on its coat of arms. Additionally, the bid committee promised to hold compact Games that would not alter Lillehammer's character, all on a frugal budget of 1.8 billion Norwegian kroner (NOK) ($280 million). Nevertheless, a Lillehammer Olympics appeared remote. Numerous presentations to the Olympic family on the city's virtues could not convince the IOC of Lillehammer's readiness for the world stage. Østersund/Åre, Sweden, and Sofia, Bulgaria, led a field of four candidates. Only Anchorage appeared to have less backing, in part due to its proximity to the 1988 Winter Olympics in Calgary.

Lillehammer's bid committee had all but conceded defeat by the time of the IOC decision at Seoul's Games in 1988. Several organizing committee leaders left Seoul prior to the vote, and the executive director told other bid cities they did not stand a chance. Surprisingly, a majority of the IOC's members failed to agree. Although IOC votes are confidential, rumors circulated that the IOC decision was influenced by an incident that tipped the scales in Lillehammer's favor. Østersund/Åre supposedly lost because of a controversy between Sweden and the Soviet Union. Prior to the vote, Sweden accused a Soviet submarine of violating its territorial waters, resulting in a retaliatory Soviet vote for Lillehammer. Sofia lost favor as other IOC members swung toward hosting the Games in smaller cities with predictable winter weather, a reaction to Calgary's size and erratic snowfall.

Lillehammer 1994—A snow block along Lillehammer's main street depicted the Olympic Aid logo, a humanitarian campaign that raised $2 million to assist children in war-torn countries. Courtesy of Larry Maloney.

Before the celebration over Lillehammer's victory faded, the immense undertaking of the city's commitment began to weigh heavily on its citizens, and the entire nation, and with just cause. The realistic cost of staging the Games surpassed every worst-case scenario; instead of a $280 million Olympic commitment, Lillehammer's residents faced a $1 billion expenditure. Local and national leaders realized the city could not absorb such a financial burden. To avoid international embarrassment, the Norwegian parliament agreed to assume financial responsibility for all cost overruns, but parliament's support came with the price of greater authority in the decision-making process. The government created the Lillehammer Olympic Organizing Committee (LOOC) to oversee preparation of the Games, with the central government retaining a majority voice in economic development issues. Two nonnegotiable government demands worked to Lillehammer's favor: site placement and personnel appointments. The central government, refusing to fund an event that would forever change Lillehammer while generating few residual benefits to the region, demanded that more venues be dispersed throughout the region, a violation of Lillehammer's original promise of a compact Games. However, the government's demand increased the likelihood that the venues would continue to be used long after the Olympic flame was extinguished. The ensuing battle for new sports facilities among the region's municipalities caused rifts in the organizing committee and finally brought about the departure of Ole Sjetne, the LOOC's president. The timing of Sjetne's resignation provided the government with the opportunity to select a new president, industrialist Gerhard Heiberg. The subsequent addition of Henrik Andenaes as managing director secured the government's control of Lillehammer '94.

Parliament's request for broader site dispersal enlarged the scope of the Games as they became a showcase event for the entire country. The LOOC capitalized on the world spotlight by creating a seamless image for the Games that promoted Norway's unique cultural heritage through architecture and design. Design teams from throughout the country worked to create some of the Olympic movement's most celebrated structures. The "Viking Ship" in Hamar, so called for its roof design resembling an overturned ship, proved to be an engineering marvel with wooden roof beams spanning more than 100 yards. Project engineers accomplished this task by developing a new laminate/glue technique for wood that surpassed the structural strength and fire safety of steel. Architects used the same technology to build the Northern Lights skating hall, the largest building in the world to use wood for structural support. Norwegian engineering prowess also made

Lillehammer 1994—The United States' 2-man bobsled team at Lillehammer. Courtesy of Ed Goldstein.

possible the world's largest in-mountain arena, the ice hockey hall at Gjøvik. Workers blasted a cave in the mountain over a period of more than nine months and removed more than 29,000 truckloads of debris. The completed space had perfect acoustics, increasing its usefulness after the Games, and remained at a constant temperature, thus saving money. Asian businessmen flocked to the mountain hall to study the feasibility of similar structures in their overpopulated nations.

The design and marketing program for the LOOC matched the boldness of the venues. The organizing committee developed a theme for the 1994 Winter Games that was distinctly Nordic and reflective of the country's heritage, yet at times they received inspiration from unlikely sources. Prior to Lillehammer's selection by the IOC, Mexican artist Javier Ramirez Campuzano, the son of IOC member Ramirez Vasquez, sent the bid committee an unsolicited drawing of a mascot he felt embodied Norway. The LOOC quickly adopted Håkon, based on a thirteenth century member of the royal family, as the Olympic mascot. The later addition of Kristin, another ancient royal personage, made the pair the first child mascots in the history of the Olympic Games. The most successful design concept, however, threatened to eclipse not only the mascots but also the striking Northern Lights Olympic logo.

A 4,000-year-old Norwegian cave drawing of a man on skis inspired the design of twelve primitive sport pictograms that took the country by storm. Unlike design themes from previous Games, the pictograms and the logo embodied Norway's love of the season and its sports. The committee guaranteed that this love would not be cheapened through the sale of plastic trinkets. The LOOC chose thirty-five companies to make higher-priced, high-quality items that served a function in daily life, and Olympic fans voiced their approval through the sounds of clanging cash registers. The LOOC budgeted $3.5 million for royalties from the sale of Olympic-related merchandise and was surprised to find it set a Winter Olympics record, when more than $250 million in sales generated a royalty payment of $23.8 million.

The extraordinary Olympic sales figures were indicative of the frenzy building among Norwegians for the Games. Early versions of Lillehammer Olympic pins sold on the black market for up to $200. Norwegians mailed 1.8 million applications for the 900,000 tickets available in that country. In the middle of the night, Olympic-crazed Norwegians surreptitiously removed special manhole covers bearing the Lillehammer Olympic logo. The most amazing indicator of Olympic hysteria, however, was the daily countdown T-shirt auction. Each day for 1,000 days, the LOOC auctioned a T-shirt bearing the number of days remaining until the Games on Lillehammer's main street. The auctions raised more than $300,000 for the LOOC, with the final T-shirt selling for a remarkable $7,500.

Lillehammer's Olympic Games encompassed more than the tangible results of T-shirts, pictograms, and mortar: a deep respect for the environment guided the development and design of the entire Olympic program to such an extent that the IOC revised its procedures for selecting future host cities. During the bidding process, Prime Minister Grø Harlem Brundtland pledged to protect Norway's environment during the Games. Her promise carried weight: she chaired the United Nations Commission on Environment and Development. Moreover, the government required Lillehammer to meet environmental guidelines before pledging to underwrite the Games. Despite this national commitment, a cosmetic environmental initiative might have resulted, if not for a standoff between the LOOC and environmental activists over the Åkersvika bird sanctuary in Hamar. Environmental groups claimed placement of the Viking Ship building on the shore of the sanctuary would disrupt migratory bird patterns, and they demanded another site for the speed skating venue. The LOOC ignored those demands, claiming that building plans were completed and construction ready to begin. Tempers had reached a flash point when IOC president Juan Antonio Samaranch arrived in Norway to review Olympic development, at which time the environmental groups accosted him in Hamar. The unrelenting stubbornness of the LOOC and the environmentalists prompted Samaranch to suggest mediation on the Viking Ship site. The resulting modifications were slight: planners moved the venue away from the shoreline and rotated the structure slightly so that visitors would not disturb the sanctuary's residents.

The most important change brought by mediation, however, was the new perception that business and environmentalists could work toward common goals. The negotiations laid the foundation for a constructive dialogue and the development of the first green Games. Environmental groups received $100,000 per year from the government to create Project Environment-Friendly Olympics as an umbrella organization to work with the LOOC. Representatives from the LOOC, the project, the region's local governments, and the Ministry of the Environment met once each week to review and discuss development issues. The LOOC hired an environmental coordinator to review all aspects of Olympic planning, a decision that affirmed their commitment to undertake large-scale building projects while also protecting natural habitats. To avoid radical alterations of the landscape, the LOOC reversed the curves at the Hunderfossen bobsled-luge track to hug the mountainside, and designers outlined a Lysgårdsbakkene ski jump that complemented the contours of the mountain. Schoolchildren helped plant Olympic forests and transplanted rare wildflowers from construction sites, while developers faced fines of up to $7,500 for felling any trees marked for protection by the LOOC and the environmentalists. All venues incorporated the latest energy-saving techniques, such as recirculation of waste heat, and computer-monitored thermostats. In all, environmental design lowered energy consumption at Olympic sites by 30 percent.

The green campaign expanded beyond the actual management at Olympic venues. The LOOC instituted a green office protocol, including recycling and the purchase of products meeting strict environmental standards. Corporate sponsors signed contracts that included environmental clauses, in which they pledged to provide services and products that minimized environmental impact. In most cases, packaging for equipment was stored and reused after the Games. Lillehammer city leaders instituted a strict ban against billboards and other visual pollution that would alter the city's character. Sponsor recognition was limited to discreet banners affixed to light poles or small signs carved from Norwegian wood. Strong efforts were made to cushion the impact of the projected 100,000 daily visitors to the Olympic region. Edible plates made of potato starch and cutlery produced from cornstarch were composted, and Coca-Cola recycled all its paper cups used during the Games. Even the Olympic torch, constructed of a specially designed recycled glass and concrete, burned propane gas. The most notable signs of the green campaign to limit waste, however, were the medals draped around athletic necks. Granite excavated from the ski jump became the core element in the unique design of the Olympic medals, the first to combine stone and precious metals.

The LOOC's environmental profile made a lasting impression on the country and the Olympic movement. More than 25 percent of Norway's municipalities adopted LOOC's green office protocol, and the IOC implemented environmental requirements for future organizers.

The LOOC's efforts to preserve the natural habitat while undertaking a development campaign of grand proportions highlighted the committee's concern that the 1994 Winter Olympic Games be more than just another athletic competition. In addition to protecting the environment, the organizing committee believed the Olympic movement had veered from the goals of the Olympic charter, which call for efforts to "contribute to building a peaceful and better world." The LOOC felt it was time not only to entertain the world but also improve humankind, particularly the lives of children living in dangerous settings.

The LOOC worked with the city of Lillehammer and Norwegian relief agencies to establish the first-ever Olympic humanitarian program. Olympic Aid became their effort to raise awareness of the plight facing children in war-torn Sarajevo, the host of the 1984 Winter Olympics. The first phase of the two-year initiative began during the closing days of Barcelona's Games. Olympic Aid distributed posters to all athletes that showed a small photograph of the Games of Sarajevo with a larger, overwhelming photograph of a Sarajevo child wrapped in bandages. The awareness and fundraising campaign continued when Olympic Aid organized a day of Olympic solidarity involving every Olympic city through Atlanta, the host of the 1996 Games. The two events raised NOK 27 million ($4 million) for the children of Sarajevo. The LOOC recognized soon thereafter that children around the globe needed the Olympic community's support too, so additional programs were established to build schools in Eritrea, to fund a rehabilitation center for the youth of Beirut, and to educate children in Guatemala and Afghanistan.

Lillehammer 1994—The ski jump venue at Lillehammer. Courtesy of Ed Goldstein.

The grand ideals of world peace and solidarity represented during the Olympic Games moved spectators and athletes alike to support Olympic Aid. Johann Olav Koss, the Norwegian speed skating champion and Olympic Aid ambassador to Eritrea, challenged his countrymen to contribute NOK 10 for each Norwegian gold medal won during the Games. The people of Norway responded to his appeal individually and through community fund-raising drives. The IOC offered to match Koss' and other athletes' contributions with equal donations to the Sarajevo campaign. In all, the generosity of visitors and the citizens of Norway helped Olympic Aid raise NOK 65 million ($9 million) for the five relief efforts.

Despite Lillehammer's noble intentions to expand the boundaries of the Olympic movement, more sensational events held the public's attention, the most famous of which involved Albertville bronze medalist Nancy Kerrigan. An attacker clubbed Kerrigan on the knee during the U.S. Olympic figure skating trials in January 1994. A police investigation later tied the assailant to figure skater Tonya Harding, who had won the Olympic trials due to Kerrigan's injury. Other Harding confidants including her bodyguard and her husband were arrested for their involvement in a plot to improve Harding's chances of winning a medal by preventing Kerrigan from competing in Lillehammer. Their efforts failed, as the U.S. Olympic Committee (USOC) selected Kerrigan for the Olympic team, and her injuries healed rapidly. The bungled conspiracy also cast suspicion on Harding's role in the plot. Despite Harding's pleas of innocence, the USOC attempted to remove her from the Olympic team. Harding's lawyers responded with a $25 million lawsuit against the USOC, resulting in a delay of any disciplinary action against Harding until after the Games.

The Kerrigan-Harding incident added a touch of sensationalism that increased the Games' visibility, but the event Norwegians called "Wounded Knee II" caused less concern for IOC members than the prospect of an icy reception from the host country. The IOC's penchant for fine living conflicted with the Norwegian preference for simple lifestyles. Many Norwegians believed that Samaranch was blatantly lobbying for the country's valued Nobel Peace Prize, specifically because of his public statements and efforts to stop fighting in Sarajevo and end apartheid in South Africa. Prior to the Games, a Norwegian poll found that 58 percent of those polled held negative views toward the IOC. Two teenagers sharing those sentiments were caught painting a message, "Samaranch Go Home," and a swastika on a downtown wall the week prior to Opening Ceremonies. Several IOC members indeed made plans for an early departure in case actions turned more hostile.

Lillehammer 1994—Jamaican and U.S. flag bearers at the Closing Ceremonies of the Lillehammer Games, 1994. Courtesy of Ed Goldstein.

When the Games opened, however, the populace's suspicions gave way to a rousing show of support for the Olympic Movement, and unfortunate pre-Olympic events were soon eclipsed by the extraordinary moments of the Games, starting with the lighting of the Olympic flame. Organizers improved upon Barcelona's archer and flaming arrow by routing the Olympic flame down the ski jump. Stein Gruben, a last-minute replacement for Ole Gunnar Fidjestøl, made a successful jump with the torch that thrilled an anxious audience, still shaken by 1988 Olympic bronze medalist Fidjestøl's skull-rattling crash during his final torch-lighting practice run. Gruben's spectacular jump acted as the precursor to equally magnificent competitions. Johann Olav Koss set the standard of excellence during the Games and cemented his destiny as a Norwegian sports icon by winning an unprecedented three gold medals in world record time in the 1,500-, 5,000-, and 10,000-meter speed skating events. Bonnie Blair became the most decorated U.S. Winter Olympic athlete with her gold medals in the 500- and 1,000-meter speed skating races, for a career total of five gold medals and one bronze. Blair also became the only American athlete to repeat gold medal performances in the same event (the 500-meter race) in three consecutive Winter Games. Her success, however, was overshadowed by the long-awaited triumph of her teammate, Dan Jansen. In his fourth Olympic Games, Jansen overcame the personal tragedy of his sister's death during the 1988 Games to win the 1,000-meter speed skating races in world record time and capture his first Olympic gold medal in his final event.

Lillehammer also produced a hockey final to rival the excitement of the United States' legendary win over the Soviet Union in 1980. Sweden and Canada battled one another to a 2-point tie after regulation play and a 10-minute overtime. The game was decided using the 1992 rules change of a shoot-out, requiring one player to attempt a goal against the opponent's goalie. The score remained tied after the first round of shoot-out play, but Sweden won the heart-throbbing game in the second round.

Skiing records also dominated these Games. Italian skier Alberto Tomba, notorious for his social life, became the first to win medals in three Olympics with his silver medal in the slalom; he also tied the record for total Alpine Olympic medals with five. Swiss Alpine skier Vrenie Schneider became the first woman to win three gold medals in that sport. Andreas Schöbächler of Switzerland and Lina Tcherjazova of Uzbekistan became the first competitors to win gold medals in the new medal sport of freestyle skiing aerials. Russia's Lyubov Egorova and Norway's Bjorn Dæhlie tied the career gold medal record for women (six) and men (five) with their performances in the women's 20-kilometer cross-country relay, the 10-kilometer pursuit, the 5-kilometer classical-style race, the men's 15-kilometer cross-country pursuit, and the 10 kilometer classical-style cross-country race, respectively.

The expectations of high drama at women's figure skating came true as well. Nancy Kerrigan was ready to compete by the opening of the Games, but Harding crumbled under the pressure of the investigation and the media's intense scrutiny. Other skaters, such as the 16-year-old orphan from Ukraine, Oksana Baiul, maintained the pressure on Kerrigan to skate the best performance of her career. Baiul's status as the favorite to win the ice skating competition was threatened the day prior to the finals when, during practice, she collided on the ice with another competitor. Despite three stitches on her shin and a back injury, Baiul skated in the finals with the assistance of an IOC-approved painkiller. Critics and spectators alike felt Baiul's performance failed to match Kerrigan's technical excellence. Artistic merit, however, indisputably belonged to Baiul. Baiul and Kerrigan tied for total points, but Baiul won with the closest margin possible due to a tenth of a point lead in the tie-breaking artistic category. The best performance Harding could manage was a broken shoelace and an opportunity to re-skate her program, leaving her in eighth place overall.

In all, Lillehammer produced a spectacular Olympic Games. Even record cold temperatures and more than 50 inches of snow failed to dampen the spirits of spectators and athletes alike, with the possible exception of the 112 individuals who suffered fractures or broken bones while maneuvering on snow-compacted surfaces. Norway's love of sport became evident by the way predominantly Norwegian crowds cheered for all athletes, not just their own. Yet as fate would have it, Norwegians cheered more for their countrymen than any other national team, as Norway won twenty-six medals, the most the country ever won at the Winter Games. Crowds surpassed all expectations and broke records with 88 percent of all seats sold, an accomplishment that aided the committee in surpassing its financial projections. The success of ticket sales and the marketing campaign helped the LOOC earn an estimated NOK 400 million ($57 million) surplus, the majority of which will be used to maintain venues. The only sector of Lillehammer's Games to lose money was the cultural festival ($1.3 million), which organizers blamed on low attendance due to record cold temperatures.

It is certain that the IOC and a majority of the sports-loving public will never again mistake Lillehammer for fictitious Hammerville. Certainly the LOOC's adroit handling of the Olympic Games enhanced Norway's reputation for management, design, and quality. The Norwegian construction industry hoped its creativity and adeptness would lead to new building contracts in other countries, and the LOOC offered the world two important gifts: greater stewardship of the environment and a system for the Olympics to assist those in need. It is too early to determine the long-term benefits the region will reap from hosting the Games, however. As Barcelona discovered, hosting a successful Olympics does not protect a community from the whims of the global economy. Lillehammer has no guarantee that the new facilities and international recognition will improve the economy sufficiently to keep its young people, particularly women, in the region. Lillhammer's city leaders have ideas, however, on the best approach to keep the world's eye on Norway. In case the region cannot sustain the magic created during sixteen days in February 1994, Lillehammer planned to bid for the 2010 Winter Olympics.

ACKNOWLEDGMENTS

I would like to thank Mr. Torstein Rudi of the LOOC's public relations department and Nita Kapoor of Olympic Aid for their assistance in locating up-to-the-minute financial figures.

BIBLIOGRAPHICAL ESSAY

Several official publications by the Lillehammer Olympic Organizing Committee documented the Games from infancy to closing ceremonies. The Norwegian publisher, J.M. Stenersens Forlag A.S., published a series of official books, beginning with Knut Ramberg, ed., *Destination Lillehammer* (Oslo, 1989). Stenersens also released *This is Norway*, Arne Bonde ed., in 1992. See also *The Official Book of the XVII Lillehammer Olympic Games* (Oslo, 1994), another organizing committee publication. The Final Report of the organizing committee was published in 1995 in a traditional four-volume report, as well as a CD-ROM version containing additional data and film clips from the Games.

In addition to larger works, several publications were used to develop this chapter, including "Building an Environmental Policy and Action Plan for the International Olympic Committee," by the Project Environment-Friendly Olympics and the Norwegian Society for the Conservation of Nature (1992); "The Olympic Environmental Message," published by the LOOC (1993); "The Greening of Sports: The Third Dimension of the Olympics," published by the Ministry of Environment (Oslo, 1994); and "An Environmentally Friendly Olympics: The Norwegian Example," also published by the Ministry of Environment (Oslo, 1993), all of which provide in-depth information into the development of the LOOC's environmental program. Small pamphlets published by the LOOC were used to develop this chapter as well, and direct communication with Olympic Aid provided supplemental information on its efforts.

Other works provide additional history on the Lillehammer experience. Among them are "Simply Too Good to be True: An Evaluation of the Lillehammer Winter Olympics," by Arild Gjerde in the autumn 1994 edition of *Citius, Altius, Fortius.*

Of particular significance for a complete review of Lillehammer's Olympic Games are the *New York Times* and the *Washington Post*, both of which carried extensive coverage of the Olympics. The *Atlanta Journal/Constitution* covered the Games in-depth in preparation for the 1996 Summer Olympics in Atlanta. National magazines such as *Time* and *Sports Illustrated* covered Lillehammer extensively during the Games.

Two videos are important to note. Filmmaker Bud Greenspan continued his series of Olympic films with the production of *16 Days of Glory: Lillehammer '94,* and CBS produced a compilation of sports highlights from the 1994 Games.

NAGANO 1998

Naofumi Masumoto

EIGHTEENTH OLYMPIC WINTER GAMES

Located 117 kilometers northwest of Tokyo, Nagano City is one of the most popular ski resort cities in Japan. On June 1, 1989, it won the domestic nomination race among the cities of Asahikawa, Yamagata, and Morioka. It had lost domestic bidding races to host the Winter Games two times previously. On February 12, 1990, a Nagano delegation visited International Olympic Committee (IOC) headquarters to present its international bid to President Juan Antonio Samaranch. Other bidding cities were Aosta, Italy; Jaca, Spain; Ostersund, Sweden; Salt Lake City, United States; and Sochi, in the former Soviet Union. On June 15, 1991, at the IOC Session in Birmingham, England, in the fifth round of voting, Nagano won 46 votes, enough to defeat Salt Lake City by 4 votes.

During the bidding campaign, the Nagano Organizing Committee (NAOC) promised that it would pay accommodation and transportation costs for the 2,000 athletes expected to compete. However, a subsequent Japanese economic depression forced the organizing committee to break its promise. Moreover, when the IOC corruption scandal was investigated in 1999, the Nagano bid committee was also investigated because of suspicions that IOC members had been bribed for their votes. In the end, Nagano bidding expense records could not be verified, because bid officials had the books burned in 1992 after Nagano was chosen to host the Games.

At the Nagano Games, a total of 2,177 athletes participated. Some 788 female athletes participated in the Games, 36.2 percent of the total, a 6.2 percent increase compared to the 1994 Lillehammer Olympic Winter Games. A total of 72 national Olympic committees participated, 6 more than in Lillehammer. Television broadcasts reached 180 countries, an increase of 50 percent over Lillehammer, and the cumulative global audience was estimated at 10.5 billion, which was 1.9 percent less than Lillehammer because of the large time difference between Japan and Europe and North America.

According to the NAOC official report, the goals for the Nagano Games were to bring about the participation of children, to pay homage to nature, and to stage a festival of peace and friendship, under the theme "Games from the Heart—Together with Love" (NAOC, *Official Report of the XVIII Olympic Winter Games*, Vol. 1 [Nagano, 1999], p. 11). A youth camp was held, with 217 youths from 51 countries in attendance. Moreover, for the first time, "One School, One Country" programs were developed in Nagano. Each of the 76 elementary, junior high, and special schools in Nagano City joined international-awareness and mutual-understanding activities while being paired with a participating country. Students learned about the cultures and customs of their partner countries and exchanged information with students from those countries. These programs were a great success and were continued at the 2000 Summer Games in Sydney and the 2002 Winter Games in Salt Lake City. The IOC has made this one of its official programs to be carried on at least until the 2008 Beijing Games.

As a goal of "homage to nature," an environmentally sensitive policy was given priority in preparing the venues and transportation system. One of the contentious environmental issues concerned the starting point for the men's Alpine downhill race. Though the International Ski Federation (FIS) asked the NAOC to raise the starting point in order to create a more challenging race, the NAOC refused in order to protect the ecosystem of a national park. This issue was resolved as a compromise only two months before the beginning of the Games.

The third goal, the promotion of peace, was an important activity for the NAOC. In November 1997, the United Nations adopted a resolution regarding an Olympic truce. The NAOC issued the Nagano Olympic Peace Appeal, which included joining the campaign to ban anti-personnel land mines. To promote this appeal for peace at the opening ceremony, the NAOC selected Chris Moon, a British anti-land-mine activist who had lost his right arm and leg to a land mine when he worked in Africa, as the one of the final torchbearers in the stadium. He ran into the stadium surrounded by many cheerful children called "Snow Children." This powerful program transmitted the message of peace worldwide.

Seven new facilities were built for the Nagano Games: Snow Harp, for cross-country skiing; M-Wave, for speed skating; White Ring, for figure skating and short-track speed skating; Big Hat/Aqua Wing, for ice hockey; Spiral, for bobsled and luge; and Hakuba ski-jumping stadium. To improve the infrastructure for the Games, a new transportation network was constructed, including a high-speed expressway, the Shinkansen Bullet Train Line, and the opening of new roads and tunnels to create easier access to venues around the Nagano prefecture. At some of these construction sites, problems concerning foreign workers arose. Japanese construction companies used illegal immigrant workers and paid them low wages in order to reduce costs. This caused human rights activists to protest in Japan.

Television revenues for the Nagano Games were $513.5 million, including the $375 million from the Columbia Broadcasting System (CBS) for U.S. television rights, the highest broadcast revenue ever for the Olympic Winter Games, and about 150 percent more than for the 1994 Lillehammer Winter Games. Because of the large time difference between Japan and the United States, much of the CBS programming was taped. American viewers were less interested in taped programming, and therefore television ratings were not high. However, the Nagano budget shows the growth of Olympic commercialism. Indeed, the NAOC donated $1 million and a 3-D high-definition theater system to the Olympic Museum in Lausanne in 1998. The largest Japanese winter resort company, Kokudo, arranged this donation, but some criticized it as a payoff to IOC President Samaranch in gratitude for winning the right to host the 1998 Games.

There were some significant changes in the format of the Games in Nagano. Curling returned to the Games after a 60-year absence and nine new events were added: women's ice hockey, men's and women's freestyle skiing aerials, men's and women's snowboard giant slalom and half pipe, and men's 500-meter and women's 1,000-meter short-track speed skating. This created a total of seven sports and 68 events. At Nagano, professionals from the National Hockey League (NHL) took part for the first time in the Olympic Winter Games as "Dream Teams." Medals were awarded every night in the central square in Nagano City, in an enthusiastic atmosphere. This practice replicated that of the 1988 Calgary Games, where athletes were presented their medals in a downtown park. Because of the popularity of this style of medal presentation, the 2002 Salt Lake City Games continued this new tradition. The relationship between athletic performance and technology was tightened in the Nagano Games, too. Use of the hinged ice skate (the clap skate) began in the Nagano Games, and the use of these special skates reduced times by an average of 5 percent.

As usual, some controversies marked the Nagano Games. First, before the Opening Ceremony of the Nagano Games, the IOC's policy of keeping the program a secret was put to the test. On the day following the dress rehearsal, some Japanese newspapers printed a picture of the final torchbearer, figure skater Midori Ito. The IOC stripped the press passes from the journalists involved and restricted the newspaper company's privileges because it had broken the IOC's policy of secrecy, which was deemed to be very important in order to sustain the interest of the worldwide television audience until the opening day. This IOC policy can be seen as based purely on commercialism, as it attempted to raise television ratings of the Opening Ceremonies.

Second, the IOC Medical Commission carried out a comprehensive doping program that included blood testing at the cross-country skiing and biathlon events. A total of 621 samples was collected. On February 8, after the men's snowboard giant slalom, the gold medalist Ross Rebagliati of Canada tested positive for marijuana. Though the IOC Executive Board stripped Rebagliati's gold medal, the Court of Arbitration for Sport (CAS) overturned the decision. The reason for the CAS decision was that the IOC medical code did not classify marijuana as a prohibited substance, nor did it clarify punishment for its usage.

Third, the U.S. Olympic hockey team, which included professional NHL players, vandalized three apartments after being eliminated from the tournament in a 4–1 quarterfinal loss to the Czech Republic. Athletes broke several chairs and emptied fire extinguishers, causing damage estimated at $3,000 and stirring controversy in the United States. U.S. Olympic hockey team coach Ron Wilson called the vandalism "a deplorable act," and NHL commissioner Gary Bettman initiated an investigative follow-up.

The 1998 Nagano Winter Olympic Games left only a limited legacy. After the great success of the Games, the Nagano prefecture government and Nagano City decided that except for the speed-skating venue (M-Wave), the ski-jumping venue, and the bobsled/luge track (Spiral), all venues would be removed because of the great costs to maintain the facilities. Moreover, although the NAOC established the Nagano Olympic Museum in the room of the M-Wave, the space and contents of the exhibition are so uninteresting that few people have visited. The most important legacy of the Nagano Games will be the "One School, One Country program," an Olympic educational program that has had a significant domestic, national, and international impact.

The transportation network around the Nagano area is also an important legacy. The Japanese government extended the Shinkansen Bullet Train Line from Takasaki to Nagano. The construction was finished five months prior to the opening of the Games. Two main expressways, Nagano expressway and Joshinetsu expressway, were constructed to improve access from Tokyo and other prefectures to Nagano and the competition venues. Moreover, a local road network linking the Olympic venues in Nagano prefecture was created, and a total of 114.9 kilometers of road was improved. In particular, the 25.2-kilometer Shiga Route created easy access to the Shiga ski resort area, provided direct access to Shiga Kogen, and reduced the overall travel time. These improvements helped the ski resort company improve its profits. Unfortunately, after the Games, many hotels in Nagano City went bankrupt and construction companies stopped working because the public facilities and utilities they had constructed were ten years in advance of what the city needed.

Olympic filmmaker Bud Greenspan of the United States made the IOC's official film of the 1998 Nagano Games, *Nagano '98 Olympics: Stories of Honor and Glory*. This conflicted with Japanese expectations that a Japanese director would make a memorable official film as had happened for the 1964 Tokyo Olympic Games and the 1972 Sapporo Winter Games. In his official film, Greenspan depicted not only the local and national messages from the Nagano area and Japanese national culture, but also the universal messages of the competing athletes, who tried to overcome past tragedies and defeats with dedicated training. Unfortunately, because this IOC official film was not available for public viewing in Japan except in the Nagano area, most Japanese people could not enjoy the historical and emotional legacy of the 1998 Nagano Winter Olympic Games.

BIBLIOGRAPHICAL ESSAY

Much information on the 1998 Nagano Winter Games is found in the NAOC's three-volume *Official Report of the XVIII Olympic Winter Games* (Nagano, 1999), published in English, French, and Japanese. The NAOC also published a *Final Report to the IOC Radio and Television Commission* (Nagano, 1998), a *Final Report to the IOC Press Commission* (Nagano, 1998), and a report, *High Technology Olympics Nagano 1998* (Nagano, 1998?), that deals with the technical advances in transportation, security, television, fiber-optic networks, and weather forecasting. The archives of the Olympic Study Center of the Olympic Museum in Lausanne are the best and most convenient place to research the materials related to the Nagano Games. The collection includes, among other things, the bid reports of all six cities. The archives of the Amateur Athletic Foundation in Los Angeles (AAFLA) also contain material on the 1998 Nagano Games.

There are not many articles in English about the Nagano Games. For the IOC corruption issue, see Douglas Booth, who researched gifts in Olympic culture, especially in the 2000 Sydney Games but also including the 1998 Nagano Games ("Gifts of Corruption? Ambiguities of Obligation in the Olympic Movement," *Olympika* VIII [1999]: 43–68). David Foster discussed the Internet's recent role in reporting the

Games, including the Nagano Games, in "A Review of Olympic Games Results on the Internet," *Journal of Olympic History* (Winter 1999): 40–42. For the marketing program in the Nagano Games, see the analysis in "Nagano Olympic Winter Games: Marketing Program Analysis," *Journal of Olympic History* (Winter 1999): 38–39. The IOC's official magazine, *Olympic Review*, is among the useful materials to research the IOC's standpoint on the Olympic management of the 1998 Nagano Games (especially volume XXVI, numbers 19–21, 1998). The IOC's official Web site has archived pages on the 1998 Nagano Games: http://www.olympic.org/uk/games/past/index_uk.asp?&OLGT=2&OLGY=1998.

SALT LAKE CITY 2002

Lex Hemphill

NINETEENTH OLYMPIC WINTER GAMES

Salt Lake City's engagement with the Winter Olympics provides persuasive evidence of the redemptive power of the Games, for no city required more redemption than did the capital city of the state of Utah. After pursuing the Winter Olympics for 30 years, Salt Lake City finally won the right to stage the 2002 Games in 1995, whereupon it embarked on what was surely the most tumultuous seven-year preparation period ever endured by an Olympic host city. In that period, the city that is headquarters to the Mormon Church had its name permanently affixed to the worst scandal in the history of the International Olympic Committee (IOC). But after that painfully bumpy ride, Utahns finally got their fortnight in the sun, literally and figuratively, when they presented a superb Olympics in February 2002. For them, those two weeks counterbalanced the scandal-filled, seven-year run-up to the Games. And it left Salt Lake City with a unique—and, yes, redemptive—story to tell about the ups and downs of hosting the Winter Olympics.

Salt Lake City's unmatched geographical asset as a potential Olympic host city—the close proximity of a major city to the magnificent Wasatch Mountains—was remarked upon as early as 1928, when Amateur Athletic Union officials idly mused upon Utah as a site for the 1932 Winter Games. But it wasn't until the mid-1960s that the city formally pursued the Olympics. In 1965, at the behest of Utah Governor Calvin Rampton, civic leaders formed a committee to seek the 1972 Winter Olympics. The goal was not so much to win the Games as to generate free publicity for Utah's ski industry, and the campaign succeeded on that score. In January 1966, Salt Lake City won the U.S. Olympic Committee's (USOC) nod as America's candidate city for 1972, but lost the IOC balloting to Sapporo, Japan. The same group of bidders stayed in the hunt for the 1976 Games, but lost the USOC candidature to Denver. Then, when Denver and Colorado voters rejected the 1976 Olympics, the USOC turned to Salt Lake City in early 1973 to try to keep the 1976 Games in the United States. But the IOC, spurned already by the Americans, opted for Innsbruck, Austria.

Olympic talk in Utah quieted for a decade until a new group of bidders, led by corporate attorney Tom Welch, came on the scene in 1985 to seek the USOC candidature for the 1992 Winter Games, a contest that late-entering Salt Lake City lost to Anchorage. But four years later, in June 1989, the Utah bidders came back and beat three other cities to become the USOC candidate for the 1998 Winter Games (and, eventually, 2002 as well). However, the American designation came with a unique requirement attached: the USOC, chastened by the weak showing of its winter athletes in Calgary in 1988, extracted a commitment from the winning city to build winter sport facilities for its athletes, whether or not it eventually won the IOC bid.

Salt Lake City's bid leaders knew they needed popular backing to make such a commitment. So, they put a measure on the statewide November ballot asking Utah taxpayers to dedicate a portion of their sales tax (1/32 of a cent) to the construction of winter sport facilities. On November 7, 1989, Utah citizens, aware they were risking the building of white elephants if the Olympics never came, approved the referendum, with 57 percent of the nearly 380,000 voters consenting. It would be the only statewide ballot ever held on the Olympic question in Utah, and voters were banking on the bidders' intent, as stated in the ballot question, to repay the state "if revenues generated by the Olympic Games are adequate." The dedicated sales tax over a 10-year period, eventually capped at $59 million, funded the construction of ski jumps and a bobsled-luge track at Utah Olympic Park, as well as the speed skating oval (not including its roof) in Kearns.

Salt Lake City 2002—U.S. skier Travis Mayer performs in the freestyle moguls competition at the 2002 Winter Olympic Games in Salt Lake City. Courtesy of Larry Maloney.

A year and a half after the 1989 referendum, Welch and his right-hand man, Dave Johnson, brought their bid to the IOC members in Birmingham, England. Already an underdog to Nagano, Japan, Salt Lake City's prospects had been further diminished in September 1990 when the IOC awarded Atlanta the 1996 Summer Olympics; it was thought unlikely that the United States would win back-to-back Olympics. On June 15, 1991, Salt Lake City indeed lost to Nagano by a 46–42 vote in the final round of balloting, after needing a win in a tiebreaker with Aosta, Italy, just to get past the first round. Salt Lake City's strong runner-up showing, despite the obstacles in its way, stamped it as the prohibitive favorite to win the bid for the 2002 Games.

Ten cities bid for the 2002 Winter Games, and for the first time, the IOC used a preliminary round to winnow the candidates to a workable number for the final vote. In January 1995, the IOC cut the field to four—Quebec, Canada; Ostersund, Sweden; Sion, Switzerland; and Salt Lake City. Then, on June 16, 1995, in Budapest, Salt Lake City won on the first ballot with 54 votes, swamping Sion and Ostersund, which had 14 each. The advantages of its geography, its advance venue construction, and its 30-year effort were sufficient explanations for Utah's overwhelming victory. But events that would unfold three and a half years later revealed that something else had played into Salt Lake City's successful bid: excessive generosity toward IOC members by the Utah bidders.

The transition from bid committee to the Salt Lake Organizing Committee (SLOC) was seamless enough. Welch remained the organization's president, although he expressed disappointment in late 1995 when he was given an annual salary of $315,000, after having worked on the bid effort for 10 years on a mostly voluntary basis. At one point, Welch proclaimed that he was better than his Atlanta counterpart, Billy Payne, who was making twice his salary. Johnson remained as SLOC's vice president.

The ink was barely dry on the bid award when SLOC received its first piece of wondrous news. In August 1995, NBC announced a package deal to broadcast the Sydney and Salt Lake City Olympics, with the rights to the latter coming in at an unexpectedly high $545 million, a record for a Winter Olympics and higher even than the rights fee NBC paid for the 1996 Summer Olympics in Atlanta. SLOC's share of that total would be $327 million, more than one-third higher than it had budgeted in its revenue projections, offering a sense of temporary relief to those Utahns who feared that a budget shortfall might leave them with a hefty post-Olympics bill.

Much of SLOC's first two years were spent on finalizing details for its sport venues. While the strength of Salt Lake City's bid was the advanced preparation of its venues, some of them changed sites after the bid. The most notable of these was the cross-country skiing and biathlon venue. The original site, Mountain Dell Golf Course, was deemed too flat and boring by international ski officials, and it did not hold snow well. After months of studying an alternate site in Salt Lake City's watershed area, the committee finally opted to go beyond Salt Lake County to Soldier Hollow, on the edge of Wasatch Mountain State Park, in late 1997.

Two other venue development plans on which SLOC worked feverishly in this period ultimately required action from the U.S. Congress for completion—the Olympic Village at the University of Utah and the downhill skiing venue at Snowbasin. To complete the former, SLOC and the university sought the transfer of 11 acres from the adjoining Fort Douglas military base, a long and tangled process that did not become final until 1998. As for the latter, the development of Snowbasin entailed a land exchange that Congress finally approved in October 1996, but it was a deal that created the most environmentalist fury in the pre-Olympic preparation period.

Snowbasin owner Earl Holding, a SLOC board member and also the owner of the Sun Valley resort in Idaho, had long sought to acquire 1,320 acres of Forest Service land in order to transform the small ski area into a four-season destination resort. After Utah won the bid, the Snowbasin forces skirted the normal land-exchange process and went straight to Congress, seeking legislation that would accelerate the swap and claiming a bit disingenuously that it was necessary for staging the Olympic downhill. Under the deal, Holding ultimately got 1,377 precious acres at Snowbasin from the Forest Service in exchange for 11,757 acres in various parcels he owned in northern Utah—equal value in the appraisers' estimation but certainly not to environmentalists. Critics were further irritated by the fact that Holding got a $15 million access road to Snowbasin paid for by the federal government.

SLOC's fairly routine existence dealing with these issues was shattered on July 17, 1997, when it was reported that Salt Lake City police were investigating a domestic dispute between Welch and his wife Alma. The incident had taken place in the garage of the family's Salt Lake City home on July 9, boiling over from a discussion over Welch's relationship with another woman, one that he would later describe as platonic. Police were summoned by a call from the couple's 11-year-old son and were told differing stories by Alma, who claimed she had been thrown into the garage wall, and by Tom, who claimed there was no struggle.

Welch, who had gone to Africa on a hunting trip shortly after the encounter and returned home early when news of the incident broke, faced a misdemeanor charge of domestic violence battery, to which he pleaded no contest (the charge was dismissed a year later after he completed family counseling). Also, after consulting with SLOC's executive board, he resigned as president of the organization. By the end of a dizzying July, Welch's 12-year Olympic adventure had been scuttled, and SLOC sought to recover from its first real crisis.

But things got worse before they got better. SLOC was poised to offer Welch a $2 million severance package, but members of the public and of the Salt Lake City Council were incensed at the proposal. Welch offered to forego recompense for his past bid committee service, and the package was eventually scaled down to $1.1 million. In addition, there was the matter of succession. Frank Joklik, chairman of the SLOC board and of the bid committee board before that, moved into Welch's position as president without a hiring search, a quick coronation that some board members opposed. Robert Garff was subsequently appointed as board chairman.

The chief highlight of Joklik's reign, which would also prove to be brief, was the solidifying of SLOC's budget. It had been set at roughly $800 million during the bid days, but after winning the bid, SLOC began operating under the assumption of a $920 million cash budget, not including undetermined value-in-kind items. Then, in the fall of 1998, after a nearly yearlong process initiated by Joklik, SLOC presented an intricately detailed budget to local public officials. The grand total: $1.45 billion. And that did not include expected federal dollars for transportation and security. The jittery part of the budget was that, with three and a half years to go before the Games, SLOC still had to generate $375 million from corporate sponsors in an uncertain economic climate—a task that would soon become even more difficult.

Just 16 months after the Welch incident, the real seismic event hit. On November 24, 1998, a Salt Lake City television reporter revealed the existence of a two-year-old draft letter from Johnson, SLOC's vice president, to Sonia Essomba, the daughter of an IOC member from Cameroon. The letter stated that an enclosed check for more than $10,000 would be the last SLOC payment toward her education at American University. The implication of the letter was clear: SLOC had made education payments to the relative of an IOC member at a time when it was seeking IOC votes for its 2002 bid. Two weeks later, after a SLOC review of bid records, Joklik responded that the bid committee had made such payments to 13 individuals, 6 of whom were relatives of IOC members, and that the payments totaled nearly $400,000. He insisted that these payments constituted humanitarian aid, in the spirit of the Olympic Solidarity program, and should not be construed as bribes.

But bribes is exactly what venerable IOC member Marc Hodler was calling them a couple of days later in Switzerland, where the IOC was preparing for a regularly scheduled meeting. Hodler then raised the rhetorical ante in between sessions of the IOC meeting on December 12, when he claimed that the Olympics were for sale, that certain agents deliver bid-city votes in exchange for a fee, that a handful of IOC members can be bought, that the last four site-selection processes had been tarnished, and that Salt Lake City was more victim than villain in the process. On that tumultuous weekend in Lausanne, the Salt Lake City scandal became an international cause célèbre. By Christmas, no fewer than four investigations had been launched into the scandal—one each by the IOC, the USOC, the SLOC, and a fourth by the U.S. Justice Department into possible unlawful activity by the Salt Lake City bidders.

Salt Lake City 2002—Women's ice hockey is a newly added event to the Winter Games. Here Canada defeats Finland at the Salt Lake City Games, 2002. Courtesy of Ed Goldstein.

As the new year of 1999 dawned, in a scandal-tinged America already consumed at the time by the impeachment of President Bill Clinton, the Olympic bribery story mushroomed. While the various investigators worked on their reports, news trickled out not only of scholarships for IOC relatives, but of other favors, including cash payments given to IOC members by bidders (IOC rules had limited bid-city gifts to a value of $150). On January 8, the scandal claimed its first casualties when Joklik and Johnson, the top two officers in SLOC's administration, submitted their resignations. Joklik, who had been chairman of the bid committee board in the early 1990s when the questionable activities occurred, said he did not know about the improper payments at the time but would step aside since the excessive gifting took place on his watch. Utah Governor Mike Leavitt, expressing disgust at the bid revelations, stepped into the state's Olympic leadership vacuum, while Salt Lake City Mayor Deedee Corradini announced that she would not seek another term in office; both had served on the bid committee but denied knowing of the improper activities.

The first of the scandal reports to be presented publicly was that of the IOC's ad hoc panel, headed by Canadian Richard Pound and focused primarily on the conduct of IOC members who "abused their positions." On January 24 in Lausanne, the IOC announced that its executive board, acting on the Pound report, was recommending the expulsion of six IOC members (three others had already resigned prior to the meeting) for accepting excessive favors from the Salt Lake City bidders. Two months later, on March 17, the whole IOC membership met to act on the recommendations and voted to expel six of its members and to issue warnings of varying degrees to nine others. Four had resigned by then, meaning that a total of 19 IOC members, more than 15 percent of the body, were disciplined in the Salt Lake City scandal. And that did not include Rene Essomba, whose daughter Sonia was the subject of the infamous leaked letter; he had died before the scandal broke.

But the IOC had to do more than police its guilty members. With sponsors becoming wary of continuing their financial support of the Olympic Movement and with American congresspeople threatening to impede the flow of U.S. corporate dollars to IOC coffers, the IOC also had to reform its process of selecting future Olympic host cities. IOC President Juan Antonio Samaranch, who received an overwhelming vote of confidence from IOC members at the March meeting, favored eliminating bid-city trips for IOC members, thus drying up the opportunities for gift-giving. He set up two commissions, one to examine bidding procedures and another to revamp the IOC's ethics code. After those panels completed their work and offered recommendations, the IOC met on the weekend of December 11–12, 1999, in Lausanne and passed 50 reform proposals, the most important of which was that site visits to Olympic bid cities were now prohibited. After getting his way, Samaranch declared the problem to be solved and then went to Washington, D.C., to subject himself to questioning by a U.S. House of Representatives subcommittee, an unfriendly barrage that he weathered reasonably well.

While the IOC's process of internal reform took almost all of 1999, SLOC's did not take nearly that long. About two weeks after the release of the IOC's Pound report, SLOC's sitting ethics committee, charged with ferreting out the bid committee's activities, released its 300-page report on February 9, 1999. It was the most complete catalogue of the Salt Lake City bidders' gifting practices from 1991 to 1995, and it placed most of the blame on Welch and Johnson—who simply became "Tom and Dave" in local lore—while only mildly chastising the bid committee's board for weak oversight. The Salt Lake City bidders had offered gifts, favors, and payments estimated at more than $1 million, including $70,000 in direct cash payments to Jean-Claude Ganga of the Republic of Congo, one of the IOC members eventually expelled. So eager was Welch to please fellow members of the Olympic family that in one instance he took $30,000 out of his own children's trust accounts to make a loan to the spouse of a Samoan IOC member. The revelations were still fresh when, two days after releasing the report, SLOC set itself on a new course and named Massachusetts venture capitalist Mitt Romney to succeed Joklik as the organization's president.

After the release of the IOC and SLOC reports, the USOC's specially created oversight commission, chaired by former U.S. Senator George Mitchell, issued its report on March 1. It placed blame on the IOC for its "culture of improper gift-giving," on SLOC for its bid procedures, and on the USOC for failing to monitor the activities of American bid cities. The Mitchell report also noted that it "strains credulity" to think that Welch and Johnson engaged in their improprieties without the knowledge of the high-profile members of Salt Lake City's bid committee board, an opinion that was shared by many Utahns. As for direct USOC involvement, one of its officials, Alfredo La Mont, the director of international relations, resigned in January due to his undisclosed relationship with Welch in assisting the

Salt Lake City bid. A year later, La Mont pleaded guilty to two federal tax fraud charges in regard to a fictitious company through which he had received payments from the Salt Lake City bidders.

The fourth investigation, that of the U.S. Justice Department, was the one that could most imperil the Salt Lake City bidders. With the exception of a guilty plea obtained from a Salt Lake City businessman on a tax fraud charge in August 1999 and the two pleas from La Mont in March 2000, the federal investigation yielded little for a year and a half. Then, on July 20, 2000, the hammer dropped on Welch and Johnson in the form of a federal grand-jury indictment on 15 felony counts of bribery, racketeering, and fraud, charges for which the two bid leaders could have received prison time. More ominously for SLOC, the prospect loomed of Utah civic leaders being called to the witness stand and questioned about their professed ignorance of the bid improprieties, all of it possibly happening in a Salt Lake City courtroom at or near the time of the Olympics themselves. Then, a year later, on July 16, 2001, U.S. District Judge David Sam dismissed four of the counts against Welch and Johnson, arguing that Utah's commercial bribery statute upon which they were based was ill-applied in this case. Finally, on November 15, 2001, less than three months before the Olympics, Sam threw out the rest of the case, much to the relief of all involved. The Justice Department filed an appeal to Sam's ruling on January 23, 2002, but at least the 2002 Olympics would proceed without the concurrent distraction of a federal trial.

In the meantime, it was left to Romney, a Mormon and the son of a former Michigan governor, to pick up the pieces in Salt Lake City. His most critical task was to eliminate the huge SLOC budget gap of roughly $375 million between revenues and expenses; he did it by paring the budget to about $1.3 billion and generating revenues by collecting commitments from previously wary sponsors. In the fall of 2000, SLOC launched its ticketing campaign and sold about $30 million worth of tickets on the first day, putting it well on its way to achieving its goal of $180 million in ticket sales. The 2000–2001 winter season featured a series of successful test events at SLOC's competition venues. The last of these to be completed was at the enclosed speed skating oval, where cracks in the concrete forced a repouring of the surface in late 2000, prior to a record-setting debut in March 2001.

In two and a half years, the charismatic Romney had restored SLOC's equilibrium, but there would be one more crisis to face. On September 11, 2001, just five months before the start of the Olympics, terrorist attacks on the World Trade Center in New York and on the Pentagon in Washington stunned the nation, and, as a footnote, called the 2002 Winter Olympics into question. Romney, who was in Washington at the time of the attacks to lobby Congress for more federal dollars for security, bravely stated that the Games would go on. Picking up that refrain in Lausanne was new IOC President Jacques Rogge, who had succeeded Samaranch just two months earlier. But the climate was too unsettled for such certainty, and when the United States began air attacks in Afghanistan in October, IOC member Gerhard Heiberg was quoted as saying that "a country at war can't organize the Olympic Games." Heiberg quickly apologized, contending that was not what he meant. Romney and IOC officials asserted a more positive message: that it was precisely in such difficult times that the Olympic dynamic of universality and friendship is most needed.

The events of September 11 naturally focused SLOC and the IOC on the issue of security. The federal government stepped up its investment in Games security to about $220 million (the total federal contribution to the Games was estimated at almost $400 million, a figure not included under SLOC's privately funded $1.3 billion budget). Athletes, media representatives, and spectators would all be exposed to greater security measures at venue access points than at previous Olympics. And there would be no commercial or private access to the airspace over Salt Lake City for the duration of the Opening and Closing Ceremonies at the open-air, 50,000-seat Rice-Eccles Stadium on the University of Utah campus. But the most important security development was that there were no other terrorist attacks after September 11 to jeopardize the Games. And, as the Olympic torch relay made its way across the country over a two-month period, beginning on December 4, a spirit of renewed patriotism fused with the Olympic spirit to heighten anticipation of the Games.

Finally, on February 8, 2002, Salt Lake City's excruciating incubation period came to an end. The Opening Ceremonies that night, which featured the moving presentation of the tattered flag that had survived the World Trade Center attacks five months earlier, launched the largest-scale Winter Olympics ever—more than 2,500 athletes from 77 countries, competing in 78 events, a 70 percent increase in the program since the last time the Winter Games visited North America in 1988. The weather, so balky in previous Winter Olympics, cooperated not just for the opening but also for most of the two weeks. A couple events were postponed by high winds early in the Games, but other than that, sunny conditions prevailed. The logistical operation of the Games was nearly flawless, and for Americans there was the added bonus of the improbable success of the home team. Never a winter sports power, the United States won an astonishing 34 medals over the Olympic fortnight, one fewer than first-place Germany and 21 more than the United States had ever won before at a Winter Olympic Games.

For all the inspirational moments, though, the event that overshadowed all others in the Olympics was the scandalous outcome of the pairs figure-skating competition. On the fourth night of the Games, reigning world champions Jamie Sale and David Pelletier of Canada skated a marvelous free program that the Delta Center crowd assumed was redeemable for a gold medal. But the judges delivered a 5-4 victory to Elena Berezhnaya and Anton Sikharulidze, the eleventh consecutive Olympic gold in pairs figure skating for Russian skaters. North American fans and media howled at the decision, but it might have stood as just another unpopular figure-skating result were it not for the controversy that emerged around the pro-Russian vote of French judge Marie Reine Le Gougne. At a review meeting of the judges and the referee the morning after the pairs free skate, an emotional Le Gougne said she had cast her vote under pressure from Didier Gailhaguet, the president of France's ice sports federation, a tale she recanted before the week was out. Her story, accompanied by rumors that the French were vote-swapping with the Russians in order to get a favorable result for their ice dancing team, threatened to overtake the Games.

Jacques Rogge, the IOC president overseeing his first Olympics, prevailed upon Ottavio Cinquanta, president of the International Skating Union, to resolve the matter quickly. Cinquanta got his ISU board members together three nights after the pairs competition, and they decided to give gold medals to the jilted Canadian pair as well. The next morning, the IOC approved the solution, and Sale and Pelletier, objects of international sympathy by now, were declared cowinners. The double-gold solution defused the tempest for the rest of the Olympic fortnight, but the Skategate mess continued long after the Games. On April 30 in Lausanne, the ISU suspended both Le Gougne and Gailhaguet for three years (and for the 2006 Olympics). Then, in June at a meeting in Kyoto, Japan, the ISU voted to overhaul its scoring system over the next two years in an attempt to restore public confidence in the sport.

But the most stunning aftershock of Skategate came on July 31, when U.S. prosecutors charged Alimzhan Tokhtakhounov, a reputed Russian organized crime figure who was then living in Italy, with conspiring to fix the figure skating results in Salt Lake City. His supposed scheme was to ensure a pairs gold for the Russian team and a gold in ice dancing for the French team of Gwendal Peizerat and Marina Anissina, a Russian native, in exchange for the personal procurement of a French visa. The allegations, which resulted in a five-count indictment handed down by a federal grand jury in New York on August 21, were based on Italian police wiretaps of Tokhtakhounov's phone conversations, including one in which he reportedly told Anissina's mother that even if the skater were to fall in her Olympic competition, "we will make sure she is number one." The Russian connection in Skategate, which the ISU had ignored in its own investigation, cast a post-Salt Lake City pall over the Winter Olympics' most popular sport.

In addition to the skating corruption at the Salt Lake City Games, there were the requisite Olympic doping stories. In the wake of the doping scandal at the 2001 Nordic ski championships in Finland, the IOC and SLOC focused on having a clean Games. To that end, 95 percent of the Olympic athletes underwent testing before coming to Salt Lake City. There was little doping news during the Olympic fortnight, but on the last day of the Games, three Nordic skiing medalists—triple gold medalist Johann Muehlegg of Spain and Russian stars Larissa Lazutina and Olga Danilova—were busted for using darbepoetin, a new stamina-boosting drug. Muehlegg and Lazutina each lost one gold medal, and much later, at an International Ski Federation meeting in June, the three skiers were each suspended for two years. In all, there were seven confirmed doping cases at the 2002 Games, more than in all previous Winter Olympics.

Still, these Olympics were distinguished more by positive stories than by positive drug tests. American Sarah Hughes's stunning performance in the women's figureskating competition washed out some of the bad taste left over from the pairs controversy. And Canada's twin hockey triumphs were notable, particularly that of the men, who ended a 50-year Olympic gold drought by winning the second Olympic tournament that featured National Hockey League players. But perhaps the most moving story of these Games was written by American Jim Shea, who won gold in the men's skeleton, an event that was making its first appearance in the Olympics since 1948. Shea became a third-generation Winter Olympian, following his father (a 1964 Nordic skier) and his grandfather (a 1932 gold-medal speed skater). What made his triumph poignant was the fact that his grandfather, 91-year-old Jack Shea, was killed in a car accident only a month before the Games, dashing his dream of joining his son and grandson in Utah.

The 2002 Olympics were an artistic and popular success, as were the Paralympics that followed in March, the first Winter Paralympics ever taken under the wing of the Olympic organizing committee. A couple of days after the Olympics ended, Romney went to the state capitol to pay Utahns their long-promised $99 million—the $59 million that they had committed to building Olympic facilities in the 1989 referendum and a $40 million legacy fund to operate them. Then, on

April 24, Romney convened his last SLOC meeting and announced that his organization finished with a $56 million surplus. With that, Romney left Utah and returned to Massachusetts (where he was elected governor in November), leaving SLOC's shutdown duties to his right-hand man, Fraser Bullock. On September 18, Bullock conducted the last SLOC board meeting, at which he estimated SLOC's final profit to be $100 million. The Utah Athletic Foundation, the entity in charge of post-Olympics operation of the main sport venues (the Utah Olympic Park, the Olympic Oval, and the Soldier Hollow Nordic skiing site), would ultimately receive $76.5 million, almost double the budgeted $40 million legacy fund. Thus, the Salt Lake City Olympics were a financial triumph, despite the stain of scandal that was attached to them.

BIBLIOGRAPHICAL ESSAY

The repository for the official records of the 2002 Winter Olympics in Salt Lake City is the Special Collections Department at the J. Willard Marriott Library at the University of Utah. The Salt Lake Organizing Committee contracted with the Marriott Library to house its records, which include minutes from board meetings, financial reports, and other materials. The SLOC did not complete the process of preparing and handing over the documents until several months after the end of the Games, at which point the library staff began the task of accessioning the files. Well before the Games, the library had inventories of SLOC records from 1985 to 1993. This 14-box collection includes bid books, correspondence, news releases, newsletters, and 4 boxes of newspaper clippings.

In addition to bid committee and organizing committee records, the Marriott Library has other pertinent collections in its Utah Ski Archives, founded in 1989 to preserve Utah's winter sports history. These archives include photographs, video footage, personal papers, and oral histories from individuals who were central to the development of skiing in Utah and, eventually, to its connection with the Olympic Games. Also, among the books documenting that history are Alan Engen, *For the Love of Skiing* (Salt Lake City, UT, 1998); Alan Engen and Gregory Thompson, *First Tracks* (Salt Lake City, UT, 2001); and Alexis Kelner, *Skiing in Utah: A History* (Salt Lake City, UT, 1980).

In addition to its archival holdings, the Marriott Library has among its western Americana resources a number of monographs on Utah's Olympic history, including material on Salt Lake City's earlier bid for the 1972 Winter Games and newspaper clippings and local magazine articles on Salt Lake City's various efforts to host the Winter Games.

Salt Lake City's two daily newspapers, the *Salt Lake Tribune* and the *Deseret News*, copiously covered the bribery scandal in 1998–1999, and during the Games themselves, both papers produced daily Olympic Games sections and subsequently published Olympic Games books. The *Tribune*'s book, *17 Remarkable Days* (Salt Lake City, UT, 2002), consolidates the paper's daily Olympic sections and is a handy reference in Games competition. Nationally, the scandal brought more pre-Olympic attention from the press than a host city would normally expect; during the Games, several newspapers besides the local ones covered the events comprehensively, and *Sports Illustrated* published a daily magazine.

TORINO 2006

John E. Findling

TWENTIETH WINTER OLYMPIC GAMES

Torino (or Turin) is located in the Piedmont region, a large area in northwestern Italy bordering on France with a population of about 4.5 million. The largest city in Piedmont, Torino boasts a city population of some 900,000 and a metropolitan population of about 2.2 million, making it the largest city ever to host a Winter Olympic Games. Torino lies just east of the Italian Alps, where the outdoor events—skiing, curling, biathlon, snowboarding, bobsled, luge, and skeleton—will take place.

In March 1998, a coalition of local organizations, the Italian National Olympic Committee, and the Italian representatives on the International Olympic Committee (IOC) announced their intention to submit a bid for the 2006 Winter Games. Other cities bidding for these Games included Sion, Switzerland; Klagenfurt, Austria; Helsinki, Finland; Zakopane, Poland; and Poprad Tatry, Slovakia. The Torino candidacy was delivered to the IOC on August 31, 1998, and IOC representatives visited the city in mid-October.

According to the bidding process reforms that the IOC enacted after the Salt Lake City scandals made headline news in 1998, IOC members were not permitted to visit the candidate cities en masse. Instead, the six candidate cities made 50-minute final presentations to the IOC on June 18, 1999, and after the presentations, a selection college was appointed to review the candidacies and announce the two finalists. The selection college, which consisted of eight members, including French skier Jean-Claude Killy and Ukrainian sprinter Valery Borzov, picked Sion and Torino as the finalists, and on June 19, the IOC voted 53–36 to award the Games to the Italian city.

Most observers thought that Sion, which had been a candidate for the Winter Games in 1976 and 2002, had the better bid from a technical standpoint but had lost support because of Marc Holder, the veteran IOC member from Switzerland. Holder was an important figure in the 1998 revelations of IOC members' corruption in the Salt Lake City scandal, and many IOC members may have voted against Sion, the Swiss candidate city, because of their resentment towards Holder. Torino's presentation, however, pointed to the size of the city and its ability to provide all the necessary amenities for athletes, officials, and visitors, while still being close to excellent venues in the nearby mountains.

The Torino Olympic Organizing Committee, better known as TOROC, was created on December 27, 1999, with Paolo Rota, an engineer and former managing director of Invicta, as its CEO and Marcello Pochettino, a former Fiat and Maserati executive, as deputy CEO. In addition, former Torino mayor Valentin Castellani is TOROC's president, and Evalina Christillin, who had been president of the bid committee, is deputy president. The organization set up offices in a renovated Fiat building not far from the center of the city and quite close to several of the Games venues.

The XX Winter Olympic Games are scheduled for February 10–26, 2006, with competition in 15 sports, three Olympic villages (at Torino, Bardonecchia, and Sestriere), and seven competition sites. TOROC estimates that the Games will attract 2,550 competitors; 1,400 officials; 2,300 representatives from the IOC, various national Olympic committees, and the international federations of the relevant sports; 650 judges and referees; and 9,600 media personnel. Torino will also host the 2006 Winter Paralympic Games from March 10 to March 19, using the same venues as for the Winter Olympics. A special TOROC committee will arrange competition in the biathlon, Alpine skiing, Nordic skiing, curling, and ice sledge hockey.

The showcase venue for the 2006 Games will be the Palasport Olimpico, located in Torino near the existing Stadio Comunale. An international competition was held to design this building (and the surrounding area) and was won by a group headed by noted Japanese architect Arata Isozeki. In addition to the construction of the Palasport, Isozeki's plan also calls for the renovation of the Stadio Comunale, where the Opening and Closing Ceremonies are to be held. The new Palasport will seat 12,800 and be ready by April 2005. Other venues in Torino include the renovated Palavela, an existing multipurpose arena built in 1961 that will host the figure skating and short-track skating events in front of 9,000 spectators, scheduled to be ready in November 2004, and a second hockey arena, a temporary facility built within the existing Giovanni Agnelli Pavilion in the Torino trade show complex, with seating for 6,000 and a completion date of February 2004.

TOROC is also overseeing the construction of a new speed-skating stadium, the Oval Lingotto, for 8,000 spectators, due to be ready by December 2004, and a new 3,000-seat venue for curling in the outlying district of Pinerolo, about 36 kilometers to the southwest. Most of the construction on these new or renovated venues commenced in the spring of 2003; the total costs of construction are estimated at more than 214 million euros.

Farther to the west, in the mountains, Alpine skiing events will take place near Sestriere on existing courses that meet International Ski Federation (FIS) standards. Some of the women's Alpine events, as well as the biathlon, are scheduled for Cesana San Sicario. The snowboarding competition will occur at the Melezet ski complex in Bardonecchia, while freestyle skiing will be contested near the village of Sauze d'Ouix-Jovenceaux. The ski-jumping events and the Nordic skiing will take place at Pragelato, and the bobsled, luge, and skeleton competition is slated for Cesana Pariol. The various mountain sites are all between 85 and 100 kilometers from Torino, and the Italian government has pledged to make the necessary improvements to the connecting roads.

As has become standard since Lillehammer, TOROC adopted policies to ensure as little environmental damage and degradation as possible, in keeping with IOC guidelines. A set of environmental plans has been drafted in conjunction with local authorities, and a system of monitoring the implementation of these plans has been devised.

The IOC's Coordination Commission, which serves as a liaison between a host city and the IOC, met with TOROC on December 12–13, 2002, to review the organizing committee's plans for the 2006 Games. The commission was pleased with the improvements that TOROC made in its organizational structure and with the hiring of 135 new employees. In addition, the commission noted the increased coordination between TOROC and local institutions and organizations. Other good news included the results of a survey indicating a high level of public support for the Games.

In December 2002, TOROC launched its licensing program for the production and sale of goods bearing Olympic trademarks exclusive to the 2006 Games, including the Torino logo and the emblem of the Italian National Olympic Committee. Official pins, always the most popular souvenir, will be produced by Trof, a Norwegian firm that has set up a branch in Torino.

BIBLIOGRAPHICAL ESSAY

At this point, two years before the 2006 Winter Games, it is uncertain where the official records for the Games will be deposited. The Organizing Committee for the Games, known as TOROC, maintains an informative Web site, http://www.torino2006.org, and the organization sends by e-mail regular bulletins of its ongoing activities in preparing for the Games. TOROC periodically publishes a *Media Update* that presents current information concerning its organization, venues for the Games, environmental concerns, and the Paralympics that will follow the Winter Games in Torino. For a contrary view, see http://nolimpiadi. 8m.com, a Web site for those opposed to the Torino Games.

Torino's unexpected success in winning the honor of hosting the Games was covered in major newspapers. See the *New York Times*, March 19, June 20, and July 4, 1999; *The Times* (London), June 17, 19, 20, and 21, 1999; and the *Chicago Tribune*, June 17 and 19, 1999. Italian readers can follow the preparations for the 2006 Games in *La Stampa*, a national newspaper in Italy that is published in Torino. Its Web address is http://www.lastampa.it.

VANCOUVER 2010

Larry Maloney

Vancouver brings the Winter Olympic Games back to North America just eight short years after the Salt Lake City Games of 2002, but the city's quest for this prize extends back to the 1960 Winter Olympics in Squaw Valley. At those Games, a group of Vancouver skiers attending the Games began to think on a grand scale and dreamt of hosting the 1968 Winter Olympics in their own city. One obstacle blocked their path to Olympic glory: Vancouver's temperate coastal climate rarely produces snowfalls one would equate with the Winter Games. Their search for a suitable mountain venue for Olympic skiing brought them to London Mountain where little but a lodge existed. From this humble beginning, Vancouver's current-day Olympic partner, Whistler, was born.

This early group of Olympic hopefuls made no bid for the 1968 Winter Olympics, but they set in motion a 43-year-old collaboration toward bringing the Olympics to British Columbia. During this time, Vancouver/Whistler attempted to win the 1976 Winter Games, and Whistler initially attempted to secure the 1980 Winter Games before withdrawing its candidacy. These early defeats deterred neither community. As they continued to grow and gain in international stature, so did their Olympic aspirations.

In 1998, Vancouver and Whistler felt the time had come to mount an all-out campaign for the 2010 Winter Olympic Games. By this time, however, the value of the Olympic enterprise as an economic development tool attracted multiple cities to the bidding process. Faced with an ever-growing list of candidate cities, the International Olympic Committee (IOC) changed its bidding rules. Beginning with the 2010 bid, the IOC established an entrance fee of $100,000 per city to defray bid evaluation costs. The cities proceeding to the final round would have to pay an additional $500,000.

In spite of the entrance fees, Vancouver faced competition from a wide field of candidates that included Sarajevo; Andorra; Bern, Switzerland; Harbin, China; Jaca, Spain; Pyeonchang, South Korea; and Salzburg, Austria. The first-round elimination left Vancouver facing the favorite, Salzburg, as well as Bern, and lesser-known Pyeonchang.

Salzburg considered its strength to be its historical reputation as a winter sport paradise. Bern based its bid on hosting an affordable Games through the use of existing sport venues and transportation networks. Pyeonchang stressed that bringing a Winter Games to Asia would promote winter sports in a region where they are lesser known. Pyeonchang also played a trump card—a South Korean Winter Olympics could accelerate reconciliation with North Korea.

Vancouver's strength, its alliance with Whistler, also proved to be its principal weakness. The Sea-to-Sky Highway connecting the two communities traversed mountainous terrain for 78 miles. The trip during winter months often became a traveler's nightmare and could take up to two hours to complete. Vancouver compensated for the distance in its bid by pledging to build two distinct Olympic centers. According to the bid plan, Whistler would have all the Olympic amenities required to be self-sustaining—its own athletes' village, media centers, and media housing. Additionally, Vancouver stated that British Columbia planned to spend $425 million to expand the highway to at least three lanes for 75 percent of the journey.

Before the strength of Vancouver's bid and distant accommodations could be tested, however, local politics led to the self-elimination of one of the final four candidates. One month after the first-round elimination, Bern held the first-ever election to determine whether the residents of a bid city supported funding for an Olympic bid. In a stunning defeat, approximately 80 percent of the city's residents voted against such support. Bern's bid secretary, Iris Huggler, responded to the defeat by saying, "I'm positive none of the other [candidate] cities could survive a vote either. The difference is that they're smart enough not to do it" ("Bern to Withdraw 2010 Games Bid," *Vancouver Sun*, September 23, 2002).

In light of the outcome of Bern's vote, it seemed unlikely any of the remaining bid cities would contradict Huggler's advice. Larry Campbell, however, made a campaign promise after the Bern vote that a similar vote would take place if he were elected Vancouver's mayor. At Mayor Campbell's first city council meeting, the council voted 8-2 to schedule a nonbinding plebiscite to determine support for the Olympics in Vancouver. The bid committee and the IOC were stunned given the potential outcome and the precedent it would set for future bids. One IOC member stated that a rejection by Vancouver's electorate could jeopardize Vancouver's bid, Toronto's bid for the 2012 Olympic Games, and any future Olympic aspirations Canada might have. Even though the outcome would be nonbinding, IOC President Jacques Rogge made it clear that anything less than a majority vote of 60 percent would mortally wound Vancouver's Olympic dream.

Supporters of the Vancouver bid rallied quickly and pulled together a $540,000 campaign that blanketed the city with building wraps, banners, and advertisements in newspapers and on radio and television stations. Even Prime Minister Jean Chrétien asked the city's voters to support the bid. The previous turnout for a plebiscite in Vancouver only reached 15 percent of registered voters. For the Olympic plebiscite, 46 percent of the electorate voted, of which 64 percent voted in favor of the Games. The members of the IOC understood the message—the Olympics are welcome in Vancouver.

When the IOC voted for the winning bid city just five months later, Vancouver remained the favorite, but politics began to play a role in the final selection. In the first round of voting, Pyeongchang received 51 of the minimum 54 votes needed to win the bid, while Vancouver received 40, and an embarrassed Salzburg limped into third with 16. IOC vote watchers believed many European IOC members threw their votes to Pyeongchang to protect the European candidate field vying for the 2012 Summer Games (Paris, London, Madrid, and Moscow). A 2010 Winter Games in Europe, particularly after Athens in 2004 and Turin in 2006, could have hurt the chances of a European candidate in 2012. Once the European candidate was eliminated, Vancouver and Whistler won over Pyeongchang 56 to 33 in the second and final round of voting.

Now that Vancouver and Whistler have secured a prize that was 43 years in the making, both communities will face the pressure to excel that has daunted every Olympic city in the modern era. In fact, the bar of achievement for Vancouver 2010 already has been raised. Gerhard Heiberg, the former president of the Lillehammer organizing committee and the chairman of the IOC evaluation commission, stated after Vancouver's victory, "I think they can put on the best Games the world has ever seen" ("Best Games World Has Ever Seen: Heiberg," *The Province*, 3 July 2003). If Vancouver can successfully stage the event described in their bid, they may achieve that goal.

Vancouver's plan calls for staging all ice events in Vancouver, including Opening and Closing Ceremonies, figure skating, ice hockey, curling, and speed skating. With the exception of freestyle skiing and snowboarding at Cypress Mountain outside Vancouver, all Alpine events, as well as luge, bobsled, and skeleton, will take place at Whistler. If Vancouver carries out its plan for two self-contained Olympic hubs, the majority of venues will be less than 15 minutes away from either the Vancouver or the Whistler athletes' village.

One aspect of the plan may be hard to achieve—maintaining the budget described in the bid. Vancouver plans to host these Games for the equivalent of $1.55 billion. This expenditure includes capital construction, such as the largest-ever venue for curling (6,000 capacity), as well as two villages totaling $171 million. As a point of comparison, the successful Games of Salt Lake City closed its books having spent $1.9 billion.

However, the federal and provincial governments plan to cover some capital expenditures off budget, which might help to keep the organizing committee on budget. For example, improvements to the Sea-to-Sky Highway will be paid by the province, while the province and the federal government will assist with the financing of an expansion of the Convention Center (to be used as the media complex) as well as construction of a rapid transit line from the airport to downtown Vancouver. The province and federal government also will provide $129 million toward security for the Games.

Expectations for a high return on investment have reached Olympic proportions already with six and a half years to go before the Opening Ceremonies. Analysts estimate the 2010 Games will generate $7.2 billion in economic activity in the region through planning, construction, and tourism, as well as create up to 228,000 jobs.

The highest expectations, however, center on Canada's Olympic team. At both the 1976 Games in Montreal and at the 1988 Games in Calgary, Canada's team failed to win a gold medal on its home soil. The federal government faces pressure to increase funding for the Canadian Olympic Corporation to as much as $85 million per year to avoid a similarly embarrassing fate in Vancouver. And the pressure will continue to grow as the time until 2010 evaporates given that studies show that it takes 10 to 12 years to groom an Olympic champion. However, the Games on Canadian soil should increase donations from its corporate community.

The Vancouver bid committee funded the first attempt to train the generation of athletes competing in 2010. The LegaciesNOW initiative provides $3.6 million seed money to engender a love of winter sports in the next generation, which the bid committee hopes will include medal contenders as well. LegaciesNOW could serve as a model for communities across Canada.

Vancouver has a stunning backdrop of sea and mountains that will play well with the world's television audiences. The Games also enjoys the support of the majority of its residents. To achieve the status of hosting the best Games ever, however, it will need to avoid the chronic construction delays that have plagued Athens 2004, and both communities will need financial support from the province and the federal government. After all, 43-year-old dreams should not be neglected just as they are coming to life.

BIBLIOGRAPHICAL ESSAY

This chapter was written shortly after Vancouver/Whistler won the bid for the 2010 Winter Olympic Games. Therefore, resources are not abundant at this time on these Games. The Vancouver bid site, http://www.winter2010.com, contains the bidding documents submitted to the International Olympic Committee. The Web site address for the organizing committee likely will change. The Web site http://www.canada.com, a collaborative effort of several of the nation's publishers, maintains a portal with information and history on the Vancouver bid. The Web site http://www.msnbc.com also provides an array of articles on the Vancouver bid, as does the *New York Times* (http://www.nyt.com) and the *Washington Post* (http://www.washingtonpost.com) Web sites.

APPENDIX A: THE INTERNATIONAL OLYMPIC COMMITTEE

Dwight H. Zakus

At the beginning of the twenty-first century, the modern Olympic Movement is marked by rapid change. This era of change began in the 1980s with Juan Antonio Samaranch's presidency and was initially one of marked expansion of all elements of the movement, but the Salt Lake City bidding scandal of 1998–1999, along with subsequent International Olympic Committee (IOC) and government inquiries, imposed even more dramatic changes in the Olympic movement. It is the presidency of Jacques Rogge that will implement these latest changes.

The IOC, described in the *Olympic Charter* as the "supreme authority of the Olympic movement," is responsible for the spread of modern Olympism, the philosophy that is basic to this global organization. This philosophy is expressed in the charter as a

> philosophy of life, exalting and combining in a balanced whole the qualities of body, will, and mind. Blending sport with culture and education, Olympism seeks to create a way of life based on the joy found in effort, the educational value of good example and respect for universal fundamental ethical principles. The goal of Olympism is to place everywhere sport at the service of the harmonious development of man *[sic]*, with a view to encouraging the establishment of a peaceful society concerned with the preservation of human dignity.

The Olympic Movement, which the IOC governs, ensures that Olympism is spread throughout the world by means of Olympic sport festivals and the various educational, artistic, and sport development programs it supports. IOC members act as trustees of the movement.

The primary way that the IOC ensures that this occurs is through the celebration of the Olympic Games. These Games are based on the fundamental philosophical principles of modem Olympism, but other publications and educational programs exist to enhance the development of Olympism. The charter is "the codification of the Fundamental Principles, Rules and By-laws adopted by the IOC. It governs the organization and operation of the Olympic movement and stipulates the conditions for the celebration of the Olympic Games." The fundamental principles remain little changed over the years; however, the charter was extensively reviewed between 1982 and 1990, and a number of changes were ratified at the 1999 Tokyo Session. The charter continues to be amended as required, often as the result of major reviews, such as those by the IOC Reforms Commission and Ethics Commission.

The charter also delineates the relationships with other members of the Olympic family. The members of the family are the international sport federations (IFs), national Olympic committees (NOCs), and the current organizing committees (OCOGs) for upcoming Summer and Winter Games. The Olympic Movement is therefore involved in a nexus of all sport, at all levels of competition, in the world.

At the second meeting of the IOC in Athens (1896), delegates voted that each nation should form its own NOC and that each NOC would be eligible to have a representative on the IOC. In addition, the powers of the IOC and its president were defined and the relationship between the IOC and the various NOCs spelled out. Many of the policies approved in 1896 remain in the current version of the charter. With this authority, the IOC is able to control the individuals (especially athletes), organizations (clubs and local/national/regional sport bodies), the Olympic Games, and other games (e.g., Universiade, Pan American) that seek recognition under its charter. This policy dates back to the founding meeting in Paris in 1894.

The Villa Mons-Repos in Lausanne, Switzerland, was Coubertin's home. It also served as IOC headquarters from 1921 to 1968. Courtesy of University of Illinois Archives, Avery Brundage Collection.

Although the presidency and headquarters of the IOC were originally to change with each Olympiad, this did not occur. During the 1901 meeting in Paris, Pierre de Coubertin, first elected in 1896, was reelected president for a 10-year term. Six years later, this term was extended for another 10 years. Therefore, the headquarters in the early years of the movement were located in Coubertin's private offices in Paris until 1915 and then in Lausanne, a beautiful city on Lake Leman and a favorite location of Coubertin. Lausanne had been the site for IOC sessions and congresses beginning in 1908. As Coubertin felt a need to ensure the administrative continuity of the movement and protect its archives, he relocated the headquarters in Lausanne, a safe haven during World War I (and subsequently World War II). The relationship between the IOC, the city of Lausanne, the canton of Vaud, and the Swiss government has evolved and is now of central importance in the operations of the IOC. In 1993 Lausanne was declared the Olympic capital.

In Lausanne, the IOC headquarters were first housed in the Casino de Montenon (1915–1921). As the staff, operations, archives, and museum grew, the Villa

Mons-Repos (1921–1968) became the headquarters and served also as Coubertin's home. Several other buildings have housed different elements of the IOC and its secretariat since 1915. Currently the Chateau de Vidy (1968–present) and its new administrative annex, Olympic House (1986–present, with an extension opened in 1998), make up the main headquarters. They house meetings, produce publications, provide translation and public and legal relations, and contain facilities for the secretariat staff, including the president's office.

On June 23, 1993, a new museum, research center, archive, and library opened in Ouchy, the port town adjacent to Lausanne. In late 1993 the IOC purchased the Guelfi Villa located next to the museum as the administrative headquarters for the museum. These new buildings replaced an older facility in downtown Lausanne and areas within Olympic House in Vidy. The IOC also has a residence (Villa Gruaz) near its headquarters, and its assistance program, Olympic Solidarity, now occupies two floors in the Villa Mons-Repos.

In June 1894 a congress was held at the Sorbonne in Paris, at the initiative of Coubertin, ostensibly to discuss sportive matters but specifically, according to Coubertin's memoirs, to establish a modern version of the ancient Greek Olympic Games. Some 78 delegates from 10 countries attended these meetings. On June 23, 1894, several decisions were accepted in a plenary session, including the establishment of a modern cycle of Olympic Games. Several rules for these Games were set, as were the first two host cities: Athens (1896) and Paris (1900). Thirteen individuals (including some not in attendance) were selected as members of the newly named Comite International des Jeux Olympiques. Demetrios Vikelas of Greece was appointed president since the first Games were to be held in Athens. Father Didon's motto of *Citius, Altius, Fortius* (faster, higher, stronger) was accepted as the official motto of the new movement. The congress closed as it had opened, with ceremonies and other festivities to celebrate both ancient and modern sport. This pomp, ceremony, and absolute adherence to protocol became a hallmark the IOC in all of its activities, as listed in the *Olympic Charter.*

In July 1894 the first *Bulletin* of the IOC was published. This publication was the main source of information about the Olympic Movement. It appeared sporadically after 1896 and has been revived under other titles, including the current one, *Olympic Review.* Generally, *Olympic Review* contains the minutes of meetings, decisions of congresses and sessions (and, after 1921, Executive Board meetings), the status of both individual and organizational members, and Olympic stories. Today, a wide variety of publications—including two journals (*Olympic Review* and *Olympic Message*), the speeches of the presidents, the charter, manuals on holding the Games, histories, as well as postcards, posters, comics, and other related items—emanate from the *IOC.*

The IOC remained a small body well into the twentieth century. It had 15 members in 1896, 25 in 1901, 48 in 1914, 65 in 1930, 73 in 1939, 95 in 1995, and 128 in 2002. The first female members, Pirjo Haggman and Flor Isava-Fonseca, were selected in 1981. In 1990 Isava-Fonseca became the first woman to be elected to the Executive Board (EB). Overall, 20 women have been members of the IOC and 3 have been on the EB as of 2002.

New members were selected at the whim of Coubertin until 1902, when a postal vote was initiated for the whole IOC to approve new members. This procedure was apparently discontinued in 1939, although many other decisions continued to be made this way well into the 1970s. When the EB was established in 1921, one of its tasks was to recommend individuals for membership. As a result of the 2000 reforms, a nominations commission now does this. It receives names of suitable members from each element of the Olympic Family and presents names to the EB to put forward to the full IOC membership for approval. A certain number of active athletes are now elected IOC members by their peers during a Summer or Winter Games. Prior to 1998–1999 there were exceptions to the membership procedure. For example, in 1992 Samaranch was given permission to appoint two members and to circumvent the rules on language, domicile, and the maximum number of members per country.

In the early years of the IOC, any country belonging to the movement could have at least one IOC member, although some had up to three. Generally, if a country had hosted a Summer or Winter Games, or had individuals serving as president of an NOC, an NOC association, an IF or an IF association (these are listed below), it had greater representation on the IOC. The size of the IOC could potentially grow to several hundred on this basis, but as a result of the 2000 reforms, the IOC now has a maximum of 115 members. Of this total, 15 members are from the winter and summer IFs or are IF association presidents, 15 are from the NOCs or are regional NOC presidents, fifteen are athletes, and seventy are individually selected members.

In 1908, at its 10th Session in London, the IOC defined the criteria for membership, length of term, and total number of members. Each member represents the IOC in his or her country, lives in that country, ensures that its NOC follows the charter, and is conversant in either English or French, the official languages. Each member takes an oath of admission to support the IOC charter. Members must attend the annual session, participate on the many permanent or ad hoc commissions of the IOC, or hold office on one of the other world sport bodies the IOC recognizes.

As of 2002 there have been 481 members on the IOC. Originally IOC members were elected for life, but currently they must retire from active participation at the age of 80. Under the 2000 reforms, transitional arrangements are in place to make the IOC less secretive and more democratic. If a member has 10 years of service (and retires or resigns for good reason), he or she becomes an honorary member at retirement. This allows former members to attend the sessions as nonvoting delegates and go to the Games. In 2000 the category of honorary member was expanded to include eminent personalities from outside the IOC who have made significant contributions to the movement. Members may also be labeled *decommissionaire*, which means they have been expelled from the IOC for not attending sessions or for "knowingly jeopardizing the interests of the IOC or acting in a way which is unworthy of the IOC." This was put into effect following the Salt Lake City scandal of 1998–1999; 6 members were expelled, 4 members resigned, and 9 others were given official warnings.

Until it was abolished at the end of 1975, members had to pay an annual membership fee that varied from 50 to 250 Swiss francs. These membership fees represented the main source of revenue for the IOC for many years. Many members failed to pay this amount and were declared *decommissionaire*. Other members, of course, died (many on the long journeys they had to make to attend the meetings, which were mainly in Europe), resigned, changed their country of residence, or lost interest. It is interesting to note that the EB and the general membership have generally refused to accept retirements and resignations, except in the case of misbehavior.

The session is the annual general meeting of the Olympic Movement. Sessions have been held every year except during the world wars. From 1936 to 1992, two sessions per year were held, but the IOC returned to the single annual meeting format after the Winter Games cycle was altered in 1994. In addition, a number of extraordinary meetings have been held. Cities around the world compete in an intense bidding process to host sessions, which are elaborate ceremonies with formal speeches, cultural activities, dinners, balls, receptions, and other social activities in addition to the business meetings. A strict protocol is followed at these meetings, based on one's position and length of service on the IOC. This protocol also applies to attendance at the Games and other IOC-related activities. This also applies to EB meetings, which are usually held in conjunction with an IF or NOC association meeting.

At the beginning of the movement, sessions of the IOC were identified as congresses, but that term is now used for separate, less regular meetings, which are concerned with particular topics or issues. Three of these congresses were held when a change of presidents occurred. The first took place in 1925 when Comte Henri de Baillet-Latour replaced Coubertin. The second was in 1972 when Lord Killanin replaced Avery Brundage. The 1981 congress was held the year after

The IOC conducts its business at periodic sessions in elegant locations such as this palace in Rome. Courtesy of University of Illinois Archives, Avery Brundage Collection.

Juan Antonio Samaranch replaced Lord Killanin. In June 1994, a Centenary Congress was held in Paris to mark the centennial of the IOC's founding. The charter now stipulates that congresses will be held every eight years.

The congresses are important in the history of the Olympic movement for two key reasons. First, they deal with fundamental issues of global sport. The IOC holds a distinctive position in that it was established during a period when few national sport bodies (now NOCs) and few international sport governing bodies (IFs) existed. Therefore, the congresses dealt with many basic issues that still take considerable organizational effort: standardization of the rules, equipment, and officiating and judging; financing and organizing the Games and their facilities; eligibility (especially the issue of amateurism); the establishing, promoting, and expansion of NOCs and IFs; sport pedagogy; sport hygiene; doping; and, most importantly and regularly, developing the program of the Summer and Winter Games. The reports of the congresses of 1921, 1925, 1930, and especially 1972, 1981, and 1994 are voluminous, attesting to this complex and difficult task.

Congresses also hear the reports of commissions. From the very first meeting, commissions have provided input for the operation of the Olympic Movement. Many of the commissions have continued to operate since the early days of the movement, although others are ad hoc. They are consultative only, except for the Games-coordinating ones (those organizing future Summer or Winter Games), which are operational in nature. In 2002, 22 commissions and 3 Games-coordinating commissions were in operation. Several of these resulted from the IOC's 2000 reforms, in particular the Ethics, Nominations, and IOC 2000 Reforms Follow-up commissions. The president now decides when a commission is needed and when its work has finished, chairs several of them, and serves ex officio on all of them. A full list of commissions is annually published in the *IOC Directory*.

Other advisory groups and individual consultants also carry out duties under the IOC's guidance. Councillors exist for the council of the Olympic Order, the council of the Olympic Movement, and the court of arbitration for sport. Advisers are also used for juridical matters, marketing, the Olympic coin and stamp programs, technical matters regarding television, preparation for the Olympic Games, relations with Switzerland and with developing countries, and with the NOCs and IFs. Clearly, this committee structure has served an important role in carrying out the IOC's work under the charter.

The workload of the IOC increased dramatically once the Games gained stability and recognition after 1912. In 1921 an Executive Board was established to meet more frequently for carrying out routine business and proposing an agenda to the annual session. The EB structure has varied over time. Other than the president, it has had from one to four vice presidents and from three to six members at large. Prior to the late 1990s crisis, the EB consisted of the president, four vice presidents, and six members at large, elected by the membership at an annual session.

According to the charter, the vice presidents and members at large must rotate off the EB every four years and are not eligible for immediate re-election, although this rule has not always been followed. In fact, it has often been ignored and is an ongoing point of contention in the IOC, especially when the Avery Brundage and Juan Antonio Samaranch presidencies were extended. Recent reforms have set EB membership limits. The president is elected for eight years, with one possible four-year extension. Vice presidents and members are elected for four-year terms and must sit out four years before being reelected (unless elected president or vice president). The terms are staggered to provide continuity. After the 2000 reforms, the EB increased to 15 members and now must include a representative from a summer IF, a winter IF, an NOC, and the athletes. The director-general, IOC administration directors, and other staff must attend EB meetings.

The EB began its work on October 1, 1921; its first recorded meeting minutes are dated November 7, 1921, in Paris. Before 1962, the EB generally met annually, although it convened more frequently in those years when Games took place. From 1962 to the present there have been more frequent meetings, with four the standard since the 1970s.

Although the session is theoretically central to the operation of the IOC, the EB has come to hold a very important power position since 1980. The IOC has a much more corporate orientation today than in its earlier history. Samaranch lived in

Lausanne and worked full-time for the IOC. Not since Coubertin did a president have such a presence in the daily operation of the movement. Current President Jacques Rogge also lives and works full-time in Lausanne, acting as a chief executive officer in his presidential position.

The secretariat (now officially the IOC Administration) is the bureaucracy that handles the IOC's daily operation. The size and elaboration of the secretariat have changed with the growth of the IOC. In the early days of the movement Coubertin was very much the key figure in ensuring that IOC business was completed. He was the secretary-general for the first meetings and wrote prodigiously about the movement in the *Bulletin/Olympic Review* and in his memoirs. The executive board of the pre-1921 period was very much that of an amateur sport club in that the members filled various roles to carry on the business operations of the body. Translators, transcribers, and other staff were initially selected on an ad hoc basis, especially for the recording of the minutes and results of the congresses, whereas regular staff members now fill those roles.

Around 1922, non-IOC members first joined the secretariat. The EB named a chancellor and secretary to assist the president with IOC business. The chancellor (later identified as secretary-general) helped organize meetings and assisted the secretary with other services and duties, such as copying the minutes of meetings. Various men filled this role: Fred Auckenthaler (1922–1924), André Berdez (1925–1940), Werner Klingeberg (1939–1945), Otto Mayer (1946–1964), Eric Jonas (1964–1965), and Johann Westerhoff (1965–1969). Lydia Zanchi, a part-time employee from 1926 to 1946, handled many of the administrative tasks in these early years. Her work in maintaining the integrity of the IOC was particularly vital during World War II, when EB members were unable to meet regularly. In 1946, Zanchi became the IOC's full-time secretary, a position she held until her retirement in 1966.

Under Westerhoff, the secretariat modernized and modestly expanded. Westerhoff worked with the city of Lausanne to obtain Vidy and then departmentalized, formalized, and professionalized operations in the headquarters. He identified a number of commissions and prepared the first budgets. Throughout his tenure he struggled with Brundage to complete and fund this modernization, only to be ousted eventually by Brundage.

In 1969 two directors were appointed to replace Westerhoff. Monique Berlioux became secretary-general and Arthur Takac technical director. Berlioux was actually the director of press and public relations and in charge of the *Olympic Review* until 1973. Through her strength of character and capacity for work, Berlioux took control of the secretariat and moved it through an expansion and rationalization process. Her reports, including suggestions for changes in the structure of the secretariat, were extensive and detailed. From her reports to the sessions and the EB meetings, it is possible to see how formalized the organization became under her guidance.

The secretariat grew from a staff of 12 in 1969, to 35 in 1978, to 83 in 1986, a year after Berlioux left the secretariat. Although there was a growing need for employees, difficulties were encountered with attracting and retaining them. A good deal of this problem had to do with obtaining Swiss work permits, but some apparently stemmed from Berlioux's leadership style. Berlioux's power in organizing and operating the IOC eventually resulted in a conflict with Samaranch that led to her removal in 1985. She was replaced by Raymond Gafner, who acted as administrative delegate until 1989, when the current director, François Carrard, was appointed, and by Françoise Zweifel as secretary-general (1985–2000).

The entire secretariat has undergone considerable change since 1980. The IOC's rapid expansion was not met with necessary organizational change, a problem that has long plagued the organization. The EB has frequently discussed it, and external consulting agencies have, from time to time, studied it. With the election of Jacques Rogge as president in 2001, both internal and external audits of the entire organization occurred. In 2002 seven external audits on all aspects of the IOC were undertaken to enhance the efficiency of its various functions. An extraordinary session in November 2002 dealt with changes indicated by these audits (see Chart 1 for this structure).

The secretariat expanded from 97 full-time equivalent positions in 1995 to 220 in early 2002. Other staff is hired on part-time or contract basis as needed. Nine departments, each with a director, work under the director-general. Each department is further divided into specialized task units common to many large organizations. The president and the director-general also have cabinet staffs.

New IOC member Juan Antonio Samaranch serving as a guide to Avery Brundage and other IOC officials in Barcelona, 1967. Courtesy University of University of Illinois Archives, Avery Brundage Collection.

This expansion will continue as the requirements of the Olympic family continue to grow. From the beginning of the movement, controversies between the IOC and NOCs and especially the IFs have increased. Because the IOC was formed when few of these organizations existed, many of the early congresses, sessions, and Executive Board meetings wrestled with the problem of establishing globally acceptable rules, regulations, and eligibility requirements, as well as the constant controversies over which sports to include in the Games and which sport organizations to recognize. Departments for relations between the IOC and NOCs and IFs have long been an organizational feature.

Members of NOCs and IFs meet regularly with the IOC. Some meetings bring together all three groups, but most are bilateral. The IOC continues to grant recognition to new NOCs as the world map changes, and to new IFs. Currently 199 NOCs are recognized, and 35 IFs (28 for summer sports, and 7 for winter sports) have status as International Olympic Federations, with 28 others (2 are provisional) retaining status as recognized international federations. All NOCs are members of regional associations, which include the Association of NOCs of Africa (ANOCA), the Olympic Council of Asia (OCA), the Pan American Sports Organization (PASCO), the Association of European NOCs (AENOC), and the Oceania

Chart 1
The IOC Administration

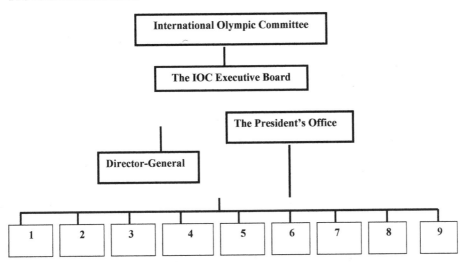

1. **Marketing Director**

2. **Communications Director**

3. **Director, Finance Logistics**

4. **Technology Director**

5. **Director, Sports, Relations with Ifs**

6. **Director, Relations with NOCs (Director of Olympic Solidarity)**

7. **Legal Director**

8. **Medical and Scientific Director**

9. **Information Management Director**

NOCs (ONOC). These regional associations belong to the Association of NOCs (ANOC), which holds a general assembly every two years, with its executive council meeting twice yearly. The regional associations meet every year, and their executives meet on a more regular basis. These NOC organizations are part of the Olympic family, as are the IF associations. These IF groups include the Association of Summer Olympic International Federations (ASOIF), the Association of the International Winter Sports Federations (AIWF), the Association of the IOC Recognized International Sports Federations (ARISF), and the IF umbrella organization, the General Association of International Sports Federations (GAISF). The IOC has also established firm relations and linkages with the International Paralympic Committee. Individuals now sit on both committees, and organizing the Paralympics is now a part of an OCOGs contractual responsibility. The IOC also

Chart 2
IOC Subsidiary Organizations

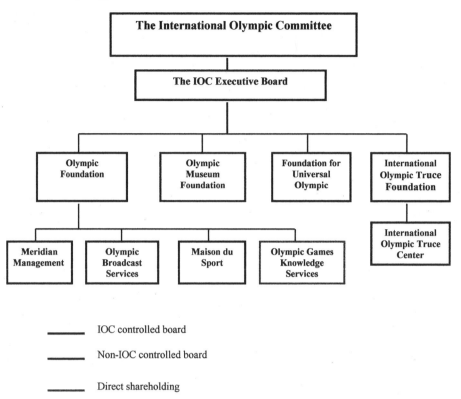

gives its sanction to a number of regional games, IF championships, and allied sport-related organizations.

Revenues increased through the 1960s as television, sponsorship, and licensing programs were refined. In the 1980s, the Olympic Partners program (TOP, formerly "The Olympic Programme") was established to court sponsorships, and lucrative television contracts were signed. Established cost-sharing agreements exist with the IFs, NOCs, and the OGOCs. During each Olympiad, billions of dollars are generated through these programs. This situation contrasts sharply with the days when member fees were virtually the only source of operating funds for the movement. Today the IOC, several NOCs, and many of the IFs have considerable incomes, assets and investments, and healthy contingency funds.

The IOC owns, manages, and wholly or partially funds a number of enterprises. The oldest is Olympic Solidarity, established in Rome in 1971 by the Italian Olympic Committee, but actually an extension of an earlier IOC program. This body moved to Lausanne in 1980 and an IOC-appointed director took charge. Olympic Solidarity is the principal way by which the NOCs share in the wealth of the Olympic movement. In 1981 a budget was approved that included funds for programs for technical courses, sport-administration courses, scholarships for coaches and athletes, sports equipment, marketing development, sport-medicine courses, and subsidies for airfares to and accommodations at the Summer and Winter Games. The budget for Olympic Solidarity rose from $4,426,000 in 1983 to $204 million for the 2001–2004 period.

Second in longevity is the International Council for Arbitration of Sport (ICAS). Initially founded in 1984 as the Court of Arbitration for Sport (CAS), it adjudicates, hears, and rules on sport-related legal matters. Until 1994 it received operating funds from the IOC and was directly under IOC control, but it now exists as a separate entity. IOC members sit on the ICAS, the Commission for CAS, and recommend members for the two CAS tribunals. The IOC Ethics Commission works closely with this body, as does the World Anti-Doping Agency (WADA). WADA, founded in 1999 during the IOC-sponsored World Conference on Doping, is headquartered in Montreal, at arm's length from the IOC, and is partially funded by the IOC. IOC members also sit on its various boards.

Other subsidiary elements of the IOC include (see Chart 2) the Olympic Museum Foundation (incorporated under Swiss law in 1992), with an IOC-appointed director and board and funded by IOC grants and operating revenues, and the Foundation for a Universal Olympic Ethic, established in 2001, to assist the IOC's Ethics Commission in its work. The

The main entrance to the Olympic Park at Quai d'Ouchy in Lausanne, Switzerland, where the new IOC museum is located. Courtesy of John E. Findling.

International Olympic Truce Foundation and Center (incorporated under Swiss law in 2000) works in cooperation with the government of Greece (and is located in Olympia and Athens) to promote international peace, friendship, and understanding through sport and the Olympic ideal. It, too, has IOC members on both its board and executive staff.

An important subsidiary is the Olympic Foundation (incorporated under Swiss law in 1993), which acts as a trust fund to ensure sound IOC financial operations in the future. The IOC wholly controls the foundation and its board. Initially it was given operating revenues, but it now must generate its own revenues through returns on capital investment. IOC budgets operate in four-year cycles although long-term budgets are prepared and contingency funds held to ensure operations should an Summer or Winter Games be canceled or be affected by terrorism. After operating costs are met, excess income can fund new programs and projects. The Olympic Foundation has sought to expand its bases for income generation.

Under the Olympic Foundation are four subsidiary organizations. In 1996 the IOC and private interests formed Meridian Management to replace International Sport and Leisure as the marketing partner for the TOP program. The IOC has a 25-percent ownership share and a 50-percent voting share in this company. Olympic marketing now has subsidiary units for its visual archives, broadcasting, and promotional activities. In 2001 the Olympic Broadcast Services was formed as a private firm. After 2008 it will provide the host broadcasting services for the Summer and Winter Games, based on knowledge gained through previous broadcasting experiences. The IOC has an 80-percent ownership share. The Maison du Sport is a new building under construction in Lausanne that will lease or sell space, starting in fall 2004, to IFs and other sport organizations that want to move their operations to Lausanne. In 2002 the Olympic Games Knowledge Services was formed at Monash University (Australia) as a separate corporate entity. The Olympic Knowledge program based on the operations of the Sydney 2000 Games was expanded. This company develops intellectual property to assist cities bid and then organize and operate Games in the most effective and efficient way possible. The IOC has a 66.6 percent shareholding in this company. An IOC member chairs the board, and other members sit on its board.

Over the years, the IOC has changed from a volunteer organization to a professionally managed corporation. The IOC had long sought legal status to provide tax relief and security for its operation. Furthermore, it has sought exclusive rights to the use of its symbol, flag, motto, emblems, and anthem. When the IOC gained legal status as an international nongovernmental, nonprofit organization from the Swiss Federation in September 1981, it brought the movement into a new phase of existence. Since 1981, the organization has grown significantly and continues to become more complex and corporately based.

BIBLIOGRAPHICAL ESSAY

The body of literature on the IOC has expanded considerably since 1994. Most published work, however, focuses on the whole movement so that one must extract and piece together elements specifically on the IOC. The basic document is the *IOC Charter* (Lausanne, 2002). It is the central source for the rules, guidelines, and policies of the movement. With this, the document *IOC 2000 Reforms* (supplement to the *Olympic Review*, December 1999–January 2000) indicates the changes to the IOC and its operations resulting from the crises of 1998–1999.

Other key IOC publications include a three-volume centennial history, Raymond Gafner, ed., *1894–1994: The International Olympic Committee, One Hundred Years* (Lausanne, 1994); Jean-Loup Chappelet, "Samaranch: From Baden-Baden to Paris," in *Olympic Congress: 1894 The Centennial 1994* (Lausanne, 1994); and *The Olympic Movement* (Lausanne, 1987). Monique Berlioux, ed., *Olympism* (Lausanne, 1972) is another in-house publication that describes the workings of the IOC to that date. Berlioux also contributed an entry to Lord Killanin and John Rodda, eds., *The Olympic Games: 80 Years of People. Events and Records* (New York, 1976) and papers to the IOA (see below). With respect to the secretariat, the best recent piece is Pierre Morath, *Le C.I.O. à Lausanne: 1939– 1999* (Lausanne, 2000).

The IOC has a vast archives that grows daily. Key among its contents are the minutes of meetings for the sessions, Executive Board meetings, and documentation on the commission meetings and activities. Swedish NOC member Wolf Lyberg has made extremely useful summaries of the sessions and EB minutes (1894– 1988), in *Fabulous 100 Years of the IOC: Facts, Figures, and Much, Much More* (Lausanne, 1996). Although they are vetted and lack, in certain cases, the detail now contained in annexes to the minutes, they allow scholars the opportunity to follow the development of the IOC. A more recent compilation of this type of information is Wolf Lyberg, comp., *The Seventh President of the IOC: Facts and Figures* (Lausanne, 2001). Former Chancellor Otto Mayer also published a monograph in French and Spanish, *A travers les anneaux olympiques* (Geneva, 1960), detailing session and EB business from 1894 to 1960. The IOC's library also contains a growing collection of periodicals and books on specific sports and games. The early copies of the *Bulletin/Olympic Review* are essential for the study of the Olympic Movement.

The IOC has published the memoirs of Coubertin, first in a small monograph and later in a three-volume boxed set, as well as the speeches of Brundage, Killanin, and Samaranch. The results of the Varna, Baden-Baden, and 1994 Paris congresses are also available. Also, a growing collection of materials from recent congresses of other members of the Olympic family is contained in the IOC research center. See also Norbert Müller, *One Hundred Years of Olympic Congresses, 1894–1994: History, Objectives, Achievements* (Lausanne, 1994). Another useful IOC reference book is *Biographies of the International Olympic Committee* (Lausanne, 2001), which contains short biographies of each member.

Nikolai Gueorguiev, a former Bulgarian NOC member, has studied the evolution of the Olympic program over the years. His unpublished manuscripts, available at the IOC archives, reveal much about the evolution of Summer and Winter Games events. His work indicates the steady growth of events and participants in the Games so that by the 1990s it had become a matter of considerable logistical and economic concern to the IOC and host cities. See Jere Longman, "Less Is More, More or Less" in the *New York Times*, January 22, 1995, for a brief discussion of the dilemma.

The International Olympic Academy (IOA) in Greece publishes English and French versions of its presentations, many of which are pertinent to the development and change in the IOC. One should also consult the IOA's descriptive pamphlet, *International Olympic Academy* (Athens, 1983). In addition, Nina Pappas, "History and Development of the International Olympic Academy, 1927–1977" is a typescript history available at the University of Illinois Archives, and Norbert Müller, *The International Olympic Academy (IOA): Through its lectures 1961–1998* (Lausanne, 1998) is a useful account of the organization.

Other larger works related to the IOC include Jean Leiper, "The International Olympic Committee: The Pursuit of Olympism 1894–1970" (Ph.D. diss., University of Edmonton, 1976); chapters in Dwight Zakus, "A Preliminary Examination of the Dialectical Change in 'Modern' Sport and of the Intervention of the Canadian State in Sport between 1968 and 1988" (Ph.D. diss., University of Edmonton, 1988); John Hoberman, "Toward a Theory of Olympic Internationalism," in *Journal of Sport History* 22, 1 (1995): 1–37, and Dietrich Quanz, "Civic Pacifism and Sports-based Internationalism: Framework for the Founding of the International Olympic Committee" in *Olympika* 2 (1992): 1–23. Key secondary works with information on the history of the IOC include John MacAloon, *This Great Symbol: Pierre de Coubertin and the Origins of the Modern Olympic Games* (Chicago, 1981); Allen Guttmann, *The Games Must Go On: Avery Brundage and the Olympic Movement* (Urbana, IL, 1984) and *The Olympics: A History of the Modern Games* (Urbana, IL, 2002); David Young, *The Modern Olympics; A Struggle for Revival* (Baltimore, 1996); and Lord Killanin, *My Olympic Years* (London, 1983).

Two key Web sites to locate research materials are the IOC page, (http://www.olympic.org/) and the Amateur Athletic Foundation of Los Angeles page (http://www.aafla.com/). Both contain a wide range of online materials that can be downloaded (in PDF).

DEMETRIOS VIKELAS

Kimberly D. Pelle

Little known and not as celebrated as Coubertin, Brundage, or other International Olympic Committee (IOC) presidents, Demetrios Vikelas (also spelled Bikelas) is no less important; he was the first president of the IOC. The creation of the IOC and his election as president in 1894 constitute the beginning of the modern Olympic Movement.

According to David C. Young, Vikelas was the most educated and the most worldly of all IOC presidents. He was born in 1835 on the island of Syros in Greece. Shortly after, his family became refugees during the Greek war of independence. As a youth, Vikelas spent time in Odessa, Constantinople, and Syros. In 1851, he left Syros and moved to England, where he joined two of his uncles who were merchants and eventually became quite wealthy. There he was able to perfect his knowledge of English. In addition to working with his uncles, Vikelas continued his education at the University of London, where he studied architecture, German, Italian, and French. At the age of thirty, he married a wealthy Greek heiress, Calliopi Jeralopolou, and shortly after became a full partner in his uncles' business. By the time Vikelas reached age 35, he was extremely wealthy, having made his fortune in the London, Athens, and Paris mercantile and banking industries.

Vikelas had not been married long when his wife developed a serious illness that would render her an invalid. Vikelas retired, and the couple moved to Paris. Here, Vikelas dedicated his time and efforts to his wife's comfort and rediscovered his first love: literature. He translated many of Shakespeare's works into Greek and found time to write a great deal about Greek affairs and educational topics.

In 1893, he created the Institut Melas outside of Athens for the creation of kindergartens throughout Greece. A loyal Greek, he sent money to nationalist insurgents on Crete and collaborated in the founding of a Greek school in London. His knowledge of and devotion to Greece and Greek culture were influential and important in regard to his handling of the negotiations and organizing the details of the 1896 Athens Games.

Vikelas, who was by no means a sport enthusiast, considered his election as IOC president to be somewhat coincidental and destined. In February 1894, Vikelas received a letter from a friend, Alexander Fokinos, asking him to take his place as a delegate representing the Panhellenic Gymnasium Club of Athens at the International Athletic Congress, which was to be held in mid-June at the Sorbonne in Paris. Vikelas's first inclination was to decline, but upon learning that the organizer of this endeavor was Baron Pierre de Coubertin, an acquaintance with whom he shared many of the same qualities—Panhellenism, patriotism, and a devotion to the cause of education—he accepted the invitation. The outcome of this congress was Vikelas's election as president of the committee to reestablish the Olympic Games. Although Vikelas was surprised at his election, he accepted the responsibility with pleasure and took his official duties seriously as he began the tedious task of setting the wheels in motion for the 1896 Games.

Accounts vary as to the extent of Vikelas's involvement in the organization of the first modern Olympic Games. According to Young, Vikelas did almost all the work.

Young states that it was Vikelas who met with officials in Athens, Vikelas who got them to agree to host the Games, and Vikelas who tended to the public relations, sent out invitations, and made arrangements to use various facilities in the city. Young also concludes that it is Vikelas who is responsible for the Olympic tradition and the Olympic spirit of goodwill that still exists today.

Although most other historians believe Coubertin deserves the credit for the idea of the Olympics and for the reestablishment of the modern Games, Young is quick to note that Coubertin was too busy with planning his upcoming wedding to participate in the organization of those first Games. Young further notes that Coubertin, who was serving the IOC as the secretary-general, failed in his attempt to recruit French and British teams and was remiss in his management of IOC officials. Most interestingly, Young notes that perhaps Coubertin would not have been the important IOC figure as he is known today if it were not for Vikelas. In early 1895, Coubertin's interest in the Olympic Movement waned and he submitted his resignation to the IOC; Vikelas refused to accept it.

Other accounts of Vikelas's Olympic involvement and tenure as IOC president depict Vikelas as a mere marionette in Coubertin's grand scheme. According to John MacAloon, Vikelas's success in implementing and organizing the early preparations for the Games was merely an illusion that Coubertin later had to rectify.

Nevertheless, historians do portray the organization of the 1896 Games as tedious, due to internal political and financial problems. Vikelas deserves recognition for his role in organizing these Games. Except for a brief absence, in which he returned to Paris to bury his wife, Vikelas was the instrumental figure throughout the development of the first modern Olympic Games. Vikelas worked well with IOC officials and fulfilled his IOC presidential duties with determination and enthusiasm. The

Demetrios Vikelas, IOC president, 1894–96. Courtesy of International Olympic Committee, IOC Museum Collections.

only controversy encountered during Vikelas's tenure as IOC president was a disagreement with Coubertin in regard to future Olympic Games. Since the 1896 Games were so successful, the Greeks decided to claim the Olympic Games as their own; they wanted all future Games to be held in Athens. This is ironic when one considers that it took great effort on Vikelas's part to convince the Greeks to host the 1896 Games. Coubertin was adamant that the Games be international in scope and as such, move around the world. Although Vikelas agreed with Coubertin that the Olympic Games should indeed be international, his Greek pride and fierce loyalty to his country led him to sympathize with his compatriots, and he lobbied in their favor. Coubertin rejected all proposals on this matter. Vikelas tried to compromise, proposing instead "in-between" games in Athens. Again Coubertin declined, determined to internationalize future Olympic Games. The two had heated debates and their relationship became strained. In late 1896, Vikelas resigned as president of the IOC, although he remained very active in the organization until 1899, and his friendship with Coubertin survived the disagreement. Interestingly, a successful "in-between" Games did take place in Athens in 1906. Coubertin gave the event the IOC's blessing, but he did not attend and labeled the games as "unofficial."

Vikelas died in July 1908. At the end of his life, Vikelas returned to the cause of Greece, locked in seemingly endless conflict with Turkey. He remained active in the literary field, writing and editing several books, and he continued to be involved with activities which promoted education. In 1904 he organized a large conference on education in Athens, out of which came an education museum. In 1905 he served as the Greek delegate to the Olympic Congress in Brussels and accepted the intermediate 1906 Games as "Jeux Olympiques Internationaux d'Athens."

Young gives a heartwarming account of Vikelas as a lover of all people and a philanthropist. Despite Vikelas's modest reputation, he was a serious man who gave all his interests his utmost consideration, especially his role as the first IOC president. His obscurity is not at all deserved.

BIBLIOGRAPHICAL ESSAY

Primary sources regarding Demetrios Vikelas are somewhat limited. Information is available at the IOC Archives in Lausanne, Switzerland, which includes correspondence between Vikelas and Coubertin, as well as Vikelas's writings. Among Vikelas's writings, two articles relate to the Olympics: "Les Jeux Olympiques Internationaux," *Estia* [Athens] (1895): 146 and "Les Jeux Olympiques dans le passé et l'avenir. Memoire présenti au Congrès de 1894 au nom de la Société Panhelleneque d'Athens," *Bulletin Officiel du CIO* 1, 2 (October 1894): 3–4.

Secondary sources of use to researchers include two in-depth and insightful articles. David C. Young gives an enlightening account in "Demetrios Vikelas: First President of the IOC," *Stadion* 14, 1 (1988): 85–102. Researchers who are able to read French may wish to consult Yves Pierre Boulongue, "Les presidencies de Demetrios Vikelas et de Pierre de Coubertin," in Raymond Gafner, ed., *Un Siêcle du Comité International Olympique: L'Idée—Les Présidents—L'Oeuvre* (Lausanne, 1994).

See also Pierre de Coubertin, "Demetrios Vikelas," *Revue Olympique* 8 (September 1908): 131–32 and brief passages concerning Vikelas's role in the 1896 Games in Allen Guttmann, *The Olympics* (Urbana, Ill., 2002) and John J. MacAloon, *This Great Symbol: Pierre de Coubertin and the Origins of the Modern Olympic Games* (Chicago, 1981).

PIERRE DE COUBERTIN

Anthony Th. Bijkerk

Pierre Fredy, Baron de Coubertin was born in Paris on January 1, 1863. His father, Charles Fredy, Baron de Coubertin, was a well-known French academic painter (1822–1908), and his mother, Marie-Marcelle Gigault de Crisenoy, baronesse de Coubertin (1823–1907), was the granddaughter of the Marquis de Mirville. Pierre's grandfather on his father's side, Julien Bonaventure, was a brilliant officer, diplomat, and musician. An ancestor, Pierre Fredy, was ennobled by King Louis XI of France in 1477. Pierre de Coubertin had two brothers, Paul

(1847–1933) and Albert (1848–1913), and one sister, Marie (1855–1942), all much older than he. Pierre spent most of his youth between the rue Oudinot in Paris, where he was born, and the house in Mirville, which belonged to his mother's family.

Pierre de Coubertin received his first schooling from a private tutor. His youth ended when he entered the Jesuit College and l'Ecole libre Saint-Ignace, in the rue de Madrid in Paris. His education in this college lasted seven years, and during this time he learned, among many other things, to love the antique world of the Greeks and Romans.

In 1872, Coubertin read Thomas Hughes's book *Tom Brown's School Days*, which captured his imagination and had a lasting influence on his life. Contrary to what others have written, Pierre never entered the Ecole Militaire de Saint-Cyr, the French military academy, although he was preparing to do so. Before taking the final step, he decided to renounce a military career and instead chose to look forward to an "era of peace." He entered law school, but stayed there only about one year. In 1880, he enrolled at the School for Political Sciences in Paris and received a bachelor of law degree in 1885, studying under such distinguished scholars as Hippolyte Taine, and reading the works of Alexis de Tocqueville and Frederic Le Play, each of whom made an indelible contribution to his personal beliefs, and from whom he learned about philosophy, sociology, education, and "how to educate oneself."

Pierre de Coubertin, IOC president, 1896–1925. Courtesy of University of Illinois Archives, Avery Brundage Collection.

Hippolyte Taine taught him to turn his gaze to the future without denying his past and, above all, about "natural education." Taine was enthralled by the British parliamentary system (in his opinion the ideal form of democracy) and the educational system of England's public schools. He was instrumental in giving Coubertin a lasting interest in the British educational system. Tocqueville's writings taught him about the value of using contemporary history and provoked his interest in American democracy, the U.S. constitution, and the enterprising spirit of the American people. From Le Play, Coubertin learned about the inevitability of classes and about new theories of sociology. These three masters formed Coubertin into the humanist that he became later in his life.

In 1883, at the age of 20, Coubertin visited England. Taine likely suggested the trip, and Coubertin made visits to various public schools, some Jesuit Catholic schools, and several universities, including Cambridge and Oxford. Of course, he visited Rugby, the setting of *Tom Brown's School Days*, where Thomas Arnold had been the headmaster. He wrote down his experiences in a report, which was first published in *La Réforme Sociale* in 1883 and later, in 1889, in *L'Education en Angleterre*.

Coubertin felt that Thomas Arnold's ideas about the system of school sport, student self-government, and postgraduate athletic associations, adapted to the French character and situations, could be dropped into the fertile ground of the French educational system, which at that time seemed prejudiced and old-fashioned. France was humiliated to have lost the Franco-Prussian war to Germany in 1870–1871, and Coubertin was convinced that the German soldiers' training in sport (gymnastics) had been the main reason for German military superiority. This notion, combined with his trip to England, gave him the idea of reforming the French school system.

Avery Brundage at the grave of modern Olympic Movement founder Pierre de Coubertin in Lausanne, Switzerland. Courtesy University of Illinois Archives, Avery Brundage Collection.

During the 1880s, school sport was slowly introduced in France, mainly in Paris. Coubertin succeeded in founding the Comité Jules Simon, named after its president, a staunch republican and conservative professor-reformer. Jules Simon, who was then 74 years old, was a kind of father figure for Coubertin, who was 26 and looked to Simon as his spiritual adviser. As a result, Coubertin became the secretary-general of the *Comité pour la propagation des exercices physiques dans l'éducation*—the official name for the Comité Jules Simon. Most of his work consisted of publishing articles and spreading his ideas through personal visits to important persons who could aid him in reaching his goals.

In 1889, Coubertin put notices in several English newspapers explaining his interest in British sport and physical education and requesting Englishmen with similar interests to contact him. Dr. William Penny Brookes from Much Wenlock in Shropshire, who had founded the Wenlock Olympian Society in 1850 and later organized the Wenlock Olympian Games and the National Olympic Games in England, sent Coubertin some of his writings. In June 1889, during the Paris Exposition Universelle, Coubertin and the Comité Jules Simon arranged the International Congress on Physical Exercise in the Sorbonne. When Coubertin spoke to the congress on June 15, 1889, he quoted freely from Brookes's documents but never acknowledged Brookes in his speech, even though Brookes had made reference to a national Olympic games in London in 1866.

Coubertin made his first trip to North America in July 1889 to attend a congress on physical education and to visit sport facilities and physical-education programs at several universities and high schools in both the United States and Canada. Coubertin was quite impressed with the excellent facilities available for students, and after his return, he wrote a very favorable report, *Universités Transatlantiques*, published in 1890.

In 1890, Coubertin and his friend Georges Saint-Clair founded the *Union des Sociétés Françaises de Sports Athlétiques* [USFSA], parallel to the British Amateur Athletes Association (AAA) and the American Amateur Athletic Union (AAU). Up to this time, Coubertin had never used the word "Olympic" anywhere in his writings. In October 1890, Coubertin paid another visit to Dr. William Penny Brookes in Much Wenlock. Invoking an old Wenlock tradition, Brookes organized a special autumn edition of the Wenlock Olympic Games to celebrate his French protégé's visit. The athletic contests were not particularly significant, but Brookes put on a great deal of pageantry for Coubertin, who was invited to plant an oak tree, which even today still thrives in Wenlock. This meeting clearly had a profound influence on the young French aristocrat and eventually became the foundation upon which he later built his modern Olympic castle. Brookes was 81 years old, and he was happy to find someone with whom he could freely discuss his longtime dreams of creating an international Olympic Games.

After his return from Wenlock, Coubertin published his experiences in an article with the title "Les Jeux Olympiques à Much Wenlock—Une page de l'histoire de l'athlétisme," in which he referred to the Wenlock games as Olympic Games and gave Brookes credit for reviving the ancient Olympics. However, in his later publications, Coubertin increasingly minimized Brookes's role, eventually claiming credit for the Olympic idea for himself, as in his 1908 book *Une Campagne de Vingt-et-Un Ans*, where he asserts that he and only he conceived the Olympic idea. But based upon the letters of the period around 1890, there can be no doubt that Dr. William Penny Brookes played a very important role in Coubertin's life by dropping his Olympic ideas right into Coubertin's lap. The two kept in contact by correspondence through the next two years. Brookes invited Coubertin to attend his regular spring Wenlock Olympics, but Coubertin declined the invitation because of other pressing business. However, he sent a gold medal to Brookes to be used as a prize at the Wenlock Olympics.

In July 1892, Coubertin wrote to Brookes about the festival the USFSA was going to organize in Paris that November to commemorate its fifth anniversary. Although he detailed his plans, he made no reference to "Olympic Games." In September 1892, a Shropshire newspaper printed a summary of Brookes's efforts in the modern Olympic revival movement and made reference to the end of a speech by Brookes: "If he lived long enough, Dr. Brookes hoped to go and witness an international festival at Athens, or upon the old spot where the Olympic Games were started." Thus, as early as September 1892, thousands of people had heard or read about Brookes's international Olympic proposal.

On November 25, 1892, during the USFSA jubilee meeting at the Sorbonne in Paris, attended by a great crowd of French and foreign dignitaries, Coubertin gave a speech about modern sport in which he stated, "It is necessary to internationalize sports. . . . It is necessary to pursue and realize . . . this grandiose and beneficent project; namely the re-establishment of the Olympic Games." To his chagrin, his audience did not comprehend the meaning of the proposal, thinking he had used the phrase symbolically. Coubertin's first effort had thus been in vain.

Early in 1893, a USFSA member proposed an international congress to be held in 1894 to discuss the problems of amateurism. Coubertin immediately seized on the idea and began to plan for a second chance to promote a revival of the Olympic Games. That fall, he visited the United States again, and during that trip he met

William Sloane of Princeton University. In Sloane, he found a kindred spirit, and with him, he discussed his plans about reviving the Olympic Games. Sloane fully supported Coubertin's ideas and agreed to serve as a commissioner for the 1894 Paris Congress. Coubertin also found Charles Herbert, secretary of the AAA in England, who was willing to serve on the secretariat for the 1894 Congress. In January 1894, Coubertin mailed out a circular advertising the International Congress of Amateurs, listing the eight items on the agenda. Seven of these concerned frequent questions raised about the concept of amateurism, but the eighth item read, "The possibility of re-establishing the Olympic Games. Under what conditions would it be feasible?" The congress was planned for June 1894 at the Sorbonne in Paris. A short time before the actual start of the Congress, Coubertin published a more detailed program, adding two more items, both related to his Olympic Games idea:

> VIII—The possibility of re-establishing [the Olympic Games]—Advantages from the athletic, moral and international point of view.
>
> IX—Conditions to be imposed on competitors.—Sports represented.—Material organization and frequency of the revived Olympic Games.
>
> X—Nomination of an International Committee responsible for preparing their re-establishment.

The congress took place under the presidency of Baron de Courcel, a senator and former French ambassador to Germany. After two plenary sessions, the delegates were divided, according to their preference, into two committees: one to solve the questions about amateurism and the other to consider the revival of the Olympic Games. The Greek delegate, Demetrios Vikelas, was, to his own surprise, elected president of the latter committee. Not surprisingly, the delegates voted for the reestablishment of the Olympic Games. Coubertin originally wanted the first Olympic Games to be held in 1900 in Paris, but the congress did not want to wait six years and thus came to another decision. After a stirring speech by Vikelas, the first international Olympic Games were unanimously awarded to Athens and were set to be held in 1896. Coubertin persuaded the congress to approve Paris as the site of the 1900 Games and requested that the delegates endorse his proposals for the new international committee. Vikelas was elected president of that committee, formally known as the International Committee for the Olympic Games, and Coubertin became its first secretary-general.

Coubertin lost no time in starting to organize the 1896 Games. He created a new magazine, *Revue Olympique*, which was published for the first time in July 1894. At the top of the first page of this bulletin was the motto: *Citius, Altius, Fortius* (faster, higher, stronger). This motto originally came from Father Henri Didon, Father Superior of the Collège Albert-le-Grand in Arcueil, near Paris. Didon was a good friend of Coubertin and was instrumental in organizing sport as part of the educational system in his school. The first issue of *Revue Olympique* contained an elaborate account of the first congress of June 1894; the names of members on the newly installed International Committee of the Olympic Games, and information about the intentions of the committee and the decisions made during the congress.

Next came the task of convincing the Greeks to organize the first Olympic Games of the modern era. Vikelas traveled to Athens and started sounding out the Greek government and other parties. He met with opposition from the Greek Prime Minister Trikoupis, who told him that the government could not support the organization of the Games because of financial problems. Vikelas, who had also talked without success to Stephanos Dragoumis, president of the Zappas Olympic Committee, had to return home to Paris because of his wife's serious illness. When he returned in Paris, he met briefly with Coubertin and advised him to visit Athens and take over the discussions with Greek authorities. Coubertin arrived in Athens on November 8, 1894, and immediately started making the rounds. He met with the Greek Crown Prince Constantine twice and was convinced that the prince was completely on his side. He also met with many Greeks who were favorably disposed towards the Olympic Games, and he gave a stirring speech to the Parnassus Literary Society. In this speech he gave a deliberately low estimate of the cost of holding the Games in Athens. Coubertin's Parnassus speech is considered to be a landmark in the history of the Olympic idea. It was of decisive importance for Coubertin himself, since it contained the body of thought from which he would develop the future Olympic structure. He also involved the local newspapers, most of which supported his plans. In a meeting at the Zappeion, Coubertin presented to his audience a draft program for the Games, which he had drawn up before leaving Paris. That same day, the organizing committee for the Games was founded, and Coubertin, after reporting to the crown prince of his success, left Athens, thinking that everything had gone well. But nothing was further from the truth, because even before Coubertin arrived back in France, his newly installed organizing committee had been disbanded. All its members, loyal to Prime Minister Trikoupis, had resigned.

During December 1894 and early January 1895, uncertainty reigned in Athens. Vikelas and Crown Prince Constantine tried to salvage the embattled Olympic proposal. Sentiment for holding the Games was growing, especially among the general public of Athens. With the help of Timoleon Philemon, secretary-general of the organizing committee, Constantine was able to raise enough money. Especially important was the donation from George Averoff, a Greek living in Alexandria, Egypt, which was used to fund the rebuilding of the stadium. Coubertin himself was not very much involved in this work, as he was planning to get married, to the utmost regret of Vikelas. Vikelas had been begging Coubertin to take a more active role in the preparations for the Games, and when he learned about Coubertin's wedding plans, he expressed fear that they would distract Coubertin from his work. During this period, Coubertin remained incommunicado for a rather long time, greatly hampering Vikelas's work. As the secretary-general of the International Committee for the Olympic Games, Coubertin was expected to do much more, and it is probably due to his distractions and inertia that so few nations came to Athens in 1896.

Following Coubertin's marriage to Marie Rothan on March 12, 1895, his work on a book on French history occupied even more of his time. Vikelas begged Coubertin to provide him with plans for a velodrome, but when Coubertin's plans finally arrived they were too late to be implemented. This proves that the Greeks really tried to involve Coubertin in the organization of the Games, contrary to Coubertin's later claims.

The Games of the First Olympiad of the modern era, which were held between April 6 and 15, 1896, were a great success, but they provoked a deep controversy between Coubertin and the Greeks. After the Games had ended, Greek Olympic leaders wanted to institutionalize them in Athens, and in this, they were supported not only by the Greek royal family and the general public, but also by many of the foreign participants, including the American team.

Coubertin, however, was totally opposed to the Greek idea, since he wanted the Olympic Games to be held all over the world. He had expressed himself in rather strong terms on this subject in a meeting with the Greek crown prince on the last day of the Games. During this meeting, he proposed the idea of staging Panhellenic Games to be held every four years in between the international Olympic Games. Coubertin also complained that the Greeks had not given him the credit he deserved for reviving the Games and that they had wanted the credit all for themselves, as his name had not been mentioned anywhere.

This dispute, especially clear in his letters to Vikelas, lasted throughout the following years, but Coubertin did not hesitate to tell everyone involved that the next Olympic Games would be held in Paris in 1900 and after that in either New York, Berlin, or Stockholm.

Shortly after the closing of the Olympic Games in Athens, Vikelas suggested that Coubertin plan another Olympic congress to complete the work begun at the 1894 congress in Paris and to ratify the holding of intermediate Olympic Games in Greece.

The second Olympic Congress was held in the French city of Le Havre in 1897. Agenda items at this congress were questions of health and education and the advancement of the cause of amateur sport. Among the speakers was Coubertin's good friend, Father Didon. One of the 59 delegates was the Reverend de Courcy Laffan, headmaster of Cheltenham College in England, who would become one of the most faithful servants of the Olympic cause.

In accordance with the decisions taken in Paris in 1894, Coubertin had taken over the presidency of the International Committee for the Olympic Games from Vikelas, since Paris was the next site of the Games. They were to be organized under the flag of the Exposition Universelle Internationale de 1900 à Paris, which was to be the biggest exposition ever staged. The commissioner of the fair, Alfred Picard, did not think much of sports. Therefore, Coubertin appointed an old childhood friend, Viscount Charles de La Rochefoucauld, president of the organizing committee. In November 1898, however, the USFSA claimed exclusive rights for all sports events organized in France in 1900. La Rochefoucauld did not want to be involved in a political fight and resigned. The organizing committee dissolved as a result of this decision and Coubertin was back to square one.

Picard appointed Daniel Mérillon as president of the sports commission, which was to organize the sports events related to the exposition. Mérillon was president of the French Shooting Association, and he took on his new job with élan. Coubertin, because of his many foreign contacts, agreed to support the new organization. But the Games were not a success, as nowhere were they referred to as "Olympic Games." There were too many events, both for amateur and professional sport, they were spread over six months, and even today it is unclear which events were approved Olympic events. Coubertin was not involved in any sports events connected with the exposition.

Both Coubertin and the other members of the IOC wanted the next Olympic Games to be held abroad, and the first choice was Chicago. However, after an internal American dispute between Chicago and St. Louis, the Games were transferred to St. Louis, to be held in conjunction with the Louisiana Purchase International Exposition. It was a decision Coubertin would regret forever.

The Games of the III Olympiad were a disaster from the Olympic point of view. Again, the Games were conducted over a period of six months and with multiple series of events. There were events such as the Anthropology Days, in which primitive tribes held "Olympic" competitions in events like mud fighting and pole-climbing. Coubertin was informed of these unusual events by one of the few IOC members who attended these Games, as he himself had remained in France, and was appalled at what had taken place in St. Louis. He vowed never again to organize the Olympic Games as a sideshow to an international exposition. And once again, the question arose as to which of the events should be awarded Olympic recognition.

The Olympic Movement could hardly sustain such an organizational disaster once again. Coubertin needed help to revive the movement, and assistance came from an unexpected source: the Greeks. In 1896, Coubertin had proposed the organizing of Panhellenic Games in between the international Olympic Games. This was done to appease those Greeks who wanted the Games permanently in Athens. However, in 1901, the IOC had received a proposal from three German members to hold a second series of Olympic Games, in between the regular series of Games. These alternate Games would be organized in Athens starting in 1906 and would be called the international Olympic Games in Athens. Coubertin reported the motion in the *Revue Olympique*, but in his *Mémoires Olympiques* (1931), he said he gave no support to this idea. He managed to keep the question of the Athens Games off the IOC agenda until the 1905 congress in Brussels. By then, Greek IOC member Alexander Merkati reported that an organizing committee had been established and was preparing to hold international Olympic Games in Athens in 1906.

Again Crown Prince Constantine served as chairman of the organizing committee. On Sunday, April 22, 1906, athletes from the participating nations marched into the stadium, thus starting a new Olympic tradition. As the host country, the Greeks came in last, another tradition that has been maintained until today. King Georgios then declared the Games open, and the Samaras Hymn was played, as in 1896. The Games were a great success and likely saved Coubertin's dream. Surprisingly, Coubertin did not come to Athens, although several other members of the IOC did.

Coubertin had instead decided to hold a conference on Arts, Letters, and Sport in Paris at the end of May 1906. He dreamed of Olympic Games that were "not just ordinary world championships, but a four-yearly festival of academic youth, 'the spring of mankind', a festival of supreme efforts, multiple ambitions." He said "that it was time to restore the Olympiads to their original beauty." Coubertin intended to include art competitions in the Olympic Games, but it took quite a few years before he could do this. Art competitions were first held at the Olympic Games in Stockholm in 1912, and then only after Coubertin's personal intervention.

At the 1904 session of the IOC in London, the Games of the IV Olympiad were awarded to Rome. However, when Rome withdrew its candidacy, the IOC awarded the 1908 Olympic Games to London. The London Olympic Games had, once again, a strong affiliation with a major exhibition, the Franco-British Exhibition, but contrary to the Games in 1900 and 1904, the organizers in 1908 were able to keep the Olympic Games on an equal footing with the exhibition. For the first time, a winter sports event, figure skating for men, women, and pairs, was organized as part of the official Olympic program. The 1908 London Olympic Games may be called a success, in spite of numerous controversies. There were protests about the rules and especially about the biased judging by the British officials,

461

which came from the French, Canadian, Swedish, and, particularly, the American teams. The feelings between the British and the Americans ran so high that it almost put an end to the Games. Only the diplomatic skills of Coubertin prevented the departure of the American team.

By 1908, Coubertin's position as president of the IOC was no longer as secure as it had been at the beginning of the movement. The American James Sullivan wanted to dissolve the IOC and start with a new international committee that had more American influence. These efforts fortunately came to naught, as Sullivan received little support for his scheming.

When the IOC met in Berlin in 1909, Stockholm was the only candidate to host the Games of the V Olympiad in 1912. Although the Swedish organizers wanted to reduce considerably the program of the Games, the IOC decided on the program itself, adding the art competitions. Coubertin took the initiative to have the decathlon and modern pentathlon added to the program. The success of 1912 Olympic Games in Stockholm may be seen as the dawn of the modern Olympic Movement, and the Games were a high point in Coubertin's career as president of the IOC.

During the IOC Session in Stockholm, the 1916 Olympic Games were awarded to Berlin, but these Games were cancelled after World War I broke out. Nevertheless, the IOC Session in 1914 deserves special mention, because Coubertin organized this session to celebrate the 20th anniversary of the revival of the modern Olympic Movement, and he used the opportunity to launch the Olympic emblem, the familiar five interlocking rings. During the opening ceremony of the session in the Richelieu Amphitheatre of the Sorbonne University on June 15, 1914, the newly designed Olympic flag was first used as a decoration. Coubertin designed both the emblem and the flag.

During World War I, Coubertin considered resigning from the IOC, but since his mandate did not expire until 1917, he decided to stay, saying, "A captain does not leave the bridge of his ship during a storm." However, he did appoint another IOC member, Godefroy de Blonay from neutral Switzerland, as president ad interim and delegated some of his official functions to him. Coubertin worked for the French army until the war ended. In 1915, Coubertin traveled to Switzerland, where he signed an agreement with the mayor of Lausanne to make the city the place where the new headquarters of the IOC would eventually be located. This did not happen until much later, in 1925, after Coubertin's resignation as IOC president.

After the signing of the armistice, Coubertin resumed his duties as IOC president, in spite of the fact that his actual mandate had expired in 1917; Blonay had renewed the mandate that year. The 16th IOC session took place in Lausanne in April 1919, and the major decisions made during this meeting were the selection of Antwerp as host for the 1920 Olympic Games and a provision that only nations with an IOC member could participate in the Games. The 1920 Olympic Games again showed innovations. For the first time the white flag with the multicolored Olympic rings was hoisted in the Olympic Stadium, though not yet in an official ceremony like today. Another first was the Olympic oath, spoken by the Belgian Victor Boin, a water-polo player and fencer.

The 18th IOC Session took place at the same time as an Olympic congress, both organized in Lausanne in June 1921. There were some very important decisions made during this session. Coubertin played a masterly coup d'état when on March

17, 1921, he circulated a letter in which he declared that it was his intention to resign the IOC presidency after the 1924 Olympic Games. He requested that his IOC colleagues award the 1924 Olympic Games to Paris, so that the Games would celebrate the 30th anniversary of their revival in the city in which they were born. At the same time, Coubertin insisted that the 1928 Olympic Games be awarded to Amsterdam and that the vote for the 1928 Olympics should be taken at the same session in 1921. The vote this time was not unanimous, because the Italians were strongly opposed to the dual proposal. The IOC first had to vote to make it possible to select host cities for two consecutive Olympiads. This vote passed, not unanimously, but with a clear majority. Then the IOC voted on the host cities in 1924 (Paris) and 1928 (Amsterdam). When the majority voted in favor of Coubertin's proposal, the angry Italians immediately left Lausanne and returned home. Coubertin also proposed the creation of an executive committee, in order to have the work of the IOC continue more regularly. This proposal was unanimously accepted and the first executive committee of the IOC was then elected, with Blonay, Jiri Guth-Jarkovsky, Henri Baillet-Latour, Sigfrid Edström, and the Marquis de Polignac.

During the IOC session in Rome in 1923, Los Angeles was chosen as host city for the 1932 Olympic Games. This session also decided that a first winter sports week would be held in Chamonix, France, in 1924, under the patronage of the IOC. Coubertin himself proposed the holding of African Games every other year. Although the proposal was accepted, it took six more years before the first African Games could be organized in 1929 in Alexandria, Egypt.

In February 1924, the Wintersports Week took place in Chamonix. Not until the 1926 session of the IOC in Lisbon was it decided to rename it as the First Olympic Winter Games.

The Paris Games of 1924 were the last Games Pierre de Coubertin personally attended. It was the first time the Olympics visited the same city for a second time, but in twenty-four years, the situation had changed dramatically for the better. This time the Olympic flag few over the stadium until the closing of the Games. At the Closing Ceremony another new tradition was introduced. The flags of Greece (paying tribute to the immortality of Hellenism), France (paying tribute to the current host country) and the Netherlands (the next host country) were raised and the three national anthems played. Coubertin wrote about this: "With this addition, the protocol of the Olympic ceremonial was finally completed; I had constructed it little by little. . . . " Coubertin also introduced the tradition to have the names of the winners engraved on small marble plaques attached to the walls of the Olympic stadium.

In 1925, an Olympic congress met in Prague, preceded by an IOC session. On May 28, 1925, the IOC elected Count Henri de Baillet-Latour as successor to Coubertin. Coubertin was appointed Honorary Life President, with the specification that this honor should never be conferred on anyone else, although it was later granted to Lord Killanin. Coubertin remained in office until September 1, 1925, and then handed over the presidency to Baillet-Latour.

In the last years of his life, Coubertin concentrated on writing his memoirs, which were published in 1931. He remained in contact with the Olympic family, although he no longer visited any Olympic Games, nor any session of the IOC. He fully supported the idea of the German IOC member, Dr. Carl Diem, for an Olympic torch relay, starting in ancient Olympia and finishing in the Olympic Stadium in Berlin during the official Opening Ceremony for the 1936 Games. His contacts with Diem were frequent, and Diem visited Coubertin several times in Lausanne in the early 1930s. Throughout his career, Coubertin had spent most of his private fortune realizing his Olympic dreams and promoting pedagogical and promotional activities. In the last years of his life, he became rather destitute. In 1936, Baillet-Latour informed the IOC of Coubertin's financial difficulties, and many personal friends donated money to a Pierre de Coubertin Fund. However, most of it came too late; on September 2, 1937, Coubertin succumbed to a massive stroke while walking in a park in Geneva. Despite his long years of work in the Olympic Movement and the many individuals he had met in his work, he died a lonely man.

Pierre de Coubertin's funeral took place on March 26, 1938, at the Church of Notre Dame du Valentin in Lausanne, and he was buried in the cemetery at Bois-de-Vaux in the same city. According to his will, his heart was placed in an urn and brought to ancient Olympia, where, on March 26, 1938, Prince Paul of Greece placed the urn in a stele, a special commemorative monument designed for this purpose.

BIBLIOGRAPHICAL ESSAY

Throughout his life, Pierre de Coubertin was a prolific writer, publishing over 1,000 articles, 30 books, 50 pamphlets, and innumerable letters. Most of his work concerned educational subjects, or subjects related to the Olympic Movement in general, and in particular the International Olympic Committee. Among Coubertin's many publications, there are several that need to be mentioned here: *Une Campagne de vingt-et-un ans [1887–1908]* (Paris, 1909) and his *Mémoires Olympiques* (Lausanne, 1931) are the most important ones in this respect. Both of these books deal exclusively with his efforts to reestablish the Olympic Games. See also the three volumes published by the International Olympic Committee on the writings of Coubertin, *Textes Choisis Pierre de Coubertin* (Lausanne, 1986). An abridged edition in English is also available: *Pierre de Coubertin – Olympism, Selected Writings* (Lausanne, 2000).

With respect to the rebirth of the Olympic Movement, consult David C. Young, *The Modern Olympics: A Struggle for Revival* (Baltimore, MD, 1996), clearly one of the most valuable additions to the history of the early period of the Olympic Games. Other noteworthy books on Coubertin's life and work are John J. MacAloon, *This Great Symbol: Pierre de Coubertin and the Origins of the Modern Olympic Games* (Chicago, 1981), the best biographical study in English; Yves-Pierre Boulogne, *La vie et l'ouevre pédagogique de Pierre de Coubertin 1863–1937* (Montreal, 1975); Marie-Therese Eyquem, *Pierre de Coubertin: l'Épopée olympique* (Paris, 1966); Carl Diem Institut, *Pierre de Coubertin – The Olympic Idea – Discourses and Essays* (Cologne, Germany, 1967); Andre Senay and Robert Hervet, *Monsieur de Coubertin* (Paris, 1956); Karl Lennartz, et al., *Die Olympischen Spiele 1896 in Athen – Erläuterungen zum Neudruck des Offiziellen Berichtes* (Kassel, Germany, 1996); and Patrice Cholley, *Pierre de Coubertin – La deuxième croisade* (Lausanne, 1996).

COUNT HENRI BAILLET-LATOUR

Edward S. Goldstein

Belgium became a modern nation in 1830, some 60 years prior to Baron Pierre de Coubertin's creation of the modern Olympic movement. While Coubertin dreamed the Olympics would promote world peace and harmony, the leaders of Belgium—a country long renowned for its culture and commerce but not for its military prowess—had the less grand objective of staying out of harm's way in a Europe set apart by hostile nations and alliances. One young Belgian whose life was intertwined with Coubertin's vision and Belgium's fate was Count Henri de Baillet-Latour. Born March 1, 1876, in Brussels, Baillet-Latour joined Coubertin's fledgling International Olympic Committee (IOC) in 1903 and gave the next four decades of his life to the organization, the last 16 years of them spent as Coubertin's successor. Baillet-Latour's custodianship of Coubertin's dream would end upon his death in 1942 with the world at war and his country occupied by the same Nazi regime that hosted Berlin's controversial 1936 Olympic Games.

Baillet-Latour, while 13 years younger than Coubertin, fit in nicely with the aristocratic gentleman's-club atmosphere that long characterized the governance of the IOC. The cigar-smoking Belgian was owner of several racehorses and was the president of the elite Jockey-Club de Bruxelles. His conception of the Olympic Movement scarcely differed from Coubertin's. Baillet-Latour helped organize the third IOC Congress, held in Brussels in 1905, an occasion "at which the idealistic spokesmen for internationalism gave voice to their dreams for a more pacific world unified by a common commitment to amateur sport" (Guttmann, *The Olympics*, p. 28). The congress also featured debate over the concept of amateurism, with the Olympic barons attempting to exclude members of the lower classes from competition, despite the universal aims of the Olympic movement. Shortly thereafter, Baillet-Latour organized Belgian participation in the 1908 London and 1912 Stockholm games.

Henri Baillet-Latour, IOC president, 1925–42. Courtesy of University of Illinois Archives, Avery Brundage Collection.

Two years after the Stockholm Games, Europe's peace was shattered; the guns of August fired in Belgium, as German armies used the small nation's countryside as an invasion route to France. The 1916 Games, scheduled for Berlin, were never held. When the war ended with Germany's defeat, the IOC voted in 1919 to place the first postwar games symbolically in Belgium's port city of Antwerp. Baillet-Latour distinguished himself by helping the Antwerp committee organize the massive undertaking, despite having only a year's lead time and a scant budget. The following year he was rewarded with a nomination to the IOC's newly formed five-member executive board. And at the IOC's 1925 Congress in Prague, following two rounds of balloting, Baillet-Latour was elected to an eight-year term as president, to succeed the retiring Coubertin.

During Baillet-Latour's first term, a major issue on the IOC's agenda was the question of women's sports. In 1929, Baillet-Latour argued before the executive board for limiting women athletes to the "suitably feminine" sports of gymnastics, swimming, tennis, and figure skating, but a decision was postponed until after the Berlin Olympic Congress of 1930. Holding to the common prejudice that participation in track and field would turn women into "masculine Amazons," Baillet-Latour proposed to track and field's governing body, the International Amateur Athletic Federation (IAAF), meeting in conjunction with the congress, that the five women's track-and-field events introduced at the 1928 Games be eliminated from the 1932 Los Angeles Games program. American delegate Gustavus Kirby angrily counterproposed that if women were banned, a special congress be summoned to consider the elimination of men's track and field. The IAAF then voted to continue supporting female inclusion, and the full Olympic Congress also followed suit.

The Berlin Congress was also fateful, as its organizers successfully pressed the IOC in 1931 to award the 1936 Summer Games to their city. On January 24, 1933, six days prior to Adolf Hitler's accession to power, the *Organisationskomittee* for the Berlin Games was formed. The Nazi Party's bitter ideological views about race and religion extended to sport, with Nazi spokesman Bruno Malitz condemning modern sports for being "infested" with "Frenchmen, Belgians, Pollacks and Jew-Niggers," who had been allowed "to start on tracks, to play on the soccer fields and to swim in the pools" (Guttmann, *The Olympics*, p. 54). Propaganda Minister Josef Goebbels convinced Hitler, however, that the Games would be an opportunity to showcase Germany's vitality and organizational expertise and to promote its particular brand of national socialism. Baillet-Latour was concerned from the start about Hitler's intentions and intervened in 1933 to force the Nazis to retain the two principal organizers of the Berlin games—Theodor Lewald and Karl Ritter von Halt—after it was disclosed that Lewald's father was a Jewish convert to Christianity and that von Halt had Jewish ancestors.

The right of Jewish athletes to participate on the German national team became the focus of worldwide attention as the IOC met for its 1933 Congress in Vienna. At the congress, which reelected Baillet-Latour to a second eight-year term by a 48–1 vote, the president pressed Germany's three IOC members for written assurance from their government that German Jews would have the right to participate in the Games. He did receive such an assurance and declared it to be "satisfactory."

Despite this promise, the Nazis moved quickly and brazenly to exclude German Jews from private German sports clubs and to deny them use of public sports facilities. Those Jewish athletes who had a chance to make the team, including world-class high jumper Gretel Bergmann, were eventually denied fair tryouts. As a result of negative publicity about the Nazi regime, a significant movement to boycott the Berlin Games arose in Great Britain, Canada, and the United States. American IOC member Ernest Lee Jahncke, who had served in the Herbert Hoover administration as assistant secretary of the navy, published an appeal in the November 27, 1935, *New York Times* calling for Baillet-Latour to meet his "duty to hold the Nazi sports authorities accountable for the violation of their pledges. . . . Let me beseech you to seize the opportunity to take your rightful place in the history of the Olympics alongside of de Coubertin instead of Hitler." Baillet-Latour was furious at this public airing of the IOC's business and promised Avery Brundage, then head of the American Olympic Association, that he was ready to come to the United States to combat the boycott campaign. He had recently visited Hitler, who had assured him that the charges against Germany were false. Baillet-Latour told Jahncke that the president's duty was to execute the will of the IOC, which was steadfastly committed to the Games. He subsequently supported Jahncke's replacement by Brundage on the IOC. Four months later, when Hitler violated the Versailles Treaty by sending armed soldiers into the demilitarized Rhineland, Baillet-Latour told a press conference that only an armed conflict would prevent the holding of the Games in Berlin. Baillet-Latour's motivation is still the subject of some historic controversy. One interpretation of his actions holds him to the mistaken belief that allowing the Germans to host the Olympics would somehow reduce Hitler's aggressive instincts. The less generous explanation is that he was so determined to have the Olympics go forward as scheduled that he willingly overlooked German violations of the Olympic code. Despite Baillet-Latour's statement that the IOC would not interfere with the internal policies of other countries, when questions were raised about the Nazi regime's discriminatory practices, he did assert IOC prerogatives in his dealings with the Nazis over the actual conduct of the Games. Shortly before the 1936 Winter Olympics in Garmisch-Partenkirchen, he personally demanded that Hitler have anti-Semitic signs around the city removed, stating that during the Olympics the host city becomes "sacred Olympic territory" of which he was the master. Astonishingly, Hitler complied. During the Berlin Games, Hitler left the Olympic stadium in order to avoid being placed in the position of having to shake the hands of the black American gold- and silver-medal-winning long jumpers Cornelius Johnson and David Albritten. Baillet-Latour subsequently told the führer that he must invite all the victors to his box or none of them. Hitler decided to save his greetings to German athletes for a post-Games celebration. Thus, Hitler did not actually refuse to shake the hand of America's four-gold-medal winner Jesse Owens, as popular myth holds.

As the Berlin Games wound down, Baillet-Latour attended a grand dinner given by Hitler for Olympic notables and sat next to the wife of the Nazi Youth leader, Baldur von Schirach. The woman remarked on how well "the great festival of youth, peace and reconciliation" was going. Baillet-Latour replied, "May God preserve you from your illusions, madame! If you ask me, we shall have war in three years." (Quoted in *New York Times*, June 15, 1986). He was absolutely right. Germany invaded Poland on September 1, 1939, and by the following spring had occupied Belgium. With the world engulfed in war, the 1940 Winter Games, originally scheduled for Sapporo, Japan, and then moved to Garmisch-Partenkirchen, were cancelled. The same fate struck the 1940 Summer Games, which were first set for Tokyo and then shifted to Helsinki. During the winter of 1940–1941, the German sports officials Carl Diem, Karl Ritter von Halt and Reichssportsfuhrer Hans von Tschammer und Osten visited Baillet-Latour and told him that Hitler had a grandiose plan for a new order in postwar sports. Coubertin's dream was to be transformed into the Nazi Olympics, which would be held "for all time" in a 450,000-seat *deutsches Stadion* built by Hitler's favorite architect, Albert Speer. Baillet-Latour never lived long enough to see the crumbling of this nightmare vision; he died of a stroke on January 6, 1942, shortly after hearing his son had died in a free Belgium army exercise in the United States and exactly two years and five months prior to the day when the Allied invasion of Normandy hastened the end of the Nazi empire.

While the events of World War I and II provide dramatic bookends to Baillet-Latour's life in the Olympic Movement, he should also be remembered for his steady leadership of the IOC after Coubertin and for keeping the basic amateur and male-oriented structure of the Games intact during the interwar period.

BIBLIOGRAPHICAL ESSAY

Count Henri Baillet-Latour may be among the least chronicled of the IOC presidents. He never wrote about his own life and experiences in the Olympic Movement, and his papers have not been collected and made public. Scattered letters to and from Baillet-Latour may be found in the IOC Archives in Lausanne and in the Avery Brundage Papers, University of Illinois Archives.

The best secondary source for a study of Baillet-Latour's regency over the IOC is Allen Guttmann, *The Olympics: A History of the Modern Games* (Urbana, IL, 2002). Guttmann's history details Baillet-Latour's involvement in early Olympic congresses and his role in organizing the 1920 Antwerp Games, which brought him into prominence within IOC circles. He also writes with knowing authority about Baillet-Latour's relationship with IOC founder Baron Pierre de Coubertin and about his role in the events leading up to the 1936 Berlin Olympics.

For more detailed insight into Baillet-Latour's involvement in the controversial 1936 Summer Games in Berlin, consult the various sources dealing specifically with those Games, especially Duff Hart-Davis, *Hitler's Games* (London, 1986). This source provides a dramatic overview of the events leading up to the Berlin Olympics and is very critical of the role of Baillet-Latour in allowing the Games to go forward, despite clear warning signs that the Nazis would use the Games as a propaganda vehicle and would violate the nondiscrimination clause of the Olympic charter.

SIGFRID EDSTRÖM

Edward S. Goldstein

On a per capita basis, no other set of countries has had greater success in the modern Olympics than Scandinavia has. Born into cultures that cherish the outdoor life, Scandinavia's sons and daughters have dominated competition in the Winter Games and more than held their own in such disparate Summer Games events as boxing, sailing, wrestling, and track and field. In the first modern Olympics in Athens in 1896, Sigfrid Edström ran the 100-meter sprint for his native Sweden. His best time in the event was an impressive 11 seconds flat. In Olympic affairs, however, Edström was more of a marathon man, as he served the International Olympic Committee (IOC) for 31 years, guiding it as acting president from 1942 to 1946 and as president from 1946 to 1952.

Like Baron Pierre de Coubertin, Edström was of aristocratic stock. He was born November 21, 1870, in Gothenburg and was educated there and in Zurich as a civil engineer. In 1899 he married Ruth Miriam Randall, an American. Edström became president of the Swedish General Electric Company in 1903. Although he remained an industrialist all his life, Edström's avocational focus turned toward athletics when the Olympics came to Stockholm in 1912. For those games, Edström was director and vice president of the organizing committee and a member of the stadium-building committee. During the Stockholm Olympics he began a lifelong friendship with American decathlete Avery Brundage. Enthused by the success of the Stockholm Games, Edström became a founder and the first president of the International Amateur Athletic Federation (IAAF), track and field's governing body.

In 1921, Edström joined future IOC president Count Henri de Baillet-Latour as a member of the first five-member executive board of the IOC. One of Edström's first significant actions was to counter traditional Scandinavian opposition to a separate Winter Olympic Games by voting to allow the IOC to give its patronage to the Wintersports Week, which was held in Chamonix, France, in 1924. Until then the Scandinavian countries feared a Winter Games would diminish the appeal of their traditional skiing competitions. At the IOC's 1925 Congress in Prague, the body voted to formally adopt the Winter Games as an official part of the Olympic program.

The IOC also debated the issue of amateurism at the Prague Congress. Edström argued that compensating athletes for the time they spend away from work would "open up the floodgates" to professionals from the lower classes. The IOC agreed but did allow for athletes to be reimbursed for their expenses for periods up to 15 days. Seven years later, just prior to the 1932 Olympic Games in Los Angeles, Edström, acting as president of the IAAF, disqualified from competition the great Finnish runner Paavo Nurmi, after allegations that Nurmi was being paid to run.

Edström also shared the prejudice of his time against the participation of women in strenuous athletic events. In 1924, his IAAF voted to sanction women's track-and-field events in general but not to advocate their inclusion in the Olympic Games. But Edström did not count on the popularity of the "Women's Olympics" put on by the fledgling Federation Sportive Feminine Internationale and its leader, Alice Milliat. In 1926 he met with Milliat and agreed to recommend to the IOC that women be allowed to compete in five athletic events, beginning with the 1928 Games in Amsterdam.

Sigfrid Edström, IOC president, 1946–52. Courtesy of International Olympic Committee, IOC Museum Collections.

In the events leading up to the controversial 1936 Berlin Olympics, Edström supported the IOC's official position that the Olympics should go on as scheduled, no matter how outrageous the actions of the Nazi government toward its people. By 1934, when it became clear that German persecution of its Jewish citizens was increasing and might lead to an international backlash against the Games, Edström wrote Brundage a letter that in part excused Germany's anti-Semitism and called for keeping Jews "within certain limits" even in the United States.

Less than four years after the Berlin Games, war engulfed Europe and IOC president Baillet-Latour found himself unable to focus on his Olympic duties from his occupied Belgian home. Edström, IOC vice president since 1938 and a neutral-country citizen, was the logical choice to supervise IOC business. When Baillet-Latour then died of a stroke in 1942, Edström became the acting IOC president. One of Edström's first actions was to recommend to the other IOC members that Avery Brundage become second vice president.

In August 1945, Edström, Brundage, and Britain's Lord Aberdare met in London to discuss the revival of the Games. While Aberdare had lost his optimism and wondered if the Games should be resumed as if the horrors of World War II had never occurred, Edström and Brundage persuaded him that the Games were more necessary than ever. Later, by a mail ballot of IOC members, London, England, and St. Moritz, Switzerland were selected as the Summer and Winter Olympic sites, respectively, for 1948.

In 1946, at the IOC's first postwar session in Lausanne, Switzerland, Edström was elected president by acclamation. The IOC members then attempted to deal with a pent-up demand for new Olympic events. They considered but rejected petitions for the inclusion of archery, baseball, gliding, team handball, polo, roller-skating, table tennis, and volleyball. (Of these sports, volleyball was accepted in 1964, table tennis in 1968, archery and team handball in 1972, and baseball in 1992.)

During the next important IOC session, held in 1951 in Vienna, delegates passionately debated whether or not IOC members who had been associated with the deposed regimes of Germany, Italy, and Japan should be allowed to remain in the organization. Edström called some of the accused members—including his long-time acquaintance from Germany, Karl Ritter von Halt—"old friends" and refused to put the matter to a vote, despite the protests of a number of members whose homelands had been occupied by German forces during the war.

Edström's reign as IOC president wound down as the cold war continued and as the athletes of the Communist world were welcomed into the Olympic Movement. As early as 1947 Edström indicated to Brundage that he was willing to allow Communist nations to compete in the Olympics, but the aging capitalist drew the line at endorsing the election of Communists to the IOC board. The Soviet Union was given permission to compete in the Games at the IOC's May 1951 Congress in Vienna. (Although czarist Russia had participated in the Olympics, the Soviet Union under Lenin and Stalin had withdrawn from the Games and sponsored its own workers' games.)

The question of Chinese Olympic participation following the bloody civil war between Mao Zedong's Communists and General Chiang Kai-shek's Nationalists was a more difficult one for the IOC leadership. On the eve of the 1952 Games in Helsinki, the mainland Communists and the Chinese Nationalists on the island of Formosa (now known as Taiwan) each claimed to be the sole legitimate representative of Chinese athletes, and both angered Edström with their political harangues. A compromise proposal to allow the individual sport federations to recognize either the Communists' or the Nationalists' athletes failed; the Nationalists boycotted the Games because the Communists were expected to be present, and the Communists arrived too late to compete.

Edström's IOC also wrestled with the classic cold-war issue of divided Germany. At the 1951 IOC Session in Vienna, the national Olympic committee from democratic West Germany was officially recognized and requested to include representatives from Communist East Germany. Years of fruitless negotiations aimed at achieving this objective followed. At a 1952 meeting in Copenhagen, a furious Edström was left waiting for nine and a half hours for a meeting to begin because the East German negotiators refused to walk 300 yards to his hotel. Eventually, the East Germans did form a common team with the West Germans from 1956 through 1964. From 1968 through 1988, the two Germanys competed as separate teams. After the Berlin Wall fell in 1989, a reunified German team appeared in the 1992 Games.

In his final official act, opening the 1952 Summer Games at Helsinki, Edström said, "We hope the Olympic Games will allow a respite from political tensions and that international understanding will increase among the youth of the world as a direct result of their intermingling and participation during the Games." Sigfrid Edström died in Stockholm on March 18, 1964, shortly after the Winter Olympics were held in Innsbruck, Austria, still under the shadow of the cold war.

In his Olympic career, Edström was both participant and administrator, competitor and rule-maker. While his faith in the Olympic Movement contributed to the expanding role of sport in world society, his inner-circle clannishness led to decisions that stressed exclusion over inclusion. In these ways, Edström reflected the fascinating times in which he was one of many memorable lords of the rings.

BIBLIOGRAPHICAL ESSAY

Neither the IOC nor the Brundage Papers at the University of Illinois Archives has extensive material relating to Edström's life and career. The IOC archives has a number of circular letters Edström wrote to IOC members during World War II as "Olympic Bulletins." These letters are also available in the Brundage Papers, as is correspondence between Brundage and Edström and an assortment of newspaper clippings from the years of Edström's presidency.

Among secondary works, the most useful is Allen Guttmann, *The Olympics: A History of the Modern Games* (Urbana, Ill., 2002), which focuses on the organization and ideology of the Olympic Movement rather than on the Games themselves. Guttmann recognizes that from the start the Games have been influenced by politics and represent an important twentieth-century social movement. His description of Edström's role in the IOC's wrangling over such issues as amateurism, women's participation, and the recognition of Communist countries is quite riveting. Much of this is further elaborated in Guttmann's biography of Brundage, *The Games Must Go On: Avery Brundage and the Olympic Movement* (New York, 1984).

AVERY BRUNDAGE

Robert K. Barney

In 2001, the International Olympic Committee (IOC) selected the organization's eighth president, Jacques Rogge. Among Rogge's predecessors, none occupied the position during more difficult times of upheaval than did Avery Brundage. Brundage, for 20 years (1952–1972) the czar of Olympic affairs the world over, at one time or another was embroiled in almost every conceivable issue that hounded the IOC: eligibility, commercialism, nationalism, race, politics, gigantism, and a good many more. On each issue, Brundage's public stance and problem-solving approach was consistent and unyielding. There was no room for compromise. It was either Avery's way or the highway, so to speak.

There is nothing in Avery Brundage's lineage that suggests an aristocratic strain. He was born in Detroit of working-class parents on September 28, 1887. Such an egalitarian background is distinctively at odds with that elitist quality consistently identified with the organization that he would come to preside over longer than any president, with the exception of the Olympic *renovateur* himself, Baron Pierre de Coubertin. Brundage's parents were Easterners from upstate New York. His father was a stonecutter by trade. The Brundages moved to Chicago when Avery was five years old. Shortly afterwards, Avery's father abandoned the family, prompting his mother to turn the family domicile into a boarding house. Though never as destitute as Horatio Alger's enterprising, youthful urban heroes, Avery "hustled a buck" just as industriously. He became a *Chicago Tribune* paperboy at twelve. When he was 13, Brundage won a citywide newspaper essay contest; his prize was an expense-paid trip to Washington to witness William McKinley's second inauguration. He enrolled at the R. T. Crane Manual Training School (popularly known as Crane Tech) where he was a solid student, mixing after-school athletics with a daily schedule of 9:00 to 5:00 classes, a seven-mile trolley ride to and from school, and a two-hour pre-dawn stint of newspaper deliveries. Clearly, young Brundage knew hard work, discipline, tenaciousness, sacrifice, and, at the same time, the need for setting priorities. While admired characteristics, his constant practice of them to an ascetic degree later made him a wearisome figure to his IOC colleagues and world sport leaders, most of whom believed that the context of a changing world had isolated Avery.

Avery Brundage, IOC president, 1952–72. Courtesy University of Illinois Archives, Avery Brundage Collection.

Brundage entered the University of Illinois in 1905. Four years later he graduated with a degree in civil engineering. By any standard of measurement, he left behind an enviable student-athlete record. His academic standing merited membership in two honor societies; his athletic pursuits in track and field earned him an Intercollegiate Athletic Conference (Big 10) discus championship in his senior year; his extracurricular student energies gained him a position on the *Daily Illini* newspaper staff, chairmanship of the Senior Stag (the university's gala annual prom), and affiliation with two literary organizations. Brundage's college life had been busy. He was driven to succeed, to prove that a poor boy could make it in the types of forums where all too often only the wealthy or politically connected succeeded. College revealed another typical characteristic of Brundage. Overly serious, genuinely zealous in the pursuit of mission, abrupt and even acerbic to those who did not subscribe to his way of doing things, Brundage did not exemplify the nature of the individual usually so actively engaged in campus life. There is evidence that Brundage was something of a loner, neither particularly well liked nor sought after by his classmates. Indeed, Brundage never did enjoy a wide circle of friends during his lifetime—business and athletic associates, yes, but close friends, no.

Almost immediately after graduation, Brundage went to work as a construction superintendent for the well-known Chicago architectural firm of Holabird and Roche. With borrowed money he established his own construction company in 1915. But once an athlete, always an athlete. Brundage joined the Chicago Athletic Association's Cherry Circle track-and-field team in 1910, trained himself to compete in what was then called the "all-around" competitions (100-yard dash, high jump, broad jump, hammer throw, pole vault, 120-yard high hurdles, mile run, 880-yard walk, and 56-pound weight throw). He placed third in the 1910 national championships for the event, fourth in 1911, and captured first place in 1914, 1916 and 1918. Brundage's skill as a "all-arounder" made him a serious candidate for two new Olympic events planned for Stockholm in 1912, the decathlon and pentathlon. In western regional trials he placed high enough in both events to be selected to the U.S. Olympic team. His Olympic performance, though an improvement over previous American achievements, by no means matched that of the legendary Jim Thorpe, who won both events with stunning performances. Brundage placed sixth in the pentathlon and failed to complete the decathlon, dropping out of the event's final test, the 1,500-meter run. For Brundage, a man of unusual discipline and willpower, failure to complete the event was not only a contradiction, but most probably a severe embarrassment, too.

Upon his return to Chicago, Brundage immersed himself in business affairs and continued his association with the Chicago Athletic Association. Leaving track-and-field competition, Brundage turned to handball, an activity for older sportsmen. Eventually, he won the city championship and was at one time ranked among the top 10 players in the nation. It was the sport of handball that launched Brundage's long and fruitful affiliation with the Amateur Athletic Union (AAU) of the United States. Following dedicated service with the Central Association of the AAU, he served as chairman of the national handball committee from 1925 to 1927. By 1926 Avery Brundage had become a recognized figure in the power venues of AAU administration. In 1928 he was elected president of both the AAU (serving until the fall of 1935, except for 1933) and its Olympic arm, the American Olympic Association (AOA). By the early 1930s, when Brundage had reached his mid-forties, he had become an American sports czar faintly reminiscent of the storied James E. Sullivan of a bygone era.

America's confrontation with Germany and the Nazi regime's trusteeship of the 1936 Summer Games in Berlin propelled Avery Brundage into the international Olympic spotlight. A festering confrontation arose between those national sports federations and AAU officials who favored American Olympic participation in 1936 and those who did not. Brundage, a staunch believer that sport should be held apart from politics, championed the participation argument. New York judge Jeremiah Mahoney, president of the AAU in 1935, led the adversarial position of non-participation. In an extremely close vote of delegates at the AAU convention held at the Commodore Hotel in New York City in December 1935, Brundage's point of view prevailed. An American Olympic team went to the Berlin Games, an occasion which showcased the track and field exploits of African Americans, particularly Jesse Owens. With the death of American IOC member Charles Sherrill in June 1936, as well as the ouster from the IOC that same year of American boycott supporter Ernest Jahncke, Brundage, the leader of the fight to keep the United States in the 1936 Games, became an obvious candidate to join William G. Garland as IOC members from the U.S. Brundage's selection (or "co-option," as the IOC terms it) was confirmed at the IOC's 35th Session in Berlin in July 1936. Though a fresh face on the IOC, Brundage lost little time in climbing its internal structure to power and authority. In 1937 he replaced the recently deceased Baron Godefroy de Blonay of Switzerland on the powerful executive board.

Avery Brundage was also making a name for himself outside of the Olympics. His construction business in Chicago flourished. Capital and influence accrued. This was fortunate, since he would need money in the years ahead. He estimated that in his position as IOC president he spent $75,000 annually on travel and administrative costs associated with Olympic duties. Brundage was also interested in politics. Reflecting his business and administrative style, his political position was almost always on the far right. He was a confirmed Republican and an isolationist in foreign policy matters. Outspoken, sometimes volatile, generally resolute, Brundage was often at odds with individuals and groups of opposing thought and action. At times he spoke publicly on boiling world issues, including his perception of Germany and Japan in the late 1930s—that Germany defended Western civilization from the onslaught of communism and that Japan was basically friendly and wanted only peace with America. Postures like those, together with a streak of anti-Semitism, often kept Brundage in hot water during the turbulent decades of the 1930s and 1940s.

Brundage's Olympic life was not dormant during the years of World War II, when both Summer and Winter Games were cancelled. Partially motivated toward keeping the United States involved in international sport during the war years, Brundage was among those who revived interest in the concept of Pan American Games, the first edition of which was planned for Buenos Aires in 1942. The Argentinian dream of organizing the first Pan American Games in 1942, however, was delayed until 1951.

Meanwhile, Count Henri Baillet-Latour had succeeded Coubertin as president of the IOC in 1925. When the Belgian aristocrat died in Brussels in 1942, Olympic leadership passed to the IOC's first vice president, Sigfrid Edström of Sweden. During the wartime years of the 1940s, Brundage helped Edström maintain contacts with IOC members, irrespective of their geopolitical allegiances. Brundage's IOC Executive Board membership and his zeal to aid in Olympic matters prompted Edström to suggest his name for the second vice president position, a distinction the Chicagoan assumed at the IOC's first postwar executive board meeting, held in London in 1945. More and more, as the decade of the 1940s passed, Brundage publicly pontificated on Olympic problems, often being viewed in the United States as the real leader of the IOC. In Lausanne in 1946, at the IOC's first postwar general session, Brundage was proclaimed first vice president. His sponsor was Edström, whose wife was not only American but a former Chicago schoolteacher. With the 82-year-old Edström voicing no desire to continue as IOC president after the Helsinki Games in 1952, Brundage became an obvious candidate to succeed him. In a rousing election that progressed through 25 rounds of balloting, Brundage prevailed over England's Lord David Burghley, an Olympic gold medalist at the Amsterdam Games and an individual who would joust continually with Brundage on all sorts of Olympic issues during the 1950s and 1960s. In the end, Brundage's election to the IOC presidency boiled down to his proven administrative expertise in American and international Olympic matters.

Brundage served as president of the IOC for a period of 20 years, passing the gavel of leadership to Michael Morris, Lord Killanin, following the tragic conclusion of the Munich Games in the summer of 1972. During that period, Brundage faced almost all of the major issues which to greater or lesser extent continue to be viewed as Olympic problem areas. The earliest issues were those surrounding the amateur-professional dichotomy, followed by problems caused by the aftermath of World War II, with the collapse of colonial empires and fracture of former Olympic countries into two or more national-political entities.

Brundage's confrontation with forces in contradiction with Rule 26 (eligibility) of the IOC statutes was perhaps the most vexing of all issues confronted in his long Olympic career. Born and bred in the turn-of-the-century atmosphere of a sporting amateur myth inherited from England, the hardworking Brundage, who claimed that his "athletic journey" had always been undertaken simply for the joy and satisfaction of it all, held no sympathy for those whose involvement in sport might be motivated by a quest for records and the payoffs that might accrue in the form of cash, goods, jobs, or the type of recognition that eventually converts into financial gain. Again and again, throughout the years of his presidency, Brundage stood astride the bridge of the Olympic ship ready to do battle with those in violation of his perception of the amateur athlete. He warmed up to the task in 1947 when he noted that an adoring Ottawa had given its Canadian figure-skating darling Barbara Ann Scott a canary-colored convertible for winning the gold medal at the world championships. He was quick to warn that Scott's amateur status for the Olympic Winter Games scheduled for St. Moritz the following year might be jeopardized. An alarmed Ottawa citizenry "temporarily reclaimed" the automobile, and the Canadian press vilified Brundage. Scott eventually won the Olympic women's figure-skating title in 1948 and shortly thereafter, as Brundage fumed, the convertible was returned to her custodianship.

For 20 years Avery Brundage warred with all challengers, including many of his IOC colleagues, on the issue of eligibility. For the most part his campaign to preserve the exclusive atmosphere of Olympic amateurism can be viewed as a grudging retreat against the forces of change. Though Brundage admonished that "broken time" payments to Olympic athletes would spell "the end of the Olympic Movement as it now exists" (and he was right), IOC members pushed for a more lenient eligibility code. Arguing that the paradox between the commensurate training time and support infrastructure necessary to pursue the Olympic motto, *Citius, Altius, Fortius,* and the requirement that athletes remain amateurs made liars, cheaters, and hypocrites out of Olympic aspirants, the IOC took the first in a series of steps that has led today to the participation of full-fledged professionals in the Games, of which the so-called U.S. "Dream Team" basketball contingent in Barcelona is the most celebrated example. Despite Brundage's condemnations against such action, the IOC's Rule 26 was modified in 1962 to allow national Olympic committees (NOCs) to administer "broken time" compensation to athletes for the support of "dependents suffering hardship." In hardly the blink of an eye, "suffering dependents" became "suffering athletes." Brundage, who continually railed against putting interpretations of important Olympic statutes in the hands of NOCs, whose very existence was rooted in nationalism, had every reason in the years ahead to say, "I told you so!"

As Brundage reached the end of his tenure as IOC president, he gathered himself for one last kick at the eligibility can. Like a petulant schoolboy, he made sure that it was one of vigorous dimensions. The sport was Alpine skiing and the issue was the constant association by most international-caliber skiers with the skiing industry's manufacturers and resort sites for remuneration in hard cash, "kind," or both. Brundage was never a vigorous enthusiast of the Winter Games. To him, the Summer Games by themselves were too big and getting even more so with each passing Olympiad. The toll on IOC resources and energies in any one Olympic year was mind-boggling, especially in those years of limited financial resources, of which the Brundage presidential years certainly were characteristic. It is a pity that Brundage never thought of alternating the Summer Games with the Winter Games in even-numbered years, a formula that was implemented in the 1990s.

Of all those Olympic athletes, in both an individual sense and a generic sport sense, whom Brundage monitored relative to encroachments on the Olympic eligibility code, none elicited his anger as much did Alpine skiers. Sojourning around the globe on the world ski circuit, brandishing ski equipment emblazoned with manufacturing logos to millions of admiring television viewers, and flaunting an athletic jet-set lifestyle was more than Brundage could tolerate. After numerous confrontations with the International Ski Federation on the issue, Brundage's frustration boiled over. He moved to delete Alpine skiing entirely from the program of the 1972 Winter Games in Sapporo. Brundage's IOC colleagues prevented such a drastic procedure from occurring, but they were persuaded to support the disqualification from the Games of Austria's Karl Schranz, the most illustrious Alpine ski performer in the world and, at the same time, the individual Brundage considered to be the most blatant violator of amateur standards. The entire Austrian ski team reacted by threatening to boycott the Sapporo Games. Schranz, now a martyr, convinced them to participate. He subsequently flew home to Vienna where he was greeted as a hero by thousands of fellow Austrians and presented with a gold medal for "service to the state." Schranz's disqualification was hardly full satisfaction for Brundage. His alienation from Alpine skiing continued for the rest of his life.

The geopolitical results of World War II presented severe problems for the modern Olympic Movement, and Avery Brundage was left to wrestle with virtually all of them. A charter member of the modern Olympic Movement, Germany was fractured into two states, East and West. Indeed, the whole of Europe was separated into eastern and western political-economic spheres. Additionally, Korea split into North and South, and China became the People's Republic of China on the mainland and the Republic of China on the island of Formosa. Following the war, too, much of the colonial empires of Germany, Italy, Portugal, Belgium, England, France, and the Netherlands in Africa, Southeast Asia and Oceania was dissolved, replaced by scores of newly independent countries. There are several ways in which new countries can be recognized internationally. One is to join the United Nations. Another is to establish a national Olympic committee and join the world sport community. For new countries this was an easy matter. For those old regimes now split in two, the task was not so easy. Although the problems concerning North and South Korea and the "two Chinas" were delayed until well after his death, Brundage could not escape the German question.

Germany, as had been the case following World War I, was excluded from participating in the first postwar Olympic Games in London in 1948. Brundage, a close friend of Germany's NOC leaders, Karl Ritter von Halt and Carl Diem, labored mightily to have Germany readmitted to the modern Olympic Movement. Following World War II, however, Germany was split into the pro-Soviet East and the Allied-sponsored West. The German Democratic Republic (East Germany, or GDR) argued for its own Olympic autonomy. The Federal Republic of Germany (West Germany, or FRG) argued that it represented all Germans. Prolonged negotiations in late 1951 and early 1952 between IOC authorities and representatives of both East and West Germany aimed at having one combined German team for the Helsinki Games resulted in stalemate and acrimony. West German athletes participated at Helsinki; East Germans did not. Under the urbane leadership of Hans

Schöbel, a noted Brundage ingratiator, East Germany was finally successful in establishing an NOC in 1955 and gaining IOC recognition but with the proviso that they would compete in combined German status with the West Germans. When the combined German Olympic team appeared for the 1956 Winter Games in Cortina d'Ampezzo, Italy, and for the Summer Games in Melbourne, its composition heavily favored West German athletes by a ratio of about three to one. Roughly the same scenario prevailed in 1960 at Rome. Shortly afterward, in August 1961, East Germany sealed itself off from its western brethren by erecting the Berlin Wall and implementing a menacing frontier along its entire western border. Despite a West German boycott of all sporting relations with the East in retaliation, the IOC continued to insist on a single team to represent all of Germany at Tokyo in 1964. Both sides were furious over this dictum. To Brundage's credit, he patiently moved each side towards compromise, but it took 14 meetings of the national Olympic committees of East and West and nearly 100 sessions of dialogue among Germany's national sports federations before a combined German team appeared in Tokyo.

By the mid-1960s more and more international sport federations were recognizing the German Democratic Republic as a separate and distinct entity at world and regional championships. This fact had some influence on the IOC allowing a separate East German team to compete at Mexico City in 1968, even though the official flag of both East and West was the Olympic banner with the familiar five ring symbol. No German, East or West, could quibble with the anthem played at medal ceremonies for German winners of gold—the "Ode to Joy" from the final movement of Ludwig van Beethoven's *Ninth Symphony*. With Brundage's friend Schöbel co-opted to the IOC in 1964, replacing West Germany's deceased Karl Ritter von Halt, the GDR finally owned the type of franchisement that could pay dividends. Partly because of Schöbel's IOC activities, partly because of Brundage's personal sponsorship, and partly because of pressure from the Soviet Union, the IOC voted 44–4 at its 67th General Session (Mexico City, 1968) for acceptance of the East Germans, an acceptance that guaranteed them their own flag, their own anthem, and, of course, their own team. It was ironic that the GDR's first appearance in a Summer Olympic Games was at Munich in 1972. The appearance at the Opening Ceremonies of the GDR team, basking in the condition of complete autonomy, provided Brundage with his most satisfying moment at his last Olympic Games.

The China question, somewhat akin to the German situation, provided Brundage with continual headaches. First, completely unlike the German case, Brundage had no cronies among Chinese Olympic personnel to whom he could relate in a convivial fashion. Second, the atmosphere for dialogue with Olympic officials from the People's Republic of China was consistently compromised by Brundage's frequently haughty and intransigent manner, a demeanor that grated against the international naïveté of Chairman Mao Zedong and his Olympic coterie. But when all was said and done, the entire issue boiled down to the argument presented by both the People's Republic of China on the mainland and the Republic of China on Formosa that each exclusively represented all Chinese on Olympic matters. Following a two-decade-long civil war, the triumph of Mao's Communist forces over Chiang Kai-shek's Nationalists in 1949 resulted in the defeated Nationalist's escape to Formosa, where "business as usual," including Olympic business, was carried out under the name of the Republic of China. On the mainland resided almost one billion Chinese, citizens of a new regime, the People's Republic of China.

The cleavage between the two Chinas rallied sharp political-economic lines in the context of global politics. All too familiar with class struggle, emerging countries in the Communist world were sympathetic to the plight of the People's Republic of China, despite its stance of self-imposed isolation. On the other hand, the United States had been a supporter of Nationalist China since early in the century. It continued political recognition of and aggressive commercial relationships with Taiwan (the Nationalists' new name for Formosa). Conversely, in its postwar strategy of containment, the United States shunned the People's Republic of China. Brundage, a personification of American capitalism, was most often viewed by Communist Chinese leaders as simply a "faithful menial of the U.S. imperialists." Every move that Brundage made to work toward a solution of the "two Chinas" problem was immediately interpreted by sports officials from the People's Republic as simply another reflection of a U.S. foreign policy aimed at aggrandizement of Taiwan. Brundage, in turn, accused the Chinese Communists of continually mixing politics with sport in their dialogue with him on the issue of Olympic Games participation. Though Communist China made a cameo appearance at the Helsinki Games in 1952 (one swimmer competed), the confrontation between Brundage and the People's Republic of China became an enduring stalemate, one which in the end forced a bitter Chinese resignation from the modern Olympic Movement in 1958.

With the crusty Brundage retired in 1972 and the more conciliatory Lord Killanin in the presidency; with the People's Republic of China's expanded representation in various international sport federations; with United Nations membership and increasing diplomatic recognition, with the death of Mao in 1976 making way for Deng Xiaoping and a China bent on entering the modern world; indeed, with the IOC's growing realization that the international Olympic Movement could not truly be called "international" if it continued to exclude almost one-third of the world's population, the People's Republic of China was admitted to the Olympic family in 1980. Taiwan was told that it might remain in Olympic good standing if it no longer insisted on being called the Republic of China and accepted the designation of Chinese Taipei. Though initially defiant at this rebuff, in the end it acquiesced. In Los Angeles in July 1984, an Olympic power of the future took its place among the competing nations. It might have been far sooner had Brundage worked as diligently on the Chinese issue as he had on the German problem.

Avery Brundage hated confrontations that mixed national or global politics with sport. Most of the time they sorely tested his patience and occupied time he would have liked to spend on other items of Olympic business. In the South African apartheid issue he met one of the few outright defeats that he experienced in his 20-year presidency. Seeking international recognition as a first order of business after ridding themselves of European colonial domination, emerging African nations joined the modern Olympic Movement in the 1950s. The nation on the African continent with the longest Olympic affiliation was South Africa, its athletes having competed since 1908. Since the days of early Dutch settlement and subsequent British stewardship, however, the country functioned under a strict racial policy called *apartheid*. Whites ruled; colored and black South Africans lived with scant social, political, and economic franchise. Only white athletes represented South Africa at the Olympic Games. Such blatant racial discrimination and resulting political hegemony angered millions of black Africans. In an effort to apply world pressure on South Africa for destruction of apartheid, African nations protested to Olympic officials that the IOC was in violation of its own fundamental principle that no athlete be excluded from Olympic competition because of race, religion, or politics. Opportunities for membership on the South African Olympic team, it was argued, were prevented by virtue of "a person's race." Remaining united in their quest, African countries gathered support from the Soviet Union and other countries in the Communist bloc, as well as many third-world countries, in an effort to exclude South Africa from the modern Olympic Movement unless its policy of apartheid was obliterated.

Brundage, a longtime friend of Reginald Honey, South Africa's IOC member, continually rebuffed the African bloc's argument, asserting over and over again that "the Olympic Games cannot be shaped by politics." As other worldwide sanctions of a social, economic, and political nature were meted on South Africa, and as it refused to budge on the issue, black Africa played its trump card, threatening a wholesale boycott of Olympic Games to which the South Africans were invited. Tokyo in 1964 and Mexico City in 1968 withdrew their invitations to South Africa in the face of possible boycott. Brundage called this action outright blackmail. Still, he procrastinated on getting tough with an Olympic country obviously in violation of family rules. With gathering world opinion and sanctions exerted against South Africa, together with rising African influence in the halls of IOC decision-making, Brundage's reluctance to take action was finally brushed aside. In 1970 the IOC voted to banish South Africa from the Olympic family. Though African nations won the battle against Avery Brundage and South Africa, they failed to win the war. A resolute South Africa continued to cling tenaciously to white hegemony. Startling domestic events in the early 1990s, in which the IOC had no role, finally brought an end to the evil doctrine. It is difficult to imagine, if Avery Brundage had still been alive, how he would have greeted the tides of change in South Africa, when he had dismissed himself from playing a role of possible great influence on the situation.

Avery Brundage, an exponent of sustaining Olympic participation only for amateurs, of trying to keep the Games from gaining unmanageable size, and of separating them from harm at the hands of both domestic and international politics, was also intent on protecting the Olympic image from contamination by commercial forces. Though an alert watchdog over liaisons between Olympic athletes and commercial firms, an action that usually elicited prompt censure from him, Brundage, nevertheless, was at last drawn to compromise his consistent hard-line stance on the subject. It was the beckoning hand of television that intruded into Brundage's austere world of divorce between amateur sport and commercialism.

Though a primitive form of television had been present in Berlin in 1936, and again in London in 1948, the happy marriage between sport and television did not really commence until television sets became commonplace in American homes by the middle of the 1950s. Networks soon realized that sporting extravaganzas were especially attractive program fare. The World Series, college football bowl games, and college basketball were early targets for the three big American television networks. Attraction to the Olympic Games followed. When Australian Olympic officials charged with organizing the Melbourne Games in 1956 argued with local and international television networks on the distinction between Olympic news coverage and Olympic entertainment programming, the result was that the Games went untelevised except for scant coverage by two local stations, and then, only at venues where the seats had been sold out.

A principle for future IOC revenue acquisition had, however, been established. If the Games were desired as entertainment viewing, that is, for television programming beyond a brief news report, then television would have to pay for the privilege. By the time of the 1960 Winter Games in Squaw Valley and the Summer Games in Rome, the IOC had enlarged its Media Statutes (Rule 49) to include television rights. The chief architect of these policies was Avery Brundage. Though a commercial relationship of this nature was decidedly repugnant to him, the thought of throwing thousands of dollars into the hands of others for absolutely no return consideration was even more repugnant. Brundage and the IOC joined with the organizing committees of the Squaw Valley Winter Games and the Rome Summer Games to negotiate the sale of television rights to CBS for $50,000 and $394,000, respectively.

How did Brundage rationalize this marriage of convenience? Despite the obvious folly of allowing American business enterprise to capitalize on the Games for little or no investment, the pragmatic Brundage knew that if a major source of revenue were not found, the future of the modern Olympic Movement was in dire jeopardy. The fact of the matter was that when Brundage assumed the presidency in 1952, the IOC operated at an annual deficit of more than $3,000. Television rights fees could solve the financial problem, and besides, television might be used to help promote a worldwide understanding of the concept and philosophy of Olympism, rather like a form of electronic religion.

Despite all this, Brundage was not particularly progressive when it came to television matters. The shrewd business mind that had earned him millions in the construction industry in Chicago was consistently outmaneuvered by the negotiating strategies of television moguls. Olympic television rights fees sold to American networks for each Olympic Games during the Brundage presidency increased at a minuscule rate when compared to the percentage increases achieved by future IOC president Juan Antonio Samaranch.

Avery Brundage died in Garmisch-Partenkirchen, Germany, on May 8, 1975. He was 87 years old and had been involved with the Olympic Movement for over 60 years. As his legacy unfolded, detractors and defenders pronounced their judgments. *Obdurate, outwardly unfriendly, dictatorial, crusty bureaucrat, cultural conservative, personification of frigidity and false cleanliness, intransigent, unswerving, obstinate,* and many more similar terms have been used to describe Avery Brundage as he led the modern Olympic Movement through the problem-laden years between 1952 and 1972. Other terms were also used to describe him: *thoroughly honest, honorable, principled, a man who dedicated himself and much of his life to serving the modern Olympic Movement.* For many who knew him and dealt with him on various Olympic issues, a positive memory of Avery Brundage will be difficult to manage. His detractors outweighed his defenders several times over. For them, unkind images of Brundage railing against enlargement of the Olympic Games due to expanded opportunities for women athletes; pernicious penalties meted out for even the most minor violations of Olympic regulations; and a consistently black-and-white approach to issues will always override anything remotely favorable one might remember. Lastly, his detractors will always point at his crass handling of the Black September massacre and its aftermath at the 1972 Munich Summer Games, the final Games under his IOC custodianship. Nevertheless, for those who decry the Olympic Movement's contemporary subservience to commercial forces, deplore the nonsense of such a happenstance as America's basketball "Dream Team," castigate the myriad instances of the Olympic Games being manipulated by politics and politicians, and carp at the ever-growing immensity of the great festival and its conversion to mass entertainment, Avery Brundage will most certainly be recalled for having been the last serious barrier of resistance in preventing such questionable character from enveloping the late-twentieth-century version of a noble 100-year-old ideal originally visualized by a dedicated Frenchman named Pierre de Coubertin.

BIBLIOGRAPHICAL ESSAY

Avery Brundage has probably elicited more serious scholarly writing than any other figure in Olympic history, including the Baron de Coubertin. One reason for this is that he saved almost every document pertaining to his life in sport. In his will he made provisions for his papers to be donated to the archives of his alma mater, the University of Illinois. Thus, when one desires to undertake research on the subject of Avery Brundage, the fundamental primary sources are to be found in the Avery Brundage Collection (ABC), the original version of which is, of course, at the University of Illinois. A microfilm copy of the ABC can be found at the Centre for Olympic Studies at the University of Western Ontario in Canada. The microfilm version of the ABC numbers some 150 reels of material, including letters, reports, IOC and USOC minutes, observations, reactions, reminiscences, and newspaper clippings of Avery Brundage's athletic and Olympic career. An absolutely indispensable index of the ABC is Maynard Brichford, comp., *Avery Brundage Collection: 1908–1975* (Cologne, 1977). Another important repository is the International Olympic Committee archives in Lausanne, Switzerland. Far less in volume and more haphazard in organization are the records of the U.S. Olympic Committee in Colorado Springs, Colorado.

Some biographical treatments of Brundage exist. The best, without question, is Allen Guttmann, *The Games Must Go On: Avery Brundage and the Olympic Movement* (New York, 1984). Of far lesser note is Heinz Schöbel, *The Four Dimensions of Avery Brundage* (Leipzig, Germany, 1968), available in both German and English editions. Many works explore the relationship between Brundage and various problem issues. Of those, the following bear the most credibility based on the record of primary sources examined. For Brundage and Olympic television matters, see Stephen R. Wenn, "An Olympian Squabble: The Distribution of Olympic Television Revenue, 1960–1966," in *Olympika: The International Journal of Olympic Studies*, 3 (1994): 27–48 and, for a more comprehensive view, Robert K. Barney, Stephen R. Wenn, and Scott G. Martyn, *Selling the Five Rings* (Salt Lake City, UT, 2002) For the best review of Brundage and his confrontation with the "two Chinas" issue from the point of view of both English and Chinese sources, see Dongguang Pei, "'A Question of Names': The Two Chinas Issue and the People's Republic of China in the Modern Olympic Movement" (master's thesis, University of Western Ontario, 1995).

For particularly enlightening observations on Avery Brundage and his entanglement with the South African, Chinese, and amateur/professional questions, written from the perspective of Brundage's successor, see Lord Killanin, *My Olympic Years* (London, 1983). For discussions of Brundage and the German question, see Christopher R. Hill, *Olympic Politics* (Manchester, 1992); Richard Espy, *The Politics of the Olympic Games* (Berkeley, Calif., 1979); and John Hoberman, *Olympic Crisis* (New York, 1986).

MICHAEL MORRIS, LORD KILLANIN

Kathy L. Nichols

Michael Morris, Lord Killanin, joined the Olympic Movement in 1951, inspired by the idealism of the founder of the modern Olympics, Baron Pierre de Coubertin. Killanin aspired to help build a system of games that reflected the values of the Olympic charter—those of fair competition without interference by politicians. Despite these ideals, his tenure as president of the International Olympic Committee (IOC) spanned eight of the most turbulent years in the history of the organization. And, in his own words, "long before that I was to become acquainted with two of the forces that have come more and more to darken the idealism inspired by Coubertin and put the whole Olympic movement at risk: politics and violence" (Killanin, *My Olympic Years*, 32).

Michael Morris, Lord Killanin, IOC president 1972–80. Courtesy of International Olympic Committee, IOC Museum Collections.

Michael Morris was born on July 30, 1914, to Lieutenant-Colonel George Henry and Dora Maryan Morris. He was, in the words of John Hennessy, a "strange mixture of patrician and commoner." The Dublin, Ireland, native succeeded to the title of third baron of Killanin in 1927 upon the death of his uncle. Killanin was educated at Eton, the Sorbonne in Paris, and Magdalene College, Cambridge. Although young Killanin was an avid amateur boxer, rower, and equestrian, he received little recognition as an athlete. At Cambridge he served as literary editor of *Varsity* and as president of the Footlights, the university drama club. After receiving a B.A. from the Sorbonne, he embarked on a career in journalism and served in the House of Lords.

Killanin was on the editorial staff of Dublin's *Daily Express-Daily Mail* from 1935 to 1939, where he served as special war correspondent during the Sino-Japanese War of 1937. Before World War II interrupted his newspaper career, Killanin was a political columnist for the *Daily Dispatch*, where he and other journalists edited a chronicle of the Munich talks entitled *Four Days*.

During World War II, Killanin served in the 30th Armed Battalion, rising in rank to brigade major in 1943. In 1945, he married Mary Sheila Chathcart, the daughter of an Anglican minister, with whom he had one daughter and three sons. Killanin continued to write, eventually publishing a total of six books and several screenplays. In addition, he directed several films, including *The Quiet Man*, working with John Ford. Killanin's interest in the film industry led to his appointment to the Government Committee on the Film Industry in 1957 and as chairman of the Dublin Theater Festival in 1958. The activity for which he is best known, however, is his involvement in the Olympic Movement, beginning in 1951 when he joined the Olympic Council of Ireland.

Killanin once said his "Olympic life began not through any prowess at sport, but by trying to resolve disputes and squabbles" (Killanin, *My Olympic Years*, 23). In 1951, Irish national sporting associations reflected the fractured political situation in the country; some associations represented a united Ireland, while others, despite claims that they represented the entire country at an international level, did not field united teams. Killanin was committed to the idea of a united Ireland, not just politically but also in sport and business. His reputation for supporting the cause of the Irish Republican Army while denouncing their methods, combined with his peerage and service during World War II, gave him credibility with all sides of the Irish conflict.

In 1951, because Killanin's political views were acceptable to all sides, Major General W. R. E. Murphy of the International Amateur Boxing Association and Patrick Carroll, president of the Irish Amateur Boxing Association, asked Killanin to become president of the Olympic Council of Ireland, a body representing all of Ireland. As president, Killanin's desire to unite all sporting events on a national basis was only partially successful; he never achieved unity in Irish track-and-field or cycling teams. Shortly after his election, Killanin was asked to replace J. J. Keane, the first president of the Olympic Council of Ireland, on the IOC. In 1952, Killanin attended his first IOC meeting in Oslo, Norway, as a nonvoting participant. He attended the 1952 Helsinki Games both as a member of the IOC and president of the Irish Olympic Council.

International politics, an issue that plagued Killanin throughout his tenure in the IOC, posed a problem during the planning of the Helsinki Games. The Eastern bloc countries, competing in the Games for the first time since World War II, requested separate quarters for their athletes. According to Killanin, the IOC granted this request because of a desire to bring these countries back into the Games. Even during his first session in the IOC, Killanin objected to the use of the Olympic Games as a political tool.

The question of professionalism on the part of Olympic athletes arose at Helsinki and followed Killanin, without resolution, throughout his IOC tenure. Killanin believed that the concept of amateurism was, by 1952, fundamentally different from the concept set forth by Coubertin. Throughout his life he continued to lobby for broader acceptance of private and governmental support for amateur athletes.

An ironic event occurred during the Helsinki Games when sportswriter Arthur MacWeeney suggested to Killanin that he might someday become president of the IOC. MacWeeney believed future presidents of the IOC should come from small countries that would not leave the IOC "fettered with its politics." Killanin took the statement in jest, because he had no desire at that time to hold the office and because he did not believe he could afford to serve in the position. In later years, however, MacWeeney's statement became prophecy; Killanin advanced through the ranks until he was elected president of the IOC in 1972.

Killanin's ability to mediate disputes and to smooth rough situations proved valuable in the posts he held during his rise to the IOC presidency. In 1966 he was appointed *chef de protocol* of the organization. He was responsible for meeting all IOC members and instructing them and their spouses on the rules of protocol for the organization. Killanin was unanimously elected to the IOC Executive Board in 1967. The same year, he was appointed chair of a commission charged with determining whether the South Africans were in compliance with IOC standards of equal treatment and facilities for all athletes regardless of race, religion or nationality. Killanin's commission discovered that although the South African national Olympic committee (NOC) tried to comply with IOC standards, the government would not allow integrated national sports teams. Appalled at the level of discrimination toward black athletes, the commission reported that South Africa was still in violation of IOC guidelines. Despite the report, members of the IOC voted to invite South Africa to compete in the 1968 Mexico City Summer Games. The vote was followed by a strong reaction against the invitation, including a threat by several nations to boycott the Games. Eventually the IOC withdrew the invitation, but only after severe criticism from several countries. Killanin resented the fact that the report from his commission had not received the attention it deserved, and he believed that the political turmoil generated over the issue severely damaged the reputation of the IOC.

Killanin's journalism experience proved helpful when, in 1969, he was appointed chairman of the press committee. He formed an easy rapport with journalists at press conferences and said he "understood what journalists required, and as I made their lives a little easier and brought some clarity out of the mystery of the way the Olympic Movement worked, I gained respect." Killanin considered the posts of *chef de protocol* and chairman of the press committee the two most important positions he held on his way to the presidency of the IOC. His tenure as vice president, however, was also instrumental in his eventual election to the presidency.

At the 1968 IOC Session before the Mexico City Olympics, Killanin was elected vice president of the IOC after turning down an invitation to run for the presidency. Immediately after his election to the vice presidency, Killanin was exposed to one of the first situations in which political controversies surrounding the Olympic Games ended in violence and threatened to disrupt the Games.

Student demonstrators, furious that the Mexican government spent enormous sums of money to host the Olympic Games while the majority of Mexican citizens lived in poverty, protested for several months before the 1968 Summer Games. On the day Killanin arrived in Mexico City, an armed battle between students and the police resulted in the deaths of 267 students and injuries to 1,200 others. IOC President Avery Brundage called an emergency session of the IOC and members discussed the possibility of canceling the Games. They voted to continue as planned, but the violence that occurred at Mexico City left a deep impression on Killanin:

> This was my first experience of violence at the Olympic Games and its sequel was exceptionally tight and oppressively visible security arrangements. The carrying of the Olympic torch to the top of the huge pyramid at Teotihuacan prior to the opening ceremony was, in itself, immensely dramatic. Yet for me it was marred by the armed guards who were stationed everywhere in full battle gear and with loaded rifles. (Killanin, *My Olympic Years*, 49)

Mexico City was also the site of nonviolent political protest. Some black athletes from the United States boycotted the Games, and two U.S. track athletes greeted their national anthem on the victory stand by wearing black and raising their fists in support of the U.S. Black Power movement. The Czechoslovakian team received a standing ovation from the crowd in response to the invasion of that country by Warsaw Pact armies. After Mexico City, political agendas were no longer covert, and the Olympics became an open forum for political issues. Unfortunately, Killanin's first experience of violence at the Olympic Games would not be his last. While Killanin was president-elect of the IOC in 1972, violence once again disrupted the festivities of the Games; this time, Olympic athletes were the victims.

Killanin was elected president of the IOC in 1972 at the IOC Congress held prior to the Munich Games. Killanin lacked the personal wealth of many of his predecessors and, in fact, declined the 1968 invitation to run for the presidency because he could not afford the position. After the 1968 Games, television revenues created a strong financial base for the organization, allowing the IOC the ability to underwrite the president's expenses. After the retirement of Avery Brundage at Munich, Killanin was elected to take office after the Games were over.

The president-elect was attending the sailing events in Kiel when he was informed that eight armed Palestinian terrorists had occupied the Israeli quarters in the Olympic Village. One Israeli athlete was dead. The terrorists executed nine other athletes and two bodyguards before the next morning. Killanin described the event as a "time of nightmare and confusion." He criticized Brundage for the way he handled the crisis, especially Brundage's refusal to inform IOC members as to how the event was unfolding. Brundage made crucial decisions without consulting or informing IOC members and, most reprehensibly to Killanin, used the memorial service to chastise African countries that were threatening to boycott the Games for political reasons. The Palestinian attack was the most heinous incident in modern Olympic history and a horrifying example of political manipulation in the Olympic Games.

Although the terrorist attack was the most extreme incident during Killanin's IOC career, political issues connected with the Games continued to plague the affable Irishman. Killanin was determined to use his presidency to build an organization that would more closely mirror the ideals espoused by Coubertin. To that end, he was instrumental in resolving a dispute over the eligibility of the People's Republic of China (PRC). After mainland China became Communist, Olympic organizations in Taipei—the capital of Taiwan, where the Nationalist Chinese had fled and established the Republic of China—as well as in the mainland cities of Nanjing and Beijing each claimed to be the NOC that had enjoyed IOC recognition before World War II. During Brundage's tenure the IOC recognized only Taipei, eliminating athletes from the PRC from Olympic competition. Under Killanin, both Chinas were participating in the IOC by 1981, despite continuing political disputes that threatened to keep both nations out of the organization.

China proved to be one of several issues that threatened the 1976 Montreal Olympic Games. The People's Republic of China had recently resumed diplomatic relations with Canada and demanded that Canada not recognize Taiwan. Killanin worked out a compromise that allowed Taiwan to compete but not to use "Republic of China" in its name. Taiwan rejected Killanin's compromise, refused to participate, and ended the problem for 1976. Killanin, disappointed that the Taiwanese would not compete, was quickly embroiled in another political situation that jeopardized the Games.

In July, days before the beginning of the Montreal Games, a number of black African nations threatened to withdraw from competition if New Zealand were allowed to participate. The prime minister of New Zealand, Robert Muldoon, had allowed his country's rugby team to compete in South Africa, angering black African nations. After several days of negotiation, 28 African nations pulled out of Olympic competition just 24 hours before the beginning of the Games. The 1976 Games also hosted a few minor demonstrations by Ukrainians against the Soviet Union, but they were nonviolent and the protestors were quickly arrested. Killanin was now primed for the Moscow Games in 1980, which would serve as a battleground for even more political controversy than in Montreal.

The IOC had voted almost unanimously to allow Moscow to host the 1980 Olympics. The Soviets agreed to allow competitors from all nations, except those with ties to South Africa, to enter. Israel, in an attempt to show that it believed in the importance of the Games, suspended diplomatic relations with Pretoria. Until late 1979, it appeared that Killanin's last Olympics would go smoothly.

In December 1979, the Soviet Union invaded Afghanistan. By the second week of January 1980, Killanin was receiving suggestions from the United States that the Games be moved. By February these suggestions turned to demands. Killanin explained to Lloyd Cutler, one of President Jimmy Carter's counselors, that the IOC had no right to dictate the foreign policy of a country and that the Games should be apolitical and not used for political manipulation. Killanin was very angry that Carter would make demands on the IOC and, for one of the few times in his IOC career, he assumed a nonconciliatory attitude toward the U.S. president. After the meeting with Cutler, Killanin asked for a meeting with the executive director of the U.S. Olympic Committee (USOC), Donald Miller, and its president, Robert Kane. Killanin then traveled to Lake Placid for the Winter Games, where he met with the two, who assured him that the USOC was autonomous and would resist political pressure. Unfortunately, Killanin and the USOC representatives learned later that the USOC was subject to U.S. laws under the Amateur Athletic Act of 1978.

Killanin continued to negotiate the IOC's position before the Games at Lake Placid began. Secretary of State Cyrus Vance gave the opening speech at the Games, infuriating Killanin because of his demand that the IOC cancel the Moscow Games. Killanin considered the speech outrageously political and offensive to the Soviet Union. He was convinced that the hard line taken by Carter toward the Moscow Games was not only because of his moral outrage at the invasion of Afghanistan, but also an attempt to bolster his sagging political popularity. Whatever his motive, Carter ordered a boycott of the Moscow Games.

When Carter's stand was buttressed by firm support from British Prime Minister Margaret Thatcher, Killanin became concerned that if other countries joined the U.S. boycott, the Games would be jeopardized. Killanin presented a firm statement to the IOC reiterating the purpose of the Olympic Games and the apolitical nature of the IOC and the NOCs. He emphasized that many NOCs were in a difficult position if their governments ordered a boycott, but that they had a duty to the amateur athletes who had trained for competition in the Games. Finally, Killanin emphasized his personal responsibility to see that the Olympic Games went on as scheduled, and in the end, they did.

Killanin agreed to serve one eight-year term when elected to the IOC presidency in 1972. Although several members of the IOC urged him to run for reelection, he refused to run for another term. After the election of Juan Antonio Samaranch as IOC president in 1980, Killanin retired to Dublin. He continued to work toward his Olympic goals as Honorary Life President of the IOC during retirement. After fighting the debilitating effects of Parkinson's disease for a number of years, Killanin died April 25, 1999.

Killanin worked throughout his IOC career to end political manipulation of the Games, but his presidency was dominated by issues tied to politics and nationalism. The violence and political manipulation that occurred during the 1972, 1976, and 1980 Olympic Games threatened to tear apart the very foundation of the Olympic Movement. Through the leadership of Killanin, however, the IOC survived and emerged a stronger, more vital organization.

BIBLIOGRAPHICAL ESSAY

In 2000, Sheila, Lady Killanin donated Lord Killanin's personal library and papers to the James Hardin Library at the National University of Ireland in Galway. Additional papers are held in the IOC archives in Lausanne, Switzerland. The Avery Brundage Collection at the University of Illinois Archives, Urbana, Illinois, contains some papers relevant to Killanin's work on the public relations and press commission between 1966 and 1971.

My Olympic Years (London, 1983) is Killanin's autobiographical description of his Olympic experience. Many of the events are corroborated in Christopher Hill, *Olympic Politics* (Manchester, 1992), which contains detailed accounts of the China controversy and the Moscow boycott. The relationship between Killanin and his predecessor, Avery Brundage, is described in Allen Guttmann, *The Games Must Go On* (New York, 1984).

Richard Espy analyzes the political controversies of the Killanin years in *The Politics of the Olympic Games* (Berkeley, CA, 1979), as does David B. Kanin, *Political History of the Olympic Games* (Boulder, CO, 1981). See also the IOC publication *The International Olympic Committee One Hundred Years; The Idea – The Presidents – The Achievements*, vol. III (Lausanne, 1996) for a description of the Killanin presidency.

JUAN ANTONIO SAMARANCH

John E. Findling

Juan Antonio Samaranch, the seventh president of the International Olympic Committee (IOC), was born in Barcelona, Spain, on July 17, 1920, the son of Francisco Samaranch Castro, a textile manufacturer, and Juana Torello Malhevy. He received a good education at business schools and at the German College before the outbreak of the Spanish Civil War. In that conflict, he was drafted into the Popular Front army of the existing government and served as a medic but apparently deserted and spent the rest of the war hiding in Barcelona, although sources differ on his activities at this time.

In 1940, Samaranch passed a state examination qualifying him to be a *perito mercantil*, or business appraiser, and he went to work in his family's business, Samaranch, S.A. During the early 1940s, he developed an interest in sport, first as a boxer fighting under the name of "Kid Samaranch" in the Catalonia championships, and then as a player and promoter of *hockey sobre patinas* (roller hockey), a variation of hockey played on roller skates. In 1943, he became coach of the Royal Spanish Athletic Club and wrote articles for *La Prensa* under the pen name "Stick." Two years later, he led the effort of the Spanish Roller Hockey Federation to be admitted to the International Federation of Roller Hockey, and in 1946, he attended the international congress of the sport in Montreux, Switzerland, at which Spain was admitted to the international federation. In 1950, he joined the executive council of the international federation, a prelude to Barcelona hosting the world roller hockey championships the following year, at which Spain won its first world title.

In 1951, Samaranch, perhaps emboldened by the Spanish roller-hockey victory, ran for the Barcelona city council but lost. He continued his association with the roller hockey federation, however, and by 1954, he had become vice president of the International Federation, president of the Spanish federation, and a Barcelona city councilman, representing the Movimiento party of the authoritarian national government of Francisco Franco. In 1955, he became a provincial deputy and also vice president of the organizing committee for the second Mediterranean Games, held in Barcelona, and in 1956, he was appointed to the Spanish Olympic Committee and headed the Spanish contingent at the Winter Games that year in Cortina d'Ampezzo, Italy.

Juan Antonio Samaranch, IOC president, 1980–2001. Courtesy of International Olympic Committee, IOC Museum Collections.

Between 1960 and 1975, Samaranch's influence increased in both the Olympic Movement and Spanish politics. He led the Spanish team to the Rome Games in 1960 and the Tokyo Games in 1964. As early as 1955, he began cultivating a close relationship with Avery Brundage through flattering letters and telegrams; he might have been named to the IOC earlier than 1966 had Spain ever hosted an Olympic Games. Brundage engineered his appointment to the IOC in 1966; the next year, Samaranch rose to the presidency of the Spanish Olympic Committee. He sought a position on the IOC Executive Board in 1968, but he had to settle for the post of *chef de protocol*. In 1970, he succeeded in joining the IOC Executive Board and in 1974, he was named vice president, making him the most likely successor to Lord Killanin, the current president.

Meanwhile, Samaranch continued to be active in Barcelona and Catalonia business and political affairs. He left the city council in 1961 but remained visible in the city by serving on the boards of several real-estate firms and banks and continuing to represent Barcelona as a provincial deputy. But sports were clearly commanding more of his time; in 1967 he left the provincial council and the following year sold the family business, which he had taken over in 1957 after his father's death. Five years later, however, political fortune came his way again when he was elected president of the deputation of Barcelona, one of the most important political posts in Catalonia and one closely tied to the Franco regime.

When Franco died in 1975, Spain returned to a democratic form of government nominally headed by King Juan Carlos. Samaranch's ties with the Franco regime brought political difficulties for him in Barcelona, and he was no doubt grateful to resign his presidency of the deputation in order to become Spain's first ambassador to the Soviet Union in 1977. His work in helping the Moscow Organizing Committee plan the 1980 Summer Games and his efforts to minimize effects of the U.S.-led boycott of those Games convinced the Soviets to swing their support to him in the IOC presidential election in 1980, which he won rather handily over Willi Daume of West Germany, James Worrall of Canada, Lance Cross of New Zealand, and Marc Hodler of Switzerland.

Under Samaranch's presidency, the IOC underwent vast changes. Its annual budget grew from 5.8 million Swiss francs in 1981 to 24.4 million Swiss francs in 1990; its assets soared from $2 million in 1980 to more than $105 million in 1990 and then $900 million in 2001. Samaranch was the first IOC president since Coubertin to work full-time at the job and maintain his primary residence is Lausanne. In many ways, Samaranch pushed the IOC into the realities of late-twentieth-century political and economic life, earning in the process heated criticism from those who believed that his policies trampled the original ideals and meaning of the Olympic Movement as Coubertin conceived it a century ago. Much of the new direction for the IOC began with the important and productive IOC Congress at Baden-Baden in 1981, the organization of which was Samaranch's first major task as president.

Politically, Samaranch did much to raise the visibility of the IOC in world affairs. He worked futilely to get the Soviet Union and other boycotting nations to come to the Los Angeles Games in 1984, but he was more successful in dealing with the political controversies that swarmed around the Seoul Games in 1988. There he was able to soothe the feelings of the North Koreans after their demand to co-host the Games was rejected; he also prevented a threatened boycott by other Communist nations that had no diplomatic relations with South Korea and had asserted that coming to Seoul would present unacceptable security risks. There was no boycott, and the Games were concluded without significant political disturbances. Samaranch's deft diplomatic touch continued throughout his tenure. At the 2000 Games in Sydney, he persuaded teams from the two Koreas to march together at the Opening Ceremonies, a gesture that no other international organization had ever been able to achieve.

Samaranch and the IOC were also closely involved in the South Africa question. When South Africa, which had been suspended from the Olympic Movement in 1964, began to move away from its strict apartheid policies, Samaranch sent a delegation to the country to help create a mixed-race sports commission there and provided $2 million for training facilities for black athletes. The IOC welcomed back South Africa in 1992, and Nelson Mandela was Samaranch's guest at the Barcelona Games that year.

As the Soviet Union and Yugoslavia both collapsed in the late 1980s and early 1990s, the IOC moved quickly to recognize the newly independent countries that resulted from the political upheaval. The IOC recognized the Baltic states of Estonia, Latvia, and Lithuania in 1991 soon after they joined the United Nations (UN) and, after they had created national Olympic committees, invited them to send teams to the Albertville Games. Other former Soviet republics, not yet part of the UN, were invited to join what was called the Unified Team, and five did so. Croatia and Slovenia, formerly parts of Yugoslavia, came to the Albertville Games, and Samaranch convinced UN authorities to lift their boycott on Serbia and Montenegro with regard to the Olympics so that athletes from those states could participate as individuals in the Games. Samaranch carried out much of the IOC's diplomacy personally by frequent travel; by the end of his tenure, he had visited more than 190 countries, including the 15 former Soviet republics.

In general, Samaranch was an able enough diplomat to put an end to the fear of widespread political boycotts, a fact that has significantly increased the competition among cities to host the Games. One of his tactics was to co-opt his adversaries. For example, when Jean-Claude Ganga of the Congo Republic became seen as a leader in the African boycott movement in the early 1980s, Samaranch had him appointed to the IOC, which put an end to the African boycott movement. Unfortunately, Samaranch's judgement was not altogether sound, as Ganga was one of the individuals implicated in the Salt Lake City bribery scandal, who then left the IOC.

An even more visible and controversial aspect of the Samaranch regime was its embrace of professionalism for the athletes and commercialism for the Games. Samaranch lobbied the international sport federations, which control eligibility rules for Olympic participants, to open the Games to professional athletes, a move he defended as only fair, since most countries without significant professional athletes give large state subsidies to their Olympic athletes, making them de facto professionals. His success in this regard was seen most dramatically by the presence of the "Dream Team" of U.S. professional basketball players at the Barcelona Games. But most other sports, including tennis and hockey, now allow professionals to compete in the Olympics.

The commercial success of the 1984 Los Angeles Games elevated the Olympic Movement into the world of big business and modern commercialism. Television rights had already demonstrated that large amounts of money could be generated for the Olympic Movement, and in 1985, Samaranch tried to take control of commercialism through the creation of TOP, The Olympic Programme, an extensive marketing effort that quickly became an important revenue producer for the IOC and lessened the dependence on the sale of television rights for income. TOP was the creation of International Sports, Culture and Leisure Marketing of Lausanne (ISL), an agency whose majority owner was Horst Dassler, the chairman of the Adidas Company, a giant sport equipment manufacturer, who was believed to have been influential in assuring Samaranch's election to the IOC presidency. By the end of the 1980s, ISL had paid some $15 million for its exclusive contract with the IOC and had developed TOP-I for the Seoul Games and the more successful TOP-II for the Barcelona Games. Although the IOC-ISL relationship ended in 1996, as the IOC developed its own marketing operation, TOP efforts continued unabated: TOP-IV, which covered the 1997–2000 years, raised some $350 million, and TOP-V, for 2001–2004, is expected to bring in $600 million. Television rights still constitute nearly 50 percent of IOC income, but the sale of sponsorships now accounts for more than 30 percent, with other income coming from licensing programs and ticket and souvenir sales.

Much of the additional money generated has gone to support Samaranch's efforts to increase the humanitarian work of the IOC. He increased IOC cooperation with the UN and its humanitarian agencies, as well as with other nongovernmental organizations, sensing that the IOC can be helpful in areas like drug education and AIDS prevention. He created a department of international cooperation, focusing on such areas as the environment, education, and economic development, and worked hard to persuade the UN to declare 1994 the International Year of Sport and the Olympic

Movement. In 1981, Samaranch brought about the creation of Olympic Solidarity, an aid program to NOCs, especially those in developing countries. Originally created in 1971 as an IOC committee to aid the newly independent countries of Africa and Asia, Olympic Solidarity became a semi-autonomous agency within the IOC, although the IOC president serves as its chairman. Between 1983 and 2000, the agency distributed $435.5 million to NOCs around the world. One of the largest recipients was the U.S. Olympic Committee, but each NOC is guaranteed enough money to send at least six athletes and two officials to an Olympic Games.

The substantial changes Samaranch brought to the IOC did not come without criticism and controversy, much of which concerned the power and authority Samaranch assumed during his years in the presidency. One telling example of this was the conflict with Monique Berlioux. Berlioux had worked for the IOC since the 1960s and had risen to the influential position of executive director. She wielded great authority in that role during the terms of Brundage and Killanin, who spent most of their time away from Lausanne. When Samaranch became president in 1980 and made the post his full-time occupation, conflict developed between him and Berlioux, who was used to running the organization with a good deal of independence. They clashed over the growing commercialism of the IOC and the contract with ISL, and they each supported their home city as host for the 1992 Games—Samaranch favoring Barcelona, Berlioux championing Paris. By 1985, the differences between the president and the director had become irreparable, and the IOC Executive Board demanded Berlioux's resignation.

Later in the 1980s, the executive board granted Samaranch the right to name two additional IOC members on his own authority, without screening or approval by the IOC, as was customary. Samaranch used this privilege to appoint Primo Nebiolo, the head of the International Amateur Athletic Federation (IAAF), to the IOC. Although there was logic in Nebiolo's appointment—the IAAF is the largest and most influential of the international sport federations—Nebiolo's selection raised much controversy, since he had recently been linked with cheating scandals in world championship track-and-field meets. Samaranch brushed off the criticism by stating that the IOC had granted him the authority to make independent appointments and that nothing had ever been proven against Nebiolo.

There was some thought that Samaranch would retire after the Barcelona Games of 1992, much as Coubertin had retired soon after the Games were held in his home country, France, in 1924. But Samaranch stood for re-election in 1993, wanting to see the Olympic Movement through its centennial observances between 1994 and 1996. He ran again for the IOC presidency in 1997 after the IOC, in 1995, amended its rules and raised the mandatory retirement age from 75 to 80. Given the crises that beset the organization during his last term, Samaranch cannot be blamed for wishing at times that he had retired in 1993 or 1997.

During his last years in office, Samaranch had to deal with both a major doping crisis and a major bribery scandal involving the bid process for the 2002 Winter Olympics. Critics claimed that Samaranch coasted through the last years of his presidency, perhaps because he wanted to minimize discord within the IOC or because he had seen so much corruption during his years as an official in the Franco government that he found the IOC's level of corruption tolerable.

It was revealed in the late 1990s that East German Olympic team officials had been regularly supplying performance-enhancing drugs to its athletes during the

1980s and that the IOC was aware of this but did nothing about it. A doping scandal in the 1998 Tour de France bicycle race led the IOC to look into its own doping problem and to create the World Anti-Doping Agency, which, among other things, approved a drug test for EPO, an endurance drug widely used in cycling, long-distance running, and swimming. The sincerity of the IOC's resolve to fight the drug problem was questioned early in 2000, however, when it influenced the IAAF, the sport federation for track and field, to lift its two-year, drug-related suspension of Javier Sotomayor, a Cuban high jumper and gold medalist at Barcelona, so that he could compete at Sydney. On the other hand, the drug-testing measures that the IOC did set in place were enough to dissuade more than 20 members of the People's Republic of China team from participating in the Sydney Games for fear that their use of drugs would be detected.

The Salt Lake City bribery scandal was first made public in December 1998 when veteran IOC member Marc Hodler of Switzerland revealed the existence of bribery agents who worked for various bidding cities, receiving between $3 million and $5 million to influence IOC members' votes. This came hard upon the news that the Salt Lake City bid committee had established a $500,000 scholarship fund for relatives of six IOC members and had doled out other favors, including a number of guns, given as gifts to IOC members and to Samaranch himself, and a free knee-replacement operation for the mother-in-law of an IOC member. Other reports implicated both the Nagano and Sydney bid committees in corrupt activities as well. In the face of overwhelmingly negative press commentary about the IOC and openly expressed concern by a number of important Olympic sponsors, Samaranch appointed IOC vice president Richard Pound to launch an investigation that resulted in the expulsion of six IOC members and the resignations of four more. In addition, the IOC established Commission 2000, a prestigious committee that included former U.S. secretary of state Henry Kissinger and former United Nations secretary-general Boutros Boutros Ghali, to formulate a new bid process. The commission recommended and the IOC approved the creation of a special committee to evaluate potential host cities and a rule barring IOC members from making official visits to contending cities. In addition, a related reform permitted eight active athletes to be chosen for membership on the IOC. Samaranch stopped short, however, of acceding to demands that the IOC enact reforms that would democratize it by making most of its membership formed of individuals elected by international sport federations and national Olympic committees. Other suggested reforms that called for placing the Olympics at a permanent site or rotating the Games among a small number of cities have not generated much enthusiasm.

Samaranch, who retired after the Sydney Games in 2000, was a highly influential president. His pragmatic policies with respect to the inclusion of professional athletes into the Games and the acceptance of corporate largesse into the organization significantly changed the character of the Olympic Games. In addition, he was the most active supporter of a greater role for women in the Olympic Movement. The number of women members of the IOC is now 13; there were none when he assumed office in 1980, and female participation in the Games rose from 21 percent in 1980 to 42 percent in 2000. While his numerous critics say he ruined the ideals of amateurism and brought the Games into the brutal and corrupt world of contemporary politics, while making himself into a kind of imperial being, his supporters maintain that he did only what was necessary in order to keep the Olympic flame alive in the modern world, a world vastly different from that in which Pierre de Coubertin kindled the modern Olympic Movement a century earlier.

BIBLIOGRAPHICAL ESSAY

The main body of Samaranch's papers is at the Biblioteca de l'Esport, Generalitat de Catalunya, Valencia 3, 08015 Barcelona, Spain. The IOC archives in Lausanne also possesses considerable material relating to the Samaranch presidency, although some material of recent origin is likely to be closed to researchers.

There have been two recent biographies of Samaranch in English, representing wildly differing points of view. David Miller, *The Olympic Revolution: the Olympic Biography of Juan Antonio Samaranch* (London, 1992) is a very favorable treatment of the life and career of the IOC president by the chief sportswriter for the *Times* of London. On the other hand, Vyv Simson and Andrew Jennings, *The Lords of the Rings* (London, 1992) is so critical of Samaranch, his political past in Spain, and his management of the IOC that he has filed suit against the authors for defaming the organization. Jennings updated the book as *The New Lords of the Rings* (London, 1996), with reports of Olympic corruption between 1992 and 1996. A more balanced biography, though one written in a traditional Spanish style often baffling to English-speaking readers, is Jaume Boix and Arcadio Espada, *El Deporte del Poder: Vida y Milagro de Juan Antonio Samaranch* (Madrid, 1991). A short sketch of Samaranch's life can be found in *Current Biography Yearbook 1994*, pp. 508–12. Wolf Lyberg, *The Seventh President of the IOC, 1980–2001* (Lausanne, 2001) is a compendium of statistics on how the IOC changed during Samaranch's presidency. It also includes summaries of executive board meetings, a log of Samaranch's travels, and discussion of the evolution of various aspects and suborganizations of the IOC.

Christopher R. Hill, *Olympic Politics* (Manchester, 1992), John A. Lucas, *The Future of the Olympic Games* (Champaign, Ill., 1992), and Allen Guttmann, *The Olympics: A History of the Modern Games* (Urbana, Ill., 2002) all contain considerable material on the progress of the Olympic Movement and the IOC under Samaranch's leadership. Articles on Samaranch and his policies include William O. Johnson, "Goodbye, Olive Wreaths; Hello, Riches and Reality," *Sports Illustrated* 66 (February 9, 1987): 168–74; Mark Mulvoy, et al., "A Presidential Pardon," *Sports Illustrated* 77 (August 3, 1992): 82–83; Andrew Jennings, "Eyes on the Prize," *New Statesman and Society* (September 17, 1993): 18–19; and Karel Wendl, "The International Olympic Committee in the Years 1980–1994," in *Proceedings*, 2nd International Symposium for Olympic Research (London, Ontario, 1994).

Finally, during Samaranch's tenure as president, the IOC significantly increased the range of its publications, which offer insight on what the organization believes its primary accomplishments to have been. Apart from the public-relations nature of the narrative, these publications often do provide statistics and illustrations not found elsewhere. The *Olympic Review* chronicles the ongoing activities of the IOC and occasionally publishes historical articles. *Message Olympique/Olympic Message* is an occasional publication of the IOC; number 37 (September 1993) is devoted to the new Olympic museum that opened in June 1993. The museum has its own publication, *Olympic Magazine*, highlighting its exhibits and also publishing some historical articles. See also *Olympic Solidarity: the Last Ten Years* (Lausanne, 1993), for a review of the first decade of the assistance program begun during Samaranch's presidency. More recent information is available at the IOC Web site, http://www.olympics.com.

The scandals of Samaranch's last term and his retirement in 2001 prompted a number of newspaper and magazine articles. See, for example, the *Observer* (London), September 6, 1998; the *Sunday Telegraph* (London), March 21, 1999; the *Salt Lake Tribune*, January 6, 1999; the *Australian*, September 11, 2000, the *New York Times*, September 10, 2000; and the *Financial Times* (London), August 26, 2000.

JACQUES ROGGE

Kimberly D. Pelle

Presently sitting at the helm of the world's most prestigious sporting organization is Jacques Rogge, the eighth president of the International Olympic Committee (IOC). That Rogge occupies such a position is fitting when one considers his well-documented medical and athletic career, not to mention a family background that consisted of very sport-minded individuals. Rogge was elected IOC president on July 16, 2001, following Juan Antonio Samaranch, who served 21 years as IOC president. He is the second Belgian to lead the IOC after Henri Baillet-Latour, who presided from 1925 to 1942, and the second former Olympian to fill the presidential position after Avery Brundage, from 1952 to 1972. Jacques Rogge has assumed his duties as president with a new Olympic motto for the new millennium: "purity, solidarity, and humanity."

Jacques Rogge was born May 2, 1942, in the city of Ghent. His grandfather was a professional cyclist and his father was a Belgian track-and-field and rowing champion, as well as a field hockey player. Rogge's love for sports was developed at the tender age of three, when his parents began taking him sailing off Belgium's North Sea coast on weekends. His passion became the sea, and when he was 17, he joined the Belgian national sailing team and was a junior world champion. He went on to compete in yachting competitions at the Mexico 1968, Munich 1972, and Montreal 1976 Olympic Games and was world champion once, runner-up twice, and Belgian national champion 16 times. In addition to sailing, Rogge was also drawn to rugby. While playing for exercise in the winter, Rogge soon found himself fascinated by the sport. He became a member of the Belgian national rugby squad, was capped ten times, and played on the Belgian national championship team on one occasion.

Jacques Rogge, IOC president, 2001–present. Courtesy of International Olympic Committee, IOC Museum Collections.

Although Rogge briefly considered discontinuing his education to become a professional athlete, his common sense told him otherwise. His education began at the Jesuit College in St. Barbara in Ghent, where he studied Greek and Latin classics. At the University of Ghent, he received a degree in sports medicine and went on to study medicine at the University Libre in Brussels, where he became an orthopedic surgeon. During his first year at medical school he met his future wife, Anne Bovijn, a radiologist, when he was 19 and she was 18. In a heartwarming account in the *Olympic Review*, "Jacques Rogge, In the Name Of Sport And Ethics," he credits her with having the greatest influence on his life. They have two children, Caroline and Philip, and in keeping with family tradition, both are very athletic.

Rogge is a quiet intellectual with exceptional diplomatic skills. He speaks five languages fluently: French, Dutch, English, German, and Spanish. He is a lover of geometrical art, is highly organized, and calls himself a workaholic. His colleagues are impressed with his honesty, forthrightness, and integrity. In addition to running successful sport medicine centers in Deinze and Ghent, where he saw about 3,000 to 4,000 patients a year and performed approximately 400 operations a year, he was also a sports-medicine lecturer at his alma mater and at the University of Ghent.

If Rogge's education and medical career is impressive, his work in the sports arena is equally notable. Although Rogge was selected to participate in the 1980 Moscow Games, at 37 he was beginning to feel as though he had lost his edge. Instead of competing, he was appointed by the Belgian Olympic committee to serve as the chief manager of the team. Thus began his love affair with the Olympic Movement. His other offices in sports administration have included president of the Belgian national Olympic committee from 1989 to 1992, president of the European Olympic Committee (EOC) in 1989, member of the IOC since 1991, executive board member in 1998, and chairman of the coordination commissions for the Sydney Games in 2000 (heralded as the "best Games ever" by Samaranch) and the Athens Games in 2004. He has been a member of the World Anti-Doping Agency Council since 1999, and he has served on the Olympic Solidarity commission since 1999. He now holds the highest appointment in sport circles: president of the IOC.

Choosing to become a candidate for president was a decision Rogge did not make lightly. He would have to give up his medical practice, relocate his family, travel constantly, become a semi-public figure, and perform his duties without a salary, but he believed he could make positive changes for the Olympic Movement. Still at the center of attention in 2001 was the Salt Lake City bribery scandal that was throwing the IOC into turmoil. Allegations of corruption within the organization and investigations of IOC members revealed that there were indeed guilty parties. Resignations and expulsions of colleagues were newsworthy, and the IOC began undergoing some major reforms. The IOC's credibility was at stake, and Rogge was up for the challenge.

Along with four other candidates, Richard Pound, a Canadian lawyer and member of the IOC since 1978; Pal Schmitt, the Hungarian ambassador to Spain and member of the IOC since 1983; Kim un-Yong, a South Korean civil servant and IOC member since 1986; and Anita DeFrantz, the IOC's American vice president, Rogge announced his candidacy for president of the IOC. In an article in *Motion – Sport in Finland*, January 2001, "Changes ahead for the IOC," Ari Pusa notes that DeFrantz and Schmitt had no chance in the election. According to newspaper and magazine accounts, Rogge was the strongest contender for the position. Although some members wondered if he was tough enough for the job, Rogge's reputation was impeccable and his career as a sport administrator was impressive. He also had Samaranch's support, as well as that of most European members. Pound, known as the "money-man," was also a strong candidate with a prestigious IOC record. He headed up the investigation into the Salt Lake City corruption (which meant disciplining colleagues), was head of the World Anti-Doping Agency, and was chairman of the television-rights negotiations commission, a vital IOC financial resource, but his outspoken manner tended to alienate many IOC members. Kim un-Yong had been the favorite up until the Salt Lake City scandal, but allegations that his son had accepted bribes resulted in a near expulsion for this powerful figure. Still, Kim, a former United Nations General Assembly delegate, did bounce back and managed to retain and rally support for his candidacy. It was, however, Jacques Rogge who emerged the victor.

On July 16, 2001, at the 112th IOC Session in Moscow, Jacques Rogge was elected the eighth president of the IOC. In light of the Salt Lake City scandal, Rogge's key themes were transparency, accountability, and the fight against drugs in sport.

As a result of the Salt Lake City debacle, reforms in the way the IOC conducts business with bidding cities had already been put in place under Samaranch's reign. An ethics commission was created, and new guidelines for the bidding process were established, but Rogge intends to continue auditing monetary transactions and administrative activities and to monitor the reforms with frequent assessments. In order for the IOC to remain credible, it needs to return to the ideals of the Olympic Movement. The Salt Lake City Games were Rogge's first as president. He was determined to be diligent and to deliver what he had promised. The scandal was the biggest disappointment of his career. He was "shocked, ashamed, and embarrassed." Although determined not to let history repeat itself, Rogge, being a team player, believes the IOC should be governed by all members, including the athletes it serves. He has said on more than one occasion that the Olympics belong to the athletes. At Salt Lake City, Rogge became the first IOC president to live with the athletes in the Olympic Village.

Doping is another issue Rogge intends to tackle. He is quick to admit the problem is worldwide and not limited only to the Olympics. In a presentation delivered at the National Press Club on November 27, 2001, Rogge asserted that doping is the number one threat to the credibility of sport, noting that "When people no longer trust a result, start to doubt their heroes, or worse, when mothers stop sending their children to play sports because they fear their kids will fall prey to the temptation to take harmful drugs, we have lost the most important game." Rogge continues to push the IOC to contribute to and support the World Anti-Doping Agency. Reforms that focus on research and education have been put in place, and prior to the Sydney Games, the IOC initiated blood testing for athletes and sponsored the procedure. Rogge is quick to note this battle will not be won easily, and that "the fight against doping is a highly complicated affair involving science, law and ethics."

Another daunting and highly political task facing Rogge as president is the downsizing of the Games. His belief is that "gigantism" contradicts the universal nature of the Games. Without affecting the quality of the Games, Rogge intends to scale down certain elements of the Games, including the budget, the number of events, technology, expenses, and the complexity of infrastructure, so that cities in developing countries and regions will also have a chance at hosting the Olympics. "If we don't descale the games," Rogge has noted, "they will forever only be organized in rich, wealthy, and sophisticated countries." Rogge believes that when a city hosts the Games it not only leaves a great legacy to that city, but it also perpetuates Olympic values. He has said, "Sport is a universal language; it teaches important social values, helps us escape daily concerns, and breaks down barriers to bring people together. The Games are more than sport; they are a celebration of humanity."

The sheer size of the Olympic Games also creates concerns for security. The political turmoil between countries that exists today and the constant threat of war and terrorism makes security the most important concern for the IOC. At the Salt Lake City Games, Rogge worked with federal and state officials to ensure the security of the athletes and spectators at the Games. Greater resources and more sophisticated security technology are being applied, and the upcoming Athens Games will benefit from these policies. An outspoken opponent against boycotting, (Rogge defied pressure from his government to boycott the Moscow Games) he believes the Games "should be an answer to violence not a victim of it."

At the helm for only three years now, Rogge intends to address many other issues and will face many other challenges. Keeping a watchful eye on the upcoming and controversial Beijing Games, opening the doors for more women athletes and more women sport administrators, and continuing the theme of universality in the Olympic Movement are just a few issues he intends to address. But Rogge, unlike some past presidents, has only 8 to 12 years to affect change and leave his mark on the Olympic Movement. Hopefully his past accomplishments will reflect his future successes.

BIBLIOGRAPHICAL ESSAY

As Rogge is new in his position as president of the IOC, most information currently available on his life and career is found on the IOC Web site (www.olympic.org) and in various newspaper and magazine articles, either in print or on Web sites. The IOC archives in Lausanne gathers much of this information together in a clippings file on Rogge.

Major newspapers, such as the *New York Times*, the *Times* (London), and the *Washington Post* covered Rogge's election as IOC president in July 2001 in some detail. An at-home profile of Rogge may be found in *Olympic Review* 27, 40 (2001): 35–38. Rogge laid out some of his thoughts in an interview with the *Australian Financial Review*, September 14, 2000. *Sport Europe*, in several of its issues during the year 2001, ran a feature article, "10 Questions for Jacques Rogge, " each dealing with a different Olympic-related issue, such as doping, the role of athletes in the movement, and universality.

APPENDIX B: THE U.S. OLYMPIC COMMITTEE

Robert P. Watson, updated by Larry Maloney

"The U.S. Olympic Committee is a dysfunctional, unhealthy organization that needs radical restructuring before it can resume its mission of serving the nation's best athletes" (*Washington Post*, 14 February 2003, reporting on testimony before the U.S. Senate Committee on Commerce, Science, and Transportation).

America's Olympic founding fathers could not have realized their experiment in international sporting competition would evolve into the cauldron of chaos that exists today within the U.S. Olympic Committee (USOC). In fact, the early years of the U.S. Olympic Movement were also steeped in chaos as the nation struggled to field teams. During the first quarter of the twentieth century, no permanent, formal organization existed to select qualified athletes for the Olympic team. That the United States competed at all was largely the result of the energy and charisma of James E. Sullivan, founder of the American Athletic Union (AAU) and later, A. G. Spalding, a prominent publisher and sporting goods manufacturer.

During this era, organization played a backseat to jockeying for control of the Olympic Games. A collage of forces including the AAU, the National Collegiate Athletic Association (NCAA), large colleges, national sport federations, and prominent individuals vied for control of the Olympic Movement in the U.S. Under the prevailing arrangement, several sports had little or no representation in matters of administration and often found themselves overlooked or underrepresented on the U.S. Olympic team. Less visible sports often suffered while popular sports, such as track and field, enjoyed a significantly disproportionate allotment of positions on the U.S. team. Conflicts often occurred between factions claiming to represent different sports and between the AAU and NCAA, resulting in protests, resignations, and ultimately the disruption of the larger objective of fielding quality American teams for the Olympic Games. The lack of structure also undermined the informal system's ability to deal effectively with issues such as the provision of adequate training facilities, the financial needs of athletes, or institutional fund-raising.

The year 1921 proved to be a turning point in Olympic sport administration thanks in part to the country's preparations for the 1920 Games in Antwerp.

Although the team performed well at those Games, it had to travel in cramped quarters aboard U.S. troop ships and had no access to training facilities. A meeting at the New York Athletic Club produced a proposal to organize the U.S. Olympic effort under a single, formal administrative structure: the American Olympic Association (AOA)—the predecessor of the USOC. In 1940 the AOA was renamed the United States of America Sports Federation; the name was again changed in 1945 to the United States Olympic Association (USOA); the current designation of the USOC came in 1961.

The establishment and growth of the USOC has been, at times, a laborious and politicized process with many events serving to shape the organization we know today. In 1950, for example, action by the federal government (PL 805) gave the then-USOA a federal charter as a private, non- profit corporation, and with this the ability to solicit, as well as receive, tax-deductible contributions. This would prove invaluable in addressing the financial demands of the U.S. Olympic Movement.

In part due to the rather poor showing of U.S. athletes against Soviet and East German competitors in the 1976 Games, attention was again focused on improving the U.S. Olympic Movement, resulting in the formation of the President's Commission on Olympic Sports. The net effect of this movement was a reformed Olympic organization. On July 1, 1978, USOC headquarters moved from New York City to its present location in Colorado Springs, Colorado. Possibly the most important public action in strengthening the USOC was the enactment of PL 95-606 in 1978. The passage of the Amateur Sports Act finally named the USOC as the official coordinating organization for athletes and sports on the Olympic and Pan-American Games programs. The act, however, did little to end the battles, which would continue throughout the century, for control of the organization.

Shortly after the USOC's restructuring, the Soviet Union invaded Afghanistan and set the stage for the first U.S. boycott of an Olympic Games. Following the Soviet invasion in December of 1979, the U.S. government condemned the hostility and moved to boycott U.S. participation in the upcoming Games. Both houses of Congress voted overwhelmingly in January 1980 not to send a team to Moscow, and the Carter Administration supported the decision. As such, in April 1980 the USOC voted by a two-to-one margin not to accept an invitation to the Moscow Games.

Even though approximately 50 countries participated in the boycott, the U.S. government led the initiative, and public opinion in America seemed to support the decision. Yet, the USOC did not come away from the boycott decision without criticism. The larger question concerning the notion of keeping the Olympic Games above the fray of politics was raised. In fact, 25 American athletes and a member of the USOC Executive Board brought suit against the USOC (*DeFrantz v. USOC*) claiming that, in preventing athletes from competing in the Games, the USOC had exceeded its statutory powers and abridged the constitutional rights of U.S. Olympic athletes.

The boycott of the Moscow Games was the most politicized and sensitive event the USOC had faced in its history, but the final years of the twentieth century would expose the USOC to scandals and events that damaged the organization's credibility. Throughout the 1990s, the USOC best resembled an amateur flyweight boxer, who by some twist of fate found himself suddenly in the ring competing for the heavyweight title. Scandals pummeled the organization, most of which it managed poorly, and the committee ended the century bloodied by one of the Olympic Movement's more embarrassing fiascoes, the Salt Lake City bidding scandal.

The 1990s began with a leadership scandal for the USOC. In 1991, Robert Helmick resigned in controversy as USOC president. The USOC Special Counsel's office eventually released a report criticizing Helmick for conflicts of interest in his personal business relationships, particularly $300,000 in payments he had received from sport federations or companies with ties to the Olympic Movement. Part of the controversy surrounding Helmick included the USOC's reluctance to openly discuss the details of his resignation. Additionally, the year before Helmick's resignation, the USOC was in the news for its high-profile buyout of two USOC officials in order to purchase the services of new USOC executive director, Harvey Schiller. Obviously, public relations of this kind did nothing but add to existing public skepticism of the USOC.

The year 1994 brought a new round of problems to the USOC with the knee whacking of figure skater Nancy Kerrigan by associates of rival skater Tonya Harding. The USOC attempted to block Harding from the team after she acknowledged knowing of the plot but doing nothing to prevent it. Harding filed a $25 million lawsuit against the organization in return. The primary evidence the USOC thought it could use to keep Harding off the team was the code of conduct all Olympic athletes sign. However, Harding's knowledge of and participation in the Kerrigan incident occurred before her selection to the U.S. Olympic figure skating team, before she was bound by the code of conduct. It took the USOC more than two years to devise a code of conduct that would provide the USOC and the national governing bodies more discretion in supervising athletes at the Games.

The code of conduct came under direct challenge at the 1998 Olympic Winter Games when the U.S. men's hockey team, straight from an abysmal performance, damaged three rooms in the Olympic Village. Team members refused to cooperate in the ensuing investigation by the USOC and the National Hockey League, although all the members of the team had signed the code of conduct, which included statements such as the following:

- Must accept accountability for my behavior and its outcomes
- Must honor my obligations and promises
- Must exercise self-control
- Must respect authority

Eventually, the USOC paid Nagano $3,000 in compensation for the damage, while the millionaire athletes who had committed the damage were denied the privilege of attending a White House ceremony for U.S. athletes.

The most damaging crisis of the 1990s, however, was the Salt Lake City bidding scandal. The Amateur Sports Act of 1978 charged the USOC with "exclusive jurisdiction" over the organization of any Olympic Games on U.S. soil. As such, the USOC had the sole responsibility of monitoring the activities of the Salt Lake City bid committee for the 2002 Games (see Salt Lake City 2002 essay for details). In December 1998, revelations of the bid committee's activities to win the Games underscored how little oversight the USOC provided. Unfortunately, further inquiries revealed a deeper involvement.

The USOC's director of international relations, Alfredo LaMont, pled guilty to tax fraud and admitted to accepting $65,000 in payments from the Salt Lake City bid committee, as well as $40,000 from the Rome 2004 bid committee, for intelligence gathering on members of the International Olympic Committee (IOC). Additional investigations revealed that the USOC provided after the vote more than $60,000 in athletic training and equipment for athletes from Turkey, Mali, Uganda, and Sudan—all countries that supported the Salt Lake City bid.

As at the beginning of the 1990s, the USOC ushered in a new decade with leadership scandals. Norm Blake became the first chief executive officer in 2000 and within months began testing his authority over the board with an ambitious plan to redistribute USOC funds to the National Governing Bodies (NGBs) of sports that had a proven track record of winning medals at the Games. Blake's plan encountered immediate obstacles from the board, the majority of whom worked for or represented organizations whose viability would be in jeopardy without committee funding. Sandra Baldwin, a board member at the time, sent a letter criticizing Blake to then President Bill Hybl, which began to turn the tide against Blake. Nine months after becoming the USOC's chief executive, Blake resigned. "This was a far more political organization than I could possibly have imagined," Blake said after realizing his plan was doomed due to "the absence of sufficient organizational resolve and commitment" (*New York Times*, October 26, 2000). Baldwin succeeded Hybl as president and was forced out in 2002 after false claims on her résumé came to light.

To complicate matters, questions began to emerge about the quality of USOC drug testing the year after the Salt Lake City scandal. Dr. Wade Exum, who served as the committee's chief of drug testing for nine years, went public in 2000 with claims that half of the athletes who tested positive for banned substances, such as synthetic testosterone, faced no repercussions, even though all should have been barred from competition. After years of negotiations with the USOC to settle a lawsuit for wrongful termination, Exum threatened to release documentation indicating specific, well-known athletes who failed drug tests. A trial date was set for April 2003.

Disarray at the USOC reached unfathomable depths by the end of 2002. The latest morass pitted the USOC president, Marty Mankamyer, against the organization's chief executive officer, Lloyd Ward, the former CEO of Maytag, who had no previous experience in sport management but had a calm demeanor and corporate training. In December 2002, the USOC began an internal investigation of Ward, who had asked a staff member to shepherd a business proposal from his brother and a friend. An internal review determined that Ward had committed two violations of the committee's ethics code. However, he was not asked to step down as a result of this breach, which led to the resignation of several members of the ethics committee. As a punitive measure, the USOC executive committee revoked his annual bonus of $184,800. Mankamyer became one of the more vocal advocates for Ward's resignation, which Ward refused to submit. Allegations surfaced that Mankamyer had a conflict of interest in her calls for Ward's resignation due to a real estate transaction involving both officers. After scrutiny from the federal government continued to grow and questions regarding the committee's leadership failed to subside, both figures resigned. As of this writing, turmoil at the leadership level had resulted in the departure of five presidents or chief executive officers since 2000.

Ward's conduct propelled this latest crisis at the USOC to the forefront of media coverage. However, the public witnessed the pervasive bureaucratic infighting within the organization as never before, infighting that is endemic due to structural imperfections in the committee's governing structure.

Currently, the USOC maintains a two-tiered governance composed of a board of directors and an executive committee, each of which vies for control of the institution. The board of directors functions much like a legislative body. In this capacity it sets forth the objectives of the USOC, votes on or confirms administrative officers, has the power to amend the USOC Constitution and By-laws, admit new members, and likewise, vote to terminate membership. It seems as if everyone has a seat at the table of the USOC board. All the Olympic/Pan-American sport organization members of the USOC have seats on the board. Additionally, the board includes USOC officers, as well as past USOC presidents, and IOC members. Moreover, other affiliated bodies such as the community- and education-based multisport organizations, the armed forces, state Olympic organizations, and the disabled in sport organizations have seats on the board. Remaining membership, which must total at least 20 percent of board seats, consists of athletes. When all representatives are tallied, more than 123 individuals representing a variety of organizations with vested interests in USOC decision making have seats on the USOC board. However, there is more than one governing council operating the USOC.

Next in the decision-making hierarchy is the executive committee, the administrative unit of the USOC. It has responsibility for the implementation of the business and operational affairs of the USOC, according to the guidelines set forth by the board of directors. The executive committee is served by an executive staff of five: the chief executive officer (CEO), deputy secretary general, the administrative assistant to the CEO, assistant executive director, and the deputy executive director.

The CEO serves as the chief administrative official of the USOC, a position that replaced the post of executive director in 2000. Elected by a majority vote of the board, the CEO is awarded a salary and benefits package and, to assist in the management of USOC business, has the services of a paid staff of more than 500. Furthermore, the executive committee is served by an executive council. Headed by the CEO, the council meets as often as is necessary to fulfill its function of administrative oversight. Membership on this council numbers 23 and includes USOC officers, IOC members, Olympic/Pan-Am sport organizations, and representatives from affiliated organizations as well as athletes.

The bureaucratic malaise at the USOC results from two internal factions, both of which have competing views and perceptions of their roles in the organization: the volunteer staff versus the paid staff. Tension between the volunteer president and the paid chief executive was pervasive for years but has grown since the USOC restructured the post of executive director into chief executive officer.

The president of the USOC served as the primary spokesperson of the committee until the creation of the chief executive officer post. The USOC created this post after an independent study concluded that the committee needed a chief executive with a professional staff supporting the position. Specifically, the study recommended allowing the volunteers to set policy but placing the staff in charge of carrying out the policy. In addition to the aims of the study, the USOC hoped to attract an executive who could speak the language of the corporate world on which the committee was so reliant for financial support.

The dichotomy between the volunteer and paid staff rests with a perception among the volunteer staff, primarily the board, that they must protect the interests of their organizations more than they protect the interests of the USOC as an entity. The paid staff, which is supposed to carry out instructions from the board, faces obstructions in running the organization efficiently. The USOC has struggled

Table B1
USOC Member Organizations

Olympic Games Sport Organizations

National Archery Association	The Athletes Congress
USA Badminton	USA Baseball
USA Basketball	US Biathlon Association
US Bobsled & Skeleton Federation	USA Boxing, Inc.
USA Canoe/Kayak	USA Curling
US Cycling Federation	US Diving, Inc.
USA Equestrian	US Fencing Association
US Field Hockey Association	US Figure Skating Association
USA Gymnastics	USA Hockey
USA Judo	US Modern Pentathlon Association
US Luge Association	US Rowing Association
US Sailing	USA Shooting
US Ski & Snowboard Association	US Soccer Federation
USA Softball	US Speedskating
USA Swimming, Inc.	US Synchronized Swimming, Inc.
US Table Tennis Association	US Taekwondo Union
US Team Handball Federation	US Tennis Association
USA Track & Field	USA Triathlon
USA Volleyball	United States Water Polo
US Weightlifting Federation	USA Wrestling

USOC Affiliated Sports Organizations

USA Bowling	USA Dancesport
USA National Karate-Do Federation	US Orienteering Federation
US Raquetball Association	USA Roller Sports
US Squash Racquets Association	USA Water Ski
Underwater Society of America	United States Sports Acrobatics Federation

Community-Based Multisport Organizations

Amateur Athletic Union	American Legion
Boy Scouts of America	Boys & Girls Clubs of Amer.
Catholic Youth Organization	Jewish Community Centers Association
National Congress of State Games	National Senior Games Association
Native American Sports Council	YMCA of the USA
YWCA of the USA	

National Association of Police Athletic Leagues
Amer. Alliance for Health, Physical Education, Recreation & Dance

Education-Based Multisport Organizations

National Association of Intercollegiate Athletics
National Collegiate Athletic Association
National Federation of State High School Associations
National Junior College Athletic Association

Armed Forces Organizations

U.S. Air Force	U.S. Army
U.S. Marine Corps	U.S. Navy

Disabled in Sports Organizations

Disabled Sports USA	Dwarf Athletic Association of America
National Disability Sports Alliance	Special Olympics International
US Association of Blind Athletes	USA Deaf Sports Federation
Wheelchair Sports USA	

Table B2
USOC Leadership

USOC Presidents	USOC Executive Directors
1900–1904 A. G. Spalding	1950–1965 J. Lyman Bingham
1904–1906 David Francis	1965–1973 Arthur G. Lentz
1906–1910 Caspar Whitney	1968* Everett D. Barnes
1910–1912 F. B. Pratt	1973–1985 F. Don Miller
1912–1920 Col. Robert M. Thompson	1985–1987 George D. Miller
1920–1924 Gustavus T. Kirby	1987–1988* Baaron B. Pittenger
1924–1926 Col. Robert M. Thompson	1988 Harvey W. Schiller
1926** William C. Prout	1988–1989* Baaron B. Pittenger
1926* Henry G. Lapham	1989–1994 Harvey W. Schiller
1926–1927 Dr. Graeme H. Hammond	1994–1995* John Krimsky
1927–1928 Maj. Gen. Douglas MacArthur	1995–1999 Dick Shultz
1928–1953 Avery Brundage	2000 Norm Blake
1953–1965 Kenneth L. Wilson	2000–2001* Scott Blackmun
1965–1969 Douglas F. Ruby	2001–2003 Lloyd Ward
1969–1970** Franklin L. Orth	2003–Open
1970–1973 Clifford H. Buch	
1973–1977 Phillip O. Krumm	
1977–1981 Robert J. Kane	
1981–1985 William E. Simon	
1985** John B. Kelly, Jr.	
1985–1991 Robert H. Helmick	
1991–1992 William J. Hybl	
1992–1996 Dr. LeRoy Walker	
1996–2000 William J. Hybl	
2000–2002 Sandra Baldwin	
2002–2003 Marty Mankamyer	
2003–* Bill Martin	

Key: * = Acting President/Executive Director
      ** = Died in office

with this dichotomy for years and continues to be a source of frustration. In 2000, former executive director Harvey Schiller said, "The volunteer leadership has to focus on what it can give, not what it can take away . . . The motto shouldn't be, 'Where's mine?'" (*New York Times*, November 26, 2000).

One thing, however, unites both factions—fiscal mismanagement. Senator Ted Stevens (R., AK), father of the 1978 Amateur Sports Act that created the USOC, said in the aftermath of the Ward investigation, "We have statements and documents that indicate moneys have been used that were not proper. It looks to me, as a former United States attorney, that it's close to criminal activity" (*New York Times*, March 1, 2003). On a grand scale, evidence exists that Ward billed the USOC for travel for his wife to events unrelated to the Olympics or Pan-American Games. Other examples include lavish relocation expenses for chief staff members and severance packages of more than $1 million to remove an executive no longer wanted.

Questions of fiscal impropriety caught the attention of at least one of the Olympic committee's premier sponsors. David D'Alessandro, chairman of John Hancock, a worldwide Olympic Sponsor, threatened to cancel his $50 million sponsorship unless the USOC institutes tighter fiscal controls. During congressional hearings in 2003, D'Alessandro testified that the USOC had filed "inconsistent and opaque tax returns" with the IRS (*New York Times*, February 14, 2003). Specifically at issue, the 2001 return, the most recent available for review, shows an itemization for revenue from worldwide corporate sponsors such as John Hancock but none of the revenue for sponsorships the USOC negotiated at the national level, which makes it difficult to determine where all of the USOC's revenue originates. D'Alessandro offered to pay for an independent review of the USOC's finances, which has yet to be accepted.

The USOC's financial management cannot be overlooked or impugned for long without the committee suffering repercussions. In 2001, the USOC received a total of $88.9 million in revenue to operate its athlete training centers, provide funding to the national governing bodies, and other activities, which makes the committee one of the wealthiest national Olympic committees in the world. Of the $88 million, the worldwide Olympic sponsors accounted for $27.9 million. Additionally, the committee received a significant share of funding from the International Olympic Committee, which the USOC negotiated on the basis that the IOC receives a majority of its funding from U.S. corporations and broadcasting companies (7 of 11 worldwide Olympic sponsors are American companies). If the USOC continues to remain unstable past the current crisis, the IOC may be unable to justify the share of revenue the committee receives. Likewise, sponsors may not want to associate with an unstable USOC as the instability shifts the public's focus from what should be the most important aspect of a national Olympic Committee—training an elite cadre of Olympic athletes.

Fortunately, the internal bickering in the USOC has not resulted in a slump in performance for the United States at the Olympic Games. The United States won more medals at the Sydney Games than any other country: 97 total. The United States experienced equally good results in Salt Lake City with 34 total medals, the most the U.S. has ever won at a Winter Olympic Games. However, questions have arisen as to whether the USOC has done enough to support its athletes' Olympic aspirations. For example, although the U.S. won the most medals at the Sydney Games, the country ranked 46th on a cost per medal basis.

The USOC provides a variety of services to maintain the performance of elite athletes. The question that will be asked in 2003 is if these services are the best at optimizing performance and medal counts. One of the services to question is the use of Olympic training centers (OTCs). The USOC operates three main centers in the United States with smaller centers throughout the country. These state-of-the-art facilities in Colorado Springs, Lake Placid, and San Diego provide a variety of training opportunities and sport medicine analysis for as many athletes as possible. According to its 2001 tax return, the USOC spent $21.2 million to operate the three facilities. However, while Norm Blake served as CEO, the USOC began a review of the training facilities to determine if there was a more efficient means of providing training services to athletes. At that time, the *New York Times* referred to the centers as "symbols for largesse but have produced few gold medals" as most athletes favor training and competing with their teams or on the European circuit (*New York Times*, November 26, 2000).

Recent developments indicate that the USOC, at least in terms of athlete performance, is looking for alternatives. After a dismal return of six medals at the Calgary Games, the USOC began the Podium Program in which the committee dedicated funds to improving the performance of U.S. athletes in specific winter sports. In the four years leading up to Salt Lake City, the USOC invested $22 million in this program, and they decided the money would be well spent searching for athletes in other sports, such as in-line skating, who could cross over to winter sports. Based on the results of U.S. athletes at Salt Lake City, the program worked, particularly in less developed sports such as skeleton and women's bobsled.

In spite of sensational headlines and disarray within the organization, results matter most, and the USOC has improved the performance of U.S. teams in the past ten years. As Bill Stapleton, chairman of the USOC athletes advisory council said, "The USOC, for all its failings, remains the best Olympic committee in the world. . . . The athletes didn't win 97 medals in Sydney in spite of us" (*New York Times*, November 26, 2000). However, the calls for reform will not abate. As of this writing, the future of the USOC remains unclear. One thing, however, is certain; the U.S. Congress will not allow America's premier sport organization to continue business as usual. Organizational reform, either from within or from Capitol Hill, will occur in 2003.

In October 2003, the USOC approved a sweeping overhaul to its governance structure. The board of directors has been cut from 123 members to 11, the 22-member executive committee has been abolished, and the 23 committees have been reduced to just four. These changes take effect in March 2004. Three bills before the U.S. Congress mandate an even more streamlined structure but have yet to be acted upon. However, it is likely that greater financial transparency will be required of the USOC in the future. Other insiders have stated that the USOC needs an executive with experience at handling a complex organization more than it needs a superstar CEO. More than anything else, however, the USOC needs to find some mechanism for the volunteers and paid staff to center all their attention on one priority—determining what is best for America's premier athletes.

BIBLIOGRAPHICAL ESSAY

For basic information on the role of the USOC, its mission, organizational structure, budget, and program operations, the USOC publishes an annual edition of the *United States Olympic Committee Fact Book*. Another source that provides an overview of the USOC is on videotape: Bud Greenspan and Nancy Beffa, *Sharing the Dream* (1990). Also, Kenneth Reich, *Making It Happen: Peter Ueberroth and the 1984 Olympics* (Santa Barbara, CA, 1986) offers a working, inside look at the many aspects of organizing an Olympic event as does the related work by Jeffrey M. Humphreys and Michael K. Plummer, *The Economic Impact on the State of Georgia of Hosting the 1996 Olympic Games* (Atlanta, GA, 1992).

Records and official sources are also available for legal, statistical, and official information on the USOC and Olympics: the *USOC Constitution and Bylaws* (1991) is available through the USOC; Bill Mallon, *The Olympic Record Book* (New York, 1988) contains statistics related to the USOC. Expenditures of the national governing bodies of Olympic sports and USOC financial information is available in *USOC Support of NGBs* (Colorado Springs, CO, 1991).

Sources on the creation and growth of the movement include C. Robert Paul, Jr., "Historical Background of the USOC," *U.S. Olympic Academy Conference Report* (Colorado Springs, 1987): 68–75.

A more detailed history of USOC leaders and key events in the organization's past, or efforts at improvement and reform may be found in several sources: Robert E. Lehr, *The American Olympic Committee, 1896–1940: From Chaos to Order* (New York, 1985); *Toward a More Effective United States Olympic Effort: Report to the United States Olympic Committee* (New York, 1965); and Allen Guttmann, *The Games Must Go On: Avery Brundage and the Olympic Movement* (New York, 1984).

Numerous books discuss political issues pertaining to the Olympics such as the process and struggle for power and leadership, money, and politics' influence on the Games. While not written directly about the USOC, these works, listed below, do highlight topics pertinent to the USOC mission.

John Huberman, *The Olympic Crisis: Sport, Politics, and the Moral Order* (New Rochelle, NY, 1986).
Christopher R. Hill, *Olympic Politics* (New York, 1992).
Richard Espy, *The Politics of the Olympic Games* (Berkeley, CA, 1979).
Martin Barry Vinokur, *More than a Game: Sports and Politics* (Westport, CT, 1988).
Vyv Simson, *The Lord of the Rings: Power, Money, and Drugs in the Modern Olympics* (New York, 1992).

The U.S. Olympic Academy's annual conference provides a forum for the discussion of themes pertaining to the Olympics. Often, among the topics presented are the USOC and issues relating to the organization. Published proceedings of the USOA sessions, in the form of scholarly papers, offer highlights from the conference and a source of information on the Olympics and the USOC. See the following USOC reports:

USOA XI, "The Olympics: Serving All People and All Nations," (1987)
USOA IX, "Olympism: A Commitment to a Better World Tomorrow through Sport," (1985).
USOA VII, "Olympism: A Movement of the People," (1983).
USOA V, "Expanding Olympic Horizons," (1981).
NOA II, "Sport and Olympism: A Way of Life," (1978).
USOA I, "Perspectives of the Olympic Games," (1977).

APPENDIX C: THE OLYMPIC GAMES AND TELEVISION

Stephen R. Wenn

The television medium fulfills two principal functions for the International Olympic Committee (IOC). First, television acts as a conduit to a global audience for the promotion of Olympism, the philosophy of the Olympic Movement grounded in principles such as fair play, equality, and international harmony. Second, the sale of Olympic television rights supplies the Olympic tripartite (the IOC, national Olympic committees [NOCs], and international sport federations [IFs]) and local organizing committees with large sums of capital. For Olympic Games staged between 1984 and 2008, the IOC negotiated television contracts worth more than $10 billion. Corporate sponsorship money raised through the Olympic Partners program beginning in the 1980s provided needed diversification of its revenue base, but television revenue still provides 50 percent of the Olympic Movement's financial resources.

Olympic athletes first appeared on television in 1936; however, the evolution of Olympic television rights in 1958, and the advent of satellite technology in the 1960s, mark the two most significant signposts in the early history of Olympic television. The first development, an effort spearheaded by IOC President Avery Brundage following the 1956 Melbourne Olympics, empowered future Olympic organizing committees (OCOGs) to negotiate the sale of exclusive Olympic television rights on a regional basis with the world's broadcasters, with the sums accrued disbursed by the IOC. The second event, a landmark development in global communications, opened the door for transoceanic, instantaneous transmission of Olympic competition in 1964 and had a catalytic effect on the value of Olympic television rights, especially in the competitive U.S. sport television market. Olympic television audiences and the value of Olympic television rights increased steadily over the past four decades. Television rights for the 2000 Sydney Olympic Games were sold for more than $1.3 billion, while the telecasts drew 3.7 billion viewers. Television rights sales for Salt Lake City yielded $738 million, and telecasts attracted an audience of 2.1 billion people.

Two central themes pervade the history of the Olympics and television: conflict and control. Money from the sale of television rights left the IOC and its partner organizations, the NOCs and IFs, at odds concerning how the money should be allocated. In the 1960s, Brundage devoted significant energy to establishing a distribution formula that would bring peace to the Olympic Movement, while protecting his vision of its ideals and the legitimate financial needs of the OCOGs. For Brundage, commercialism was a slippery slope. He knew that the revenue could facilitate better promotion of Olympic ideals through expansion of the IOC's Lausanne headquarters but he worried about the impact on the IOC's image resulting from a marriage with commercial entities. The IOC could manage this situation, Brundage believed, if it exerted complete control over the distribution of the money.

When television money prompted pitched battles between administrators of purportedly amateur sport organizations, Brundage's views progressively hardened. "I have deplored on more than one occasion," observed Brundage, "the idea of financial considerations being introduced into Olympic affairs. For the first time serious arguments have been provoked and I do not like it!" (Barney, et al, *Selling the Five Rings* [2002], 99). In 1966, Brundage shepherded the Rome formula, the IOC's first formal distribution formula for television revenue, through the IOC General Session. Given the increasing capital budget demands facing OCOGs, Brundage directed 66 percent of the television money to the local organizers. However, the OCOGs wanted more, and some IF leaders were dissatisfied with their allotted 11 percent, which fell well short of their previous demand for 33 percent.

By the time he retired in 1972, Brundage favored transferring complete control of the television portfolio to the OCOGs with a modest sum directed to the IOC to cover its administrative budget. By that time, however, it was not possible to close Pandora's box as NOC and IF leaders, as well as some IOC members, understood the medium and long-term impact of satellite technology on the value of Olympic television rights. After having conducted their businesses on shoestring budgets for years, they coveted the financial possibilities and dismissed Brundage's advice. "Distressed and disillusioned," commented Allen Guttmann, "Brundage watched as the IOC first adopted the financial procedures and then the fiscal attitudes of a modern corporation." (Barney, *Five Rings*, 100).

In 1955, Avery Brundage pondered the financial possibilities of Olympic telecasts for the Olympic Movement. He informed members of the IOC Executive Board that "the International Olympic Committee has always kept itself free from financial entanglements, so free, in fact, that it has never had money enough to do the useful work it could be doing if it had a larger staff. I am not sure we should ever get into 'business,' but on the other hand certainly we should not give millions of dollars away" (Barney, *Five Rings*, 59). It was not the first time that Brundage considered television's financial possibilities. He had tried to sell the television rights to the U.S. Olympic track-and-field trials in 1948 (in order to offset the United States Olympic Committee's [USOC] costs for the upcoming London Games) and U.S. television rights to the 1952 Helsinki Olympics (a portion of the sale would have flowed to the USOC). He was unsuccessful in both ventures. The IOC Executive Board held preliminary discussions concerning the question of television money in Cortina, Italy, in the early months of 1956.

Meanwhile, the Melbourne Organizing Committee wrestled with budget issues for the upcoming 1956 Summer Olympics. One means of offsetting its costs involved the sale of a commercial film of the Games following their conclusion.

However, television and cinema newsreel networks also desired an opportunity to provide daily updates to their audiences, especially in Europe and North America. The television networks sought royalty-free access to nine minutes of footage tailored to their domestic audiences. Wilfrid Kent-Hughes and fellow members of the Melbourne Organizing Committee desired remuneration for any footage exceeding three minutes, claiming that any other approach would compromise sales of the official Olympic film.

With satellite technology still six years away, the networks were limited to the use of delayed footage (in the case of the U.S., the footage would be three days old before it would be televised in conjunction with morning, midday, and evening newscasts). Television executives countered that such footage possessed little value, certainly nothing comparable to that accorded to sport events televised on a live basis. Also, and more importantly, they refused to pay for footage to be used for news purposes. The impasse proved impossible to resolve.

Brundage engaged in a two-year consultative process with international television executives in order to craft policy that would protect the television networks' access to footage for news coverage, while also providing OCOGs with an opportunity to raise funds through the sale of television rights. The widescale television blackout of events in Melbourne could not be repeated. In 1958, Brundage's action plan was passed in the form of extensive revisions to the IOC's Rule 49 on Publicity. Television networks were granted access to nine minutes of daily footage for news purposes; however, a network that wished to schedule more extensive programming would have to pay for exclusive rights. Brundage ceded complete control of the negotiation process to the OCOGs, but the IOC retained control over the distribution of the money.

This plan did not meet with the approval of the 1960 Squaw Valley and Rome Olympic committees that had been charged with the responsibility for staging the Winter and Summer Games respectively in 1955. They strongly resisted Brundage's attempt to exert control over television revenue retroactively. Troubled by these arguments over commercial revenue, Brundage withdrew the IOC's claim to 1960 television revenue, and in ensuing years issued claims for minimal sums payable to the IOC from the organizing committees of the 1964 and 1968 Olympic festivals. While this arrangement satisfied organizing committee officials, especially in an era when new satellite technology portended spiraling television rights fees, representatives of the NOCs and IFs chafed under this policy.

In the early 1960s, Avery Brundage was confronted by the financial ambitions of leaders of the international sport federations. While Bunny Ahearne, an official with the International Ice Hockey Federation, was their most vociferous advocate, he was supported by Berge Phillips (swimming), Roger Coulon (wrestling), and Oscar State (weight lifting), who similarly minced few words in their condemnation of the IOC's television policy. In 1964 and 1968, the IOC divided its share of television revenue evenly with the federations. Ahearne and his colleagues resented the limited amounts of money accruing to the federations. For the Mexico City Olympics (1968) the federations shared a paltry $100,000 (the U.S. television rights alone sold for $4.5 million). They also opposed Brundage's appointment of IOC Executive Board member David Cecil, the Marquess of Exeter, who served as president of the International Amateur Athletics Federation (IAAF), as the individual who determined the division of the federations' money. Exeter resisted their call for equal shares payable to all the federations, and he employed a formula based, in part, on attendance at events sponsored by the individual federations at prior Olympic festivals. Naturally, this formula favored Exeter's federation and worked against lower-profile sports.

While Brundage grew tired of the IFs' incessant lobbying, and questioned their devotion to amateurism and increasingly commercial tendencies, the NOCs also proffered their hands for a share of the television money. IOC members Armand Massard (France), Guru Dutt Sondhi (India), and Giulio Onesti (Italy) questioned why the NOCs received no television money at all. Television money for the NOCs, stated Massard, would reduce their dependence on government funding, a situation that compromised their autonomy in some countries. Massard concluded that the IFs "have no real needs," in light of their ability to raise sums through their respective world championships. Onesti agreed. The federations' demand for one-third of all Olympic television revenue, noted Onesti, was "out of line with their principles of function [that] would appear to me to be purely that of a technical nature and the control over the regularity of sport events" (Barney, *Five Rings*, 92). When Sondhi learned that some IFs threatened to ban Olympic telecasts of their events if their financial demands were not met, he told Brundage that the federations "have assumed too much power and dignity to themselves and covertly, if not overtly, try to overawe the IOC" (Barney, *Five Rings*). Brundage, locked in an extended struggle with the federations over amateur regulations on numerous fronts, could not argue with Sondhi's analysis. Yes, Brundage could rationalize ceding some television money to the NOCs because one of their functions involved promoting Olympic ideals. However, the Olympic Games could not be staged without the cooperation of the federations.

Brundage arrived at an inspired solution. He delegated the challenge of constructing a distribution formula acceptable to all three parties (IOC, NOCs, and IFs) to a working committee headed by Giulio Onesti and Exeter. As the two heavyweights on the committee, Exeter, who championed the federations, and Onesti, who supported the NOCs (and had also served as president of Rome's organizing committee in 1960), would be forced to deal with the financial claims of both parties. Compromise was their obvious mandate. In effect, Brundage put the two men in a room, and refused to unlock the door until they offered a solution. Their efforts resulted in a distribution formula that recognized the claims of the IFs and NOCs. The IOC Executive Board made a few minor alterations to the Onesti/Exeter formula, and Brundage gained IOC support for the plan at the IOC's General Session in April 1966. OCOGs, beginning in 1972, would receive 66 percent of the television money, while the IOC, IFs, and NOCs would share equally the remaining 33 percent

"Technical services fee, what is a technical services fee?" When alerted to the plans of the Sapporo and Munich Olympic Organizing Committees to deduct a technical services fee from the sum negotiated for U.S. television rights, thereby lowering the amount of money subject to the Rome formula, one can imagine this question being asked by incredulous IOC officials. Sapporo officials eventually backed away from this position and agreed to subject all U.S. television money to the Rome formula, but Munich held firm. Munich Organizing Committee President Willi Daume refused to yield and eventually received the IOC's permission to deduct $6 million from the $13.5 million U.S. contract with ABC, leaving $7.5 million subject to division according to the terms of the Rome formula. Daume argued that the Rome formula did not take into account the burgeoning costs borne by organizing committees in providing the infrastructure necessary not only to stage, but also to televise the Olympic Games to an international audience. The IOC accepted Daume's terms only after having obtained guarantees that the Innsbruck and Montreal Olympic Organizing Committees would not follow Daume's lead.

As IOC president, Lord Killanin delegated much authority in television matters to IOC Finance Commission Chairman Jean de Beaumont (France) and IOC Executive Director Monique Berlioux; however, he closely monitored negotiations and IOC/OCOG dealings with respect to television. When the Innsbruck, Montreal, Lake Placid, and Moscow Organizing Committees opted for similar tactics to those employed by Willi Daume, Killanin charted a different path for the IOC. The IOC made special arrangements with all of the aforementioned that enhanced their respective shares of television revenue. However, rather than remaining the absent partner in the television negotiations process in the future, Killanin prepared the ground for the IOC to take a more active role in negotiating contracts, and protecting its financial interests.

Killanin used a twofold strategy to achieve this goal. First, he established a television subcommittee, under Berlioux's leadership, to learn more about the television industry and the television rights negotiations process. Second, he accepted the concept of a joint negotiation policy. In 1977, the IOC determined that it would jointly negotiate television contracts with the 1984 and future organizing committees. Both initiatives demonstrated two realities for the Olympic Movement. First, the IOC, under Killanin, was not shackled by Brundage's philosophical aversion to commercialism. Second, the IOC, now dependent upon television revenue for in excess of 90 percent of its operating budget, had little choice but to assume a higher profile in the negotiations process to safeguard its financial interests.

Over the course of the next decade, the joint negotiation policy proved problematic for the IOC and its television negotiators, Monique Berlioux (1984) and Richard Pound (1988). The Sarajevo and Los Angeles Organizing Committees resisted any loss of autonomy in television negotiations. Stymied in her efforts to ensure that the IOC played a role in the negotiation of the U.S. television contract, Berlioux effectively assumed control of negotiations with television representatives from the other major markets, in the process pushing disgruntled Yugoslavian officials to the sidelines. Peter Ueberroth, president of the Los Angeles Organizing Committee, ignored the new policy and claimed exclusive control of the negotiations process, given his organization's lack of public sector money. The IOC officials, including Berlioux, were reduced to advisor status. Ueberroth understood that the IOC was willing to seek maximum revenue in television negotiations with U.S. networks. However, he knew that the European Broadcasting Union, the only viable option for European television from the IOC's perspective, had not been forced to pay what he and many other observers considered market value for television rights in the past. He would negotiate with EBU, and other potential television rights holders, not the IOC. The IOC granted Ueberroth this authority in the waning days of Killanin's presidency. Richard Pound and the Calgary Organizing Committee officials collaborated successfully on the negotiation of a record $309 million U.S. television contract and relations between the IOC and Calgary officials concerning television were generally positive. However, Pound's frustrations with the Seoul Organizing Committee officials prompted the IOC to assume complete control of television negotiations for the 1992 Olympic Games and beyond. Relations were especially strained with respect to the U.S. television contract when the Koreans expected between $600 and $700 million, but the best offer received (from NBC) was $325 million. In short, in keeping with past tendencies, the OCOGs sought maximum television revenue without regard for the fact that the IOC needed to maintain a long-term relationship with the television networks.

Soon after Juan Antonio Samaranch's arrival in Lausanne in 1980, his relationship with Monique Berlioux deteriorated. It has been speculated that philosophical differences over Samaranch's decision to align the IOC with major multinational corporations through a worldwide sponsorship program played a contributory role in this process. As a means of reducing Berlioux's power base, Samaranch removed Berlioux as the IOC's point person in television negotiations and appointed Canadian tax lawyer Richard Pound in her place. Even though Pound had no experience in negotiating television contracts, Samaranch appreciated Pound's intellect and energy. In hindsight, Pound's appointment proved to be one of Samaranch's most astute actions as IOC president. Pound provided the IOC with sound, competent leadership of the television portfolio, and later corporate sponsorship, for 18 years.

Pound, like Samaranch, adopted a pragmatic view concerning the IOC's link with commercialism. With the expansion of the Olympic program, and the unwillingness of local, regional, and federal governments to bankroll Olympic festivals in the post-Montreal (1976) period, the development of a second lucrative revenue stream through television was essential. Even though Pound and Samaranch had their differences on certain issues, they functioned well together, and from the perspective of revenue generation, their partnership was wildly successful.

One critical area in which they differed, and which guided events involving Olympic television negotiations in the 1990s, was the different negotiating models employed in the U.S. and European territories. Pound sought maximum revenue from U.S. television networks by leveraging the competitive nature of the U.S. market and the attractiveness of the Olympic television property. With three primary options (ABC, CBS, and NBC) and the Fox network's arrival on the bidding scene, Pound's negotiating position was enviable, but subject to the health of the U.S. sport television market. The results of Pound's efforts are shown in Table C1. Samaranch, who retained exclusive control of European negotiations with executive board member Marc Hodler, dismissed the possibility of a collaborative telecast effort on the part of emerging European private television networks, in favor of pursuing contractual arrangements with EBU. EBU, stated Samaranch, offered the IOC with the only opportunity for blanket coverage in Europe. EBU officials were not moved to elevate the sums offered for Olympic television rights in any meaningful way until they faced competing bidders. They also maintained that their government-funded status precluded offering more money. Pound agreed with Samaranch's view with respect to blanket coverage and EBU's good track record in covering the Olympics. He did not agree with Samaranch's decision not to employ competing bids in negotiations with EBU representatives.

When Pound and Calgary obtained $309 million from ABC for U.S. television rights for the 1988 Winter Games, and Samaranch and Hodler reported that $5.7 million was EBU's best offer for television rights in Western Europe for the same festival, Pound campaigned for a different negotiating approach with EBU. U.S. television executives, warned Pound, took a dim view of EBU's favored status. When U.S. television executives collaborated with Congressman Tom McMillen (R., MD), on a proposed Olympic Television Broadcast Act in 1990, Pound had something tangible to offer as evidence of potential troubles for the IOC. U.S.

Table C1
A Comparison of U.S. Television Networks and European Broadcasting Union Contracts for Winter and Summer Festivals, 1998–2008.

	United States	European Broadcasting Union
1988 Winter	$309,000,000	$ 5,700,000
1988 Summer	300,000,000	28,000,000
1992 Winter	243,000,000	18,106,560
1992 Summer	401,000,000	75,000,000
1994 Winter	295,000,000	24,000,000
1996 Summer	456,000,000	247,000,000
1998 Winter	375,000,000	72,000,000
2000 Summer	715,000,000	350,000,000
2002 Winter	555,000,000	120,000,000
2004 Summer	793,000,000	394,000,000
2006 Winter	613,000,000	135,000,000
2008 Summer	894,000,000	443,360,000

All figures in U.S. Dollars

Figures include rights and technical fees or other considerations

television executives had lost their patience with the sums negotiated for the U.S. television contract relative to Europe and other markets. If Congress passed the legislation, live U.S. Olympic coverage could not be interrupted by commercial advertising and the networks would be provided with an exemption from the Sherman Anti-Trust Act, thereby permitting them to submit a pooled bid. Both initiatives spelled a diminution of the value of U.S. television revenue. Thankfully, from an IOC perspective, Pound convinced McMillen to withdraw the bill.

The proposed Olympic Television Broadcast Act, alone, did not move Samaranch to modify his approach. Pound's persistence and a whopping $300 million offer for U.S. television rights to the 1996 Atlanta Games from Universum-Film AG (a German network) forced Samaranch's hand. EBU still received the contract, but the $250 million it was required to pay made inroads against the disparity of the value of U.S. and European television rights.

A second challenge Pound faced in managing the television file involved the IOC's relationship with the Olympic Movement's most powerful NOC, the U.S. Olympic Committee. In 1985, the USOC announced its plans to invoke ownership of the Olympic rings in the U.S. territory as outlined in the Amateur Sports Act, a U.S. federal statute passed in 1978. In short, the USOC claimed compensation from the 1988 U.S. Olympic broadcasters (ABC—Calgary, NBC—Seoul), and future Olympic broadcasters from their advertising time sales to companies planning to use the Olympic logo during their commercials.

The USOC asserted that its own domestic sponsorship program was compromised by the networks' ability to sublicense the use of the Olympic rings to commercial advertisers. IOC legal advice confirmed that U.S. law trumped the Olympic Charter. Pound was forced to reach an agreement to protect the financial interests of ABC, NBC, the IOC, and the organizing committees. Without the possibility of employing the Olympic five-ring logo, commercial advertisers would seek much lower advertising rates. In early 1986, the IOC signed the Broadcast Marketing Agreement with the USOC. The USOC received a lump sum payment of $15 million (shared equally by the IOC and the 1988 Seoul and Calgary OCOGs) in exchange for granting ABC and NBC the right to sublicense the Olympic logo. The USOC also received 10 percent of all U.S. television rights fees beginning in 1992 for the same concession to Olympic broadcasters in the future.

Relations between the IOC and USOC were strained in the 1990s due to the IOC's desire to maintain the terms of the Broadcast Marketing Agreement and the USOC's persistent lobbying for 20 percent of the revenue from all future U.S. television contracts. The USOC crafted elements of the Olympic Television Act. Specifically, the USOC convinced McMillen to include a clause in the bill that would have transferred the right to negotiate U.S. television agreements from the IOC to the USOC. This clause permitted the USOC to determine the distribution of the U.S. television revenue. In 1996, the USOC tried without success to have this same negotiating arrangement buried in a Senate bill. An alert NBC staff member alerted the IOC to the situation, and the USOC yielded to the IOC's demand to withdraw this element of the legislation. The IOC's decision to pursue a long-term television agreement (2004–2008) for the U.S. territory in 1995, without input from the USOC, prompted the USOC's second legislative foray in Washington.

Pound and Samaranch explored the possibility of multifestival television agreements in the summer of 1995. NBC Sports executive Dick Ebersol floated the idea to Pound and Samaranch, and the $1.25 billion offered for the rights to the Sydney and Salt Lake City festivals was too attractive to turn down. With direction from the executive board, Pound held further secret talks with Ebersol about the 2004, 2006, and 2008 Olympic festivals. Pound and Ebersol referred to these discussions as the Sunset Project. They exchanged ideas on an acceptable year-over-year increase based on an anticipated inflation rate and how to deal with the issue that they were negotiating a deal for festivals for which the sites were not yet known. Ebersol and his boss, General Electric CEO Jack Welch, viewed long-term ownership of the Olympic property positively. Samaranch and Pound considered the financial security that such an arrangement offered to the Olympic Movement, as well as the benefit to future bid committees that would have more accurate revenue data with which to plan their bids. The template was eventually used for negotiation of long-term agreements in the world's other television markets in 1996 and 1997.

Pound, no doubt, also appreciated consummating this deal while the USOC was still locked into receiving 10 percent of the U.S. television contracts. In December 1995 Pound and Ebersol announced a second $2.3 billion television deal. For his part, Pound thought that $230 million was more than sufficient compensation for the USOC. USOC officials fumed, and pursued their agenda quietly in Washington.

When their wanderings on Capitol Hill were discovered, Samaranch, who had entered into personal negotiations with USOC officials about effecting a change to the 10 percent clause in the Broadcast Marketing Agreement, felt betrayed. Pound, a veteran of a number of skirmishes with the USOC, was not surprised. Samaranch, Pound, and IOC Director General François Carrard confronted the USOC's Dick Schultz in Atlanta during the 1996 Summer Olympics. Schultz complied with Samaranch's demand that the USOC abandon its legislative efforts in Washington.

Samaranch, agitated by the USOC's activities, called a summit meeting of IOC and USOC officials in October 1996 to address the matter. He was blunt. The USOC, stated Samaranch, could play by the IOC's rules or withdraw from the Olympic Movement. It was, at best, a veiled threat given the importance of the U.S. market to the Olympic Movement's finances. Samaranch was willing to concede 15 percent of U.S. television revenue to the USOC for 2004 and beyond before the Washington episode, but the best he was willing to offer now was 12.75 percent. USOC officials accepted the offer. This summit meeting demonstrated the substantial rift between the two organizations over Olympic television revenue. Since 1997, USOC and IOC officials have worked, with some success, to improve their working relationships. How these improved relations fare when television negotiations for Olympic festivals in 2010 and beyond are held in 2003, will be a subject of some interest to Olympic observers.

Television answered two needs for the Olympic Movement during the course of the last 40 years. From a promotional standpoint, television has carried Olympic events to an ever-increasing number of television viewers. Record audiences of 3.7 and 2.1 billion people witnessed Olympic events from Sydney and Salt Lake City respectively. Television executives, especially those situated in the United States, have provided the Olympic Movement with a steady source of revenue that has offset substantial revenue previously drawn from public treasuries in host communities. Athletes' development in developing nations, one of the IOC's mandates, requires a more focused and efficient approach on the part of the organization. Television revenue (and other commercial revenue) can be more effectively employed in pursuit of this objective. It remains a major challenge for Olympic officials.

Questions have been raised about television's control over event scheduling, what is seen and not seen, and decisions concerning the addition of new sports to the Olympic program. Concessions to U.S. television executives annoyed some television officials (and viewers) abroad, but the IOC answered that these concessions simply recognized the magnitude of U.S. television's financial investment in the Olympic Movement. The issue has been less debated in recent years, given NBC's predilection to tape Olympic events for telecast in prime time in the United States. Some Americans resent NBC's approach, but the hue and cry is not sufficient to alter Dick Ebersol's mindset.

And, indeed, television viewers are captive to the vision of Olympic production teams. Will the network provide an international perspective or play the nationalism card, focusing on domestic athletes, to the exclusion of fascinating stories involving foreign athletes? Television executives, having expended millions of dollars for rights fees, must generate audiences for their advertisers. And, the executives maintain that the best way to generate large audiences is to focus on domestic athletes. Olympic television producers are both blessed and cursed. They have one of the dream jobs in sport television when one considers the scope of the challenge. But, they also have decisions to make on a minute-by-minute basis as to which events to cover, and it stands to reason that not all viewers will be satisfied with those decisions. NBC's collaboration with MSNBC and CNBC was designed to create more hours of Olympic coverage, but also to provide an avenue for satisfying more elements of NBC's audience that might prefer access to coverage of lower-profile sports. The Canadian Broadcasting Corporation (CBC), Canada's Olympic broadcaster through 2008, has taken the same approach through its alliance with The Sports Network (TSN).

When the IOC considers the efforts by IFs to add new sports to the Olympic program, there are issues such as universality and gender balance to ponder, but the individual sport's telegenic qualities and potential audience demographics are considered. Snowboarding and beach volleyball owe their admission not just to their growing popularity, but also the ability of these sports to generate audiences that advertisers seek to tap into with the presentation of their products or services. This reality is the source of lament for some Olympic observers.

However, when all of these issues are considered, what must be remembered is that without television, broadcast advertisers, and corporate sponsorship, the scale of the Games would be much smaller than that to which we have grown accustomed, and the debt of host cities would be even more pronounced. Granted, there is much logic in reducing the size of the Olympic program as a means of controlling costs in host cities and reducing the pressure placed on host cities with respect to the scope (and cost) of their security plans. This question will consume the time of the newly appointed Olympic Games Study Commission headed by Richard Pound. Still, those hoping for a less commercialized Olympic spectacle will be disappointed. The emergence of a symbiotic relationship between Olympic sport and commercial entities paralleled similar developments in professional sport in the last 50 years, and has proven far too lucrative for national Olympic committees, international sport federations, organizing committees, and the IOC itself, for the IOC to turn back the clock.

BIBLIOGRAPHICAL ESSAY

The subject of sport television is explored in a number of works by academics including, Joan Chandler, *Television and National Sport: The United States and Great Britain* (Urbana, IL, 1988) and Ben Rader, *In Its Own Image: How Television Has Transformed Sports* (New York, 1984). Interesting analyses of the same subject have been provided by sport television executives Terry O'Neil and James Spence. See Terry O'Neil, *The Game Behind the Game* (New York, 1989) and Jim Spence (with Dave Diles), *Up Close and Personal: The Inside Story of Network Television Sports* (New York, 1988). One of the more enjoyable books on sport television is David Klatell and Norman Marcus, *Sports for Sale: Television, Money, and the Fans* (New York, 1988). For information on this subject from a British perspective, see Steven Barnett, *Games and Sets: The Changing Face of Sport on Television* (London, 1990).

The most comprehensive analyses to date on the subject of Olympic commercialism has been provided by Robert Barney, Stephen Wenn, and Scott Martyn, *Selling the Five Rings: The IOC and the Rise of Olympic Commercialism* (Salt Lake City, UT, 2002). The authors detail and assess the efforts of IOC officials in administering the television and corporate sponsorship portfolios in the twentieth century. Overviews of Olympic television can be found in Robert Joseph Lucas, "A Descriptive History of the Interdependence of Television and Sports in the Summer Olympic Games," (master's thesis, San Diego State University, 1984) and Stephen R. Wenn, "A History of the International Olympic Committee and Television, 1936–1980," (Ph.D. diss., Pennsylvania State University, 1993).

Recent developments in Olympic television have been placed in the broader context of sport, media, and culture by David Andrews. See David L. Andrews,

"Sport," in Richard Maxwell, ed., *Culture Works: Essays on the Political Economy of Culture* (Minneapolis, MN, 2001): 131–62. An alternative, and valuable read on this subject is Gary Whannel, "The Television Spectacular," in Alan Tomlinson and Gary Whannel, ed., *Five Ring Circus: Money, Power, and Politics at the Olympic Games* (London, 1984). Olympic television has been examined in the context of specific festivals. For example, see James F. Larson and Heung-Soo Park, *Global Television and the Politics of the Seoul Olympics* (Boulder, CO, 1993) and Miquel de Moragas Spa, Nancy K. Rivenburgh, and James F. Larson, eds., *Television in the Olympics* (London, 1995). The latter work explores telecasting decisions regarding the 1992 Barcelona Olympics.

Olympic television negotiations provided the grist for a number of authors including Richard Alasckiewicz, John McMillan, Robert Lawrence, and Stephen Wenn. See Richard K. Alasczkiewicz and Thomas L. McPhail, "Olympic Television Rights," *International Review for the Sociology of Sport* 21, 2/3 (1986): 211–28; John McMillan, "Bidding for Olympic Broadcast Rights: The Competition Before the Competition," *Negotiation Journal* 7 (July 1991): 255–63; Robert Z. Lawrence (with Jeffrey D. Pellegrom), "Fool's Gold: How America Pays to Lose in the Olympics," *Brookings Review* (fall 1989): 5–10; Stephen R. Wenn, "Lights! Camera! Little Action: Television, Avery Brundage, and the 1956 Melbourne Olympics," *Sporting Traditions* 10 (November 1993): 38–53; Stephen R. Wenn, "An Olympian Squabble: The Distribution of Olympic Television Revenue, 1960–1966," *Olympika: The International Journal of Olympic Studies* 3 (1994): 27–47; Stephen R. Wenn, "Growing Pains: The Olympic Movement and Television, 1966–1972," *Olympika: The International Journal of Olympic Studies* 4 (1995): 1–22; Stephen R. Wenn, "Television Rights Negotiations and the 1976 Montreal Olympics," *Sport History Review* 27 (November 1996): 111–38; Stephen R. Wenn, "Richard Pound's Dilemma: Sub-Saharan Africa Television Rights and the 1992 Barcelona Olympics," *Olympika: The International Journal of Olympic Studies* 6 (1997): 25–50; Stephen R. Wenn, "A Turning Point for IOC Television Policy: U.S. Television Rights Negotiations and the 1980 Lake Placid and Moscow Olympic Festivals," *Journal of Sport History* 25 (spring 1998): 87–118; Stephen R. Wenn, "Conflicting Agendas: Monique Berlioux, Ahmed Karabegovic, and U.S. Television Rights Negotiations for the 1984 Sarajevo Olympic Winter Games," in Robert K. Barney, Kevin B. Wamsley, Scott G. Martyn, and Gordon H. MacDonald, eds., *Global and Cultural Critique— Problematizing the Olympic Games: Fourth International Symposium for Olympic Research* (London, Ontario, 1998): 115–27; and Stephen R. Wenn, "Riding into the Sunset: Richard Pound, Dick Ebersol, and Long-Term Olympic Television Contracts," in Kevin B. Wamsley, Scott G. Martyn, Gordon H. MacDonald, and Robert K. Barney, eds., *Bridging Three Centuries: Intellectual Crossroads and the Modern Olympic Movement—Fifth International Symposium for Olympic Research* (London, Ontario, 2000): 37–50.

APPENDIX D:
OLYMPIC FEATURE
FILMS

Scott A. G. M. Crawford

In terms of the athletic genre, there seems little doubt that film critics hold the view that boxing and baseball have provided sport movies with their most artistically pleasing moments. *The Pride of the Yankees* (baseball) in the World War II era and the *Rocky* quintet (boxing) in contemporary cinema are frequently described as great movies. Other critics have praised the monumental aesthetics of *The Natural* (baseball) and the brash and uncompromising muscularity of *Raging Bull* (boxing). And then of course there is the classic 1997 documentary *When We Were Kings*. The reason for inserting it here, in the midst of a discussion about feature films, it that this vehicle—a celebratory revisiting of the Ali-Foreman epic world heavyweight fight—serves to highlight the theatrical mannerisms and mercurial persona that made Ali perfectly engaging and just right as a fit for the Hollywood cinema screen. Will Smith's very deserved 2002 Oscar nomination (for Best Actor) for his portrayal of Ali, in *Ali*, serves as a reminder that the one time Louisville Lip has been an actor par excellence throughout the whole of his life. Carrington quotes Spike Lee: "Ali was a beautiful specimen, a fighting machine. He was handsome, he was articulate, he was funny, charismatic, and he was whipping ass too!"

With respect to Olympic films, the works of Leni Riefenstahl, Mashiro Shinoda, Kon Ichikawa, and Bud Greenspan have elevated the documentary feature to great heights, but very little attention has been given to the Olympic feature film. In fact, while there have been few feature films made with significant Olympic content, some of them epitomize classic filmmaking. After more than 20 years, *Chariots of Fire* (1981) is assuming the celebrity status of a film classic as it appears increasingly in the top choices of leading critics.

The definitive source in terms of identifying Olympic feature films is Harvey M. Zucker and Lawrence Babich, eds., *Sports Films: A Complete Reference* (1987), which describes a number of films of varying quality that focus on the Olympics. *Jim Thorpe—All American* (aka *Man of Bronze*), released in 1951, tells the story of America's greatest track-and-field athlete. Instead of merely chronicling Jim Thorpe's athletic versatility, its canvas goes from his days on the Indian reservation to the loss of his Olympic gold medals because of his playing professional baseball. The casting of Burt Lancaster as Thorpe was perfect in terms of physicality. Lancaster had begun his career as a gymnast/acrobat, and with his sculpted physique and passionate personality, he personified the athlete-as-actor folk hero. However, it should be stressed that in terms of ethnicity the film is a monumental failure. Jim Thorpe was unquestionably the greatest Native American athlete of the twentieth century, and Warner Brothers's decision to cast a white man taking on the mantra of this stellar athlete has to be seen as exploitative and racist.

Three years later Allied Artists brought out *The Bob Mathias Story* (aka *The Flaming Torch*), starring Bob Mathias playing himself. Despite clever editing, with real footage from the 1948 and the 1952 Olympics, the film failed because Mathias was undistinguished as an actor, and the screenplay failed to capture the magnetism that Mathias communicated in real life.

Cary Grant continues to be recalled and revered as a charming actor with a rare gift of being funny without seeming to be a clown or a buffoon. Sadly his last movie, *Walk, Don't Run* (1966), was disappointing and very forgettable. However, it does have an Olympic connection. The story is about a businessman visiting Tokyo, Japan, during the 1964 Olympics. There are no available hotel rooms, because of the number of Olympic visitors, so Grant eventually rents a room from a British Embassy secretary played by Samantha Eggar. They then meet a member of the U.S. track team, a race walker played by Tim Hutton. Grant assumes the role of matchmaker. The film elicited little response on its release and is sustained by little more than the fact that it marked Grant's cinematic swan song.

Perhaps the most disappointing of the Olympic feature films was Twentieth Century Fox's *The Games*, released in 1970. It had all the elements for success, including a star-studded international cast (Michael Crawford, Stanley Baker, Ryan O'Neal, Jeremy Kemp, Charles Aznavour) and a screenwriter (Erich Segal) who had enjoyed enormous success with *Love Story*. The story line deals with four runners from different countries (Great Britain, United States, Czechoslovakia, and Australia) as they prepare for the 1960 Rome Olympics. The result was a cinematic disaster. An absence of character development, unreal acting performance (only Crawford looked as if he was a runner), and a weak plot doomed *The Games*.

If *The Games* marked the nadir of the Olympic feature film, *Goldengirl* (1979) fared nearly as badly. Nevertheless, *Goldengirl* deserves watching because its polemical thesis calls attention to the moral and ethical conflicts that are part of Olympic sport. Coaches need to be committed, and athletes must train ferociously to succeed. *Goldengirl* is the story of a female American runner who sets out to win triple sprint medals (in the 100-, 200-, and 400-meter races) at the 1980 Olympics. Susan Anton was miscast as a muscular athlete but James Coburn, Curt Jurgens, and Robert Culp are interestingly assembled as the Machiavellian troupe determined to win at all costs. It should be stressed that 20 years later, as the scale and severity of the institutionalized doping of Olympic athletes carried out in the former East Germany becomes public knowledge, films such as *Goldengirl* begin to assume the prophetic clout of *1984* or *2001: A Space Odyssey*.

One of the most controversial contemporary sport films was the 1982 Warner Brothers feature, *Personal Best*, a brave effort at setting out a lesbian relationship against a background of Olympic track-and-field athletics. Mariel Hemingway did look as if she could run quickly and sprint hard, and her relationship with Patrice Donnelly attempted to raise serious questions about issues of gender and sexuality in the competitive sport arena. Scott Glen as the hard driving coach strikes a familiar chord in Olympic studies. Just how far should coaches go in pushing athletes to become Olympic champions?

Lost among these titles is a delightful vignette film that too often has been seen as trite and superficial. *Wee Geordie* (released in Great Britain as *Geordie*) is a 99-minute British Lion/Times Film Corporation comedy. It tells the story of a gamekeeper's weak son in the Scottish Highlands who finds fame and a new physique by sending off for a mail-order physical culture program. Bill Travers, in the starring role, develops into a towering Celtic giant, specializes in the hammer throw, and represents Great Britain at the 1956 Melbourne Olympics. There is a love interest with another athlete at the games (remember that at the 1956 Games, Hal Connolly, the American hammer thrower, had a celebrated romance with an Eastern European athlete), but Travers comes home and lives happily ever after in his Scottish village. Positive points should be stressed. The film had no pretension; it set out only to popularize and caricature the quaintness of Scotland. The original novel by David Walker is a quintessential romance, but Walker had a fine eye for the nuances of athletic competition. Director Frank Launder used an actual Highland Games setting to give a sense of

Nigel Havers, Daniel Gerroll, Ian Charleson and Nick Farrell in the 1981 film *Chariots of Fire*. © 20th Century Fox/Allied Stars/Enigma/The Kobol Collection.

credibility and reality to a variety of athletic events featuring heaving and tossing. The film in style and tenor is reminiscent of the work of Sir Compton Mackenzie who, despite being English born, developed into an iconoclastic and rabid supporter of Scottish nationalism.

The greatest Olympic feature films is the Twentieth Century Fox release *Chariots of Fire* (1981). The story concerns the successes of an evangelical Protestant Scot, Eric Liddell, and an English Jew, Harold Abrahams, at the 1924 Paris Olympics. Abrahams won the 100-meter race, upsetting the favored Americans, and Liddell, normally a dash man, raced the 400 meters to take the gold medal. Critics speak of memorable track sequences, and researchers have a wonderful treasure trove for exploring a myriad of Olympic issues. Tom McNab, a distinguished British track-and-field coach and sport historian, was a consultant for the film, and his many contributions helped to elevate it to a work of generally accurate artistry. Winner of the Academy Award for Best Film in 1982, *Chariots of Fire* to a great extent recreated the flavor and substance of the Abrahams and Liddell lifestyles, the ethos of Cambridge, the aristocratic administration of British track and field, and the events of the 1924 Olympics. Although some critics bemoaned *Chariots of Fire*—Pauline Kael in the *New Yorker* thought the slow-motion running sequences artificial and staged—Roger Ebert considered *Chariots* a great film because it went beyond the story line to make important statements about human nature. Without doubt *Chariots of Fire* will continue to demand analysis and examination for many years to come.

Two years after *Chariots of Fire*, Buena Vista films released *Running Brave*, the story of Cree Indian Billy Mills who, in a magnificent final-lap dash, won the 10,000-meters gold medal at the 1964 Olympics. Despite a sincere and sympathetic portrayal of Mills by Robby Benson, the film saw limited runs and quickly was sold to video markets. This is a great pity because the film focuses on important issues about sport, minority groups, and the roles of both in American society. Once again a question needs to be raised by the selection of a Caucasian rather than a Native American actor in the star role. Hopefully, happily, the 2002 Oscar successes by African Americans Denzel Washington and Halle Berry will consolidate the future central place and position of minorities in film.

Billy Crudup portrays Steve Prefontaine in the 1998 drama *Without Limits*. © Warner Bros./The Kobol Collection/Chen, Linda R.

Much work needs to be done identifying and classifying Olympic feature films made outside the United States. Australia, a country justly acclaimed for movies such as *Gallipoli*, *Breaker Morant*, and *Picnic at Hanging Rock*, is also the country in which *Dawn* was produced. The fascinating story of swimmer Dawn Fraser, who won gold medals in the 100-meter freestyle at the 1956, 1960, and 1964 Olympics, sadly did not translate successfully into a film despite the selection of Bronwyn Mackay-Payne, an outstanding athlete, for the lead role. The South African film *My Way* (aka *The Winners*) appeared in 1974, with actor Joe Stewardson in the role of the 1948 Olympic marathon winner who becomes obsessed with victory. He marries and then subjects his children to draconian training philosophies. The film addresses the survival of humanitarian values in the face of an excessive commitment to sporting success. The 1977 German comedy *Ties to the Olympics* develops the scenario of a firm's winning the shoe contract for the West German Olympic team. It is intriguing to view, knowing that when the film was released, the German firms of Adidas and Puma dominated the world and Olympic market in sport shoes.

Olympic feature films have been around for a long time and have explored virtually every facet of human behavior. In 1925 the American Charles Paddock appeared in *Nine and Three-Fifths Seconds*. This sprinter, who had been upset by Harold Abrahams of Great Britain in the 1924 Olympic 100-meter final, appears as the hero who outruns a horse and chases a villain who had kidnapped his girlfriend. The 1977 Aragon movie *2076 Olympiad* was a science fiction feature that stretched the bounds of credulity even further. The year is 2076, and the Olympic Games are being televised by a cable network that specializes in erotica. Instead of athletic skills, the Games focus on sexual performance.

Other modern films with an Olympic flavor have been equally dismal. Olympian gymnast Kurt Thomas of the United States appeared in the 1985 martial arts movie *Gymkata*, and Dorian Harewood as Jesse Owens in the 1984 Paramount film *The Jesse Owens Story* looked wooden and dull. This film tried the old formula of using documentary footage of Owens racing in the 1930s.

The Olympic feature film, apart from the exceptional *Chariots of Fire*, does not emulate the many brilliant documentaries on the Olympics. Nevertheless, in the last decade there have been a handful of promising attempts at Olympic feature films and the best of them deserve repeat viewings and merit intelligent assessment. Some examples are *Breaking the Surface*, which tells the Greg Louganis story. While the intense focus on an overbearing father and an abusive lover makes for a bleak scenario, the issues of homosexuality and athletics, and the complexities involved in a HIV-positive athlete continuing a career in athletics, are Olympic topics that need to be addressed. Two contrasting 1996 films that also deserve a critical audience are *Rowing Through* and *Run for the Dream*. The former spotlights a male sculler at Harvard who trains obsessively for a place on the U.S. team at the 1980 Moscow Olympics. America's boycott at those Olympics means that the rower had to wait and train for four more years. As the 1984 Los Angeles Olympics approaches, the once unbeatable sculler finds himself pressed, and stressed, by younger rivals. *Run for the Dream* tells of the extraordinary success enjoyed by Gail Devers with her 1992 Barcelona Olympics gold medal in the 100 meters. She achieved this amazing performance despite the fact that 17 months earlier she suffered a debilitating thyroid condition known as Grave's Disease that very nearly crippled her. Alfre Woodward is well cast as Devers and supporting actors—Louis Gossett Jr. and Robert Guillaume—craft a drama which makes for compelling viewing untouched by either melodrama or sentimentality.

However, the best of this 1990s crop of Olympic films is one that has been largely ignored by critics and sport studies specialists alike. *Without Limits* (1998), a study of the Oregon track star Steve Prefontaine, showcases the Olympics as one act in a series of acts that make up the life and times of an athlete once called by the popular press as the "James Dean of track and field." Nevertheless, this act shines and sparkles and just may be the best ever single episode of a Hollywood Olympic film. The stage is the 1972 Munich Olympics, the event the 5,000 meters in which the short, cocky, arrogant, impetuous Prefontaine takes on the lanky, linear Flying Finn, Lasse Viren. Director Robert Towne has in actor Billy Crudup, a young man who could win any Prefontaine-look-alike contest. Towne's genius is that he faithfully recreates the seesaw battle—literally lap after lap—of the 5,000 meters and the accuracy, reliability, and credibility of this reenactment is a superior work of art and craft. When integrated with the authentic track-and-field jargon from screenwriters Towne and Kenny Moore (Moore was an Olympian who ran the 5,000 meters and later wrote track essays for *Sports Illustrated*), *Without Limits* emerges as a minor cinematic gem. Donald Sutherland as coach and mentor Bill Bowerman gives a finely wrought performance and the harrowing events of the 1972 Munich Olympics, with the deaths of the Israeli athletes, are inserted as stark reminders that despite the Games going on there was a sense of sadness and tragedy that had an impact on every performer at the 1972 Olympics.

The horror of the terrorist attacks of September 11, 2001, on the United States created, most understandably, a strong antipathy towards what were once popular action movies. That said, the 1972 Munich Olympic deaths are a testament to an Olympic arena not being divorced from an external world in which good and evil, confrontation and collegiality, vice and virtue are competing forces. Two Olympic films that consider terrorism and protest are *21 Hours at Munich* (1976) and *Blast* (1996). The first of these films reviews the 1972 Olympic massacre, and the gloomy narrative is buoyed up by the gravitas displayed by the actors, William Holden, Franco Nero, and Anthony Quayle. In *Blast*, the plot deals with terrorists taking spectators hostage at the 1996 Atlanta Olympics. Unfortunately, neither film is well made nor well acted, although Rutger Hauer, the villain in *Blast*, is constantly intimidating. *Sword of Gideon* (1986) describes an elite commando group that sets out to avenge the Munich Olympic killings. *Pentathlon* (1994) charts the story of a star East German athlete, played by Dolph Lundgren, who defects to the United States a year before the tearing down of the Berlin Wall. The specter of German police persecuting family members because of the defection is given a marked degree of contemporary resonance by the fact that recent investigations show the Stasi (the East German secret police) were key players in controlling vast sections of the national sport structure from the 1970s to the early 1990s.

Two other sport films with an Olympic focus have to do with winter sports. In *The Cutting Edge* (1992), a former hockey player tries to win Olympic glory as a figure skater in pairs competition. Robin Cousins, the 1980 gold medallist in figure skating, choreographed the skating sequences. The 1993 film *Cool Runnings*, a comedy starring John Candy, was based loosely on the experience of the Jamaican bobsled team at the 1988 Calgary Games.

Olympic feature films of the twenty-first century will, hopefully, continue the odyssey so promisingly initiated by *Chariots of Fire* and *Without Limits*. There are compelling screenplays just waiting to be fleshed out on such topics as the Ben Johnson saga, Florence Griffith Joyner's sensational successes, the phenomenon of male and female African distance runners, and the aura of chemical championing achieved by Irish and Dutch elite female swimmers. In short, the potential for Olympic feature films of the future is limitless.

BIBLIOGRAPHICAL ESSAY

An important source with which to begin the study of Olympic feature films is Harvey M. Zucker and Lawrence J. Babich, eds., *Sports Films: A Complete Reference* (Jefferson, NC, 1987). Judith A. Davidson and Daryl Adler, eds., *Sport on Film and Video* (Metuchen, NJ, 1993) does not include feature films. For analyses of *Chariots of Fire*, see the British Cultural Studies and Sport issue of *Sociology of Sport Journal* 9, 2 (June 1992). For an unusual source on British film, consult Peter Lovesey and Tom McNab, eds., *The Guide to British Track and Field Literature, 1275–1968* (London, 1969). It is a valuable Olympics source inasmuch as Lovesey wrote *Goldengirl* and McNab was a consultant in the making of *Chariots of Fire*. Roger Ebert, *The Movie Home Companion—1994* (Kansas City, MO, 1993), is typical of video guides prepared annually by movie critics, containing brief sketches of many hundreds of films. For a critique of *When We Were Kings* see the Carrington-Crawford tandem essay in *International Review for the Sociology of Sport* 33, 1 (March 1998): 75–81. For some historical speculations on *Chariots of Fire* see S. A. G. M. Crawford, "Another Type of Chariots of Fire," *Track and Field Quarterly Review*, vol. 92, no. 2 (summer 1989): 60–62.

OLYMPIC FEATURE FILMS

1925 *Nine and Three-Fifths Seconds* (United States). Director: Lloyd B. Carleton.
1928 *Olympic Hero* (United States). Director: R. William Neill.
1936 *One in a Million* (United States). Director: Sidney Lanfield.
1937 *Charlie Chan at the Olympics* (United States). Director: H. Bruce Humberstone.
1951 *Jim Thorpe—All American* (aka *Man of Bronze*) (United States). Director: Michael Curtiz.
1954 *The Bob Mathias Story* (United States). Director: Francis D. Lyon.
1955 *Wee Geordie* (Great Britain). Director: Frank Launder.
1962 *It Happened in Athens* (United States). Director: Andrew Marton.
1966 *Walk, Don't Run* (United States). Director: Charles Walkers.
1969 *Downhill Racer* (United States). Director: Michael Ritchie.
1970 *The Games* (United States). Director: Michael Winner.
1974 *My Way* (aka *The Winners*) (South Africa). Director: Joseph Brenner.
1975 *The Other Side of the Mountain* (United States). Director: Larry Peerce.
1976 *21 Hours at Munich* (United States). Made for Forbes Television.
1977 *2076 Olympiad* (United States). Director: James P. Martin.
1977 *The Greatest* (United States/Great Britain). Director: Tom Grier.
1977 *Ties to the Olympics* (West Germany). Director: Stefan Lukschy.
1977 *Wilma* (United States). Director: Bud Greenspan.
1979 *Dawn* (Australia). Director: Ken Hannam.
1979 *Goldengirl* (United States). Director: Joseph Sargent.
1979 *Ice Castles* (United States). Director: Donald Wrye.
1979 *Running* (United States). Director: Steven Hilliard Stern.
1980 *Olympiade 40* (Poland). Director: Andrzej Kotkowski.
1981 *Miracle on Ice* (United States). Director: Stephen Hilliard Stem.
1981 *Chariots of Fire* (Great Britain). Director: Hugh Hudson.
1982 *Personal Best* (United States). Director: Robert Towne.
1983 *Running Brave* (United States). Director: D. S. Everett.
1984 *The First Olympics: Athens 1896* (United States). Director: Alvin Rakoff.
1984 *The Jesse Owens Story* (United States). Director: Richard Irving.
1985 *Going for the Gold: The Bill Johnson Story* (United States). Director: Don Taylor.
1986 *American Anthem* (United States). Director: Albert Magnoli.
1986 *Sword of Gideon* (United States). Director: Michael Anderson Sr.
1988 *Blades of Courage* (United States). Director: Randy Bradshaw.
1992 *The Cutting Edge* (United States). Director: Paul Michael Glaser.
1993 *Cool Runnings* (United States). Director: Jon Turteltaub.
1994 *Pentathlon* (United States). Director: Bruce Malmuth.
1996 *Breaking the Surface* (United States). Director: Steven Hilliard Stem.
1996 *Blast* (United States). Director: Albert Pyun.
1996 *Run for the Dream* (United States). Director: Neema Barnette.
1996 *Rowing Through* (United States). Director: Masato Harada.
1996 *Prefontaine* (United States). Director: Steven James.
1998 *Without Limits* (United States). Director: Robert Towne.
2000 *The Loretta Claiborne Story* (United States). Director: Lee Grant.

APPENDIX E: INTERNET SOURCES ON OLYMPISM AND THE OLYMPIC GAMES

Richard Cox

INTRODUCTION

Recent years have witnessed a revolution in the world of information with the development of the Internet and more specifically the World Wide Web (WWW). Without going into the finer details of what the Internet is, does, and can potentially do, it is worth noting two main facilities for the sharing and delivery of information via the Internet. These are electronic discussion groups, which provide a forum for debate and the exchange of ideas and information, and the WWW for its collection and display of information. Examples of listservs devoted to the subject of the Olympic Games and Olympism are *SportHist* (http://www.umist.ac.uk/ sport/ishpes.html), devoted mainly to the academic discussion of sport, including the Olympic Games, and Sport-Culture-Society (sport-culture-society at http:// www.jiscmail.ac.uk/), which is more concerned with sociopolitical aspects of sport from a sociological point of view. A useful source for identifying listservs is http://www.jiscmail.ac.uk/.

Via the WWW, many sources of information once only locally accessible can now be accessed from almost anywhere in the world provided one has connectivity to the worldwide network, be it via cable or satellite from a desktop computer, handheld personal organizer, or mobile telephone. (For further information on this, see R. W. Cox, *Sport and the Internet* [Frodsham, UK: Sports History Publishing, 1995]; R. W. Cox and M. Salter, "The IT Revolution and the Practice of Sport History: An Overview and Reflection on Internet Research and Teaching Resources," *Journal of Sport History* 25, 2 [summer 1998]: 283–302.) The ease with which information can now be published on the WWW has provided the spur for many institutions and individuals to post information for worldwide public consumption, information that sometimes would not have reached more than a select few. The problem with this phenomenon is that there is now a wealth of information that is variable in quality and content and for the newcomer, this can be confusing, misleading, and even daunting. In this essay, the key objective has been to illustrate the broad range of information that is available and to identify the more useful information sources within these spheres. Not all Web sites are accessible without first registering; some require the payment of a fee.

WORLD WIDE WEB

Searching the WWW

The WWW hosts millions of separate sites and is growing rapidly. Anyone with access to a server can post information and many do. This ranges from individuals representing official organizations and posting official documents to hobbyists posting information of their own choosing, sometimes generated by themselves, occasionally without any real academic credibility. At worst these sites can be misleading. Discovering resources on the WWW can be difficult although many search engines now exist to assist in the process. Each has its own methods for searching, identifying, and informing. Some have a particular bias and are better at identifying information in some areas than others based on location, language, timeliness (some go back further back in time than others, for example), or scholarship. Among the better known and more popular ones are Jeeves and Google, although many other useful ones exist. A helpful listing, indicating the specific strengths of each one of the search engines and direct links can be seen at http://www.hero.ac.uk/reference_resources/internet_search_facilities473.cfm.

A simple search using the term Olympi* found 1.5 million sites through Google. Obviously this included many sites using the word Olympic, irrespective of whether it had anything to do with sport (such as Olympic Dry Cleaning) or the Games themselves, so searches need to be as specific as possible using Boolean operators such as "and," as well as wild cards. Many of the individual Web sites have their own search facilities that help locate very specific items.

Gateways and Portals

Often more helpful to the academic researcher are subject portals, hubs, and gateways. In slightly different ways, these attempt to list useful links on a particular subject or provide their own searchable database of resources.

SPORTQuest is an online search engine and directory of sport and fitness-related Web sites (http://www.sportquest.com/index.html). It is produced by SIRC, whose bibliographic database is described separately below. A search on Olympics revealed the following topics with the number of links in parantheses.

Administration (1)	Associations—International (2)
Associations—National (25)	Biography (8)
Ceremonies (1)	Collecting (1)
Countries and Regions (7)	Directory (2)
Documentation (4)	Facility (1)
FAQs (1)	General (24)
Hall of Fame and Museum (1)	History (11)
News (25)	Newsgroups/Listservs—Directories (1)
Sponsorship (2)	Statistics (3)
Statistics—Results (2)	Training (1)
Visitor Information (3)	Women (3)

Altis, at http://www.altis.ac.uk, is a portal for Internet sources on sport and leisure designed for the academic community in Great Britain but accessible universally free of charge. It is part of the Resource Discovery Network (http://www.jisc.ac.uk/) funded by JISC (Joint Information Systems Committee), whose purpose is to provide ready access to quality sites for staff and students working within the higher education community in the United Kingdom. This is a new service and as of August 2003, it had identified only about 100 Olympic sites. Another useful listing of sport Web sites is maintained by Gretchen Ghent at the University of Calgary. *Scholarly Sport Sites* can be found at: http://www.ucalgary.ca/library/ssportsite/.

There are no major portals aimed specifically at the Olympics so far, but there are a number of gateways ranging from reading lists provided by instructors for students on their courses, through librarians pointing out Olympic contents to their users, to sites developed by universities with Olympic Studies Centers. Examples include the following:

Olympic Games Links—http://www.sirlinksalot.net/olympics.html

Olympic Links—http://www.palmdps.act.edu.au/olympic/olympic.htm

Olympics Virtual Library—http://www.library.unisa.edu.au/vl/olympic/olymwelc.htm

The Olympic Documentation Highway—http://www.efdeportes.com/efd10/moragi1.htm

It is important to note the purpose, range, and currency of each of these sites in order to make an accurate assessment of their value in relation to one's needs.

BIBLIOGRAPHIC DATABASES

SIRC

SPORTDiscus is produced by the Sport Information Resource Centre, Ottawa (http://www.sirc.ca/) and claims to be the world's leading sport, fitness, and sports medicine bibliographic database. For more than 30 years, SIRC has been providing access to full-text and bibliographic references in such areas as sport medicine, physical education, coaching and training, arts and history, corporate wellness, engineering, and health and safety. It currently boasts over 600,000 qualified references from thousands of international periodicals, books, e-journals, conference proceedings, theses, dissertations, and Web sites, and it has direct links, where they exist, to full-text articles. Inside *SPORTDiscus* the researcher will find many references to the Olympic Games, the Olympic Movement, and Olympism. In many cases, it can provide ready access to the full article through SIRCExpress, a document delivery service. Other *SPORTDiscus* services include SIRCRetriever, which searches through thousands of article references added to *SPORTDiscus* each month. The user establishes a subject-specific profile and customized results are sent monthly directly to the user's email address. These services are now accessible via the WWW but require an account with the company before access is granted.

The Olympic Games: A Bibliography, compiled by A. J. Veal and K. Toohey, which can be accessed through the National Library of Australia (http://pandora.nla.gov.au/pan/), is a web-based bibliography containing some 1,400 entries, which is periodically updated. It is not meant to be comprehensive, but it is arranged in alphabetical order by author, with a separate section at the end listing official Games reports. The original version of the bibliography, with some 600 entries, was published in a printed format in 1995.

For specific publications of a historical nature on Olympism, the Olympic Movement, and the Olympic Games, Richard W. Cox compiles an annual bibliography that is currently published by Frank Cass (the first edition was *International Sport 2000*, published in 2001). This bibliography is also published as a supplement to the *International Journal of the History of Sport* (http://www.frankcass.com/jnls/ihs.htm). Prior to 2000 the annual listing was published in *Sport in History*, accessible free of charge via the British Society of Sports History Web site at http://www.umist.ac.uk/sport/bsshsh2.html.

Facts, Statistics, and Results

The quantifiable nature of sport has always attracted the interest of fact-gatherers and statisticians. Although many sites include information that might be reasonably included under this heading, researchers specifically interested in facts and figures on the Olympic Games might find the information they need more readily at http://www.factmonster.com/ipka/A0114094.html. Sponsored by the Family Education Network, this site provides considerable information on the Olympic Games, as well as special features on various aspects of the Games, including the beginnings of the modern Olympics and the latest IOC reforms. Within each article there are links to additional information. There is also information about previous Games from 1896 on, including medal winners and results. It is possible to search by country, sport, or event. There are links throughout the resource to additional information and also some quizzes and crossword puzzles for light relief.

Groups of enthusiasts have produced more specialized lists such as the United Kingdom Track and Field All-Time Lists. This provides a complete list of medalists in all sports at both Summer and Winter Olympic Games. Their Web site can be found at http://www.gbrathletics.com/olympic/. Other reference Web sites of a more general nature include *Hickok's Sports Encyclopedia* (http://www.hickoksports.com/history/olympix.shtml) and *Encyclopedia Britannica* (http://www.britannica.com/).

Quizzes

The popularity of sport quizzes has resulted in a number of sites devoted to questions and answers, an example being *Olympic Almanac* (http://www98.pair.com/msmonaco/Almanac/). Many others of the sites mentioned below, especially the educational ones, also have tests and quizzes to assist learning and test knowledge.

INDIVIDUAL WEB SITES

Web Sites of Official Olympic Bodies

A—International

The most important of these Web sites is the official site of the International Olympic Committee (IOC) (http://www.olympic.org/uk/index_uk.asp). This site, with English and French language options, contains profiles of athletes and sports, past and present, and details of the Games held since 1896, searchable by date or location. There is a multimedia gallery, which requires the use of a Windows Media Player or RealPlayer for access to audio and video files. The site contains information about the organization of the IOC and the Olympic Movement, as well as documents, including the Olympic Charter and current Olympic records. The news section includes issues of the IOC journal, *Olympic Review*, from February 2001 onwards; earlier issues are available via the Web site of the Amateur Athletic Foundation of Los Angeles (AAFLA), described separately below. The art and culture section contains links to the Olympic Museum at Lausanne.

Paralympics

The official Web site of the International Paralympic Committee, the international organization of elite sports for athletes with disabilities, is at http://www. paralympic.org/. It organizes, supervises, and coordinates the Paralympic Games and other multidisability competitions at elite sport levels. The site contains the International Paralympic Committee Handbook, a current affairs section, the anti-doping code, an events calendar, a media section, useful links, and the free quarterly newsletter, *The Paralympian*, available either online or in printed form. There is information on the Paralympic Games, past and present, and on individual sports, featuring rules, classifications, results, and records.

Special Olympics

The Web site address of the Special Olympics, the organization responsible for the worldwide organization of training and athletic competition for people with mental retardation, is at http://www.specialolympics.org/. This includes details of forthcoming events, results of past events, coaching, and volunteer programs.

Deaf Olympics

The Web site for Deaflympics, the major Olympic-equivalent event for the deaf, is at http://www.deaflympics.com/. The site contains information about the Games and details of past and future Deaflympics.

B—National

Nearly all national Olympic committees (NOCs), such as the United States Olympic Committee (USOC) (http://www.usolympicteam.com/) have a Web site that aims specifically at their own involvement in the Games. These vary in quality and the amount of information they include. Some are designed to attract sponsorship and media interest, others to inform athletes, and still others to do both. The British Olympic Association site (http://www.boa.org.uk/) provides historical and current information about the Olympic Movement. There are separate sections covering the various Olympic sports and details of both the Summer and Winter Games. Below is a listing of selected official committees that have sites.

- Australia: Australian Olympic Committee (AOC)
- Austria: Osterreichisches Olympisches Comite/Austrian Olympic Committee
- Belgium: Belgian Olympic and Interfederal Committee (in English, French, and Dutch languages)
- Bermuda: The Bermuda Olympic Association
- Canada: Canadian Olympic Association (COA)

- Croatia: Hrvatski Olimpijski Odbor/Croatian Olympic Committee (COC)
- Cyprus: Cyprus National Olympic Committee (CNOC)
- Denmark: Danmarks Idraets-Forbund/Danish Olympic Committee
- Estonia: Estonian Olympic Committee (EOC)
- Finland: Suomen Olympiakomitean verkkosivut
- Italy: Comitato Olimpico Nazionale Italiano (CONI)
- Japan: Japanese Olympic Committee (JOC)
- Kenya: National Olympic Committee of Kenya
- Lithuania: National Olympic Committee of Lithuania (NOCL)
- New Zealand: New Zealand Olympic Committee
- Norway: Norwegian Olympic Committee (NOC)
- Slovakia: Slovensky Olympijsky Vybor/Slovak Olympic Committee (SOC)
- Slovenia: Olimpijski Komite Slovenije/Olympic Committee of Slovenia (OCS)
- Spain: Comite Olimpico Espanol
- Switzerland: Swiss Sports Server (in German, English, French, and Italian languages)
- Ukraine: Olympic Committee of Ukraine

A useful index to national organizations is maintained at http://www.olympic. org/uk/organisation/noc/index_uk.asp. More specifically devoted to European nations is the Web site of the European Olympic Committees (http://www.euroly mpic.org/index.html).

Some countries have Web sites devoted to specific centers, such as the U.S. Olympic Training Center in Colorado (http://www.olympic-usa.org/about_ us/visitor_ctr.html) or an institution's involvement in the Olympic Games; see, for example, the University of Michigan (http://www.umich.edu/~bhl/bhl/olymp2/ oltitle.htm) or Pennsylvania State University Olympians (http://www.psu.edu/sports/ olympics/family.html).

Similarly, the national organizations involved with special Olympic festivals also frequently have Web sites, such as the one for the UK (http://www.para lympics.org.uk/).

C—Games Sites

Sites both past and present, for both Winter and Summer Games can be identified at http://www.princeton.edu/%7Ewpfau/olympics/olympics.html. A selection of these, including sites for future games (confirmed and potential), is listed below. This includes sites devoted to specific aspects of the Games such as conservation or economic impact. Another useful site that has links to Salt Lake City and future Games sites, as well as to various historical and sport-specific sites, is www. sirlinksalot.net.

2000

Sydney—Much information on all aspects of the Sydney Games may be accessed through www.gamesinfo.com.au, which contains archived sites from the Games. A site prepared by PriceWaterhouseCoopers for the New South Wales Department of State and Regional Development, this report documents the business and economic benefits of the Sydney Olympics 2000. The site gives a brief summary of the paper, but the whole report is available for download, free of charge, with Adobe Acrobat Reader. It may be accessed at www.games info.com.au/pi/ARPICOE.html.

2002

Salt Lake City—www.saltlake2002.com, is the official site of the Salt Lake City 2002 Winter Olympics.

2004

Athens—http://www.athens2004.com is the official Web site of the 2004 Summer Olympic Games.

2006

Torino—http://www.torino2006.org is the official Web site of the 2006 Winter Olympic Games.

2008

Beijing—http://www.beijing-2008.org is the official Web site of the 2008 Summer Olympic Games.

2010

Vancouver—http://www.winter2010.com/ and http://www.mcaws.gov.bc.ca/2010/index.htm, prepared in January 2002 by the Ministry of Competition, Science and Enterprise, Province of British Columbia, this report analyzes the economic impact of winning the 2010 Olympic bid. The Web site provides the entire report in both HTML and PDF formats and is available free of charge. There are also links to news items, report updates, and 2010 Olympic bid information.

2012: Bid City Sites

Leipzig—http://www.leipzig2012.de/

London—http://www.parliament.the-stationery-office.co.uk/pa/cm200203/cmselect/cmcumeds/268/26802.htm. Rather than a promotional site, the Web site deals with an inquiry into the UK government's decision-making process about whether to support a London bid for the 2012 Olympic Games. The report contains some useful income and expenditure figures related to the staging of the Olympic Games. It also includes, as an annex, a summary of a public opinion poll on the merits of the 2012 bid. There are many other sites complementing this one ranging from the host city's site (by the Greater London Council), to the sites of the major political parties' reactions to the British Olympic Association and other support groups.

New York City—http://www.nyc2012.com/

Sport Organizations

Several international and national sport organizations have sections on their Web sites devoted to the involvement of their sport in the Olympic Games. Examples include the International Badminton Federation (http://www.intbadfed.org/)

and the International Tennis Federation site of Olympic Tennis (http://www. tennisgold.com/). These include a selection of news items, results, and photographs.

Research Centers, Organizations, and Learned Societies

Among the most notable centers of academic research with Web sites are the Centre for Olympic Studies, University of New South Wales, Australia (http://www.arts.unsw.edu.au/olympic/); the Centre for Olympic Studies, University of Western Ontario (http://www.uwo.ca/olympic/); and the Centre of Olympic and Sports Studies, Universitario Autonoma, Barcelona (http://blues.uab.es/ olympic.studies).

The University of Western Ontario Centre produces a scholarly journal, *Olympika*, and also publishes the proceedings of its biennial *Olympic Research Symposium*. Details of the contents can be seen on its Web site and back copies of full-text articles at the AAFLA Web site (http://www.aafla.org/). The Barcelona Centre Web site includes *The Olympic Games Directory*, a database containing detailed information on the academic activities relating to the Olympics and the scholars undertaking such research (http://olympicstudies.uab.es/main.asp).

Among academic organizations not tied to specific institutions is the International Society of Olympic Historians (http://www.olykamp.org/isoh/). It produces the *Journal of Olympic History*, which also has a Web site detailing its contents. Full-text articles are available at the AAFLA Web site. *Olympic Review*, published quarterly by the International Olympic Committee, along with more general sport history journals such as the *Journal of Sports History* and *The Sports Historian*, can also be found in digitized form on the AAFLA Web site.

A general listing of sport historians is maintained by the North American Society for Sport History (NASSH), which has a Web site at http://www.nassh.org/. There is a link to their scholars' list that indicates the specific research and teaching interests of those included, many of whom have a keen interest in Olympism, the Olympic Movement, and/or the Olympic Games.

Museums and Halls of Fame

There are several museums of Olympism, the most famous being the IOC Olympic Museum in Lausanne (http://www.olympic.org/uk/passion/museum/ home_uk.asp).

This Web site provides an insight into the activities of the museum, its collections, current displays, and special exhibitions. There are also many other museums and sport halls of fame with specialized collections and/or exhibitions devoted to the Olympic Movement. The Powerhouse Museum in Sydney, for example, in association with the Ministry for Hellenic Culture in Athens mounted a special exhibition of the Ancient Olympic Games (http://www.phm.gov.au/ancient_greek_olympics/) to coincide with the 2000 Olympic Games. Although the exhibition is no longer on view at the museum, a Web site devoted to the exhibition enables visitors to see what the exhibition was like and access the learning materials. This is a very entertaining and informative multimedia production. Another such site is at http://sunsite. anu.edu.au/mirrors/olympics/.

Web Sites of Library Collections

Again, the most well known library devoted to Olympism is that of the IOC Study Centre in Lausanne, which houses a considerable collection and has a Web site at http://www.olympic.org/uk/passion/studies/index_uk.asp. This site outlines the services it offers, details of access, and the collections it holds. Close on its heels in terms of both size and profile is the library of the Paul Ziffren Sports Resources Center at the Amateur Athletic Federation of Los Angeles. Its library catalogs can be accessed via the WWW at http://www.aafla.com/4sl/over_frmst.htm.

In the year 2000, the Library of Congress developed an excellent Web site (http://www.lcweb.loc.gov/rr/main/olympics/). It included the following headings:

- Catalogs
- Indexes and Abstracts
- Directories
- CD-ROMs
- Official Reports
- Dissertations
- Newspapers
- Prints and Photographs; Maps; Main Reading Room Vertical File
- Selected Images from the Library of Congress Collections
- General Bibliography
- Olympic Rules
- History and Politics
- Biographical Directories and Results
- Hosting the Games—Administrative Issues

Archives of Primary Source Material

With respect to primary source material, the IOC has a large archive at its Lausanne headquarters (http://www.olympic.org/uk/passion/museum/home_uk.asp). It is a treasure trove for researchers on many sport-related subjects. The archives house 450 linear meters of documents dating back to 1894, including correspondence of IOC presidents and members, IOC correspondence with NOCs and international sport federations, administrative correspondence, reports of sessions and executive board meetings, documents on the organization of the Summer and Winter Games, and material relating to host-city candidates. A 30-year rule applies to most documents; a 50-year rule applies to personal files. Most of the administrative records are in English or French (or both). Most national Olympic associations maintain their own archives. For an overview of the archives see Cristina Bianchi, "Memoria Olympica: Apercu des archives historique du Comite International Olympique," *Memoire vive* 8 (1999): 101–16.

An important manuscript collection is the Avery Brundage Collection, housed at the University of Illinois, Champaign. The Brundage Collection contains files on all aspects of the Olympic Games, including details of delicate negotiations through some very turbulent and difficult times between 1936 and 1972, when Brundage was involved in the Olympic Movement. Former archivist Maynard Brichford has described the collection in *Avery Brundage Collection, 1908–1975* (Schorndoff, Germany: Hofmann, 1977) also available on microfilm at the AAFLA library and other study centers. Manuscripts relating to the Olympic Games exist in many other general collections and may be identified via the online catalogs accessible over the WWW. Documents relating to Britain's involvement with the Olympic Games Movement can be found in Cabinet papers, records of the Home Office (regarding public order at the 1908 and 1948 Olympic Games), and the records of the Foreign Office (regarding diplomatic issues). See http://www.pro.gov.uk/.

An interesting oral history project in Great Britain is the creation of a sound archive of memoirs of all surviving British Olympians (see http://www.umist.ac.uk/sport/) and several Web sites contain oral recordings (e.g. http://www.olympicwomen.co.uk/).

The Olympic Games have always attracted considerable media interest and a helpful resource for the scholar of this subject will find the Web site of the Olympic Television Archive Bureau (OTAB) (http://www.otab.com/) helpful.

More specific sources, such as films on the Olympic Games, are listed at http://www.runningmovies.com/olympic.htm.

Media

The Olympic Games have flourished as a result of media interest in the events, and many media companies have used the Olympics to promote themselves and sell their sponsors' wares, so it is no surprise to find that many major newspapers and broadcasting organizations have Web sites with specific sections devoted to the Olympic Games. Perhaps two of the best known ones are CBS Olympic Sports (http://cbs.sportsline.com/u/olympics/) and the BBC (http://news.bbc.co.uk/sport1/hi/other_sports/3068323.stm).

There are also Web sites that have collated newspaper reports relevant to events or organizations (e.g. the Web site of the U.S. Olympic Committee at http://www.usolympicteam.com/) and there are newspaper organizations themselves that have created Web sites specifically documenting their own coverage of particular Games. An example is the *Times* (London) and *Sunday Times* (http://www.times-olympics.co.uk/). This site has copies of all the reports published by the two newspapers on the Sydney Olympics, providing an invaluable resource for the researcher of media reporting.

The WWW has now been around since the mid-1990s and is itself becoming an important primary source for researchers. The National Library of Australia has archived a number of Web sites relating to the Sydney 2000 Games. This includes the official site which was archived at various stages of its existence and provides access to complete results of the Games. A number of other sites related to the Games have also been archived including the torch relay site and sites about other aspects of the Games including transport, tourism, and government involvement.

Criticisms and Scandals

Not all the world is enamored by the Olympic Games and there are Web sites attacking the movement. Examples include *The Great Olympic Swindle* (http://www.ajennings.8m.com/) and criticism of the Salt Lake City Games (http://greennature.com/article837.html). Indeed no Olympic Games appear to have escaped some form of irregularity, and one can find many news stories on the Web pages of the various news agencies and newspapers as they break into the public domain. A useful listing of current news stories can be found on the Olympic Games links site mentioned above (http://www.sirlinksalot.net/ olympics.html).

Education, Teaching, and Learning

The idea of Olympism as a way of achieving world peace and harmony is one that many have sought to teach and promote. The International Olympic Truce Foundation was set up for this purpose and has a stimulating multimedia Web site at http://www.olympictruce.org/. The International Olympic Academy, which is affiliated with the IOC, hosts a biennial congress in Olympia. Delegates from around the world attend and present papers on all aspects of the Olympic Movement. The academy's recent proceedings can be consulted on the WWW at http://www.ioa.leeds.ac.uk/. In addition, there is an association of past participants (International Olympic Academy Participants Association) who exchange information and ideas and who have a Web site at http://www.ioapa.org/.

There are other centers and organizations devoted to the teaching of Olympism with Web sites. See, for example, the Institute for Olympic Education at the University of Alberta (http://www.olympiceducation.org/) and the Foundation for Sport and Olympic Education (http://virtuals.compulink.gr/fose/index_en.htm).

There are several Web sites devoted to teaching what the Olympic Games are about, how they came into being, and how they have changed. The story and timeline of Olympics told through historical photographs and presentations about athletes and key Olympic moments is at http://www.musarium.com/kodak/ olympics/ olympichistory/.

Specifically devoted to the ancient Olympic Games are the following sites: Dartmouth College's Ancient Olympic Games Virtual Museum (http://minbar. cs.dartmouth.edu/greecom/dympics/); Tufts University's *Ancient Olympics* (http:// www.perseus.tufts.edu/Olympics/); the University of Pennsylvania Museum of Archaeology and Anthropology's *The Real Story of the Ancient Olympic Games* (http://www.museum.upenn.edu/new/research/Exp_Rese_Disc/Mediterranean/Ol ympics/olympicintro.shtml); the Hellenic Ministry of Culture's *The Olympic Games* (http://www.culture.gr/2/21/211/21107a/og/games.html); and *The Olympic Games of Ancient Greece* (http://education.nmsu.edu/webquest/wq/olympics/olympicwq. html).

Other Web sites are concerned with more specialized topics such as the involvement of women in the Games (http://www.olympicwomen.co.uk/). This site includes the recorded memories of some of the world's oldest women Olympians as well as a brief history of women in the Olympic Games and a range of useful statistics. Another notable site concerned with women's issues is at http://www. feminist.org/archive/olympics/intro.html. Part of the Feminist Majority Web site, this section commemorates 96 years of women's participation in the Olympics, including profiles of athletes, facts about women in the Olympics, and an interview with a feminist Olympics expert.

Environmental issues have been important in several recent bid processes; examples of Web sites devoted to this theme can be found at http://www.oca. nsw.gov.au/html/conservationresources.stm.

Some sites use Olympism as a popular theme to teach other subjects such as mathematics. For a good example of this see http://www.ex.ac.uk/cimt/data/olympics/olymindx.htm.

Collectors and Memorabilia

Popular interest in the Olympic Games spawned a whole industry of merchandising displaying Olympic Games logos, mascots, pins, posters, and much more. Many of these have become collectors' items

The IOC established the Olympic Collectors Commission in 1992. It embraces the International Federations of Olympic Philately (FIPO), Olympic Numismatics (FINO), and Olympic memorabilia collectors. Its Web site (http://www. collectors. olympic.org/) aims to bring Olympic collectors together, encourage the exchange of ideas, communicate the results of historical research, and, above all, to facilitate the trading and selling of Olympic collectibles. Via this Web site collectors can keep abreast of events such as fairs, discover historical information, and identify Web sites of individual clubs and federations. The Society of Olympic Collectors has its own Web site at http://www.societyofolympiccollectors.org/, and there is a specific site devoted to Olympic pin collectors (http://home.earthlink. net/~zola/ pin.html).

Details of Olympic logos can be seen at http://www.aldaver.com/. Examples of traders specializing in Olympic memorabilia include Harvey Abrams (http://www.harveyabramsbooks.com/). Details of Olympic collectors auctions can be viewed at http://www.coubertin.com/ and reports on fairs, such as the International Olympic Collectors Fair in South Korea in 2001, are available at http://www.collectors.olympic.org/e/fino/fino_foire_collect_intro_e.html. Current prices of memorabilia such as Olympic coins are available at http://www.24carat.co.uk/olympicgames.html or at http://www.ebay.com/.

Last, but of course by no means least, is a Web site for Olympians themselves. The World Olympians Association Web site can be found at http://www.woa.org/.

Other Electronic Sources

Finally, it is worth noting that there are also other electronic formats used to publish material on the Olympic Games. The first official report to be issued on CD-ROM simultaneously with a print edition was that of the Lillehammer Winter Games in 1994. The CD-ROM includes some visual footage from the competition.

In 1996, the Amateur Athletic Association of Los Angeles produced a CDE, *Women and the Olympics*, which traces the historical involvement of women in the Olympic Games and includes much photographic material. Most of the bid organizations since the mid-1990s have produced CD-ROMs, and there are also CD-ROMs covering specific sports in the Olympic Games as well as related topics such as the architectural plans of Olympic buildings.

The IOC library has produced a list of nearly 100 of these CD-ROMs at http://multimedia.olympic.org/pdf/en_report_124.pdf.

Many of the indexes and bibliographies mentioned above are also available on CD-ROM as well as online. CD-ROMs have the advantage of being easily transferable and transportable if network connection to the WWW does not exist or is slow or frequently interrupted. However, this technology has now been superseded by DVD and is not developing at a rate commensurate with Web technology. What is more, Web sites can be constantly updated as new information comes to light, mistakes are corrected, and new links are established.

IMPORTANT NOTE

Not all Web sites exist in perpetuity. Even if the address remains the same, the content might not. Some of the sites identified above may have changed even by the time this chapter goes to press, but, if they are well managed, an automatic link or referral address will be included. Long URLs quoted above are sometimes the addresses of Web pages generated by the database sitting behind the Web site and may not be directly loadable. In such instances the user is advised to shorten the address to a more generic form and use the links to get the site to generate the appropriate pages. An example would be finding the URL for the library of the Olympic Studies Centre at the IOC. One cannot access it directly by entering the address http://www.olympic.org/uk/passion/studies/index_uk.asp in one's Web browser. Entering this address will direct one's browser to the generic page for the IOC Olympic Studies Centre from where one will see a link to the library, which one will then need to click on.

GENERAL
BIBLIOGRAPHY

This general bibliography describes major archival collections with Olympic-related holdings as well as books and articles that deal with more than one Olympics or that are topical in nature. While we have tried to be as comprehensive as possible, space does not permit the listing of every one of the hundreds of books and articles that have been published on the Olympics, and we urge readers to pursue the published bibliographical guides noted below, as well as the many fine bibliographies included in the better books and articles on various aspects of the Games. Many other titles can be found by searching online at the various Web sites hosted by Olympic studies centers or sport information and documentation projects.

PUBLISHED BIBLIOGRAPHICAL GUIDES

Richard Mandell, a historian who has written much on the Olympic Movement, published the first important article dealing with the availability of research materials for the study of the Olympics, "The Modern Olympic Games: A Bibliographical Essay," *Sportwissenschaft* 6, 1 (1976): 89–98. This article sets out the state of Olympic study in 1976, noting that most of the available material is in German, and identifying two extensive bibliographies, both in German: Karl Lennartz, *Bibliographie: Geschichte der Leibesubungen* (Cologne, 1971), which lists only German-language works, and the 43-page bibliography in H. Lenk, *Werte, Ziele, Wirklichkeit der modernen Olympischen Spiele* (Stuttgart, Germany, 1964; expanded ed., 1972). Although Mandell is quite critical of Lenk's bibliography (and much else about the state of Olympic Games history), he does lay out the problem as a challenge to future researchers.

Bill Mallon remedied the lack of a thorough bibliographical guide in English in *The Olympics: A Bibliography* (New York, 1984). This very useful work lists all of the Games organizing committee official reports and other publications, IOC and national Olympic committee publications, and hundreds of other publications in over 30 different languages. Sections on theses and dissertations and on Olympic films are also included. Unfortunately, the citations are not annotated, so researchers have no clear idea of the content or quality of any book, but the citations are complete, allowing one to request a title on interlibrary loan or through other library services. Mallon's book is now more than 20 years old as well, and for more recent titles, researchers must rely on computerized databases or CD-ROM publications dealing with sports.

To learn about libraries and archives with extensive Olympics holdings, a useful place to start is with the *World Directory of Sport Libraries, Information, and Documentation Centres* (Belconnen, Australia, 1994). The information in this book was supplied by the libraries themselves and compiled by the National Sport Information Centre, a part of the Australian Sport Commission, for the International Association for Sport Information (IASI), a group that promotes access to sport information resources around the world. The *World Directory* lists just over 100 libraries, not all of which, of course, have relevant Olympic materials. Unfortunately, the *World Directory* has not been updated since 1994, but the IASI maintains a Web site titled *World Directory of Sports Information Centres and Experts*. It can be found at http://www.directory-iasi.org/.

ARCHIVES WITH SIGNIFICANT OLYMPIC HOLDINGS

The International Olympic Committee (IOC) library and archives is the most logical place to begin. The archives, which contain material dating back to the founding of the modern Olympic Movement and the IOC in the 1890s, is located at the IOC headquarters in Lausanne, Switzerland. Much of the material deals with the operations of the IOC itself over the years, and the collection is arranged topically, with sections devoted to the various Olympic Games and their organizing committees, international sport federations, national Olympic committees (NOC), IOC presidents and members, non-Olympic sport organizations, other international organizations, and non-IOC individuals. Correspondence is embargoed for 50 years and IOC minutes for 10 years, although waivers may be granted to researchers who fill out an application and have a genuine need for access to these records. In general, researchers should notify the IOC well in advance of their planned visit and provide a letter of recommendation from their NOC or university. The director of the Olympic Study Centre is Fernando Riba and the archivist is Cristina Bianchi; they may be contacted at the Olympic Research and Studies Centre, International Olympic Committee, Quai d'Ouchy 1, 1001 Lausanne, Switzerland.

The IOC also maintains an important library and museum at its Lausanne headquarters. The library, open to museum visitors, contains 18,000 volumes and 250 current periodicals, nearly all of which relate in some fashion to the Olympic Movement. Items in the collection are accessible through a computerized catalog, and the classification system is logical and easy to learn. The museum, which reopened in new quarters in June 1993, contains extensive exhibits on both Summer and Winter Games, interactive exhibits on a variety of topics from notable Olympians to training tips, and Olympic art. A separate room in the museum accommodates several temporary exhibits each year. The IOC's Web address is http://www.olympic.org/.

The International Olympic Academy in Olympia, Greece, operates seminars for Olympic scholars and students annually, and it maintains a collection of more than 15,000 books, 250 journals, as well as video and photographic resources. Its Web site is http://www.ioa.org.gr/.

The U.S. Olympic Committee (USOC), located in Colorado Springs, Colorado, also maintains archives of more limited use to researchers. The USOC archives is an unaccessioned and unclassified collection of materials that document the history and activities of the USOC. While there are no finding aids available at this time, known strengths of the collection include minutes of the executive committee dating back to 1919; final reports issued by the organizing committees of most of the Games; periodical publications of the USOC and IOC, such as newsletters; and U.S. Olympic Academy and International Olympic Academy proceedings. In addition, the archives contain the following materials, but it is not known whether a full set is available, or which issues are missing: USOC team media guides; USOC constitutions; Olympic Festival programs and media guides; miscellaneous Olympic Trials programs and results; and miscellaneous booklets, pamphlets, and brochures on each of the Games. Also included are the collections of Herb Weinberg, radio announcer and historian, and Harold Friermood, Olympic committee and volleyball association member.

Qualified researchers may use the archives upon approval of a completed application indicating the purpose and nature of the project, the type and quantity of materials needed, the types and quantity of other resources used, and the projected time frame. The contact person is Cindy Slater, Director of Information Resources, Archives, U.S. Olympic Committee, One Olympic Plaza, Colorado Springs, CO 80909.

Other useful archival collections in the United States include the Amateur Athletic Foundation of Los Angeles, established after the 1984 Summer Games in that city. Its collection includes more than 40,000 printed volumes, 6,000 microform volumes, 400 periodicals, 90,000 photo images, 600 video volumes, and the Avery Brundage Collection (see below) on microfilm. Among the most valuable documents in the collection is every official report of organizing committees of the modern Games since 1896, or, for Games for which no such report was published, the most reliable account of those Games. In addition, the collection includes other primary documents for each Games, including programs, U.S. and British Olympic committee reports, media guides, and, for the more recent Games, the multivolume U.S. television network research manuals used by announcers for background information. In 2000, the useful National Track and Field Hall of Fame Research Library transferred its holdings from Butler University in Indianapolis to the Amateur Athletic Foundation. This collection contains about three cubic feet of clippings, arranged by Games, copies of the IOC *Bulletin* and *Olympic Review*, and assorted other materials, in addition to a comprehensive assortment of books on the Olympics.

The foundation archives also contains a wide variety of magazines and newsletters pertinent to the Olympic Movement, an ongoing Southern California Olympians oral history project, numbering some 100 transcribed interviews, and a substantial video collection, including complete U.S. television network coverage of all Games since 1988.

There is no fee to use the library. Appointments are recommended, and the contact person is Dr. Wayne Wilson, Amateur Athletic Foundation of Los Angeles, 2141 W. Adams Blvd., Los Angeles, CA 90018. The Web site is http://www.aafla.com/.

The University of Illinois archives houses the Avery Brundage Collection, an extensive archival record of the individual who was president of the IOC from 1952 to 1972. The papers fill 310 archive boxes, 109 scrapbooks and photograph albums, and several boxes of photographs, films, tapes, and microfilm. In addition, Brundage donated a collection of more than 1,500 books, many on the Olympics, which are kept in a special room in the Applied Life Sciences library. Fortunately, there is an excellent published finding aid for the Brundage papers: Maynard Brichford, comp., *Avery Brundage Collection, 1908–1975* (Cologne, 1977). The Brundage Collection has been supplemented by another Olympic collection that includes material on the Games since 1972. This collection includes published material from organizing committees of the Games beginning with Montreal 1976. The archives also contains the Frederick J. Ruegsegger Collection. Ruegsegger was Brundage's business manager and adviser for many years, traveling with him and frequently translating for him. This collection contains letters and clippings related to Brundage as well as 24 boxes of audiotapes of IOC meetings between 1969 and 1972. The contact person is William J. Maher, University Archives, 19 Main Library, University of Illinois, Urbana, IL 61801.

At the Gerald R. Ford Library, Ann Arbor, Michigan, are the records of the President's Commission on Olympic Sports, 1975–1977, which looked into the USOC and related sport organizations with respect to the manner in which U.S. athletes were being prepared for Olympic competition. A printed finding aid for these papers is available. For more information, write to Stacy Davis, Archivist, Gerald R. Ford Library, 1000 Beal Avenue, Ann Arbor, MI 48109.

The Douglas F. Roby Papers are at the University of Michigan Archives. Roby was a member of the IOC from 1952 to 1985 and president of the USOC from 1965 to 1969. He was also president of the Amateur Athletic Union (AAU) in 1951 and tried to bring the Olympic Games to Detroit at various times between 1944 and 1972. His papers include material on those efforts as well as his work on behalf of the AAU, IOC, and USOC. In addition, there are pamphlets, reports, directories, and serials published by the IOC and cities that hosted Games between the 1960s and 1990s. A finding aid is available. Contact the head of reference and instruction, Barbara MacAdam, at 209 Harlan Hatcher Graduate Library, University of Michigan, Ann Arbor, MI 48109-1205 or at bmacadam@umich.edu.

In Canada, researchers should start at the Centre for Olympic Studies at the University of Western Ontario in London. A relatively new repository for Olympic materials, the center contains copies of the daily IOC press reviews from 1993, summaries of the minutes of IOC sessions and executive committee meetings, IOC academy reports, various Canadian Olympic Association reports, official reports and other publications related to the 1976 Montreal Summer Games and the 1988 Calgary Winter Games, photocopied material from earlier Olympic Games, and the scrapbook of 1932 Canadian Olympian Alda Wilson, the fifth-place finisher in the 80-meter hurdles. In addition, the center's holdings include a substantial slide collection, a microfilm copy of the Avery Brundage papers, and a number of theses and dissertations on Olympic topics as well as a representative collection of books on the Olympic Movement. The center publishes *Olympika: International Journal of Olympic Studies*, which contains scholarly articles on the Games. Other Olympic material is housed in the special collections department of the university library, including a number of official reports and organizing committee publications, Canadian Olympic Association meeting minutes (1934–1949) and publications, scrapbooks and clippings from a Canadian who participated in the 1906 and 1912 Games, and a fairly extensive Olympic stamp collection. The center also sponsors an International Olympic Symposium every other year and publishes the proceedings; these contain many articles of diverse interest to Olympic scholars. The contact person is Dr. Kevin Wamsley, Director, Alumni Hall, Faculty of Kinesiology, University of Western Ontario, London, Ontario N6A 3K7, Canada. The center's Web site is http://www.uwo.ca/olympic/.

In Germany, there are several sport history centers containing significant collections of Olympic-related material. The most extensive of these is the Deutsche Sporthochschule Köln (Cologne), where Olympic study is centered in the Carl-Diem-Institut. The centerpiece of this collection is the papers and letters of Diem, who was active in the German Olympic Movement for well over 50 years, spanning the period from Coubertin to Brundage. Over 90,000 letters form the basis of this collection, and to these are added Diem's many publications, 10,000 sport photographs, his library of 3,000 books, and the papers of his wife, Liselot, a professor of sport methodology who was active in the German national Olympic committee and the World Women's Federation of Sport and who wrote more than 20 books. The school houses the largest general sport library in Europe with over 100,000 books and 300 journals. Arrangements to conduct research should be made in advance. For more information, write Dr. Karl Lennartz, Director of Archives, Carl-Diem-Institut, Deutsche Sporthochschule Köln, Carl-Diem-Weg 6, 50933 Köln, Germany.

The Institut für Sport-Wissenschaften at Georg-August-Universitat in Göttingen, Germany, contains a library of 22,000 volumes and 300 journals but no original archival material. It has a computerized index of its own holdings, as well as those of the Carl-Diem-Institut, and also possesses a microfilm copy of the Brundage papers. The institute's holdings in sport medicine are particularly strong. Contact the institute at Georg-August-Universität, Sprangerweg 2, 37075 Göttingen, Germany. Not too distant from Göttingen is the Lower Saxony Institute for Sport History (Niedersächsisches Institut für Sportgeschichte), whose collection also contains a substantial number of published works (especially of German origin) about the Olympics. For more information, write Niedersächsisches Institut für Sportgeschichte Hoya e. V., Hasseler Steinweg 2, 27318 Hoya, Germany.

The Deutsches Olympisches Institut is located in Berlin, where it was founded in 1990 as an academic research center that also does consulting work for the national Olympic committee of Germany. Its address is Am Kleinen Wannsee 6A, 14109 Berlin, Germany, and its Web site is http://www.doi.de/.

Near the site of the 1972 Games in Munich is the Technische Universität, whose sport library contains 36,000 volumes and 190 journals. Although not Olympic-specific, the library has an extensive section on the Olympic Movement, including, of course, a great deal on the 1972 Games. For more information, write to Dr. Ulrike Mertz, Sportbibliothek, Technische Universität, Zentrale Hochschulesportanlage in Olympiapark, Connollystrasse 32, Munich, Germany.

In Spain, the Centre d'Estudis Olímpics is located at the Universität Autonomade Barcelona, on the outskirts of the city. The center was established in 1989 and maintains a library, sponsors conferences, often in conjunction with the IOC, and hosts visiting scholars in Olympic studies. Its library, or documentation center, contains 5,000 books, 60 periodicals, a good collection of visual material and is particularly rich in holdings for the 1992 Barcelona Games. The director is Dr. Miquel de Moragas, and he may be contacted at Universität Autonoma de Barcelona, 08193 Bellaterra, Barcelona, Spain. The center's Web site is http://blues.uab.es/olympic.studies/.

In Italy, a small research facility is the Centro Italiano Studi Olimpici Sportivi located at Via Rati 66, Sport Division (Olympic C.), Gogoleto, Italy. Founded in 1998, this center operates under the aegis of the Comitato Italiano Pierre de Coubertin and organizes Olympic-related academic activities around Italy and maintains a library. Its Web site is http://www.coubertin-olympicstudies.org/.

Australia's Olympic heritage is documented in several repositories. Apart from the library of the Sydney organizing committee for the 2000 Games (see essay on those Games), researchers will find useful information at the Centre for Olympic Studies at the University of New South Wales in Sydney. This center, like others in Canada, Spain, and Argentina, offers researchers a comprehensive library on Olympic matters and some documentary and photographic material, and sponsors occasional conferences and colloquia. Not surprisingly, the center is particularly strong on material related to the Sydney 2000 Games, with 62 boxes of documentation from those Games. Interested researchers should write its director, Richard Cashman, or access the Web site http://www.arts.unsw.edu.au/olympic/. The National Library of Australia has 4 manuscript collections and 25 oral histories related to the Olympics, as well as pictorial files on the Games from 1952 onwards, more than 30 films and videos, and extensive clippings files from 1956 onwards. The contact person is Elizabeth Dracoulis, Director, Reader Services, Australian National Library, Canberra, ACT, 2600 Australia.

Three separate centers at the Melbourne Cricket Club offer research material on the Games. The Australian Gallery of Sport and Olympic Museum has a general collection of material from the 1956 Melbourne Games; the Beaurepaire Collection, containing scrapbooks, albums, photographs, and a diary documenting that family's long involvement with the Olympic Movement; and two smaller Olympic collections. For more information, write Judy Hansen, Collections Curator, Australian Gallery of Sport and Olympic Museum, Melbourne Cricket Club, P.O. Box 175, East Melbourne 3002, Australia. The Melbourne Cricket Club Museum has a collection of correspondence relating to the management of the 1956 Games, part of which were held at the club. For more information, write the Secretary, M.C.C., at the address above. Finally, the Melbourne Cricket Club Library, separate from the museum, contains about 200 Olympic-related books. More information is available from David Studham, Librarian, at the same address.

The only research center devoted to Olympic studies in South America is the Centro de Estudios Olimpicos y Ciencias del Deporte Jose Benjamin Zubiaur, located at the Universidad Nacional de San Luis, in San Luis, Argentina. This center was founded in 1996 and works to document and facilitate research on the Olympics, with particular attention to Latin American participation in the Olympic Movement. Among its research projects are the unofficial Olympics in Buenos Aires in 1910 and the international meeting of NOCs in Buenos Aires in 1975. Dra. Bernardita Zalisnak is the head of research, and the Web site of the center is http://linux0.unsl.edu.ar/~squiroga/.

Sport institutes and research centers exist in many other countries, but few of them specialize in Olympic studies. However, the following may be useful to researchers: in France, L'institut national du sport et de education physique, 11 avenue du Tremblay 75012 Paris, France; in Finland, the Sport Library of Finland (SUK), Stadion, Helsinki 00250, Finland; in Monaco, the archives of the International Amateur Athletic Federation, 17 rue Princesse Florestine, BP 359, MC-98007, Monaco Cedex, Monaco; in New Zealand, the library of the New Zealand Olympic and Commonwealth Games Association, P.O. Box 2251, Wellington, New Zealand.

BOOKS AND ARTICLES

General Histories

There are many general histories of the modern Olympics. Most are either pictorial histories or journalistic accounts; most concentrate almost exclusively on the athletic performances at the Games themselves and treat their political, social, and cultural context, if at all, in a very perfunctory manner. One notable exception to the above is Allen Guttmann, *The Olympics: A History of the Modern Games* (Urbana, IL, 2002). Guttmann, who has also written a biography of Avery Brundage, emphasizes the political maneuvering behind the Olympics and notes only briefly the outstanding athletic achievements. Unlike most general histories, *The Olympics* does not have a separate chapter for each Olympic Games; rather, its 13 chapters touch on disparate stages of Olympic history, including the tenure of IOC president Juan Antonio Samaranch and the impact of professional athletes and a greater number of women on athletic performance since 1990. The book also contains a good bibliographical essay.

Among the pictorial histories of the Olympics, one of the more recent is a *Sports Illustrated* publication, *The Olympics: A History of the Games* (New York, 1992), published after the Albertville Winter Games but before the Barcelona Summer Games of 1992. One of the earliest such histories, but still very worthwhile, is Richard Schaap, *An Illustrated History of the Olympics* (New York, 1963). Schaap, who was a longtime sports journalist, touched on both the highlights and the controversies of the Games in his text, and the photographs are well chosen to capture the dramatic moments of the Games. A statistical appendix is included. John Rodda and Lord Killanin, *The Olympic Games: 80 Years of People, Events, and Records* (London, 1976), written while Killanin headed the IOC, is a reliable pictorial history with more text than most such books; Lee Benson et al, *Athens to Atlanta: 100 Years of Glory* (Salt Lake City, UT, 1993), is the U.S. Olympic Committee's view of the Olympic Games; Nicolaos Yalouris, *The Olympic Games* (Athens, 1976), is a coffee-table book covering both the ancient and modern Games, with roughly equal space devoted to each. The modern Games are covered on a Games-by-Games basis. Yalouris does present some information on the fine arts competitions accompanying each Olympic Games as well, noting that competitive exhibitions were dropped after 1948 because of the mediocre quality of the work and controversies over its judging. Paul Lecia, *Sport Shots* (New York, 1937), is an older book that is all pictures. Researchers of the history of the Winter Games should not overlook Ossi Brucker, *Titel, Tranen und Triumphe: die Olympische Winterspiele von 1924–1992*

(Kassel, Germany, 1992), a pictorial survey, but one of the very few general histories of the Winter Games, with an informative chapter on the background and origin of those Games. Another pictorial survey is the U.S. Olympic Committee, *Chamonix to Lillehammer: The Glory of the Olympic Winter Games* (Salt Lake City, UT, 1994), quite possibly published in conjunction with Salt Lake City's bid to host the 2002 Winter Games.

General histories in which text is emphasized over pictures include Bill Henry, *An Approved History of the Olympic Games* (New York, 1948), written by an individual who worked at the 1932 Los Angeles Games and had for many years close ties with the U.S. Olympic Committee; Alexander M. Weyand, *The Olympic Pageant* (New York, 1952), by a retired military officer who was a wrestler in the 1920 Games; R. D. Binfield, *The Story of the Olympic Games* (London, 1948), which is organized by event rather than by Games, as is Nicolaos Yalouris, *The Eternal Olympics* (New Rochelle, NY, 1979). Another general history is Hugh Harlan, *History of the Olympic Games: Ancient and Modern* (Los Angeles, 1964), which has a section on the origins of the modern Olympics. A shorter history is Xenophon L. Messinesi, *History of the Olympic Games* (New York, 1973), which also contains a chapter on the International Olympic Academy. A more recent brief history is Kristine Toohey and A. J. Veal, *The Olympic Games: A Social Science Perspective* (New York, 1999); its topical organization includes chapters on nationalism, economics, the mass media, and drugs, with Barcelona, Atlanta, and Sydney highlighted as case studies. A very recent book is Geoffrey M. Horn and Catherine Gardner, eds., *Olympism: A Basic Guide to the History, Ideals, and Sports of the Olympic Movement* (Torrance, CA, 2001). Finally, Bill Henry's daughter, Patricia Henry Yeomans, has written *Five Olympiads: Sixteen Years of Olympic Games History* (Los Angeles, 2001), which focuses on the Games during Samaranch's tenure.

John Lucas, a respected academic historian of the Games, has written "The Modern Olympic Games: Fanfare and Philosophy, 1896–1972," *The Maryland Historian* 4 (fall 1973): 71–87, which he expanded into *The Modern Olympic Games* (Cranbury, NJ, 1980). Another important Lucas article is "From Coubertin to Samaranch: The Unsettling Transformation of the Olympic Ideology of Athletic Amateurism," *Stadion* 14, 1 (1988): 65–84. Two publications that relate the ancient Games to their modern counterparts are Paul J. Wade, "Greece and the Olympic Games," *Gourmet* (March 1984): 28–32, 68–76, an article without scholarly pretension, and Roland Renson et al., eds., *The Olympic Games Through the Ages: Greek Antiquity and Its Impact on Modern Sport* (Athens, 1991). This publication contains the proceedings of the 13th International Congress of HISPA, held in Olympia, Greece, in May 1979. Finally, Norbert Muller and Joachim K. Rühl, eds., *Olympic Scientific Congress 1984 Official Report: Sport History* (Niedernhausen, Germany, 1985), contains many articles of significance about Olympic history.

Two recent publications discuss the relationship between the Olympic Games and other mega-events, such as world's fairs. Maurice Roche, *Mega-Events and Modernity: Olympics and Expos in the Growth of Global Culture* (London, 2000) discusses the impact of these events on such things as national identities, power elites, and tourist culture. Matthew Burbank, *Olympic Dreams: The Impact of Mega-Events on Local Politics* (Boulder, CO, 2001) deals with the way that Olympic Games and similar events have changed the politics and economics of host cities.

The centennial of the modern Olympic Games in 1996 brought out many new works on the history of the Games. The official IOC centennial history is Willi P.

Knecht, ed., *100 Years of the Olympic Games of Modern Times*, 11 vols. (Munich, 1990–95). Ten volumes deal with the history of the Games from 1896 to 1996; the 11th (1994) treats various cultural themes associated with the Games. This set of heavily illustrated, large-format books was published in six languages. An official history of the IOC is Raymond Gafner, ed., *The International Olympic Committee–One Hundred Years*, 3 vols., (Lausanne, 1994–96). One of the most useful IOC-sponsored publications is Wolf Lyberg, *Fabulous 100 Years of the IOC: Facts, Figures, and Much, Much More* (Lausanne, 1996). An IOC publication, this book surveys in an informal manner the history of the movement, with much information on IOC members, IOC sessions and executive board meetings, and on Olympic symbols and traditions. Norbert Muller, *One Hundred Years of Olympic Congresses* (Lausanne, 1994), summarizes the 12 congresses that have been held since the founding of the IOC in 1894. Muller is also the editor of *Coubertin and Olympism: Questions for the Future* (Lausanne, 1997), a collection of articles derived from presentations at the Olympic Congress held in Le Havre, France, in 1997. Among other publications, researchers may want to consult Sue Leonard, ed., *Chronicle of the Olympics, 1896–1996* (London, 1996), which devotes nearly 100 pages to lists of medal winners. Another IOC-sanctioned publication is Henri Charpentier and Euloge Boissonade, *La Grande Histoire de Jeux Olympiques: Athenes 1896–Sydney 2000* (Paris, 2000), which includes chapters on doping scandals, bribery affairs, and the IOC presidents. A contrarian viewpoint is presented in Rod Beamish, "Pierre de Coubertin's Shattered Dream," *Queen's Quarterly* 10, 3 (fall 1996): 489–501, which argues that contemporary Games no longer represent what Coubertin originally intended. Finally, it is impossible to overlook *The Olympic Century*, a mammoth multi-authored 24-volume project of the World Sport Research and Publications organization and published in 2000. Each volume covers a particular Olympiad, excluding the three lost to world wars, as well as the ancient Olympics. Illustrated coffee-table books, they cover the bid process and preparations for the Games, as well as the athletic events and other relevant topics.

General histories in German include Friedrich Mevert, *Olympische Spiele der Neuzeit-von Athens bis Los Angeles* (Niederhausen, Germany, 1983), a survey history; Klaus Ulrich, *Olympische Spiele* (Berlin, 1978), which touches on some of the political and ideological issues of the Games; Manfred Blodorn, ed., *Sport und Olympische Spiele* (Reinbek, Germany, 1984), an anthology of essays on Olympic ideas and ideals, with essays on the 1936 Berlin Games, women and the Olympics, and amateurism, among others. Willi Knecht, *100 Jahre Olympische Spiele der Neuzeit, 1896–1996* (Munich, 1990), is a four-volume pictorial history honoring the centennial of the Games. It contains short essays on the Games in four languages and an abundance of outstanding illustrations with captions in six languages. A more recent publication is Wolfgang Decker, Georgios Dolianitis, and Karl Lennartz, *100 Jahre Olympische Spiele--Der Neugriechische Ursprung* (Wurzburg, Germany, 1996), which contains articles on the pre-Olympic Games in Greece, the 1896 and 1906 Games in Athens, and much more touching on the early history of the modern Games. A general history, published near the centennial of the Games, is Karl Adolf Scherer, *100 Jahre Olympische Spiele: Idee, Analyse und Bilanz* (Dortmund, Germany, 1995), which contains short chapters on each of the Games, along with lists of medal winners, IOC members, international sport federations, and national Olympic committees.

French readers may consult Gaston Meyer, *Le Phemonene Olympique: Athenes—Rome* (Paris, 1960), a general account, which includes a separate chapter on Coubertin and appendixes with the IOC constitution and Olympic records. For the earliest of the modern Games, see Otto Mayer, *Retrospectives Olympiquex: Athenes 1896—Rome 1960* (Geneva, Switzerland, 1961), which discusses the organization and staging of the first two Games. A general history of the Winter Olympics in French is the IOC-sanctioned *Un siecle d'Olympisme en Hiver: De Chamoniz a Salt Lake City* (Meolans-Revel, France, 2001). Eric Monnin, the author, devotes a chapter to winter sport festivals prior to Chamonix, but most of the book deals with athletic achievements at the Winter Games.

There are a number of books that deal specifically with one or another Olympic function, such as the bid process and site selection. The troubles over the Salt Lake City bid have generated a number of new publications in this area, some of which are mentioned in the bibliography following the Salt Lake City essay. Other, more general works include Pieter de Lange, *The Games Cities Play* (Monument Park, South Africa, 1998) and Peter Schollmeier, *Bewerbiengen um Olympische Spiele: Von Athen 1896 bis Athen 2004* (Cologne, 2001) on the bid process, and Alain Lunzen-fichter, *Athenes . . . Pekin (1896–2008): Choix Epiques das Villes Olympiques* (Anglet, France, 2002) on site selection. Lunzenfichter's book emanated from the unsuccessful bid of Paris for the 2008 Games. Other books deal specifically with various Olympic traditions. Miquel de Moragas et al., eds., *Olympic Ceremonies: Historical Continuity and Cultural Exchange* (Barcelona, 1996) is the proceedings of an international symposium that explores the historical background of a variety of Olympic Games ceremonies. Walter Borgers, *Olympic Torch Relays, 1936–1994* (Kassel, Germany, 1996), describes the origins of the torch relays for the Berlin Games and presents highlights of later torch relays, while Janet Cahill, *Running Toward Sydney: The Olympic Flame and Torch* (Petersham, NSW, Australia, 1999) focuses on the Melbourne Games and plans for the Sydney Games relays. Olympic Villages and their impact on urban planning is the subject of Miquel de Moragas et al, eds., *Olympic Villages: Hundred Years of Urban Planning and Shared Experiences* (Lausanne, 1997), the proceedings of another international symposium. Finally, a 1999 symposium on the role of volunteers at the Olympics resulted in Miquel de Moragas et al., eds., *Volunteers, Global Society, and the Olympic Movement* (Lausanne, 2000).

REFERENCE BOOKS

Olympic record books abound, as many are published by television networks or corporate sponsors prior to each Olympics, but two books devoted almost entirely to Games statistics stand out above the rest. Erich Kamper and Bill Mallon, *The Golden Book of the Olympics* (Milan, 1992) is an exhaustively complete statistical review of Olympic performances. Not content to list the medal winners in each event of each Games, Kamper and Mallon have recorded virtually every combination and permutation of Olympic records conceivable. Thus, a researcher can learn who the oldest and youngest gold medal winner was at each Games, the number of medals athletes from each country and the number of records they have set, and the winners of the arts competitions, of discontinued sports, and of demonstration sports. The book also contains the birth and death dates of each nation's medalists and much more. More modest in scope but more accessible is David Wallechinsky, *The Complete Book of the Olympics* (Woodstock, NY, 2000), which contains the records of the first eight finishers in each Olympic event. Arranged on a sport-by-sport basis, the book also includes some commentary about most events at most

Games, pointing out something unusual or remarkable about each event. The book also has a brief general history of the Games, a listing of national medal totals for each Games, and four sections of action photographs. Wallechinsky has also published *The Complete Book of the Winter Olympics* (Woodstock, NY, 2001). Yet another record book is Stan Greenberg, *Olympic Facts and Feats* (Enfield, UK, 1998), a publication of the Guinness Book of Records factory. A more theoretical book about record-setting performances is A. B. Johnson Jr. and Melinda Johnson, *Olympic Trends: A New Look at the Modern Olympics* (New York, 1991). The authors use statistics and graphs to demonstrate the evolution of improved performance over the history of the Games. A more specialized book is David E. Martin and Roger W. H. Gynn, *The Olympic Marathon* (Champaign, IL, 2000), which tells the reader everything he or she might want to know about that prominent Olympic event. And a reference book that is far more than a record book is Ian Buchanan and Bill Mallon, *Historical Dictionary of the Modern Olympics*, 2d ed. (Lanham, MD, 2002). This book contains short entries on the history of all Olympic events, traditions, organizations, and contemporary issues, as well as biographical sketches of many prominent Olympians.

THE OLYMPICS AND POLITICAL ISSUES

As the Olympics have become more embroiled in international political issues, writers have risen to the bait and published books on the subject. Two books that cover the political ground of the post-World War II Olympics are Richard Espy, *The Politics of the Olympics* (Berkeley, 1979) and David B. Kanin, *Political History of the Olympic Games* (Boulder, CO, 1981). Peter Graham and Horst Ueberhorst, eds., *The Modern Olympics* (West Point, NY, 1976) and Jeffrey O. Segrave and Donald Chu, eds., *The Olympics in Transition* (Champaign, IL, 1988) are both anthologies containing articles on the Olympics; many touch on the politics of the Games. Uriel Simri and Sarah Lieberman, eds., *Sport and Politics* (Netanya, Israel, 1984), is a collection of articles that deal with such topics as the 1980 Moscow Games, the 1984 Los Angeles Games, issues related to China and South Africa, and the participation of Israel in the Asian Games. A book that is very critical of the politicization of the Olympic Movement in recent years is Helen Jefferson Lenskyj, *Inside the Olympic Industry: Power, Politics, and Activism* (Albany, NY, 2000). Another critical book, though more focused on amateur sport in the United States and the USOC in the 1980s, is David F. Prouty, *In Spite of Us* (Brattleboro, VT, 1988). Prouty was the executive director of the U.S. Cycling Federation. John Lucas, mentioned earlier, may have the last word with *Future of the Olympic Games* (Champaign, IL, 1992), in which he tackles the difficult contemporary issues facing the Olympic Movement: nationalism, commercialism, drugs, and the role of women.

Other important publications with a political bent include John Hoberman, *The Olympic Crisis: Sport, Politics, and the Moral Order* (New Rochelle, NY, 1986), a study of the IOC and the Olympic Movement as an international institution which has survived the twentieth century by accommodating distasteful political regimes and issues rather than resisting them, a doctrine Hoberman calls amoral universalism, where universal participation sometimes calls for the sacrifice of moral standards. A more recent book is Kay Schaffer and Sidonie Smith, *The Olympics at the Millennium: Power, Politics, and the Games* (New Brunswick, NJ, 2000). A more journalistic view of recent Olympic politics is found in Geoffrey Miller, *Behind the Olympic*

Rings (Lynn, MA, 1979). Miller, the European sports editor for the Associated Press, discusses such issues as amateurism, television, and the IOC presidencies of Brundage and Killanin. Similar themes are echoed in John Sugden, "The Power of Gold: The Course and Currency of the Political Olympics," *Physical Education Review* 4 (1981): 65–78. See also Joel Thiver, "Politics and Protest at the Olympic Games," in Benjamin Lowe, David Kanin, and Andrew Strenk, eds., *Sport and International Relations* (Champaign, IL, 1978). One book and two articles deal specifically with the apartheid question and South Africa: Richard Lapchick, *The Politics of Race and International Sport* (Westport, CT, 1975); March L. Krotee and Luther C. Schwick, "The Impact of Sporting Forces on South African Apartheid," *Journal of Sport and Social Issues* 3 (1979): 33–42; and Peter Hain, "The Politics of Sport and Apartheid," in Jennifer Hargreaves, ed., *Sport, Culture, and Ideology* (London, 1982). Recent concerns about terrorism and security are the subject of Tod Hoffman, "Munich 1972, Atlanta 1996," *Queen's Quarterly* 10, 3 (fall 1996): 477–87.

On the important connection between the Olympic Movement and television, which can also have political ramifications, see the relevant parts of Benjamin Rader, *In Its Own Image: How Television Has Transformed Sports* (New York, 1984). Even more to the point is Stephen Wenn, "A History of the International Olympic Committee and Television, 1936–1980" (Ph.D. diss., Pennsylvania State University, 1993). Wenn's work and much more information about television and the general commercialization of the Olympic Games may be found in Robert Barney, Stephen Wenn, and Scott Martyn, *Selling the Five Rings: The IOC and the Rise of Olympic Commercialism* (Salt Lake City, UT, 2002).

COUNTRY-SPECIFIC OLYMPIC HISTORIES

There are a number of books that trace the Olympic history of a particular country. Max and Reet Howell, *Aussie Gold* (Albion, Queensland, 1988), traces the long history of Australian participation in the Olympics, as do Gary Lester, *Australians at the Olympics: A Definitive History* (Melbourne, 1984), Harry Gordon, *Australia and the Olympic Games* (St. Lucia, Queensland, 1994), and *Australia's Olympic Century: All the Games in Pictures* (Sydney, 1998). Henry Roxborough, *Canada at the Olympics* (Toronto, 1963) summarizes Canadian performance at the Games from 1896 through 1960, along with some general history, and includes appendixes on Olympic literature, stamps, symbols, and Canadian medalists. A book published in conjunction with the 1988 Calgary Games, *Canada at the Olympic Winter Games: The Official Sports History and Record Book* (Edmonton, Alberta, 1987), by Wendy Bryden, traces the history of winter sports in Canada and the background of the Calgary Games. The book also includes information on Canadian athletes in the Winter Games.

For the People's Republic of China, see Rolf von der Laage, *Sport in China: Gestern und Heute* (Berlin, 1977), which surveys sport in mainland China, including developments back to 1913 and China's participation in past Olympics. The Republic of China Olympic Committee has published *Amateur Sport in the Republic of China* (Taipei, 1984), which includes material on Taiwan at the Olympics. Cuba's recent Olympic history is profiled in Raymond Pointu and Roger Fidani, *Cuba: Sport en Revolution* (Paris, 1975). For Czechoslovakia, there is Jan Kotrba et al, *Czechoslovakia and Olympic Games* (Prague, 1984). The history of early twentieth-century sport in France is chronicled in Emmanuel de Waresquiel, *De Roland Garros a Marcel Cerdan, 1900–1945* (Paris, 1995), which includes good coverage of the Olympic Games. Arnd Kruger has detailed Germany's long association with the Olympic Movement in a two-volume work: *Deutschland und die olympische Bewegung (1918–1945)* (Berlin, 1982) and *Deutschland und die olympische Bewegung (1948–1980)* (Berlin, 1982). Kruger devotes much space to the 1936 Berlin Games but relatively little to the 1972 Munich Games. More about Germany and the Olympic Movement can be learned from four biographical studies of Olympic leaders: Carl Diem's autobiography, *Ein Leben für den Sport* (Ratingen, Germany, 1974); Arnd Kruger, *Theodor Lewald: Sportfuhrer ins Dritte Reich* (Berlin, 1975); Eerke Hamer, *Willibald Gebhardt: der erste deutsche Treuhander des olympische Gedankens* (Cologne, 1970); and Klaus Huhn, *Der vergessene Olympier: das erstaunliche Leben des Dr. Willibald Gebhardt* (Berlin, 1992). East Germany's strong showing in recent Olympics is examined in Yuri Brokhin, *The Big Red Machine* (New York, 1978). For a survey of the postwar sporting relationship between the two Germanys, see G. A. Carr, "The Involvement of Politics in the Sporting Relationships of East and West Germany, 1945–1972," *Journal of Sport History* 7, 1 (spring 1980): 40–51.

For Hungary, see Jenoe Boskovits, *Die Geschichte des ungarischen Sports* (Budapest, 1983), a general sport history that includes information on Hungary's participation in the Olympics. Saradindu Sanyal traces India's participation in the Games in *Olympic Games and India* (Delhi, 1970). Mexico's Olympic experience is described in Antonio Lavin, *Mexico en los Juegos Olimpicos MCMLXVIII* (Mexico, 1968), written for the 1968 Games. Monaco's National Olympic Committee is celebrated in Alain Manigley, *Comite Olympique Monagasque, 1907–1992* (Monaco, 1993). Jerzy Jabrzemski, *Sport in Poland* (Warsaw, 1956), mercifully translated into English, is an older book that highlights Poland's efforts at the Olympics and includes many illustrations, as well as sections on winners and Polish women at the Games. The Romanian Olympic Committee published *Liebeserziehung und Sport in Rumanien* (n.p., n.d.) to highlight that country's role in the Olympics. South Africa's turbulent relationship with the Olympic Movement is detailed in Rudolf W. J. Opperman, *Africa's First Olympians: The Story of the Olympic Movement in South Africa, 1907–1987* (Johannesburg, 1987). An authorized history of the Spanish National Olympic Committee is Conrado Durantez, *El Comite Olimpico Espanol: Origines y Naturaleza Juridica* (Madrid?, 1999). For Spain, see also Angel A. Magdalena, *Los Pioneros Espanoles del Olimpismo Moderno: Adolfo Buylla, Aniceto Sela, Adolfo Posada* (Asturias, Spain, 1992), a history of Olympic sport in Spain that focuses on three of Samaranch's predecessors. Several books have been published on sport in the Soviet Union. Among those that deal with the Olympics, James Riordan, *Soviet Sport: Background to the Olympics* (New York, 1980) discusses the evolution, structure, and organization of Soviet sport, its application in gymnastics and soccer, and the problems of women in sport. A separate chapter traces Soviet Olympic history. See also Riordan's article, "The USSR and the Olympic Games," *Stadion* 6 (1980): 291–314. Norman Schneidman, *The Soviet Road to Olympus* (Toronto, 1978) touches on similar themes. German readers can also consult Martinus van den Heuvel, *Rusland en de olympische spielen* (Haarlem, Germany, 1980). For the United States, consult Fred G. Jarvis, *From Vision to Victory: America's Role in Establishing the Modern Olympic Games* (New York, 1996), a USOC-sponsored publication with good information on the contribution of the New York Athletic Club in the early years, and Mark Dyreson, *Making the American Team: Sport, Culture, and the Olympic Experience* (Urbana, IL, 1998). Dyreson's book looks at the broad concept of the United States as a sporting republic and incorporates American experiences in the early Olympic Games into that concept. Finally, Ali Ramos discusses Venezuela's Olympic experiences in *Venezuela Olimpica* (Caracas, 1980).

OLYMPIC BIOGRAPHIES

A substantial number of resources are available for those wishing to study the biographies of Olympians. By far the most comprehensive source is Erich Kamper, *Lexicon der 12000 Olympioniken* (Graz, Austria, 1975), published also in an English edition, *Who's Who at the Olympics*. The 1975 edition was updated to include 14,000 Olympians in a 1983 edition, and updated again in a 1992 edition, with Bill Mallon as co-author. Entries in this publication are very brief, including just hometown, birth and death dates, and a record of Olympic participation. Mallon has published a book dealing only with U.S. Olympic medalists, *Quest for Gold: The Encyclopedia of American Olympians* (New York, 1984), which has longer sketches for many subjects. A similar work is Gennadi Martichev, *Who Is Who at the Summer Olympics, 1896–1992*, 4 vols. (Riga, Latvia, 1996). This book lists Olympic athletes by sport, with their birth and death dates and information on their Olympic performances. See also the Buchanan and Mallon book noted above, *Historical Dictionary of the Modern Olympics*, for short biographies of some Olympic participants.

Other collective biographies include Dimiter Mishev, *Meet the Olympians* (Sofia, Bulgaria, 1964), which contains data on Olympic athletes between 1896 and 1960 and essays on early specialization and sports longevity; Lewis H. Carlson and John J. Fogarty, *Tales of Gold: An Oral History of the Summer Olympic Games Told by America's Gold Medal Winners* (Chicago, 1987), containing 58 oral histories of athletes representing a variety of Olympic events between the 1912 and 1984 Games; William O. Johnson, *All That Glitters Is Not Gold: An Irreverent Look at the Olympic Games* (New York, 1972); Erich Kamper and Herbert Saucel, *Olympischen Heroen: Portraits und Anekdoten von 1896 bis Heute* (Erkrath, Germany, 1991), a collection of short essays and anecdotes of Olympic highlights and biographical sketches of 64 Olympic heroes; Stan Tomlin, ed., *Olympic Odyssey: The Olympic Story as Told by the Stars Themselves from 1896 to 1956* (Croydon, England, 1956), a collection of essays on each Games from 1896 to 1952, as told by participants such as Fanny Blankers-Koen. The book includes many photographs and the program for the Melbourne Games. General books on women in the Olympics include Siobhan Drummond and Elizabeth Rathburn, *Grace and Glory: A Century of Women in the Olympics* (Washington, D.C., 1996); Stephanie Daniels, *"A Proper Spectacle": Women Olympians 1900–1936* (Petersham, New South Wales, Australia, 2000); Uriel Simri, *Women at the Olympic Games*, 2d ed. (Netanya, Israel, 1979); Adrianne Blue, *Faster, Higher, Further* (London, 1988); and relevant parts of Allen Guttmann, *Women's Sports: A History* (New York, 1991). Sheila Mitchell, "Women's Participation in the Olympic Games, 1900–1926," *Journal of Sport History* 4, 2 (summer 1977) analyzes the relationship between the IOC and the international sport federations that led to an increase in women's events at the Olympic Games.

Olympic champions from down under are the subject of Graeme Atkinson, *Australian and New Zealand Olympians: The Stories of 100 Great Champions* (Canterbury, Victoria, 1984). Ian Buchanan provides short biographies of British winners in

British Olympians: A Hundred Years of Gold Medallists (Enfield, England, 1991); see also Sam Mullins, *British Olympians: William Penney Brooks and the Wenlock Games* (London, 1986), a British Olympic Association publication. Bulgarian athletes are profiled in Nikolai Kolev, *Bulgaria's Olympic Champions* (Sofia, Bulgaria, 1988). For Canadian athletes, see Frank Cosentino and Glynn Leystion, *Olympic Gold: Canada's Winners in the Summer Games* (Toronto, 1975) and *Winter Gold: Canada's Winners in the Winter Olympic Games* (Markham, Ontario, 1987). French Olympic champions are highlighted in Raymond Marcillac, *Champions Olympiques* (Paris, 1967), while Hungarian winners through 1952 receive their due in Ferenc Mezo, *The Golden Book of Hungarian Olympic Champions* (Budapest, 1955). Jimmie Carnegie chronicles Jamaican athletes in *Great Jamaican Olympians* (Kingston, Jamaica, 1999). For Soviet medalists, see Valerii Shteinbakh, *638 Olympic Champions: Three Decades in the Olympic Movement* (Moscow, 1984).

Somewhat more specialized are James Page, *Black Olympian Medalists* (Englewood, CO, 1991), which deals with African American winners, and Michael D. Davis, *Black American Women in Olympic Track and Field* (Jefferson, NC, 1992), which surveys African American women's performances at various Games from 1932 to 1988, and includes biographical sketches and a short appendix on chromosome sex testing. Another recent book on African American women at the Olympics is Martha Ward Plowden, *Olympic Black Women* (Gretna, LA, 1996), which contains biographical sketches of a number of recent Olympians, mostly competitors in track and field. Dennis H. Phillips, *Australian Women at the Olympic Games, 1912–1992* (Kenthurst, New South Wales, 1992) is a chronological survey of Australian women's participation in the Summer Games, based in part on interviews.

An older work is K. Silberg, *The Athletic Finn: Some Reasons Why the Finns Excel in Athletics* (Hancock, MI, 1927), which profiles the great Finnish runners Hannes Kolehmainen, Willie Ritola, Paavo Nurmi, and Albin Stenroos. See also Martti Jukola, *Athletic in Finland* (Helsinki, 1932), a profile of the Finnish teams in the 1932 Winter and Summer Games, but which emphasizes track and field, and includes a lengthy sketch of Nurmi and shorter sketches of Lauri Lehtinen, Volmari Iso-Hollo, and several other track-and-field athletes.

Biographies and autobiographies of individual Olympic athletes must be used with great care. Although we have tried to avoid including those which would fall into the juvenile literature category, others meant for an adult readership are frequently so highly adulatory (or self-congratulatory) that one is forced to question their factual accuracy. Nonetheless, there are those that are honest treatments of the subject's life and career and present useful insights into what it means to compete (and, often, win) at the Olympics.

In addition to the biographies mentioned in some of the bibliographies following the essays on each of the Games, the following books are a representative sampling of what is available. Needless to say, most biographies deal with the greatest of the Olympic heroes, many of whom went on to successful careers in professional sport, film, or broadcasting.

Track and field, the most popular event (for most Americans, at least) on the Summer Olympic program, has produced the largest number of biographies. Jim Thorpe, the Native American athlete who won a gold medal at the 1912 Games in Stockholm and later had it stripped for having violated the amateur code, had his story told by Robert W. Wheeler, *Jim Thorpe: World's Greatest Athlete* (Norman,

OK, 1975) and by Brad Sieger and Charlotte Thorpe, *Thorpe's Gold* (New York, 1984), which recounts the family's fight to get his medals returned. Eric Liddell, the Scottish runner at the 1924 Paris Games who later went on to a missionary career in China, where he died in 1945, is the subject of D. P. Thomson, *Eric H. Liddell: Athlete and Missionary* (Barnock, Perthshire, Scotland, 1971), and Sally Magnusson, *The Flying Scotsman* (New York, 1981). Interestingly, his teammate Harold Abrahams, who with Liddell was memorialized in the 1981 film *Chariots of Fire* and who went on to a long and distinguished career in the British Olympic Movement, has not been the subject of a significant biography. For Paavo Nurmi, the best distance runner of the 1920s, consult the heavily illustrated, celebratory biographies by Sulo Kolkka and Helge Nygren, *Paavo Nurmi* (Helsinki, 1974) and Risto Taimi, *Paavo Nurmi 100–1997* (Turku, Finland, 1997).

Jesse Owens, the African American who won four gold medals at the 1936 Berlin Games, is the subject of William J. Baker's fine biography, *Jesse Owens: An American Life* (New York, 1986). Hank Nuwer, *The Legend of Jesse Owens* (New York, 1998) is newer but less academic than Baker's book. Owens also published an autobiography, *Jesse: The Man Who Outran Hitler* (New York, 1983). Another runner at the Berlin Games, 1,500-meter champion Jack Lovelock of New Zealand, is the subject of two biographies: Norman Harris, *The Legend of Lovelock* (London, 1964) and Christopher Tobin, *Lovelock, New Zealand's Olympic Gold Miler* (Dunedin, New Zealand, 1984). Bob Mathias, the 17-year-old decathlon winner at the 1948 London Games and later a U.S. congressman, found biographers in Jim Scott, *Bob Mathias: Champion of Champions* (n.p., 1952); Myron Tussin, *Bob Mathias: The Life of an Olympic Champion* (New York, 1983); and Chris Terrence, *Bob Mathias: Across the Fields of Gold* (Lenexa, KS, 1998). Mathias also played himself in a poorly received film biography. Emil Zatopek, the Czech distance runner at the 1948 and 1952 Games, is the subject of Frantisek Kozik, *Der Marathon- Sieger* (Prague, 1953) and Pierre Naudin, *Zatopek: Le Terrasier de Prague* (Paris, 1972). Harold and Olga Connolly, whose love affair at the 1956 Melbourne Games breached the Iron Curtain, told their story in *Rings of Destiny* (New York, 1968). In 1964, the late Bob Hayes was considered the fastest man in the world after his victory in the 100-meter sprint. His autobiography, *Run, Bullet, Run: The Rise, Fall, and Recovery of Bob Hayes* (New York, 1990), tells of the difficulties he faced after the Games were over. Kip Keino, the celebrated Kenyan distance runner who won medals in the 1964, 1968, and 1972 Games, is the subject of Francis Noronha, *Kipchoge of Kenya* (Nakura, Kenya, 1970). Alberto Juantorena, the Cuban middle-distance runner who won two gold medals at the 1976 Montreal Games, is made into a role model for Cuban youth in E. Montesinos, *Alberto Juantorena* (Havana, 1980). And the tragic life of the Ethiopian marathoner Abebe Bikila is told in Tsige Abebe, *Triumph and Tragedy: A History of Abebe Bikila and His Marathon Career* (Addis Ababa, Ethiopia, 1996).

Bob Beamon, who set the world long jump record at the 1968 Mexico City Games, has his due in Bob Beamon and Walter Milana Beamon, *The Man Who Could Fly* (Columbus, MS, 1999). Bruce Jenner, the telegenic 1968 decathlon winner, told his life's story in *The Olympics and Me* (Garden City, NY, 1980), while Frank Shorter, the marathon champion four years later at Munich, wrote his autobiography, *Olympic Gold: A Runner's Life and Times* (Boston, 1984). Lasse Viren, the Finnish distance runner who won gold medals in the 5,000- and 10,000-meter runs in both the 1972 and 1976 Games, published an autobiography, *Lasse Viren:*

Olympic Champion (Portland, OR, 1978). The two-time decathlon winner, Daley Thompson, one of Britain's most popular sport heroes, wrote *Daley: The Last Ten Years* (London, 1986) and was the subject of Skip Rosin, *Daley Thompson: The Subject Is Winning* (London, 1983). Carl Lewis, the American athlete who dominated the sprints and long jump during the 1980s, wrote, with Jeffrey Marx, *Inside Track: My Professional Life in Amateur Track and Field* (London, 1990). For another view of Lewis, see the *New York Times Magazine*, 17 June 1984, a special issue on the 1984 Summer Games, which contains an article, "Carl Lewis: The Quest for Olympic Greatness." Lewis's great rival in the 1988 Seoul Games, Ben Johnson, is the subject of James R. Christie, *Ben Johnson: The Fastest Man on Earth* (Toronto, 1988), which was written before Johnson's drug-induced downfall. Later, Johnson's coach, Charles Francis, sprang to his runner's defense in *Speed Trap: Inside the Biggest Scandal in Olympic History* (New York, 1990), written with Jeff Coplon. Another Lewis rival was Linford Christie, whose autobiography, *To Be Honest with You* (London, 1995), discusses his encounters with Lewis. To get a sense of what it was like to coach Olympic track and field, consult Bud Spencer, *High above the Olympians* (Los Altos, CA, 1966), a biography of Robert Lyman (Dick) Templeton, longtime Stanford University track coach and coach of many Olympic athletes.

There are fewer works on women track-and-field athletes, but a few recent publications are beginning to correct the imbalance. Susan E. Cayleff has published *Babe: The Life and Legend of Babe Didrickson Zaharias* (Urbana, IL, 1995), an excellent scholarly biography of the heroine of the 1932 Los Angeles Games. Zola Budd, with Hugh Eley, *Zola* (London, 1989) recounts her spectacular collision with American runner Mary Decker at the 1984 Games in Los Angeles. American marathoner Joan Benoit wrote her autobiography with Sally Baker, *Running Tide* (New York, 1987). And one of the dominant figures at the 2000 Games in Sydney, Cathy Freeman, the Australian runner, was the subject of Adrian McGregor's biography, *Cathy Freeman: A Journey Just Begun* (Milsons Point, NSW, Australia, 1998) that was published well before the Sydney Games.

Boxing and swimming are the other Summer Games events that have produced subjects for biographies. The best of several biographies of Muhammad Ali, who as Cassius Clay won a gold medal at the 1960 Rome Games, is probably Thomas Hauser, *Muhammad Ali: His Life and Times* (London, 1991). The Cuban boxing champion Teofilo Stevenson is the subject of Mariolo Cabale Ruiz, *Teofilo Stevenson, grande entre los grandes* (Havana, 1985). For swimmers, consult Narda Onyx, *Water, World, and Weissmuller: A Biography* (Los Angeles, 1964); Don Schollander and Duke Savage, *Deep Water* (London, 1971); and Mark Spitz and Mickey Herkovitz, *Seven Golds: Mark Spitz' Own Story* (Garden City, NY, 1984). The great Russian swimmer of the 1990s Alexandre Popov has collaborated with Alain Coltier to write his autobiography, *Nager dans le Vrai* (Paris, 2001). Perhaps the most outstanding woman swimmer in the Olympics was Dawn Fraser, whose autobiography, *Below the Surface: Confessions of an Olympic Champion* (New York, 1965), recounts her record performance at the 1956 Melbourne Games. Greg Louganis, the diving champion, tells his story in *Breaking the Surface* (New York, 1995). A different perspective on Olympic swimming is found in Jean M. Henning, *A Sports Odyssey: Journal of an Olympic Wife* (Fort Lauderdale, FL, 1998). Henning was the wife of Dr. Harold (Hal) Henning, who coached American swimmers at the Olympic Games from 1968 through 1984. Finally, synchronized swimming is featured in Sylvia Frechette, with Lilianne Lacroix, *Gold at Last* (Toronto, 1994), which tells the story of a Canadian synchronized swimmer who won a gold medal at the Barcelona Games amidst a swirl of controversy.

Books treating Olympic histories of other sports are scarce. For equestrian sports, see Pierre Jonqueres d'Oriola, *A cheval sur cinq Olympiques* (Paris, 1969), written by a member of the French equestrian team in every Olympic Games between 1952 and 1968. English-speaking equestrian enthusiasts will want to consult Jennifer O. Bryant, *Olympic Equestrian: The Sport and the Stories from Stockholm to Sydney* (Lexington, KY, 2000), with its many illustrations, and Barbara Wallace Shambach, *Equestrian Excellence: The Stories of Our Olympic Equestrian Medal Winners* (Boonsboro, MD, 1996), a collection of biographical sketches of the 38 medal winners from the United States.

Nearly all the major biographies of Winter Games athletes focus on figure skating champions. A number of biographies have been published on Sonja Henie, gold medalist in the 1928, 1932, and 1936 Games, who later had an important film career. The most recent is Raymond Strait, *Queen of Ice, Queen of Shadow: The Unsuspected Life of Sonja Henie* (New York, 1985). Heine's autobiography is *Wings on My Feet* (New York, 1940), which covers her Olympic years and her early film career. Most of the later women's champions have been the subject of biographies: see Clay Moore, *She Skated Into Our Hearts* (Toronto, 1948), on Barbara Ann Scott; Luanne Pfeifer, *Gretchen's Gold* (Missoula, MT, 1996), on Gretchen Fraser; Robert Parker, *Carol Heiss: Olympic Queen* (Garden City, NY, 1961); Dorothy Hamill, *Dorothy Hamill On and Off the Ice* (New York, 1983); and Bernard Heimo, *Katarina Witt* (Altstatten, Germany, 1985). Men have not been so celebrated, but see Dick Button, *Dick Button on Skates* (London, 1956) and Keith Money, *John Curry* (New York, 1978). American speed skaters Eric Heiden and Dan Jansen are the subjects of Suzanne Munshower, *Eric Heiden: America's Olympic Golden Boy* (New York, 1980) and Dan Jansen, with Jack McCallum, *Full Circle* (New York, 1994). Finally, see Jayne Torvill and Christopher Dean, *Torvill and Dean: The Autobiography of Ice Dancing's Greatest Stars* (Secaucus, NJ, 1996).

Traditional European dominance in skiing events has led to a number of biographies and autobiographies about Olympic champions. An interesting skiing autobiography is Franz X. Gabl, *Franz II* (Missoula MT, 2000), about the 1948 gold medal winner who returned to competitive skiing after four years on the Russian front as a World War II infantryman. Toni Sailer, *Mein Weg zum dreifacher Olympiasieg* (Salzburg, Austria, 1956) is the autobiography of Austria's greatest skier, who won three gold medals at the Cortina Games in 1956. A French edition is also available. Rosi Mittemaier, one of Europe's top women skiers of the 1970s tells her story in *Ski-Zirkus: Meine 10 Jahre im Hochleistings-sport* (Frankfurt, 1976). Herman Maier, winner of two gold medals at Nagano, is profiled in Hans Pruller, *Hermann Maier und das weisse Wunderteam* (Vienna, 1998).

SPORT-SPECIFIC HISTORIES

A few scholarly books and articles that deal with one sport at the Olympics have been published. For Olympic swimming, see Kelly Gonsalves, *First to the Wall: 100 Years of Olympic Swimming* (Poole, Dorset, UK, 1999), a popular history that includes lists of medal winners. Heiner Gillmeister, *Olympischen Tennis: Die Geschichte der olympischen tennisturniere (1896–1992)* (Augustin, Germany, 1993) describes the feud between the IOC and the Federation Internationale du Lawn

Tennis over the use of re-amateurized professionals in the 1920s that led to tennis being dropped from the Olympic program. In 1968, the International Skating Union published *The Olympic Games: Results in Figure Skating 1908, 1920, 1924–68; Results in Speed Skating 1924–1968* (n.p., 1968), whose title is self-explanatory. A National Rifle Association publication, Jim Crossman, *Olympic Shooting* (Washington, D.C., 1978), does much the same for that event. Curling merits two books: Warren Hansen, *Curling: The History, the Players, the Game* (Westport, CT, 2000), a general account written by an enthusiastic competitor, and Jean Sonmor, *Burned by the Rock: Inside the World of Men's Championship Curling* (Toronto, 1991), which deals with the history of Canadian curling but also includes information about the sport's reintroduction at the 1988 Calgary Games. Even more specialized is John D. Fair, "Olympic Weightlifting and the Introduction of Steroids: A Statistical Analysis of the World Championship Results, 1948–72," *International Journal of the History of Sport* 5, 1 (1988): 96–114, which concludes that steroids are not solely responsible for the record-breaking performances of recent years. While no comprehensive history of Olympic track and field has been published, Charlie Lovett, *Olympic Marathon: A Centennial History of the Games' Most Storied Race* (Westport, CT, 1997), traces the history of that event. An official history of Olympic wrestling is Rayko Petrov, *100 Years of Olympic Wrestling* (Budapest, 1997), a publication of FILA, wrestling's international federation.

OLYMPIC MISCELLANEA

Still other books touch on miscellaneous aspects of the Olympic Movement. Barclay F. Gordon, *Olympic Architecture: Building for the Summer Games* (New York, 1983), surveys the architecture and design utilized in Olympic venues, with separate chapters on the 1936 Games and each of the Games from 1952 through 1980. The book is well illustrated with drawings and photographs. A study of the Olympic art competitions between 1908 and 1952 is found in Richard Stanton, *The Forgotten Olympic Art Competitions* (Victoria, British Columbia, 2000). Stanton also includes biographical sketches of many of the medal-winning artists. Giulio Andreotti, *Sport et Arte* (Rome, 1960) surveys the art and architecture displayed at the 1960 Games in Rome. Olympic music is the subject of William K. Giegold, *100 Years of Olympic Music: Music and Musicians of the Modern Olympic Games, 1896–1996* (Mantua, OH, 1996). The IOC also published a book, *The Olympic Games and Music* (Lausanne, 1996) on the same topic. Takis Doxas, *Light of Olympia* (Athens, 1980), presents in several languages the poem, "Light of Olympia," recited at each Games. Information on the medical side of Olympic sport may be found in A. Dirix, H. G. Knuttgen, and K. Tittel, *The Olympic Book of Sports Medicine* (Oxford, 1988), and, much more extensively, in *Encyclopedia of Sports Medicine*, 9 vols., (Oxford, 1988–2000), a publication sponsored by the IOC Medical Commission in collaboration with the International Federation of Sports Medicine. The recent Olympic Games have been marked by revelations of illegal drug use; these form the basis of Wayne Wilson and E. Derse, eds., *Doping in Elite Sport: The Politics of Drugs in the Olympic Movement* (Champaign, IL, 2001). William J. Baker, *If Christ Came to the Olympics* (Sydney, 2000), analyzes the links between the Olympics and religion, ranging from shared rituals to evangelical Olympians.

It is now standard for the Paralympics, Olympic-style Games for physically challenged athletes, to be held at the Summer Games site a few weeks after the Games close. Joan Scruton, *Stoke Mandeville Road to the Paralympics: Fifty Years of History* (Brill, Aylesbury, United Kingdom, 1998), provides the first comprehensive history of these Games, which began at the Stoke Mandeville Hospital in Aylkesbury, England, in 1942, as part of a rehabilitation program for patients with spinal cord injuries. The IOC sanctioned these Games in 1960, and in 1976, athletes with other disabilities were invited to participate. See also R. D. Steadward and Cynthia Peterson, *Paralympics* (Edmonton, Alberta, Canada, 1997), a coffee-table size pictorial history of the Paralympics, including biographical sketches of prominent disabled athletes.

Many philatelists view the Olympic Games with special delight because since 1896, many countries have issued commemorative stamps honoring the Games. Among books that deal with Olympic stamps are Vsevolod Foorman, *Olympic Stamps* (Moscow, 1981), which treats stamps thematically rather than by Games or issuing country. An IOC publication, *Philatelique Olympique/Olympic Philately* (Barcelona, 1982?) also focuses on themes, while another IOC publication, *Postes, Philatelie et Olympisme/Post, Philately and Olympism* (Barcelona, 1984), includes a summary of stamps issued for each Games between 1896 and 1928, special Olympic postal markings, illustrated postcards and labels, as well as stamps and special postmarks commemorating IOC Congresses up to 1930. Collectors may also wish to consult *Philatelie und Olympia* (Munich, 1972), published by Schwaneberger Verlag, which also publishes stamp catalogs for German collectors. This book is an anthology, with a number of illustrated articles on the various stamps and postmarks created for the 1972 Munich Games. A recent contribution to the field of Olympic philately is Umesh V. Shenoy, *Olympic Origins to Centenary: A Philately Journey through the Eras* (Mumbai, India, 2000). Robert J. DuBois, *Catalog of Olympic Labels, 1894–1985* (Pottstown, PA, 1986) deals with the stamp-like commemorative labels that have been issued for most Games. Michele Menard, *Coins of the Modern Olympic Games* (Rockcliffe, ON, Canada, 1991) covers Olympic coins issued by host countries, often to raise funds. A projected second volume will treat coins issued by countries not hosting a Games. Mary A. Danaher, *The Commemorative Coinage of Modern Sports* (New York, 1978), focuses primarily on the many coins minted for the 1976 Montreal Games.

DOCUMENTARY FILMS

While documentary films produced for each Olympic Games are included in the bibliographies following each of the Games, there are a number of other video resources and books about filmmakers that do not confine themselves to just one Olympics. Leni Riefenstahl, the late centenarian producer of the classic film on the Berlin Games of 1936, *Olympia*, has been the focus of a considerable (and growing) body of scholarship. One might start with Riefenstahl's own version of her life, first published in German as *Memoiren, 1902–1945* (Munich, 1987), and in English as *The Sieve of Time: The Memoirs of Leni Riefenstahl* (London, 1992) or *Leni Riefenstahl: A Memoir* (New York, 1993). Incredibly detailed and self-adulatory, Riefenstahl's writing is viewed skeptically by most critics but contains much information on the filming and editing of *Olympia*. Researchers should also consult Cooper Graham, *Leni Riefenstahl and Olympia* (Lanham, MD, 2001), originally published in 1986 and probably the best secondary account; Glenn B. Infield, *Leni Riefenstahl: The Fallen Film Goddess* (New York, 1976), a popular account but one based on archival sources; Renata Berg-Pan, *Leni Riefenstahl* (Boston, 1980), part of Twayne's Theatrical Arts series; and Taylor Downing, *Olympia* (London, 1992), a publication of the British Film Institute, which offers a close examination of the film.

As Riefenstahl approached her hundredth birthday in 2002, four new books appeared: Angelika Taschen, ed., *Leni Riefenstahl: Five Lives* (London, 2000), a pictorial book that focuses more on Riefenstahl's post-Olympic career as a photographer in Africa and underwater; and Rainer Rother, *Leni Riefenstahl: The Seduction of Genius* (London, 2002), an illustrated biography originally published in German; Jurgen Trimborn, *Riefenstahl: eine deutsche Karriere* (Berlin, 2002); and Lutz Kinkel, *Die Scheinwerferin: Leni Riefenstahl und das "Dritte Reich"* (Hamburg, 2002).

Two articles are also worth consulting. Frank DeFord, "The Ghost of Berlin," *Sports Illustrated*, August 4, 1986, 48–64, is a lengthy, sensitive biographical sketch that includes much on Riefenstahl's later life, and Cooper Graham, "'Olympia' in America, 1938: Leni Riefenstahl, Hollywood, and the Kristallnacht," *Historical Journal of Film, Radio, and Television* 13 (October 1993): 433 *ff.*, examines the reception Riefenstahl and *Olympia* received in the United States on the eve of World War II.

Bud Greenspan, the current official documentary filmmaker of the Olympic Games, has produced films dealing with different aspects of the Olympic Movement since 1964. A total of 22 films comprise *The Olympiad* series, released together as a video package in 1988. Among these episodes are *Great Moments at the Winter Games*, which many critics consider his greatest work; *Those Who Endured*, which profiles four winners who had suffered earlier defeats; and *The Immortals*, featuring Sonja Henie, Toni Sailer, Birger Ruud, and Billy Fiske.

Other parts of Greenspan's *The Olympiad* include *The Australians* (1975); *The Big Ones That Got Away* (1975); *The East Europeans* (1980); *The 800 Meters* (1979); *The Fastest Men in the World* (1980); *The 1,500 Meters* (1980); *The Incredible Five* (1975); *Jesse Owens Returns to Berlin* (1964); *The Magnificent Ones* (1979); *The Marathon* (1974); *The Persistent Ones* (1975); *The Rare Ones* (1979); and *Women Gold Medal Winners* (1975).

Greenspan has also produced a made-for-television film biography of track-and-field champion Wilma Rudolph called *Wilma* (1977) as well as *America at the Olympics* (1984); *An Olympic Dream* (1988); *For the Honor of Their Country* (1991); and *Measure of Greatness* (1992).

Greenspan has published three books: *Play It Again, Bud* (New York, 1973), which deals with his early work, including that on *The Olympiad* series, and *100 Greatest Moments in Olympic History* (Los Angeles, 1995), which includes written versions of many of the Olympic performances that have appeared in his films, and a partner book, *Frozen in Time: The Greatest Moments at the Winter Olympics* (Los Angeles, 1997). John Brant describes Greenspan's early career in "The Games According to Greenspan," *Runner's World* 19 (July 1984): 50–54.

JOURNALS AND ORGANIZATIONS

A number of journals dedicated to sport studies frequently publish articles of interest to Olympic historians. Among them are the *Journal of Sport History*, the publication of the North American Society for Sport History (NASSH); *Stadion; Canadian Journal of the History of Sport; International Journal of the History of Sport;* and *Olympic Review*, the journal of the IOC. Special mention should be made of the

Journal of Olympic History, formerly known as *Citius, Altus, Fortius,* the journal of the International Society of Olympic Historians (ISOH). Founded in 1991, ISOH is the only group dedicated solely to the study of Olympic history. Bill Mallon, a founder of ISOH, has compiled a list of Olympic-related dissertations and theses; for information about the list or ISOH, write Mallon at 303 Sutherland Court, Durham, NC 27712.

INDEX

Index

ABOUT THE EDITORS AND CONTRIBUTORS

CARLY ADAMS is a Ph.D. candidate working under the supervision of Kevin Wamsley at the University of Western Ontario. Her primary areas of interest are Canadian sport history and gender issues, with a focus on the twentieth century. She spent six weeks at the International Olympic Academy in the spring of 2002, attending the Tenth International Postgraduate Seminar on Olympic Studies.

JOSEPH L. ARBENA is a professor of history at Clemson University. He has a Ph.D. from the University of Virginia and has published on the aspects of sports across Latin America. He is the author of *An Annotated Bibliography of Latin American Sport* (1989). He has also been the editor of the *Journal of Sport History*. He believes that he is living proof that a sound mind does not require a sound body.

TIM ASHWELL teaches in the sport management program at the University of Massachusetts, Amherst. A longtime sports broadcaster and journalist, he earned his Ph.D. in history at the University of Massachusetts, Amherst, and studies the connections between political culture and popular culture in the twentieth-century United States.

NORMAN BAKER was born about the time of Berlin, married by the time of Rome, received his Ph.D. from University College London before Mexico, and moved to the United States shortly thereafter. Around Barcelona, he switched his research interests from eighteenth-century London politics to sport history, specifically Britain after World War II. He retired from the history department of the University at Buffalo before Sydney but continues to research and write in the field.

C. ROBERT BARNETT is a professor and director of graduate studies in the Division of Exercise Science, Sport, and Recreation at Marshall University in Huntington, West Virginia. He became interested in the 1904 Olympic Games when helping a student who was having difficulty with the topic. He has a sense of humor that no one seems to appreciate as much as he does.

ROBERT K. BARNEY is professor emeritus in the Faculty of Kinesiology at the University of Western Ontario and is the director of the center for Olympic studies there. He is the editor of *Olympika* and has written extensively on both the ancient and modern Games as well as on Canadian sport, baseball, and the Turner movement.

ANTHONY TH. BIJKERK was born in what is now Indonesia and entered the Dutch Royal Naval Academy in 1950. He was a naval officer from 1953 to 1965, when he became director for sports and recreation for the city of Leeuwarden, Netherlands, a position he held until 1990. His interest in the Olympic Movement began in 1960, and since then he has done extensive research in the history of Dutch participation in the Olympic Games and has created a valuable database on Dutch Olympians. He is a member of the International Society of Olympic Historians and has served as its secretary-general and as editor of its journal.

MAYNARD BRICHFORD is emeritus university archivist at the University of Illinois in Urbana-Champaign. He prepared the finding aid for the Avery Brundage Collection and supervised its processing in the University Archives. He has presented more than ten papers on aspects of Brundage's career.

DOUGLAS BROWN worked among a bounty of bureaucrats who tried to organize Canada's amateur athletes so that they would perform better at the Olympic Games. After working closely with the Canadian Olympic Association and a number of other International Games Organizations, Doug's idealism was duly challenged. He then switched vantage points and turned to an academic life, studying the phenomenon of international sport rather than being its handmaiden. As an assistant professor at the University of Calgary, Doug continues to research, write, and teach on the culture of Olympic Games and modern sport.

RICHARD CASHMAN is an associate professor in history and director of the Centre for Olympic Studies at the University of New South Wales. He is the author and editor of a number of monographs on the Sydney Olympic Games, including *Staging the Olympics* (coedited with Anthony Hughes). He has written extensively on Australian sport. His most recent book, *Sport in the National Imagination*, was published in December 2002 by Walla Walla Press. During the Sydney Olympic Games he helped organize a number of conferences, facilitated the visits of international Olympic scholars, and contributed to the official Post Games Report. He was runner number 53, day 99 (the day before the Opening Ceremony) in the torch relay.

JAMES COATES is an energetic bundle of muscle mass. He was born in Annapolis, Maryland, and received his degrees from the University of Maryland. He is the director of student teaching at the University of Wisconsin at Green Bay. He loves listening to old soul music, dancing, lifting weights, and having fun. He's the little man with the big voice.

SANDRA COLLINS is a student of Professor John MacAloon and is writing her dissertation about the never-held Tokyo Games of 1940. She was chosen by the IOC study center in 1999 to conduct research at the IOC archives in Lausanne in order to acquire information for her dissertation.

RICHARD COX founded the British Society of Sports History (1982) and is the co–founding editor of the *International Journal of the History of Sport* (1984) and the *Sports Historian* (1992; now *Sport in History*). He has authored 10 books on sport, including the recent *Encyclopedia of British Sport* (2000) and the *Encyclopedia of British Football* (2002). His three-volume *Bibliography of British Sports History* was published in 2003. He is currently vice president of the International Society of the History of Physical Education and Sport (ISHPES). After 17 years as director of sport at the University of Manchester Institute of Science and Technology, he sought a career change and is now working for the Modern Pentathlon Association of Great Britain, looking after international athletes living in northern England. He has a lifelong involvement in the sports of swimming and kayaking, in which he still trains, coaches, and competes.

SCOTT A. G. M. CRAWFORD is a Scottish New Zealander who is a professor and graduate coordinator in the Department of Physical Education, College of Education and Professional Studies, Eastern Illinois University, Charlestown. He has been a longtime book review editor for the *International Journal of the History of Sport*. He collects assorted toy lead soldiers, all manner of lapel pins, and postage stamps from the British Empire and Commonwealth countries.

JOHN DALY is professor emeritus at the University of South Australia and lectures on the history and sociology of sport and Australian history. He is the author of numerous books and articles, including *Quest for Excellence* (1991). Dr. Daly has been associated with the Australian athletic team for more than twenty years as either head coach or manager, and he managed the national track-and-field team at the Barcelona Games—his fifth Olympics representing Australia. For his services to Australian sport, he was awarded the medal of the Order of Australia in 1991.

ANDRE DREVON, a former professor at the National Sports Institute in Paris, France, now produces documentary films on the topic of sports history. He has also published articles and books on the subject. Two of his films are *Georges Demeny and the Sportive Origin of Cinematography* and *The Forgotten Olympic Games, Paris, 1900.*

ROBERT DUNKELBERGER received master's degrees from Bowling Green State University in Ohio and the University of Illinois at Urbana-Champaign and is currently University Archivist at Bloomsburg University of Pennsylvania. He has written articles and presented papers dealing with the history of intercollegiate football, basketball, and baseball and is a longtime fan of the Cincinnati Reds.

WILLIAM DURICK, while earning his doctorate degree at Penn State University, worked closely with Olympic authority John Lucas and renowned sports historian Ron Smith. He has published a number of articles in scholarly journals, including "The Gentleman's Race: An Examination of the 1869 Harvard–Oxford

Boat Race" in the *Journal of Sport History*. Durick teaches history at the secondary level and enjoys coaching track and football.

MARK DYRESON earned his Ph.D. at the University of Arizona and teaches in the Department of Kinesiology at Penn State University. He has done extensive research in the relationship between the United States and the Olympic Movement in the early twentieth century and published *Making the American Team: Sport, Culture, and the Olympic Experience* in 1998. In 2002, he was elected vice president of the North American Society for Sport History.

ASTRID ENGELBRECHT is a doctoral student in sport studies at Georg-Augus-Universitat in Gottingen, Germany. At last report, however, she was somewhere deep in the jungles of Peru.

JOHN FEA is assistant professor of American history at Messiah College in Grantham, Pennsylvania. He has found teaching and writing about history to be a wonderful consolation prize after his dream of being a member of the 1984 U.S. Olympic hockey team was shattered when he realized that he couldn't skate.

JAMEY J. FINDLING teaches philosophy at Newman University in Wichita, Kansas. He earned his Ph.D. at Villanova University and spent a year studying at the University of Freiburg in Germany. He is a devoted Grateful Dead fan and a past winner of the Chimay Cup.

JOHN E. FINDLING is professor of history at Indiana University Southeast in New Albany. He has written and edited several books on world's fairs and expositions, most recently *Fair America* (2000), coauthored with Robert W. Rydell and Kimberly D. Pelle. With Kimberly Pelle, he coedited *Historical Dictionary of the Olympic Movement* (1996). In his spare time, he helps manage a stamp and postcard business in Louisville, Kentucky, and frets constantly about the inability of the Chicago Cubs to reach the World Series.

JANICE FORSYTH is a Ph.D. student at the International Centre for Olympic Studies at the University of Western Ontario, although much of her research focuses on ideas about race and gender in contemporary Aboriginal sport practices in Canada. She is also interested in various issues dealing with the history of the modern Olympic Movement.

EDWARD S. GOLDSTEIN is a senior speechwriter at NASA headquarters. He was a press volunteer for the Los Angeles Olympic Committee in 1984 and was a member of the USOC's Education Committee in 1999. He fell in love with Holland, host country of the 1928 Summer Olympics, during a student exchange to the University of Groningen in 1988.

JOHANNA HACKNEY earned a B.A. with honors at Indiana University Southeast, with a double major in French and economics and a minor in international studies. ULF HAMILTON is a senior officer at Nordiska Museet in Stockholm and is responsible for the collection of sport and leisure. Hamilton has a Ph.D. from

Stockholm University in history and an M.S. from Chalmers Technical Institute in Gothenburg. He has several publications on the history of technology and history of sport.

LEX HEMPHILL worked for the *Salt Lake Tribune* for 25 years in several roles, including sportswriter, editorial writer, and Olympic writer. He covered seven Olympic Games for the *Tribune*, including, of course, the 2002 Games in his hometown.

ANNETTE HOFMANN holds a master's degree in American studies and physical education from Eberhard Karls Universitat in Tubingen, where she also received a doctoral degree on German Turnen in the United States. Since 1999 she has been a research assistant (assistant professor) in the department of sports science at Westfalische Wilhems Universitat in Munster. Dr. Hofmann serves as a council member of the International Society for the History of Sport and Physical Education (ISHPES). Her research interests include ethnicity and sport, cross-national sport studies, and sport and health.

IAN JOBLING is an associate professor in sport history and director of the Center for Physical Activity and Sport Education in the Department of Human Movement Studies at the University of Queensland, Australia. He was the inaugural chair of both the Oceania Olympic Academy in Australia and the Education Commission of the Australian Olympic Federation. He is a member of the editorial review board of *Olympika: International Journal of Olympic Studies* and the president and a member of the editorial review board of *Sporting Traditions: Journal of the Australian Society for Sports History.*

JOHN J. KENNEDY JR. earned his Ph.D. in history at Temple University. His dissertation research focused on the environmental history of colonial America. He has done research on the Rocky Flats nuclear weapons plant in Colorado, on Denver's attempt to secure the 1976 Winter Games, and on the USOC's procedures in selecting a site to put forward for the 1998 Winter Olympics.

BRUCE KIDD wanted to be a professional hockey player until his father brought home inspiring film footage and stories from the 1952 Olympics in Helsinki (where he was the entire Canadian Broadcasting Corporation TV production team) and turned his athletic interests completely around. Kidd has followed the Olympics ever since.

MICHAEL KRUGER has been a professor of sports science and director of the Department of Sports Science at the Westfalische Wilhlems Universitat in Munster since 1999. Majoring in German studies, history, pedagogy, and physical education, he graduated from Tubingen, where he also received his doctoral degree and later became a lecturer. In 1995–96, he was a visiting fellow at the University of Leicester, Great Britain. His research interests include sport pedagogy, sport history, and especially the history of German Turnen.

DOMINIQUE LEBLOND teaches in the department of education and science at the University of Parix XII in Creteil, Cedex, France. Among her publications is "The Sacralization of the American deserts in the WRA [War Relocation Authority] Concentration Camps," *American Studies in Scandinavia* (1999).

MICHELLE LELLOUCHE is an employee benefits attorney, with a law degree and a master's degree in history from Florida State University. When not working at becoming the next Scott Turow, she is a very amateur figure skater.

KARL LENNARTZ is senior lecturer at the German Sport University Cologne, head of the Olympic research institute (Carl and Liselot Diem Archive) at the German Sport University, and a sport historian with expertise in the history of the Olympic Movement. He has published numerous works on the history of the Olympic Movement and sport history in general and is vice president of the International Society of Olympic Historians (ISOH) and the chief editor of the *International Journal of Olympic History*.

GORDON MACDONALD received his Ph.D. from the University of Western Ontario. He has done research on a number of Olympic-related topics, including the history of the Canadian Olympic Committee and the conflict over German representation in the IOC after World War II.

LARRY MALONEY resides in Washington, D.C., and received a master's degree in international service from American University. His particular interest in the Olympic Movement centers on the economic and political ramifications of the Games on host cities. He contributed several essays to the *Historical Dictionary of the Modern Olympic Movement* (1996), and he has attended six Winter and Summer Olympic Games.

BILL MALLON is the current president of the International Society of Olympic Historians (ISOH). He has authored or coauthored over twenty books on the history of the Olympic Games and international sport. His day job is as an orthopedic surgeon specializing in shoulder surgery. He is with Triangle Orthopedic Associates in Durham, North Carolina, and he is a clinical associate professor in the Division of Orthopedic Surgery at Duke University Medical Center.

MARTIN MANNING was born and raised in Boston, Massachusetts, a city that has never hosted an Olympics. He has degrees from Boston College and from Catholic University. He is presently archivist for the United States Information Agency, Washington, D.C., and curator of its historical collection, which includes records of the agency's involvement in sports exchanges. He has contributed entries to the *Dictionary of American Biography* and the *American National Biography*, wrote the entry on the 1970 Osaka exposition for the *Historical Dictionary of Worlds Fairs and Expositions, 1851–1988* (1990), and is presently completing a book on American propaganda for Greenwood Press.

NAOFUMI MASUMOTO is an associate professor in the Department of Kinesiology at Tokyo Metropolitan University and teaches a sport culture course including Olympic issues. He received his Ph.D. from University of Tsukuba, Japan. He has written a Japanese book, *The Epistemology of Sport Films* (2000), that includes the interpretation of the IOC's official Olympic films. He has presented five papers on the interpretation of sport films at the International Olympic Symposiums held at the University of Western Ontario, Canada, from 1994. He has been a lecturer of the International Olympic Academy in Olympia in 1999 and an executive member of Japan Olympic Academy since 2001. His favorite Olympic film is *Tokyo Olympiad* (1964) by Kon Ichikawa.

FLORIS J. G. VAN DER MERWE was born in Cape Town, South Africa, and studied physical education and history at Stellenbosch University, where he received his B.A. with honors and a Teachers Diploma. He went to Potchefstroom to complete his master's and doctorate degrees. His M.A. thesis was on South Africa's participation and the British Empire and Commonwealth games from 1930 to 1958, and his dissertation dealt with South Africa's participation in the Olympic Games from 1908 to 1960. This is where and how the author's specialization in sport history started. A teaching post at Stellenbosch University was awaiting him in 1979 and another master's degree in history followed. At present Dr. van der Merwe is a senior lecturer in the Department of Sports Science.

MIQUEL DE MORAGAS is director of the Centre d'Estudis Olimpics I de l'Esport at the Universitat Autonoma de Barcelona. He is the author or coauthor of several Olympic-related publications, including *Los Juegos de la Communication* (1992) and *Television and the Olympics* (1995). His center maintains a directory of Olympics scholars and hosts frequent conferences on Olympic issues.

YVES MORALES was born in Oran, Algeria. He began teaching physical education and sport at the secondary level in 1985 and received a Ph.D. in 1999. His dissertation dealt with the history of winter sport. He has taught at René Descartes University and is presently a lecturer at Paul Sabatier University in Toulouse, France. In his spare time, he has managed to get married, raise several children and a dog, and pursue an avid interest in skiing and snowboarding.

JIM NENDEL is a Ph.D. candidate and graduate assistant in the Department of Kinesiology at Penn State University. He has done research on a number of Olympic-related topics, including the famous Hawaiian swimmer Duke Kahanamoku, gold medalist at the Stockholm Games of 1912.

KATHY L. NICHOLS is assistant site manager at Farmington, a historic home in Louisville, Kentucky. She was assistant editor on a book-length project involving the editing of physics texts used in colonial America and has studied rural-urban migration in Kentucky. She bakes wedding cakes in her spare time.

RON PALENSKI is one of New Zealand's most experienced sports writers with about 30 books to his credit, including the definitive work on New Zealanders competing in the Olympic Games. Increasing age meant an increasing knowledge of sports history, and he set up, designed, and operates the New Zealand Sports Hall of Fame.

MORGAN PATRICK is a professional historian from Bergen County, New Jersey. He earned his B.A. from William Patterson College and his M.A. from Monmouth University. His thesis dealt with the New Jersey home front during the American Civil War. In addition, he is an active reenactor of the American Revolutionary War and Civil War eras.

KIMBERLY D. PELLE earned an M.S. in education in 2000 and works as a counselor in the Office of Admissions at Indiana University Southeast. She and John E. Findling have collaborated on a number of projects, including *Historical Dictionary of World's Fairs and Expositions, 1851–1988* (1990), *Historical Dictionary of the Modern Olympic Movement* (1996), and with Robert W. Rydell, *Fair America* (2000). An excellent cook and dancer, she has developed a considerable reputation for her crawfish etouffe and "knock-you-naked" margaritas.

DORIS PIEROTH is an independent historian in Seattle working in Northwest regional history. A foray into Washington State aquatic history led to her book on women in the 1932 Olympic Games and provided her with the "unforgettable bonus of talking with eleven of those marvelous people." She received her doctorate degree from the University of Washington.

ROLAND RENSON was born in Sint-Truiden in occupied Belgium in 1943 and liberated one year later by the U.S. Army. He studied physical education, physical therapy, and social anthropology in Leuven. He is a professor at K.U. Leuven on the faculty of physical education and physical therapy, where he teaches sport history, comparative physical education, and sociocultural aspects of sports and games. He has been president of the International Society for the History of Physical Education and Sport (ISHPES).

JAMES RIORDAN is emeritus professor at the University of Surrey and honorary professor in sports studies at Stirling University, Scotland. He is currently president of the European Sports History Association. Having lived for five years in the Soviet Union, where he played football for Moscow Spartak, he wrote extensively on communist sport, including the books *Sport and Soviet Society* (1977), *Soviet Sport* (1980), and *Sport, Politics, and Communism* (1991). His most recent book is the edited *European Cultures and Sport* (2003).

JOACHIM K. RÜHL, sport historian, is a senior lecturer and academic advisor at the Olympic Research Centre of the German Sport University in Cologne. After having treated Robert Dover's Olympic Games in his dissertation (1969), which he considered to be the only Olympic Games *before* Coubertin, he fell over backward when he found out that there are at least fourteen others, of which seven are outlined in his essay.

SWANTJE SCHARENBERG is expert of artistic gymnastics at the German Gymnastics Union. She studied sports, journalism, and ethnology and received her Ph.D. from Goettingen University. There she taught sport journalism, gymnastics, and circus. She has also taught at Queensland University in Brisbane, Australia, and in the Department of Sport Sciences at the University of Mainz, Germany. Her main focus of research is the interwar.

SUSAN SAINT-SING is a second-year doctoral candidate at Penn State University. She was a member of the 1993 U.S. National Rowing Team that went to the World Championships in the Czech Republic. She is the author of five books.

CHRISTINE SELL is a former Olympic aspirant whose life has finally come together. As a young person, swimming and the Olympics constituted reality. As an adult, theatre and directing have been her preoccupations. She received her M.A. in theatre studies from the University of Akron and taught for 18 years. A professional director, her productions span many genres—from the staging of classical works to modern comedies, from musical theatre to chamber opera.

JOHN SLATER lived on the Miura Peninsula south of Yokohama in Kanagawa prefecture and traveled extensively in the western Pacific from 1962 to 1964. He now lives in the Great Smoky Mountains of North Carolina, where he studies the relationship between the mass media and the Olympic Games and teaches at Western Carolina University. He still remembers all the words to "Sakura, Sakura," which he sometimes sings in the shower, and he invariably removes his shoes when he enters the house.

JON W. STAUFF, associate professor of history at St. Ambrose University, Davenport, Iowa, wrote his dissertation on German sport and political culture during the 1920s and 1930s. He has done further research into a variety of topics related to the German working class in the 1920s and to the peace movement.

JUNKO TAHARA is an associate professor in Chukyo Women's University in Japan. Her interest is Olympic studies, especially on the various aspects of relationship between Japan and the international community. She was a Lawn Bowls World Championship (England) player in 1996. She is expected to be one of the first Olympic athletes among the few Olympic studies scholars in Japan.

VESA TIKANDER holds a master's degree in history from the University of Helsinki and works as a researcher at the sports library of Finland, located at the Olympic stadium of Helsinki.

KEVIN B. WAMSLEY is director of the International Centre for Olympic Studies at the University of Western Ontario, London, Ontario. He received his Ph.D. in 1992 from the University of Alberta. His research interests include leisure, sport, cultural activities, nineteenth-century Canada, hegemony, gender construction, and international sport festivals. He has published articles in *Social History* and the *Canadian Journal of History of Sport* and has recently edited a book on research methods in sport and cultural history.

STEPHEN WASSONG is a scientific assistant at the German Sport University in Cologne. He has published works about the history of the Olympic Movement and about the American influence on Pierre de Coubertin and cultural aspects of U.S.-American sport, and he won the Junior Scholar Award of the European Committee for the History of Sport (CESH). He is chief editor of the *International Journal of Olympic History*.

ROBERT P. WATSON teaches government at Northern Arizona University and is the author of numerous articles on topics such as environmental protection, bureaucracy, women in politics, and U.S. foreign aid. He is the coeditor of *Latin America and the Caribbean in Transition*.

PAULA D. WELCH is professor emeritus of exercise and sport sciences at the University of Florida in Gainesville. She is a member of the board of directors of the U.S. Olympic Committee and is a trustee of the U.S. Olympic Foundation. She has written numerous articles on the Olympic Games.

STEPHEN B. WENN is an associate professor of kinesiology and physical education at Wilfrid Laurier University in Waterloo, Ontario, Canada. He obtained his B.A. and M.A. degrees in physical education from the University of Western Ontario in 1986 and 1988, respectively. He concluded his Ph.D. studies at the Pennsylvania State University in 1993. Stephen is one of the coauthors of *Selling the Five Rings: The IOC and the Rise of Olympic Commercialism* (2002), a book that details the rise of the IOC to its status as a corporate entity. He enjoys recreational ice hockey, jogging, spending time with his family, and serving as the "Shadow GM" of his favorite professional sport franchise, the Toronto Maple Leafs. Stephen, his wife, Martha, and their children, Timothy and Lily, live in Waterloo, Ontario.

HAROLD E. (RUSTY) WILSON JR. holds a Ph.D. in sport history from Ohio State University. Currently employed at Ohio State, he also announces for Buckeye swimming and gymnastics events. His areas of interest are Olympic politics, biographical studies of Olympic athletes, and oral histories. He has published articles on George S. Patton in the 1912 Olympics and Romania's participation in the 1984 Los Angeles Olympic Games. A founding member of the International Olympic Academy Participants Association, he is a member of the executive board and newsletter editor. In 1996 he was a guest of the Hellenic Olympic Committee for the Greek leg of the Olympic flame relay, a discussion coordinator at the International Olympic Academy, and a gymnastics announcer at the Atlantic Olympic Games. He also collects historical Olympic items.

WAYNE WILSON is director of research and library services for the Amateur Athletic Foundation library in Los Angeles. He received his Ph.D. in sport studies from the University of Massachusetts and has published and edited several articles on sports culture.

YING WUSHANLEY (formerly Ying Wu) was born in Shanghai and received his Ph.D. from Penn State University. He is an associate professor at Millersville University in Pennsylvania and a former council member of the North American Society for Sport History. He has published in the *Journal of Sport History, Sport History Review, International Journal of the History of Sport,* and *International Review for the Sociology of Sport* and has contributed entries to the *International Encyclopedia of Women and Sport* and the *Scribner Encyclopedia of American Lives.*

DWIGHT H. ZAKUS is a senior lecturer in sport management at the Gold Coast Campus of Griffith University in Bundall, Queensland, Australia. Other than an academic interest in the Olympic Movement, he enjoys cross-disciplinary studies in all aspects of human movement.